D0365680

For Reference

Not to be taken from this room

American
Jewish
Year Book

The American Jewish Committee acknowledges with appreciation the foresight and wisdom of the founders of the Jewish Publication Society (of America) in the creation of the AMERICAN JEWISH YEAR BOOK in 1899, a work committed to providing a continuous record of developments in the U.S. and world Jewish communities. For over a century JPS has occupied a special place in American Jewish life, publishing and disseminating important, enduring works of scholarship and general interest on Jewish subjects.

The American Jewish Committee assumed responsibility for the compilation and editing of the YEAR BOOK in 1908. The Society served as its publisher until 1949; from 1950 through 1993, the Committee and the Society were co-publishers. In 1994 the Committee became the sole publisher of the YEAR BOOK.

American

Jewish

Year Book 2005

VOLUME 105

Editors
DAVID SINGER
LAWRENCE GROSSMAN

THE AMERICAN JEWISH COMMITTEE
NEW YORK

ISBN 0-87495-135-6

Library of Congress Catalogue Number: 99-4040

PRINTED IN THE UNITED STATES OF AMERICA
BY MAPLE-VAIL BOOK MANUFACTURING GROUP, BINGHAMTON, N.Y.

Preface

Volume 105 of the AMERICAN JEWISH YEAR BOOK covers the events of the year 2004.

On the occasion of the 350th anniversary of Jewish life in North America, historian Jack Wertheimer, in a specially commissioned article, surveys the current state and future prospects of the institution that has always been, and still remains, most central to the American Jewish community—the synagogue.

Momentous long-term shifts in Jewish population patterns in the U.S., Israel, and around the world are described by the eminent demographer Sergio DellaPergola in his article on world Jewish population.

The YEAR BOOK's coverage of American Jewish life includes articles on national affairs, anti-Semitism, and Jewish communal affairs.

The article on Israel describes in detail the diplomatic, political, economic, and social developments during 2004, with much attention to the Israeli government's controversial "disengagement" initiative.

Manifestations of anti-Semitism in many countries—vandalism, physical attacks, verbal abuse, hostile editorials, and biased reporting—continued to be linked to opposition toward Israel. These disturbing events are carefully described in the YEAR BOOK's regular articles on individual countries, as are important events and trends within the Jewish communities of these countries.

Carefully compiled directories of national Jewish organizations, periodicals, and federations and welfare funds, as well as obituaries and religious calendars, round out the 2005 AMERICAN JEWISH YEAR BOOK.

We gratefully acknowledge the assistance of our colleagues, Cyma M. Horowitz and Michele Anish, of the American Jewish Committee's Blaustein Library, and the contribution of Rachel Arnold, our assistant, in preparing the index.

THE EDITORS

Contributors

TOBY AXELROD: Correspondent, Jewish Telegraphic Agency and *Jewish Chronicle* (London); Berlin, Germany.

JEROME A. CHANES: Faculty Scholar, Brandeis University; adjunct professor, sociology and Jewish communal issues, Yeshiva University; former national affairs director, National Jewish Community Relations Advisory Council.

SERGIO DELLAPERGOLA: Professor and head, Division of Jewish Demography and Statistics, Avraham Harman Institute of Contemporary Jewry, Hebrew University of Jerusalem, Israel; senior fellow, The Jewish People Policy Planning Institute.

RICHARD T. FOLTIN: Legislative director and counsel, Office of Government and International Affairs, American Jewish Committee.

ELISE FRIEDMANN: Editor in chief, *Nieuw Israelitische Weekblad;* Amsterdam, Holland.

LAWRENCE GROSSMAN: Editor, AMERICAN JEWISH YEAR BOOK; associate director of research, American Jewish Committee.

RUTH ELLEN GRUBER: European-based American journalist and author, specialist in contemporary Jewish affairs; Morre, Italy.

LIONEL E. KOCHAN: Historian; Wolfson College, Oxford, England; deceased September 25, 2005.

MIRIAM L. KOCHAN: Free-lance journalist and translator; Oxford, England.

LEV KRICHEVSKY: Bureau chief, Jewish Telegraphic Agency, Moscow, Russia.

COLIN L. RUBENSTEIN: Executive director, Australia/Israel and Jewish Affairs Council; honorary associate, Monash University, Melbourne, Australia.

GEORGES SCHNEK: President, Jewish Museum of Belgium; former president, Jewish Central Consistory of Belgium; emeritus professor, biochemistry, Free University of Brussels, Belgium.

MILTON SHAIN: Professor, Hebrew and Jewish studies, and director, Kaplan Centre for Jewish Studies and Research, University of Cape Town, South Africa.

HANAN SHER: Senior editor, *The Jerusalem Report;* Jerusalem, Israel.

MURRAY GORDON SILBERMAN: Adjunct professor, Austrian Diplomatic Academy, Vienna, Austria.

BRIGITTE SION: Former secretary general, CICAD, the Committee against anti-Semitism and Defamation; Geneva, Switzerland.

MEIR WAINTRATER: Editor in chief, *L'Arche,* the French Jewish monthly, Paris, France.

HAROLD M. WALLER: Professor, political science, McGill University; director, Canadian Centre for Jewish Community Studies, Montreal, Canada.

JACK WERTHEIMER: Provost, Joseph and Martha Mendelson Professor of American Jewish History, Jewish Theological Seminary of America.

Contents

OTHER COUNTRIES

DIRECTORIES, LISTS, AND OBITUARIES

Special
Article

The American Synagogue: Recent Issues and Trends*

By Jack Wertheimer

$\mathbf{B}$Y THE CLOSING DECADE of the twentieth century, the synagogue had become the great reclamation project of the American Jewish community. Jewish foundations poured new money into synagogue renewal efforts, hoping to teach congregational professionals and lay leaders how to create a more welcoming and religiously inspiring environment. National "outreach" programs were launched to attract unaffiliated Jews to synagogues, often

*I acknowledge with appreciation the generous assistance of the following academic colleagues, rabbis, and other knowledgeable observers of American congregations who graciously took the time to inform my thinking and answer my questions. *Synagogues generally:* Chancellor Ismar Schorsch, Jewish Theological Seminary; Professors Michael Berenbaum, University of Judaism; Lawrence Hoffman, Hebrew Union College, N.Y.; Shawn Landress, University of Judaism; Sara Lee, Rhea Hirsch School of Jewish Education, Hebrew Union College; the late Charles Liebman, Bar Ilan University; Michael Meyer, Hebrew Union College, Cincinnati; David N. Myers, UCLA; and Ron Wolfson, University of Judaism; and Dr. Alisa Rubin Kurshan, UJA-Federation of New York. *Reform temples:* President David Ellenson, Hebrew Union College; Rabbis Herbert Bronstein, Chicago; Mitch Chefitz, Miami; Stanley Davids, Jerusalem; Daniel Freelander, Union for Reform Judaism (URJ); Elyse Frishman, New Jersey; Laura Geller, Los Angeles; Samuel Karff, Houston; Robert Levine, New York; Jeffrey Salkin, Atlanta; Herman Schaalmann, Chicago; and Lance Sussman, Philadelphia. *Conservative synagogues:* Rabbis Morris Alan, Minneapolis; Aaron Brusso, Minneapolis; Richard Cameras, Los Angeles; Jerome Epstein, United Synagogue of Conservative Judaism; Ed Feinstein, Los Angeles; Felipe Goodman, Las Vegas; Joel Meyers, Rabbinical Assembly (RA); Daniel Nevins, Detroit; Paul Plotkin, Margate, Florida; Elliot Schoenberg, RA; Harold Schulweis, Los Angeles; Michael Siegel, Chicago; Elie Spitz, Los Angeles; and several dozen others who invited me to spend Shabbat in their congregations and in the process enabled me to observe their synagogues. *Orthodox synagogues:* Dr. Steven Bayme, American Jewish Committee; Rabbis Jeffrey Fox, Englewood, New Jersey; Asher Lopatin, Chicago; Avi Shafran, Agudath Israel of America; Mayer Waxman, Union of Orthodox Jewish Congregations of American (OU); and Harvey Well, Associated Talmud Torahs, Chicago; Professors Benjamin Gampel, Jewish Theological Seminary; Jacob J. Schachter, Yeshiva University; and Chaim I. Waxman, Rutgers University. *Reconstructionist synagogues:* Rabbi Richard Hirsh, Reconstructionist Rabbinical Association, Philadelphia. *Congregational trends in American religion:* Presidents William McKinney, Pacific School of Religion, and Barbara G. Wheeler, Auburn Theological Seminary; Professors Nancy T. Ammerman, Boston University; Jackson Carroll, Duke University; Carl Dudley, Hartford Seminary; Penny Edgell Becker, University of Minnesota; Nancy Eisland, Emory University; and E. Stephen Warner, University of Illinois.

targeting specific subgroups such as singles, empty-nesters, inter-married families, and homosexuals and lesbians. Federations of Jewish philanthropy created commissions designed to improve synagogue life. Individual congregations, too, were caught up in efforts at self-reform, hiring professional consultants to guide their "re-visioning" of themselves as "caring communities."

Much of this activity was prompted by a barrage of criticism from communal leaders and rabbis bemoaning the sorry condition of Jewish congregations. "I don't like going to synagogue," confessed Edgar M. Bronfman, head of the World Jewish Congress. "I generally find the atmosphere stultifying, the services overly long, boringly repetitive, and mostly without meaning to the young Jews of today."[1] Writing in a less confessional vein from their perch at a major family foundation, Rabbi Irving (Yitz) Greenberg and his late son, Jonathan J. Greenberg, concluded:

> The last three decades have been a bear market for shuls [synagogues]. Membership and participation rates have dropped significantly. Complaints of boredom and irrelevance fill the air. Shul life has been criticized for excessive factionalism and small-mindedness . . . . Rabbis complained that they were shoved aside by the emergent lay leadership and blamed it all on "checkbook Judaism," i.e., Jewish life run by money instead of values. Yet the lay leaders complained that rabbis were uninspiring, acting like politicians but neglecting their constituents'—and their own—spiritual lives. The Havurot groups, which first emerged in the sixties, . . . blamed the soulless institutional synagogues and their Hebrew schools for the traumas which scarred their Jewish souls and turned off so many of their peers.[2]

Professor Lawrence Hoffman, who cofounded a major synagogue transformation project, challenged congregations to take a hard look at themselves. Noting the boast of a rabbi that some 200 members of his congregation attend synagogue on a weekly basis, Hoffman asked, "What does the figure of 200 attendees out of 3,000 congregants mean? [It amounts to] 7 percent of the 30 percent of all Jews who claim an affiliation, [a] figure equivalent to

---

[1]Edgar M. Bronfman, "A New Synagogue for a New Era," *Contact* 2, Autumn 1999, p. 5.

[2]Rabbi Yitz Greenberg and J.J. Greenberg, "The Synagogue: A Time for Tearing Down & a Time for Building Up," ibid., p. 3.

only 2 percent of the total population[;] only one person out of every 50 Jews" attends synagogue weekly.[3]

Even established leaders within the synagogue world joined the chorus of criticism. Rabbi Eric Yoffie, president of the Union for Reform Judaism (URJ), sorrowfully conceded his disappointment with the quality of religious services in many of his movement's synagogues: "All of us — rabbis, cantors, lay leaders — seem ready to admit that, far too often, our services are tedious, predictable, and dull. Far too often, our members pray without fervor or concentration. Far too often, our music is dirge-like and our Torah readings lifeless, and we are unable to trigger true emotion and ascent."[4] An ordained Conservative rabbi did not shrink from confessing in print that, "like the majority of American Jews, despite my personal commitment to tradition, I had simply decided to write off synagogue involvement."[5] A Reconstructionist rabbi sweepingly announced his "frustration with hundreds of synagogues across America that have yet to understand the needs of today's Jews . . . . America's synagogues serve hundreds of thousands of Jews . . . but most are in crisis."[6] And lest one assume that Orthodox Judaism enjoys immunity from the problem, Rabbi Tzvi Hersh Weinreb, executive director of the Union of Orthodox Jewish Congregations, reported that many Orthodox Jews around the country told him that their services lacked "emotional power," leaving them spiritually "arid and numb."[7]

It would be hard to think of any other American Jewish institution that has been subjected to such cold scrutiny and withering criticism — with the possible exception of the so-called Hebrew schools, the supplementary religious programs run *by synagogues.*

---

[3]Lawrence A. Hoffman, "From Common Cold to Uncommon Healing," *CCAR Journal* 41, Spring 1994, p. 7.

[4]Eric H. Yoffie, "Realizing God's Promise: Reform Judaism in the Twenty-First Century," presidential sermon delivered at the Union of American Hebrew Congregations General Assembly, Dec. 18, 1999, and published under the title "The Worship Revolution," *Reform Judaism* 28, Spring 2000, p. 24. More recently, Yoffie has expressed satisfaction with the positive changes in his movement's congregations. See Yoffie, "False Prophets," ibid. 29, Spring 2001, pp. 23–28.

[5]Richard A. Marker, "Beyond Renewal — A Call for Transformation," *Sh'ma* 30, Sept. 1999, p. 1.

[6]Sidney Schwarz, *Finding a Spiritual Home: How a New Generation of Jews Can Transform the American Synagogue* (San Francisco, 2000), pp. xxiv–xxv.

[7]Zvi Hersh Weinreb, "Orthodox: Imbue Ritual with Spirituality," *Forward,* Mar. 14, 2003, p. 9.

The motive of these critics—as they all hasten to point out—is not to denigrate synagogues but to spur them to take remedial action. To one extent or another, all would agree with Dr. Ismar Schorsch, chancellor of the Jewish Theological Seminary, that "the synagogue, generically speaking, is the bedrock institution of the total Jewish community. It alone is the aquifer for the social capital that nourishes and drives the vaunted organizational structure that marks American Jewry . . . . While its ritual is a bridge to the divine, it is also a force for cohesion and the language of social values."[8] Most everyone would acknowledge that the membership figures of synagogues are unequaled by any other Jewish institution, and thus the sheer human traffic making its way through congregations, in addition to their special capacity to mobilize Jews, make them unique. And yet, as Dr. David Gordis, president of Boston Hebrew College, observed, "the very focus on synagogue transformation suggests a degree of ambivalence: it stipulates the continuing dependence of the Jewish community on a flourishing synagogue at its center for the continued vitality of Jewish life even as it questions whether the synagogue is capable of playing the required role."[9]

Despite widespread skepticism about the possibility of salvaging the synagogue, a slew of new initiatives have been launched to address the criticism. These, and the dissatisfaction that prompted them, suggest the need for some stocktaking. The pages that follow will consider whether the contemporary synagogue is indeed in crisis, the factors that have contributed to the perception that it needs radical revamping, and the various programs in place to redefine the synagogue for a new generation.

THE POSTWAR SYNAGOGUE

The first step in assessing current plans for the renewal of the American synagogue is to examine the suburban synagogue that emerged after World War II. That institution, after all, is the bête

---

[8]Ismar Schorsch, "The Centrality of the Synagogue," commencement address, Hebrew Union College, New York City, May 9, 2002, www.jtsa.edu/about/communications/speeches/20020513.shtml.

[9]David M. Gordis, "Changing the American Synagogue," *Tikkun* 16, May-June 2001, p. 74.

noire of contemporary critics, who think that much of what is wrong with congregational life today is directly traceable to its missteps and failings.

Growth and Expansion

The saga of the mid-twentieth-century synagogue is frequently told as a story of stunning growth and expansion that yielded only meager religious results. While new synagogues mushroomed across the landscape, the claim is made that Jews "seldom came to them and even more seldom identified with what was going on inside."[10] Contemporaries celebrated "the flourishing state of the American Jewish community's religious bodies," but later observers would declare that "what was revived was not so much religious belief as belief in the value of religion," and that the 1950s revival was "more show than substance."[11] "In sum," wrote one analyst of mid-century American Jewry, "the [synagogue] model for the 1950s was nonreligious religion."[12]

It was, indeed, a time of explosive quantitative growth for the American synagogue. In 1957, the Synagogue Council of America estimated a "grand total of 4,200 congregations," more than double the number 50 years earlier, and about 1,000 more than immediately before World War II. The Reform movement's Union of American Hebrew Congregations (UAHC, predecessor of the URJ) grew from 290 temples in 1937 to 698 in 1970, and in the same period the Conservative movement's United Synagogue (US) increased from 250 member congregations to 832.[13] During just one two-year period of the 1950s, 131 new congregations joined the US and 50 affiliated with the UAHC.[14]

This frenetic growth was fueled primarily by Jewish geographic mobility. Like their fellow Americans, Jews were on the move in

---

[10]Samuel C. Heilman, *Portrait of American Jews: The Last Half of the 20th Century* (Seattle, 1995), p. 31.

[11]Jonathan Sarna, *American Judaism: A History* (New Haven, 2004), p. 277.

[12]Hoffman, "From Common Cold to Common Healing," p. 10.

[13]Arthur Hertzberg, "Communal Affairs," *American Jewish Year Book 1958* (New York, 1958), p. 114; Nathan Glazer, *American Judaism* (Chicago, 1957), p. 12; Wolfe Kelman, "The Synagogue in America," in David Sidorsky, ed., *The Future of the Jewish Community in America* (New York, 1973), p. 157.

[14]Jack Wertheimer, "Recent Trends in American Judaism," *American Jewish Year Book 1989* (New York, 1989), p. 65.

the postwar era. Huge numbers abandoned urban neighborhoods, moving from the Bronx and Brooklyn in New York City to Queens and then Long Island or Westchester, from Newark to the Oranges in New Jersey, from Baltimore to the near suburb of Pikesville, from urban Roxbury in Boston to suburban Chestnut Hill and Newton, from Philadelphia and Chicago to their greener suburbs.[15] And growing numbers made their way to warmer regions of the country, settling in the beckoning "golden cities" of Los Angeles and Miami.[16]

In these new settings, the children and grandchildren of East European immigrants found themselves in an unfamiliar environment. No longer anchored in the Jewish, largely immigrant neighborhoods that had nurtured them, they eagerly sought a new central address for Jewish activities on the lonely suburban frontier. As one prototypical synagogue brochure of the time put it: "The community needs a place for our children and we adults need some place to carry on our social lives. What better place can there be than our synagogue?"[17]

Here in a nutshell were the dual expectations set by suburban Jews for their postwar synagogues. First, they sought a place near home for social interaction with fellow Jews because, as one new suburbanite put it, "My real close friends, my after-dark friends, are mostly Jewish; my daytime friends are Gentile."[18] Second, they needed a facility to socialize and educate their children as Jews. The following excerpt from a contemporary synagogue fund-raising brochure sought to capitalize on this need:

Are not all our dreams and hopes centered around our children? . . . Do not wait until the moment when they will come home to us say-

---

[15]Some particularly evocative accounts of how this transplantation process affected synagogue life are Morris Freedman, "New Jewish Community in Formation: A Conservative Center Catering to Present-Day Needs," *Commentary* 19, Jan. 1955, pp. 36–47; Lucy Dawidowicz, "Middle-Class Judaism: A Case Study," ibid. 29, June 1960, pp. 492–503; and Paula E. Hyman, "From City to Suburb: Temple Mishkan Tefila in Boston," in Jack Wertheimer, ed., *The American Synagogue: A Sanctuary Transformed* (New York, 1988), pp. 185–205.

[16]Deborah Dash Moore, *To the Golden Cities: Pursuing the American Jewish Dream in Miami and L.A.* (New York, 1994).

[17]Albert I. Gordon, *Jews in Suburbia* (Boston, 1959), p. 98.

[18]Quoted in Herbert J. Gans, "Park Forest: Birth of a Jewish Community," in Elliot E. Cohen, ed., *Commentary on the American Scene: Portraits of Jewish Life in America* (New York, 1953), p. 217.

ing: It is your fault that I did not make the right friends. It is your fault that I have to spend time in places that you don't like. It is your fault that my adolescent years were guided by the wrong people. It is your fault that my love and loyalty can be shaken by the slightest wind. Let's not wait for this moment—too much is at stake. Join in a sincere effort to build a Community Center where our children will meet the right friends in dignity, be guided by the right leaders and grow up to be good Americans and Jews.[19]

One would hardly know from this that religion was to play any role in such an institution, let alone that what was being promoted was a synagogue.

The priorities clearly lay elsewhere. As Lawrence Hoffman has noted astutely, the synagogues' "floor plans tell the tale." Suburban congregations typically built "huge school wings, but small sanctuaries."[20] Moveable partitions enabled congregations to carve out meeting-room spaces and classrooms. Their primary users were children enrolled in religious school programs prior to bar and bat mitzvah.[21] In contrast to the early decades of the twentieth century, when Jewish schooling was often housed in communal institutions or separate educational settings, the synagogue now assumed predominant responsibility for Jewish education. In the late 1950s, it was estimated that the congregational school accounted for almost four-fifths of all students receiving a Jewish education.[22] These supplementary schools began to absorb an increasingly high percentage of synagogue budgets, a necessary investment in light of the new reality of congregational membership: most people who joined synagogues did so in order to secure a Jewish education for their children.[23] In one suburban community studied in-

---

[19]Quoted in Gordon, *Jews in Suburbia,* pp. 105–06.

[20]Hoffman, "From Common Cold to Common Healing," p. 10.

[21]A growing literature traces the evolution of the bat mitzvah, an American innovation that has caught on elsewhere as well, especially in Israel. See Paula E. Hyman, "The Introduction of the Bat Mitzvah in Conservative Judaism in Postwar America," *YIVO Annual* 19 (1990), pp. 133–46, and "Bat Mitzvah," in Paula E. Hyman and Deborah Dash Moore, *Jewish Women in America* (New York, 1998), vol. 1, pp. 126–28; Jenna Weissman Joselit's discussion of "Red-Letter Days" in *The Wonders of America: Reinventing Jewish Culture, 1880–1950* (New York, 1994), pp. 89–133; Regina Stein, "The Road to Bat Mitzvah in America," in Pamela Nadell and Jonathan Sarna, eds., *Women and American Judaism* (Hanover, N.H., 2001), pp. 223–34; and Ora Wiskind Elper, ed., *Traditions and Celebrations for the Bat Mitzvah* (Jerusalem, 2003).

[22]Hertzberg, "Communal Affairs," p. 114.

[23]On these developments see Jack Wertheimer, "Jewish Education in the United States: Recent Trends and Issues," *American Jewish Year Book 1999* (New York, 1999), pp. 10–16.

tensively during this period by Marshall Sklare, "most Jews wait[ed] until their children reach[ed] school age" before joining a synagogue. Whereas "a mere 19 percent of families in which all the children are under school age belong to a synagogue," Sklare reported, "the affiliation rate triples to 56 percent in the early-school phase and spurts to 87 percent when there is a child in the peak years of religious education."[24] Congregations had clearly assumed a pediatric mission.

Simultaneously, synagogues also sought to involve adults in a range of activities. Men virtually monopolized synagogue governance in this period, particularly the realms of financial decision-making and board leadership. Women tended to be involved as volunteers in "helping" the male decision-makers and as the overwhelming majority of participants in educational programs.[25] "Synagogues, like churches," Hoffman observes, developed "a shopping list of programs for suburbanites avoiding loneliness or seeking social services like welcome wagons and book clubs. Religious schools for the children and sisterhoods for the mothers soon dominated the landscape."[26]

Surging enrollments in congregational schools and active social programming produced spectacular increases in synagogue membership. Although hard numbers are difficult to come by, it was estimated in the late 1950s that some 60 percent of American Jews affiliated with a synagogue and that another 20 percent turned to the synagogue for specific "sacramental events in life." This suggested that "the synagogue was a matter of real concern to perhaps 4,000,000 American Jews."[27] The laments of overextended rabbis

---

[24]Marshall Sklare and Joseph Greenblum, *Jewish Identity on the Suburban Frontier: A Study of Group Survival in the Open Society* (Chicago, 1967; 2nd edition, 1979), p. 181.

[25]Albert Gordon concluded that "the women of suburbia are the enthusiastic 'students' in both day and evening classes," but that they "complain that they cannot get their husbands to attend formal classes." Gordon, *Jews in Suburbia*, pp. 124–25.

[26]Hoffman, "From Common Cold to Common Healing," p. 10.

[27]Hertzberg, "Communal Affairs," p. 115. To be sure, there were disparities between communities. In the Midwestern suburban community they named Lakeville, Sklare and Greenblum (*Jewish Identity on the Suburban Frontier*, p. 97) found that 83 percent were "past or present members" of synagogues, a figure that rose to 93 percent when families with children over age 18 were counted. Albert Gordon (*Jews in Suburbia*, pp. 248–49) surveyed some 78 local communities and correlated overall Jewish population estimates with membership figures supplied by synagogues, and his tables showed wide fluctuations. In Burbank and Whittier, California, for example, less than 35 percent affiliated, whereas in Swampscott, Massachusetts, 86 percent of Jews were synagogue members.

further confirmed that synagogue membership was booming. As one rabbi ruefully observed of his once "small congregation," "I reckoned without due consideration to the likelihood that my quiet suburban community would grow and grow and grow. It has reached such proportions that I can hardly serve all my congregants adequately.... The congregation has grown too large—and there seems nothing that I can do about it."[28]

Even if the 60-percent affiliation figure is inflated, synagogue membership in the postwar era certainly dwarfed rates prevalent earlier in the century. A 1919 estimate suggested that less than a quarter of Jewish families were members of congregations, and the 1926 *Census of Religious Bodies* counted only one synagogue per 1,309 Jews. Affiliation was undoubtedly even lower during the Great Depression, when membership in all American religious congregations declined; according to historian Jonathan Sarna, "synagogues and Jewish educational institutions suffered particularly from the economic downturn."[29] Thus, membership in synagogues during the postwar era represented a high-water mark compared to previous decades—and, as we shall see, compared to subsequent ones as well.

Attendance at religious services, by contrast, did not keep pace with membership growth. A survey conducted by the National Opinion Research Center (NORC) in 1945 found that only 24 percent of Jews claimed to attend religious services at least once a month, compared to 81 percent of Catholics and 62 percent of Protestants; and a mere 9 percent of Jews claimed to attend at least once a week.[30] According to a Gallup survey conducted a decade later, the figure for Jewish once-a-week synagogue attendance rose to 18 percent, as compared to 74 percent for Catholics and 40 percent for Protestants, but research in local communities suggested that the Jewish figure was inflated.[31] By 1970, the National Jewish Population Survey determined that only 8 percent of Jewish house-

[28]Gordon, *Jews in Suburbia,* pp. 95–96. This rabbi's honest self-appraisal stands in marked contrast to the mythologizing in which many of his colleagues engaged, when they aimed to convince themselves and their congregants that their exceptional talents largely accounted for congregational growth.
[29]Sarna, *American Judaism,* pp. 356–57.
[30]Marshall Sklare, "The Ethnic Church and the Desire for Survival," in Peter I. Rose, ed., *The Ghetto and Beyond: Essays on Jewish Life in America* (New York, 1969), p. 110.
[31]Hertzberg, "Communal Affairs," p. 118.

hold heads attended religious services 50 times a year or more, whereas 55 percent attended fewer than four times a year.[32]

It was precisely the disparity between climbing membership figures and sparse attendance at worship services that evoked such scornful criticism of the mid-century synagogue even during its period of explosive growth. Mordecai Kaplan, for one, pronounced "Jewish spiritual life in this country [as] only skin deep. Jewish life is social rather than spiritual . . . . One half of Jewish identity is the product of Gentile exclusiveness and the other half is the product of Jewish association."[33]

An Evolving Institution

In the view of contemporaries, the sterility of the services repelled religiously sensitive people. "The modern temple suffers from a severe cold," observed Rabbi Abraham Joshua Heschel, "the services are prim, the voice is dry, the temple is clean and tidy . . . no one will cry, the words are stillborn." Rabbi Harold Schulweis understood these remarks to be "directed against the metallic services, against the lugubrious tones of the ritual master of ceremonies intoning the siddur pagination."[34] "Uniformity came to characterize American decorum," writes anthropologist Riv-Ellen Prell. "Reform Jews, and the most acculturated and suburbanized Conservative Jews . . . thought decorum should govern how people prayed and who legislated the tone, volume, and pace of prayer. These more acculturated communities encompassed all of religious life into an aesthetic of uniformity and order."[35]

Indeed, to one extent or another, synagogues across the denominational spectrum—with the exception of the Hasidic and ultra-Orthodox sectors of the Orthodox community—insisted upon decorous services and formality. This entailed the maintenance of

---

[32]Fred Masarik and Alvin Chenkin, *Jewish Identity: Facts for Planning* (New York, 1974), p. 4. Women, in all likelihood, attended at a higher rate, but they generally would not have been counted as "household heads."
[33]Jacob Neusner, "Religion," *American Jewish Year Book 1960* (New York, 1960), p. 57.
[34]Harold W. Schulweis, "Restructuring the Synagogue," *Conservative Judaism* 27, Summer 1973, p. 13.
[35]Riv-Ellen Prell, *Prayer and Community: The Havurah in American Judaism* (Detroit, 1989), p. 62.

social and spatial distance between the rabbis, cantors, and other synagogue officiants, on the one hand, and the average member, on the other. Rabbis were expected to deliver formal sermons on the Sabbath and holidays. Formal attire was de rigueur: synagogue functionaries in most Conservative and Reform congregations wore black robes, and a few Modern Orthodox synagogues required top hats or cutaways. A corps of ushers supervised the proceedings to insure that all ran smoothly. Women, as noted above, though active in a voluntary capacity, rarely officiated or even appeared on the pulpit.

Still, there were important denominational variations. Reform congregations were typified by what Lawrence Hoffman has called a "common aesthetic." Services were primarily in English; all prayer was recited in unison, so that congregants did not serve as prayer leaders; and prayer was read rather than sung or chanted — singing was the preserve of the (mainly Gentile) choir, and few temples even employed a cantor.[36] The ideal Reform religious service included "an inspirational sermon, organ music, and [a] choir"; these "contributed to . . . the esthetic beauty, and a certain grandeur that marked the service."[37] Friday night services were the weekly centerpiece of the worship experience, but only a small minority of members attended even that with any regularity.

Conservative synagogues, in contrast, generally employed a cantor and included congregational singing; prayers were primarily in Hebrew, albeit with some selections read in English. Late Friday evening services were primary for Conservative Jews.

This service was scheduled at an untraditional hour, after dinner on Friday evening, rather than at dusk. This was meant to facilitate attendance by a generation that could neither hope to take off early from work on Friday nor to stay home on Saturday. The service was directed to the broad membership, not just those who equated prayer with "davening." The rabbi gave a formal sermon, rather than a d'var torah, applying Jewish insights to political, social or cultural issues of the day. The service, lasting about an hour, featured a com-

---

[36]Interviews with Rabbis Herman Schaalmann (June 23, 2003) and Lawrence Hoffman (June 11, 2003). For an ethnographic portrait of such a congregation as late as the 1970s, see Frida Kerner Furman, *Beyond Yiddishkeit: The Struggle for a Jewish Identity in a Reform Synagogue* (Albany, 1987).

[37]Jeffrey A. Summit, *The Lord's Song in a Strange Land: Music and Identity in Contemporary Jewish Worship* (New York, 2000), p. 63.

bination of cantorial settings and English unison or responsive readings.[38]

Some Conservative synagogues incorporated organ or piano music into this service, and used it on other occasions, too. Generally, however, services not held on Friday night hewed closely to the traditional Hebrew liturgy. Only gradually in this period was the annual Torah cycle replaced in some synagogues with the shorter triennial portions—the entire Torah being read over the course of three years instead of one. Otherwise, innovation was confined to English translations and newly composed English meditations added to the services. Many congregations continued to employ Orthodox prayer books and Torah commentaries (as well as rabbis with Orthodox training).

Orthodox services were, of course, more traditional, retaining Hebrew and the received *nusach*—the words and melody of prayer as handed down from earlier generations. But in the Modern Orthodox sector, which was dominant at the time, rabbis, like their non-Orthodox counterparts, delivered formal sermons, synagogues made an effort to enforce decorum, and it was not unusual for some prayers to be read in English. In the immediate postwar era such synagogues serviced a significant population of nonobservant members who attended irregularly. Especially outside the New York area, many Modern Orthodox and so-called Traditional synagogues provided for mixed seating of men and women, turned a blind eye to the reality that congregants drove to synagogue on the Sabbath, and followed the example of the Conservative movement by scheduling late Friday evening services.[39] To be sure, a recently arrived wave of Holocaust-era refugees—some Hasidic, others what would become known as *haredi* or "yeshivish"—established

---

[38]Michael Panitz, "Completing a Century: The Rabbinical Assembly since 1970," in Robert E. Fierstien, ed., *A Century of Commitment: One Hundred Years of the Rabbinical Assembly* (New York, 2000), pp. 124–25.

[39]Lawrence H. Schiffman, "When Women and Men Sat Together in American Orthodox Synagogues," *Moment* 14, Dec. 1989, pp. 40 ff. On the existence of Orthodox congregations in this period with many nonobservant members see Jeffrey S. Gurock, *From Fluidity to Rigidity: The Religious Worlds of Conservative and Orthodox Jews in Twentieth Century America,* David W. Belin Lecture in American Jewish Affairs no. 7 (Ann Arbor, 1998), pp. 27–37; and also Charles S. Liebman's contemporaneous account of what he called "residual" and "nonobservant" Orthodox Jews, "Orthodoxy in American Jewish Life," *American Jewish Year Book 1965* (New York, 1965), pp. 30–38.

a range of new synagogues striving to transplant European ways of prayer on American soil, but this was a marginal phenomenon at the time.

Yet despite the considerable evidence that the postwar synagogue was formal and decorous, it is inaccurate to portray it as static and unchanging. Contemporary observers, in fact, were struck by the *experimental* quality of what was unfolding around them. For one thing, a very high percentage of Jews joining congregations were doing so for the first time. Writing of the "new suburbanites" of the 1950s, Harry Gersh marveled at the novelty of the situation: while "the average metropolitan Jew is not a synagogue member . . . move this average Jew to Suburbia and the chances are he'll join up." One rabbi told Gersh that "most of my new congregation are new to synagogue experience. In the city it takes an effort to become a member. You have to make a decision, go find a synagogue, walk in, and join. Usually, no one helps you, even at the last stage. So it's easier not to join. But out here it's the path of least resistance to join." Gersh conceded that in all the joining "there is little mention of those who come to the synagogue because this is the place where Torah lives. But they are the minority in Suburbia, as they are everywhere."[40] Even so, these first-time synagogue members were engaged in a novel experiment in which synagogue participation played a central role.

This emerging new form of Jewish life was rich with possibilities. In his study of suburban Judaism, Rabbi Albert Gordon noted a remarkable transformation taking place before his eyes. He quoted the president of the Levittown Jewish Center expressing amazement at the growth of his congregation: "Do you realize that 90 percent of these people haven't been in a synagogue since they were bar mitzvah? And look at them now, working like beavers. I guess it's just that there's a lot we don't know, and we want to know — we're hungry for Jewish learning and Jewish life."[41] This hunger prompted a range of experimental and imaginative programs to teach Judaism to families and young people lacking Judaic knowledge.

Writing about a congregation founded in the postwar years, Morris Freedman captured the spirit of innovation:

---

[40]Harry Gersh, "The New Suburbanites of the 50's: Jewish Division," *Commentary* 17, Mar. 1954, pp. 218, 219, 221.

[41]Gordon, *Jews in Suburbia*, p. 101.

Almost the chief impression I carried away with me was its air of improvisation and its great fluidity. Educational and youth directors seem to come and go; organization and content of class and group work do not always conform to the spit-and-polish standards the national organizations are trying to set. But perhaps this is just what the . . . public is buying right now—grandeur in the externals, undemanding informality and trial and error in substance . . . . It is clear . . . that the patterns for the future have by no means been fixed; and that what will finally emerge may show only the thinnest connection with what we see today. At any rate, a close and sober look now may offer an opportunity for those deeply concerned to help shape those patterns before the mold hardens.[42]

This contemporaneous description of how new congregations improvised hardly conforms to the stereotype of the complacent suburban synagogue any more than does the claim of the Levittown Jewish Center's president that people were eager to learn.

From a comparative perspective, historian James Hudnut-Beumler captures the spirit that animated American houses of worship at the time, synagogues and churches alike, their membership consisting predominantly of young families:

Suburbanization resulted in homogeneous communities that, far from being the sterile wastelands their worst critics feared, became the locus of incredible vitality . . . . These were times and places when and where everything was possible; veritable utopias in which death, cancer, and poverty appeared to have been banished. A typical suburban church or synagogue could go years without a funeral or memorial service. On the other hand, the joyful, life-affirming rituals of baptism, first communion, confirmation, bar mitzvah and now bas mitzvah, were frequently celebrated in the local houses of worship. Moreover . . . the prospects for the future were bright: ecclesiastical budgets were ever on the rise, never in descent or tied to the declining incomes of aging and retiring members; building programs were underway (the family proud of their new split-level home would soon be attending a church equally new and worthy of pride); and the typical suburban church or synagogue had exactly what most prospective members were looking for in a religious home—people exactly like themselves.[43]

True, as Hudnut-Beumler observes, there was an insular, naive, and perhaps even self-satisfied quality to these congregations,

---

[42]Freedman, "New Jewish Community in Formation," p. 47.

[43]James Hudnut-Beumler, *Looking for God in the Suburbs: The Religion of the American Dream and its Critics, 1945–1965* (New Brunswick, N.J., 1984), p. 7.

but that was an understandable consequence of the rapid upward mobility and unexpected success attained by the new suburbanites who had grown up during the hard years of the Great
Depression.

To be sure, no sooner had the baby-boomer children raised in
these suburban congregations come of age than they subjected
their synagogues to severe criticism, bemoaning their cold and im-
personal atmosphere; their rigid division between performing functionaries and passive membership audience; their failure to enact
equality for women; and their oligarchic structure of governance.
Emerging in the late 1960s and early 1970s, this critique was part
of a much broader youthful onslaught against all American es-
tablishments.

What is truly remarkable in the Jewish community is how rapidly
congregations responded to the criticism. Take, for example, the
question of women's participation. A national study of congregational practices carried out in 1978 found that almost all Reform
congregations permitted women to give sermons, lead services,
and be called up to the Torah. Almost half of the Conservative synagogues counted women for a minyan and allowed them to lead
services, while more than three-quarters of them had women delivering sermons. Most Reform congregations and two-thirds of
Conservative ones called upon women to open the ark and chant
kiddush and havdalah. In the Orthodox world, women had only
made inroads in sermon-making (7 percent of synagogues) and
chanting kiddush and havdalah (2 percent).[44]

Congregations also innovated in other areas in the late 1960s and
1970s. Encompassing the feminist critique but going beyond it was
the *havurah* movement, the expression of a new generation that insisted not only on more involvement of women but also on a dramatic change in the aesthetics and decorum of prayer: greater lay
participation and engagement, less hierarchy and formality, and
the active presence of children.[45] In response to the creation of

---

[44]These data are reported in Sylvia Barack Fishman, *A Breath of Life: Feminism in the
American Jewish Community* (New York, 1993), p. 153.

[45]This is the overarching theme of Prell, *Prayer and Community*. On the trajectory of
American congregations more generally in the 1950–90 period, see E. Brooks Holifield,
"Toward a History of American Congregations," in James P. Wind and James W. Lewis,
eds., *American Congregations: New Perspectives in the Study of Congregations* (Chicago,
1994), vol. II, pp. 43–47.

fledgling independent *havurot* at the grassroots level, many synagogues established their own *havurot* to provide settings for more
intimate religious experience.[46] And even in congregations that
maintained the old structure, rabbis and cantors experimented
with less formal ways of carrying out their roles. Many Reform and
Conservative congregations, for example, replaced the Ashkenazi
pronunciation of Hebrew, associated with the old formal way of
doing things, with an Israeli-style Sephardi accent, creating an
ambience that evoked the Zionist renewal of Jewish culture.

Contrary to the common assumption, then, synagogue life in the
second half of the twentieth century was not impervious to change.
It was, in fact, in a constant state of remaking.

THE SYNAGOGUE TODAY

By the end of the twentieth century, a new synagogue aesthetic
had emerged that crossed denominational boundaries even as the
contents of the service and nature of the liturgy continued to vary.
Before looking at the situation more closely, a review of basic data
about the world of the American synagogue today is in order.

The Demography of Synagogue Life

According to a recent report in the *American Jewish Year Book,*
there were 3,727 synagogues in the United States in 2001, 40
percent of them Orthodox, 26 percent Reform, 23 percent Conservative, and the rest falling into far smaller groupings: Reconstructionist (3 percent); Sephardi (3 percent); Traditional (1 per-
cent); Humanistic (1 percent); Gay/Lesbian (0.5 percent); and
Jewish Renewal (0.4 percent).[47] This breakdown is not necessarily
indicative of each movement's actual membership base: the percentage of Orthodox Jews is far smaller than that of their houses
of worship, since Orthodox synagogues are generally smaller and
have far fewer congregants than those affiliated with the other
major denominations.

---

[46]Harold Schulweis, "Restructuring the Synagogue," especially p. 19.
[47]Jim Schwartz, Jeffrey Scheckner, and Laurence Kotler-Berkowitz, "Census of U.S. Synagogues, 2001," *American Jewish Year Book 2002* (New York, 2002), p. 117.

Jewish congregations are spread unevenly across the United States. They are most densely concentrated in middle-sized communities of the Northeast and Midwest, where Jewish settlement has been continuous for a long time and the population has remained stable. Synagogues are sparsest in the Sunbelt and other communities where recent transplants have settled, and where the broader local culture does not encourage joining. As demographer Ira Sheskin has explained, migrating American Jews quite often "break their institutional ties with the community in which they were raised and . . . [fail] to re-establish ties in their new community."[48]

Synagogue membership varies considerably by region. The National Jewish Population Survey (NJPS) of 2000–01 found an overall adult membership rate of 46 percent, with Jews in the Midwest (53 percent) and Northeast (50 percent) having the higher rates of affiliation, and Jews in the South (44 percent) and West (36 percent) claiming lower rates. These differences match similar regional variations in overall patterns of Jewish connectedness. Jews in the Midwest tend to engage in Jewish civic life — giving to federations, joining Jewish organizations, volunteering for Jewish agencies, and participating in adult Jewish education — at higher rates than Jews in other parts of the country; Jews in the West report the lowest levels of Jewish engagement. The *household* rate of affiliation was only 40 percent overall, with a high of 47 percent of Midwestern Jewish households and a low of 30 percent of Western households.[49]

Since roughly half the Jews of the United States live in the three largest metropolitan areas — Greater New York, Greater Los Angeles, and the southeastern coast of Florida — the differing congregational membership patterns in these communities underline the gap between the Northeast and the Sunbelt. In the New York area, 43 percent of Jewish households are synagogue-affiliated; in Greater Los Angeles the figure stands at 34 percent; and in

---

[48]Ibid, pp. 118–25; Ira M. Sheskin, "Jewish Demographics on the Local Level," *Contact* 5, Spring 2003, pp. 5–6.

[49]*The National Jewish Population Survey 2000–01: Strength, Challenge and Diversity in the American Jewish Population* (New York, 2003), pp. 7–8. It must be emphasized that these figures cover only the estimated 4.3 million Jews who are most Jewishly engaged, leaving out another million or so less engaged Jews, and thus inflating the overall percentages.

the southeastern counties of Florida, all the individual communities have synagogue affiliation rates that fall within a 27-to-37-percent range.[50]

Synagogue members tend to share certain social characteristics. An analysis of the 1990 NJPS found that baby-boomers were, on average, less likely than their elders, who were born before World War II, to attend synagogue once a month or more (23.6 percent versus 27.9 percent). But the reverse was true for the Orthodox. Close to half of Orthodox baby-boomers claimed to attend services a few times a week, a figure three times greater than Orthodox Jews born before the war.[51] Almost half of all married couples in the "core" Jewish population that had children belonged to a synagogue, as compared with only a quarter of couples with no children. At the other end of the spectrum, "single-parent families with or without other adults present in the household proved to have the lowest rate of synagogue affiliation, only about one in three." A family's synagogue affiliation was shown to be linked especially to the presence of children in the pre-bar/bat mitzvah years. Sixty-two percent of "core" Jewish households with children in the 10–14 age cohort were members, as compared to just 39 percent of households with children aged 0–4. The NJPS data also substantiated the important connection between Jewish education and synagogue membership, as 90 percent of families that included children enrolled in some form of Jewish education joined a synagogue.[52] Jews of a higher socioeconomic status were more likely than others to affiliate with synagogues, and this was especially the case for Conservative and Reform Jews. Similarly, levels of general

---

[50]*The Jewish Community Study of New York 2002: Highlights* (New York, 2003), p. 45; Sheskin, "Jewish Demographics," p. 6. In Florida, Dade County reported a 37-percent affiliation rate; Broward County, 27 percent; and South Palm Beach, 36 percent.

[51]Chaim I. Waxman, *Jewish Baby Boomers: A Communal Perspective* (Albany, 2001), pp. 89–91. Reconstructionist respondents to the 1990 NJPS also claimed a very high rate of frequent synagogue attendance, close to two-thirds reporting attendance once a month or more. Impressionistic evidence of a sharp decline in the number of men who actually attend Reform temples raises the question of whether the self-reporting of individuals accurately gauges attendance. Rabbi Jeffrey K. Salkin, for example, has written of the "great, unspoken crisis facing modern Judaism . . . the disengagement of men in large numbers. . . . Men are increasingly distancing themselves from congregations—as worshipers, as students of Torah, as trustees." Salkin, "Jewish Macho," *Reform Judaism* 26, Spring 1998, pp. 28–29.

[52]Ariela Keysar, Barry A. Kosmin, and Jeffrey Scheckner, *The Next Generation: Jewish Children and Adolescents* (Albany, 2000), pp. 42–45.

educational attainment were higher among synagogue-affiliated Jews than among nonmembers.[53]

Initial findings of the 2000–01 NJPS suggest a significant shift underway in the fortunes of the various denominations, and the prospect of even greater change in the decades to come. Adherents of Reform now constitute the plurality of synagogue members (39 percent of affiliated households), supplanting membership in Conservative synagogues (now 33 percent of affiliated households).[54] But Reform's position as the largest synagogue movement will probably be short-lived, as high fertility rates in the Orthodox community are likely to catapult Orthodox Judaism into the lead. Today, 21 percent of households affiliated with a synagogue are Orthodox, but their children represent 40 percent of youngsters in synagogue-affiliated families, as compared to 27 percent in affiliated Conservative households and 33 percent in Reform households. If Orthodoxy can retain the allegiance of its younger generation, the Orthodox synagogue will replace the Reform temple as the congregation of choice for the plurality of synagogue members in the near future.[55]

Membership does not necessarily translate into attendance, and it has long been acknowledged that the large majority of synagogue members attend infrequently. According to the 2000–01 NJPS, 27 percent of Jews claimed to attend a Jewish religious service at least monthly. The same regional variation seen in synagogue membership applies to attendance, with 30 percent of Jews in the Northeast saying they attend at least once a month as compared to 22 percent in the West.[56] Nationally, the denominational differences are stark, with the Orthodox far ahead: 58 percent of synagogue-affiliated Orthodox adults claim to attend religious services *at least once a week,* compared with 37 percent of Conservative synagogue

---

[53]Bernard Lazerwitz, "Denominations and Synagogue Membership: 1971 and 1990," in David M. Gordis and Dorit P. Gary, eds., *American Jewry: Portrait and Prognosis* (West Orange, N.J., 1997), pp. 199–219.

[54]"National Jewish Population Survey 2000–01: Conservative Jews," Feb. 2004 posting on the United Jewish Communities Web site, www.ujc.org.

[55]These data are from an unpublished paper by Steven M. Cohen, "The Changing Contours of Conservative Jewry and Other Major American Jewish Denominations: Evidence from the National Jewish Population Studies, 1990 and 2000," pp. 6–7. I thank the author for sharing a draft of his work with me.

[56]*National Jewish Population Survey 2000–01,* pp. 7–9.

members and 24 percent of Reform members who claim to attend *at least monthly.*[57]

As is the case with synagogue membership, more Jews in the 35–54 age bracket claim to attend monthly (32 percent) than Jews aged 55–64 (25 percent), probably because the former are more likely to have pre-bar/bat mitzvah children at home. This difference holds for Conservative and Reform Jews, but not for the Orthodox, among whom there is virtually no difference in attendance rates between members below age 55 and those above it. Clearly, the great majority of Orthodox Jews decide whether to attend services on grounds other than the ages of their children.[58]

Frequency of synagogue attendance has been found to correlate with the contribution of time and money to Jewish institutions and causes beyond the congregation itself, as well as to participation in broader civic matters. A team of scholars at Brandeis University concluded:

> In the case of Jews, religious involvement seems to lead both to involvement in Jewish organizations and to participation in other general organizations. In other words, the synagogue socializes American Jews into further voluntary participation in other Jewish organizations, which in turn socializes them into participation in general voluntary associations. Synagogue membership and frequency of synagogue attendance have been found to be strong predictors of philanthropic contributions to non-Jewish organizations. Frequency of attendance at synagogue services is one of the strongest predictors of volunteering for Jewish organizations.[59]

As such findings have become public knowledge, federations of Jewish philanthropy and other Jewish bodies have drawn the ob-

---

[57]"National Jewish Population Survey 2000–01: Orthodox Jews" and "National Jewish Population Survey: Conservative Jews," both at www.ujc.org. On Reform Jews I am using unpublished data analyzed by Steven M. Cohen, "Denominational Variations in Jewish Identity Characteristics: Evidence from the National Jewish Population Survey, 2000–01," dated Nov. 20, 2003, table 10. In a survey of Conservative synagogue members in North America (including Canada) conducted in the mid-1990s, 45 percent of respondents claimed to attend religious services at least once a month. See Jack Wertheimer, ed., *Conservative Synagogues and Their Members: Highlights of the North American Survey of 1995–96* (New York, 1996), p. 38.

[58]Cohen, "Denominational Variations," table 11.

[59]Gary A. Tobin and Gabriel Berger, *Synagogue Affiliation: Implications for the 1990s,* Research Report 9, Cohen Center for Modern Jewish Studies, Brandeis University, ed. Sylvia Barack Fishman, Sept. 1993, p. 3. Waxman (*Jewish Baby Boomers,* p. 92) has found this correlation especially true for Jews of the baby-boom generation.

vious conclusion that organized Jewish life is largely sustained by congregational activity, and have been paying greater attention to synagogues.

When examined in the broad framework of American religious life, these Jewish patterns are anomalous in a number of ways. Roughly two-thirds of Americans claim to be members of a house of worship, at least 25 percentage points higher than Jewish synagogue membership. Whereas the highest regional affiliation rates for Americans are found in the South, for Jews they are found in the Northeast, and even Jews in the Midwest affiliate to a greater degree than those in the South (Jews, like other Americans, are least likely to belong to a house of worship if they live in the West). In the general population, Americans join churches in rising percentages as they get older, whereas Jewish rates of synagogue affiliation drop after children have left the house.[60]

The Jewish/non-Jewish difference in membership patterns is also true of attendance at religious services. Surveys of American religious behavior have consistently reported that at least two out of every five adults say they attend church weekly. The high point of church attendance occurred during the 1950s, when 49 percent reported attending on a weekly basis; by the 1990s the figure had fallen to around 40 percent. American Jews, in contrast, have consistently reported far lower rates. According to a Gallup poll conducted in 1998, 46 percent of Catholics, 42 percent of Protestants, and just 27 percent of Jews claimed to have attended a religious service during the previous week. Surveys conducted by the National Opinion Research Center (NORC), which yield lower numbers for all groups, also have Jews at the bottom of the list: 7 percent of Jews claim to attend services weekly, as compared with 27 percent of non-Jewish Americans — 22–26 percent of liberal-to-moderate Protestants, 31 percent of Catholics, and 36 percent of fundamentalist Protestants.[61] As was the case for membership, church attendance in the East lags behind rates in the South, but patterns of synagogue attendance are just the reverse. And while

---

[60]George Gallup, Jr., and D. Michael Lindsay, *Surveying the Religious Landscape: Trends in U.S. Beliefs* (Harrisburg, 1999), p. 12. Self-reported church membership rates fluctuated between 65 and 71 percent from the mid-1960s through the 1990s.

[61]Ibid., p. 15; Tom Smith, *Jewish Distinctiveness in America: A Statistical Portrait* (New York, 2005), p. 9.

church attendance is strongly correlated with age, older Jews, their children grown, are less likely than their middle-aged coreligionists, whose youngsters are still home, to attend services.[62] As for denominational patterns, Orthodox Jews outpace every other American religious group when it comes to reported rates of regular attendance at worship services; the percentage of Conservative Jews who say they attend is roughly comparable to that of liberal Protestants; and Reform Jews score below every other American religious group in their self-reported frequency of attendance.[63]

Why Don't They Join?

The generally low rates of synagogue affiliation and attendance have elicited no small amount of anguished hand-wringing in the American Jewish community, as well as attempts to determine the causes. A standard culprit is the high cost of synagogue membership.[64] Most churches support themselves through voluntary offerings, such as cash donations when the plate is passed, or tithing. Synagogues, however, usually charge fixed membership dues to

---

[62]Gallup, Jr., and Lindsay, *Surveying the Religious Landscape,* p. 12.

[63]Bernard M. Lazerwitz and Ephraim Tabory, "A Religious and Social Profile of Reform Judaism in the United States," in Dana Evan Kaplan, ed., *Contemporary Debates in American Reform Judaism: Conflicting Visions* (New York, 2001), pp. 19–38; J.J. Goldberg, "People and Politics," *New Jersey Jewish News— MetroWest,* Apr. 20, 2000, p. 37. The accuracy of these surveys has been challenged by a small-scale study that compared self-reporting about church attendance with an actual count of the number of Protestants and Catholics attending church one Sunday in two counties in Ohio. The head count found that only half the number of people who claimed to attend weekly actually appeared in church, leading the authors to conclude: "Too much trust in survey data has produced a distorted image of religion in America by masking declines in church participation. Church attendance is less strong and stable than pool data shows." Since figures for synagogue attendance are also based on self-reporting, the question remains why roughly half as many Jews as Christians claim to attend weekly. See C. Kirk Hadaway and Penny L. Marler, "Did You Really Go to Church This Week? Behind the Poll Data," *Christian Century* 115, May 6, 1998, pp. 472–75.

[64]A poll in Los Angeles concluded that synagogue membership is higher among "parents, more affluent and more educated Jews, and more observant Jews." This led the survey researchers to suggest that "cost may be a factor for less affluent Jews." *L. A. Times/Yediot Aharonot* poll, March/April 1998, "LA Times Poll Alert," April 23, 1998 – Study #407/408, p. 3. The case for viewing the entire problem as a matter of "sticker shock" and for throwing billions of dollars at the problem is made by J.J. Goldberg, "Jewish Sticker Shock," *New York Jewish Week,* Feb. 26, 1999, pp. 2–3. A useful overview of the subject is Jeffrey K. Salkin, "The Jews We Don't See: What To Do about the Unaffiliated," *Reform Judaism* 20 (Winter 1991), pp. 4–6, 39–40.

pay for expenses, such as salaries for the rabbi(s), cantor, educators, office and custodial staff, and the costs of electricity, phones, and office equipment. Some congregations also fold the costs of synagogue schooling into the membership dues, rather than charging a separate tuition. Recent surveys indicate that such dues currently range from a few hundred dollars to over $3,000 per family.[65] The dues generally fall short of covering the synagogue's entire budget.[66]

The annual dues are collected in the weeks before the Jewish New Year, as those charges entitle families to have seats for High Holy Day services, when synagogues attract their largest crowds. That is why Jewish newspapers in late summer are invariably filled with articles bemoaning the practice of requiring Jews "to pay to pray." And just as routinely, synagogue officials defend the practice of charging dues as a necessary means for congregations to finance their activities, even as they claim never to turn anyone away who cannot afford the expense. In some cases, congregations do indeed erect monetary barriers that are too high; in other instances, the process of applying for lower membership dues is onerous, or members are unwilling to bare their personal financial data.[67] Often, though, people simply do not regard the synagogue as a service worth paying for. As one rabbi has summarized the attitudes he has encountered: "I have other priorities in my life. My spare money goes to vacations. I'm still Jewish, whether I belong to a synagogue or not."[68]

To address the concerns of those who genuinely cannot afford high dues, a number of congregations have experimented with alternative fee structures. It has become common for synagogues to

---

[65]Julie Wiener, "Redefining the Synagogue: Temple Tries Voluntary Dues to Get Rid of Shul Sticker Shock" Jewish Telegraphic Agency Daily News Reporter, Aug. 15, 2000.

[66]In an interview with the author, Rabbi Daniel Freelander, a professional at the URJ, estimated that 80 percent of the budget of Reform temples is covered by membership dues.

[67]Lani Harac, "Paying To Attend Services—A High Holiday Staple," *Baltimore Jewish Times,* Sept. 14, 2001, www.jewishtimes.com/1666.stm; Ami Eden, "Synagogues: How Much is Too Much? The Cost of Jewish Living," *Philadelphia Jewish Exponent,* Aug. 19, 1999, p. 6. Prof. Ron Wolfson offers a defense of congregations in Eryn Brown, "An Experience Worth the Price of Admission," *Los Angeles Jewish Journal,* Sept. 14, 2003, Web edition. For a report on 15 congregations in the San Francisco Bay area that offer free High Holy Day services see Aleza Goldsmith, "From Vallejo to Nob Hill, Free Holy Day Services Abound," *Jewish Journal of Northern California,* Sept. 9, 2001, www.jewishsf.com/bk010907/1b.shtml.

[68]Salkin, "Jews We Don't See," p. 5.

offer discounts of varying degrees, and even free membership, to young adults, singles, widows, widowers, divorced people, and families headed by a single person. Quite a few congregations have stratified fee structures pegged to the separate needs of over a dozen different subpopulations.[69]

Such variations in dues structures have important implications for the marketing of congregations. One of the factors driving experiments in pricing is the heightened competition between the many congregations, as each seeks to create a "market niche" for itself and to develop "name recognition" in an age when quite a few potential synagogue members "shop around" before joining, just as consumers of other services do.[70]

The Reform movement has devoted the most sustained attention to the fee structure of its congregations. In the late 1980s, over 300 Reform congregations signed on to a "privilege card" program that reduced or eliminated fees for Jews under the age of 30.[71] Others offer a first year of free membership as an inducement—in marketing parlance, a "trial membership." For more established members, a fair number of Reform temples offer a system of dues geared to the ability to pay, the money "collected according to an honor system" so that no one at the temple checks tax forms to ensure that people are honestly reporting their incomes. Some congregations report considerable success in bringing in new members at discount prices who eventually go on to pay full freight when asked, or even before being asked. To be sure, some cheat, like the family that bought a home for $5 million while it was underpaying its synagogue dues.[72]

---

[69]To illustrate the lengths to which synagogues go to accommodate younger Jews, we cite the example of Temple Chai in Phoenix, which introduced a new rate structure in 2000: singles under age 25 were asked to pay $20, and those between 26 and 30, $120, with the amount rising by another $120 each successive year. Young couples had to pay double these sums. "Temple Offers Reduced Rates to Young Adults," *Jewish News of Greater Phoenix,* www.jewishaz.com/jewishnews/970822/rates.shtml.

[70]The commodification of houses of worship is discussed in Donna Gehrke-White, "Selling God—Churches Lure Flock with Madison Avenue Flair," *Miami Herald,* July 22, 2001, p. 1A. A good survey of ad campaigns run by congregations is provided in Walter Ruby, "Get It While It's Hot," *Manhattan Jewish Sentinel,* Oct. 31–Nov. 6, 1997, pp. 8 ff.

[71]Salkin, "Jews We Don't See," p. 6.

[72]Julie Wiener, "Redefining the Synagogue: Reform Movement Most Aggressive in Synagogue Transformation Efforts," Jewish Telegraphic Agency, Aug. 15, 2000, p. 1. See also Mark Jacobson, "How to Make Temple Fees Fair," *Reform Judaism* 22, Spring 1994, p. 53.

One Jewish community whose congregational fees have been systematically studied is Philadelphia. A survey of synagogues there found that Orthodox and Conservative synagogues dealt with the challenge of financing their operations somewhat differently than Reform. The Reform temples followed the system described above, relying on members to assess themselves based on a scale provided by the congregation. In addition, some charged a special fee for those who wanted to purchase High Holy Day seats without joining, while others insisted on additional payment for "those who do *not* come on the High Holidays." Six out of the seven Reform congregations also required members to contribute toward a building fund. The Orthodox synagogues, in contrast, charged a fixed annual amount, between $300 and $650, with no extra fees. Two reasons were offered for this policy: first, the congregations, relatively small and employing few professionals, needed less money,[73] and second, allowance was made for the large tuition costs being shouldered by member families, virtually all of which were sending children to Jewish day schools. Conservative synagogues (and the Reconstructionist ones as well) employed a stratified dues structure based on family and life-cycle status, with single members under 35 charged less, and families with children in the pre-bar/bat mitzvah years charged more. Another factor in calculating fees in the Conservative synagogues was the location of one's reserved seats.[74]

But contrary to the claim that "sticker shock" is at the root of the contemporary synagogue's problems, sheer cost is hardly the only factor. It is not so much that dues are high, but rather, as the late sociologist Egon Mayer put it, "The full sentence is: 'for an institution I'm not using, that's a lot of money to pay.'"[75] Many Jews have gotten used to viewing synagogue membership as a form of insurance, bought just in case they will actually need the services of the congregation for a life-cycle event. As such, it is ex-

---

[73]Quite a few Orthodox pulpit rabbis supplement their income by working outside the congregation, a practice far less common in the other denominations. In Chicago, for example, every single Orthodox rabbi with a pulpit also has other employment. Interview with Rabbi Harvey Well, Associated Talmud Torahs of Chicago, Feb. 3, 2005.

[74]Rela Geffen Monson and Ruth Pinkenson Feldman, "The Cost of Living Jewishly in Philadelphia," *Journal of Jewish Communal Service* 68, Winter 1991–92, pp. 148–59. The dollar figures reflect fees levied during the late 1980s.

[75]Quoted by Salkin, "Jews We Don't See," p. 39.

tremely expensive, and under this calculus it is hardly surprising that fewer Jews join.[76]

When synagogue affiliation was at its peak, in the postwar years, an estimated 60 percent of American Jews belonged to a synagogue at any one point in time.[77] This was, we recall, the period that Jews newly arrived in the suburbs needed the social outlet the synagogue provided. Furthermore, the large baby-boomer generation was approaching bar/bat mitzvah age, and parents needed the services of the congregational supplementary schools. By 2000, however, membership rates had dropped to 46 percent of households. This was largely because Jewish adults now had many social opportunities outside the synagogue, and there were far fewer families with small children. With little perceived need for what the synagogue provided, there was widespread reluctance to spend money on a membership that was rarely used.[78]

Interestingly, despite the fall in levels of affiliation, there is no evidence that attendance by members has dropped. Indeed—if the self-reporting of synagogue members is to be believed—Jews who join synagogues today are attending with greater frequency than before.

According to the National Jewish Population Survey (NJPS) of 1971, 18 percent of Jews claimed to attend services at least once a month.[79] Surveys conducted in Boston and New York in the mid-1960s concluded that 17 percent and 20 percent of Jews, respectively, could be counted as "frequent" synagogue attenders, defined in the Boston study as "more than once a month" and in the New York study as "once a month or more."[80] The 2000–01 NJPS,

---

[76]Sociologists Jackson Carroll and Wade Clark Roof, speaking about Jews, found that "this kind of calculating, consumerist approach to involvement . . . is particularly evident in some of the younger families, Xers and young boomers." Jackson W. Carroll and Wade Clark Roof, *Bridging Divided Worlds: Generational Cultures in Congregations* (San Francisco, 2002), p. 158.

[77]During the late 1950s, almost two-thirds of "Lakeville's" Jews claimed to be synagogue members (Sklare and Greenblum, *Jewish Identity on the Suburban Frontier*, p. 97). Surveys, of course, take a snapshot in time when they ask about current membership; the majority of American Jews do affiliate with a synagogue, at some point in their lives.

[78]In the mid-century years, as noted above, a staggeringly high 87 percent of "Lakeville's" Jews affiliated with a synagogue in the years immediately before a child in the family was reaching bar/bat mitzvah age. Ibid., p. 181.

[79]Ira Sheskin, *How Jewish Communities Differ: Variations in the Findings of Local Jewish Population Studies* (New York, 2001), p. 89.

[80]Marshall Sklare, *America's Jews* (New York, 1971), pp. 118–22. Sklare and Greenblum, *Jewish Identity on the Suburban Frontier*, p. 60, concluded that only 13 percent of Jews in "Lakeville" attended twice a month.

by contrast, indicates that 27 percent of Jews say they attend at least once a month.[81] A separate recent survey of the New York area had 29 percent of respondents claiming to attend at least monthly.[82]

If anything, then, congregations appear to be more successful today at attracting their members to participate in religious services with some frequency. But they are less successful than synagogues during the halcyon years in the mid-twentieth century at recruiting new families to join and at ensuring that affiliated families maintain their membership.[83]

Making Changes

Seeking to heighten their appeal to unaffiliated Jews—and also to attract more of their current members to prayer services—congregations of all stripes have worked hard over the last two decades to improve their programs, and especially to rethink aspects of their religious worship. Every movement within American Judaism has issued newly revised prayer books, Bible commentaries, and, most recently, a plethora of weekly *divrei Torah,* pages discussing the portion of the Pentateuch read in congregations that week, distributed free of charge over the Internet and also available in hard copy at synagogues. Congregations in all of the movements have been reconfiguring the roles of rabbi and cantor, and have experimented with music and dance as central features of the worship service. There is increased emphasis on individual petitionary prayer—for healing, for comfort, to celebrate personal milestones. Congregations set aside more time during regular services for such prayer, and may also conduct specially designated services just for such petitions. The cumulative effect of these changes has broken down much of the formality of the mid-century synagogue, making what goes on more participatory and personalized.

---

[81] *National Jewish Population Survey 2000–01,* p. 7.

[82] Jacob Ukeles and Ron Miller, *Jewish Community Study of New York: 2002* (New York, 2004), p. 125. While the increase of the Orthodox group is certainly a major factor in New York, the more punctilious religious practice of the preexisting Orthodox element and the disappearance of the old "nonobservant Orthodox" category also contribute to the increase in the overall frequency of synagogue attendance.

[83] According to the *Los Angeles Times* poll mentioned above (note 64), some 23 percent of respondents nationally claimed they had dropped their synagogue membership.

REFORM

The transformation has been most dramatically evident in Reform temples. The formal, clergy-dominated religious services they used to provide are now largely a thing of the past, replaced by a far more participatory style of worship. Some of the more ambitious congregations have accomplished this by encouraging every member to "re-imagine" the congregation "literally from the ground up." At Oheb Shalom in Baltimore, for example, a reporter noted that "literally everything is changing"—the use of space, governance structure, dues policies, delivery of services to youth and families, not to mention the style and content of the worship services.[84]

The push for change usually comes on the congregational level, from members or synagogue professionals. The long-time spiritual leader of Oheb Shalom, Rabbi Donald Berlin, launched "Project Joseph"—what he called "a visionary exercise"—in response to complaints from younger members that the "congregation of my parents and my grandparents . . . doesn't speak to me."[85] At Temple Israel in Miami, congregational decline was the motivating factor: the rabbi and cantor felt they had to develop a new approach to worship because membership had dropped so precipitously that there was little to lose in taking a gamble.[86] At Temple Israel in Boston, a new style of worship evolved after its recently hired rabbi, Bernard Mehlman, discovered that his new congregation offered no Friday evening service during the summer; the experimental service he initiated, held in the synagogue atrium, proved immensely popular.[87] Congregation Shir Tikva in Troy, Michigan, started without a rabbi, and the members created a lay-led service. Later, when they got around to hiring a full-time rabbi, he was careful not to do "anything to lessen lay involvement in worship."[88] In the last quarter of the twentieth century it became common for Reform temples to

[84]Adam Stone, "Redefining Oheb," *Baltimore Jewish Times*, May 11, 2001, www.jewish times.com/1444.stm.

[85]Ibid.

[86]Interview with Rabbi Mitchell Chefitz, cantorial soloist Karina Zilberman, congregational president Jane Kahn Jacobs, and Robert Glazier, an officer, at Temple Israel, Miami, March 4, 2005.

[87]Summit, *The Lord's Song in a Strange Land,* pp. 54–58.

[88]Janet R. Marder, "Worship that Works," *Reform Judaism* 25, Spring 1997, pp. 18–19.

compile their own prayer books to fit congregational needs, using the new technology of desktop publishing to usher in an "era of . . . customizing and greater localism."[89]

Given the longstanding tradition of congregationalism in American religion, it is hardly surprising that Reform worship has remade itself through the initiatives of individual synagogues. Somewhat more surprising is the extent to which the movement's national leadership—the UAHC and then the URJ—has pushed for such changes, so that the pressure for innovation came not only from the bottom up, but also from the top down. The process began under the UAHC presidency of Rabbi Alexander Schindler in the 1980s, when the issue was pressing congregations to hire cantors who would introduce congregational singing. The current president of the URJ, Rabbi Eric Yoffie, escalated the rhetoric to urge nothing less than "a new Reform revolution" in worship.[90] He has prodded congregations to innovate, and chastised those that let themselves get mired in turf battles:

> We Reform Jews are, on the whole, quite conservative in our worship patterns. We say we want prayer that is authentically Reform, but this usually means "what I remember from *my* temple when I was growing up." And no two of us ever seem to remember the same thing. Generational differences are particularly pronounced. Our congregations, therefore, often confront a multiplicity of conflicting worship demands. Older members threaten to vote with their checkbooks if worship is changed, while younger members threaten to vote with their feet if it is not.[91]

Moreover, the URJ uses its biennial conventions to model a variety of different styles of worship service, in the hope that participants will take those ideas back to their home congregations.[92]

One innovation that has caught on among many congregations is the reconfiguration of the synagogue building to create a more intimate ambience. The changes were already beginning in the 1970s and 1980s, when newly constructed temples were "built with

---

[89]Peter S. Knobel, "The Challenge of a Single Prayer Book for the Reform Movement," in Dana Evan Kaplan, ed., *Platforms and Prayer Books: Theological and Liturgical Perspectives in Reform Judaism* (Lanham, Md., 2002), especially pp. 185–89.

[90]Quoted in Debra Nussbaum, "This Year, No Christmas Wreaths; UAHC Biennial a Time for Quiet Reflection," *Intermountain Jewish News,* Dec. 24, 1999, p. 9.

[91]Eric H. Yoffie, "The Worship Revolution," pp. 24–25.

[92]For a good overview of the changes see Dana Evan Kaplan, *American Reform Judaism: An Introduction,* (New Brunswick, N.J., 2003), pp. 79 ff.

[weekly] Shabbat worship in mind" rather than, as was the case before, with an eye only to the two High Holy Days. The new setup often allowed rabbis to sit or stand in the center of a circle rather than occupy a platform situated away from, and on a higher plane than, the rest of the congregation.[93] Daniel Freelander describes the new type of Reform temple:

> To encourage congregational participation and make the worship leaders more accessible, the bimah is built low and open, and seats are often arranged in a "U" or semicircle so worshipers can see one another. Sound systems are rarely necessary, as discussions and Torah dialogues have often replaced formal sermons. Organs and choir spaces rarely exist; members prefer a cappella singing or the use of electronic keyboards or guitar as accompaniment.[94]

Also, some already existing congregations rebuilt their spaces to achieve the new feeling. An observer of congregational trends reported that it had become impossible to keep count of the number of congregations "that are lowering their bimah or removing their fixed seats so that people can sit in a semicircle and see one another, rather than sitting in long, straight rows." One temple replaced its sanctuary, which had once seated 2,000 members, with two large rooms that would work well on ordinary Sabbaths. But this required a major rethinking of High Holy Day services, since neither room seated more than 800 after the renovation.[95]

Even a number of congregations that did not undertake new construction have moved their smaller services into rooms that allow for informal seating arrangements. Thus has emerged another innovation: providing a variety of types of religious services within one congregation—in the words of one such temple, affording "multiple worship opportunities." This reflects a desire to cater to the different tastes and needs of individual members.[96] As we shall see, Reform temples are not unique in this regard.

---

[93]Diane Winston, "Searching for Spirituality: Reform Judaism Responds" *Moment* 17, June 1992, p. 34.

[94]Daniel Hillel Freelander, "Why Temples Look The Way They Do," *Reform Judaism* 23, Fall 1994, pp. 35–37. Freelander also notes the "economic pragmatism" driving these changes: "Congregations could not afford to heat or air-condition massive social halls used only four or five times a year, or classrooms used once or twice a week. Sanctuaries with high ceilings were seen as an energy nightmare" (p. 37).

[95]Stone, "Redefining Oheb."

[96]For a run-down of the seven services sponsored by Congregation Emanu-El of San Francisco, see Kaplan, *American Reform Judaism*, pp. 92–93.

The "alternative" Shabbat morning session, separate from the main service (which tends to be dominated by bar/bat mitzvah celebrations), is often arranged so as to maximize face-to-face interaction, such as meeting in the round. "It's very important that we're able to face one another," said one participant in such a service in San Diego. "It means that the minyan is not a theater. You can see people's eyes rather than the backs of their heads. Dressing casually helps people feel at home. And most important is the sense of participation."[97]

Indeed, personalization of the service, a major departure from the high degree of anonymity that characterized the Reform temple of old, is a hallmark of much of the movement today. Here is a description of a typical Friday evening service at Temple Isaiah in Lexington, Massachusetts:

> Before the congregation rises to recite the kaddish together, those who are observing a *yahrtzeit* [anniversary of a relative's death] or are mourning a recent death are invited to stand as the name of the deceased is read. "It's important for people to stand as individuals," explains one rabbi. "How else will congregants know who is hurting that evening, so they can reach out and offer support? This is particularly important for women, whose names have been changed through marriage; without asking them to stand, we'd have no way of knowing they are mourning."[98]

Other occasions for providing a public forum to recognize the individual include the Torah reading, when members are called up to celebrate joyous personal and family occasions, and the old but newly popular prayer for the sick, *mi sheberach l'cholim,* when members may publicly name people close to them who are ill.

A new emphasis on study and discussion has added to the participatory atmosphere. Rather than rely upon the rabbi to deliver formal sermons, congregants today are more apt to engage in discussions with one another, with the rabbi playing the role of facilitator. Not only does such a system enable members to express their views, but, in the process, rabbis are relinquishing control over who may speak publicly and over what may be said. A particularly successful example of this was a program launched at the Jewish Community Center of White Plains, New York. Over the course

---

[97]Marder, "Worship that Works," p. 14.
[98]Ibid., p. 15.

of nine years, 120 regulars have met for a weekly service they call "Shabbat Morning Lift," centering on a line-by-line discussion of the Torah text. "Everyone offers a different perspective, and all questions are encouraged — even irreverent and challenging ones," comments Rabbi Shira Milgrom. "Each participant is both giver and receiver, including me."[99] This is an approach to synagogue life that few Reform rabbis of an earlier generation would have contemplated.

The modernization of synagogue music has become so central to contemporary Reform that Rabbi Eric Yoffie, the URJ president, has identified it as "the single most important key to the success or failure of our revolution."[100] In the pages of the *American Jewish Year Book,* Mark Kligman has provided a detailed discussion of how the traditional cantorial repertoire has been replaced by popular music imported from Reform summer camps and composed by homegrown musicians such as Debbie Friedman and Jeff Klepper.[101] Congregations are also experimenting with various combinations of musical instruments to accompany the services, and with changing the rhythm and style of performance. There might be the folk-music sound, jazz improvisations, 18-piece orchestras, klezmer music, African-American gospel, or Jamaican reggae.[102] Thus there is great variation from one congregation to another, and even from one Friday night to the next in the same temple. Fidelity to a fixed liturgy is the farthest thing from anyone's mind. Rather, the common denominator in today's Reform temple is engaging people in active, full-throated singing, often accompanied by clapping, foot-stomping, or dancing, a far cry from the reserved Reform worship of the past.[103]

---

[99]Ibid., p. 17.

[100]Yoffie, "The Worship Revolution," p. 26.

[101]Mark Kligman, "Contemporary Jewish Music in America," *American Jewish Year Book 2001* (New York, 2001), pp. 115–25.

[102]The range of musical styles to be found in Reform temples is nicely captured in Beth Gilbert, "Worshiping With Joy," *Reform Judaism* 31, Winter 2002, pp. 50–54. Kaplan, *American Reform Judaism,* p. 60, describes the "Rock 'n Roll Rabbi" who plays Jewish songs set to the melodies of Bob Dylan, the Grateful Dead, and the Beach Boys.

[103]For a good overview of Reform services in the early 1980s that suggests the gradual evolution of new musical tastes, see Ronald N. Ashkenas and Todd D. Jick, *Coping With Change: The Reform Synagogue and Trends in Worship,* published in 1984 by the Joint Commission on Worship: American Conference of Cantors, Central Conference of American Rabbis, and Union of American Hebrew Congregations, especially pp. 10–11. On the debate over the desirability of these shifts in musical tastes, see David Mermelstein, "Is Popular Culture Defining Synagogue Music?" *Reform Judaism* 24, Spring 1996, pp. 42–49.

The Reform cantor is no longer a classically trained singer. Baltimore's Oheb Shalom, for example, replaced its long-time cantor—whose expertise was in formal renditions of the classical *nusach* either solo or accompanied by a choir—with a successor who defined herself as "a song-leading cantor" who offered "approachable music." In line with this populist approach, the somber tones of the organ have been replaced by guitar strumming, keyboard music, and the sounds of a flute. Thus was effected a "change from aria to folk music, [which] mirrors a transition in the cantor's role from ambassador to God, chanting on behalf of the flock, to a leader who helps members pray directly to God."[104]

The turn to participatory singing is just one example of how Reform temples are going back to once rejected forms. The most recent survey of congregational practices conducted by the URJ documented the growing receptivity to traditional usages. Over 90 percent of responding congregations placed *kippot* (skullcaps) in a visible and accessible place for congregants wishing to don them, and 65 percent did the same for *talitot* (prayer shawls); 78 percent of rabbis and cantors claimed to wear both these ritual garments by choice. Greater traditionalism is also evident in the recitation of *slichot* (penitential) services in the period before the High Holy Days by 85 percent of congregations, the celebration of two days of Rosh Hashanah by 44 percent, and the sponsorship of *tashlich* (symbolic casting of sins into the water on Rosh Hashanah) by 69 percent.[105]

Since only 38 percent of Reform congregations responded to the survey questionnaire, the URJ did not publish it, and the results should be treated with caution. Nevertheless, the findings are in line with an earlier survey, conducted in 1994, that had a response rate of over 50 percent.[106] The 1994 data showed 51 percent of temples conducting services on the second and last days of Passover and Sukkot, which had not been celebrated by earlier generations of Reform Jews, 66 percent reciting the *yizkor* memorial service on the last days of festivals, and a marked increase in the incorporation of at least a modicum of Hebrew into the services. In addi-

---

[104]Kimberly A.C. Wilson, "Congregation Sings a New Song," *Baltimore Sun,* June 29, 2003, Internet edition.

[105]Union for Reform Judaism, "Worship Survey 2000 Summary," unpublished report. I am grateful to Rabbi Daniel Freelander for sharing this with me.

[106]Daniel Freelander, Robin Hirsh, and Sanford Seltzer, *Emerging Worship and Music Trends in UAHC Congregations* (New York, 1994).

tion, as a sign of the decline in formalism, growing percentages of congregations reported that they turned to face the back of the sanctuary to welcome the Sabbath during the singing of *Lecha Dodi* on Friday evenings, carried the Torah scrolls around the sanctuary before and after they were read, and called mourners to rise in place to recite the kaddish. These seemingly small gestures represented, in fact, a sharp break from the choreography of the Classical Reform temple, and, in many cases, were introduced only after serious and sometimes heated congregational debate.

"Inclusiveness" is a relatively new priority of which Reform congregations are exceptionally proud. Reform has been at the forefront of efforts to equalize the status of women and men in the synagogue. By 1975, virtually every American Reform temple counted women as members of the minyan (ten-person prayer quorum) and involved them in the Torah service. Hebrew Union College, which trains Reform synagogue professionals, has been ordaining women as rabbis since 1972 and as cantors since 1973.[107] Another target of Reform outreach has been the gay and lesbian community. Reform performs commitment ceremonies for them in the synagogue, calls such couples up to the Torah together, and ordains openly homosexual rabbis and cantors.[108] Reform temples have also aggressively courted intermarried families, so much so that the NJPS 2000–01 found that some 20 percent of members either were at the time, or had previously been, intermarried.[109] Efforts to address the needs and interests of these different populations have clearly affected the contemporary Reform temple, placing new strains on the clergy to address what one cantor called "the

---

[107]Mark Slobin, *Chosen Voices: The Story of the American Cantorate* (Urbana, 1989), p. 120.

[108]Kaplan, *American Reform Judaism,* chap. 10, "The Acceptance of Gays and Lesbians." The URJ has prepared a handbook to help congregations welcome them, *Kulanu (All Of Us): A Program for Congregations Implementing Gay and Lesbian Inclusion* (New York, 1996).

[109]Kaplan, *American Reform Judaism,* chap. 8, "The Outreach Campaign." For the percentage of intermarried Jews in Reform temples see Bruce Phillips, "American Judaism in the Twenty-First Century," in Dana Evan Kaplan, ed., *The Cambridge Companion to American Judaism* (New York, 2005), p. 411. On the challenges that this population poses to temples, see Michael A. Meyer, "The Place and Identity of the Non-Jew in the Reform Synagogue" [Hebrew], *Gesher* 146, Winter 2002, pp. 66–74; and Fran Chertok, Mark Rosen, Amy Sales, and Len Saxe, "Outreach Families in the Sacred Common: Congregational Responses to Interfaith Issues, Summary Report," Cohen Center, Brandeis University, and UAHC-CCAR Commission on Reform Jewish Outreach, Nov. 2001.

competing interests." She went on: "It means that I have to try to appeal to many constituencies. I have to offer a smorgasbord so people are comfortable." One frequent result, given the menu of different kinds of worship services available in the synagogue, "is that families often go to just the monthly service that appeals to them."[110]

Nothing dramatizes the unresolved tensions generated by the transformation of Reform Judaism more than the long-delayed publication of a new Reform prayer book. The Reform movement replaced its standard *Union Prayer Book* in 1975 with *Gates of Prayer,* and then issued a second version of the latter that provided gender-neutral translations of the prayers. But *Gates of Prayer* has attracted criticism within the movement for the confusing inclusion of numerous alternative prayer services (ten different ones for the Friday evening service alone), the absence of transliteration of Hebrew for those who do not read that language, retention of masculine language in describing God, reliance upon prayers recited in unison rather than sung together, and the mere smattering of excerpts from the traditional liturgy.[111] The availability of *Gates of Prayer* did not bring greater liturgical coherence to Reform, and the popular trend of individual congregations devising their own prayer books continued.

After conducting a study to ascertain "what was working or not working," the Central Conference of American Rabbis (CCAR) resolved in 1998 to publish a new prayer book "to maintain a sense of movement identity." Since then, various draft versions of *Mishkan T'fila,* the projected new prayer book, have been tried out in over 300 congregations. Now scheduled for publication in 2006, *Mishkan T'fila,* with prayers for weekdays, the Sabbath, and holidays, will strive to encompass varying points of view within the movement while also creating commonalities between Reform congregations — no easy task. It will appear in two versions: a single volume without transliterations, and a two-volume set with

---

[110]Debra Nussbaum Cohen, "Reform Jews Pursue Quest to Find New Religious Balance," *Jewish Telegraphic Agency Daily News Bulletin,* Dec. 21, 1999.

[111]"*Gates of Prayer*: Ten Years Later — A Symposium," *Journal of Reform Judaism* 32, Fall 1985, pp. 13–38; and Elyse D. Frishman, untitled forthcoming article to be published in the *Journal of Reform Judaism.* Rabbi Frishman, who chaired the publication committee for the new *Mishkan T'fila* prayer book, not only graciously shared an advance draft of this article with me, but also consented to an interview that provided much useful information about prayer book revision in the Reform movement.

transliterations of all Hebrew texts. Both will feature pages facing the Hebrew liturgy that will provide reflections on key themes "of Reform Judaism and Life: social justice, feminism, Zionism, distinctiveness, human challenges." *Mishkan T'fila* will include a variety of theological positions, with God portrayed variously as "transcendent . . . naturalist . . . mysterious, [a] partner . . . [an] evolving God."[112]

The protracted debates over the new prayer book suggest that the process of remaking worship in the Reform temple has not been accomplished without serious internal tensions. For one thing, Classical Reform still has its supporters. Despite the manifest enthusiasm in many quarters for revolutionizing the synagogue, there remain champions of the more formal and decorous worship service who feel alienated by current trends, which they see as too insularly Jewish. As two long-time members of a prominent temple in Los Angeles put it in a letter of complaint to their rabbi, for the past seven generations their families had worshiped at Reform temples that had urged them "to participate in community affairs and to fully appreciate all that America offered. Today it seems all they want us to do is learn Hebrew so we can understand the service and music."[113] Another point of friction can be found in lay/rabbinic relations. The more the CCAR/URJ, the lay arm of the movement, has pressed for changes in worship, the more rabbis have found themselves under the threat of displacement by lay leaders, who want to participate and make decisions in all spheres, including the religious.

Truth to tell, the efforts to break down the stiff formalism of Reform worship services have proved only partially successful. Many temples still have not freed their prayer services of the need to recite or sing everything in unison. And for all their success in increasing attendance levels at various types of services, the temples still attract no more than 10–25 percent of their members to worship on a regular basis.[114] Still, no one can gainsay the fact

---

[112]On this background, see Knobel, "The Challenge of a Single Prayer Book," pp. 185–89.

[113]Letter dated Oct. 11, 2004, sent also to the top leadership of the Reform movement. Names withheld.

[114]This discussion of tensions and unresolved issues is distilled from my interviews with Reform rabbis, as is the estimate of regular attendees. See also the observation of Lawrence A. Hoffman, who claims that the likelihood of average Reform temple members attending a Sabbath morning service with a sharp focus on a bar or bat mitzvah if they do not know

that a scant five years after hearing a call for a "revolution" in the synagogue, Reform Judaism has taken enormous strides in a new direction.

CONSERVATIVE

Conservative synagogues also transformed themselves in the closing decades of the twentieth century.[115] Like their Reform counterparts, they have sought to encourage greater participation by all members, a less formal style of worship, and an ambience that takes diversity of needs into account. But they have done so in their own fashion, developing a particular "Conservative" style. Indeed, there is probably greater uniformity of Sabbath worship, particularly on Saturday mornings, in Conservative synagogues than in the other synagogue movements.

While someone entering a Reform temple during services will likely find the congregation using a self-published prayer book composed by congregants and the professional staff, "no matter whether one attends a Conservative synagogue in Seattle or Miami, Boston or San Diego," one peripatetic observer noted, "the Sabbath morning service is virtually identical."[116] This uniformity is due to the adoption of a common prayer book and *Chumash* (Pentateuch) within the movement. In the mid-1990s, approximately half of the Conservative synagogues employed the *Sim Shalom* prayer book, and 94 percent the so-called Hertz *Chumash,* a commentary written by Joseph Hertz, a former chief rabbi of Great Britain who was the first rabbi ordained by the Jewish Theological Seminary, and whose orientation to biblical scholarship was

---

the celebrating family "is only slightly higher than the probability that they will be found at a randomly selected funeral where they know neither the mourner nor the deceased." Quoted in Marc Lee Raphael, *Judaism in America* (New York, 2003), p. 105.

[115]Journalists and scholars have lavished a good deal of attention on Conservative synagogues in the closing decade of the twentieth century. Among the former are Paul Wilkes, *And They Shall Be My People: An American Rabbi and His Congregation* (New York, 1994); and Stephen Fried, *The New Rabbi: A Congregation Searches for its Leader* (New York, 2002). An academic research project I directed on Conservative synagogues produced a series of five pamphlets and an edited volume, Jack Wertheimer, ed., *Jews in the Center: Conservative Synagogues and Their Members* (New Brunswick, 2000). See also Martin Laskin, *An Ethnographic Study of an American Conservative Synagogue* (Lewiston, N.Y., 2002).

[116]Raphael, *Judaism in America,* p. 98. In preparing this book, Raphael visited over 100 congregations of all denominations.

Orthodox.[117] Since then, the Conservative movement has issued a revised version of *Sim Shalom* (1998)—the two most important additions, both optional, were a reference to the biblical matriarchs along with the patriarchs at the opening of the *amidah,* and the long abandoned priestly benediction—and a new *Chumash* commentary, *Etz Hayim* (2001).[118] By 2005, some 669 out of the 750 Conservative congregations (belonging to the United Synagogue) in North America had adopted *Etz Hayim,* and the vast majority of Conservative congregations were using one or another version of *Sim Shalom.*[119]

The liturgical music employed in Conservative congregations is also fairly uniform. The Conservative movement has not produced innovative liturgical composers and performers comparable to Debbie Friedman (Reform) or Shlomo Carlebach (Orthodox),[120] though some rabbis report that the latter's tunes have recently become popular at Friday evening services.[121] Insofar as any American congregations still adhere to the traditional tunes and include nineteenth- and early-twentieth-century compositions, Conservative synagogues are most likely to do so. Conservative services have also been influenced by Israeli music and even more by so-called "camp music," melodies introduced for educational

---

[117]Wertheimer, *Conservative Synagogues and Their Members,* p. 13. The data are for the 750 out of 860 Conservative synagogues that belong to the United Synagogue.

[118]*Siddur Sim Shalom,* edited by Jules Harlow, was published in 1985. It was then issued in a revised format for Shabbat and Festivals in 1998 (edited by Leonard Cahan and others); and for weekday services (edited by Avraham Reisner). Both the latter strove for "gender sensitive language." *Or Hadash,* a commentary on *Sim Shalom* by Reuven Hammer, was issued in 2003. *Etz Hayim: Torah and Commentary* was published in 2001. *Mahzor for Rosh Hashanah and Yom Kippur: A Prayer Book for the Days of Awe,* edited by Jules Harlow, appeared in 1972. All were copublished by the Rabbinical Assembly and the United Synagogue of Conservative Judaism. On the various publications, see Ami Eden, "Conservatives Taking a Page From Orthodox Prayer Book," *Forward,* Mar. 28, 2003, Internet edition.

[119]Communication from Rabbi Joel Meyers, executive vice president of the Rabbinical Assembly, May 3, 2005. Over 200,000 copies of the *Etz Hayim* Torah commentary were sold in the four years after its initial publication.

[120]Max Wohlberg, cantor and professor at the Cantorial Institute of the Jewish Theological Seminary, fulfilled such a role in the last generation. His liturgical music was widely adopted in Conservative synagogues, even though few worshipers could identify the composer. Charles S. Davidson, *From Szatmar to the New World: Max Wohlberg, American Cantor* (New York, 2001).

[121]Through an Internet search, I learned of the proliferation of such Friday evening services. Rabbis Paul Plotkin of Margate, Florida, and Aaron Brusso of Minneapolis shared their experiences with me via e-mail. Both indicated that such services had increased attendance on Friday evenings.

purposes at the Ramah summer camps, run by the Jewish Theological Seminary. While camp alumni have brought this music into the synagogue, many Conservative congregants are ignorant of its origins.[122]

In contrast to Reform temples, which are still heavily oriented to the Friday evening service as the primary worship experience of the week, Conservative synagogues now attract their largest numbers of worshipers on Sabbath and festival mornings. The impetus for this shift came, among other factors, from younger families with children that found attendance on Friday evenings burdensome, and rabbis eager to free up their own Friday evenings for a leisurely dinner with their families. In 1990, the Conservative rabbinate responded to this groundswell: the Rabbinical Assembly passed a resolution encouraging congregations to move toward a reemphasis on Shabbat morning prayer.[123] Indeed, a survey of congregational practices conducted in the mid-1990s found that nearly half of Conservative congregations offered a Friday evening service at the traditional time of sundown, which varies with the seasons of the year, as an alternative to the late service. Smaller congregations and those with many older members still favored the late service, while large synagogues and those with younger congregants opted for the early time.[124]

The Sabbath morning service has not only replaced the late Friday evening service through much of the Conservative movement, but also differs from it in being less formal and more traditional. On Shabbat morning there is very little of the recitation of English prayers in unison that was characteristic of the Friday evening service. As noted by Rabbi Robert Fierstien, "with the exception of the abbreviation of the Torah reading to the triennial cycle, popularized by the 1980s, the Shabbat morning service remained essentially traditional in length and in its focus on Hebrew. The re-

---

[122]This phenomenon has been analyzed—and excoriated—in Boaz Tarsi, "Voices in the Sanctuary: Musical Practices of the American Synagogue," *Conservative Judaism* 35, Fall 2002, pp. 61–73; and Pinchas Spiro, "Ramah—A Blessing and a Curse," *Journal of Synagogue Music,* 25, 1995, pp. 5–8.

[123]Robert E. Fierstien, *A Century of Commitment: One Hundred Years of the Rabbinical Assembly* (New York, 2000), p. 125.

[124]Quantitative data are available in Jack Wertheimer, ed., *Conservative Synagogues and Their Members: Highlights of the North American Survey of 1995–96* (New York, 1996), p. 43.

focus on Shabbat morning meant that, for the typical synagogue-going Conservative Jew, prayer now meant a more traditional activity than had previously been the norm."[125]

To be sure, the triennial cycle "exception" noted by Fierstien—completing the reading of the Torah in three years instead of one, as is done in Orthodox congregations—has the very untraditional effect of abbreviating the length of the Sabbath morning service. In every region of the country a majority of Conservative congregations employ the shortened readings, with a high of 88 percent of congregations in the West and a low of 56 percent in the Northeast.[126] Quite a few congregations have also adopted another means to shorten the service: eliminating the prayer leader's complete repetition of the entire *amidah* either for the morning service or for the additional service that directly follows it.

The turn to traditional observance has also found expression in the continuing practice of celebrating the second days of the festivals, which, according to Jewish law, is required only outside of Israel. Beginning in the 1960s, there was considerable rabbinic agitation to eliminate the second day on the grounds that, with the creation of the State of Israel, Jews around the world should follow the calendar of coreligionists in the Jewish state, and also because attendance on festivals that fell out on weekdays was quite low. The Conservative rabbinate, in fact, sanctioned the option of eliminating the extra day, but most congregations continue to observe it.[127]

As in the case of Reform, Conservative congregations offer a wide selection of concurrent religious services on Sabbath mornings. Over two-thirds say they have a Shabbat program for toddlers and a junior congregation for older children; others also have teen services.[128] There are so-called learners' services for those with minimal background, and intimate *havurah* services, in addition to the main service.[129] Obviously, the availability of many different types of services depends heavily on the size of the congregation.

---

[125]Fierstien, *Century of Commitment,* p. 125.

[126]Wertheimer, ed., *Conservative Synagogues and Their Members,* p. 21.

[127]Ibid.

[128]Ibid., p. 45.

[129]For an account of how one Conservative congregation developed a thriving alternative service that attracts an average of 180 weekly attendees, many of whom are Jewishly knowledgeable, see Joel E. Rembaum, "A Venture in Synagogue Spiritualities," *Sh'ma* 21, Jan. 25, 1991, pp. 45–48.

It is not at all unusual for large congregations—those with over 600 members—to sponsor three or four simultaneous prayer services every Shabbat morning, some targeted at people with particular needs or interests.[130]

The participation of ordinary lay members in leading parts of the service is a noteworthy feature of the Conservative synagogue. They routinely lead the morning services. Quite a few congregations encourage the laity to deliver *divrei Torah*—their thoughts on the week's Torah portion. In many congregations laypeople take turns reading the Torah, and it is not uncommon, in larger synagogues, for dozens, if not hundreds, to participate. Often, these Torah readers did not have this skill before, but were trained in synagogue programs. Anthropologist Riv-Ellen Prell describes such a program at Beth El, in Minneapolis, where the cantor not only teaches this skill to congregants, but also recognizes those who have read at least seven Torah sections during the previous year with an annual Shabbat dedicated to their accomplishments. "In 1995," Prell writes, "at their Shabbat service recognition, Beth El's *bimah* was filled with young adults and men and women who had met this goal, some for as many as ten years."[131]

Like Reform and Reconstructionist congregations, Conservative synagogues have become overwhelmingly egalitarian: women and men partake equally in the services.[132] A survey conducted in the mid-1990s indicated that 83 percent of Conservative congregations in North America counted women in the minyan and allowed them to read from the Torah, 78 percent reported that women led services, and 79 percent had had a female president.[133] Similarly, bar mitzvah boys and bat mitzvah girls are treated the

---

[130]For examples of how this works in several Conservative and other kinds of synagogues, see E.J. Kessler, "Rabbis Bucking for Friday Nights at the 'Synaplex': Trend Sees Practice of Holding Several Smaller Minyans Within a Synagogue," *Forward,* June 5, 1998, p. 1.

[131]Riv-Ellen Prell, "Communities of Choice and Memory," in Wertheimer, ed., *Jews in the Center,* p. 277.

[132]The Federation of Jewish Men's Clubs, an umbrella for some 275 men's auxiliaries in Conservative synagogues, has labored to strengthen the participation of Jewish men in religious life. One of its most noteworthy programs, "World Wide Wrap," aims to raise the number of men donning phylacteries (tefillin) during weekday prayer. See Pauline Dubkin Yearwood, "Teaching Tefillin: They Aren't Your Father's Men's Clubs Anymore," *Chicago Jewish News,* Jan. 26–Feb.1, 2001, pp. 14–15; and Aleza Goldsmith, "S.F. Men's Club Gets All Wrapped Up in Ties that Bind," *Jewish Bulletin of Northern California,* Feb. 2, 2001, Internet edition.

[133]Wertheimer, ed., *Conservative Synagogues and Their Members,* p. 16.

same way in the large majority of congregations.[134] Since this survey included Canadian congregations, which tend to be less friendly to gender equality than those in the U.S., and the trend toward egalitarianism has undoubtedly accelerated in the decade since the data were gathered, it is likely that egalitarianism is all but universal today in Conservative congregations throughout the United States.

Like their counterparts in the other movements, Conservative rabbis have, both literally and figuratively, sought "to come down off the *bimah.*"[135] Many younger rabbis sit or stand among the congregants rather than on a pulpit above them. Except for the High Holy Days, rabbis are apt to engage in a discussion or study session with congregants about the Torah portion, and not deliver a full-blown sermon. These interactions with the laity, often interspersed between the portions of the Torah reading, generally take the form of brief observations about the text, sometimes with the opportunity for questions and reactions from the pews.

A number of Conservative synagogues have also followed the example of Reform and Reconstructionism in the use of musical instruments in the service, a practice contrary to rabbinic law and therefore generally avoided in earlier generations. Geography makes a great difference: Conservative synagogues on the West Coast are more likely to allow instrumental music during Shabbat and festival services than those in other regions.[136]

The success of Sinai Congregation in Los Angeles in drawing up to 2,000 singles to its monthly "Friday Night Live" is undoubtedly due to the popularity of Rabbi David Wolpe and the central location of the synagogue. But the music of Craig Taubman and his band is also a major draw. "It's a very musically oriented service," commented a neighboring rabbi, "which makes people very comfortable who are not normally used to going to synagogue, because the tunes are catchy."[137] With Sinai Congregation providing a model for emulation, Conservative synagogues on the West Coast

---

[134]Ibid., p. 17.

[135]Sarah Blustain, "A New Generation of Rabbis Is Coming Down Off the Bimah," *Moment* 24, Dec. 1999, pp. 61–65, 76–79. As this article makes clear, the trend is common among rabbis of all denominations.

[136]Wertheimer, ed., *Conservative Synagogues and Their Members,* p. 21.

[137]Michael Aushenker, "Will Friday Nights Ever Be the Same?" *Jewish Journal of Greater Los Angeles,* Nov. 22, 2004, Internet edition; Angela Aleiss, "Friday Night Live Draws

that do not employ instrumental music at Friday evening services are at a great disadvantage in attracting worshipers.[138] The technique also draws crowds on Shabbat morning: another congregation in Los Angeles now sponsors a monthly event called "One Shabbat Morning," also featuring Taubman's band and music, which attracts many hundreds of worshipers to its two-hour service.[139] In other parts of the country, where Conservative congregations remain averse to such practices on the Sabbath, some are experimenting with Friday night services that utilize musical instruments only before the Sabbath begins,[140] while many more have adopted the melodies composed by the late Shlomo Carlebach, in the expectation that the spirited singing and dancing can have the desired effect without the instrumental music.

The most influential Conservative congregation during the 1990s was B'nai Jeshurun of Manhattan, whose combination of instrumentation, lively singing and dancing, exclusively Hebrew prayers, and facilitated discussions has been widely discussed and admired by other Conservative synagogues.[141] Attending Friday evening services at "BJ," as it is affectionately known, became an almost required pilgrimage for rabbis across the denominational spectrum, and especially for those who are Conservative. Under the leadership of the charismatic Rabbi Marshall Meyer, a community activist who had previously rebuilt Jewish institutional life in Argentina, "BJ" was transformed from a small, failing congregation — albeit one with a history dating back to the 1820s — to a powerhouse that packed in between one and two thousand wor-

---

Young Jews to Their Faith," *Religious News Service,* June 8, 2000, Internet edition. For a more extensive analysis of the phenomenon see J. Liora Gubkin, "Friday Night Live: It's Not Your Parents' Shabbat," in Richard W. Flory and Donald E. Miller, eds., *GenX Religion* (New York, 2000), pp. 199–210.

[138]The use of instrumental music by Conservative congregations in the Bay area is surveyed by Abby Cohn, "Rock Services Bring New Sprit, Controversy to Conservative Synagogues," *Jewish Bulletin of Northern California,* Aug. 22, 2002, www.jewishsf.com/bk020822/la.shtml.

[139]Julie Gruenbaum Fax, "New Stamp on Service," *Jewish Journal of Greater Los Angeles,* Oct. 22, 2004, Internet edition.

[140]Adat Shalom of Detroit, for example, sponsors Shabbat Rocks, featuring music performed by the clergy prior to the onset of the Sabbath. See Shelli Liebman Dorfman, "Shabbat Just Keeps on Rockin'," *Detroit Jewish News,* Nov. 29, 2002, p. 57.

[141]Sara Moore Litt, "BJ: A Model for a Revitalized Synagogue Life. A report based on research by Dr. Ayala Fader and Dr. Mark Kligman," Congregation B'nai Jeshurun and Synagogue, May 2002.

shipers every Friday evening, and many hundreds on Sabbath morning. Its liberal politics[142] also endeared it to many New Yorkers, as did the attractiveness of Meyer's successors, Rabbis J. Rolando Matalon and Marcelo Bronstein.

But the style of the service was vital to its success: keyboard music accompanied by other instruments; joyous singing and dancing in the aisles; and an air of informality modeled by rabbis and congregants alike. While most Conservative congregations have concluded that the "BJ" model cannot be adopted wholesale, aspects of its service have been widely emulated.[143]

ORTHODOX

Orthodox Jews, constituting less than 20 percent of synagogue-affiliated Jews but maintaining more synagogues (some 1,500) than any other branch of American Judaism, are the Jewish group most likely to attend synagogue weekly, with many attending daily. Orthodox synagogues are highly autonomous, with no single overarching umbrella organization. Slightly under a quarter of Orthodox synagogues are affiliated with the Union of Orthodox Jewish Congregations of America (popularly known as the OU), which is the largest Orthodox congregational body. Smaller numbers of synagogues belong to the National Council of Young Israel, Agudath Israel of America, Chabad-Lubavitch, and other Hasidic groups. Over one-third (more than 500) are not affiliated with any congregational arm.[144] This diffusion means that systematic data are not available for Orthodox synagogues in the way they are for

---

[142]Although it was one of the founding members of the United Synagogue, the congregation no longer identifies with the Conservative movement, preferring a postdenominational label. Part of the reason for the break was the status of gays and lesbians in Conservative Judaism: at "BJ" they are fully integrated into the community. See Walter Ruby, "Growing Pains," *Manhattan Jewish Sentinel,* Oct. 30–Nov. 5, 1998, pp. 20–21.

[143]For one of many examples of a Conservative congregation explicitly trying to adapt this model for its Friday evening services, see Mara Dresner, "Ruach Shabbat Services Big Draw at Emanuel Synagogue," *Connecticut Jewish Ledger,* Feb. 2, 2001, p. 6.

[144]Schwartz, Scheckner, and Kotler-Berkowitz, "Census of U.S. Synagogues," pp. 117–18. Nearly 100 of these are non-Ashkenazi, usually consisting of recent immigrants from Syria, Iran, Iraq, or elsewhere in the Middle East, or from Muslim republics of the former Soviet Union. While tending to fly under the communal radar screen, they deserve careful study both because of the interesting ways they have adapted to America, and because their second generation will enrich many other congregations. For reports on two such congregations in the Los Angeles area, one Baghdadi and the other Farsi-speaking, see Gaby Wenig,

those of the other denominations, making it more difficult to generalize about trends within Orthodoxy.[145]

There are a number of reasons why Orthodox synagogues tend to be smaller than those of the other branches. For one thing, Orthodox Jews must live within walking distance of a synagogue, limiting the number of potential congregants to residents of the immediate neighborhood. They also do not use microphones on the Sabbath or holidays, and therefore need a smaller setting than the average Reform and Conservative congregation. In addition, Orthodox Jews maintain the traditional view of the synagogue as not just a place for prayer but as a manifestation of community, and therefore prefer a more intimate setting. In the last few decades, this search for intimacy has accelerated. There was much discussion, toward the end of the twentieth century, of the "shtiebelization" of Orthodoxy, as earlier, relatively large Orthodox synagogues gave way, in many neighborhoods, to small, informal prayer settings, sometimes in private homes, storefronts, schools, or rented facilities.[146] A major factor propelling this trend was the growing popularity of yeshiva education.

Indeed, Orthodoxy generally has been profoundly reshaped by the high percentages of its young people attending Jewish day schools at least through the high school years, and then, for many, continuing on in some form of post-high-school study. For thousands of young Modern Orthodox men and women, this means spending a year or two before college at an Israeli yeshiva.[147] In the

---

"Kahal Joseph's New Beginning," and "Nessah Seeks Younger Crowd," *Jewish Journal of Greater Los Angeles*, Aug. 27, Sept. 2, 2002, www.jewishjournal.com/hom/preview.php?id= 9093 and 9145.

[145]My discussion of Orthodox synagogues draws heavily upon interviews I conducted with Rabbis Avi Shafran of Agudath Israel of America and Mayer Waxman of the OU, May 3, 2005. Due to the paucity of research on the subject and the tendency of newspaper articles to focus on "out of the box" trends and efforts at religious liberalization that are favored by journalists, my description of Orthodox developments is inevitably impressionistic.

[146]*Shtiebel* is a Yiddish word meaning a small room. For a description of such a prayer group—albeit one in Canada—that tries to recreate the ambience of a yeshiva, see Simcha Fishbane, "Back to the *Yeshiva:* The Social Dynamics of an Orthodox Sabbath Morning Service," in Jack N. Lightstone and Fredrick B. Bird, eds., *Ritual and Ethnic Identity: A Comparative Study of the Social Meaning of Liturgical Rituals in Synagogues* (Waterloo, Ontario, 1995).

[147]There are separate schools for men and women, and the latter, which do not call themselves yeshivas, generally do not teach Talmud, which is the primary subject of study at the men's yeshivas. On long-term trends in Orthodox life see Haym Soloveitchik, "Rupture and

more strictly Orthodox and Hasidic worlds, where college is shunned or attended reluctantly and only part-time for the purpose of preparing for a career, young men and women are likely to spend several years mainly in yeshivas and women's seminaries, both in the U.S. and Israel.

Yeshiva attendance has not only raised the literacy of these Jews, insuring their easy participation in worship services conducted entirely in Hebrew, but has also shaped their expectations of synagogues. The yeshiva has gotten them used to praying three times a day, every day, and Orthodox synagogues, which a generation ago might have had trouble rounding up ten men for a weekday minyan, may have a hundred or more attendees for morning and afternoon/evening prayers.[148] Many young women, having adopted the same regimen, now attend weekday services, a phenomenon virtually unheard of in previous generations, and this sometimes requires rearrangement of the prayer room to provide a screened-off space for the female participants.

Furthermore, prayer may be intense in the typical yeshiva, but it is not prolonged, since the students' focus is on their regimen of study. This experience has now come to define the style and pace of Orthodox synagogue worship, as congregants look for a service that is speedy, yet cuts no corners. There is little patience for the formality and slow pace of Sabbath prayers found at larger Orthodox synagogues, and hence the attractiveness of the *shtiebel*. Conventional Orthodox congregations, feeling the need to compete, have created alternative Sabbath and festival services on the premises. Some meet in a smaller room than the main sanctuary to impart a sense of intimacy; others are geared to specific subpopulations with common interests, such as young families. Most popular is the so-called *hashkamah* minyan that begins at 7:30 or 8:00 on Sabbath morning, an hour or more before the regular service (*hashkamah* literally means getting up early). Dispensing with sermons and other time fillers and zipping along at a brisk pace, the *hashkamah* minyan resembles the yeshiva prayer service.

Reconstruction: The Transformation of Contemporary Orthodoxy," *Tradition* 28, Summer 1994, pp. 64–130; Chaim I. Waxman, "The Haredization of American Orthodox Jewry," *Jerusalem Letter/Viewpoints* 376, Feb. 15, 1998; and Samuel C. Heilman, *Sliding to the Right: The Contest for the Future of Orthodox Judaism in America* (Berkeley, 2005).

[148]Afternoon prayers are generally followed immediately, or after a short break, by evening prayers, so that all three daily services can be recited in two visits to the synagogue.

Explaining why his congregation sponsors seven different Shabbat morning services attracting 1,300 worshipers on a regular Sabbath, and five separate services on weekday mornings, the rabbi of the Young Israel of Woodmere explained: "People come from different homes, different traditions. People studied in different schools. Some people like a smaller minyan. Some people like a bigger minyan. Some people like a quicker minyan," a perspective shared, as we have seen, by many rabbis of the other denominations today.[149] The availability of so many options within the synagogue, of course, also serves to limit the incentive to abandon the congregation in favor of a *shtiebel*.

The yeshiva experience has also influenced the roles played by synagogue professionals. Gone are the days when Orthodox synagogues conducted their Sabbath and festival services with pomp, relied upon star cantors, and featured a sermon with suitable oratorical pyrotechnics.[150] Today, laymen rather than professional cantors lead the prayers, generally in the style of the yeshiva world. And, given the Judaic sophistication of many of the members, pulpit rabbis can no longer get away with conventionally edifying sermons, and so they either deliver talks that are highly textually based, or offer critiques of what are perceived as pervasive problems in the community, such as the evils of gossip and the dangers of family strife.

Similarly, in their capacity as teachers, the rabbis are under great pressure to offer high-level classes (*shiurim*) several times a week, hopefully emulating the intensity of what synagogue members experienced in the yeshiva. Both the number of classes per week and the intellectual demands they make of the rabbi and his congregants are unique in the history of the American synagogue. In the more modern congregations, men and women may attend these classes together (though women rarely study Talmud), while in more strictly Orthodox communities study is segregated by sex. To augment both the variety of classes and their quality, Orthodox synagogues have harnessed new technologies such as the Internet

[149]Rabbi Hershel Billet quoted in Steve Lipman, "A Place for Everyone," *New York Jewish Week,* Apr. 7, 2000, p. 16.

[150]For a description of such services in several Manhattan congregations during the first half of the twentieth century, see Jenna Weissman Joselit, *New York's Jewish Jews: The Orthodox Community in the Interwar Years* (Bloomington, Ind., 1990). Actually, there are a few synagogues in Manhattan and elsewhere that still adhere to this model.

and satellite television to bring prominent teachers virtually into the congregation. Some 44 institutions, mainly synagogues, are hooked up to the Torah Conferencing Network, which beams in the presentations of leading rabbis, thanks to the miracle of dish TV.[151] *Daf Yomi* classes, the daily study of a page of the Talmud that has caught on throughout the Orthodox world, are facilitated through use of the telephone—"dial a *daf*"—and Internet sites. And yeshivas in the U.S. and Israel deliver analyses and study packets on the weekly Torah reading through e-mail and the World Wide Web.

The Orthodox synagogue has also benefited from a highly sophisticated publishing enterprise, Mesorah Publications/ArtScroll, which has issued many different versions of the prayer books for the daily service, Sabbath and festivals, and High Holy Days; Torah commentaries; and the complete Talmud with the original Aramaic and English translation on facing pages. These handsomely produced volumes appear in different sizes, formats, and with varying amounts of elucidation and commentary, albeit from a strictly Orthodox perspective that ignores modern critical scholarship. These publications are ubiquitous in Orthodox synagogues across the spectrum, including the most modern. The prayer book alone, for example, had sold some 800,000 copies by 2003, more than one for every Orthodox Jew in the land![152]

Like their counterparts in other denominations, Orthodox synagogues have experimented with different musical styles. Hasidic *nigunim* (wordless melodies), which have made their way into all types of American congregations, have taken particular hold in Orthodox ones, which have also been at the forefront of incorporating neo-Hasidic compositions by the late Rabbi Shlomo Carlebach. Quite a few Carlebach services have sprung up. The Carlebach Shul on the West Side of Manhattan—where the rabbi often officiated when he was alive—and the so-called "Happy Clappy Minyan" at Beth Jacob Congregation in Beverly Hills are particularly renowned, but Friday night Carlebach services are featured

---

[151]See www.torahconferencing.net. On the broader phenomenon, see Jonathan Rosenblum, "Technology in Torah's Service," *Hamodia*, Feb. 16, 2005, www.jewishmedia resources.com/article/808.

[152]The sales figures are reported in Ami Eden, "Conservatives Taking a Page From Orthodox Prayer Book," *Forward*, Mar. 28, 2003, Internet edition.

at modern Orthodox synagogues across the country, indeed, all over the world.[153]

And also like their non-Orthodox counterparts, Orthodox communities have developed a new mode of engaging their members in petitionary prayer, especially for healing. In addition to the traditional custom of mentioning the names of sick people and praying, in the course of the Torah reading, for their recovery (a practice that most non-Orthodox congregations have adopted), many Orthodox synagogues have instituted so-called *Tehillim* clubs. These are groups of women who gather weekly in private homes to pray for the recovery of the sick through recitation of the biblical Psalms. Orthodoxy's continuing ban on calling women up to the Torah reading, when the standard prayer for the sick is recited, undoubtedly has spurred this phenomenon. With an eye to this potential market, ArtScroll published a *Women's Siddur* in 2005 that pays particular attention to prayer practices relevant to women, reproduces Psalms "in an easy-to-read font size," and includes "hard-to-find prayers" for those looking to find a marriage partner, for marking one's wedding day, for "pregnancy and childbirth," and for "raising children."[154]

While seeking to maintain the guidelines of Jewish law, Orthodox congregations have expanded the role of women in other ways as well. In Modern Orthodox synagogues, women have been elected to the board beginning in the 1970s, and have more recently served as presidents of congregations. The propriety of board membership was first addressed in a 1976 responsum, "Women on Synagogue Boards" by the noted authority Rabbi J. David Bleich. He left it up to pulpit rabbis to decide the issue, concluding that "given a spirit of good will and cooperation, substantive accommodation of the needs and desires of women can be achieved even within existing parameters."[155] Less than 20 years later, a Modern Orthodox rabbi in the Midwest reported: "our shul in Chicago is on its fourth woman president."[156] It has also become common-

---

[153]For a vivid description of a Sabbath morning service in the Carlebach mode, see Gaby Wenig, "C'mon Get Happy," *Jewish Journal of Greater Los Angeles,* Feb. 7, 2003, pp. 35, 38. Some observers believe that the Carlebach phenomenon has already peaked in Orthodox circles.

[154]www.artscroll.com; and *Jewish Press* (Brooklyn, N.Y.), July 8, 2005, p. 25.

[155]J. David Bleich, "Women on Synagogue Boards," *Tradition* 15, Spring 1976, p. 67.

[156]Communication from Rabbi Asher Lopatin, May 5, 2005.

place for Orthodox synagogues to celebrate the bat mitzvah of 12-year-old girls, albeit not as part of the service. Some provide for the girl to deliver a speech to the congregation after the conclusion of services, or at a party in a room separate from the sanctuary. In the more strictly Orthodox and Hasidic sectors, the bat mitzvah is relegated to a party for family and friends, but it is surely noteworthy that a girl's Jewish coming-of-age is acknowledged at all, something that would not have happened 50 years ago.[157]

A very small number of Modern Orthodox synagogues have experimented with ways to involve women in leading the synagogue service. One approach is the creation of a separate women's *tefilla* (prayer) group, which is entirely led by women and omits those prayers that require a quorum of males.[158] Other congregations maintain one unified service with women and men sitting separately, but allow women to come forward and lead certain parts of the service. An Orthodox rabbi from Chicago described to his congregation what he witnessed at a number of such synagogues in the U.S. and Israel, where women led

> *kabbalat shabbat* [welcoming the Sabbath], but not *ma'ariv* [the evening service], *p'sukei d'zimra* and *hotza'at sefer torah* [preliminary psalms and taking out the Torah], but not *shacharit* nor *musaf* [the morning service proper and the additional Sabbath or festival service]. Women read Torah, *haftara* [the prophetic reading] and get *aliyot* [are called up to the Torah] equally with men. There are some differences from minyan to minyan: the D.C. minyan . . . apparently is fully egalitarian, and, while having separate seating, does not have a *mehitzah* [separation between the sexes]. Some services wait for ten men and ten women to come before starting (Shira Chadasha in Jerusalem, and Tehilla in Chicago), while others will start with just ten men. Some try to always give to women the limited parts they

---

[157]For a brief survey of practices in different sectors of the Bay area Orthodox community, see Rachel Sarah, "Public Bat Mitzvahs Come to Orthodoxy," *Jewish Journal of Greater Los Angeles*, Mar. 11, 2005, www.jewishjournal.com/home/searchview.php?id= 13770. On national trends, see Sylvia Barack Fishman, "Women's Transformation of Public Judaism: Religiosity, Egalitarianism, and the Symbolic Power of Changing Gender Roles," in Eli Lederhendler, ed., *Who Owns Judaism? Public Religion and Private Faith in America and Israel*, Studies in Contemporary Jewry 17 (New York, 2001), p. 141.

[158]About 45 groups across the country belong to the Women's Tefilla Network. For a listing see www.edah.org/tefilla.cfm. These groups have sparked considerable controversy in the Modern Orthodox sector. On one particularly intense confrontation in Queens, New York, see Elicia Brown, "The Politics of Prayer," *New York Jewish Week*, Jan. 31, 1997, p. 14, and Jeff Helmreich, "Rabbinical Supervision: Did a Ruling on Women's Prayer Groups Go Too Far?" *Manhattan Jewish Sentinel*, Feb. 6, 1997, p. 3.

can do; others will just choose the person — man or woman — who they feel fits the role for that Shabbat.[159]

These represent a tiny number of congregations within the larger synagogue world of Orthodox Judaism, and it is still too early to tell whether they represent a vanguard or a fringe phenomenon.[160]

NICHE SYNAGOGUES

As one of the dominant synagogue trends of the late twentieth century was the creation of religious services tailored to the needs of subgroups within larger congregations, it is hardly surprising that freestanding niche synagogues have sprung up across the land aimed at particular clientele. These types of congregations still attract a relatively small minority of synagogue members, but they speak to the changing needs of American Jews and a continuing dissatisfaction with larger congregations. Their purpose is to create a setting for populations of Jews who claim to be underserved by mainstream synagogues, much as niche churches perform the same function for American Christians.[161] Whether or not they actually draw significant numbers of unaffiliated Jews to the synagogue — a claim they make, but which is hard to substantiate — their very existence generates competitive pressure upon mainstream congregations, and these are forced to pay greater heed to previously overlooked Jewish subpopulations.

Orthodox Outreach: The largest niche-congregation sector is that of the Orthodox. Within this group, Chabad has the most congregations (some 346),[162] followed by Aish HaTorah, and other outreach groups. Even though these synagogues are organized by entrepreneurial Orthodox rabbis and attract mainly "seekers" who

---

[159]Rabbi Asher Lopatin of Chicago described these synagogues in an open letter to his congregation dated July 31, 2003.

[160]The Tehilla Minyan in Chicago bills itself as "a minyan *shivyoni hilkhati*—a minyan committed to following a Modern Orthodox perspective of Halakhah while enabling women to participate in leading *tefilla.*" See www.tehilla.org.

[161]Sociologist Nancy T. Ammerman, in *Congregation and Community* (New Brunswick, N.J., 1996), pp. 130–31, defines niche churches as congregations that "do not serve a specific locale. They reach beyond an immediate neighborhood to create an identity relatively independent of context . . . . The implications of a mobile, cosmopolitan culture where congregational choice is the norm make such religious sorting more and more likely."

[162]Schwartz, Scheckner, and Kotler-Berkowitz, "Census of U.S. Synagogues," p. 128.

are drawn to the Orthodox ambience, many of the rabbis, especially those representing Chabad, have no illusions that their congregants are, or will become, observant Orthodox Jews, and a good number of the major donors belong to the non-Orthodox movements.

Most outreach synagogues begin as storefronts or in modest dwellings, but some, especially those identified with Chabad, develop into major institutions. In 1994, Chabad opened a $10-million synagogue in Bal Harbour, Florida. In Solon, outside Cleveland, some 500 "Reform and Conservative families" put up a $3-million Chabad synagogue. In Aspen, Colorado, the local Chabad rabbi purchased a plot for $6.3 million that will be the site of a synagogue. In Weston, Florida, a 16,000-square-foot Chabad Center was opened in early 2004.[163] In 2005, 20 new Chabad centers were scheduled to open on the West Coast alone, bringing the number in that region up to 180.[164] Chabad has been particularly active on or near campuses, attracting young Jews of many backgrounds to religious services, Shabbat meals, and Jewish study at some 67 colleges and universities across the country.[165] The scope and seriousness of Chabad's foray into synagogue life is also illustrated by its publication of a new prayer book for weekdays, the Sabbath, and holidays. It reproduces "an emended text" of the standard Chabad prayer book, a full English translation, "transliterated essentials, like Kaddish and Borchu," "instructions for sitting, standing, and other customs," and ample English explanations and diagrams for those unfamiliar with the services.[166]

Chabad's extraordinary success is due to the overriding sense of mission that animates its *shluchim* (emissaries) and the minimal de-

---

[163]Sue Fishkoff, *The Rebbe's Army: Inside the World of Chabad-Lubavitch* (New York, 2003), p. 34; Ellen Harris, "Building Their Congregation 'One Family at a Time,'" *Cleveland Jewish News,* Sept. 10, 2004, www.clevelandjewishnews.com/articles/2004/09/10/news/local/achabad0910.prt; Chris Leppek, "Chabad Buys $6.3 Million Aspen Resort," *Intermountain Jewish News,* Sept. 12, 2003, www.ijn.com; "New Jewish Community Center Opens in Florida," Mar. 22, 2004, www.lubavitch.com/Article.asp?Article=427&Section=50&Month=3&Year=2004.

[164]West Coast Chabad Lubavitch, www.chabad.com/communityoutreach03.cfm.

[165]Shlomo Shamir, "The Lubavitcher Rebbe's Legacy Keeps Rolling Across America," *Haaretz,* Jan. 8, 2004, www.haaretz.com/hasen/objects/pages/PrintArticleEn.jhtml?itemNo=380719.

[166]Nissan Mangel, ed., *Siddur Tehillat Hashem—Nussach Ha-Ari Zal, With English Translation, Annotated Edition* (New York, 2003), advertised at http://store.kehotonline.com/prodinfo.asp?number=EP-STH.AB.

mands it makes on those it serves. In the words of Professor Michael Berenbaum, "Those who attend come from all backgrounds and all places—socioeconomic, religious, spiritual and psychological . . . . They are warmly welcomed and the service, however traditional, is tailored to their needs, without compromising Orthodox standards or principles. How the Jews get to the synagogue or what they do after Shabbat services is less important than their presence at services."[167]

For the most part, Chabad synagogues make no pretense of being Orthodox. As one of their rabbis put it: "We don't serve Orthodox people here . . . . We're not looking to build an Orthodox community. We're looking to build a strong Jewish community."[168] The attraction for non-Orthodox Jews, both to Chabad and to other outreach facilities, comes from the intimate community they find, the personal attention they get, and the few demands made on them—most charge little or nothing for dues; children can celebrate their bar/bat mitzvah without fulfilling any minimum requirement of school attendance; and celebrations can be informal and inexpensive.[169]

While these outreach synagogues claim to address otherwise unaffiliated Jews, quite a few of their people maintain dual memberships or are dropouts from the mainstream congregations.[170] There is every reason to expect the continuing expansion of this sector of synagogues, particularly as Chabad, Aish HaTorah, and

---

[167]Michael Berenbaum, "To Change But Not Be Changed," *Jewish Journal of Greater Los Angeles,* Sept. 10, 2004, www.jewishjournal.com/home/preview.php?id=12818.

[168]Leppek, "Chabad Buys Resort." See also the statement of a Chabad rabbi in Alpharetta, Georgia, who acknowledged that at a Chabad center "most of the people will not be Orthodox and will not be very religious." Vivi Abrams, "Marketing Judaism in Suburbia," *Atlanta Jewish Times,* May 17, 2002, www.atljewishtimes.com/coverstory.htm.

[169]The low expectations are an ongoing source of friction with Conservative and Reform rabbis, who feel that Chabad is poaching on their turf and competing unfairly. See Fishkoff, *Rebbe's Army,* pp. 123–31, and Bob Keeler, "The Lubavitchers of Long Island," a multipart series in *Newsday* (Long Island), especially "The Debate Over Chabad," Oct. 25, 2000, pp. B6–B9.

[170]This vastly complicates the challenge of measuring the relative memberships of the different denominations. A leading Chabad spokesman in California observed that fewer than 100 Sabbath-observant Jews live in Orange County, but nearly 2,000 had attended High Holy Day services at the six Chabad centers and one Modern Orthodox synagogue. See David Eliezri, "Undercounting the Orthodox," *Forward,* Nov. 12, 1999, p. 12. The task of counting participants in Chabad programs is also made more difficult by the movement's tendency to inflate figures, as noted in Fishkoff, *Rebbe's Army,* p. 204.

a growing number of yeshivas have instituted training programs to prepare young rabbis for outreach work.[171]

"Progressive" Synagogues: At the other end of the ideological spectrum are several hundred fellowships and congregations that describe themselves as liturgically and socially progressive. That is, they compose their own prayers, resist the "corporate" culture of conventional synagogue life,[172] pride themselves on their openness to previously marginalized groups such as gays and lesbians, the intermarried, and singles, and embrace the causes of the political left. Unlike Orthodox outreach congregations, founded by rabbis looking to recruit congregants, the progressive groups are a grass-roots phenomenon: Jews in a particular locality band together without professional assistance, often intentionally eschewing rabbinic leadership.[173] Some 120 of them affiliate with the National Havurah Committee,[174] approximately 100 are linked to the Federation of Reconstructionist Congregations and Havurot,[175] and another 35 to Aleph: Alliance for Jewish Renewal. Structurally, these three bodies are not easy to disentangle, and a number of congregations belong to more than one. For quite a while their leaders were also intertwined: many Renewal and Havurah people were either ordained at the Reconstructionist Rabbinical College or taught there, and their members still attend retreats together at places such as Elat Chayyim in Accord, New York.[176]

The Reconstructionist movement is the best known of these groups. It has, in fact, the infrastructure of a Jewish denomination — an umbrella organization for synagogues, a rabbinical seminary, and an association of rabbis. Reconstructionism also has the most defined ideological positions, originating in the views of its

---

[171]Adam S. Ferziger, *Training American Orthodox Rabbis to Play a Role in Confronting Assimilation* (Ramat Gan, Israel, 2003).

[172]This theme has been central to the writing of Rabbi Sidney Schwarz. See, for example, his "The Rabbi as Spiritual Leader," *Reconstructionist* 64, Fall 1999, pp. 24–33.

[173]See the description of the Shir Hadash Reconstructionist *havurah,* with its emphasis on the pride and self-reliance of the members, in Susie Davidson, "Shir Hadash Includes Jews of All Types," *Boston Jewish Advocate,* Sept. 5–11, 2003, p. 2.

[174]www.havurah.org/directory.

[175]www.jrf.org.

[176]The former president of the Reconstructionist Rabbinical College has stated that "the furthest left people, spiritually and intellectually, produced by [his college] . . . find their home in Aleph." David Teutsch quoted in Eric Caplan, *From Ideology to Liturgy: Reconstructionist Worship and American Liberal Judaism* (Cincinnati, 2002), p. 349.

founder, Rabbi Mordecai Kaplan (1881–1983), although the clarity and direction of the movement became murkier in the decades since his death, just as all the movements have become less ideological. Many of the congregations meet in their own buildings, and approximately two-thirds have rabbis. In the more established congregations, the Sabbath morning service is the focal event of the week, whereas in the smaller *havurot,* twice monthly Friday evening services are central. Reconstructionism proudly embraces an especially large percentage of intermarried families. The 2000–01 NJPS found that 44 percent of self-identified Reconstructionist adults were intermarried. While that figure may be exaggerated by the small size of the Reconstructionist sample, the movement's own internal survey a decade ago put the figure at 30 percent for members under age 40, higher than any other movement.[177]

A sampling of mission statements put out by Reconstructionist congregations highlights their overall direction. Congregation Dor Hadash in San Diego describes Reconstructionism as "ritually traditional and socially liberal." It goes on:

> Reconstructionist congregations are based on the belief that each generation of Jews is charged with the responsibility for envisioning the Judaism of its own time and then creating it. Congregation Dor Hadash offers its members a community-based environment in which to learn, pray and make friends. . . . [I]ts doors are open to all — singles, marrieds, gays, lesbians, interracial, interfaith. The members are a diverse and varied group of people from all walks of life. A significant portion of Dor Hadash households are interfaith families who have decided to keep a Jewish home.[178]

The Ann Arbor Reconstructionist Havurah "requires commitment to building a participative [sic] inclusive Jewish community." Furthermore,

> We depend upon shared leadership among a broad range of members and the active participation of all members in community life. Because participation extends beyond formal group activities, we

---

[177]The NJPS data are cited by Phillips, "American Judaism in the Twenty-First Century," p. 412. For results of the survey conducted by the Reconstructionist movement in 1996, see Carol Towarnicky, "Boundaries and Opportunities: Report on the Role of the Non-Jew in Reconstructionist Synagogues," *Reconstructionism Today,* Spring 1998; and Elaine Kahn and Debra Nussbaum Cohen, "Reconstructionist Survey Finds Inclusiveness Attracts," *MetroWest Jewish News,* Dec. 12, 1996, pp. 8, 19.

[178]www.dorhadash.org/aboutus.htm.

make a commitment to support each other in our efforts to integrate Jewish principles and practice into our daily lives. As an inclusive community, we recognize that barriers come in many forms and we are committed to pluralism and gender equality. Events will be held in wheelchair-accessible locations. Non-traditional households are welcomed. While not imposing on the prerogatives of parents, we take a share of responsibility for our Havurah's children. Finally, we each agree to provide funds within our means so that economic hardship will not hinder participation.[179]

A third congregation, the Reconstructionist Synagogue of the North Shore (Long Island, N.Y.), affirms in its mission statement the centrality of "the democratic process . . . to the functioning of a Reconstructionist synagogue," and therefore,

> The Rabbis and Cantor are the resource persons, the guides, the facilitators. With this guidance and the cooperation of the Ritual Committee, the congregation participates actively, offering readings, songs, performing rituals such as candlelighting and kiddush. Congregational singing plays a large role in our services, as the rabbis, cantor and congregation come together for meaningful, responsive worship experiences.[180]

Reconstructionist congregations assume that members have some familiarity with the traditional services but are prepared to experiment with the liturgy and jettison aspects that do not speak to them. They are outspokenly left-wing in their political and social orientation. Rejecting hierarchy, they have reinterpreted the role of the rabbi, making him/her a facilitator of democratic decision-making rather than the decision-maker. The emphasis on inclusion of groups that are allegedly excluded from other synagogues, such as the handicapped and indigent, is a point of pride. But it has created some discomfort in Reconstructionist synagogues that have undertaken capital campaigns to build permanent structures, since raising the necessary money entails breaking with their "anti-hierarchical approach to fund-raising," and potentially embarrassing people who cannot pay their share.[181]

From its inception, the Reconstructionist movement has issued a steady stream of innovative liturgical publications. Since 1999 it

---

[179]www.aarecon.org.

[180]www.rsns.org/html/worship.html.

[181]Julie Wiener, "Are the Reconstructionists Becoming More Mainstream?" Jewish Telegraphic Agency Internet edition, Nov. 7, 2000, www.jta.org/index.exe?0011075.

has released a series of new prayer books called *Kol Haneshamah* and a new Passover Haggadah, and these have become ubiquitous in Reconstructionist congregations. They contain a considerable amount of transliteration to enable nonreaders of Hebrew to participate in the services, and use gender-neutral language. While retaining Mordecai Kaplan's naturalistic understanding of the Torah's origins and his removal of references to miracles and to a personal messiah, these works are more open than earlier Reconstructionist liturgy to a mystical understanding of God, and affirm the legitimacy of reinterpreting rather than rejecting the concept of the chosenness of the Jewish people.[182]

Jewish Renewal and the network of *havurot* share the Reconstructionist niche, but differ primarily in the liturgical realm. Reconstructionist congregations follow their movement's prayer book; the others experiment both with the content of the prayers and with deportment during prayer. From the Renewal perspective, the large quotient of Hebrew and traditional liturgy in Reconstructionist synagogues and the cerebral approach taken to Judaism render the services stiff and staid. Renewal congregations favor body movement, meditation, wordless song, and the like. The point was driven home by a reporter who visited Makom Ohr Shalom in Woodland Hills, California, where the Yom Kippur services were led by the guru of Renewal, "Reb Zalman" Schachter-Shalomi: "Picture 20 massage tables, with people lying down and being gently touched, with music playing in the background. On Yom Kippur."[183] To be sure, Renewal has become somewhat less touchy-feely under the recent leadership of Rabbi Daniel Siegel, but it nevertheless remains highly experimental.

Both Renewal congregations and *havurot* tend to be small fellowships that meet a few times a month, lack large congregational structures, and focus on prayer, education, or social causes.[184] Jewish Renewal groups involve themselves with Jewish mysticism, neo-

---

[182]Reconstructionism's evolving liturgy is treated in Caplan, *From Ideology to Liturgy,* especially chap. 5.

[183]Gaby Wenig, "Stand-up, Sit-down, See the Light," *Jewish Journal of Greater Los Angeles,* Sept. 14, 2002, www.jewishjournal.com/hom/preview.php?id=9229.

[184]Because most *havurot* do not have their own buildings but usually meet either in member's homes or in rented facilities, they struggle to gain visibility. See the letter to the editor from Mark Frydenberg, incoming chair of the National Havurah Committee, *Boston Jewish Advocate,* Aug. 29–Sept. 4, 2003, p. 15.

Hasidism, and meditation. Convinced that only "a paradigm shift" will "develop a spirituality through which Judaism can transform itself,"[185] they incorporate aspects of Eastern religions into their prayers, proudly borrowing "openly and liberally from other faith traditions and speak[ing] of ourselves as JuBus, Jufis, and Hinjews."[186] The Renewal movement has issued a prayer book, *Ohr Chadash: New Paths for Shabbat Morning*.[187] Independent *havurot* are liturgically eclectic, using works and performing practices that originate in various religious movements.[188]

Gay and Lesbian: Another niche is occupied by the 19 gay and lesbian synagogues that have been founded around the country since 1972, when the first, Beth Chayim Chadashim, was organized in Los Angeles.[189] Eleven of these are independent, seven identify as Reform and belong to the URJ, and one affiliates with the Reconstructionist Federation.[190] Prayer services in gay and lesbian synagogues tend to follow Conservative or Reform practice, and therefore the congregations tend to employ the prayer books of these denominations. As the rabbi of Bet Mishpachah in Washington, D.C., put it: "When people come to our synagogues they're coming for the same reasons that any other Jews come to synagogue. With few exceptions, we say the same prayers. It's not really different in content."[191]

Even so, these synagogues have developed their own liturgical and theological responses to issues of particular concern to their

---

[185]"Four Worlds, Eighteen Affirmations, One Covenant: Aleph Statement of Principles," www.aleph.org/principles.htm. Also included is a commitment "to consult with other spiritual traditions, sharing with them what we have found in our concerned research and trying out what we have learned from them, to see whether it enhances the special truths of the Jewish path."

[186]That is, Jewish Buddhists, Jewish Sufis, and Hindu Jews. See Rami Shapiro, "Jewish Renewal Makes It to Film," *Tikkun* 16, Nov./Dec. 2001, pp. 72–73.

[187]*Ohr Chadash* is discussed by Caplan, *From Ideology to Liturgy,* pp. 350–64.

[188]Given the far-flung and unaffiliated status of many *havurot,* it is hard to generalize about their ideologies. Quite a few are defined less by social and political outlook than by their goal of creating an intimate community; others are simply serving small groups of Jews in remote places that have no synagogues. But the leadership of the National Havurah Committee is heavily drawn from the so-called progressive community.

[189]Melissa Minkin, "Celebration of 'Life': The First Lesbian and Gay Synagogue Marks Its 30th Anniversary," *Jewish Journal of Greater Los Angeles,* July 1, 2002, www.jewishjournal.com/hom/preview.php?id=8708.

[190]Schwartz, Scheckner, and Kotler-Berkowitz, "Census of U.S. Synagogues," p. 129.

[191]Debra Nussbaum Cohen, "Rabbis Explore Uniqueness of Gay Shuls," *New York Jewish Week,* June 9, 2000, p. 49.

members, ranging from prayers acknowledging discrimination to meditations on the ravages of AIDS, from attention to gender neutrality to the inclusion of non-Jewish partners in the services.[192] Since the number of their members' children is steadily growing, these synagogues are increasingly grappling with the tension between demands for congregational supplementary schools and the resentment of older members, who say that they established these synagogues as "adult places in an era when gay couples didn't often have kids."[193]

Humanistic: Still another niche is occupied by so-called Humanistic communities and congregations, which are dedicated to secular Judaism. Beginning with the founding of the first of these in a suburb of Detroit by Rabbi Sherwin Wine in 1963, the movement has grown to some 30 communities, under the umbrella of the Society for Humanistic Judaism.[194] Humanistic congregations draw upon the traditional liturgy as well as other Jewish texts when they engage in communal gatherings, but, as committed secularists, they do not pray, although they do celebrate lifecycle passages so as to "allow the family and community to reinforce their unity and to articulate the values that make life worthwhile."[195] One Humanistic congregation in Washington, D.C., eventually withdrew from the society because it was partial to a more traditional liturgy, and accepted as members Jews who believed in God. This congregation pushed the envelope by saying the Shema, a central prayer of traditional Judaism that affirms belief in one, indivisible God. To be sure, the recitation was prefaced with the words: "In concert with what Jews have said for thousands of years, let's rise and say the *sh'ma.* We are doing this as a tradition, not as a prayer."[196]

Gen X and Gen Y: Rounding out the picture are a small number of Gen X and Gen Y congregations established by and for young

---

[192]The most detailed study of one such synagogue, Congregation Beth Simchat Torah in Manhattan, is Moshe Shokeid's, *A Gay Synagogue in New York* (New York, 1995). Its discussion of the prayer service is on pp. 100–117.

[193]Cohen, "Rabbis Explore Uniqueness," p. 10.

[194]Its Web site is www.shj.org.

[195]"What Do Humanistic Jews Do?" www.shj.org/do.htm.

[196]"Beth Chaim Leaves National Movement," *Washington Jewish Week,* Jan. 19, 2003, www.washingtonjewishweek.com/localstory.html?/wjw/279687396775336.html. This congregation is now a member of the National Havurah Committee.

Jews—that is, those born since the end of the baby boom, both singles and young couples. Insofar as these groups appeal self-consciously to Jews of a specific age group, they are the contemporary analogue to the independent *havurot* of the 1970s, although they draw a far more upscale clientele than the graduate students who established the first *havurot*.

Thus the Soho Synagogue, which is Orthodox, seeks "successful, religious twenty- and thirtysomething Jews interested in being cool and kosher, too." One of the founders pronounced the synagogue's goal to "appeal to Jews who want an alternative but nothing too out-there."[197] Kehillat Hadar, perhaps the largest of the Gen X congregations, is an egalitarian, traditional minyan of several hundred that is entirely led by its members and meets in various places on the Upper West Side of Manhattan. Its participants are heavily drawn from Conservative synagogues, but the group eschews a denominational label.[198] By contrast, the Ma'alot Minyan meets in a large Conservative synagogue on the East Side of Manhattan, receives assistance from the United Synagogue of Conservative Judaism, and openly recruits alumni of Camp Ramah, Koach, the Solomon Schechter day schools, and other specifically Conservative institutions. And in nearby Park Slope, Brooklyn, a Reform congregation houses a minyan with no name that is lay-led and conducts services entirely in Hebrew. These, and others scattered around the country, have been described as "very pragmatic and self-sufficient . . . . They emphasize lay leadership, and are less interested in rabbinic authority and in creating superstructure buildings than they are in building their community."[199]

---

[197]Shana Liebman, "Can a Shul Be Cool?" *New York Magazine,* Apr. 25, 2005, p. 17; and Liel Leibowitz, "Hip With a Mechitza," *New York Jewish Week,* June 24, 2005, pp. 8–9.

[198]For a description of Hadar by one of its founders, see Elie Kaunfer, "Attracting Young People to Jewish Life: Lessons Learned from Kehillat Hadar," *Jewish Education News* 26, Spring 2005, pp. 1–2.

[199]These New York minyanim for the post-baby-boom generation are surveyed in Debra Nussbaum Cohen, "The New Gen-X Judaism," *New York Jewish Week,* Aug. 2, 2002, www.thejewishweek.com/news/newscontent.php3?artid=6503&print=yes. On the Ma'alot minyan, see Elianna Baslaw Goldman, "Building Young Adult Infrastructure: Manhattan's Ma'alot Minyan Project," *United Synagogue Review* 57, Spring 2005, pp. 18–19. Another effort in New York, Tikvat Yisrael, seeks to emulate the multiple minyanim held at Harvard Hillel that then join together after services for a communal Shabbat dinner and joint study. Eli Sachs, "Alumni Replicate Hillel Community in Manhattan," *Harvard Hillel Newsletter,* Spring 2005, p. 8.

Whether these congregations will still exist once their members have married, borne children, and moved out is doubtful.[200]

Postdenominational: Cutting across several types of niche congregations is a small but growing movement toward the creation of postdenominational synagogues. As distinct from unaffiliated congregations, these not only reject a movement label, but also revel in their eclecticism in an age when ideology is looked upon with suspicion or dismissed as irrelevant. As one Jewish Renewal rabbi, Gershon Winkler, sees it, most American Jews are "turned off by the rigidity of established 'standards' found in every Jewish denomination." Instead, Jews might be more attracted to "the broader spectrum of Judaism that shines far beyond and above the particular party-line versions they have been fed by every denomination."[201] Younger Jews seem especially attracted to this approach since, says one of them, Rabbi Leon Morris, they "resist categorization. We don't want to be labeled. We seek a model of Jewish life that is self-designated."[202] One such community in Los Angeles, named Ikar, has been touted as a vanguard institution that will inspire others to imitate its vibrancy, attractiveness to younger families, and eclecticism.[203]

In fact, not only are many of the Gen X and Gen Y synagogues postdenominational, but so are a considerable number of *havurot* and Renewal groups, which do not view themselves as belonging to denominations. Even Orthodox outreach synagogues speak the same language of inclusiveness, scornfully rejecting denominational labels. As an advertisement for one such outfit puts it: "Conservative? Orthodox? Reform? Labels are for clothes . . . not for

---

[200]Congregations around the country have invested, either sporadically or in a more sustained fashion, in special singles' or young people's services aimed at Gen X and Y Jews. Friday Night Live at Sinai Temple in Los Angeles is perhaps the best known of these, as described above, p. 44. Even more remarkable is the phenomenon of members of this age cohort founding their own synagogues. For an early effort, see Alan Silverstein and Bob Rubin, "Serving Jewish Singles in Suburbia," *Conservative Judaism* 38, Fall 1985, pp. 71–76. A survey of efforts by Reform congregations to engage with this age group is discussed in Sue Fishkoff, "New Jew Cool," *Reform Judaism* 33, Fall, 2004, pp. 20–27, 32.

[201]Andrew Silow-Carroll, "Crossing Over," *New York Jewish Week,* Dec. 15, 1999, pp. 46–49.

[202]Leon A. Morris, "Beyond, or Mixing Denominations," *New York Jewish Week,* Mar. 7, 2003, p. 26.

[203]For the program of this congregation, see its Web site, www.ikar-la.org/vision.html. Aitz Hayim Center for Jewish Living in Chicago explicitly advertises its postdenominational approach. *JUF News,* Sept. 1996, p. 17.

fellow Jews." And this sort of rhetoric emanates from Chabad and Aish HaTorah networks, which, for all of their tolerance of variations in religious behavior, would not think of breaking with Orthodox norms. In an age of "seekers," postdenominational congregations are attractive because they reject what are perceived as artificial boundaries between Jews and because they draw freely from many traditions of Judaism. Instead of setting up boundaries that read people out, they affirm community, celebration, and personal meaning.[204]

Synagogue Renewal Efforts

As synagogues have rethought their programs and approaches to worship over the past 15 years, there has been no shortage of advisors eager to guide their work. A veritable cottage industry has sprung up that seeks to "reengineer the shul," engender "synagogue change initiatives," encourage congregations to "re-vision" themselves, and offer help with "strategic planning." What follows is a thumbnail survey of the major initiatives.[205]

SYNAGOGUE 2000

This is the best known renewal initiative. Founded in 1995 by Professors Lawrence Hoffman of the Hebrew Union College in New York and Ron Wolfson of the University of Judaism in Los Angeles, this program has, to date, worked with some 195 congregations around the country. It is funded by private foundations and local federations of Jewish philanthropy. Synagogue 2000 operates interdenominationally, bringing professional and lay leaders of different local congregations together, in part to demonstrate to them that they share many common challenges, and in part "to build community across denominations."[206]

---

[204]An unknown number of congregations are independent of any organized umbrella groups, and thus fly below the radar of anyone studying synagogue life. For an "inside look at the world of independent shuls," see Walter Ruby, "Saturday, the Rabbi Stayed Home," *Moment* 22, Oct. 1997, pp. 37–44.

[205]For a complete listing, see the Databank of Community-Based Synagogue Change Initiatives compiled by the Jewish Education Service of North America, www.jesna.org/cgi-bin/dbroundtble.php3.

[206]Lawrence A. Hoffman, "Synagogue 2000: Lessons for the Future," *Contact* 7, Autumn 2004, p. 9. Information on Synagogue 2000 is available at its Web site, www.s2k.org/About/about.html.

Synagogue 2000 workshops try to get synagogues to work on six key areas of congregational life: (1) providing meaningful and participatory worship; (2) engaging members of all ages in Jewish learning; (3) developing the congregation as a locus for performing good deeds (social action); (4) converting synagogues into places for people to give and receive comfort and support; (5) encouraging synagogues to operate in a way that reflects Jewish values; and (6) creating an ambience of a welcoming community.[207]

Those in charge of Synagogue 2000 have candidly noted the two major obstacles they face: the inertia of denominational institutions—seminaries and movement organizations—that allegedly "work programmatically, providing short-term 'fixes' without addressing underlying systemic impediments," and the unwillingness of some congregations and their leaders to consider change seriously because they are continuing to attract members even as they do business as usual.[208] Synagogue 2000 has worked especially to sensitize congregational leaders to the importance of welcoming newcomers, and has distributed tapes and CDs to teach synagogues how to utilize liturgical music in new ways. The program's workshops aim to "reboot synagogue life," particularly by "sweating the details"—to imagine how the service looks to an outsider, and to find ways to involve members actively.[209] In line with its efforts to shake up the status quo, Synagogue 2000 held a huge event in Los Angeles for 6,000 lay and professional leaders. They gathered for a program called Hallelu, which used stars of stage and screen to fire up participants to "act on behalf of their own synagogues and on behalf of . . . the Jewish people."[210]

SYNAGOGUE TRANSFORMATION AND RENEWAL (STAR)

The STAR initiative has been funded to the tune of $18 million by a consortium of donors interested in helping synagogues reach more Jews. Its two main programs are "PEER: Professional Education for Excellence in Rabbis" and "Synaplex." PEER offers a

---

[207]Elliot Fein, "Synagogue 2000: Seeking Change. An Interview with Dr. Ron Wolfson," *Jewish Spectator* 66, Winter 2002, p. 24.

[208]Hoffman, "Synagogue 2000," p. 9.

[209]Gary Stern, "Synagogues Study Ways to Reform," *Journal News* (Westchester), Dec. 1, 2002, pp. 1B–2B.

[210]"Six Thousand Jews Strong," and "Sacred Connections," Synagogue 2000, Dec. 2002, www.s2k.org.

form of in-service training for rabbis already in the field, bringing them together for mentoring and mutual support in those areas of the profession for which their rabbinic training did not prepare them.[211] Synaplex focuses on involving ever larger numbers of Jews in a range of programs held in the synagogue on the Sabbath. While the provision of multiple services is one aspect of Synaplex, other programs seek to attract people to educational and recreational activities. "We are calling on the original functions of a shul as a *beit tefillah* (house of prayer), *beit midrash* (house of study), and *beit knesset* (house of gathering) during Jewish prime time—Shabbat," contends Rabbi Hayim Herring, executive director of STAR.[212] The program does not necessarily seek to attract Jews to worship. In the words of one participating rabbi, "Even if people come on Shabbat and never open a prayer book, it's fine." Accordingly, some participating congregations run everything from Saturday yoga groups, to classes on psychology, to bike rides and bird-watching excursions.[213] Strong emphasis is placed on marketing techniques to get people involved. Traditionalists may blanch, and even people in the synagogue-renewal business have their doubts. Ron Wolfson of Synagogue 2000 cautioned that "programming is essential but not the core of building a synagogue," since one must "address the issue of engagement with synagogue life."[214] Filling the synagogue on the Sabbath with people who are not there for Jewish worship or study may not be the way to create a religious community.

EXPERIMENTS IN CONGREGATIONAL EDUCATION (ECE)

Begun in 1992, ECE has worked with 41 congregations around the country, most of them Reform but also some that are Conser-

[211]Eric Fingerhut, "Torah, Talmud—and Management: Program Teaches Rabbis Skills to Run a Nonprofit," *Washington Jewish Week,* Jan. 20, 2005, www.washingtonjewishweek.com/localstory.php?wjw2/2886; Stacey Dresner, "PEER Program Helps Rabbis Learn Practical Skills," *Jewish Ledger of Western Massachusetts,* Sept. 15, 2004, www.jewishledger.com/articles/2004/09/15/news12.txt; Lisa Goddard, "New Twists on Old Faith: Young Rabbis Learn Novel Approaches to Worship and Business Affairs," *Sun Sentinel* (South Florida), Dec. 10, 2004, www.sun-sentinel.com.
[212]Danielle Haas, "Playing at a Shul Near You," *Jerusalem Report,* Dec. 2004, p. 30.
[213]Ibid, pp. 30–31; Gabrielle Birkner, "Stretching the Shul," *New York Jewish Week,* June 24, 2005, pp. 6–7.
[214]Ellen Jaffe-Gill, "Emanuel's Jumpin' at the Synaplex," *Jewish Journal of Greater Los Angeles,* Mar. 26, 2004, www.jewishjournal.com/hom/print.php?id=12016.

vative or Reconstructionist. Based at the Los Angeles campus of the Reform movement's Hebrew Union College, ECE, as its name implies, works mainly to develop the educational programs of synagogues so as to create a "congregation of learners." This is to be accomplished by engaging congregants of all ages "in some form of Jewish learning on a weekly basis in which the study of Jewish texts is woven into worship, social action, and all committee meetings." Facilitators, who are Jewish educational professionals, help congregational leaders "reflect on their current situation and consider alternative courses of action."[215] ECE also developed the Re-Imagine Project to help synagogues rethink their delivery of supplementary education, and to understand how that schooling fits into the life of the congregation. Participating synagogues benefit from a curriculum as well as a Web site where they "can take 'virtual visits' to congregations with a variety of innovative educational models already in place."[216]

FEDERATION PROJECTS

Federations of Jewish philanthropy became involved on a large scale in the wake of the 1990 NJPS, which was interpreted as showing a worrisome crisis of "Jewish continuity." Previously disengaged from synagogue life, which they considered sectarian and therefore divisive, local federations now sought to work with congregations, since strong synagogues were vital for building Jewish life. In the words of the Chicago federation's task force, "Synagogues [serve] as a portal or entry point for services . . . offered by the Jewish Federation and the agencies it supports."[217]

Indeed, since 1990 federations have come to recognize that the old division between "synagogue Jews" and "federation Jews" had

[215]Isa Aron and Robert M. Weinberg, "Experiments in Congregational Education," *Contact* 7, Autumn 2004, p. 10. See also two books by Isa Aron, *Becoming a Congregation of Learners: Learning as a Key to Revitalizing Congregational Life* (Woodstock, Vt., 2000), and *The Self-Renewing Congregation: Organizational Strategies for Revitalizing Congregational Life* (Woodstock, Vt., 2002). For a report on the impact of ECE in one Reform congregation, see Richard Jacobs, "Forsaking the Status Quo in Scarsdale," *Reform Judaism* 29, Summer 2000, pp. 51–59.

[216]Gabrielle Birkner, "Re-Imagine the Possibilities: A New Program Allows Congregations to Examine Educational Change," *New York Jewish Week,* June 24, 2005, pp. 14–15.

[217]*"Hazak V'Amatz:* Be Strong and Have Courage: Strengthening *Kehilla.* The Report of the Synagogue/Federation Long-Range Planning Task Force," July 2001.

collapsed, as federation supporters now tended to be people affiliated with a synagogue. Communities across the country established joint commissions on synagogue-federation relations, bridging the old divide between the two institutions. Federations have also lent their expertise to congregations, helping them with everything from bulk purchases of supplies to management training. Some federations have also underwritten the costs associated with participation in national projects such as Synagogue 2000 and the ECE so as to enable their local congregations to benefit from these revitalization programs.

And federations have channeled funds to congregations. In Boston, the federation pays for youth workers who develop synagogue programs for teens, helped establish Meah, an adult-education program in congregations, and supports family educators working in congregations.[218] Philadelphia's federation has funded programs to develop synagogue leadership and to weld together a consortium of congregations offering combined programs of Jewish education.[219] In New York, the UJA-Federation runs a management-assistance program under which congregational leaders of all denominations participate in eleven months of workshops run by the consulting firm McKinsey and Co. A separate program of "continuity grants" has enabled New York-area synagogues to develop initiatives to engage their members more actively.[220] Federations in communities as diverse as Atlanta, Chicago, Houston, and Los Angeles have experimented with new ways to deliver funding and other support to congregations.[221]

PRIVATE FOUNDATIONS

In a few communities, private foundations have funded efforts to strengthen synagogue life. In San Francisco, for example, the

---

[218]www.cjp.org/section_display.html?ID=192; Amy L. Sales, Annette Koren, and Susan L. Shevitz, *Sh'arim: Building Gateways to Jewish life and Community: A Report on Boston's Jewish Family Educator Initiative* (Boston, 2000).

[219]Brian Mono, "The Buzzword on the Bimah: Consulting," *Philadelphia Jewish Exponent,* Sept. 14, 2000, www.jewishexponent.com/Zoom.asp?stroyID=3949&pubID=67& subact=Cover.

[220]Stewart Ain, "The Ties That Bind," *New York Jewish Week,* Oct. 22, 1999, p. 8.

[221]These are surveyed in the Databank of Community-Based Synagogue Change Initiatives, www.jesna.org/cgi-bin/dbroundtble.php3. On programs launched in Houston, see Arlene Riesenfeld, "Houston Congregations Make Sabbath Come Alive," *Jewish Post and Opinion,* Sept. 6, 1995, p. 1.

Koret Foundation sponsored its own initiative, which "tested the hypothesis" that the presence in the synagogue of a program director or assistant rabbi with programming responsibilities would strengthen the Jewish identity of members and nonmembers.[222] In New Jersey, a similar effort to aid local congregations was supported by the Taub Foundation.

SYNAGOGUE PROGRAMS

Individual synagogues have launched their own strategic-planning initiatives. As synagogue boards are ever more likely to include members drawn from corporate sectors of American society, business models are finding their way into synagogue life — sometimes to the dismay of rabbis. The latter are now under far more pressure than before to act as chief executive officers rather than pastors or teachers, and their portfolio of responsibilities has been reshaped accordingly.[223] Synagogue boards are far more apt now to engage in McKinsey-style strategic planning to clarify their congregational mission and strengthen its delivery system.

DENOMINATIONAL BODIES

The congregational organizations of each movement have played a role in stimulating new thinking in their synagogues. Reform has been the most aggressive, promoting the ECE process and also involving some 80–100 congregations in a project called "Creating Learning Congregations."[224] Perhaps most interestingly, Reform has invested considerable energy in developing guidelines for improving "the sacred partnership" between professional and volunteer leadership in congregations.[225] The other denominations have developed new programs for congregational change as well. One prominent Orthodox rabbi, Saul Berman, has predicted that,

---

[222]Databank of Community-Based Synagogue Change Initiatives.

[223]For one rabbi's lament, see Allen I. Freehling, "Chief Executive Reform Rabbis: A Disturbing, Damaging Imbalance," *Jewish Spectator* 66, Winter 2002, pp. 21–23. On the larger phenomenon, see Jill Davison Sklar, "The Corporate Look Comes to the Synagogue World: And the Bottom Line Isn't Always Rosy," *Long Island Jewish World,* May 12–18, 1995, pp. 23 ff; and Jeffrey Levick, "Reinventing the Rabbi," *Cleveland Jewish News,* Dec. 4, 2000, Internet edition.

[224]Julie Wiener, "Charging Into Change," *Long Island Jewish World,* Sept. 29, 2000, p. 8.

[225]UAHC, "Brit Kodesh: Sacred Partnership: Readings and Exercises for Self-Study on the Relationship Between the Professional and Volunteer Leadership in Reform Congre-

as transformation efforts spread across the land, "the Orthodox community will be deeply engaged in the same process."[226] Two major Orthodox congregational bodies recently launched synagogue-renewal programs for their congregations. In May 2005, the OU offered grants of up to $20,000 to member synagogues that would develop "innovative programming," and six months earlier, in December 2004, Agudath Israel formed a National Tefilla Initiative encompassing 400 congregations for the purpose of revitalizing prayer—and this in the sector of the American Jewish community most routinely engaged with public prayer.[227]

Heralding a New Approach

It is still too early to assess the impact of these myriad efforts. The STAR initiative boasts a 78-percent increase in participants at Synaplex congregations on Friday evenings, and a 61-percent jump for Shabbat mornings. These programs have been in existence for only a few years, and it is anyone's guess how long those numbers will hold up. Everyone involved in these renewal projects acknowledges just how labor-intensive the task is, and for that reason alone all the programs combined have worked directly with only a small fraction of American congregations. But their impact transcends the individual synagogues directly served. Not only do they channel new thinking and new funding to synagogues, which, in the past, were left to fend for themselves, but they also send a strong message that the larger Jewish community is paying attention to what happens in synagogues. Whether new, more effective approaches have been developed, or whether, alternatively, "best practices" have been identified, is less important than the contribution these initiatives have made to the spirit of the age, which is to encourage systematic synagogue revitalization.[228]

gations," 2001. See also "The Rabbi-Congregation Relationship: A Vision for the 21st Century, Report of the Reconstructionist Commission on the Role of the Rabbi," Jan. 2001.

[226]Wiener, "Charging into Change," p. 16. Berman is the director of the Modern Orthodox group Edah.

[227]www.ou.org/oupr/2005/grants265.htm; Jennifer Siegel, "Seeking a 'New Way to Daven,'" *Forward,* May 13, 2005, p. 10.

[228]Zachary I. Heller, ed., *Re-Envisioning the Synagogue* (Hollis, N.H., 2005) is a recent volume that brings together the views of 17 rabbis and academics on the revitalization endeavor.

THE TWENTY-FIRST-CENTURY SYNAGOGUE

Common Themes

As is evident from the extensive initiatives for synagogue change, the American Jewish community at the beginning of the twenty-first century is eager to draw more people into congregations and to provide those who attend with a more positive experience. For all their differences of ideology, liturgy, and style, American synagogues have moved in similar directions, some with greater speed and comprehensiveness, some more slowly and haltingly, but few have been unaffected by the new spirit. Conversations with rabbis and other professionals in the denominational offices reveal a common language. Synagogues of all stripes share the following ten tendencies:

1. CREATING A "CARING COMMUNITY"

Congregations across the board are paying far more attention than in the past to the needs of individual members, and hence all the talk about "inclusiveness," a term that has different meanings depending on the setting. Reform and Reconstructionist synagogues strive to welcome Jews thought to have been marginalized — singles, gays and lesbians, intermarried Jews, Jews of non-Caucasian appearance. Conservative synagogues strive primarily to insure the involvement of women and multiple generations. And Orthodox synagogues address populations within their membership that come from different backgrounds and with different experiences, and therefore have varying sets of expectations about the style and pace of religious services.

To implement this outreach, congregations in all the denominations have expanded their activities for mutual support. Synagogues now have teams of members in the health-care field who serve as consultants for fellow congregants in need; they have organized members to visit the sick and prepare meals for the bereaved; and *hevra kadisha* groups (burial societies) have proliferated beyond the Orthodox community. A survey of congregations in Atlanta, for example, reported on synagogue programs that offered "gifts to new babies . . . support groups for divorced people, and . . . a 'member to member' group so congregants can seek out others who have undergone similar life experiences."[229]

Another dimension of the widespread effort to build caring communities is a new emphasis on hospitality and attentiveness. We have already noted the organization of welcoming squads for newcomers and the carefully organized practice of getting attendees at services to greet one another. Some synagogues go further. A Conservative congregation in Detroit sets aside time for a *"simcha* moment," when "everyone has the opportunity to tell the congregation something good that happened to them during the prior week." Congregants "bless each other at the end of services. It's not quite a group hug, but it's important that you are not ignored when you come to the synagogue."[230] And at a Reform temple in Maryland, a number of services over the course of the year are set aside as "Sacred Story Shabbats," when, instead of the usual talk about a topic in the Torah portion, members relate to the group their personal spiritual journeys. Each member focuses on a theme, such as "A Sanctuary in My Life," or "When I Have Experienced the Presence of the Divine in My Life." At the end of services, the congregation breaks into groups of ten to talk about themselves.[231] The common thread here is the attention given to individual experience in a very public setting.

2. SERVICING THE NEEDS OF MANY SUBGROUPS

Related to the emphasis on the individual is the willingness of congregations to sponsor multiple prayer services tailored to different elements of the community. "It may be stating the obvious, but different people have different spiritual needs," reports the rabbi of a Conservative congregation in suburban Philadelphia, which has three separate Sabbath morning services for adults. "If I had more space to start more minyanim, I would start them," he said. "We could have five different davening groups going on

---

[229]Todd Leopold, "Caring Communities," *Atlanta Jewish Times,* May 19, 2000, Internet edition. This article surveys the mutual-aid activities of half a dozen Atlanta congregations.

[230]Don Cohen, "Sacred Space," *Detroit Jewish News,* Oct. 1, 2004, www.detroit.jewish. com/modules.php?name=News&file=print&sid =1693.

[231]Warren G. Stone, "A Place of Jewish Personal Revelation," *Reform Judaism* 25, Winter 1996, pp. 70–71.

here."[232] In fact, the Synaplex model promoted by STAR seems to be pushing more congregations in this direction.

There are some downsides to the multiplication of services under one roof. For one thing, fragmentation can diminish allegiance to the synagogue, in turn affecting the cohesiveness of the entire congregation, not to speak of making it more difficult to raise money. "The fund-raisers can't give the same pitch. It's easier for people to say, 'I gave at the other minyan.' There's not that critical mass," argues one observer. Also, rivalries can erupt between competing services. Still, many synagogues have concluded that the risk is worth taking because members enjoy the intimacy of smaller services and the enhanced opportunities for active lay participation. To counter the dangers, some congregations have instituted a kiddush buffet after services to bring everyone together and maintain a sense of common purpose.[233] In an era when Americans are seeking options, multiple minyanim provide multiple points of entry.

3. THE REVIVAL OF PETITIONARY PRAYER

Petitionary prayer, asking God to fulfill one's needs, especially for healing, has become so important that synagogues of all denominations have reworked their worship services to allow special opportunities for it. Such prayers have always been part of the traditional liturgy, but over the past decade or so congregations of every stripe have come to emphasize one particular prayer—the *mi sheberach* for the sick. Matters were not always so. In Reconstructionist and Reform synagogues the prayer had long been anathema—in the former because the movement's theology denied the prayer's underlying assumption that a personal God is directly involved in the lives of people, and in the latter because classical Reform services had no place for individual prayers. But with the setting of the *mi sheberach* to the music of Debbie Friedman, it has now become ubiquitous in Reform temples and even among Reconstructionists. Today, even in most Orthodox congregations, worshipers line up to insure that a synagogue functionary will in-

---

[232]E.J. Kessler, "Rabbis Bucking for Friday Nights at the 'Synaplex': Trend Sees Practice of Holding Several Smaller Minyans Within a Synagogue," *Forward*, June 5, 1998, p. 1.
[233]Ibid., p. 2.

clude the names of friends and relatives who are ill in the communal prayer, or, as is the practice in virtually every Conservative synagogue, members stand at their seats and state the name of the sick person at the appropriate spot in the communal prayer. It would make for a fascinating ethnographic study to understand why this once fairly obscure prayer has assumed such importance and ubiquity: Are more people living with illness? Has research on the efficacy of prayer inspired people to participate? Is the *mi sheberach* popular precisely because it is both highly personal and universal? Is it a further expression of the quest for "meaning" in congregational worship?[234] What is beyond dispute is that the prayer for healing has profound meaning for many congregants in all kinds of synagogues.[235]

4. THE SPIRITUAL USES OF MUSIC

Music has become crucial to the American synagogue service. We noted above the emphatic insistence of Rabbi Eric Yoffie, president of the URJ, that a "prayer revolution" is dependent upon the appropriate use of music during worship. The exact same position was espoused by a Modern Orthodox rabbi, who wrote:

> nothing . . . comes close to the power of communal song. The energy that fills the room when all of the voices have joined as one is incomparable. Achieving this does require a rigid insistence that all of those who want to lead services comply with the communal singing standard, and the synagogue must provide opportunities for training. But the benefit in terms of renewal of interest and active participation in prayer is enormous.[236]

Few who are engaged in synagogue revitalization would disagree, and thus congregations all across the spectrum have developed

---

[234]Congregations do not confine themselves to this one prayer; some support the expressions of their congregants' Jewish needs "in health, spirituality, family relationships, education and social life." See, for example, the survey of new synagogue initiatives in Sun Valley (Phoenix) described in Barry Cohen, "Seeking Meaning: Synagogues Offer Cornucopia of Opportunities for Adults 35–55," *Jewish News of Greater Phoenix,* Sept. 22, 2000, www.jewishaz.com/jewishnews/000922/seek.shtml.

[235]It is not easy to ascertain how many synagogues offer healing services, but a network of some 30 healing centers, mostly based in Jewish family-service agencies, is affiliated with the National Jewish Healing Center. See its Web site, www.ncjh.org/centers.php.

[236]Rabbi Yosef Kanefsky, "Orthodoxy and Synagogue Renewal," *Contact* 2, Autumn 1999, pp. 8–9.

new approaches to music in order to overcome sterility and rote renditions of the prayer service.

For some congregations on the more traditional end of the spectrum, the music of Shlomo Carlebach has offered a new way: "Call it Modern Orthodoxy meets the holy rollers — a joyous, some say ecstatic, Judaism," wrote two journalists of Carlebach's "heartstirring melodies."[237] Others outside Orthodoxy, and not constrained by traditional opposition to the use of musical instrumentation in the services, have introduced complete bands or combinations of instruments chosen for their effects on worshipers. All are aimed at "bringing back that loving feeling."[238]

5. RETHINKING SPATIAL ARRANGEMENTS

As we have seen, some congregations have embarked on new construction to create more suitable spaces for prayer, and rabbis and cantors, in many cases, now place themselves within the congregation rather than in front of or far above it. In 1989, the chancellor of the Jewish Theological Seminary urged congregational leaders of the Conservative movement to "take a fresh look at the nature of our main services, so heavily dependent on the frontal orientation of the sanctuary . . . . The erecting of a new synagogue should encourage those responsible to consider a design that would restore the reading of the services and the Torah to the center of the sanctuary, and would underscore the role of the cantor as agent and facilitator."[239] Similar themes have been sounded in all the movements, so that even when congregations cannot afford to rebuild, they are moving services into rooms permitting flexible seating arrangements. Synagogue architects have designed light-weight pews and *mehitzahs* that can be moved easily; ramps and other conveniences to allow the disabled to get around; and environmentally sensitive arrangements to connect worshipers with nature.[240]

---

[237]Herb Keinon and Marilyn Henry, "Music to Their Ears," *Jerusalem Post*, Oct. 29, 1999, p. 19.

[238]Miriam Shaviv, "Bringing Back That Loving Feeling," *Jerusalem Report*, Oct. 2, 1997, pp. 50–51.

[239]Ismar Schorsch, "A Synagogue Is Not a Temple," delivered at the United Synagogue convention, Nov. 8, 1989, and published in Schorsch, *Polarities in Balance*: *Essays of Ismar Schorsch* (New York, 2004), p. 45.

[240]Sandee Brawarsky, "Rearranging the Synagogue: When It Comes to Shul Re-Design

6. REVOLUTIONIZING THE CHOREOGRAPHY OF WORSHIP

Congregants are less apt today to view themselves as an "audience" and more as participants. They are no longer docile, but move around during prayer, clapping and sometimes dancing; even in Reform temples it is not uncommon for the Torah to be carried around the synagogue and for congregants to turn around to greet the Sabbath on Friday night. An increasing number of people are able to read the Torah publicly, rather than relying on the cantor. Rabbis and cantors, in turn, are now far more facilitative than priestly; they work to involve congregants in the service, not to enact it for them.

7. THE ACTIVE PARTICIPATION OF WOMEN

Aside from Orthodox synagogues, virtually all congregations treat women and men equally. Bar mitzvah boys and bat mitzvah girls assume the exact same roles during their rites of passage, and that egalitarianism extends into adulthood. Women play equal roles in board leadership, and congregations of all stripes (even Orthodox) have elected women as presidents. While there is still talk of a glass ceiling for female rabbis, change appears to be in the offing in this realm too: females outnumber males as students in most rabbinical schools that accept women, a phenomenon that is even more pronounced in cantorial schools. Particularly on the West Coast, some of the largest Reform temples are now led by women rabbis, a trend that will undoubtedly make its way eastward.

The exception proves the rule: Orthodox synagogues still maintain a physical partition between the seating areas for women and men, and the focal points of worship activity—the prayer leader and the Torah reading—are situated in the men's section. It is nonetheless noteworthy, as noted above, how Orthodox congregations have struggled to involve women in ways that are permissible within the framework of Orthodox Jewish law.

---

the New Buzz Words Are Community and Inclusiveness," *New York Jewish Week,* June 24, 2005, pp. 18–20.

8. Focusing on Adult Study

Across the spectrum of congregations, far more educational courses are offered by congregations than in previous generations, and it has become part of accepted synagogue culture for people of all ages to engage in learning. This may take the form of building skills, such as reading Hebrew, Torah cantillation, kosher cooking, or crafting Jewish ritual objects. Reform and Conservative synagogues offer intensive adult bar/bat mitzvah programs for those who did not receive a strong education when they were young. And congregations of all kinds offer a multiplicity of textual study, with classes on the Torah portion, Talmud, Jewish history, and Jewish customs and practices among the most popular.

A recent study of adult Jewish education found that the synagogue is the most commonly utilized site for such classes, followed by the Jewish community center. Why, the authors ask, is this so?

> Aside from all their other assets, synagogues are numerous and widely scattered; generally at least one is found very near where most Jews live. Nearly two-thirds of American Jews (64 percent) live within 15 minutes of a synagogue. More than two-fifths (41 percent) live within 10 minutes of one. The comparable figures for JCCs are 37 percent for 15 minutes, and 19 percent for ten minutes or less. Synagogues are quite accessible, local institutions, often surrounded by concentrated congregants who encounter one another outside the temple, thereby organically reinforcing their bonds of community. . . . Congregations are also the loci of the most important family lifecycle transitions, a place where Jews come to pray, and are professionally headed by Jewish education professionals whose very title refers to the educational role ("rabbi"="my teacher").[241]

Not surprisingly, some of the nationally franchised Jewish adult education programs, such as Meah and the Florence Melton Adult Mini-School, offer courses in synagogues.

9. Serving as the Venue for Social Action

Congregations sponsor activities designed to engage their members in programs to aid other Jews and/or the larger communities

---

[241]Steven M. Cohen and Aryeh Davidson, *Adult Jewish Learning in America: Current Patterns and Prospects for Growth* (New York, 2001), pp. 27–28.

in which they are situated. In the more traditional congregations, these generally take the form of providing clothing and food to impoverished Jews, organizing visits to those who are ill, and raising money for Jewish institutions in the U.S. and abroad. As one moves across the spectrum from the Orthodox to the more liberal synagogues, congregational programming becomes less parochial and more universalistic: synagogues might involve their members in helping out at soup kitchens, shelters for battered women, and agencies for the sick and needy, or creating a market for the sale of organic food.

Rabbis and lay leaders freely concede that they are intentionally widening the scope of their work in order to bring in Jews who are not interested in prayer and Jewish study, the synagogue's traditional priorities. "For better or worse," said one thirtysomething rabbi, "American Jews of my age have for the most part not grown up davening." Yet even in congregations where prayer is not a foreign experience, a range of social action programs, often going under the rubric of *tikkun olam* (repairing the world), are sponsored in the clear understanding that they build social capital, and in turn strengthen the fabric of the synagogue community.[242]

10. FOOD, THE WAY TO A JEW'S HEART

Although it appears nowhere in the foregoing study, food is a basic ingredient of community-building in synagogues. Late Friday evening services routinely include a "collation" of coffee (always decaf) and pastries. On Shabbat mornings, study groups in Reform temples begin over bagels and lox. And in most synagogues, there is a kiddush after Sabbath and festival morning services, as well as *seudah shlishit* ("third meal") on late Sabbath afternoon. Increasingly, congregations are introducing a "break-fast" for the community of worshipers at the end of Yom Kippur. Every synagogue offers a kiddush in its sukkah on the holiday of Sukkot. After the reading of the Scroll of Esther on Purim evening, *haman-*

---

[242]A survey of such activities sponsored by synagogues in New York is provided by Steve Lipman, "The Multitasking Shul," *New York Jewish Week,* June 24, 2005, pp. 4–5. Robert Putnam, *Bowling Alone: The Collapse and Revival of American Community* (New York, 2000), chap. 4, discusses the role of religious congregations in building social capital.

taschen and drinks are provided, and refreshments and alcoholic beverages are to be had on Simchat Torah.[243] The communal seder is a commonplace at many synagogues on Passover night. And then there are the light spreads available, before and after committee and board meetings, educational and other programs, and the more elaborate meals prepared by women's auxiliaries for the entire congregation at all kinds of festive occasions.

All of this is the source of much humor, but in truth it is hard to find a congregation that does not use food as a lubricant for community-building. More than anything else, food is the common denominator of all contemporary American synagogues.

The Synagogue in the Context of American Religious Trends

None of this would come as great news to informed observers of Christian (and perhaps other non-Jewish) congregations in America. To begin with food, note how a student of Protestant churches describes "food-centered social events":

> Church dinners and coffee hours . . . are crucial to the religious life of many Americans. For these people participating in a community is often the most important motivation for attending church, and shared meals are often more important to creating community than are shared worship experiences. The meals are a place where religious identity is shaped, community is built, and memories are created. They may not be religious, but they're not just another meal.[244]

Beyond the specific issue of food, what is noteworthy is the extent to which building community is a central preoccupation of churches, and is now driving synagogue transformation as well.

Churches, too, have grown far more interested in the choreography of services, the uses of space, and, of course, music. This is how Robert Wuthnow, one of the leading students of contempo-

---

[243]Of late, some Orthodox congregations have innovated unofficial "kiddush clubs" that make available high-quality liquor after the Shabbat Torah reading. The OU grew so concerned about the potentially embarrassing disruptions of the service that could ensue that it has tried to ban the clubs. See Gabriel Sanders, "Orthodox Union Sets Ban on Clubs for Scotch Tipplers," *Forward,* Jan. 28, 2005, pp. 1–2; and Steve Lipman, "Whiskey Rebellion," *New York Jewish Week,* Feb. 18, 2005, pp. 8–9.

[244]Daniel Sack, *Whitebread Protestants: Food and Religion in American Culture* (New York, 2000), p. 62.

rary American religious life, has described changes in Christian worship:

> Some of the nation's fastest-growing churches attribute their success to what leaders enthusiastically refer to as contemporary worship. This is a distinctive innovation that has emerged largely since the mid-1970s. Pioneered by young pastors and lay volunteers at fledgling nondenominational churches, it has grown to the point that many traditional churches have started borrowing from it as well. Contemporary worship lives up to its name. It incorporates musical instruments (such as electric guitars and keyboards) and lyrics unheard of in churches a generation ago and makes use of new communication technologies such as home-produced videos and the Internet. It is meant to attract people with little interest in historic approaches to worship. Some of its advocates further distinguish it by arguing that it offers immediacy, relevancy, and intelligibility, rather than permanence, and that it is an expression of a new generation trying to find its voice in the church.[245]

It is not difficult to find strong parallels between most new trends in synagogue life and prevailing patterns in churches, from the concern with women's equality and gender-neutral language to the harnessing of new technologies for worship and study; from the quest for inclusiveness[246] to less formal styles adopted by clergy; from the creation of niche congregations to serve specific age groups, people of the same sexual orientation, or like-minded political views, to the goal of creating "caring communities."

A recent study reports on Christian congregations that make "community building . . . an explicit focus, a subject of conversation not left to chance but carried out through organized programs":

> Beyond making some effort to care for those members who are experiencing a personal crisis, and beyond the informal groups of friends that are found in all congregations, these congregations engage in a conscious attempt to provide members with experiences of community and an opportunity to discuss what that means. There is an explicit language of community-building employed here, an elab-

---

[245]Robert Wuthnow, *All in Sync: How Music and Art Are Revitalizing American Religion* (Berkeley, Cal., 2003), p. 151.

[246]To be sure, inclusiveness has a very different connotation in churches than in synagogues, as the former are primarily concerned with ensuring racial and ethnic diversity in the membership. A fascinating ethnographic study of how one church achieved this goal is Gerardo Marti, *A Mosaic of Believers: Diversity and Innovation in a Multiethnic Church* (Bloomington, Ind., 2005).

orated discourse about what it means to be a community. This is in contrast to the family congregations, where "family" as a term is used frequently, but what it means to be a family is seldom explicitly articulated.[247]

Members of such community-building churches self-consciously refer to themselves as a "community of like-minded people" or "a caring community."[248] Is this not precisely what efforts at synagogue change are promoting? It is difficult to avoid agreeing with Heinrich Heine, who wrote over 175 years ago about his former coreligionists, *"Wie es sich christelt, so jüdelt es sich"*—as do the Christians, so do the Jews. Only, perhaps, in their heavy emphasis on textual study do synagogues depart very far from emerging church norms.[249]

A Final Word

There is much to admire in the recent drive to revitalize American Jewish congregations. Many concerned Jewish communal leaders, as we noted at the outset, regard the revival of synagogue life as vital for the health and growth of the entire Jewish enterprise. Yet even as congregations experiment with the liturgy, music, and choreography of worship services, a note of caution is in order. Perhaps synagogues have struggled to attract more regular worshipers because prayer itself is difficult, particularly for highly educated American Jews. In their study of moderately affiliated Jews who maintain some formal attachment but are not engaged actively in Jewish life, Arnold M. Eisen and Steven M. Cohen identify the gap between private and public prayer as a primary challenge. They summarize their research as follows:

> The most striking finding of our study in connection with God and the synagogue is that, for the most part, the Jews we interviewed do not make any straightforward connection between the two. They be-

---

[247]Penny Edgell Becker, *Congregations in Conflict: Cultural Models of Local Religious Life* (New York, 1999), pp. 104–05.

[248]Ibid., p. 104.

[249]Nancy T. Ammerman has commented on the divergent approaches to learning taken by synagogues and churches both in terms of subject matter and the purpose of study. She also demonstrates significant differences in the study of the Bible between the different Christian groups. See her book, *Pillars of Faith: American Congregations and Their Partners* (Berkeley, Cal., 2005), pp. 30–34, 47–49.

lieve in God far more than we expected, or than survey data about American Jews led us to believe. They are also surprisingly content with, and even fondly attached to, their synagogues. They told us time and again that they do not come to synagogue expecting to find God there, or stay away because they do not. The words in the prayer book do not particularly interest them. The God described and invoked in those prayers is very different from the one in which they believe—too commanding, for one thing, and . . . far too "Jewish." They are distinctly uncomfortable with the act of prayer. And yet, they pray. This combination of unease and devotion, enthusiasm and disquiet, came through repeatedly in our interviews—making for patterns of alienation and belonging not easily unraveled or reversed.[250]

Here, then, is the deeper dilemma facing synagogues and their members: a great many Jews have difficulty engaging in public prayer and finding it personally meaningful. Like their Christian counterparts, Jews have moved away from what sociologist Robert Wuthnow has called "a traditional spirituality of inhabiting sacred places" to a "new spirituality of seeking," exchanging the sublimity of churches and synagogues for "the new spiritual freedom" to be found through privatized, inner experiences.[251] If that is a correct diagnosis, none of the current synagogue revitalization programs will make large numbers of contemporary Jews comfortable with public prayer.[252]

Moreover, dual-earner families have to make hard decisions about how to use their limited time most efficiently. Synagogues feel compelled to make allowances for what one rabbi has called the "McDonald's generation, fast food for the soul," which is impatient with religious services that stretch on.[253] Many congregations have sharply curtailed services to fit into neat packages of an hour on Friday night or two hours on Shabbat morning, but whether such a step can make for a more satisfying synagogue experience, let alone allow for a meaningful reading of the Torah and serious prayer, is another matter.

---

[250]Steven M. Cohen and Arnold M. Eisen, *The Jew Within: Self, Family, and Community in America* (Bloomington, Ind., 2000), pp. 155–56.

[251]Wuthnow's study, *After Heaven: Spirituality in America Since the 1950s,* is cited ibid, p. 178.

[252]Perhaps for this reason, the STAR initiative urges congregations to offer alternatives to worship services so as to bring in people who cannot relate to public prayer.

[253]Steve Lipman, "Timing Is Everything," *New York Jewish Week,* June 2, 2000, p. 12.

In the years to come, American synagogues will undoubtedly continue to address the difficulties Jews experience when they engage in public worship, and in the course of doing so will engage in further experimentation. What should be clear from our survey of recent trends in synagogue life is that no matter how we judge the efforts of congregations as they have negotiated the challenges of the past decades, no fair-minded observer can accuse them of having been moribund, static, or unchanging. Surveying the world of the American synagogue at the end of the twentieth century, anthropologist Riv-Ellen Prell concluded as follows:

> Since the 1970s, the synagogue has been anything but an uncontested bedrock of American Jewish life . . . . Synagogues . . . have been responsive to cultural and social change and the challenges posed. Rabbis have fought aggressively on all sides of issues to allow their synagogues to reflect passionately held principles about gender equality, the rights of homosexual Jews, access of the intermarried, and the maintenance of Halakhah. Thus, there has been nothing bland about American synagogues. To the contrary, they have become important testing grounds, even battlegrounds, for shaping American Judaism . . . .[254]

Synagogues will surely continue to serve as such testing grounds—as indeed they must, given their centrality to Jewish life—just as they have responded with creativity and innovation to the altered religious landscape of the past half-century.

© JACK WERTHEIMER 2005

---

[254]Riv-Ellen Prell, "Communities of Choice and Memory," p. 271.

Review
of
the
Year

DEMOGRAPHY

World Jewish Population, 2005

T HE WORLD'S JEWISH POPULATION was estimated at 13.034 million at the beginning of 2005—an increase of about 44,000 over the previous year's revised estimate.[1] World Jewry continues to be close to zero population growth. Israeli Jews constituted 40.2 percent of world Jewry.

The new figures reflect updated information on Jewish population that became available following the major round of national censuses and Jewish population surveys in countries with large Jewish populations over the period 1999–2005. This new evidence generally confirmed our previous estimates, but sometimes suggested upward or downward revisions. Over the last decade, a significantly expanded database has become available allowing for the critical assessment of the worldwide Jewish demographic picture.

Figures on population size, characteristics, and trends are a primary tool in the evaluation of Jewish community needs and prospects at the local level and internationally. The estimates for major regions and individual countries reported in this overview reflect a prolonged and ongoing effort to study scientifically the demography of contemporary world Jewry.[2] Data collection and comparative research have benefited from the collaboration of scholars and institutions in many countries, including replies to direct inquiries regarding current estimates. It should be emphasized, however, that the elaboration of a worldwide set of estimates for the Jewish populations of the various countries is beset with

---

[1] The previous estimates, as of January 1, 2004, were published in AJYB 2004, pp. 489–521. See also Sergio DellaPergola, Uzi Rebhun, and Mark Tolts, "Prospecting the Jewish Future: Population Projections 2000–2080," AJYB 2000, pp. 103–46; and previous AJYB volumes for further details on earlier estimates.

[2] Many of these activities are carried out by, or in coordination with, the Division of Jewish Demography and Statistics at the A. Harman Institute of Contemporary Jewry (ICJ), the Hebrew University of Jerusalem. The collaboration of the many institutions and individuals in the different countries who supplied information for this update is acknowledged with thanks. Thanks are due in particular to Yaacov Rubel (Buenos Aires), Ellen Rubinstein (Frankfurt a.M.), Lina Filiba (Istanbul), David Saks (Johannesburg), Marlena Schmool (London), Mauricio Lulka (Mexico City), Vivian Klaff (Newark, Delaware), Laurence Kotler-Berkowitz (New York), René Decol (São Paulo), Ira Sheskin (Miami), Gary Eckstein (Sydney), Benjamin Anderman, Erik H. Cohen, Judith Even, Norma Gurovich, Uzi Rebhun, Dalia Sagi, and Mark Tolts (Jerusalem).

difficulties and uncertainties.[3] Users of Jewish population estimates should be aware of these difficulties and of the inherent limitations of our data.

DETERMINANTS OF JEWISH POPULATION CHANGE

Major geopolitical and socioeconomic changes have affected the world scene since the end of the 1980s, particularly the political breakup of the Soviet Union, Germany's reunion, the European Union's gradual expansion to 25 states (including the addition of ten new members on May 1, 2004), South Africa's transition to a new regime, political and economic instability in several Latin American countries, and the volatile situation in Israel and the Middle East. Jewish population trends were most sensitive to these developments. Large-scale emigration from the former USSR (FSU) and rapid population growth in Israel were the most visible effects, accompanied by other significant Jewish population transfers. Reflecting geographical mobility and increased fragmentation but also new consolidation of the global system of nations, over 80 percent of world Jewry live in two countries, the United States and Israel, and 95 percent are concentrated in the ten largest country communities. Six of the G8 countries[4] (the United States, France, Canada, the United Kingdom, the Russian Republic, and Germany) comprise 87 percent of the total Jewish population outside of Israel. The aggregate of these major Jewish population centers virtually determines the assessment of world Jewry's total size and trends.

One fundamental aspect of population in general and of Jewish population in particular is its perpetual change. Population size and composition reflect a continuous interplay of three major determinants. Two of these are shared by all populations: (a) the balance of vital events (births and deaths); and (b) the balance of international migration (immigration and emigration). Both of these factors affect increases or decreases in the physical presence of individuals in a given place. The third determinant consists of identificational changes (accessions and secessions), and applies only to populations—usually referred to as subpopulations—that are defined by some cultural, symbolic or other specific peculiarity, as is

---

[3] For overviews of the subject matter and technical issues see Paul Ritterband, Barry A. Kosmin, and Jeffrey Scheckner, "Counting Jewish Populations: Methods and Problems," AJYB 1988, pp. 204–21; and Sergio DellaPergola, "Demography," in Martin Goodman, ed., *The Oxford Handbook of Jewish Studies* (Oxford, 2002), pp. 797–823.

[4] The eight leading economies in the world, also comprising Japan and Italy.

the case with Jews. The latter type of change does not affect people's physical presence but rather their willingness or ability to identify with a particular religious, ethnic or otherwise culturally defined group. Some of these passages receive formal sanction through a religious ritual ceremony of one sort or another. However, the emotional and quantitative significance of passages recorded in individual perceptions, devoid of any ceremonial, cannot be undervalued.

The country figures presented here for 2005 were updated from those for 2004 in accordance with the known or estimated changes in the interval — vital events, migrations, and identificational changes. In our updating procedure, whether or not exact data on intervening changes were available, we consistently applied the known or assumed direction of change, and accordingly added to or subtracted from previous Jewish population estimates. If there is evidence that intervening changes balanced each other off, Jewish population remained unchanged. This procedure proved highly efficient in the past. Most of the times when improved Jewish population figures became available reflecting a new census or survey, our annually updated estimates proved on target.

The more recent findings basically confirm the estimates we reported in previous AJYB volumes and, perhaps more importantly, our interpretation of the trends now prevailing in the demography of world Jewry.[5] Concisely stated, these involve a positive balance of vital events (Jewish births and deaths) in Israel and a negative one in nearly all other Jewish communities; a positive migration balance for Israel, the United States, Germany, Canada, Australia, and a few other Western countries, and a negative one in Latin America, South Africa, Eastern Europe, Muslim countries, and some Western European countries as well; a positive balance of accessions and secessions in Israel, and an often negative, or, in any event, rather uncertain balance elsewhere. While allowing for improvements and corrections, the 2005 population estimates highlight the increasing complexity of the sociodemographic and identificational processes underlying the definition of Jewish populations, and hence the estimates of their sizes. This complexity is magnified at a time of perva-

---

[5] For historical background, see Roberto Bachi, *Population Trends of World Jewry* (Jerusalem, 1976); U.O. Schmelz, "Jewish Survival: The Demographic Factors," AJYB 1981, pp. 61–117; U.O. Schmelz, *Aging of World Jewry* (Jerusalem, 1984); Sergio DellaPergola, "Changing Cores and Peripheries: Fifty Years in Socio-demographic Perspective," in Robert S. Wistrich, ed., *Terms of Survival: The Jewish World since 1945* (London, 1995), pp. 13–43; and Sergio DellaPergola, *World Jewry beyond 2000: Demographic Prospects* (Oxford, 1999).

sive international migration, often implying bi-local residences and double counts of people on the move. Consequently, the analyst has to come to terms with the paradox of the *permanently provisional* nature of Jewish population estimates.

SOURCES OF DATA

In general, the amount and quality of documentation on Jewish population size and characteristics is far from satisfactory. In recent years, however, important new data and estimates became available for several countries through official population censuses and Jewish-sponsored sociodemographic surveys. National censuses yielded results on Jewish populations in Ireland, the Czech Republic, and India (1991); Romania and Bulgaria (1992); the Russian Republic and Macedonia (1994); Israel (1995); Canada, South Africa, Australia, and New Zealand (1996 and 2001); Belarus, Azerbaijan, Kazakhstan, and Kyrgyzstan (1999); Brazil, Mexico, Switzerland, Estonia, Latvia, and Tajikistan (2000); the United Kingdom, Hungary, Croatia, Lithuania, and Ukraine (2001); and the Russian Republic and Georgia (2002). Permanent national population registers, including information on the Jewish religious, ethnic or national group, exist in several European countries (Switzerland, Norway, Finland, Estonia, Latvia, and Lithuania), and in Israel.

In addition, independent sociodemographic studies have provided most valuable information on Jewish demography and socioeconomic stratification, as well as on Jewish identification. Surveys were conducted over the last several years in South Africa (1991 and 1998); Mexico (1991 and 2000); Lithuania (1993); the United Kingdom and Chile (1995); Venezuela (1998–99); Israel, Hungary, the Netherlands, and Guatemala (1999); Moldova and Sweden (2000); France and Turkey (2002); and Argentina (2003 and 2004). In the United States important new insights were provided by two large surveys, the National Jewish Population Survey (NJPS, 2000–01) and the American Jewish Identity Survey (AJIS, 2001). Several further Jewish population studies were separately conducted in major cities in the United States (notably in New York City in 2002) and in other countries. Additional evidence on Jewish population trends can be obtained from the systematic monitoring of membership registers, vital statistics, and migration records available from Jewish communities and other Jewish organizations in many countries or cities, notably in the United Kingdom, Germany, Italy, Buenos Aires, and São Paulo. Detailed data on Jewish immigration routinely collected in Israel help in the assessment of changing Jewish population sizes in other countries. Some of this ongoing research is part of a coordinated effort aimed at updating the profile of world Jewry.[6]

DEFINITIONS

A major problem with Jewish population estimates periodically circulated by individual scholars or Jewish organizations is a lack of coherence and uniformity in the definitional criteria followed—when the issue of defining the Jewish population is addressed at all. Simply put, the quantitative study of Jewish populations can rely only on operational, not normative, definitional criteria. Three major concepts must be considered in order to put the study of Jewish demography on serious comparative ground.

In most countries outside of Israel, the *core Jewish population*[7] includes all those who, when asked, identify themselves as Jews; or, if the respondent is a different person in the same household, are identified by him/her as Jews. This is an intentionally comprehensive and pragmatic approach reflecting the nature of most available sources of data on Jewish population. In countries other than Israel, such data often derive from population censuses or social surveys where interviewees have the option to decide how to answer relevant questions on religious or ethnic preferences. Such a definition of a person as a Jew, reflecting *subjective* feelings, broadly overlaps but does not necessarily coincide with Halakhah (rabbinic law) or other normatively binding definitions. Inclusion does *not* depend on any measure of that person's Jewish commitment or behavior in terms of religiosity, beliefs, knowledge, communal affiliation, or otherwise.

---

[6]Following the International Conference on Jewish Population Problems held in Jerusalem in 1987, initiated by the late Roberto Bachi of the Hebrew University and sponsored by major Jewish organizations worldwide, an International Scientific Advisory Committee (ISAC) was established. See Sergio DellaPergola and Leah Cohen, eds., *World Jewish Population: Trends and Policies* (Jerusalem, 1992). An Initiative on Jewish Demography, sponsored by the Jewish Agency under the chairmanship of Sallai Meridor, led to an international conference held in Jerusalem in 2002 and to an effort of data collection and analysis implemented over the years 2003–05. The Jewish People Policy Planning Institute (JPPPI), chaired by Ambassador Dennis Ross, provides a framework for policy analyses and suggestions, including Jewish population issues. See Sergio DellaPergola, *Jewish Demography: Facts, Outlook, Challenges*, JPPPI Alert Paper 2 (Jerusalem, 2003); and *The Jewish People Policy Planning Institute Assessment 2005*, Executive Report 2 (Jerusalem, 2005).
[7] The term was initially suggested in Barry A. Kosmin, Sidney Goldstein, Joseph Waksberg, Nava Lerer, Ariela Keysar, and Jeffrey Scheckner, *Highlights of the CJF 1990 National Jewish Population Survey* (New York, 1991).

The *core* Jewish population includes all converts to Judaism by any procedure, as well as other people who declare they are Jewish. Also included are persons of Jewish parentage who claim no current religious or ethnic identity. Persons of Jewish parentage who adopted another religion are excluded, as are other individuals who in censuses or surveys explicitly identify with a non-Jewish group without having converted out. In the State of Israel, personal status is subject to the rulings of the Ministry of the Interior, which relies on criteria established by rabbinical authorities. In Israel, therefore, the *core* Jewish population does not simply express subjective identification but reflects definite legal rules, those of Halakhah. Documentation to prove a person's Jewish status may include non-Jewish sources.

The question whether Jewish identification according to this *core* definition can or should be mutually exclusive with other religious corporate identities emerged on a major scale in the course of the 2000–01 NJPS. The solution chosen—admittedly after much debate—was to allow for Jews with multiple religious identities to be included under certain circumstances in the standard definition of Jewish population.[8] A category of Persons of Jewish Background (PJBs) was introduced: some of these were included in the Jewish population count and others were not. By the same token, Jews with multiple ethnic identities were included in the standard Jewish population count in Canada. The adoption of such extended criteria by the research community tends to stretch Jewish population definitions further than had usually been done in the past and beyond the abovementioned typical *core* definition. These procedures tend to limit actual comparability of the same Jewish population over time and of different Jewish populations at the same time.

The *enlarged Jewish population*[9] includes the sum of (a) the *core* Jew-

---

[8] In the latter survey, at least in the version initially processed and circulated by UJC, "a Jew is defined as a person whose religion is Judaism, OR whose religion is Jewish and something else, OR who has no religion and has at least one Jewish parent or a Jewish upbringing, OR who has a non-monotheistic religion and has at least one Jewish parent or a Jewish upbringing." See Laurence Kotler-Berkowitz, Steven M. Cohen, Jonathon Ament, Vivian Klaff, Frank Mott, and Danyelle Peckerman-Neuman, with Lorraine Blass, Debbie Bursztyn, and David Marker, *The National Jewish Population Survey 2000–01: Strength, Challenge, and Diversity in the American Jewish Population* (New York, 2003). See also *Contemporary Jewry* 25, 2005, which is devoted to critical essays and analyses of NJPS methods and findings. This publication, the scholarly journal of the Association for the Scientific Study of Jewry, is edited by Samuel Heilman.

[9] The term *enlarged Jewish population* was initially suggested by Sergio DellaPergola, "The Italian Jewish Population Study: Demographic Characteristics and Trends," in

ish population; (b) all other persons of Jewish parentage who—by *core* Jewish population criteria—are *not* Jewish currently (or at the time of investigation); and (c) all of the respective further non-Jewish household members (spouses, children, etc.). Non-Jews with Jewish background, as far as they can be ascertained, include: (a) persons who have themselves adopted another religion, even though they may claim to be also Jewish by ethnicity or religion—with the caveat just mentioned for recent U.S. and Canadian data; and (b) other persons with Jewish parentage who disclaim being Jews. As noted, some PJBs who do not pertain to the *core* Jewish population naturally belong under the *enlarged* definition.[10] It is customary in sociodemographic surveys to consider the religio-ethnic identification of parents. Some censuses, however, do ask about more distant ancestry. For both conceptual and practical reasons, the *enlarged* definition does not include other non-Jewish relatives who lack a Jewish background and live in exclusively non-Jewish households.

The *Law of Return,* Israel's distinctive legal framework for the acceptance and absorption of new immigrants, awards Jewish new immigrants immediate citizenship and other civil rights. According to the current, amended version of the Law of Return, a Jew is any person born to a Jewish mother or converted to Judaism (regardless of denomination—Orthodox, Conservative, or Reform), who does not have another religious identity. By ruling of Israel's Supreme Court, conversion from Judaism, as in the case of some ethnic Jews who currently identify with another religion, entails loss of eligibility for Law of Return purposes. The law as such does not affect a person's Jewish status—which, as noted, is adjudicated by Israel's Ministry of Interior and rabbinical authorities—but only the specific benefits available under the Law of Return. The law extends its provisions to all current Jews, their children, and grandchildren, as well as to the respective Jewish or non-Jewish spouses. As a result of its three-generation and lateral extension, the Law of Return applies to a large population, one of significantly wider scope than *core* and *enlarged* Jewish populations defined above.[11] It is actually quite difficult to estimate what the total size of the *Law of Return* population

---

U.O. Schmelz, P. Glikson, and S.J. Gould, eds., *Studies in Jewish Demography: Survey for 1969–1971* (Jerusalem-London, 1975), pp. 60–97.

[10] See Kotler-Berkowitz et al., *National Jewish Population Survey 2000–01.*

[11] For a concise review of the rules of attribution of Jewish personal status in rabbinic and Israeli law, including reference to Jewish sects, isolated communities, and apostates, see Michael Corinaldi, "Jewish Identity," chap. 2 in his *Jewish Identity: The Case of Ethiopian Jewry* (Jerusalem, 1998).

could be. These higher estimates are not discussed below systematically, but some notion of their possible extent is given for the major countries. The significant involvement of major Jewish organizations in Israel and in the U.S.—such as the Jewish Agency and the United Jewish Communities (UJC)—in sponsoring data collection tends to complicate research issues. Organizations are motivated by the needs of their constituencies rather than by sharp analytic criteria. The understandable interest of organizations to continue functioning and securing budgetary resources tends to bring them to favor viewing Jewish populations closer to the *enlarged* than to the *core* definition.

The following estimates of Jewish population distribution in each continent (table 1 below), country (tables 2–9), and major metropolitan areas (table 10) consistently aim at the concept of *core* Jewish population. The *core* is indeed the necessary starting point for any admittedly relevant elaboration about the *enlarged*.

PRESENTATION AND QUALITY OF DATA

Until 1999, Jewish population estimates presented in the *American Jewish Year Book* referred to December 31 of the year preceding by two the date of publication. Since 2000 our estimates refer to January 1 of the current year of publication. Efforts to provide the most recent possible picture entail a short span of time for evaluation and correction of available information, hence a somewhat greater margin of inaccuracy. Indeed, where appropriate, we revised our previous estimates in the light of newly accrued information on Jewish populations (tables 1 and 2). Corrections were also applied retrospectively to the 2004 figures for major geographical regions so as to ensure a better base for comparisons with the 2005 estimates. Corrections of the latest estimates, if needed, will be presented in future volumes of the AJYB.

We provide separate figures for each country with approximately 100 or more resident *core* Jews. Residual estimates of Jews living in other smaller communities supplement some of the continental totals. For each of the reported countries, the four columns in tables 3–7 provide an estimate of midyear 2004 total population,[12] the estimated 1/1/2005 Jewish population, the proportion of Jews per 1,000 of total population, and a rating of the accuracy of the Jewish population estimate.

---

[12] Data and estimates derived from Population Reference Bureau, *2004 World Population Data Sheet* (Washington, D.C., 2005).

There is wide variation in the quality of the Jewish population estimates for different countries. For many Diaspora countries it would be best to indicate a range (minimum–maximum) rather than a definite figure for the number of Jews. It would be confusing, however, to be confronted with a long list of ranges; this would also complicate the regional and world totals. The figures actually indicated for most of the Diaspora communities should be understood as being the central value of the plausible range of the respective core Jewish populations in these countries. The relative magnitude of this range varies inversely to the accuracy of the estimate.

The three main elements that affect the accuracy of each estimate are the nature and quality of the base data, how recent the base data are, and the method of updating. A simple code combining these elements is used to provide a general evaluation of the reliability of the Jewish population figures reported in the detailed tables below. The code indicates different quality levels of the reported estimates: (A) Base figure derived from countrywide census or relatively reliable Jewish population survey; updated on the basis of full or partial information on Jewish population movements in the respective country during the intervening period. (B) Base figure derived from less accurate but recent countrywide Jewish population data; partial information on population movements in the intervening period. (C) Base figure derived from less recent sources, and/or unsatisfactory or partial coverage of a country's Jewish population; updating according to demographic information illustrative of regional demographic trends. (D) Base figure essentially speculative; no reliable updating procedure. In categories (A), (B), and (C), the year in which the country's base figure or important partial updates were obtained is also stated. For countries whose Jewish population estimate for 2005 was not only updated but also revised in the light of improved information, the sign "X" is appended to the accuracy rating.

One additional tool for updating Jewish population estimates is provided by a recent set of demographic projections developed at the Hebrew University of Jerusalem.[13] Such projections, based on available data on Jewish population composition by age and sex groups, extrapolate the most likely observed or expected Jewish population trends over the first decades of the twenty-first century. Even where reliable information on the dynamics of Jewish population change is not immediately available,

---

[13] See DellaPergola, Rebhun, and Tolts, "Prospecting the Jewish Future."

the powerful connection that generally exists between age composition of a population and the respective vital and migration movements helps provide plausible scenarios of the developments bound to occur in the short term. Where better data were lacking, we used indications from these projections to refine the 2005 estimates as against previous years. On the other hand, projections are clearly shaped by a comparatively limited set of assumptions, and need to be periodically updated in the light of actual demographic developments.[14]

WORLD JEWISH POPULATION SIZE

The size of world Jewry at the beginning of 2005 was assessed at 13,034,100. World Jewry constituted 2.04 per 1,000 of the world's total population of 6,396 millions. One in about 490 people in the world is a Jew. According to the revised figures, between January 1, 2004, and January 1, 2005, the Jewish population grew by an estimated 44,100 people, or about 0.3 percent. This compares with a total world population growth rate of 1.3 percent (0.1 percent in more developed countries, 1.5 percent in less developed countries). Despite all the imperfections in the estimates, world Jewry continued to be close to zero population growth, with increase in Israel (1.3 percent) slightly overcoming decline in the Diaspora (−0.4 percent).

Table 1 gives an overall picture of Jewish population for the beginning of 2005 as compared to 2004. For 2004 the originally published estimates are presented along with somewhat revised figures that take into account, retrospectively, the corrections made in certain country estimates in the light of improved information. These corrections resulted in a net increase of the 2004 estimated size of world Jewry by 300. Explanations are given in the text below of the reasons for these minimal corrections.

The number of Jews in Israel rose from 5,165,400 in 2004 to 5,237,600 at the beginning of 2005, an increase of 72,200 people, or 1.4 percent. In contrast, the estimated Jewish population in the Diaspora diminished from 7,824,600 (according to the revised figures) to 7,796,500—a decrease of 28,100 people, or −0.4 percent. These changes reflect the continuing Jewish emigration from the FSU and other countries, but also the internal decrease typical of the aggregate of Diaspora Jewry. In 2004, the estimated Israel-Diaspora net migratory balance (immigration minus em-

---

[14] A new round of population projections currently undertaken in the light of the latest data helped in the current assessment.

TABLE 1. ESTIMATED CORE JEWISH POPULATION, BY CONTINENTS AND MAJOR
GEOGRAPHICAL REGIONS, 2004 AND 2005[a]

Region	2004 Original Abs. N.	Revised[b] Abs. N.	Percent[c]	2005 Abs. N.	Percent[b]	Yearly % Change 2004–2005
World	12,989,700	12,990,000	100.0	13,034,100	100.0	0.3
Diaspora	7,824,300	7,824,600	60.2	7,796,500	59.8	−0.4
Israel	5,165,400	5,165,400	39.8	5,237,600	40.2	1.4
America, Total	6,059,000	6,059,000	46.6	6,049,500	46.4	−0.2
North[d]	5,661,000	5,661,000	43.6	5,652,000	43.4	−0.2
Central	52,000	52,000	0.4	51,900	0.4	−0.2
South	346,000	346,000	2.7	345,600	2.7	−0.1
Europe, Total	1,535,800	1,536,100	11.8	1,519,600	11.7	−1.1
European Union[b]	1,121,600	1,122,900	8.6	1,121,000	8.6	−0.2
Other West	19,800	19,800	0.2	19,700	0.2	−0.5
Former USSR[e]	360,000	359,000	2.8	344,800	2.6	−4.0
Other East and Balkans[e]	34,400	34,400	0.3	34,100	0.3	−0.9
Asia, Total	5,206,000	5,206,000	40.1	5,277,100	40.5	1.4
Israel	5,165,400	5,165,400	39.8	5,237,600	40.2	1.4
Former USSR[e]	21,300	21,300	0.2	20,300	0.2	−4.7
Other	19,300	19,300	0.1	19,200	0.1	−0.5
Africa, Total	81,000	81,000	0.6	78,800	0.6	−2.7
North[f]	5,400	5,400	0.0	4,800	0.0	−11.1
South[g]	75,600	75,600	0.6	74,000	0.6	−2.1
Oceania[h]	107,900	107,900	0.8	109,100	0.8	1.1

[a]January 1.
[b]Including European Union's ten new entries.
[c]Minor discrepancies due to rounding.
[d]U.S.A. and Canada.
[e]Asian regions of Russia and Turkey included in Europe. Baltic countries included in European Union.
[f]Including Ethiopia.
[g]South Africa, Zimbabwe, and other sub-Saharan countries.
[h]Australia, New Zealand.

TABLE 2. WORLD JEWISH POPULATION, ORIGINAL AND CORRECTED ESTIMATES, AND TOTAL POPULATION, 1945–2005

Year	Jewish Population			World Population		Jews per 1000 of Total Pop.
	Original Estimate[a]	Corrected Estimate[b]	Yearly % Change[c]	Total Millions	Yearly % Change	
1945, May 1	11,000,000	11,000,000		2,315		4.75
1950, Jan. 1	11,303,400	11,297,000	0.57	2,524	1.87	4.48
1960, Jan. 1	12,792,800	12,079,000	0.67	3,027	1.83	3.99
1970, Jan. 1	13,950,900	12,585,000	0.41	3,702	2.03	3.40
1980, Jan. 1	14,527,100	12,819,000	0.18	4,447	1.85	2.88
1990, Jan. 1	12,810,300	12,868,000	0.04	5,282	1.74	2.44
2000, Jan. 1	13,191,500	12,900,000	0.02	6,000	1.30	2.15
2001, Jan. 1	13,254,100	12,914,000	0.11	6,055	1.50	2.13
2002, Jan. 1	13,296,100	12,935,600	0.17	6,137	1.35	2.11
2003, Jan. 1	12,950,000	12,948,200	0.10	6,215	1.27	2.08
2004, Jan. 1	12,989,700	12,990,000	0.32	6,314	1.59	2.06
2005, Jan. 1	13,034,100		0.34	6,396	1.30	2.04

[a]As published in *American Jewish Year Book,* various years. Some of the estimates reported here as of Jan. 1 were originally published as of Dec. 31 of previous year.
[b]Based on updated, corrected, or otherwise improved information. Original estimates for 1990 and after, and all revised estimates: Division of Jewish Demography and Statistics, The A. Harman Institute of Contemporary Jewry, The Hebrew University of Jerusalem..
[c]Based on revised estimates, besides last year.
[d]Midyear estimate of preceding year. Source: Population Reference Bureau.

igration) amounted to a gain of 5,200 core Jews for Israel.[15] This calculation includes Israeli citizens born abroad who entered Israel for the first time. Therefore, internal demographic evolution (including vital events and conversions) produced nearly all of the growth among the Jewish population in Israel, and most of the decline in the Diaspora.

Recently, instances of accession or "return" to Judaism can be observed in connection with the absorption in Israel of immigrants from Eastern Europe and Ethiopia, and the comprehensive provisions of the Israeli Law of Return. The return or first-time access to Judaism of some of such previously unincluded or unidentified individuals contributed to slowing down the pace of decline of the relevant Diaspora Jewish populations and some gains for the Jewish population in Israel.

[15] Israel Central Bureau of Statistics, *Monthly Bulletin of Statistics* (Jerusalem, 2005).

As noted, corrections should be introduced in previously published Jewish population estimates in the light of new information that has become available. Table 2 provides a synopsis of the world Jewish population estimates relating to the period 1945–2005, as first published each year in the *American Jewish Year Book* and as corrected retroactively, incorporating all subsequent revisions. These revised data correct, sometimes significantly, the figures published until 1980 by other authors and since 1981 by ourselves. Thanks to the development over the years of an improved database, these new revisions are not necessarily the same revised estimates that we published year by year in the AJYB based on the information that was available at each date. It is likely that further retrospective revisions of these numbers may be necessary reflecting ongoing and future research.

The revised figures in table 2 clearly portray the slowing down of Jewish population growth globally since World War II. Based on a post-Shoah world Jewish population estimate of 11,000,000, a growth of 1,079,000 occurred between 1945 and 1960, followed by growths of 506,000 in the 1960s, 234,000 in the 1970s, 49,000 in the 1980s, and 32,000 in the 1990s. While it took 13 years to add one million to world Jewry's postwar size, over 46 years were needed to add another million. Table 2 also outlines the slow Jewish population growth rate versus total population growth globally, and the declining Jewish share of world population. In 2005 the share of Jews per 1,000 world population was less than half what it was in 1945.

POPULATION DISTRIBUTION BY MAJOR REGIONS AND COUNTRIES

Over 46 percent of the world's Jews reside in the Americas, with over 43 percent in North America. Over 40 percent live in Asia, including the Asian republics of the former USSR (but not the Asian parts of the Russian Republic and Turkey)—most of them in Israel. Europe, including the Asian territories of the Russian Republic and Turkey, accounts for about 12 percent of the total. Fewer than 2 percent of the world's Jews live in Africa and Oceania. Among the major geographical regions listed in table 1, the number of Jews in Israel—and, consequently, in total Asia—increased in 2005. Moderate Jewish population gains were also estimated in Oceania (Australia and New Zealand). We estimate that Jewish population size diminished to variable extents in North, Central, and South America, the European Union (EU) and other European countries, the former Soviet republics in Europe and Asia, and Africa. These re-

TABLE 3. ESTIMATED CORE JEWISH POPULATION DISTRIBUTION IN THE AMERICAS, 1/1/2005

Country	Total Population	Jewish Population	Jews per 1,000 Population	Accuracy Rating
Canada	31,900,000	372,000	11.7	B 2001
United States	293,600,000	5,280,000	18.0	B 2001
Total North America[a]	325,627,000	5,652,000	17.4	
Bahamas	300,000	300	1.0	D
Costa Rica	4,200,000	2,500	0.6	C 1993
Cuba	11,300,000	600	0.1	C 1990
Dominican Republic	8,800,000	100	0.0	D
El Salvador	6,700,000	100	0.0	C 1993
Guatemala	12,700,000	900	0.1	A 1999
Jamaica	2,600,000	300	0.1	B 1995
Mexico	106,200,000	39,800	0.4	B 2001
Netherlands Antilles	215,000	200	0.9	B 1998
Panama	3,200,000	5,000	1.6	C 1990
Puerto Rico	3,900,000	1,500	0.4	C 1990
Virgin Islands	115,000	300	2.6	C 1986
Other	24,770,000	300	0.0	D
Total Central America	185,000,000	51,900	0.3	
Argentina	37,900,000	185,000	4.9	B 2003 X
Bolivia	8,800,000	500	0.1	C 1999
Brazil	179,100,000	96,700	0.5	B 2001
Chile	16,000,000	20,800	1.3	C 1991
Colombia	45,300,000	3,300	0.1	C 1996
Ecuador	13,400,000	900	0.1	C 1985
Paraguay	6,000,000	900	0.2	B 1997
Peru	27,500,000	2,300	0.1	C 1993
Suriname	400,000	200	0.5	C 1986
Uruguay	3,400,000	19,500	5.7	C 2001
Venezuela	26,200,000	15,500	0.6	B 1999
Total South America[a]	365,000,000	345,600	0.9	
Total	875,627,000	6,049,500	6.9	

[a]Including countries not listed separately.

gional changes reflect the trends apparent in the Jewish population in each of the major countries, with some notable exceptions within regions, such as the growth of Germany within the EU. We now turn to a review of recent trends in the largest Jewish populations.

North America

In the United States (table 3), two major studies were recently undertaken, the 2000–01 National Jewish Population Survey (NJPS)[16] and the 2001 American Jewish Identity Survey (AJIS).[17] The NJPS was sponsored the United Jewish Communities (UJC), the coordinating body for the local Jewish federations in the U.S., and advised by a National Technical Advisory Committee chaired by Profs. Frank Mott and Vivian Klaff. A national stratified random-digit-dialing (RDD) sample covered the whole of the U.S., subdivided into seven strata based on pre-survey estimates of Jewish population density, with sampling probabilities proportional to Jewish density in each stratum. Over 175,000 households were screened for possible inclusion, based on four questions: (1) What is your religion (or that of other adults in the household), if any? (2) Do you or does any other adult in the household have a Jewish mother or a Jewish father? (3) Were you or any other adult in the household raised Jewish? (4) Do you, or does any other adult in the household, consider your/him/herself Jewish for any reasons? Answers to these questions included options other than yes or no, thus allowing for a nondichotomous resolution of Jewish population definition. From the beginning, such screening criteria were expected to produce results not strictly comparable with the 1990 NJPS.

The final unweighted sample included 4,220 Jewish respondents and 303 people of Jewish background (PJB), for a total of 4,523 Jewish households; 625 non-Jews of Jewish background; and 4,027 non-Jews, for a total of 9,175 respondent households. The 4,027 non-Jewish households were interviewed for a National Survey of Religion and Ethnicity (NSRE) to collect data necessary for weighting and thus estimating the size of the Jewish population, and to provide comparative data to Jews and PJBs on

---

[16] Kotler-Berkowitz et al., *National Jewish Population Survey 2000–01.*

[17] Egon Mayer, Barry Kosmin, and Ariela Keysar, *American Jewish Identity Survey 2001 — AJIS Report — An Exploration in the Demography and Outlook of a People* (New York, 2002). See also Barry A. Kosmin, Egon Mayer, and Ariela Keysar, *American Religious Identification Survey 2001* (New York, 2001).

sociodemographic topics. The rate of response to the screening interview was 28 percent. Weights were directly or indirectly estimated and applied to adjust for the number of telephone lines in the household, and to match sample household and respondent data to the U.S. Census totals for sampling strata, age, gender, and region.[18]

Following claims of excessively low respondent rates, selective population undercounts, and other inappropriate procedures during and following fieldwork, the NJPS was submitted to independent professional scrutiny. It was concluded that the study—although handicapped by several methodological shortcomings such as low response rates, inconsistent survey coverage of relevant subpopulations, and loss of documentation—stood within the range of professionally acceptable research standards and biases.[19]

The total U.S. Jewish population was estimated at 5.2 million, including 4.3 million with clearly Jewish connections, 800,000 persons of Jewish background but whose Jewish identification was less clear, and over 100,000 persons in institutions. (The actual NJPS total number was below 5.1 million, but a round estimate of 5.2 million was arrived at by including persons in institutions and persons who did not report their age). Respondents from the first group, the 4.3 million, were administered a long-form questionnaire, while most respondents from the second, the 800,000, were administered a short-form questionnaire that covered a limited selection of the survey's variables. The total number of Jews plus non-Jews of Jewish background (including those with no Jewish connections) was estimated at 6.7 million. The total number of individuals in the 2.9 million households with at least one Jewish member was estimated at 8.7 million, significantly higher than in 1990.

Even as one major national Jewish population survey (the NJPS) was being undertaken, an alternative one (the 2001 AJIS) was being developed, testifying to substantive disagreements within the Jewish community and among its researchers about how to go about such a project. AJIS was based on a national RDD sample. Out of all successful contacts, a total of 50,238 respondents agreed to be interviewed. After a se-

---

[18] Kotler-Berkowitz et al., *National Jewish Population Survey 2000–01*. See also Charles Kadushin, Leonard Saxe, and Benjamin Phillips, "More Nevuchim (A Guide for the Perplexed) for NJPS 2000–01" (Waltham, Mass., 2004).

[19] Mark Schulman, "National Jewish Population Survey 2000–01: Study Review Memo," prepared for the United Jewish Communities, 2003.

ries of screening questions quite similar to those of NJPS 1990, 1,668 respondents qualified to be included in a survey of American Jewish households. The response rate was 18 percent.[20] The estimated core Jewish population, including Jews with no religion and Jews by choice, as well as Jews in institutions, was 5,340,000. Of these, 3,460,000 were born Jews whose religion was Judaism, 170,000 were converts to Judaism/Jews by choice, and 1,710,000 were born Jews with no religion. The total of Jews and others of Jewish origin was 7,690,000. The total of individuals in all households surveyed, including those without any current "core" Jew, was 9,740,000, excluding persons in institutions. The AJIS data (and not those of the 2000–01 NJPS) conceptually match the 1990 NJPS figures.

Combined reading of these two major current surveys suggests a core Jewish population in the range of 5.2–5.35 million. Assuming an intermediate value of 5.3 million, the revised 2001 estimate was at least 400,000 short of the 5.7 million we had projected for 2002 based on the 5.515 million estimated for mid-1990 by the previous NJPS.[21] There had reportedly been a Jewish influx during the 1990s of at least 200,000 new immigrants—from the former Soviet Union, Israel, Latin America, South Africa, Iran, and Western Europe. However, continuing low Jewish fertility rates, the consequent aging in population composition, and comparatively weak propensities to identify with Judaism among younger adults of mixed Jewish–non-Jewish ancestry apparently led to a significantly lower total core population size. In the historical perspective of Jewish population research in the U.S. over the last 50 years, the new findings appeared quite consistent, and more likely to be the product of actual demographic trends than an artifact of insufficient data.[22]

A 2002 study of the Jews in New York, the largest U.S. metropolitan community, pointed to a stable Jewish population of 1.4 million in the extended eight-borough area, but, for the first time in over three-quarters of a century, fewer than one million Jews lived in New York City's five boroughs.[23]

Our national U.S. estimate for 2005 assumes that the lack of growth—

---

[20] Mayer, Kosmin, and Keysar, *American Jewish Identity Survey;* and Barry A. Kosmin, personal communication to the author.

[21] See Kosmin et al., *Highlights of the CJF 1990 National Jewish Population Survey.*

[22] Sergio DellaPergola, "Was It the Demography? A Reassessment of U.S. Jewish Population Estimates, 1945–2001," *Contemporary Jewry* 25, 2005, pp. 85–131.

[23] See http://www.ujafedny.org/site/PageServer?pagename=jewishcommunitystudy.

in fact, actual population decrease—manifested, despite continuing immigration, through the 2001 surveys, is now a well-established trend. As a result, U.S. Jewry is characterized by an aging population composition, and its effectively Jewish fertility levels are significantly below its virtual demographic potential even with the inclusion of all the children of outmarriages. Under the present circumstances we estimate an annual total of about 50,000 Jewish births and nearly 60,000 Jewish deaths in the U.S. We therefore suggest a further reduction by 10,000 from our 2004 estimate of 5,290,000 million, to 5,280,000, still the largest Jewish population on Earth.

In Canada, the 2001 population census[24] indicated a decrease in the number of Jews according to ethnicity (including those declaring a religion other than Judaism) from 369,565 in 1991 to 348,605 in 2001 (−20,960, or 5.7 percent). Of the ethnic Jews in 2001, 186,475 indicated that Jewish was their sole ethnicity, and the other 162,130 mentioned it as one of their several ethnic identities. The percentage with an exclusively Jewish ethnicity thus amounted to only 53 percent of all those reporting a Jewish ethnicity, as compared to 66 percent in 1991 and 90 percent in 1981. On the other hand, the number of Canada's Jews according to religion increased from 318,070 in 1991 to 329,995 in 2001 (+11,925, or 3.7 percent). It should be noted that 22,365 Jews entered the country during the ten-year interval between the two censuses, and consequently the Jewish population would have decreased by 10,440 (3.3 percent) were it not for this immigration.

Keeping in mind that some ethnic Jews are not Jewish by religion and that an even greater number of Jews by religion do not declare a Jewish ethnicity, a combined estimate of 370,520 obtained for Canada's Jewish population, up 4 percent from 356,315 in 1991.[25] Assuming continuing immigration to Canada, we evaluate the 2005 Jewish population at 372,000, the world's fourth largest. This figure was not strictly comparable with the concept of *core* Jewish population as it included some individuals for whom Jewish was only one among multiple ethnic identities. Some of these would better be included in the *enlarged* Jewish population. Taking into account all ethnic Jews who profess a non-Jewish religion, and other non-Jewish household members, an enlarged Jewish population of above 450,000 would probably obtain.

---

[24] See http://www.statcan.ca.
[25] Charles Shahar, *The Jewish Community of Canada* (Toronto, 2004).

Latin America

In Latin America, the Jewish population was generally in decline, reflecting recurring economic and local security concerns. In Argentina, nearly 6,000 Jews emigrated to Israel in 2002—the highest figure ever in a single year from that country—due to the dire economic conditions and special incentives offered on the Israeli side. In 2003 the economic situation eased somewhat and Israel suspended its incentives. About 1,500 Jews emigrated from Argentina to Israel in 2003, declining to 458 in 2004.[26] Based on the experience of previous years, approximately 20 percent of these migrants were non-Jewish household members in the enlarged population. Partial evidence from different sources indicated that less than half of total Jewish emigration from Argentina went to Israel. Contrary to some rumors, the official data pointed to high permanence rates in Israel of the new immigrants, at least during the first year, and an expected attrition of about 10 percent leaving within the first three years.[27] We consequently assessed Argentina's Jewish population at 185,000 in 2005, the world's seventh largest.

In 2004 and 2005 two new Jewish population surveys were undertaken in the Buenos Aires metropolitan area (AMBA). Initial claims of a Jewish population of 244,000[28] appeared to be founded on significantly inconsistent definitional criteria. Of that 244,000, 64,000 reported to be of Christian religion, and another about 20,000 reported some Jewish ancestry but did not consider themselves Jewish. Overall, 161,000 people in the AMBA considered themselves as totally or partly Jewish—consistent with our 2004 estimate of 165,000. This figure for the large urban concentration appeared coherent with our 185,000 countrywide *core* estimate. The 244,000 figure would be a good estimate of the *enlarged* Jewish population in Greater Buenos Aires. Another survey limited to the City of Buenos Aires pointed to the aging composition of the core population, also reflecting the emigration of younger households over recent years.[29] The current situation implies a yearly loss of about 1,000 through a negative balance of Jewish births and deaths.

---

[26] See Israel Central Bureau of Statistics, http://www.cbs.gov.il.

[27] Shmuel Adler, *Emigration among Immigrants from Argentina that Arrived During the Period 1.1.89–31.12.02* (Jerusalem, 2004).

[28] Adrian Jmelnizky, Ezequiel Erdei, *Estudio de Población Judía en Ciudad de Buenos Aires y Gran Buenos Aires (AMBA)* (Buenos Aires, 2005).

[29] Yaacov Rubel, *La Población Judía de la Ciudad de Buenos Aires, Perfil Socio-Demográfico* (Buenos Aires, 2005).

The 2000 census of Brazil indicated a rather stable Jewish population of 86,828, up from 86,416 in 1991.[30] Considering the possible noninclusion of individuals who did not answer the census question on religion, we assessed Brazil's Jewish population at 97,000 in 2003 and, allowing for moderate emigration, 96,700 in 2005, the world's tenth largest. This appeared to be consistent with a systematic documentation effort undertaken by the Jewish Federation of São Paulo,[31] and an assumption that about one half of Brazil's Jews live in that city. Brazil's enlarged Jewish population (including non-Jewish members of Jewish households) was assessed at 132,191 in 1980 and 117,296 in 1991[32] and presumably exceeded 120,000 in 2000.

In Mexico, the 2000 census indicated a Jewish population of 45,260 aged 5 and over.[33] Of these, 32,464 lived in the metropolitan area of the capital, Mexico City, while—consistent with erratic figures in past censuses—a most unlikely 12,796 were reported in states other than the Federal District and Mexico State. Allocation of the 0–4 age group based on a 2000 Jewish survey determined a corrected estimate of about 35,000 Jews in Greater Mexico City, and 40,000 nationwide. A Jewish population survey undertaken in 2000 provided a countrywide estimate of 39,870 Jews, of which 37,350 were in Mexico City.[34] This confirmed the results of a previous 1991 survey.[35] In 2005, allowing for minor emigration, we estimated the Jewish population at 39,800, the world's 14th largest.

The fourth largest Jewish community in Latin America is located in Chile,[36] whose relatively stable Jewish population is now larger than those

---

[30] See http://www.ibge.br; and René D. Decol, "Brazilian Jews: a Demographic Profile," unpublished paper delivered at the International Conference on Jewish Demography, Jerusalem, 2002.

[31] FISESP (Federação Israelita do Estado de São Paulo), *Recadastramento comunitário 2000–01* (São Paulo, 2002).

[32] René D. Decol, *Imigraçoes urbanas para o Brasil: o caso dos Judeus,* unpublished Ph.D. dissertation, Universidade Estadual, 1999.

[33] See Instituto Nacional de Estadistica, Geografia e Informatica, *XII Censo General de Poblacion y Vivienda 2000* (Mexico City, 2002).

[34] Comunidad Judía de México, *Estudio socio-demográfico 2000* (Mexico City, unpublished tables, 2000).

[35] Sergio DellaPergola and Susana Lerner, *La población judía de México: Perfil demográfico, social y cultural* (México/Jerusalén, 1995). The project, conducted in cooperation between the Centro de Estudios Urbanos y de Desarrollo Urbano (CEDDU), El Colegio de Mexico, and the Division of Jewish Demography and Statistics of the A. Harman Institute of Contemporary Jewry, The Hebrew University, was sponsored by the Asociación Mexicana de Amigos de la Universidad Hebrea de Jerusalén.

[36] Gabriel Berger et al., *Estudio Socio-Demográfico de la Comunidad Juíia de Chile* (Santiago/Buenos Aires, 1995).

of Uruguay[37] and Venezuela.[38] Both of the latter countries experienced significant Jewish emigration in recent years. Around 2000, about 20 percent of the former pupils of Jewish schools in Uruguay and over one-third of the adult children of Caracas Jews lived in a different country.

European Union

Jewish population in Europe (table 4) tended to be increasingly concentrated in the western part of the continent, and within the European Union. On May 1, 2004, the EU expanded from 15 to 25 countries, incorporating the three Baltic countries that had been part of the Soviet Union (Estonia, Latvia, and Lithuania), another five that had been part of the Soviet area of influence in Eastern Europe (the Czech Republic, Hungary, Poland, Slovakia, and Slovenia), and two southern European insular countries (Cyprus and Malta). The EU thus reached an estimated total of 1,122,000 Jews, comprising 74 percent of the continent's total Jewish population. The other former Soviet republics in Europe outside the EU comprised 344,800 Jews, or 23 percent of European Jewry. All other European countries comprised 53,800 Jews, or 3 percent of the Jews of Europe. The EU's expanded format symbolized an important historical landmark: the virtual boundary between Western and Eastern Europe was erased, while further Eastern European countries such as Romania, Bulgaria, and Croatia were bound for future incorporation within the EU. Ongoing debates about the possible incorporation of Turkey in the longer term pointed to the further blurring of Europe's traditional cultural and geopolitical boundaries.

The largest Jewish community in Europe was in France, where a new countrywide survey undertaken at the beginning of 2002 suggested a downward revision to 500,000 core Jews plus an additional 75,000 non-Jewish members of Jewish households.[39] Before the survey, our Jewish population estimate stood at 519,000. The difference, cumulated over several years, was primarily due to a growing pace of Jewish emigration

---

[37] Nicole Berenstein and Rafael Porzecanski, *Perfil de los egresados de la Red Formal de Educación Judía Urguaya* (Montevideo, 2001).

[38] Sergio DellaPergola, Salomon Benzaquen, and Tony Beker de Weintraub, *Perfil sociodemográfico y cultural de la comunidad judía de Caracas* (Caracas, 2000). The survey was sponsored by the Asociación Israelita de Venezuela, the Union Israelita de Caracas, and the Asociación de Amigos de la Universidad Hebrea de Jerusalén.

[39] See Erik H. Cohen with Maurice Ifergan, *Les Juifs de France: Valeurs et identité* (Paris, 2002).

TABLE 4. ESTIMATED CORE JEWISH POPULATION DISTRIBUTION IN EUROPE, 1/1/2005

Country	Total Population	Jewish Population	Jews per 1,000 Population	Accuracy Rating
Austria	8,100,000	9,000	1.1	B 2001
Belgium	10,400,000	31,200	3.0	C 2002
Denmark	5,400,000	6,400	1.2	C 2001
Finland	5,200,000	1,100	0.2	B 1999
France[a]	60,000,000	494,000	8.2	B 2002
Germany	82,600,000	115,000	1.4	B 2004
Greece	11,000,000	4,500	0.4	B 1995
Ireland	4,100,000	1,200	0.3	B 2001
Italy	57,800,000	28,700	0.5	B 2002
Luxembourg	500,000	600	1.2	B 2000
Netherlands	16,300,000	30,000	1.8	B 2000
Portugal	10,500,000	500	0.0	C 1999
Spain	42,500,000	12,000	0.3	D
Sweden	9,000,000	15,000	1.7	C 1990
United Kingdom	59,900,000	297,000	5.0	B 2001
[Total European Union 15]	383,300,000	1,046,200	2.7	
Estonia	1,300,000	1,900	1.5	B 2001 X
Latvia	2,300,000	9,500	4.1	B 2001 X
Lithuania	3,400,000	3,300	1.0	B 2001
Czech Republic	10,200,000	4,000	0.4	C 2001
Hungary	10,100,000	49,900	4.9	C 2001
Poland	38,200,000	3,300	0.1	C 2001
Slovakia	5,400,000	2,700	0.5	C 2001
Slovenia	2,000,000	100	0.1	C 1996
Other[b]	1,300,000	100	0.1	D
Total European Union 25	457,500,000	1,121,000	2.5	
Gibraltar	25,000	600	24.0	B 1991
Norway	4,600,000	1,200	0.3	B 1995
Switzerland	7,400,000	17,900	2.4	A 2000
Total other West Europe[c]	12,485,000	19,700	1.6	

TABLE 4.—*(Continued)*

Country	Total Population	Jewish Population	Jews per 1,000 Population	Accuracy Rating
Belarus	9,800,000	21,000	2.1	B 1999
Moldova	4,200,000	4,800	1.1	C 2000
Russia[d]	144,100,000	235,000	1.6	B 2002 X
Ukraine	47,400,000	84,000	1.8	B 2001
Total FSU Republics	205,500,000	344,800	1.7	
[Total FSU in Europe][e]	212,500,000	359,500	1.7	
Bosnia-Herzegovina	3,900,000	500	0.1	C 2001
Bulgaria	7,800,000	2,100	0.3	C 2001
Croatia	4,400,000	1,700	0.4	C 2001
Macedonia (FYR)	2,000,000	100	0.1	C 1996
Romania	21,700,000	10,300	0.5	B 2001
Serbia-Montenegro	10,700,000	1,500	0.1	C 2001
Turkey[d]	71,300,000	17,900	0.3	B 2002
Total other East Europe and Balkans[c]	125,000,000	34,100	0.5	
Total	800,485,000	1,519,600	1.9	

[a]Including Monaco.
[b]Cyprus and Malta.
[c]Including countries not listed separately.
[d]Including Asian regions.
[e]Including Baltic countries.

not only to Israel—amounting to 2,000 in 2004—but also to Canada and other countries. Jewish emigration tended to respond to increasing manifestations of anti-Jewish intolerance, including physical violence. A survey of Jewish tourism from France to Israel unveiled a remarkable estimate of 125,000, or more than 30 percent of all French Jews aged 15 and over, who had visited the Jewish state.[40] Of these, 23 percent (about 29,000) affirmed their intention to move to Israel in the near future. A

[40] Erik H. Cohen, *Les touristes de France en Israël 2004* (Jerusalem, 2005).

distant second candidate for possible emigration was the U.S. Although migration intentions are not a proxy for actual migration decisions, the attrition in the feelings of security among French Jewry is undisputable. Our 2005 estimate for French Jewry therefore slightly shrinks to 494,000, the third largest in the world.

In the United Kingdom, the 2001 national population census provided detailed data about religion, for the first time since the nineteenth century.[41] The total Jewish population of 266,741 for England, Wales, Scotland, and Northern Ireland closely approximated our 273,500 estimate for 2002. However, considering that 22.8 percent of the UK population indicated that they had no religion and that another 7.3 percent did not answer the question—at a time when much of the organized Jewish community publicly supported participation in the census—we suggested raising the estimate to 300,000 for 2001. More detailed data from the same census for Scotland (some of its questions were different from those asked in the rest of the UK) indicated 6,448 people currently reporting Jewish religion, as compared to a total of 7,446 who said they were raised as Jews—a net loss of 13 percent.[42] Vital statistics routinely collected by the Board of Deputies Community Research Unit show a continuing excess of Jewish deaths (3,670 in 2002, 3,592 in 2003, and 3,257 in 2004) over Jewish births (2,665 in 2002, and the same in 2003).[43] The diminishing number of deaths is an obvious symptom of a shrinking population which loses about 1,000 people yearly through a negative vital balance. Taking into account some minor emigration as well, we estimated the UK's total Jewish population at 297,000 in 2005, the world's fifth largest.

In Germany, significant if slightly diminished Jewish immigration continued. In 2004, 4,757 immigrants from the former Soviet Union were recorded as new members of German Jewish communities, as compared to 6,224 in 2003 and 6,597 in 2002.[44] Admission criteria in the community follow Jewish rabbinical rules. The total number of core Jews regis-

---

[41] The census is available at http://www.ons.uk. See also Barry Kosmin and Stanley Waterman, *Commentary on Census Religion Question* (London, 2002), a publication of the JPR (Institute for Jewish Policy Research).

[42] Also see *JPR/News,* Spring 2003, p. 6.

[43] The Board of Deputies of British Jews, Community Research Unit, *Report on Community Vital Statistics 2004* (London, 2005). See also Stephen Miller, Marlena Schmool, and Antony Lerman, *Social and Political Attitudes of British Jews: Some Key Findings of the JPR Survey* (London, 1996).

[44] Zentralwohlfahrtsstelle der Juden in Deutschland (ZWJD), *Mitgliederstatistik; Der Einzelnen Jüdischen Gemeinden und Landesverbände in Deutschland* (Frankfurt a.M., 2005).

tered with the central Jewish community grew to 105,733 at the beginning of 2005, versus 102,472 one year earlier. Of the current total, fewer than 12,000 were part of the initial pool of 28,081 members that existed at the end of 1990, and the rest were recent immigrants. Since 2002, the enlarged total of Jews and non-Jewish family members who came to Germany from the FSU was larger than the respective number of FSU migrants to Israel. The age composition of the Jewish old-timers—and even more so of the newcomers—was extremely skewed to the elderly. In 2004 there were 139 Jewish births and 1,095 Jewish deaths recorded by the Jewish community in Germany, as well as 79 conversions to Judaism and 408 conversions from Judaism. This explains why the growth of the Jewish community is significantly less than the total number of new immigrants. Allowing for delays in joining the organized community and a preference on the part of some members of a minority not to identify officially with its institutions, we assess Germany's *core* Jewish population at 115,000, the world's eighth largest. The *enlarged* Jewish population, inclusive of the non-Jewish relatives of immigrants, must be approaching 200,000, and creates an entirely new framework for Jewish social and cultural life in Germany.[45]

In Hungary, our core estimate of just below 50,000 (the world's 13th largest) reflects the unavoidably negative balance of Jewish births and deaths in a country where the total population's vital balance has been negative for several years in a row. Indeed, a Jewish survey in 1999[46] indicated a conspicuously larger enlarged Jewish population. However, a demographic extrapolation based on the usually accepted number of post-Holocaust core Jewish survivors and accounting for the known or estimated numbers of births, deaths, and emigrants since 1945 closely matches our assessment. It should be noted that in the 2001 Hungarian census a scant 13,000 people reported themselves Jewish by religion.

Belgium's Jewish population was estimated above 30,000, the 15th largest worldwide. Quite stable numbers reflected the presence of a traditional Orthodox community in Antwerp and the growth of a large European administrative center in Brussels. Local Jewish population estimates were quite obsolete in comparison with most other EU countries. The next two largest Jewish communities in the EU were those in the

---

[45] Julius H. Schoeps, Willy Jasper, and Bernard Vogt, eds., *Ein neues Judentum in Deutschland. Fremd und Eigenbilder der russisch-jüdischen Einwanderer* (Potsdam, 1999).

[46] András Kovács, *Zsidók és Zsidóság a Mai Magyarországon: Egy szociológiai kutatás eredményei* [Jews and Jewry in Contemporary Hungary: Results of a Sociological Survey] (Budapest, 2002).

Netherlands and Italy. In the Netherlands, a survey in 2000 estimated a Halakhic Jewish population of 30,072, of which perhaps as many as a third were immigrants from Israel, and an enlarged Jewish population of 43,305.[47] In Italy, total Jewish community membership—which historically comprised the overwhelming majority of the country's Jewish population—declined from 26,706 in 1995 to 25,143 in 2001.[48] Our estimate, slightly below 29,000, adequately accounts for nonmembers.

Former Soviet Union

In the former Soviet Union, rapid Jewish population decrease continued, reflecting an overwhelming surplus of Jewish deaths over births, high rates of outmarriage and low rates of Jewish identification of the children, and conspicuous though diminishing emigration. Our 2005 assessment of the total core Jewish population in the aggregate of the 15 former Soviet Republics was 379,800, of which 359,500 lived in Europe and 20,300 in Asia. At least as many non-Jewish family members were part of the respective enlarged households. The ongoing process of demographic decline was compensated to some extent by the revival of Jewish cultural and religious activities, including Jewish education.[49]

In the Russian Republic, the October 2002 census indicated 233,600 Jews as against our core Jewish population estimate of 252,000 for the beginning of 2003 (derived from the February 1994 Russian Microcensus estimate of 409,000 Jews).[50] Allowing for some census undercounts

---

[47] Hanna van Solinge and Marlene de Vries, eds., *De Joden in Nederland Anno 2000: Demografisch profiel en binding aan het joodendom* (Amsterdam, 2001). The survey was undertaken as a collaborative effort between the Stichting Joods Maatschappelijk Werk and NIDI (Netherlands Interdisciplinary Demographic Institute). See also C. Kooyman and J. Almagor, *Israelis in Holland: A Sociodemographic Study of Israelis and Former Israelis in Holland* (Amsterdam, 1996).

[48] Unione delle comunità ebraiche italiane, *IV Congresso, relazione del consiglio* (Rome, 2002); and Yaakov Andrea Lattes, *Sull'assimilazione in Italia e i metodi per affrontarla* (Ramat Gan, 2005).

[49] Zvi Gitelman, "Becoming Jewish in Russia and Ukraine" in Zvi Gitelman, Barry Kosmin, and András Kovács, eds., *New Jewish Identities: Contemporary Europe and Beyond* (Budapest/New York, 2003), pp. 105–37.

[50] Mark Tolts, "Demographic Trends among the Jews of the Former Soviet Union," paper presented at the International Conference in Honor of Professor Mordechai Altshuler on Soviet and Post-Soviet Jewry, Jerusalem, 2003, German translation available in *Menora: Jahrbuch für deutsch-jüdische Geschichte* 15, 2004 (Berlin/Wien, 2005), pp. 15–44; Mark Tolts, "The Post-Soviet Jewish Population in Russia and the World," *Jews in Russia and Eastern Europe* 1 (52), Summer 2004, pp. 37–63.

after the compulsory item on ethnicity (*natsyonalnost*) on identification documents was canceled, and the option not to state an ethnicity was allowed for the first time, we estimate the Jewish population at 235,000 in 2005 (including a minor upward revision), the sixth largest in the world. The size of Russian Jewry was clearly more stable and resilient than in the other former Soviet republics. This was partly a consequence of Jewish migrations between the various republics and also the lower emigration propensities from Moscow and some of the other main urban areas.[51] Nevertheless, the striking imbalance of Jewish births and deaths, and ongoing emigration meant continuing population decline and an elderly age composition. The decline in the number of births to at least one Jewish parent could be estimated at 8,006 in 1988 and 2,177 in 1998. Recorded Jewish deaths were 13,826 in 1988 and 9,103 in 1998. As a result, the estimated negative balance of these vital events was −5,820 in 1988 and −6,926 in 1998.[52]

In the Ukraine, the population census undertaken on December 5, 2001, yielded 104,600 Jews, whereas we had expected 100,000 on January 1, 2002. Considering that our baseline for the latter estimate were the 487,300 Jews counted in the previous census of January 1989, the fit between expected and actual results was quite remarkable.[53] Taking into account the dramatic pace of emigration since 1989, the other major intervening changes among Ukraine's Jews, and the continuing emigration at the end of 2001, the census fully confirmed our previous assessment of ongoing demographic trends. Adding continuing emigration in 2003 and 2004, we assess the 2005 core Jewish population at 84,000, the 11th largest in the world.

Of the other former Soviet republics in Europe, after the accession of the three Baltic states (with a total Jewish population of 14,700 after minor revisions for Estonia and Latvia) to the European Union, the main Jewish population was in Belarus, now assessed at 21,000. Pending a new census, a survey in Moldova found an enlarged Jewish population of 9,240 in 2000.[54] We assess the core Jewish population at 4,800 in 2005.

---

[51] Mark Tolts, "Mass *Aliyah* and Jewish Emigration from Russia: Dynamics and Factors," *East European Jewish Affairs* 33, Winter 2003, pp. 71–96.

[52] Tolts, "Demographic Trends."

[53] Ukrainian Ministry of Statistics, *Population Census 2001* (Kiyev, 2002); Mark Tolts, *Main Demographic Trends of the Jews in Russia and the FSU* (Jerusalem, 2002).

[54] Malka Korazim and Esther Katz, "Patterns of Jewish Identity in Moldova: The Behavioral Dimension," in Gitelman, Kosmin, and Kovács, eds., *New Jewish Identities*, pp. 159–70.

Rest of Europe

After Hungary—the largest Jewish community in the rest of Central and Eastern Europe— joined the EU together with Poland (whose latest census indicated a Jewish population of 1,100), the Czech Republic, Slovakia, and Slovenia, only 34,400 Jews remained in non-EU East Europe and the Balkans, primarily in Turkey. A survey in Istanbul pointed to widespread aging in a community that has experienced significant past emigration. In Istanbul, 14 percent of the Jewish population was under age 18, versus 18 percent above 65.[55]

Asia

Jewish population in Asia is mostly affected by the trends in Israel (table 5). At the beginning of 2005, Israel's core Jewish population reached 5,237,600, forming an enlarged Jewish population of 5,529,300 when combined with 291,700 non-Jewish members of Jewish households.[56] Most of the 1,730 people who in 2004 underwent conversion to Judaism (as compared to 919 in 2003 and 3,533 in 2002) were new immigrants from Ethiopia, while a few hundred were immigrants from the FSU.[57] In 2004, 24,800 new immigrants arrived in Israel, of whom 14,200 were Jewish.[58] Current Jewish emigration reduced this to a net migration balance of 5,200. Israel's Jewish fertility rate continued to be stable, even rising slightly to 2.7 children per woman, higher than that of every other developed country and probably twice or more the effective Jewish fertility level across Diaspora Jewish communities. In 2004, for the first time ever, more than 100,000 Jewish babies were born in Israel, helping to determine a net natural increase of 67,300. Of the 5,237,600 core Jews in 2005, 5,000,600 lived within the pre-1967 borders plus East Jerusalem and the Golan Heights, where they formed 75.4 percent of the total legally permanent population, and 237,000 lived in the West Bank and Gaza, where they formed 6.6 percent of the total.

---

[55] Data provided through the courtesy of the Jewish Community Council.

[56] Israel Central Bureau of Statistics, *Statistical Abstract of Israel* 56 (Jerusalem, 2005). See also http://www.cbs.gov.il.

[57] Raly Sa'ar, "Family members of converts not allowed to immigrate with them to Israel," *Ha'aretz*, June 3, 2004.

[58] These data include about 4,000 immigrant citizens, the foreign-born children of Israelis on their first-time entrance in the country. Not included are foreign workers and illegal residents.

TABLE 5. ESTIMATED CORE JEWISH POPULATION DISTRIBUTION IN ASIA, 1/1/2005

Country	Total Population	Jewish Population	Jews per 1,000 Population	Accuracy Rating
Israel[a]	6,632,500	5,000,600	754.0	A 2005
West Bank and Gaza[b]	3,587,000	237,000	66.1	A 2005
Total Israel and Palestine	10,219,500	5,237,600	512.5	
Azerbaijan	8,300,000	7,000	0.8	B 1999
Georgia	4,500,000	3,600	0.8	B 2002
Kazakhstan	15,000,000	3,800	0.3	B 1999
Kyrgyzstan	5,100,000	600	0.1	B 1999
Turkmenistan	5,700,000	300	0.1	C 2000
Uzbekistan	26,400,000	5,000	0.2	C 2000
Total former USSR in Asia[c]	74,800,000	20,300	0.3	
China[d]	1,307,300,000	1,000	0.0	D
India	1,086,600,000	5,100	0.0	B 1996
Iran	67,400,000	10,800	0.2	C 1986
Japan	127,600,000	1,000	0.0	C 1993
Korea, South	48,200,000	100	0.0	C 1998
Philippines	83,700,000	100	0.0	D
Singapore	4,200,000	300	0.1	C 1990
Syria	18,000,000	100	0.0	C 1995
Thailand	63,800,000	200	0.0	C 1998
Yemen	20,000,000	200	0.0	C 1995
Other	890,986,000	300	0.0	D
Total other Asia	3,717,786,000	19,200	0.0	
Total	3,802,800,000	5,277,100	1.4	

[a]Total population of Israel, including Jews in West Bank and Gaza, 1/1/2005: 6,869,500.
[b]Total Palestinian population in West Bank and Gaza: 1/1/2005: 3,350,000 (revised).
[c]Including Armenia and Tajikistan. Not including Asian regions of Russian Republic.
[d]Including Hong Kong and Macao.

Jews represented 76.2 percent of a total population of 6,869,500 in the State of Israel, including East Jerusalem, the Golan Heights, and the Jewish but not the Palestinian population in the West Bank and Gaza. Jews comprised 6.6 percent of the total inhabitants in the West Bank and Gaza. Considering the total legal population resident in the State of Israel, the West Bank, and Gaza, evaluated at 10,219,500, Jews represented 51.2 percent, or slightly more than half. All of the preceding figures relate to the core Jewish population. If the 291,700 non-Jewish members of Jewish households are added to the Jewish side, the enlarged Jewish population thus obtained represented 80.5 percent of Israel's population (as defined above), and 54.1 percent of the total population of Israel and the Palestinian territories. On the other hand, with the further addition of about 190,000 non-Jewish foreign workers residing in Israel, core and enlarged Jews diminished, respectively, to 50.3 and 53.1 percent of the total population of 10,409,500 present in Israel and the Palestinian territories.

These estimates were significantly affected by the assessment of the total Palestinian population of the West Bank and Gaza. The latter were the subject of a high-profile debate in the media following the assertion by a group of American and Israeli investigators that current population estimates from Palestinian sources were inflated.[59] The Palestinian Central Bureau of Statistics, after a downward revision of over 100,000 to account for expected immigration that did not materialize, estimated the population in the Palestinian territories including East Jerusalem at 3,762,005 by July 1, 2005.[60] Our own independent assessment, allocating 237,000 East Jerusalem Arabs to the Israeli side and taking into account an actually negative migration balance of Palestinians and further corrections, was 3,350,000 on January 1, 2005.[61] The faster pace of population growth among Palestinians, assessed at over 3 percent annually, unquestionably generated a gradual attrition in the extant Jewish majority over the whole territory between the Mediterranean Sea and the Jordan River, and within the State of Israel itself.[62]

---

[59] Bennett Zimmerman, Roberta Seid, Michael Wise, Yoram Ettinger, David Shahaf, Ezra Sohar, David Passig, and Avraham Shvout, *Arab Population In the West Bank & Gaza: The Million-and-a-Half-Person Gap* (Washington, 2005); Bennett Zimmerman, Roberta Seid, and Michael L. Wise, "Battle of numbers: What Demographic time bomb?" *Jerusalem Post*, May 17, 2005.

[60] See www.pcbs.org.

[61] Sergio DellaPergola, "Battle of numbers: Jewish minority by 2020," *Jerusalem Post*, May 17, 2005.

[62] For an extensive discussion of the background, thrust and implications of past and current population changes see Sergio DellaPergola, "Demographic Trends in Israel and Palestine: Prospects and Policy Implications," AJYB 2004, pp. 3–68. See also Arnon Sofer

The Jewish population in the rest of Asia consisted mainly of the rapidly declining communities in the FSU's eight Asian republics, the largest of which was Azerbaijan (7,000 Jews), followed by Uzbekistan (5,000), Kazakhstan (3,800) and Georgia (3,600).[63] The largest Jewish population in a single country in Asia besides Israel was in Iran. Our estimate there, 10,800, reflects an effort to monitor widespread emigration since the Islamic revolution of the late 1970s.

Africa

Jewish population in Africa was mostly concentrated in South Africa (table 6). According to the 2001 census,[64] the white Jewish population amounted at 61,675. After factoring in the national nonresponse rate of 14 percent, a corrected estimate of 72,000 obtained. Allowing for a certain proportion of actual Jews reported among South Africa's nonwhites (11,979 blacks, 1,287 coloreds, and 615 Indians), we assessed the total size of the Jewish community at 75,000. Allowing for a moderate continuation of emigration, we estimate South Africa's Jewish population at 72,500 in 2005, the world's 12th largest.

Our revised estimates for North Africa acknowledge the ongoing reduction in the small Jewish population remaining in Morocco and Tunisia, now assessed at 4,600 overall.

Oceania

Continuing immigration produced some increase in the size of Jewish populations in Oceania (table 7). Australia's 2001 census indicated a Jewish population of 83,500, up about 4,000 from 1996.[65] Taking into account both nonresponse and the community's rather old age composition, we estimate the core Jewish population at 102,000 in 2005, the ninth largest in the world. The 2001 census also pointed to some Jewish population increase in New Zealand.

---

and Yevguenia Bistrow, *Israel Demography 2004–2020 in the Light of Disengagement* [Hebrew] (Haifa, 2004).

[63] Tolts, "Demographic Trends."

[64] See David Saks, "Community Stable, Ageing—Census," *South African Jewish Report* (Johannesburg, 2003). See also Barry A. Kosmin, Jaquelin Goldberg, Milton Shain, and Shirley Bruk, *Jews of the New South Africa: Highlights of the 1998 National Survey of South African Jews* (London, 1999).

[65] Australian Bureau of Statistics, *Population Census 2001* (Canberra, 2002). See also Gary Eckstein, *Demography of the Sydney Jewish Community 2001* (Sydney, 2003).

TABLE 6.   ESTIMATED CORE JEWISH POPULATION DISTRIBUTION IN AFRICA, 1/1/2005

Country	Total Population	Jewish Population	Jews per 1,000 Population	Accuracy Rating
Egypt	73,400,000	100	0.0	C 1998
Ethiopia	72,400,000	100	0.0	C 1998
Morocco	30,600,000	3,500	0.1	C 2003 X
Tunisia	10,000,000	1,100	0.1	C 2003
Total North Africaª	263,700,000	4,800	0.0	
Botswana	1,700,000	100	0.1	C 1993
Congo D.R.	58,300,000	100	0.0	C 1993
Kenya	32,400,000	400	0.0	C 1990
Namibia	1,900,000	100	0.1	C 1993
Nigeria	137,300,000	100	0.0	D
South Africa	46,900,000	72,500	1.5	B 2001
Zimbabwe	12,700,000	400	0.0	B 2001
Other	330,100,000	300	0.0	D
Total other Africa	621,300,000	74,000	0.1	
Total	885,000,000	78,800	0.1	

ªIncluding countries not listed separately.

DISPERSION AND CONCENTRATION

Reflecting global Jewish population stagnation along with growing concentration in a few countries, 97.4 percent of world Jewry lives in the largest 15 communities, and, excluding Israel from the count, 95.6 percent lives in the 14 largest communities of the Diaspora, of which 67.7 percent are in the U.S. (table 8). In 2005, there were at least 100 Jews in 93 different countries (table 9). Two countries had Jewish populations above 5 million each (the U.S. and Israel), another seven had more than 100,000 Jews, three had 50,000–100,000, five had 25,000–50,000, ten had 10,000–25,000, and 66 countries had less than 10,000. These 66 communities overall accounted for 1 percent of world Jewry. In only seven

TABLE 7. ESTIMATED CORE JEWISH POPULATION DISTRIBUTION IN OCEANIA, 1/1/2005

Country	Total Population	Jewish Population	Jews per 1,000 Population	Accuracy Rating
Australia	20,100,000	102,000	5.1	B 2001
New Zealand	4,100,000	7,000	1.7	A 2001
Other	8,800,000	100	0.0	D
Total	33,000,000	109,100	3.3	

TABLE 8. COUNTRIES WITH LARGEST CORE JEWISH POPULATIONS, 1/1/2005

| | | | | % of Total Jewish Population | | |
| | | | | In the World | In the Diaspora | |
Rank	Country	Jewish Population	%	Cumulative %	%	Cumulative %
1	United States	5,280,000	40.5	40.5	67.7	67.7
2	Israel	5,237,600	40.2	80.7	=	=
3	France	494,000	3.8	84.5	6.3	74.1
4	Canada	372,000	2.9	87.3	4.8	78.8
5	United Kingdom	297,000	2.3	89.6	3.8	82.6
6	Russia	235,000	1.8	91.4	3.0	85.7
7	Argentina	185,000	1.4	92.8	2.4	88.0
8	Germany	115,000	0.9	93.7	1.5	89.5
9	Australia	102,000	0.8	94.5	1.3	90.8
10	Brazil	96,700	0.7	95.2	1.2	92.1
11	Ukraine	84,000	0.6	95.9	1.1	93.1
12	South Africa	72,500	0.6	96.4	0.9	94.1
13	Hungary	49,900	0.4	96.8	0.6	94.7
14	Mexico	39,800	0.3	97.1	0.5	95.2
15	Belgium	31,200	0.2	97.4	0.4	95.6

TABLE 9. DISTRIBUTION OF THE WORLD'S JEWS, BY NUMBER, AND PROPORTION
(PER 1,000 POPULATION) IN EACH COUNTRY, 1/1/2005

Number of Jews in Country	Jews per 1,000 Population					
	Total	0.0-0.9	1.0-4.9	5.0-9.9	10.0-24.9	25.0+
Number of Countries						
Total[a]	93	62	23	4	3	1
100–900	35	31	3	-	1	-
1,000–4,900	22	20	2	-	-	-
5,000–9,900	9	3	6	-	-	-
10,000–24,900	10	5	4	1	-	-
25,000–49,900	5	2	3	-	-	-
50,000–99,900	3	1	2	-	-	-
100,000–999,900	7	-	3	3	1	-
1,000,000 or more	2	-	-	-	1	1
Jewish Population Distribution (Absolute Numbers)						
Total[a]	13,034,100	304,900	925,400	912,500	5,652,600	5,237,600
100–900	11,000	9,200	1,200	-	600	-
1,000–4,900	52,100	46,900	5,200	-	-	-
5,000–9,900	58,800	17,100	41,700	-	-	-
10,000–24,900	160,700	66,500	74,700	19,500	-	-
25,000–49,900	179,600	68,500	111,100	-	-	-
50,000–99,900	253,200	96,700	156,500	-	-	-
100,000–999,900	1,800,000	-	535,000	893,000	372,000	-
1,000,000 or more	10,517,600	-	-	-	5,280,000	5,237,600
Jewish Population Distribution (Percent of World's Jews)						
Total[a]	100.0	2.3	7.1	7.0	43.4	40.2
100–900	0.1	0.1	0.0	0.0	0.0	0.0
1,000–4,900	0.4	0.4	0.0	0.0	0.0	0.0
5,000–9,900	0.5	0.1	0.3	0.0	0.0	0.0
10,000–24,900	1.2	0.5	0.6	0.1	0.0	0.0
25,000–49,900	1.4	0.5	0.9	0.0	0.0	0.0
50,000–99,900	1.9	0.7	1.2	0.0	0.0	0.0
100,000–999,900	13.8	0.0	4.1	6.9	2.9	0.0
1,000,000 or more	80.7	0.0	0.0	0.0	40.5	40.2

[a]Grand total includes countries with fewer than 100 Jews, for a total of 1,100 Jews. Minor discrepancies due to rounding. Israel includes West Bank and Gaza.

TABLE 10. METROPOLITAN AREAS WITH LARGEST CORE JEWISH POPULATIONS,
1/1/2005

Rank	Metro Area[a]	Country	Jewish Population	Share of World's Jews %	Cumulative %
1	Tel Aviv[b,c]	Israel	2,707,000	20.8	20.8
2	New York[d]	U.S.	2,051,000	15.7	36.5
3	Los Angeles[d]	U.S.	668,000	5.1	41.6
4	Jerusalem[e]	Israel	660,000	5.1	46.7
5	Haifa[b]	Israel	656,000	5.0	51.7
6	Southeast Florida[d,f]	U.S.	498,000	3.8	55.5
7	Be'er Sheva[b]	Israel	347,000	2.7	58.2
8	Philadelphia[d]	U.S.	285,000	2.2	60.4
9	Paris[g]	France	284,000	2.2	62.6
10	Chicago[d]	U.S.	265,000	2.0	64.6
11	Boston[d]	U.S.	254,000	2.0	66.6
12	San Francisco[d]	U.S.	218,000	1.7	68.2
13	London[h]	United Kingdom	195,000	1.5	69.7
14	Toronto[i]	Canada	180,000	1.4	71.1
15	Washington[j]	U.S.	166,000	1.3	72.4
16	Buenos Aires[k]	Argentina	165,000	1.3	73.6
17	Baltimore[j]	U.S.	106,000	0.8	74.5
18	Detroit[d]	U.S.	103,000	0.8	75.2
19	Moscow[l]	Russia	95,000	0.7	76.0
20	Montreal[i]	Canada	93,000	0.7	76.7
21	Cleveland[d]	U.S.	86,000	0.7	77.4
22	Atlanta[j]	U.S.	86,000	0.7	78.0

[a]Most metropolitan areas include extended inhabited territory and several municipal authorities around central city. Definitions vary by country. Some of the estimates may include non-core Jews.
[b]As newly defined in the 1995 Israeli Census.
[c]Includes Ramat Gan, Bene Beraq, Petach Tikvah, Bat Yam, Holon, Rishon Lezion, Netanya, and Ashdod, each with a Jewish population above 100,000.
[d]Consolidated Metropolitan Statistical Area (CMSA).
[e]Revised estimate. Includes the whole Jerusalem District and parts of Judea and Samaria District.
[f]Miami-Ft. Lauderdale and West Palm Beach-Boca Raton CMSA.
[g]Departments 75, 77, 78, 91, 92, 93, 94, 95.
[h]Greater London and contiguous postcode areas.
[i]Census Metropolitan Area.
[j]Metropolitan Statistical Area (MSA).
[k]Capital Federal and Gran Buenos Aires Partidos.
[l]Territory administered by city council.

communities outside of Israel did Jews constitute at least about 5 per 1,000 (0.5 percent) of their country's total population. In descending order by the relative weight (not size) of their Jewish population, they were Gibraltar (24.0 Jews per 1,000 inhabitants), the U.S. (18.0), Canada (11.7), France (8.2), Uruguay (5.7), Australia (5.1), and the UK (5.0).

By combining the two criteria of Jewish population size and density, we obtain the following taxonomy of the 26 Jewish communities with populations over 10,000 (excluding Israel). There are five countries with over 100,000 Jews and at least 5 Jews per 1,000 of total population: the U.S., France, Canada, the UK, and Australia; another three countries with over 100,000 Jews and at least 1 per 1,000 of total population: Argentina, Russia, and Germany; one country with 10,000–100,000 Jews and at least 5 per 1,000 of total population: Uruguay; nine more countries with 10,000–100,000 Jews and at least 1 per 1,000 of total population: Ukraine, South Africa, Hungary, Belgium, the Netherlands, Chile, Belarus, Switzerland, and Sweden; and eight countries with 10,000–100,000 Jews and less than 1 per 1,000 of total population: Brazil, Mexico, Italy, Turkey, Venezuela, Spain, Iran, and Romania.

The overwhelmingly urban concentration of Jewish populations globally is evinced by the fact that in 2005, 51.7 percent of world Jewry lived in only five metropolitan areas—Tel Aviv, New York, Los Angeles, Jerusalem, and Haifa—and another 25 percent lived in the next 15 largest metropolitan areas (table 10).[66] The Jewish population in the Tel Aviv urban conurbation extending from Netanya to Ashdod now exceeds by far that in the New York Standard Metropolitan Area extending from New York State to parts of Connecticut, New Jersey, and Pennsylvania. Of the 22 largest metropolitan areas of Jewish residence, 12 were located in the U.S., four in Israel, two in Canada, and one each in France, the UK, Argentina, and Russia.

SERGIO DELLAPERGOLA

---

[66] For Israel estimates see Israel Central Bureau of Statistics, *Statistical Abstract of Israel* 56 (Jerusalem, 2005), table 2-15. For U.S. estimates see The Editors, "Jewish Population in the United States, 2003," AJYB 2004, pp. 111–42.

Review
of
the
Year

UNITED STATES

United States

National Affairs

Ａs this was a presidential election year, that contest became the prism through which the concerns of the day were focused. The election turned not only on vital issues of national security and foreign policy, but also on the uncertain state of the economy and the social and lifestyle values that divided American society. A measure of how critical these issues were to the American public was the record turnout at the polls: voter participation in 2004 was the highest of any presidential election since 1960. For the Jewish community in particular, this played out in a public drama, as the nation's political parties sought the right mix of messages that might appeal to a Jewish electorate that, though small, was more likely to vote and contribute money than other groups, and that was concentrated in a handful of closely contested states with many electoral votes.

THE POLITICAL ARENA

Seeking the Jewish Vote

The arrival of another presidential election year was accompanied by what was by now familiar speculation about a possible shift of the Jewish vote away from its historically Democratic bent. In January, even before the first primary, partisans and analysts were afforded grist for this mill when the American Jewish Committee released its annual survey of the attitudes of American Jews. In a series of theoretical matchups pitting incumbent President George W. Bush against five Democratic contenders for the nomination, the 1,000 Jews who had been polled in late 2003 remained strongly Democratic overall. Even so, the president's percentages were higher than his 19-percent share of the Jewish vote in 2000. Bush garnered 31 percent against Sen. John Kerry of Massachusetts, former Vermont governor Howard Dean, and Rep. Richard Gephardt of Missouri, 29 percent when pitted against retired general Wesley Clark, and 24 percent against Sen. Joseph Lieberman of Connecticut. Republicans took comfort in the overall rise in Jewish support so early in the campaign, but Steve Rabinowitz, a Democratic political consultant, told the Jewish Telegraphic Agency that "all this poll does is reinforce that Jews vote Democratic."

Both the Democratic primary cycle and, subsequently, the Bush-Kerry general election witnessed extraordinary efforts to appeal to a Jewish community that made up some 2 percent of the American population. This outreach reflected the fact that Jews voted in disproportionately high numbers, they tended to live in such 2004 battleground states as Florida, Pennsylvania, Ohio, and Michigan—in addition to their outsized presence in the high-electoral-vote states of New York, New Jersey, California, and Illinois—and they donated money to both political parties far in excess of their numbers.

Former Vermont governor Howard Dean, still battling the perception that he was less than firm in his commitment to Israel (see AJYB 2004, pp. 39–40), took steps to underline his personal connections to the Jewish community (including a Jewish wife and children who were being raised as Jews) and his pro-Israel bona fides. As the year began, Leon Fuerth was named Dean's chief foreign-policy adviser; Fuerth, who had served as national-security adviser to Al Gore both as senator and as vice president, was highly regarded by the pro-Israel community, and Jewish leaders hailed the appointment. Nevertheless, Dean never managed to convince Jews that he identified emotionally with their concerns, just as he could not get the majority of Democrats to believe that he had broad enough appeal to win the general election.

Neither did Jewish Democrats move in great numbers toward support for their coreligionist, Sen. Joseph Lieberman (D., Conn.), who sought to build on his 2000 star turn as Al Gore's running mate. On the night of February 3, having failed to garner victory in a single state—even coming in a distant second to Kerry in the Delaware primary, which Lieberman had designated a "must win"—the senator bowed out of the race. His supporters, particularly those who were Jewish, speculated as to why so many Jewish Democrats had looked elsewhere. Some suggested that the community was simply not yet comfortable with one of its own aspiring to the presidency. Others pointed to Lieberman's "centrist" stance on a number of issues, which might have made him marketable in the general election but did not play well with Democratic primary voters, including the Jews among them, who tended to be more ideologically liberal. This analysis seemed particularly cogent in a year marked by considerable anger among many Democrats at the administration's Iraq policy, which Sen. Lieberman had generally supported.

As the primary season progressed, Sen. Kerry built momentum with party voters, including, to all appearances, Jewish Democrats, as he came to be seen as the candidate best suited to take on President Bush. Once the nomination was clinched and continuing thereafter, the Kerry campaign took steps to convince the Jewish community that he was a reliable friend of the State of Israel.

In the general election campaign, both Democrats and Republicans employed Jewish outreach advisors and deployed armies of prominent Jewish surrogates for their respective candidates. Each side could boast an unusual Jewish surrogate: Sen. Kerry's brother, Cameron Kerry, a convert to Judaism, for the Democrats, and former New York mayor Ed Koch, a Democrat who backed Bush. The two parties also distributed specialized Jewish-issues briefing papers and pamphlets (including a White House document showcasing the president's meetings with, and messages of support from, Jewish leaders); organized myriad fund-raising events targeting Jewish givers; and slammed each other with paid advertising in Jewish community newspapers (and, at least in parts of Florida, with ads directed at Jewish readers of general-circulation papers).

Notwithstanding a Senate voting record of unblemished support for Israel, Kerry was targeted by negative messages from the Bush campaign and the president's supporters aimed at Jewish audiences, including one that depicted the senator as a supporter of Yasir Arafat and of former Malaysian prime minister Mahathir Mohamad, notorious for claiming that "Jews rule the world by proxy." For his part, Kerry sought to appeal to Jewish audiences by charging President Bush with coddling Saudi Arabia—an echo of Michael Moore's film *Fahrenheit 911*—and failing to address the Iranian nuclear threat. Aware of Jews' generally liberal outlook, Kerry and his aides also stressed the prospect of erosion of the church-state barrier, the likelihood that the next chief executive would have the opportunity to fill Supreme Court vacancies, and other possible domestic consequences of a second Bush term.

On the sidelines of the Democratic and Republican national conventions, held during the summer, the nonpartisan American Jewish Committee (AJC), Anti-Defamation League (ADL), and American Israel Public Affairs Committee (AIPAC) conducted receptions, as well as sessions on selected topics for the benefit of campaign officials, candidate surrogates, and delegates. AJC also held events at each convention focusing on the relationship of the pertinent political party—and of the Jewish community—with selected non-Jewish ethnic constituencies. Each convention was also marked by a gala opening day reception hosted by United Jewish Communities (UJC), AIPAC, and the local Jewish community relations council. The National Jewish Democratic Council and the Republican Jewish Coalition also held receptions at the convention with which each was, respectively, affiliated. The attention that these "Jewish" events received underlined once again how important this small constituency loomed in the eyes of party leaders and activists.

Just as the Republican national convention was about to begin, word broke that that officials at AIPAC were under criminal investigation arising out of allegations that they had passed on classified Pentagon documents to Israel (see below, p. 171). The matter remained a brooding presence throughout the convention. To be sure, AIPAC's events were well attended, with public officials affirming their support both for the organization and for Israel, but there was no end of discussion and conjecture as to the meaning and implications of this developing story.

Election Day 2004

When the smoke cleared after the election, President Bush had won a second term, with 286 electoral votes to Senator Kerry's 252 (in the certified count, Kerry garnered only 251 because a "faithless elector" cast his vote for John Edwards). Critically important for a president who had first reached the Oval Office with a minority of the popular vote, Bush's Electoral College victory was accompanied by a modest but convincing popular-vote majority of about 3.5 million, 51 percent as compared to 48 percent for Kerry. Thus Bush became the first president to receive an absolute majority of the popular vote since his father's election in 1988.

As anticipated, the Jewish vote tilted heavily to the Democratic side. But the majority was not as lopsided as four years earlier, and there were enough interesting nuances in the details to give Republican partisans some hope for the future. In 2000, Bush had gotten 19 percent of the Jewish vote. According to a *Washington Post* exit poll, he won 22 percent in 2004, while CNN set the figure at 24 percent. In Florida, CNN reported 20 percent of Jews voting for Bush, less than the national norm but a significant uptick from 2000, when he received only 12.1 percent.

Frank Luntz, a Republican strategist with experience in analyzing Jewish voting behavior, said that both CNN and the *Washington Post* had understated the Jewish Bush vote; in his sampling of Jewish voters in Ohio and Florida, Luntz found 25 percent going for Bush. Moreover, Luntz broke down the Jewish figures into subcategories. Following trends prevalent among non-Jews, 40 percent of Jews who attended synagogue weekly voted for the president. The more traditionally observant a Jewish voter was, the more likely he or she was to vote for Bush; more than two-thirds (69 percent) of Orthodox Jewish voters, according to Luntz, voted for the president, as compared to 23 percent of Conservative and 15 percent of Reform Jews. Going against general trends, however, young Jews, particularly young Jewish men, were more likely to vote for President Bush than the Jewish population as a whole. In contrast, exit polls of the general population found young voters more likely to support Kerry.

But Luntz's analysis was not widely shared outside Republican circles. The day after the election, the Los Angeles *Jewish Journal* ran a story captioned "GOP Could Not Improve on Their Poor Showing in 2000." Pointing to the president's reported 24 percent share of the national Jewish vote, the article noted that this "was only 5 points above his weak 2000 showing, and came after an extensive and expensive campaign by Jewish Republican groups and a big pro-Bush turnout by the Orthodox community, which strongly approved of the President's Mideast policies."

Not surprisingly, the Democratic-affiliated National Jewish Democratic Council agreed, terming Bush's increased Jewish vote "a margin with no statistically significant difference from [his] historically small Jewish vote in 2000." It also asserted that Kerry's showing "dramatically exceed[ed] the average Jewish Democratic vote" in the 1970s and 1980s, when, NJDC asserted, the Republican percentage had been 34.6 percent. NJDC executive director Ira Forman commented, "The GOP used every scare tactic, every bit of fear mongering that they could throw at John Kerry in the Jewish community. But they failed miserably."

President Bush's victory was enhanced by increased Republican majorities in both houses of Congress, vanquishing Democratic hopes of a change of control at least in the Senate. Republicans gained four Senate seats, so that their previous majority of 51-48-1 now stood a 55-44-1 (the one independent, former Republican Jim Jeffords of Vermont, generally voted with the Democrats). On the House side, Republicans netted three additional seats.

The 2004 election did not bring any alteration in the number of Jewish members of Congress: the 109th Congress, like the 108th, would include 26 Jewish representatives and 11 Jewish senators. But while the numbers did not change, some of the cast of characters did, as two long-time Jewish representatives left the scene, and two newcomers entered.

Six-term Rep. Peter Deutsch (D., Fla.) vacated his seat at year's end, a consequence of his decision to seek his party's nomination for an open Senate seat, a bid that proved unsuccessful (see below). Also departing was Rep. Martin Frost (D., Tex.), the second-longest-serving Jewish Democrat in the House (13 terms) and a former member of the Democratic leadership. Frost was one of several Texas congressmen facing district lines redrawn to favor Republican candidates, the result of an unusual mid-decade redistricting developed by House Majority Leader Tom DeLay of Texas and carried out by the state legislature. The plan worked, leading to Frost's defeat in a hard-fought race against fellow incumbent Pete Sessions, a conservative Republican (as well as the defeat of three other incumbent Texas Democrats).

All other incumbent Jewish representatives were handily reelected, as were incumbent Jewish senators Barbara Boxer (D., Calif.), Russ Feingold (D., Wis.), Charles Schumer (D., N.Y.), Arlen Specter (R., Pa.), and Ron Wyden (D., Oreg.). The reelected Jewish representatives were Gary Ackerman (D., N.Y.), Shelley Berkley (D., Nev.), Howard Berman (D., Calif.), Eric Cantor (R., Va.), Benjamin Cardin (D., Md.), Susan Davis (D., Calif.), Rahm Emanuel (D., Ill.), Eliot Engel (D., N.Y.), Bob Filner (D., Calif.), Barney Frank (D., Mass.), Jane Harman (D., Calif.), Steve Israel (D., N.Y.), Tom Lantos (D., Calif.), Sander Levin (D., Mich.), Nita Lowey (D., N.Y.), Jerrold Nadler (D., N.Y.), Steven Rothman (D., N.J.), Bernard Sanders (I., Vt.), Jan Schakowsky (D., Ill.), Adam Schiff (D., Calif.), Brad Sherman (D., Calif.), Henry Waxman (D., Calif.), Anthony Weiner (D., N.Y.), and Robert Wexler (D., Fla.). Incumbent Jewish senators not up for reelection were Norman Coleman (R., Minn.), Dianne Feinstein (D., Calif.), Herbert Kohl (D., Wis.), Frank Lautenberg (D., N.J.), Carl Levin (D., Mich.), and Joseph Lieberman (D., Conn.).

The two new Jewish representatives, both female state legislators, were well known to, and active in, their respective Jewish communities. Florida state senator Debbie Wasserman Schultz took the House seat vacated by Deutsch. Promising to focus on homeland security, Israel, and human services, Wasserman Schultz told the Jewish Telegraphic Agency that she reflected her heavily Jewish and politically liberal Fort Lauderdale-area district. Her Jewish affiliations included membership on the regional board of the American Jewish Congress and a role in the founding of the

National Jewish Democratic Council. Pennsylvania state senator Allyson Schwartz took the Philadelphia-area seat vacated by Democratic representative Joseph Hoeffel, who gave it up to wage an unsuccessful effort against Senator Specter. Schwartz too came to Congress with longstanding ties to the Jewish community and strongly held views on homeland security and social justice.

Other Jewish Democratic candidates who sought freshman seats in the House were not as successful. Jan Schneider failed in her second run against Florida Republican representative (and former Florida secretary of state) Katherine Harris, as did Paul Hodes in his effort to unseat Republican New Hampshire congressman Charles Bass, and Iraq War veteran David Ashe in his bid to assume the Virginia seat formerly held by Republican Ed Schrock. On the Senate side, former U.S. representative Eric Fingerhut failed to unseat Sen. George Voinovich (R., Ohio); Voinovich had long been a leader in the battle against global anti-Semitism in his role as cochair of the Helsinki Commission.

There were a number of other interesting Senate races. Rep. Jim DeMint, a Republican, defeated Democrat Inez Tenenbaum, whose Jewish husband was a pro-Israel activist and a member of the AIPAC board, in the election to determine who would take the South Carolina seat vacated by Democrat Fritz Hollings. DeMint was expected to be a supporter of Israel, as would have been expected of Tenenbaum, but his views on a number of domestic issues were at odds with those of much of the organized Jewish community.

After a long night of vote-counting, former University of South Florida president Betty Castor, a Jewish Democrat, conceded to former HUD secretary Mel Martinez in the contest to determine who would occupy the Florida Senate seat vacated by Democrat Bob Graham. Earlier, Castor had defeated Rep. Peter Deutsch in the Democratic primary, but only after Deutsch focused attention on Castor's alleged failure to take vigorous action when, during her tenure as university president, it was discovered that USF professor Sami al-Arian was linked to the Palestinian terrorist organization Islamic Jihad. Martinez then used that issue against Castor in the general election. The victorious Martinez became the first Cuban-American to serve in the Senate.

Arlen Specter's convincing win over Hoeffel in Pennsylvania followed a much closer call in the Republican primary, where he prevailed over a challenge from the right by Rep. Pat Toomey, thanks in part to the support of President Bush and Pennsylvania's far more conservative junior senator, Rick Santorum. Specter, a relative liberal, emphasized his conservative credentials in the primary to win over the party's base, and then moved to the political center in the contest against Hoeffel.

Several races in which there was no Jewish candidate were watched closely by Jewish leaders. Rep. Brad Carson, a Democrat, went down to defeat against former Republican congressman Tom Coburn in the context for an open Senate seat in Oklahoma. Coburn, an obstetrician who had kept a pledge to limit himself to three terms in the House, and retired in 2000, was known as a strongly ideological conservative. His positions on social issues, joined with antipathy to federal spending even when it benefited Oklahoma, raised concern that he might oppose foreign aid for Israel. But statements made by Coburn in the course of the campaign suggested an understanding of the importance for the U.S. of such aid. In a profound disappointment for many in the Jewish community, Senate minority leader Tom Daschle (D., S.D.), a strong supporter of Israel and a liberal on domestic issues, was unseated by former representative John Thune, a Republican, and thus became the first Senate leader since 1952 to be defeated for reelection. Thune was expected to be a strong ally of Israel. Another friend of Israel, Lisa Murkowski (R., Alaska), won a full Senate term, surviving a challenge that had gained momentum over her appointment by Alaska governor Frank Murkowski—her father—to the seat he vacated two years earlier.

Also on the Senate side, Democrats acceded to open seats in two closely watched races. In Colorado, state attorney general Ken Salazar, a Democrat viewed as strongly pro-Israel, won the seat vacated by Ben Nighthorse Campbell. In Illinois, in what was practically a coronation following his star turn at the Democratic national convention, Democratic state senator Barack Obama was elected to the Senate with more than 70 percent of the vote. While serving in the Illinois legislature, Obama promoted black-Jewish relations and a constructive U.S. role in the Israeli-Palestinian conflict.

Two new Republican senators—Johnny Isakson of Georgia and Richard Burr of North Carolina—were regarded as having good records on Israel. That could not be said of Cynthia McKinney (D., Ga.), a former representative who was elected overwhelmingly to her old seat after a two-year absence. During her previous tenure, McKinney became known for strongly anti-Israel views as well as for conspiracy theories that, among other things, imputed foreknowledge of the 9/11 terrorist attacks to the Bush administration. During the campaign, House minority whip Steny Hoyer (D., Md.) distanced himself and his party from

McKinney, saying, "I don't know whether she has modified her views, but they are not shared by anybody I know in the Democratic caucus today."

Post-Election Implications

There was some speculation following the election that a second-term President Bush, with the benefit of a strengthened Republican majority in Congress, might seek to enhance his legacy through a more conciliatory approach to the minority Democrats. Although, in a post-election news conference, he sounded a bipartisan note, there was, however, no reason to believe that his earnest commitment to his domestic agenda had diminished, or to doubt the determination of social conservatives to seek their political due. Moreover, the 2004 election had witnessed the departure of moderate voices from Washington and the advent of several new very conservative Republican senators (Coburn, DeMint, Thune, and David Vitter of Louisiana).

The most likely scenario, as of the end of 2004, was that the 109th Congress would provide heightened challenges to the organized Jewish community's domestic agenda. Indeed, while Senate rules requiring 60 votes to end a filibuster mean that a united Democratic minority could stop action if it determined to do so, in the new Senate, the Republican majority would need to pick off only five Democrats to stop a filibuster. It was thus much more likely that measures opposed by much of the organized Jewish community would become law.

Shortly before the election, it was reported that Chief Justice William Rehnquist was undergoing treatment for thyroid cancer. The news underlined the profound implications for domestic policy of the president's power to nominate federal judges, most particularly, justices of the Supreme Court. With a second term before him, it was likely that President Bush would eventually appoint to the bench a large number of federal trial and appellate jurists, including one or more Supreme Court justices, with far-reaching impact in a host of areas, such as church-state relations, reproductive rights, the authority of Congress to enact civil rights legislation, and much more. And with their reduced strength in the Senate, the Democrats would probably become more selective as to which nominees they would go to the mat to oppose.

Soon after his reelection in November, Sen. Specter, slated to chair the Senate Judiciary Committee, suggested that President Bush reach out to Democrats in considering whom to nominate for the Supreme Court. But countervailing pressures from social conservatives quickly entered the equation, as groups from the right, dismayed by Specter's comments, pressed the Senate leadership to pass over Specter and name someone else to head the Judiciary Committee. At year's end, it seemed likely, but not certain, that the new Congress would elect Specter to the chairmanship, but only after he had given assurances that he would seek to move judicial nominees to the Senate floor for an up-or-down vote.

The election results seemed barely in before a round of cabinet-level resignations and new appointments began. First to go was Attorney General John Ashcroft, who had drawn criticism from varied sectors of the Jewish community (and, from some quarters, praise) for his views on church-state separation and his drafting and implementation of the USA-Patriot Act and other counterterrorism measures. In contrast to the staunchly conservative Ashcroft, his designated successor—White House counsel and former Texas Supreme Court justice Alberto Gonzales—was greeted even by Jewish groups at odds with much of the administration's domestic agenda as likely to bring to the table a more moderate and less ideological perspective. To be sure, it was understood that, whatever his personal predilections, he would be carrying out the president's agenda.

Gonzales, though, was not a man free of controversy. He had helped craft a Justice Department memo in 2002 arguing that laws prohibiting torture did not apply to the detention and interrogation of "enemy combatants"—a memo that, many contended, led directly to the abuses at Abu Ghraib prison in Baghdad. On the other hand, his personal history as the son of Mexican migrant workers who rose from poverty and the fact that he would be the first Latino to serve as attorney general appealed to the Jewish community as well as to other minority groups.

Within a few days of Ashcroft's resignation, Secretary of State Colin Powell announced his own imminent departure, eliciting generally positive grades from the Jewish community for his role as America's face to the world. Nevertheless, Powell's approach to Israel-related issues flowed from an inclination to look to State Department career officers for guidance, leading to a more evenhanded stance between Israelis and Palestinians than many Jewish advocates thought appropriate, given the Palestinian role in commencing and waging a war of terror. Similarly, Powell felt comfortable operating within an internationalist framework, and therefore sought to cooperate with the UN, EU, and other nations more than much of the pro-Israel community preferred. In an administration with strong pro-Israel leanings that did not feel impelled to work on a multilateral basis, Middle East policy came to be driven more by the White House than by Foggy Bottom. For Jews, Powell's shining moment was his refusal to attend the UN World Conference Against Racism, held in Durban in 2001, when it became a forum for fervently anti-Israel and even anti-Semitic rhetoric.

The appointment of National Security Adviser Condoleezza Rice as secretary of state, with her deputy, Stephen Hadley, moving up to fill her vacated position, suggested that the State Department would fall more in line with the White House approach to the Middle East. Rice, who had developed good relations with both the American Jewish leadership and the government of Israel during the president's first term, had been the main figure in dealing with the Israeli-Palestinian conflict on a day-to-day basis. The Jewish Telegraphic Agency characterized her as the one "who backpedaled on criticisms of Israel issued by Powell's State Department," and it was Hadley who was credited with a key role in drafting the well-received April 14 letter recognizing that a final resolution of the conflict could not include a Palestinian "right of return" to Israel proper, and that final boundaries would have to reckon with post-1967 realities (see below, p. 215).

THE POLICY ARENA

Terrorism

Within the Jewish community, as within American society generally, debate continued as to whether the federal government had encroached too far on civil liberties in the battle against terrorism. Although much of the concern turned on administration actions that had nothing to do with the USA-Patriot Act, enacted by Congress in the wake of 9/11, that legislation was often invoked by civil libertarians as the poster child for all that was wrong with how the war on terrorism was being waged. To be sure, a number of specific provisions of the USA-Patriot Act continued to draw critics' attention, while the administration, for its part, insisted that national security required maintaining the law in its totality, that provisions scheduled to expire ("sunset") at the end of 2005 be made permanent, and that additional authority be granted to law-enforcement and security personnel.

One proposed set of amendments, the Security and Freedom Ensured ("SAFE") Act, introduced in both houses of Congress in 2003, drew relatively wide interest and support through 2004, possibly because it was seen as a moderate response to the concerns raised by the 2001 legislation. The SAFE Act would address civil liberties concerns by implementing additional safeguards on the use of roving wiretaps and "sneak and peek" search warrants allowed by the USA-Patriot Act. Additionally, the proposed legislation would require the FBI to provide additional background information when seeking to obtain library or other personal records about individuals, and would modify standards for the issuance of national security letters. The SAFE Act also subjected to expiration additional provisions of the USA-Patriot Act not already set to "sunset," absent new congressional action, at the end of 2005.

By the end of the 108th Congress, the House bill had a bipartisan roster of 71 cosponsors, and the Senate bill, sponsored by Sen. Lisa Murkowski (R., Alaska), had one cosponsor, Sen. Ron Wyden (D., Oreg.), but no action had been taken in either house. The American Jewish Committee endorsed the SAFE Act, describing the measure as an appropriate balancing of the need for heightened security and enforcement capabilities with respect for fundamental privacy protections.

On October 18, 2004, President Bush signed into law the Homeland Security appropriations bill (H.R.4567), which included, among much else, $25 million in funding, to be disbursed by the Department of Homeland Security (DHS) for states to assist nonprofit organizations at high risk from terrorist threats. By year's end, state officials had begun distributing the money to high-risk nonprofits—including synagogues, day schools, and other Jewish organizations—for security enhancements such as concrete barriers and "hardening" of window and doors, as well as for technical assistance to assess needs, develop plans, and train personnel. The funding represented an advance on the High-Risk Nonprofit Security Enhancement Act, a proposed package introduced in April with bipartisan support in both houses by Sen. Barbara Mikulski (D., Md.) and Rep. George Nethercutt (R., Wash.). A House cosponsor, Rep. Jerrold Nadler (D., N.Y.), succeeded in having the initiative passed by the House Judiciary Committee as an amendment to another bill in June, and the Senate Governmental Affairs Committee passed its companion measure in July, but neither version moved any further.

Both bills, in fact, had been conceptualized by the United Jewish Communities (UJC) in response to the perceived ongoing terrorist threat to Jewish and other nonprofit institutions. UJC then played a leading role in bringing together a broad coalition of eleemosynary organizations to urge passage.

As introduced, the Mikulski-Nethercutt initiative—reflecting the drafters' desire to bring on board members of Congress and organizations concerned about possible church-state problems—provided that the subsidized security enhancements could only address risks associated with terrorism and not any others, and could only be put in place through contracts between the state government and independent contractors, with no funds flowing directly from the government to the religious institutions. The bill also prescribed that the organizations to be aided by these enhancements would be determined based on an objective assessment of level of risk.

When Mikulski-Nethercutt failed to move toward passage, the coalition worked with Sen. Mikulski, Majority Leader Bill Frist (R., Tenn.), Minority Leader Tom Daschle (D., S.D.), House chief deputy whip Eric Cantor (R., Va.), and Senators Arlen Specter (R., Pa.) and Thad Cochran (R., Miss.) to include at least a portion of the contemplated funds in the Homeland Security appropriations bill. But that bill, as enacted, did not include the provisos explicitly limiting use of the funds and prescribing the structure within which they were to be disbursed.

It became evident in the course of the year that despite the efforts to draft a measure acceptable to both sides of the church-state policy divide, the organized Jewish community was split on the advisability of the initiative even with the original safeguards against direct government aid to religious institutions. Unsurprisingly, Mikulski-Nethercutt garnered support from the Union of Orthodox Jewish Congregations (OU) and Agudath Israel of America, since they did not share the "strict separation" perspective of their sister Jewish organizations; indeed, the OU made no secret that it would have preferred a bill providing straight funding from government to the religious organizations. The United Synagogue of Conservative Judaism, the American Jewish Congress, and the American Jewish Committee also came out in support of the initiative as addressing a palpable security threat to Jewish and other nonprofit institutions; AJCommittee legislative director and counsel Richard Foltin asserted that the contemplated church-state safeguards adequately met First Amendment concerns when viewed "in the context of the severe threat to life and limb posed by the threat of terrorism."

The ADL and the Religious Action Center (RAC) of Reform Judaism, however, considered Mikulski-Nethercutt deficient in protecting the wall of church-state separation, particularly given a range of practical problems, not the least of which was whether there would ever be adequate funds to address threats to the entire nonprofit community in any meaningful way. Their concerns were echoed by Senators Carl Levin (D., Mich.) and Frank Lautenberg (D., N.J.), and when the bill came before the Senate Governmental Affairs Committee in July, they proposed an amendment requiring that physical security enhancements might be purchased and installed only to the extent that the property to be improved would not be used for religious instruction or worship, unless and until the security enhancements had no value. Opposing that amendment were Senators Specter and Lieberman, the former asserting that separation of church and state did not mean that government could not protect religious institutions that were "at risk because they are religious institutions." The amendment failed 10-6, and the committee then approved the bill by a voice vote, but, as noted above, no further congressional action ensued.

Jewish organizations that had favored Mikulski-Nethercutt applauded the inclusion of $25 million for security enhancement purposes in the Homeland Security appropriations law, with the UJC promising to continue to work in the next Congress toward enactment of the High Risk Nonprofit Security Enhancement Act with full funding, as well as to urge DHS to adopt regulations ensuring that the money already allocated "can only be used for protection from terrorist attacks." AJCommittee stressed the need for a push in the 109th Congress to ensure that all funding conform to the church-state safeguards of Mikulski-Nethercutt. The RAC urged Reform congregations not to apply for or accept the Homeland Security funds, both on church-state grounds and because of the danger to religious autonomy.

As the 108th Congress moved toward adjournment of its lame-duck session, the last piece of business in both houses was the Intelligence Reform and Terrorism Prevention Act (H.R.10/S.2845), legislation intended to restructure the national intelligence agencies pursuant to recommendations for combating terrorism included in the 9/11 Commission's final report, issued in July 2004. After months of debate, the House passed the bill by 336-75 on December 7, and the Senate passed it the next day by 89-2. President Bush signed it into law on December 17. Its most controversial aspect was the bill's creation of the position of national intelligence director, who would oversee and coordinate the nation's 15 spy agencies and run a newly created National Counterterrorism Center. Following a dispute over this issue that nearly stymied passage, this restructuring was ultimately included in the final bill.

Legislators contended as well over whether the final bill would include changes affecting immigrants and asylum seekers championed by Rep. James Sensenbrenner (R., Wis.), chairman of the House Judiciary Committee. The provisions advanced by Sensenbrenner were termed the

"REAL-ID Act" because they included a section precluding the federal government from accepting a driver's license as identification if issued by a state that allowed such licenses to be issued to illegal immigrants. Another portion of the Sensenbrenner initiative, denominated "Section 101," sought to impose onerous new obstacles on legitimate asylum seekers and refugees from persecution; in particular, it imposed a heightened burden of proof for asylum seekers and provided an expansion of expedited removal procedures, so that low-level immigration officials might turn away asylum seekers without a full and fair opportunity for their claims to be considered. The version of the bill initially passed by the House included the REAL-ID provisions, while the Senate-passed version did not.

In October, 12 Jewish organizations, spearheaded by the Hebrew Immigrant Aid Society (HIAS), wrote to the conferees on the bill urging that the REAL-ID provisions be left out of the final bill because of Section 101. The groups argued that its sweeping measures could expose asylum seekers and refugees to an increased danger of deportation back into the hands of those who sought to harm them; went beyond the 9/11 Commission's recommendations; and not only would not enhance national security, but would be detrimental to it.

The overall bill nearly foundered when Sensenbrenner insisted on the inclusion of his provisions. He only withdrew his objection to the bill moving forward after obtaining assurances that he would be given an opportunity in the next Congress to bring his initiative up for a vote (Jewish groups were expected to continue to oppose it in the next Congress). Although the final legislation did not include the Sensenbrenner's language, it did establish certain minimum standards for state-issued driver licenses, while leaving in place the existing situation whereby states determined issuance criteria, including whether a license may be issued to an undocumented alien.

In another piece of late-session business, on December 8, President Bush signed into law a year-end omnibus-spending package, tucked into which was a provision that took a significant step toward seeking a measure of justice for American citizens murdered by terrorists anywhere in the world. The so-called Koby Mandell Act (H.R.401/S.684) was named for a 13-year-old American murdered by Palestinian terrorists on the West Bank more than three-and-a-half years earlier. It had been introduced in the House by Rep. Robert Andrew (D., N.J.) on January 28, 2003, and in the Senate by Sen. Gordon Smith (R., Oreg.) on March 21 of that year. The bill called for the creation of an Office of Justice for

Victims of Overseas Terrorism within the Justice Department, to assure that perpetrators of violence against Americans were pursued, prosecuted, and punished, whatever their country of origin or place of residence. It arose out of concern that the State Department, which was responsible for apprehending such terrorists, was not taking action against Palestinian perpetrators as energetically as it did against others guilty of such this kind of violence.

The omnibus spending bill did not, in the end, incorporate the Koby Mandell Act completely. Rather, the language was general and non-binding, simply alluding to the Koby Mandell Act as guidance for creation of a new Justice Department office. The Zionist Organization of America, which played a leading role in promoting the measure, pronounced itself satisfied, its president, Morton Klein, asserting, "We are looking forward to this office taking as the central focus of its existence the prosecution of Palestinian Arabs who kill Americans."

Congress also acted on two fronts relating to Israel's troubled relationship with international organizations that acted unfairly toward Israel. In July 2004, following the ruling of the International Court of Justice (ICJ) against Israel's security fence (see below, pp. 228–29), Reps. Mike Pence (R., Ind.), Shelley Berkley (D., Nev.), and Ileana Ros-Lehtinen (R., Fla.) introduced a resolution condemning the issuance of the ruling and urging nations not to take action based upon it. It went on to deplore the UN's manipulation of the ICJ for political purposes, the ICJ's acquiescence, and the attempt to infringe upon Israel's right to self-defense in the face of the Palestinian Authority's failure to stem terrorist attacks against Israelis. The resolution also warned that any action by the international community pursuant to the ICJ judgment could impede efforts to move the peace process forward.

And in November, Rep. Eliot Engel (D., N.Y.) circulated a congressional sign-on letter to Secretary of State Powell expressing shock at comments made by Peter Hansen, Commissioner General of the United Nations Relief and Works Agency (UNRWA), that UNRWA employed members of the terrorist organization Hamas, and that he did not "see that as a crime" (see below, p. 244). The letter also noted that, under Hansen, UNRWA had long been accused of looking the other way or accepting no responsibility when Palestinian terrorists operated in its refugee camps, and of failing to deal with UNRWA schools that used textbooks containing anti-Semitic material.

The congressional letter urged Powell to suspend U.S. funding for UNRWA until all members of Hamas or other terrorist organizations were off the payroll, pointing out that UN Security Council Resolution 1373(1)(d) prohibited making funds available to anyone directly or indirectly involved in terrorism. And it asked the secretary to use U.S. leverage to seek new UNRWA leadership that would be verifiably committed to countering terrorism and incitement to violence, and would cease working with terrorists. (Historically, the U.S. has contributed about a quarter of UNRWA's annual budget, the largest share by far of any donor nation.)

There were also legal steps taken in the war against terrorism. In July, criminal charges were filed against the Holy Land Foundation for Relief and Development and seven of this tax-exempt charity's officers, alleging that they had conspired to provide material support to the Hamas terrorist organization. The next month, Attorney General Ashcroft announced another indictment, this time under the federal Racketeer Influenced and Corrupt Organizations (RICO) Act, of three men charged with fund-raising on behalf of Hamas. Two of them were arrested on August 19; the third, Mousa Mohammed Abu Marzook, had been deported in 1997 and was located, at the time of the indictment, in Syria.

This was an innovative use of RICO, which had been enacted in 1970 as a tool for prosecuting mob-related activities; reliance on RICO enabled the Justice Department to bring these charges based on actions that preceded the designation of Hamas as a terrorist group in 1995. Muslim organizations, joined by some civil liberties groups, protested such use of RICO and of material support legislation, maintaining that prosecutors' reliance on these statutes criminalized politics and violated First Amendment protections of freedom of association and speech. But Attorney General Ashcroft rejected this criticism, saying, "The United States makes no distinction between those who carry out terrorist attacks and those who knowingly finance, manage or supervise terrorist organizations." Jewish and pro-Israel organizations applauded these steps.

In another move directed at stopping financial support for terror organizations, in early December, a federal civil jury sitting in Chicago issued a $52-million award in favor of David and Joyce Boim, the Israeli-American parents of a young man who had been killed in a 1996 attack in the West Bank. The amount was automatically trebled to $156 million by the judge, pursuant to applicable federal law. The award against the Quranic Literacy Institute, the Islamic Association for Palestine, the Holy Land Foundation, and an individual, Muhammad Salah, followed findings—by the jury with respect to the institute, and by a magistrate with respect to the others—that these defendants had directed funds to

Hamas. The case constituted the first use of provisions of federal antiterrorism legislation enacted in 1996 that allowed victims to go after the assets of organizations and individuals implicated in supporting a terrorist group. Jewish organizations hailed the precedent, echoing the words of the Boim family's attorney during closing arguments that the defendants and others like them were "the oxygen that keeps the terror support system going."

Soviet Jewry, Refugees and Immigration

On January 7, 2004, President Bush proposed a new temporary-worker program to match willing foreign workers with willing U.S. employers for jobs that no Americans could or would fill. In addition to new foreign workers, the program would be open to undocumented men and women currently employed in the U.S. Workers participating in the program would receive a three-year work visa, potentially renewable for an undetermined but limited period. Framed only in general terms, the proposal omitted an element of key concern to pro-immigration groups, including Jewish organizations, which had been pressing for comprehensive immigration reform—permanent earned legalization for undocumented immigrants with a demonstrated work history in the U.S. who had been in the country for a substantial time. Some observers viewed the omission as an attempt to forestall opposition from Republican restrictionists, who were sure to claim that any such provision constituted an unacceptable "amnesty"; if that was the purpose, the strategy was unsuccessful, as restrictionists were quick to attack even the modest vision outlined by President Bush as just such an "amnesty."

Initial reaction to the proposal from pro-immigrant groups was mixed. Some groups were unabashedly critical, while others—including Jewish groups that signed on to a statement spearheaded by HIAS—commended President Bush for putting these issues on the agenda for public debate and also taking a step in the right direction. In the end, the latter approach became the motif for the larger movement. AJCommittee joined with 23 other religious, ethnic, and immigrant advocacy organizations in signing an ad published in the April 21 Roll Call stating, "We agree with President Bush that the immigration system is broken and needs to be fixed . . . .We have different views on some aspects of the President's proposal, but we are united in our call to the leaders of both political parties to come together in a bipartisan fashion to enact balanced comprehensive immigration reform as soon as possible." Most crucially, in the view of these groups, it was yet to be seen whether the president and Congress would provide a clear path to citizenship for undocumented aliens who had lived in the country for an extended period of time.

Neither the president's proposal nor any other comprehensive immigration bill became concrete enough for introduction in 2004, but there were more limited measures already on the table intended to provide relief for selected, discrete groups.

On April 9, 2003, Reps. Chris Cannon (R., Utah) and Howard Berman (D., Calif.) introduced H.R.1684, the Student Adjustment Act. The Senate version, the Development, Relief, and Education for Alien Minors Act (DREAM Act), S.1545, was introduced on July 31 of that year by Sen. Orrin G. Hatch (R., Utah). Under this legislation, states would have the flexibility to determine that certain students who were undocumented aliens qualified as "state residents," and were therefore eligible for in-state college tuition rates; earned adjustment to permanent residence would be provided for an estimated 50,000 undocumented children; and the secretary of homeland security would have the authority to cancel the removal and adjustment of status of certain alien students who were long-term U.S. residents. Various Jewish groups endorsed the DREAM Act, maintaining that minors who were brought to this country illegally should not be penalized for decisions made by their parents, and that students who had participated in the American educational system and demonstrated a strong desire to contribute to American society should be able to benefit from this legislation.

On September 23, 2003, Senators Larry Craig (R., Idaho) and Edward Kennedy (D., Mass.), and Reps. Cannon and Berman introduced S.1645/H.R.3142, the Agricultural Jobs, Opportunity, Benefits, and Security Act of 2003 (AGJOBS). Under this legislation, an estimated 500,000 undocumented agricultural workers could earn legal status through their past work in the U.S. and a prospective work requirement. The program would require background checks for security purposes. Applicants would be denied permanent-resident status and be subject to removal if they failed to meet the work requirements, were inadmissible under immigration law, or had been convicted of a felony or at least three misdemeanors. A number of Jewish groups supported this legislation as well, seeing it as a proactive step to protect the civil rights of highly vulnerable workers and place them on a path towards eligibility for legalization and citizenship.

Some of these same Jewish groups continued to make known their opposition to another immigration-related measure, the Clear Law Enforcement for Criminal Alien (CLEAR) Act (H.R. 2671), introduced by Rep. Charlie Norwood (R., Ga.) on July 9, 2003. The Senate version of the legislation, the Homeland Security Enhancement Act of 2003 (S.1906), was introduced on November 20, 2003. The bill would expand the role of state and local authorities in the enforcement of federal immigration standards, convert some civil immigration violations into criminal violations, and allow the National Crimes Information Center database to be used for the enforcement of immigration violations. The Jewish groups asserted that rather than increasing security, the CLEAR Act would divert resources to the enforcement of immigration law and potentially harm relationships between law-enforcement authorities and community members.

The omnibus spending bill that passed both the House and Senate on November 20, 2004, and that President Bush signed into law on December 8, included an amendment offered by Sen. Arlen Specter (R., Pa.)— an extension of the longstanding "Lautenberg Amendment"—that continued to facilitate entry into the U.S. for Jews and evangelical Christians who were refugees from the former Soviet Union, as well as Iranian refugees who were members of religious minorities, such as Jews, Christians, Ba'hai, Zoroastrians, and Mandeans.

Advocates for refugees continued their ongoing effort to roll back portions of the 1996 welfare law that reduced legal immigrants' access to a number of public benefit opportunities. Of particular concern was that law's alteration of the Supplemental Security Income (SSI) program providing a basic monthly income to individuals 65 or older, the disabled, and the blind. Under the 1996 law, refugees entering the country or reaching age 65 after August 22, 1996, would be eligible to receive such benefits only during their first seven years in the country—but numerous factors, often technical or systemic challenges, could well bar refugees from obtaining citizenship before that cut-off point. President Bush's fiscal year 2005 budget request proposed a one-year extension for deserving refugees who were about to reach the seven-year limit. On March 25, 2004, Representatives Benjamin Cardin (D., Md.), Phil English (R., Pa.), Amo Houghton (R., N.Y.), Nancy Johnson (R., Conn.), and Sander Levin (D., Mich.), introduced the SSI for Elderly and Disabled Refugees Act (H.R.4035), a bill to provide a two-year extension of eligibility. A similar piece of legislation, S.2623, was introduced by Senators Herb Kohl (D., Wis.), Richard Lugar (R., Ind.), and Gordon Smith (R., Oreg.) on July 9.

The president's budget request for fiscal year 2005, submitted on February 2, 2004, included $730 million for the Migration and Refugee Assistance (MRA) account, the principal State Department budget account for refugee admissions and overseas assistance. This figure was $25 million lower than the previous year's appropriation. The proposal also included $20 million for the Emergency Refugee and Migration Assistance (ERMA) account—nearly $10 million less than the prior appropriation. The budget assigned $473 million to the Office of Refugee Resettlement (ORR) to provide for refugees once they arrived in the U.S.—including $399 million for resettlement, $10 million for victims of trafficking, $10 million for victims of torture, and $54 million for unaccompanied alien minors. The final package, approved by Congress, allocated $763.6 million for MRA, including $29.8 million for ERMA and $484.3 for ORR.

As of the close of fiscal year 2004 (September 30), the U.S. had admitted 52,895 refugees, short of the 70,000 target set by the president but a significant increase over the previous two years.

Foreign Aid and U.S.-Israel Relations

Congress concluded action on foreign aid funding for fiscal year 2004, which had already begun on October 1, 2003, in early 2004. The final bill appropriated $26.7 for international affairs, $1.8 billion below the administration's original request, but $1.4 billion above the amount Congress had appropriated for fiscal year 2003—and this in a year of extraordinarily tight budget constraints. The appropriation included $17.4 billion for foreign operations—$1.4 billion less than the president had requested, but $1.3 billion more than Congress had appropriated the previous year. Congress approved the president's full request for $2.64 billion in aid to Israel—$2.16 billion of it in military aid and $480 million in economic aid.

Earlier, in November 2003, Senators DeWine (R., Ohio), Feinstein (D., Calif.), Smith (R., Oreg.), and Durbin (D., Ill.) had sponsored a letter to President Bush "urging a robust increase in the U.S. International Affairs Budget for FY 2005." Reps. Houghton (R., N.Y.) and Berman (D., Calif.) put forward a similar letter in the House. The president did ask for an increase, issuing a budget for fiscal year 2005 in January 2004 that called for $31.5 billion for international affairs, including $21.4 billion for foreign operations.

The Senate improved on the president's bid by budgeting $31.8 billion, whereas the House allocated only $26.9 billion. In April 2004, Senators Lugar (R., Ind.) and Feinstein (D., Calif.) delivered a letter, cosigned by

31 colleagues, to the Senate Appropriations Committee chair and ranking member, calling for "at least the president's request" for the overall international affairs budget. On November 20, both houses approved an omnibus appropriations bill that provided for $29.7 billion in international affairs funding, including $19.7 billion for foreign operations. The bill was awaiting the president's expected signature at the end of 2004.

As the year closed and—following what had become an unfortunate precedent—before the overdue work on fiscal year 2005 (which began on October 1, 2004) had been concluded, Senators DeWine (R., Ohio), Feinstein (D., Calif.), Smith (R., Oreg.), and Durbin (D., Ill.), were circulating a letter to President Bush expressing "strong, bipartisan support for a robust increase in the FY06 International Affairs Budget as an essential investment in America's fight against terrorism and efforts to build global stability through promoting economic prosperity and expressing the compassion of the American people for those in need around the world." Representatives Jim Leach (R., Iowa) and Howard Berman (D., Calif.) circulated a similar letter in the House. Supporters of vigorous funding for foreign affairs, including groups in the Jewish community, urged members of Congress to sign on, with some noting that the report of the bipartisan 9/11 Commission, issued that summer, had strongly endorsed investment in the international affairs budget as vital to protecting America. The two letters to the president, sent December 15, were signed by a record total of 156 members of the House and Senate.

The Foreign Relations Authorization bill for FY 2004 and 2005 (H.R.1950) included language introduced by Rep. Ileana Ros-Lehtinen (R., Fla.) intended to address incitement against the U.S., the West, Israel, and Jews that was pervasive in the Muslim world. While the House passed the bill, including the incitement provisions, on July 16, 2004, the Senate took no action during the 108th Congress, and so the initiative died with the failure to enact the larger bill. The incitement provisions— which the American Jewish Committee, working in partnership with Rep. Tom Lantos (D., Calif.), had played a major role in promoting—would have directed the State Department to monitor "hateful misinformation or hostile propaganda" disseminated by government-controlled sources abroad, to recommend and carry out appropriate U.S. responses, and to submit an annual report to Congress.

Another legislative response to the rising number of anti-Semitic incidents both in Europe and the Muslim world came from Sen. George Voinovich (R., Ohio), who introduced S.2292, the Global Anti-Semitism Review Act, on April 7, 2004. It directed that not later than December

31, 2004, the secretary of state should deliver to the Senate Committee on Foreign Relations and the House International Relations Committee a one-time report on acts of anti-Semitism around the world (see below, p. 182). Accompanying legislation in the House, introduced by Rep. Lantos, called for the establishment of an office within the State Department to monitor and combat anti-Semitism. The Senate bill was passed on May 7, the House version on October 8, and President Bush signed a reconciled version of the bill into law on October 16.

Pursuant to this law, a comprehensive report on anti-Semitic incidents around the world was submitted to Congress on December 30. The report highlighted not only acts of vandalism and assault, but also the growing problem of anti-Semitic invective in the European media, and in publications, textbooks, and television programming in the Middle East and North African countries, especially Egypt and Saudi Arabia. Included under the category of anti-Semitism were cases of criticism of Israel that went beyond objections to policies and instead indulged in demonization, dehumanization, and the invocation of comparisons between Israelis and Nazis.

On May 11, President Bush signed an executive order implementing sanctions against Syria pursuant to the Syria Accountability and Lebanese Sovereignty Restoration Act of 2003. The White House cited Syria's support for terrorist groups, continued military presence in Lebanon, pursuit of weapons of mass destruction, and actions to undermine U.S. and international stabilization and reconstruction efforts in Iraq. The sanctions imposed included substantial reductions in U.S. exports to Syria, limitations on Syrian landing rights in the U.S., and restrictions on Syrian assets in the U.S.

In the aftermath of President Bush's March 14 meeting with Israeli prime minister Ariel Sharon, at which the two leaders laid out a set of principles for resolution of the Palestinian-Israeli conflict, House Majority Leader Tom DeLay (R., Tex.) and Democratic Whip Steny Hoyer (D., Md.) introduced, in June, a resolution (H.Con.Res.460) strongly endorsing those principles. It was adopted by the House on June 23 by a vote of 407-9, with three representatives voting "present." The Senate acted in a similar vein on November 19, before adjourning for recess, passing S.Res.477 by unanimous consent. The Senate resolution endorsed "a vision of two democratic States, Israel and Palestine, living side by side in peace and security," as well as a commitment to the "road map" "as a realistic and widely recognized plan for making progress toward peace" (for the American Jewish community's role in the passage of these resolutions, see below, pp. 190–91).

On March 29, Sen. Santorum (R., Pa.) introduced S.Res.325, a resolution deploring the violations of human rights and religious freedoms that Jews and other minority populations had suffered in Arab countries. The resolution, which did not move further before the close of Congress, called on the U.S. to make sure that any settlement of Palestinian refugee claims would be matched by a similar settlement of the claims of Jews from Arab countries.

Anti-Israel Bias in Education

On October 21, 2003, the House of Representatives passed the International Studies in Higher Education Act, H.R.3077, to reform Title VI of the Higher Education Act. The Senate did not pass counterpart legislation during the 108th Congress, and the bill died as 2004 ended.

Title VI provides federal funds to selected international-studies and foreign-language centers at universities across the country. It had been established to help meet vital national needs—in particular, training experts for national security and other government service, and educating the public on international affairs. Proponents of H.R.3077 maintained that the program had largely failed to meet government needs: there was no mechanism for ascertaining such needs, and few Title VI graduates entered government service. But the most significant problem, according to the critics, was that a significant number of Middle East studies centers funded by Title VI were highly politicized, with scholars uncritically promoting a positive image of Palestinians, Arabs, and the Islamic world, while ignoring or denigrating Israel. Scholars with other perspectives, the critics asserted, were excluded and discourse on critical issues stifled. Substantial Saudi and other foreign funding to some of the Title VI centers also cast doubt on their independence and objectivity.

H.R. 3077 would have responded to these concerns by requiring the secretary of education to take into account whether the activites of a center considered for funding advanced national interests and fostered debate from diverse perspectives, and by providing for the creation of a bipartisan advisory board. Although supported by a broad spectrum of Jewish organizations as consistent with academic freedom, some in the higher education community attacked it for interfering with the autonomy of academic institutions. An effort to move an endorsing resolution at the plenum of the Jewish Council for Public Affairs, held in February, was tabled for further study.

INTERRELIGIOUS RELATIONS

Catholic-Jewish Relations

Despite the widely publicized tensions between some Catholics and Jews over Mel Gibson's film *The Passion of the Christ* and the Vatican's decision to beatify the German nun whose vision of the Crucifixion underlay the movie's portrayal of Jews (see below, pp. 160–63), a major positive step was taken as well. The first international meeting of Vatican officials and Latin American Jews, held in Buenos Aires in early June, was the 18th in a series of International Liaison Committee meetings between Jewish and Catholic intellectuals and religious leaders. It concluded with an unprecedented statement, a "total rejection of anti-Semitism in all its forms, including anti-Zionism as a more recent manifestation of anti-Semitism." Pope John Paul II had already defined anti-Semitism as a sin. Signing the statement were members of the Vatican Commission for Religious Relations with the Jews and the International Jewish Committee for Interreligious Consultation (IJCIC), a coalition including the ADL, the World Jewish Congress, the American Jewish Committee, and the Orthodox, Conservative, and Reform synagogue movements.

Mainline Protestant-Jewish Relations

The year was marked by a growing rift between the mainline Protestant and Jewish communities over the Israeli-Palestinian conflict, leaving some to wonder whether a decades-long partnership on domestic policy and other international issues would survive.

For years, even as the Jewish and mainline Protestant communities worked closely together in coalitions dealing with a myriad of religious liberty, public education, civil rights and other matters, communications on the Middle East often seemed to take a place in a parallel universe, Jewish groups reacting with angry press releases to what were seen as unbalanced, double-standard statements on the Middle East that emanated from the National Council of Churches and many of its constituent churches. By 2004, however, it became clear to many leaders of the Jewish community that the problem had to be addressed head-on.

This perception was dramatically affirmed when, at a meeting in Richmond, Virginia, in July, the General Assembly of the Presbyterian Church (U.S.A.) voted 431-62 for a resolution comparing Israeli treatment of

Palestinians to South African apartheid and calling for the church to undertake a "phased selective divestment" that did more than a certain amount of business with or in Israel. The church, representing more than 3 million members, held approximately $7 billion in assets, much of that dedicated to pensions, and it was not known how much was actually invested in companies with an Israeli connection. Announcement of the resolution's adoption brought vehement condemnations from virtually the entire Jewish community. Insult was added to injury when, at the same meeting, the assembly voted 260-233 to reject a proposal to halt the funding of messianic "Jewish" congregations that targeted Jews for proselytizing activities.

In an effort to stem a trend that could easily spread to other denominations, representatives of Jewish groups met with church officials in New York in late September. Speaking of that meeting, Dr. David Elcott, national interreligious affairs director for the American Jewish Committee, told the Jewish Telegraphic Agency, "The conversations crossed each other. The Jewish community vented all of the arguments in support of the State of Israel and explained the failures of the Palestinians. The Presbyterians spoke of the powerlessness of the Palestinians and the power of Israel over the Palestinians." A second meeting took place in Washington in October that included a broader array of churches that belonged to the National Council of Churches.

In a move that Jewish groups attributed to progress made at the Washington meeting, in early November, the executive council of the Episcopal Church approved a course of action distinctly more balanced than that of the Presbyterians, even though it still raised concern among Jews. The council voted to review the church's corporate investments in order to take appropriate action with respect to both "companies that contribute to the infrastructure of Israel's ongoing occupation of the West Bank and the Gaza Strip" and "companies that have connections to organizations responsible for violence against Israel." It remained unclear what those actions might be. Jewish groups, while noting the penchant of the mainline churches to single out the Israeli-Palestinian conflict among all of the conflicts in the world, commended the Episcopalians for at least recognizing that the Palestinians, and not just the Israelis, had responsibilities.

As if to underline its more one-sided stance, less than a week later the Presbyterian Church (U.S.A.) issued guidelines for implementing that body's earlier resolution for a "phased selective divestment." No similar divestment from support for Palestinian perpetrators of violence was advanced, nor was any reference to Palestinian terrorism added to the citation of "the continued occupation of Palestinian land by Israel as the major impediment to the creation of a just peace."

Evangelical-Jewish Relations

The growing rift between the mainline churches and the Jewish community over Israel was underlined by continuing affirmations of support for the Jewish state by evangelical Christians. More than 4,000 evangelicals traveled to Israel from around the world in the fall for a Sukkot-season demonstration of solidarity organized by the Jerusalem-based International Christian Embassy, the world's largest Christian Zionist organization. David Parsons, a spokesman for the embassy, denied the common allegation that support for the State of Israel was grounded in an End of Days scenario whereby Christians supported the ingathering of Jews only as a prelude to Armageddon, in the course of which the Jews would be destroyed. "We believe God will protect this nation no matter what," Parsons said.

The Israeli government, as well as many Israelis and American Jews, welcomed this and other evangelical demonstrations of support at a time when Israel seemed under unfair and one-sided attack, and anti-Semitism was on the rise. Nevertheless, there was considerable sentiment in Israel and the American Jewish community for maintaining distance, based both on the suspicion of evangelical missionizing and on concern that the eschatological role of the Jews remained a core aspect of evangelical support. That alleged role could have baleful implications, some felt, should evangelicals come to conclude that Jews and the Jewish state were not playing their assigned role. For American Jews, abiding differences between the two communities over controversial issues of social policy heightened their apprehension.

CHURCH-STATE MATTERS

The "Faith-Based Initiative"

The "charitable choice" debate continued, as various cabinet departments and federal agencies proceeded with implementation through administrative action of key elements of President Bush's faith-based initiative. The sides of this argument were by now familiar. The administration sought to use government funds for the provision of social services by houses of worship and other pervasively religious institutions, and to permit those institutions to make employment decisions on the basis of religion, just as they had the right to do when hiring with private funds. Much of the Jewish community, however, committed to a strict separation of church and state, opposed the faith-based initiative as an establishment of religion, although a minority, largely in the Orthodox community, defending the initiative as a legitimate response to discriminatory treatment of religious institutions.

On the legislative side, advocates of "charitable choice" recognized that a sweeping bill covering all federal social services programs would not fly, and focused instead on including elements of the initiative in bills reauthorizing specific programs as they came up for consideration. They also sought to remove from long-standing legislation provisions they viewed as inconsistent with the faith-based initiative, and this, more than anything else—at least as the 108th Congress moved through its second and final year—tended to stall reauthorization of those programs altogether. Thus, although the Workforce Investment Act, H.R.1261, passed in varying forms in 2003, this bill to renew a federally funded job-training program failed to move to passage in either 2003 or 2004 because the House-passed version would have repealed a prohibition on religious-employment discrimination in the program that applied to any participating organization, including churches. H.R.2210, the School Readiness Act of 2003, which passed in the House by only one vote at the end of July 2003, also never moved to passage—or even consideration by the Senate—because it would have added new provisions allowing faith-based organizations that ran Head Start programs to make hiring decisions on the basis of religion.

Vouchers

Another perennial church-state dispute was over vouchers. When the Omnibus Appropriations bill, H.R.2673, was signed into law by President Bush on January 23, 2004, it included an appropriation of $14 million per year, for five years, to provide vouchers of up to $7,500 for low-income children in the District of Columbia to attend private and religious schools. This was, as far as anyone was aware, the first federal law providing for such vouchers. The city went on to implement the program, although opponents, including a number of national Jewish organizations, contended that Congress was foisting it on unwilling D.C. residents.

One month later, on February 25, the U.S. Supreme Court announced its ruling in *Locke v. Davey*. With Chief Justice William Rehnquist writing for the majority, the Court held, 7-2, that Washington State's denial of scholarship funds to students studying devotional theology did not violate the Free Exercise Clause of the First Amendment. The state, the court found, was entitled to make a determination that its constitution forbade students to use a state scholarship, established to assist academically gifted students with postsecondary education expenses, to pursue a degree in devotional theology. This ruling that not everything that is constitutionally permissible is constitutionally required — in effect, allowing the states to have some play in the joints — was a rebuff to those who had argued, after the court's decision in *Zelman v. Harris* (2002) upholding the constitutionality of a vouchers program, that religious schools and programs could not be constitutionally excluded from otherwise generally available government funding programs (see AJYB 2003, pp. 105–06).

Among those making that last argument was the Union of Orthodox Jewish Congregations (OU). Nathan Diament, director of its Institute for Public Affairs, commented after the court's decision: "Today is a sad day for America's 'first freedom' of religious liberty. Our nation's highest court has approved state action which denies a person a government benefit solely upon the basis that the person is engaged in what the court acknowledges is a constitutionally protected religious exercise." Separationist groups, including the vast bulk of the Jewish organizations, had supported the state of Washington, and so had the opposite response, as typified by the American Jewish Committee's observation that the court had "adopted an unremarkable perspective that simply to say a religious activity may be funded [by the state] is not to say it must fund all programs."

Pledge of Allegiance

The lines within the Jewish community were drawn in somewhat unusual form as the Supreme Court convened in March 2004 to hear argument in *Elk Grove Unified School District v. Newdow,* a case brought by the atheist father of a San Francisco public school student challenging the inclusion of the words "under God" in the Pledge of Allegiance. Many of the Jewish groups usually associated with strict interpretation of the First Amendment's prohibition on government establishment of religion took a pass on the case, viewing the language as a benign exercise in ceremonial deism.

Indeed, the American Jewish Congress, heir to a strong legacy of separationism, went so far as to file a brief in opposition to the challenge, arguing that a lower court's striking of the pledge with the objectionable words went against historical experience, and that the words themselves had no coercive effect. AJCongress counsel Marc Stern also had a pragmatic concern, telling the Jewish Telegraphic Agency, "in the political real world, a decision to ban the phrase would lead to a fast-track constitutional amendment." The ADL stood alone among Jewish groups in endorsing the lower court's ruling, saying in its brief that the words in dispute subjected students to subtly coercive pressure at an age when they were too young to reflect critically on what they were saying.

In the end, the matter was mooted, at least for the time being, when the Supreme Court ruled that the plaintiff, not being the legal custodian of the child, never had the authority to bring the suit in the first place.

Religious Accommodation

On April 11, 2003, Sen. Rick Santorum (R., Pa.) and Sen. John Kerry (D., Mass.) introduced S.2893, the Workplace Religious Freedom Act (WRFA), legislation clarifying the requirement of Title VII of the Civil Rights Act of 1964 that employers reasonably accommodate their employees' religious practices, unless doing so would cause undue hardship. The bill was a response to a judicial interpretation of this requirement, dating back to the 1970s, that defined anything more then a minimal expense or difficulty as an "undue hardship." WRFA would require that an expense or difficulty must be substantial in order to be considered an "undue hardship." By the close of the 108th Congress, the bill had a bipartisan roster of 23 cosponsors in the Senate. It was expected to be reintroduced in both houses early in the 109th Congress.

HOLOCAUST-RELATED MATTERS

Restitution

Several threads of the multi-front battle for Holocaust survivors' reparations seemed to be moving toward a close during 2004.

Over the course of the year, the Conference on Jewish Material Claims Against Germany (Claims Conference) distributed some $1 billion — the largest amount paid by the conference in a single year in its history — mostly for compensation and restitution to Holocaust survivors and heirs in 78 countries, with additional payments in support of organizations caring for impoverished survivors and for Holocaust research, education, and documentation. The largest 2004 payment, approximately $461 million, was made by way of the second and final installment of the $1.1 billion that the German government, joined by 6,000 German businesses, had agreed to pay in resolution of claims made by former Jewish slave and forced laborers. (This latter fund was itself part of $5 billion paid in compensation of slave labor, the great bulk of the proceeds going to non-Jewish victims.)

Other Claims Conference payments made in 2004 included those to survivors residing in Central and Eastern Europe and victims of Nazi medical experiments, as well as the further disbursal of money from the $1.25-billion settlement of claims against the Swiss banks, encompassing not only claims based on dormant Swiss bank accounts, but also those of refugees denied entry into Switzerland and of former slave laborers, based on the Swiss banks' role in facilitating Nazi profits from the use of slave labor.

These payments notwithstanding, resolution of the Swiss fund remained far from settled, as 2004 saw the Claims Conference turn resources that had been focused on assessing slave labor claims to locating the owners of Holocaust-era Swiss bank accounts. As a result of an agreement reached in late July among the conference, the banks, and the U.S. district court charged with administering the settlement, it was expected that an additional 5,000 names of Holocaust-era account owners would be released, and the conference would be allowed access to bank records that might help it identify accounts that had Jewish owners. This project was expected to take 12 to 18 months.

In December, Hungarian Holocaust survivors and the U.S. government announced settlement of a claim—following a referral for mediation earlier in the year—that U.S. troops had mishandled looted Hungarian Jewish property at the conclusion of World War II. While details of the settlement and the mode of distribution remained to be finalized, the Israeli newspaper *Ha'aretz* reported that U.S. authorities had agreed to pay $25 million—a fraction of a loss valued at $2 billion in current dollars. The funds would be distributed among living Hungarian survivors whether or not they had property on the train, and not just to the original owners or their heirs.

The claim arose out of the seizure by U.S. troops, in October 1945, of a train loaded with 24 boxcars of looted property that Nazi officials had intended to transport to Germany. Virtually none of it made its way to the owners; instead, as the Presidential Advisory Commission on Holocaust Assets in the United States concluded in a 1999 report, various portions of the lucre—which included art masterpieces and expensive housewares—went to governments, the wrong parties, and even to high-ranking U.S. troops. The suit, brought in federal court in Miami (where a large concentration of Hungarian survivors resided) in 2001, sought only $300 million, far less than the actual value of the assets—$10,000 each for an estimated 30,000 victims with property aboard the train—based on the maximum compensation per individual of $10,000 allowed under U.S. law.

Negotiators pointed to several factors as having led to the settlement: difficulties of proof for the plaintiffs; the fact that—while the payment was a small fraction of the loss—the U.S. was at last acknowledging responsibility; and, perhaps most crucially, concern that the case might devolve, as other Holocaust cases had, into a dispute about the worth of Jewish lives lost in the Shoah.

A less satisfying result for survivors and their advocates came in October, when a New York federal district court judge dismissed claims for payment on Holocaust-era life insurance policies against the company Assicurazoni Generali. Ruling on 20 class-action and individual lawsuits that had been consolidated for consideration in his court, Judge Michael Mukasey found that the president and the executive branch, not the courts, had jurisdiction over Holocaust-related claims against foreign companies and governments, and that claimants therefore had to acquiesce to the U.S. government's determination that insurance claims be resolved through procedures established by the International Commission on Holocaust Era Insurance Claims (ICHEIC). The ruling reflected a legal landscape that had shifted in 2003, when the U.S. Supreme Court ruled that a California law favoring survivors' claims amounted to an unconstitutional interference in foreign affairs.

The district court's ruling, following nearly 60 years of claims and ten years of litigation, immediately drew sharp criticism from plaintiffs and their advocates, who had long considered ICHEIC little more than a dilatory front for the insurance companies. Promising to appeal the decision, William Shernoff, attorney for 18 survivor families, commented, "Holocaust survivors cannot understand how their simple lawsuits against a private company can possibly interfere with President Bush's ability to conduct foreign affairs with Italy." Generali's view was, unsurprisingly, quite the opposite, the insurance company endorsing the view that "courts are not the place to revisit the tragedies of the Holocaust," while promising "offers of payments to claimants . . . in accordance with its participation in [the commission]."

Office of Special Investigation

The Justice Department's Office of Special Investigation (OSI), known for its inexorable pursuit and deportation of former Nazis living in the U.S., seemed on the verge of going out of business as the march of time slowly but surely brought the death of war criminals who had entered the country under false pretenses. In 2004, the OSI commenced only two proceedings for removal.

At year's end, however, President Bush gave the OSI a new lease on life when he signed the intelligence reform bill, which included a provision expanding OSI jurisdiction to include seeking the deportation of any former alien involved in severe human-rights violations, not just those associated with Nazi crimes. Rep. Mark Foley (R., Fla.) and Rep. Gary Ackerman (D., N.Y.) were responsible for the change. Foley, speaking of the OSI, said: "It's a phenomenal office, it's done yeoman's work. They're up and ready, and I didn't want to create new bureaucracy to do something they're so good at doing."

RICHARD T. FOLTIN

Anti-Semitism

I N 2004, THE 350TH ANNIVERSARY of Jewish life in America, anti-Semitism remained a marginal phenomenon that it no way threatened the security of American Jews. Furthermore, the U.S. government, on numerous occasions during the year, used its influence to counter anti-Semitic manifestations abroad. Nevertheless, a number of events gave cause for anxiety. The one that received most attention came early in the year—the opening of the film *The Passion of the Christ,* with its negative portrayal of Jews and its implication that they were responsible for the death of Jesus. Other flash points concerned anti-Israel actions that, in the eyes of many Jews, spilled over into anti-Semitism, such as campaigns to divest from Israel, and pro-Palestinian bias on some college campuses. Most ominous was the FBI's decision, late in the year, to investigate AIPAC, the premier pro-Israel lobby.

Assessing Anti-Semitism

One baseline criterion for measuring anti-Semitic trends in the U.S. is the annual *Audit of Anti-Semitic Incidents,* prepared by the Anti-Defamation League (ADL), which tallies up and categorizes expressions of hostility toward Jews. Its usefulness is limited, however, since inconsistencies in reporting reduce the level of accuracy, and its quantitative approach sheds little light on the overall security of Jews in a population exceeding 250 million.

The 2004 *Audit* reported 1,823 anti-Semitic incidents, an increase of 17 percent over the 2003 total of 1,557, and the highest number since 1995. Particularly notable in the 2004 data was an increase of 27 percent in the "harassment" category, to a total of 1,178 cases. The incidence of "vandalism" was virtually unchanged since 2003. Analysts suggested that aggressive law enforcement and enhanced security measures to protect synagogues and other Jewish property had kept vandalism from rising. Nonetheless, the *Audit* noted that the vandalism level in 2003 and 2004 was higher than in 2001 and 2002, a trend that bore watching. Acts of vandalism accounted for 35 percent of the overall 2004 total, and harassments—less violent, but more direct and personal—constituted the other 65 percent reported. The comparable percentages in 2003 were, respectively, 40 and 60 percent. Harassments have predominated each year since 1991; during the 1980s, vandalism was more common.

The increase in harassment was particularly evident in several states with large Jewish populations, a trend that had been going on for some time. New York—as always the state with the largest number of incidents—showed a 45-percent increase in harassments, Florida 80 percent, California 62 percent, New Jersey 30 percent, and Massachusetts 38 percent.

Anti-Semitic incidents on campus increased marginally, from 68 in 2003 to 74, still substantially fewer than the 106 reported in 2002. In the three-year period 2000–02, campus incidents increased by over 50 percent, but, by 2003, more effective counteraction and educational efforts by pro-Israel students helped reduce the number of incidents (see below, p. 195).

The ADL announced it would continue its series of surveys of U.S. and European attitudes toward Jews, conducted since 1992 by the Marttila Communications Group, Inc. (formerly Marttila and Kiley). Results of the latest polls were scheduled for release in 2005. Serious reservations had been expressed about the American survey, which used questions developed in the 1960s that might not fairly or reasonably measure anti-Semitism in the 2000s.

Justice Department data gathered under the federal Hate Crime Statistics Act (HCSA), which required an annual report on crimes motivated by prejudice, cast some light on anti-Semitism in the U.S. The 2003 statistics, which were released in 2004, indicated that of the 7,489 bias-motivated criminal incidents that year, 3,844 were motivated by race; 1,026 by ethnicity/national origin; 1,239 by sexual orientation; 1,343 by religion; and 33 by disability. Of the incidents motivated by religious bias, 927, or 69 percent, were directed against Jews and/or Jewish institutions, up from 65.3 percent in 2002. The 927 cases in 2003 constituted 12.37 percent of the total number of reported hate crimes.

Another aspect of anti-Semitism assessment was the measurement of Jewish perceptions. Reflecting the salience of anti-Semitism in the minds of many Jews, the *2004 Annual Survey of American Jewish Opinion,* conducted for the American Jewish Committee (AJC) by Market Facts, Inc., included no fewer than 25 questions on the topic. The survey found that 27 percent of the sample of American Jews said that anti-Semitism was a "very serious problem," and 67 percent said it was "somewhat of a problem." This compared with 37 percent and 60 percent in the two categories, respectively, in 2003, and 29 percent and 66 percent in 2002. The 2003 "spike" in the "very serious problem" category was believed to have been a response to the large number of anti-Jewish incidents in Europe the year before. Nine percent of those surveyed in 2004 said that anti-Semitism would "increase greatly," 33 percent said it would "increase somewhat," and 45 percent said it would "remain the same"—numbers virtually unchanged from 2003. Asked specifically about Europe, American Jews were far more alarmed—the AJC poll found that 55 percent believed that anti-Semitism was a "very serious problem" there.

Intergroup Relations and Anti-Semitism

CHRISTIANS, JEWS, AND *THE PASSION*

The public debut of Mel Gibson's film, *The Passion of the Christ,* about the final hours of the life of Jesus, took place in movie houses across the country on January 26, Ash Wednesday, reigniting the heated controversy that surrounded the lead-up to the film in 2003 (see AJYB 2004, pp. 75–76). Jews—and some others—who had seen versions of the film before its release found the depiction of Jewish characters and the emphasis on their role in the execution of Jesus to be stereotypically anti-Semitic. This came as no surprise to those who were aware that Gibson adhered to the ultra-conservative "traditionalist" Catholic splinter group that rejected the reforms of the Second Vatican Council, including the seminal document *Nostra Aetate* that absolved Jews from the charge of deicide and repudiated the anti-Semitism that flowed from Christian "teachings of contempt." Gibson's father, Hutton Gibson, who had a history of publicly expressed Holocaust denial, said, a week before the film's opening, that the Holocaust was a "fiction" and that Jews sought to take over the world. Mel Gibson then reiterated that he did not espouse his father's views, and noted that "many people died during World War II, including many Jews."

As had been the case in 2003, the organized Jewish community overwhelmingly believed *The Passion* to contain anti-Semitic themes, but disagreed about how to address the issue. While some Jewish groups complained vocally, others believed that harsh rhetoric would do nothing but harm relations with Christians. Complicating the intergroup tensions and sensitivities was the fact that although Gibson was Catholic, the most enthusiastic proponents of the film were evangelical Protestants, precisely the Christian group most supportive of Israel and antagonistic toward Islamic fundamentalism.

Representing the hard-line Jewish view was the ADL and its national director, Abraham H. Foxman, who expressed "sadness about Gibson resurrecting a debate we thought we had resolved 50 years ago. [The film] blames the vengeful Jews for the Crucifixion." He insisted that an assertive Jewish posture was bearing fruit, noting that had it not been for pressure from Jewish groups, liberal Protestants and Catholics would not, in the wake of the controversy, have publicly reiterated their view that the Jews were not collectively responsible for the death of Jesus. At the other end of the Jewish continuum was Rabbi Yechiel Eckstein of the International Fellowship of Christians and Jews—a supporter of closer ties between evangelicals and Jews—who suggested, "The hysteria of the Jewish response is uncalled for," and movie critic Michael Medved, who wrote, "Sadly, the battle over *The Passion* may indeed provoke new hatred of Jews." Medved, in fact, citing "the reckless maneuvering of real-life Jewish leaders," suggested that the villain of the affair was not Gibson but rather his Jewish organizational critics. Also in agreement was Rabbi Daniel Lapin, head of the small but vocal Seattle-based group, Toward Tradition, who declared on Pat Robertson's "700 Club" television show that the ADL and its allies were "dangerous organizations driving a wedge between American Jews and Christians."

More moderate voices were heard as well, suggesting that the religious fault lines revealed by the release of the movie should encourage the renewal and deepening of Jewish-Christian dialogue. But even those Jewish organizations that took this more hopeful position, such as the American Jewish Committee, worried about the potential erosion of four decades of progress in Christian-Jewish relations. Rabbi A. James Rudin, senior interreligious advisor to the AJC, asserted, "This movie is a defining moment for Christian leadership. If they don't speak out and point out the distortions, errors, and anti-Jewish stereotypes, this movie will be the benchmark for the Passion story for the next decades." Rudin, in fact, prepared a 47-page resource guide for Christians and Jews to be used as a basis for discussing the film.

Among American Catholics, the reception of *The Passion* was mixed, complicated by conflicting accounts of what Pope John Paul II thought about it. (His personal aide, Archbishop Stanislaw Dziwisz, denied reports that the pope, after seeing *The Passion,* asserted, "It is as it was.") Catholic sociologist Andrew Greeley of the National Opinion Research Center, commenting on the fickle nature of American Catholics when it came to both religion and public affairs, said, "Catholics who don't accept [the pope's] official teaching on birth control are hardly likely to rush off to the local multiplex to see a film that he may, or may not, have liked." Catholic responses, in fact, tended to fall into two categories: either joining with Jews in condemning the movie, or seeing and liking it, but not because of its portrayal of the Jews.

The U.S. Conference of Catholic Bishops (USCCB), the top Roman Catholic Church body in America, issued a much anticipated review of *The Passion* in early March, which dismissed claims made by Jewish and Christian scholars, as well as by professional film critics, that the movie blamed the Jews collectively for the death of Jesus. On the contrary, the review stated: "Concerning the issue of anti-Semitism, the Jewish people are at no time blamed collectively for Jesus' death, rather Christ himself freely embraces his destiny." This drew immediate and harsh criticism from the ad hoc interfaith scholars group assembled in 2003 to analyze an early version of Gibson's script, which had criticized the film exactly because it blamed the Jews (see AJYB 2004, p. 75). At the same time, the Bishops Conference drew wide praise for distributing to dioceses and parishes *The Bible, the Jews, and the Death of Jesus,* a collection of key documents on Catholic teachings about Jews and the "sin" of anti-Semitism.

In mid-March, the Institute for Jewish and Community Research released findings of a poll that suggested that seeing the movie actually changed Christian attitudes toward Jews for the better. Twelve percent of those surveyed said the film made them "less likely" to blame Jews for the crucifixion, while 5 percent said they were "more likely" to blame Jews. According to a survey in April by the Pew Research Center for the People and the Press, the percentage of Americans who believed Jews were responsible for killing Jesus had grown in recent years, although it remained a minority view. Twenty-six percent of respondents thought Jews were to blame for the Crucifixion, up from 19 percent in an ABC News poll in 1997. Pew found that the greatest increases were among young people and blacks. Thirty-four percent of those under age 30 now believed Jews were responsible, compared to 10 percent in 1997. Among blacks, the percentage had gone from 21 to 42. The Pew survey made no effort to determine the impact of *The Passion.*

By the end of 2004 there was no indication that the film—one of the highest grossing of the year—had brought an increase in American anti-Semitism, and there was not a single recorded case of anyone harming or vilifying Jews after viewing it. As Eugene Fisher of the USCCB suggested, "[The film] would not foster anti-Semitism in anyone who is not already anti-Semitic." The same seemed to be the case in Europe, even in predominantly Catholic countries with historical traditions of Christian-based anti-Jewish expression. Notwithstanding reviews that were mixed to poor, *The Passion* broke box-office records in the weeks following its European release in early April. By year's end there was no evidence that the film had contributed to anti-Semitism. In fact, most of the few statements citing *The Passion* as proof of Jewish culpability came from Muslim sources.

There was significant discussion of the movie in journals of opinion. Thus Leon Wieseltier, in *The New Republic* (March 8), suggested that whatever the abominable anti-Jewish stereotypes that pervaded the film, even worse was its "pornographic" glorification of blood and gore: "Its loathing of Jews is subsumed in its loathing of spirituality, in its loathing of existence." Historian David Berger of Brooklyn College, writing in the May issue of *Commentary,* said that the observation that Jews and Christians have been seeing different movies "is the beginning and perhaps the middle of wisdom," but even more crucial was that the film "exacerbated tensions among Christians themselves—and among Jews—as well as confrontations between secular and religious Americans."

A footnote to *The Passion* story was the fact that the actress portraying the Virgin Mary, Maia Morgenstern, was a Romanian Jew and daughter of Holocaust survivors.

Tangentially related to the Gibson film was the beatification (the penultimate step to sainthood), on October 4, of a German nun who died in the early nineteenth century, Sister Anne Catherine Emmerich. Gibson reportedly borrowed heavily from Sister Emmerich's mystical book, *The Dolorous Passion of our Lord Jesus Christ,* which presented her own "eyewitness" account of the Crucifixion and contained virulent anti-Jewish imagery and rhetoric. Jewish groups, noting that the most objectionable parts of Gibson's film flowed directly from her writings, expressed considerable distress, but Rabbi David Rosen, AJC's director of international interreligious affairs, warned against overreaction. Rosen pointed out that "beatification does not mean that the person is 100 percent kosher, only that the actions attributed . . . are worthy of emulation."

The Catholic Church, in fact, took a strong and unambiguous stand against anti-Semitism. At a July meeting of the International Catholic-Jewish Liaison Committee in Buenos Aires, this international group of Catholics and Jews issued a joint declaration in which, for the first time, Catholics condemned "anti-Semitism in all its forms, including anti-Zionism." While not carrying the weight of a papal encyclical, the declaration could not have been issued without Vatican sanction.

MAINLINE PROTESTANTS AND DIVESTMENT

The defining issue in relations between the mainline Protestant denominations and Jews in 2004 was one that straddled the vague and highly permeable boundary between criticism of Israel and anti-Semitism — divestment: withdrawing funds invested in Israel, Israeli companies, and firms doing business with Israel.

Two major Protestant communities took divestment initiatives during the second half of 2004. The Presbyterians were first, becoming the Christian group ever to decide to divest from Israel. In mid-July, the General Assembly of the 3-million-member Presbyterian Church (U.S.A.) voted to equate Israel with apartheid South Africa, and to withdraw its Israel-related investments in a "phased selective manner." (That the Presbyterian move came at the same time that the Catholic Church was condemning both anti-Semitism and anti-Zionism was not lost on the Jewish community.) A September 28 meeting between Jewish and Presbyterian leaders failed to sway the church leadership.

Divestment seemed to gather momentum as the 2.2-million-member Episcopalian Church announced at the end of September that it too was considering such a policy. But the leadership had second thoughts following a series of intensive talks with Jewish leaders in October, and seemed to back away from divestment, at least for the time being.

The major concern of the organized American Jewish community was the possibility that divestment by the largest denominations would trigger similar action by other groups, raising the possibility of a solid Protestant mainline anti-Israel front. While proponents of divestment justified their position as an attempt to change specific Israeli policies toward the Palestinians, their Jewish interlocutors sought to convince them that steps against the Jewish state that were not taken against other countries, some of them guilty of far worse actions, smacked of anti-Semitism, which, in turn, risked compromising the gains made over decades of Christian-Jewish dialogue.

BLACKS AND JEWS

Minister Louis Farrakhan, leader of Nation of Islam (NOI), had long expressed anti-Semitic and anti-white rhetoric, but a perception had developed in recent years that he had moderated his views, and the mainstream black community did not shun him. He gave numerous speeches at NAACP events and participated in a radio conversation with Rev.

Jesse Jackson in November 2004. Russell Simmons continued to invite Farrakhan to speak at his hip-hop summits, and honored him at the Source Magazine Awards in November 2004.

In fact, Farrakhan ratcheted up his anti-Semitism in 2004, focusing nearly every major speech on alleged Jewish and Israeli conspiracies. Jews, he claimed, had been Atlantic slave traders and Caribbean plantation owners. The "racist Jews who control Hollywood and the media" and were responsible for negative movie and TV stereotypes of blacks were now attacking Mel Gibson for *The Passion.* In his only address to a national audience during the year, delivered at the National Press Club in May, he blamed Israel for the war in Iraq and claimed that "American soldiers were dying for Israel." Reiterating this theme in December, in the course of a speech in Newark, New Jersey, he stated: "The war in Iraq is not your war; that's Israel's war." The NOI newspaper, *The Final Call,* ascribed mainstream media attention to the terrible suffering in Darfur, in western Sudan, to an alleged Zionist need to "control the Black agenda." NOI continued to sell *The Secret Relationship between Blacks and Jews,* an anti-Semitic book, on its Web site.

Malik Shabazz, national chairman of the New Black Panther Party (NBPP), a racist and anti-Semitic black nationalist group (see AJYB 2004, p. 74), continued to make racist and anti-Jewish statements at public events throughout 2004. After drawing well under 1,000 participants to what was supposed to be its Million Youth March in September 2003, the NBPP organized smaller protests across the country in 2004. In his search for mainstream acceptance, Shabazz appeared on MSNBC and Fox programs five times. In four of the appearances he was introduced as a member of Black Lawyers for Justice; only Fox's Sean Hannity noted Shabazz's affiliation with the New Black Panther Party. In July, Shabazz and other party members attempted to disrupt an interfaith vigil in Washington, D.C., organized by the local Jewish community council, religious leaders, and elected officials.

Lemrick Nelson, Jr.—convicted in 2003 of violating the civil rights of Yankel Rosenbaum during the 1991 Crown Heights riots, when he stabbed Rosenbaum, who subsequently died—was released from federal prison on June 2. He would serve the nine remaining months of his sentence in a halfway house. But the black-Jewish tensions emanating from those riots were revived that same month with the staging of a play, *Crown Heights,* which blamed the Jews for the riots ("There's a black boy bleeding, and the rabbi just runs"), and portrayed the murder of Yankel Rosenbaum as a tragic accident. The play was produced by All Stars Project, Inc., an organization associated with Lenora Fulani, a fringe New York City politician, who, according to Jewish defense agencies, had a history of anti-Semitism, and was coauthored by Fulani's associate, Fred Newman, an alleged cult leader. The ADL characterized the play as "distorting history and refueling hatred."

An op-ed article jointly penned by hip-hop mogul Russell Simmons and Rabbi Marc Schneier, president of the Foundation for Ethnic Understanding, appeared in a number of American Jewish newspapers, timed for the commemoration of Martin Luther King Day. It called on African-Americans "to embrace [Dr. King's] legacy and to join us in defeating anti-Semitism."

HISPANICS AND JEWS

The Nation of Aztlan, a small California-based Latino group, continued to distribute, as its only known activity, virulently anti-Semitic material. Throughout 2004, Hector Carreon and Ernesto Cienfuegos, editors of the group's publication, *La Voz de Aztlan,* blamed Jews and Israel for almost every negative event affecting Mexico or the Mexican community in the U.S. The group's Web site posted the *Protocols of the Elders of Zion,* and made frequent reference to it and to other anti-Semitic works. The site carried allegations that Israel poisoned Yasir Arafat, that Mexico was in danger of being taken over by "an International Jewish Cabal" led by Jorge Castañeda (referred to by a "Jewish" name, George Gutman), and explained suicide bombings as Mossad tricks to garner world sympathy for Israel. Some of this material was reproduced by Iranian and other Middle East news agencies.

MUSLIMS AND JEWS

At the end of June, the ADL issued a retraction and apology for suggesting that Islam's declaration of faith, the Shahada, was an "expression of hate" and "closely identified with terrorism." The dispute emerged after Jewish students at the University of California, Irvine, learned that Muslim students were planning to wear green scarves or stoles inscribed with the Shahada at the graduation processional, and alerted the ADL. Despite its acknowledgement that the Shahada was not itself objectionable, the ADL and other Jewish groups continued to charge that the wearing of green scarves was itself an expression of support for terror.

The Campus

COLUMBIA

"The committee will hear all complaints brought to it, investigate those it thinks require investigation, and deliver a factual report," wrote Columbia University president Lee Bollinger to the Columbia community on December 8. By announcing the creation of a committee to hear and assess complaints of anti-Israel and possibly anti-Jewish bias on the part of faculty members, he was hoping to bring closure to a series of events that revealed deep fissures in a university whose student body, faculty, board of trustees, and donor base included many Jews.

Since 2002, some students at Columbia College had complained about anti-Israel comments and harassment of Jewish students in a number of courses offered by the Department of Middle East and Asian Languages and Cultures (MEALAC). In 2003, the university administration announced a review of the academic content of all courses relating to the Middle East (see AJYB 2004, pp. 83–84). In May 2004, the six-person review committee reported no evidence of any problems.

But 2004 brought a new crisis, the release of a film, *Columbia Unbecoming,* produced by the David Project, a Boston-based organization devoted to promoting pro-Israel positions. It consisted of interviews with ten present and former Columbia students who spoke of instances of harassment, intimidation, and discrimination from professors, particularly those associated with MEALAC, when they expressed pro-Israel views; Israeli students, particularly, recounted incidents in which they were belittled in class or in extracurricular activities. One MEALAC professor, Joseph Massad, whose published work was heavily critical of Israel, was singled out by a number of students for abusive tactics in the classroom; two others, Hamid Dabashi and George Saliba, were mentioned as well.

The film came to public attention in mid-October, when the New York *Sun* carried a report about it. Almost immediately, Rep. Anthony Weiner (D., N.Y.), who represented a district in Brooklyn and Queens in Congress, called upon Columbia to fire Massad. The accused teachers, for their part, charged the students with fabricating conversations, misunderstanding lectures, and neglecting schoolwork, and asserted that their academic freedom was being threatened. Massad called the film "a racist witch-hunt of Arab and Muslim professors." A number of Jewish MEALC students also disputed the allegations in *Columbia Unbecoming,* asserting that Massad and the others, while highly critical of Israel, were brilliant, balanced, and provocative teachers.

A public screening of *Columbia Unbecoming* took place on October 27 as part of a press conference with David Project president Charles Jacobs and several of the students interviewed in the film. Jacobs and the students insisted that they were not calling for the firing of any professor; rather, they wanted the university to institute a "zero-tolerance" policy on anti-Semitism, increase diversity of viewpoints within MEALAC, and hold mandatory sensitivity training for incoming students. Immediately following the screening, President Bollinger said that Columbia would formally investigate the accusations, and assigned Provost Alan Brinkley to conduct the inquiry.

The ensuing brouhaha roiled the Columbia campus for many weeks, prompting at least three front-page stories—and several editorials—in the *Spectator,* the respected student-run newspaper, on the question of how to balance academic freedom with academic responsibility. Bollinger's view, already stated in March 2003, was that professors were entitled to express themselves freely in the classroom, but not to intimidate or "indoctrinate" students.

On December 8, Brinkley announced the creation of another six-member ad hoc committee to carry out the investigation. Almost immediately, it was charged with bias: one member had been Professor Massad's Ph.D. advisor, and two others had signed a petition in October 2002 calling for the university to divest from any firm that was involved in the manufacture for or sale of arms to Israel. Questions about the appointment to the committee of Lisa Anderson, dean of Columbia's School of International and Public Affairs, went back to events earlier in the year, when Columbia solicited a group of donors to fund the Edward Said Professorship in Modern Arab Studies and Literature. The late Professor Said had been a distinguished and highly anti-Israel professor of English. The list of donors, released by the university in April, contained names of individuals, and even a foreign government—the United Arab Emirates—that were actively hostile to Israel and Zionism. Dean Anderson was in charge of the establishment of the new chair as well as the accompanying fund-raising.

At year's end, the committee, chaired by the respected First Amendment lawyer Floyd Abrams, had not yet begun its work. Meanwhile, speculation was rife about a puzzling aspect of the media coverage: in contrast to the other New York daily newspapers, the *New York Times* virtually ignored the story.

OTHER CAMPUSES

In July, Harvard University announced that it was returning a $2.5-million gift from the president of the United Arab Emirates (UAE), Sheik Zayed bin Sultan al-Nahyan. It did so because the UAE president, through a policy research center he funded, sponsored lectures that blamed Jews for the September 11 attacks, claimed that Jews used human blood to bake pastries, and generally promoted intolerant attitudes toward Israel. Rachel Fish, the former Harvard Divinity School student who was serving as New York regional director of the David Project, helped provide information to Harvard about the sheik, and led the campaign to have the university return the gift. Two other universities, Columbia and Georgetown, also recipients of the sheik's largesse, had yet to give back their gifts.

On the first day of classes at Duke University in late August, the student newspaper, the *Duke Chronicle,* published an unsigned editorial praising the school for allowing the Palestine Solidarity Movement (PSM) to hold its annual conference at the school's Durham, North Carolina, campus, October 15–17. This conference, the organization's fourth, was titled "Divestment from Israel," and drew about 600 people.

The peaceful nature of the conference belied the heated atmosphere on the Duke campus during the weeks leading up to the event. After the organizers announced that high on their agenda was a call for universities to drop their investments in Israeli companies, Duke reiterated its policy against divestment, but said it would permit the conference to take place as an expression of free speech. Duke's Hillel affiliate, the Freeman Center, did not try to prevent the conference; instead, Jewish students crafted a response attuned to what they believed was a broad-based campus consensus—the condemnation of terrorism. Their goal was not achieved. Two resolutions were presented to the conference that condemned Palestinian attacks against civilians, but neither received the two-thirds majority required for passage. Even so, Jews on campus were gratified and relieved that the event was not marred by hate speech or anti-Jewish incidents.

The day after the conference ended, however, an opinion piece in the student newspaper reignited passions. Entitled "The Jews," it accused Jews of exploiting the "Holocaust industry," and said, "[I]t is impossible to ignore the unprecedented outpouring of pro-Jewish, pro-Israeli support in defiance of free speech at Duke." The paper received some 500 responses criticizing the column, and the student editor explained that the views expressed were not those of the paper. In early November, the student who wrote the article, Philip Kurian, apologized.

In late October, Jewish students at Stanford University were outraged by comments about Israel that were made at a talk, "Surviving the Holocaust: Witnessing History Repeated," by an anti-Israel Holocaust survivor and a pro-Palestinian activist. The event was promoted with fliers comparing Jews in Nazi Germany to Palestinians at Israeli checkpoints.

In an academic skirmish over Israel, more than 500 professors signed an on-line letter addressed to Hebrew University president Menachem Magidor asking "the Israeli academic leadership where it stands on the issue of current Israeli policy." The signatories represented themselves as "defenders of academic freedom and supporters of the academic boycott against Israel." As attempts to organize such boycotts, like the efforts to push divestment from Israel, had largely failed in recent years, the purpose of the letter was apparently to set the stage for another try. "This is boycott by stealth," said Martin Kramer, a monitor of anti-Israel activity, "to build a constituency that will come into play at the next big Palestinian-Israeli crisis."

Anti-Semitism and Politics

In May, Senator Ernest "Fritz" Hollings (D., S.C.)—no stranger to controversy with Jewish groups—found himself again in hot water as he prepared to end his 38-year Senate career, when he blasted the American Israel Public Affairs Committee (AIPAC), the pro-Israel lobby widely recognized for its clout on Capitol Hill, saying, "You can't have an Israeli policy other than what AIPAC gives you." Jewish organizations complained that Hollings, by scapegoating the Jewish community, was providing ammunition for anti-Semitism. Instead of retreating from his remarks, Hollings reiterated his charge and claimed that the Iraq war was being fought for Israel's benefit.

On the counteraction front, Sen. Rick Santorum (R., Pa.), the third-ranking Senate Republican, worked with the AJC, the ADL, and the Union of Orthodox Jewish Congregations to organize a special session on the floor of the Senate, in September, devoted to global anti-Semitism. In addition, Santorum distributed to Republican lawmakers a briefing book on the subject.

Both overt expressions and charges of anti-Semitism surfaced as the 2004 political campaigns shifted into high gear during the summer and early fall. In the presidential race, independent candidate Ralph Nader, the consumer advocate, faced criticism over his campaign's flirtation with individuals associated with Lenora Fulani, the New York-based radical activist whom Jewish defense agencies had long identified as anti-Semitic. Nader had been the featured speaker at a January conference in New Hampshire convened by Fulani, and some of her associates were engaged by Nader's campaign to help him get on the ballot in Texas. Fulani mounted an effort to "build bridges" to Jewish groups in New York, but the latter were not impressed.

In July, President George W. Bush's reelection campaign refused to withdraw an ad containing Nazi imagery from its Web site, despite severe criticism from Jewish groups and from the Republican chairman of the United States Holocaust Memorial Council, Fred Zeidman. The ad juxtaposed pictures of a shouting Adolf Hitler with images of former vice president Al Gore and other prominent Democrats.

Two congressional contests resulted in victories for candidates considered hostile to the Jewish community. One was Democrat Cynthia McKinney, who had represented the fourth congressional district in Georgia for ten years before losing to Denise Majette in 2002, and won back her seat in 2004. McKinney had been one of the most vocal opponents of Israel in the House of Representatives, and people close to her attributed her defeat to "Jewish money." An incumbent House Democrat, Jim Moran, of Virginia's eighth district, also won. In 2003 he had blamed Jews for the Iraq war.

Reports surfaced in early September that the FBI was investigating the American Israel Public Affairs Committee (AIPAC), the pro-Israel lobby widely recognized for its clout on Capitol Hill. Allegedly, Pentagon analyst Larry Franklin disclosed classified information to an AIPAC staffer about Iranian policy toward Iraq. As it had implications for Israel, the staffer then gave the information to the Israeli embassy in Washington. In early December, the FBI raided AIPAC offices in Washington, and four top AIPAC officials were subpoenaed by a federal grand jury.

The role of AIPAC was so central to the pro-Israel cause that any threat to its ability to function aroused trepidation in the organized Jewish community. Furthermore, Jewish leaders wondered about the possible role of anti-Semitism in the FBI probe and the potential anti-Semitic fallout that might result. "All it needs is a legitimate complaint that there was a violation of law," said Abraham H. Foxman, national director of the ADL, on December 30, "to fuel charges of dual loyalties against Jewish groups." At year's end, Jews maintained a wait-and-see attitude on the AIPAC matter.

Extremist Groups

Far-right extremists continued their activities during 2004, despite a dearth of leadership resulting from the recent deaths of such prominent figures as William Pierce and Richard Butler, and the imprisonment of others (see AJYB 2004, p. 68). One concern flowing from the absence of cohesive leadership was that more individual "lone wolves" in the extremist community were willing to take action on their own, outside of the organizational structures.

Extremist groups continued to use "white-power" music as a recruiting tool. A neo-Nazi record company, Panzerfaust, launched a major, well-publicized campaign to distribute CDs with racist and anti-Semitic lyrics to school children across the country, and other extremist groups volunteered to participate in the project. Racist skinhead groups continued to hold concerts that attracted large audiences.

Even more alarming, extremists expanded their presence on the Internet during 2004, creating new and sophisticated sites to promote hatred. Virtually every major U.S.-based extremist group had an Internet presence. There were now hundreds of anti-Semitic, anti-Israel, and Holocaust-denial Web sites, many incorporating up-to-date technologies such as streaming audio, video, and e-commerce sections, flash videos, background music, original artwork, and cartoons. However, international terrorist groups such as Hamas, Hezballah, and Al Qaeda-affiliated factions, which targeted Jews and Israel, found American Internet providers less willing than before to host their sites.

A major theme articulated by extremist groups was adamant opposition to any government action against racism or anti-Semitism, such as proposals for hate-crimes legislation (see below, p. 000). Extremist publications condemned all such policies for threatening to increase government control over the personal freedom to think and say what one wished, and blamed Jews—the alleged "world Zionist conspiracy"—for masterminding the proposed legislation. Indeed, some saw initiatives against anti-Semitism as part of an ongoing conspiracy to destroy white Christian society.

Even though right-wing extremists were generally anti-Arab on racial grounds, some, in 2004, expressed support for Muslims and the Palestinian cause. Several arguments were used in this connection: that the extremists and the Muslims shared a common Jewish enemy; that traditional Islamic values, such as the subservient role of women, were shared by conservative Christians; and that Muslims, unlike Jews, venerated Jesus.

The largest neo-Nazi group in the U.S. was still the National Alliance (NA), based in Hillsboro, West Virginia. It had been led by William

Pierce from 1974 until his death in July 2002, when Erich Gliebe, former head of NA's Ohio chapter and manager of the group's white power music company, Resistance Records, assumed control. In 2003, the group was plagued by infighting. Although accusations about the leadership's mishandling of finances continued in 2004, Gliebe and his associates maintained power. Membership in 2004 was near 1,000, a 33-percent decline since the death of Pierce. The group sought to attract young recruits through its musical recordings, leafleting campaigns, and billboards around the country. Active in the area of Holocaust denial, it sponsored lectures by the British denier David Irving, and assisted in organizing a conference dedicated to denier Ernst Zundel.

The second largest neo-Nazi group, the National Socialist Movement (NSM), was more blatantly Nazi than the NA, its members dressing and acting as if they were living in the Third Reich. NSM membership apparently grew, profiting from the NA's decline, but the organization was relatively quiet in 2004. It did hold significant gatherings in Pennsylvania, Nebraska, and North Carolina, and participated in a number of other racist events.

The virulently anti-Semitic, white-supremacist Creativity Movement, formerly the World Church of the Creator (WCOTC), promoted the idea of an all-white nation and, ultimately, an all-white world, rejecting Christianity outright in favor of its whites-only Creativity religion. It had been led since 1996 by Matt Hale, who called himself pontifex maximus, or supreme leader. In April, Hale was convicted of solicitation of murder and obstruction of justice. He remained in jail awaiting sentencing, which would undoubtedly entail many years behind bars (see below, p. 181). Without his leadership, the movement lost numbers and influence.

The Christian "Identity" movement promoted a racist, anti-Semitic agenda through the manipulation of religious themes. It taught that people of white European ancestry descended from the Lost Tribes of Israel, making them the "chosen people" of the Bible. Identity's "two-seed-line" theory asserted that only whites descended from Adam and Eve, and that Jews originated from a sexual union between Eve and Satan. Among notable Identity groups in 2004 were America's Promise Ministries of Sandpoint, Idaho; Dan Gayman's Schell City, Missouri, Church of Israel; Pete Peters' Scriptures for America Worldwide in Laporte, Colorado; and Kingdom Identity Ministries in Harrison, Arkansas. In May 2004, Peters held an event in Branson, Missouri, that attracted 500 followers. In July, three different Identity groups held events in the Pacific Northwest on the same weekend.

Aryan Nations, a paramilitary neo-Nazi group formed in the mid-

1970s and based in Hayden Lake, Idaho, also espoused Identity ideology. It was forced to declare bankruptcy in 2000, and with its leader, Richard Butler, in failing health, Aryan Nations lost members and split into four factions, although Butler remained a revered figure and a featured speaker at white supremacist gatherings. One of the splinter groups, in Louisiana, disassociated itself from Aryan Nations in March 2004. Aryan Nations hosted a three-day Aryan World Congress in Coeur d'Alene on July 16–18, with Butler and 40 other white supremacists conducting a racist parade through the city. Butler died on September 8 at the age of 86. Some of his loyalists moved the organization's headquarters from Idaho to Alabama, with a four-person leadership assuming control.

Formed in Dallas in the late 1980s, the neo-Nazi skinhead Hammerskin Nation was composed almost exclusively of young white males. With local chapters scattered worldwide (there were 18 in the U.S.), the Hammerskins claimed to represent the working class of the white racist movement, and advocated violence to achieve their goals. During 2004, three members were sentenced to prison for the racially motivated stabbing of a black man in Springfield, Missouri. Although Hammerskin Nation was in decline during 2004, it continued to sponsor rock concerts promoting group hatred, and had several popular racist bands affiliated with it. At the same time, a splinter group, the Outlaw Hammerskins, expanded its membership.

Liberty Lobby, created in 1955 by Willis Carto, was for years the most influential anti-Semitic propaganda organization in the U.S., with considerable impact on right-wing extremism generally. In recent years it had become much weaker, although its publication, the *American Free Press,* continued to peddle anti-Semitic and anti-Israel conspiracy theories. In 2004, it frequently accused Israel, influential American Jews, and "international Zionism" of initiating the war in Iraq. Liberty Lobby regularly advertised Holocaust denial literature.

The Ku Klux Klan was collectively much smaller than it had been decades earlier, but it was still the largest hate group in the U.S. In 2004, there were approximately 50 different Klan groups, ranging from small single-chapter bodies to larger organizations with chapters in many states. Most were located in the South and Midwest. In October 2004, a North Carolina Klan leader was charged with murder for allegedly helping to kill a fellow Klansman. On November 18, Bobby Frank Cherry, the Klansman who had been convicted in 2002 for the 1963 church bombing in Birmingham that killed four black girls — an event that galvanized the civil-rights movement — died at the age of 74.

So-called "militia" groups, which were stridently anti-government, continued to conduct paramilitary training in relative secrecy during 2004. According to an ADL report, these groups got a new lease on life from the various anti-Jewish conspiracies that developed following the events of September 11, 2001, and were "growing and reorganizing." The militias also sought to exploit fear of immigrants and anger at the Patriot Act and other counterterrorism measures, which militia members were sure would be directed against American citizens. In June, two Michigan militia members were charged with possessing illegal machine guns in an alleged plot to kill police officers, in retaliation for the 2003 death of a fellow member. Also in June, the Kentucky State Militia took part in border patrolling in Arizona with Ranch Rescue, an extreme anti-immigration group that conducted vigilante border patrols. In Pennsylvania, two militia leaders were charged with illegal weapons violations. Rick Stanley of Colorado, former leader of the Mutual Defense Pact Second American Revolution Militia, was found guilty in June on two felony counts of attempting to influence a public official.

David Duke, the former Louisiana Ku Klux Klan leader who was sent to jail in 2003 for financial crimes, completed his sentence and was freed in 2004. During his incarceration, Duke continued to send letters to right-wing publications and Web sites expressing contempt for the federal government, Israel, Jews, and other minorities, and promoting his book, *Jewish Supremacism*. After his release from prison, Duke's organization, EURO (European American Unity and Rights Organization), held a major rally in New Orleans, May 29–30, with the goal of promoting unity among white supremacist groups. High-ranking racist figures attending the conference signed the "New Orleans Protocol," a three-point document advocating nonviolence, collegiality, and a "high tone in our arguments." While the agreement was unlikely to maintain harmony between the myriad extremist organizations and personalities, it put Duke once again at the center of the white-supremacist movement. Duke proceeded actively to recruit new EURO members, and another book, *For Love of My People*, was slated for publication in 2005. Duke had a weekly live Internet question-and-answer program on Don Black's Stormfront forum, which featured prominent extremist guests.

Another goal of Duke's New Orleans conference was to forge strong links between white supremacists and Holocaust deniers. Highly significant was the presence on the program of Germar Rudolf, a fugitive from Germany who had established himself as the leading publisher of Holocaust-denial books in the U. S. Rudolf had long denied any connection to ideological racism, a contention now belied by involvement with Duke and his associates.

Also noteworthy was the International Revisionist Conference, held in Sacramento, California, in April. It was convened jointly by the Holocaust-denying Institute for Historical Review (IHR) and the neo-Nazi National Alliance, with the participation of a smaller "denial" group, the European American Cultural Council. IHR president Mark Weber frankly acknowledged that the collaboration with a neo-Nazi group—news of which was posted on the IHR Web site—represented a break from the IHR's previous portrayal of itself as dedicated to disinterested historical research. The Sacramento conference, originally scheduled to convene at the facilities of the Turn Verein, a German social and sports club, had to move elsewhere when, two days before the opening session, the Verein learned the nature of the program and barred the conference from using its premises.

One of the speakers in Sacramento was veteran Holocaust denier Bradley Smith. Smith's major focus in 2004 was a campaign to "decriminalize Holocaust history," that is, to legitimize the dissemination of Holocaust denial through the claim of free speech. To this end, Smith set up a new Web site and an electronic mailing list. He also managed to obtain speaking engagements at several college campuses in California.

Other Holocaust-denial activities during 2004 included speaking tours by British denier David Irving, who resided part of the year in Key West, Florida. Also, as he had done annually since 1999, Irving conducted another "Real History" conference in Cincinnati. Ingrid Rimland, who ran the on-line Holocaust-denial site known as Zundelsite, continued her efforts to draw attention to the plight of her husband, the German Holocaust denier Ernst Zundel, who was held in Canadian custody during 2004 while courts sought to resolve his legal status there (see below, p. 000). In May 2004, Rimland published *Setting the Record Straight,* consisting of letters by her husband about constructing a "cultural center" in Tennessee to promote the renaissance of the "Aryan race."

An ad placed by the IHR in the May 3 issue of the *Nation* magazine, an influential liberal weekly, generated protests both from individuals associated with the magazine and from Jewish groups. The ad, promoting a book entitled *The Founding Myths of Modern Israel,* had been scheduled to run for six issues, but was pulled after its first appearance. Although the *Nation* did not have a policy on running Holocaust-denial ads, it decided that certain claims in this one violated the magazine's policy not to print "patently fraudulent" ads. Publisher Victor Navasky noted that his magazine had a "presumption in favor of taking ads where we politically disagree," but added that all publications had the legal right to refuse any advertisement.

And finally, Bobby Fischer, the brilliant and erratic one-time world chess champion, long known, despite his own Jewish roots, for expressions of anti-Semitism and Holocaust denial, took another jab at Jews and Judaism in mid-July. After he was taken into custody in Tokyo for extradition to the U.S., Fischer's Web site announced: "Bobby Fischer does not wish to return to the Jew-controlled U.S.A. where he faces a kangaroo court and ten years in prison."

The Debate over the "New" Anti-Semitism

Several books and articles had appeared in 2003 on the question of whether there was a "new" anti-Semitism at loose in the world, largely consisting of anti-Israel rhetoric and action (see AJYB 2004, pp. 77–78). A valuable comprehensive anthology on the topic was published in 2004, *Those Who Forget the Past: The Question of Anti-Semitism,* edited by Ron Rosenbaum, who also contributed an original introduction. While all points of view were represented in the volume, Rosenbaum's own position was that there was indeed good reason for Jews to be apprehensive about the increasingly blurred line between criticism of Israel, on the one hand, and anti-Semitism, on the other. Agreeing with him was historian Omer Bartov, who wrote, in *The New Republic* (Feb. 2), "There is a Hitlerite quality to the new anti-Semitism, which now legitimizes . . . the resurrection of the myth of world domination." *Midstream,* a journal of Jewish concerns, devoted two issues to the question, "The Old and New Anti-Semitism" (February/March), and "The Old and New Anti-Semitism Revisited" (November/December).

The furor generated in 2003 by New York University historian Tony Judt's *New York Review of Books* article, "Israel: An Alternative," in which Judt called Israel a political anachronism that ought to be replaced by a binational state in Palestine (see AJYB 2004, pp. 79–80), continued into 2004. Among the most trenchant responses to Judt's thesis was Daniel Gordis's open letter to him, "My Anachronistic Home," which appeared in the January issue of *Midstream.* Gordis charged that Judt knew full well that Jews would be submerged, both politically and culturally, in a binational state. Clearly, Judt had no qualms about the disappearance of the Jewish people, and therefore he and others who agreed with him, wrote Gordis, were guilty of anti-Semitism.

Philip Roth's new novel *The Plot Against America,* which appeared in

September, was an exercise in historical fiction whose theme was American anti-Semitism. The book examined what might have happened had the isolationist and anti-Semitic aviator hero Charles A. Lindbergh had been elected president in 1940. A number of reviewers suggested that Roth, after raising hackles in the Jewish community over the years with unsympathetic portrayals of Jewish characters, had, with *The Plot Against America,* emerged as a champion of Jews against their detractors. Others claimed that the book was meant to draw parallels between a fictional Lindbergh administration and the current Bush presidency. But the work, which presented anti-Semitism as pervading the central institutions of power in America, found resonance with some in the Jewish community who believed they saw signs of exactly such a scenario in the investigation of AIPAC, anti-Semitism on the campus, and other worrying portents. Roth himself wrote (*New York Times Book Review,* Sept. 19), "All I do is defatalize the past. . . . In the 30's there were many of the seeds for [a Nazi-type regime] happening here, but it didn't . . . . It is not my point that this can happen and will happen; rather it's that at the moment when it should have happened, it did not happen."

An important conference on anti-Semitism in the U.S. and around the world in 2004 was "Anti-Semitism and the Contemporary Jewish Condition," convened in Los Angeles, October 17–19, by the University of Judaism's Sigi Ziering Institute.

A 2004 Library of Congress lecture, "Anti-Semitism in America, Past and Present: Realities and Myths," delivered by Jerome A. Chanes, was held in conjunction with the library's exhibition on the 350th anniversary of Jews in America, "From Haven to Home." This was the first Library of Congress lecture ever devoted to the topic of anti-Semitism. Chanes also authored, in 2004, the first comprehensive reference work on the subject, *Anti-Semitism: A Reference Handbook.*

Media and the Arts

The return of Shylock to popular culture—in this case, a film version of *The Merchant of Venice,* released late in 2004, directed by Michael Radford, and featuring Al Pacino as Shylock the Jew—aroused renewed concerns about anti-Semitism, particularly in the aftermath of the controversy over *The Passion of the Christ.* But most observers found that while the film could hardly escape the stereotypes of the original play—the Jew as alien, vengeful, and money hungry; Old Testament cruelty contrasted to New Testament kindness—the portrayal of Shylock was sympathetic, and the anti-Jewish elements were placed within a historical context. Kenneth Jacobson, associate national director of the ADL, which had been one of the leading critics of the Gibson film, was impressed that "[T]hey put on the screen how there was anti-Semitism, how Jews were put in ghettos, and how Jews were forced into the profession of money-lending."

The vexed question of whether works of art were exempt from criticism on the grounds of anti-Semitism came up at the beginning of the year in the case of an installation at Stockholm's Museum of Antiquities that portrayed a smiling suicide bomber. It was the work of an Israeli-born Swede, Dror Feiler, and his wife, Gunilla Skold Feiler, for an exhibition to accompany an upcoming conference on genocide. At the opening, on January 16, Avi Mazel, Israel's ambassador to Sweden, was so outraged that he committed an act of vandalism on the work. Efraim Zuroff, director of the Simon Wiesenthal Center's Israel office, characterized the installation as "a classic example of the new anti-Semitism . . . done by someone who was born in Israel, which gives it a *hekhsher* [seal of Jewish approval]." Clearly, the boundaries between freedom of artistic expression, anti-Semitism, and good taste were still bitterly contested.

Jewish viewers who saw the August 1 episode of "Da Ali G Show" on HBO were probably perplexed about a portrayal by Sasha Baron Cohen, one of television's hottest and most irreverent comedians. His character, Borat, in an effort at irony, sung at one point, "The Jew/he take everybody's money," and the chorus responded, "Throw the Jew down the well/so my country can be free/you must grab him by the horns/and then we have a big party." The ADL complained: "We are concerned that the irony may have been lost on some of your audience . . . in attempting to expose bigotry and prejudice you also bear a responsibility to be sensitive." But HBO responded: "Cohen delivers an obvious satire that exposes people's ignorance and prejudice."

In early March, the executive director of the Academy of Motion Picture Arts and Sciences—which awards the "Oscars"—defended its decision to honor Nazi movie propagandist Leni Riefenstahl during the forthcoming Academy Awards ceremony. The recognition of Riefenstahl, dubbed "Hitler's filmmaker," had been heavily criticized by some in the movie industry, prominent Holocaust scholars, and Jewish organizations. "Her art was directly linked to politics," observed Michael Berenbaum, a Holocaust scholar and professor at the University of Judaism. "To let that pass without mention is to presume that art is valueless, and that's an abomination."

180 / AMERICAN JEWISH YEAR BOOK, 2005

On the media front, Bill O'Reilly, the controversial host of "The O'Reilly Factor" on the Fox TV News Channel and on national radio, offended many Jews when he suggested, on December 3, that a Jewish caller who expressed anger that Christmas was celebrated in public schools should "go to Israel" where he would not have to submit to public acknowledgement of that holiday. When ADL national director Abraham Foxman, among others, demanded an apology, O'Reilly called Foxman "a nut." Rep. Nita Lowey (D., N.Y.) sent a letter to congressional colleagues on December 15 calling for an O'Reilly apology.

In a little-noticed book review in a major magazine, the well-known author and literary critic John Updike resorted to a combination of old-fashioned Protestant anti-Semitism and modern anti-Zionism to express his feelings about what Christians call the Old Testament. Reviewing Robert Alter's translation of *The Five Books of Moses* in the *New Yorker* (Nov. 1), Updike objected to what he considered the angry and vengeful God of the Hebrew Bible, as well as the xenophobic tribalism inherent in the idea of a chosen people. He went on, "The Israelites' effort to claim and maintain their Promised Land fuels a contemporary crisis. It is still cruelly true that, as we read in Alter's version of Numbers, 'If you do not dispossess the inhabitants of the land . . . they will be foes to you . . . .'"

Responses to Anti-Semitism

LEGISLATION AND LAW-ENFORCEMENT

As of 2004, 46 states and the District of Columbia had hate-crime laws that punished crimes motivated by group bias more severely than the same acts performed without such motivation. There was no evidence that these laws reduced the incidence of bias crime, but supporters nevertheless felt it crucial that government, as a central institution of society, should send a forthright message that such activity was unacceptable. Georgia's law was struck down during the year, the state supreme court ruling 7-0 that the statute was too broad.

Little progress was made during 2004 in passing a comprehensive federal hate-crime law. The existing federal Hate Crime Statistics Act (HCSA) required the Justice Department to gather data on crimes that manifested prejudice based on race, religion, sexual orientation, disability, or ethnicity from law-enforcement agencies across the country, and to publish an annual summary of its findings (see above, p. 159). Also, a federally mandated and funded initiative to prevent hate crime by young people, Partners Against Hate, continued to conduct training and education programs.

Legislation was introduced in April barring insurance companies from denying coverage to Americans based on their lawful travel to Israel or any other country. Taking the hint, Allstate, one of the largest insurance underwriters in the country, announced in early July that it would no longer "redline" passengers traveling to Israel. The company had been accused of refusing to sell insurance policies to those who were planning to visit Israel or other nations subject to U.S. State Department travel advisories.

Twenty-seven years after the event, the U.S. State Department and American intelligence agencies acknowledged in January that the Israeli attack on the *USS Liberty* during the Six-Day War was a mistake, and "not made in malice." The *Liberty* incident had long been used as fodder for anti-Semitic and anti-Israel expression.

In April, white supremacist leader Matt Hale was convicted in Chicago of soliciting the murder of a federal judge. Hale, leader of the former World Church of the Creator, now the Creativity Movement, was found guilty of one count of solicitation of murder and three counts of obstruction of justice. He faced a maximum penalty of 20 years in prison and a maximum fine of $250,000.

Three American members of the so-called "Virginia Jihad Network" were sentenced to long prison terms in U.S. District Court in June, for conspiring to fight alongside a Pakistani-based terrorist group and engaging in paramilitary training in the Virginia woods. Masoud Khan, a Maryland native who had traveled to Pakistan to train with Lashkar-e-Tayyaba — designated as a foreign terrorist group by the U.S. — was sentenced to life in prison on charges of conspiracy to levy war against the U.S. and providing material support to the Taliban and Al Qaeda. Seifullah Chapman was sentenced to 85 years and Hammad Abdur-Raheem to eight. The lengthy terms of Khan and Chapman resulted from mandatory minimum sentences for related weapons convictions.

Former national guardsman Duane Braden was arrested in October for allegedly planning to blow up a synagogue and a National Guard armory in Tennessee. Federal agents found bombs, weapons, and neo-Nazi paraphernalia at Braden's residence, along with notes in which he threatened to kill a rabbi and children. Authorities charged him with two federal counts of attempting to destroy an armory and possession of an unregistered firearm.

RESPONDING TO ANTI-SEMITISM ABROAD

In light of the shocking numbers of anti-Semitic incidents in Europe and the Muslim world since 2000, Senator George Voinovich (R., Ohio) introduced S.2292, the Global Anti-Semitism Review Act, on April 7, 2004. Cosponsored by Senators George Allen (R., Va.) and Joseph Biden (D., Del.), the bill directed the secretary of state to deliver to the Senate Committee on Foreign Relations and the House International Relations Committee, by December 31, 2004, a one-time report on anti-Semitic acts around the globe. Rep. Tom Lantos (D., Calif.) introduced the legislation in the House. Despite opposition from the State Department, which objected that the law would single out Jews for special treatment, it passed the Senate on May 7 and the House on October 8, and President Bush signed it into law on October 16.

Pursuant to the new law, the State Department submitted a comprehensive and detailed "Report on Global Anti-Semitism" to Congress on December 30. It defined anti-Semitism to include criticism of Israel that, going beyond principled objection to policies, indulged in demonization and dehumanization, such as invoking grotesque comparisons between Israelis and Nazis. The report highlighted not only acts of vandalism and assault, but also the growth of anti-Semitic rhetoric in the European media, and in publications, textbooks, and television programming found in the Middle East and North African countries, especially Egypt and Saudi Arabia.

Following up on their June 2003 meeting in Vienna that identified anti-Semitism as a human-rights issue, the U.S. joined with the other 54 member countries of the Organization for Security and Cooperation in Europe (OSCE) for a second meeting on the subject, which took place in Berlin in April 2004. There, these countries denounced anti-Semitism and pledged both to monitor and combat it. U.S. secretary of state Colin Powell—whose presence added significant star-power to the proceedings—emphasized that some anti-Zionist criticism of Israel was also anti-Semitic. Nobel Laureate Elie Wiesel, one of the speakers, called for a "manifesto" against hatred of Jews, and that this document should be taught in schools. Following the conference, a number of resolutions were introduced in the U.S. Congress urging all the OSCE member nations to implement the commitments they had made.

The OSCE led the way in government-level actions against anti-Semitism. In December 2003, following the Vienna meeting, the foreign ministers met in Maastricht, where they mandated the Office of Democratic Institutions and Human Rights (ODIHR) to act as a collection point for hate-crime information from governments and NGOs, and designated an official to oversee the task. ODIHR would also evaluate and disseminate "best practices" on how to gather data about hate crimes, the training of law enforcement agencies to deal with them, and educational efforts to fight prejudice. At Sofia in December 2004, the foreign ministers appointed three special representatives on tolerance issues, including one specifically to investigate instances of anti-Semitism. They also agreed to hold a third conference on anti-Semitism in June 2005, in Cordoba. American Jews groups welcomed the OSCE moves.

On a related front, in June, the OSCE convened in Paris for the first conference dedicated specifically to examining hate on the Internet. What emerged was a document, "Promoting Tolerance and Media Freedom on the Internet," which was carefully crafted to take into account the varying legal proscriptions on "hate" materials in the different OSCE nations. The member states agreed to examine Internet content in their respective countries so as to determine the level of anti-Semitism and other forms of intolerance, to investigate and prosecute criminal threats of violence based on such content, and to establish educational programs for children about the dangers of Internet hate sites.

Perhaps even more significant that the OSCE process was the historic UN conference in June entitled "Confronting Anti-Semitism: Educating for Tolerance and Understanding." This event, held at UN headquarters in New York, was the first time that organization had ever confronted the topic of anti-Semitism head-on. UN officials—and most emphatically, Secretary General Kofi Annan—acknowledged that the world body's record on this issue had fallen short of its ideals. Annan called upon the General Assembly to adopt a resolution on anti-Semitism modeled on that of the OSCE in Berlin. The UN's Third Committee, on November 22, specified "anti-Semitism" in a call for the "elimination of all forms of religious intolerance," the first time that anti-Semitism had been included in the annual "intolerance" resolution. General Assembly action was expected to follow. Felice Gaer, director of the AJC's Jacob Blaustein Institute for Advancement of Human Rights, suggested that the UN would never have taken this step had the OSCE not done so first. "When the European countries take leadership, things can change at the UN," said Gaer.

Columbia University law professor Anne Bayefsky authored two noteworthy articles on the UN in 2004. In "The UN and the Jews," which appeared in the February issue of *Commentary,* Bayefsky frankly described the anti-Semitic rhetoric expressed over the years by representatives of member states and UN officials. And the November/December issue of *Midstream* carried Bayefsky's address to the UN conference on anti-Semitism, in which she challenged the world body to confront its anti-Jewish bias.

A long-awaited report on anti-Semitism by the European Monitoring Center on Racism and Xenophobia (EUMC) was released in April. The 344-page document confirmed that anti-Semitism was a growing danger across the continent, but danced around the politically sensitive question of responsibility. The mere passing reference to Muslim perpetrators of acts against Jews was deeply disappointing to Jewish observers.

The Ford Foundation had come in for criticism in 2003, when it was learned that large financial grants from the foundation had enabled Palestinian groups virtually to hijack the 2001 UN Conference Against Racism, held in Durban, and thereby make it into a forum for verbal attacks on Israel and Jews. As leaders in Congress considered legislation authorizing the investigation of the accountability of tax-exempt groups, the foundation, after consultation with Jewish organizations, adopted a new policy requiring grant recipients to eschew support for terrorism, bigotry, and anti-Semitism, and hired Stuart Eizenstat, a former Clinton administration official with strong ties to the Jewish community, to advise on its implementation.

Finally, the banning by the French government of al-Manar, the Lebanese satellite television station controlled by the terrorist organization Hezballah, triggered calls for an examination of al-Manar's operations in the U.S.

JEWISH ORGANIZATIONAL RESPONSES

National Jewish community-relations organizations continued to invest significantly in prejudice-reduction programs, such as "Hands Across the Campus" managed by the American Jewish Committee, and "A World of Difference," an ADL program. Also, the ADL ran a series of television ads in Europe and billboard ads in the U.S. with the theme, "Anti-Semitism is Anti- All of Us."

Such initiatives—in use since the 1950s—were aimed at moderating and even eliminating prejudicial attitudes, and thereby affecting behavior. The consensus among social scientists, however, was that such changes in attitude, with few exceptions, were doubtful, raising questions about whether the large expenditures involved were worthwhile. Indeed, little evaluative research had been done to test the efficacy of these programs; such an evaluation of "A World of Difference," commissioned by the ADL and conducted in 2000, had yet to be released, notwithstanding calls for its publication by scholars and community professionals.

In February, the Simon Wiesenthal Center officially opened its Tolerance Center in New York, for professional development and prejudice reduction.

A sharp critique of Jewish "defense" organizations came from Jack Wertheimer, historian and Jewish Theological Seminary provost. In "Jewish Security and Jewish Interests," published in *Commentary* in October, Wertheimer argued that the traditional politically liberal stance of these agencies has led them, in an era of declining anti-Semitism in the U.S., to take upon themselves an increasingly diverse array of issues having little or nothing to do with "Jewish interests," defined by Wertheimer as "the defense of Jewish security." Wertheimer's article reignited the perpetual debate about Jewish communal priorities, as those who disagreed with him suggested that Jewish security was not necessarily limited to physical security, and that involvement in general social issues, such as the civil-rights struggle in the 1950s and 1960s, made Jews more secure.

The Union of Orthodox Jewish Congregations (OU) had to deal with a threat to kosher slaughtering procedures that some viewed as tinged with anti-Semitism. In early December, People for the Ethical Treatment of Animals (PETA), an animal-rights group, claimed to have videotaped proof that the kosher-slaughter practices of AgriProcessors, Inc., a plant in Postville, Iowa, were needlessly cruel to animals. On first gaining access to the video, the OU, which ran the largest kosher certification operation in the country, asserted that it "was testimony that it was done right," that the slaughterhouse did not violate laws of kashrut or any statute. Within a week, however, the OU reversed itself and raised questions about AgriProcessors' practices. Apparently, the organization's original defensive reaction reflected the memory of repeated efforts on the part of animal-rights and anti-Semitic groups to legislate "humane slaughter," a code word for the outlawing of kosher slaughter. It appeared, however, that in this case PETA was not attacking Jewish slaughtering practices, but rather only a particular firm's procedures.

A case that had dogged the ADL for a decade finally came to an end on March 1, when the U.S. Supreme Court, without explanation, declined to review a jury verdict ordering the organization to pay more than $10 million to William and Dorothy Quigley for defaming them. In 1994, when the coupled lived in Evergreen, Colorado, they had an argument with their Jewish neighbors, the Aronsons. Afterward, those neighbors used a police scanner to hear and record anti-Semitic comments the Quigleys made on a cordless phone. The Aronsons presented the recordings to the local ADL director, who denounced the Quigleys as anti-Semites at a press conference, and county prosecutors charged them with hate crimes. But it turned out that the recording had been illegal, and the charges were dropped. The Quigleys, meanwhile, pursued a defamation suit against the ADL, which they won in 2000. With the Supreme Court's refusal to intervene, the affair was over and the ADL had to pay. "But through the entire process we have continued to serve the community," said the ADL Mountain States director. "We do remain committed to our fight against hatred and racism and bigotry and extremism and anti-Semitism."

JEROME A. CHANES

Jewish Communal Affairs

American Jewry and the Middle East

A YEAR OF DEBATING DISENGAGEMENT

The American-sponsored "road map" for resolution of the Israeli-Palestinian conflict (see AJYB 2003, pp. 212–16) stalled in late 2003 as neither side seemed willing to take the steps laid out by the plan. The Palestinian Authority (PA) would not or could not quell violent acts against Israelis, while Israel did little or nothing to dismantle illegal outposts in the territories or to limit population growth in existing settlements to "natural" increase. Israel continued to build its security fence on the West Bank and to conduct targeted attacks on known terrorist leaders.

As 2004 began, left-of-center American Jewish leaders and organizations placed much of the blame for the stalemate on what they considered the Bush administration's failure to use diplomatic muscle to advance the peace process. As evidence that the matter had been relegated to the back burner, they cited the president's failure even to mention the "road map" either in his State of the Union Address in January or in the administration's new "Greater Middle East Initiative" unveiled in February. These critics, hostile in any case to the administration on matters of domestic policy, hoped that the Democrats would use this foreign-policy issue against President Bush in the 2004 election campaign. Many knowledgeable observers, however, doubted that either major party would risk alienating Jewish voters by proposing a diplomatic initiative that would be perceived as pressuring Israel.

Americans for Peace Now, however, claimed that a telephone poll it sponsored in January 2004 indicated that the mainstream Jewish organizations, which favored giving Israel a free hand, did not represent grassroots Jewish opinion. Conducted by Zogby International, the poll surveyed the views of a random sample of 500 Jews and found that 71.6 percent would be more likely to vote for a presidential candidate committed to active diplomatic engagement, and that 67.8 percent wanted the U.S. to be more evenhanded in brokering the Israeli-Palestinian conflict.

Israeli prime minister Ariel Sharon's call for unilateral disengagement from Gaza and part of the northern West Bank (see below, pp. 214–15)

188 / AMERICAN JEWISH YEAR BOOK, 2005

played havoc with the previous ideological divisions in the Jewish community. The mainstream leadership, which ordinarily deferred to the judgment of the Israeli government, was not quite ready to do so this time. Members of a delegation visiting Israel from the Conference of Presidents of Major American Jewish Organizations, the umbrella body of organized American Jewry, were briefed about the plan early in March. On their return, some told the *Forward* (Mar. 19) that it was "confusing" and "half-baked." Malcolm Hoenlein, executive vice president of the conference, said, "There is a lack of clarity about what it means and how it will be implemented and what will happen with security. Nobody knows yet what it really means."

The right-leaning and Orthodox groups, which had long considered Sharon their champion, were split. The Zionist Organization of America (ZOA) and Americans for a Safe Israel immediately denounced the withdrawal initiative as tantamount to rewarding terrorism. So did one Orthodox synagogue body, the National Council of Young Israel, which urged its congregations to telephone Likud MKs and urge them to vote against their prime minister's program. But the Union of Orthodox Jewish Congregations (OU), the largest Orthodox synagogue group, and the Religious Zionists of America (RZA) refrained from taking a position, although some of their leaders openly stated their misgivings.

Similar confusion abounded on the left-leaning flank of American Jewry. Its adherents were just as skeptical about disengagement as the right-wingers, but for opposite reasons, claiming that its unilateral nature did not take into account the needs of the Palestinians, and that it could very well turn out to be a way of staving off any further concessions on the West Bank—a suspicion reinforced by statements coming from people close to Sharon. But some on the left saw the new Israeli approach as a giant step toward peace. The most prominent exponent of this position was Rabbi Eric Yoffie, president of the Union for Reform Judaism (URJ), who declared, "When it comes to Israel and the Middle East, I am a dove and a peace activist. And my hero right now is Prime Minister Ariel Sharon" (*Forward*, Apr. 16).

Despite some concern that Israel's assassination of Hamas leader Sheikh Ahmed Yassin in Gaza City (see below, p. 234) might draw the ire of the U.S. and complicate coordination between the two countries over the Gaza withdrawal plan, Sharon had a very successful meeting with Bush in Washington on April 14. The American president announced his support for unilateral disengagement on the understanding that the "road map" would be followed afterwards; his acceptance of "changing realities on the ground" in "any final settlement" was understood as legitimizing Israel's hold on certain West Bank settlement blocs; and he rejected a Palestinian "right of return" to Israel proper (see below, p. 215).

Whatever their private doubts about unilateral disengagement, the mainstream American Jewish leaders applauded the administration's strongly pro-Sharon stand, while the left-leaning groups drew what solace they could from Bush's insistence on maintaining the "road map" framework, a position likely to prevent Israel from limiting its territorial withdrawals to those already announced. But the right-leaning elements of the community—and, more important for electoral purposes, their evangelical Christian allies—blasted Bush for approving the uprooting of Jewish settlements, and noted that his vague reference to "realities on the ground" was no guarantee that the U.S. would approve of Israel keeping any specific West Bank territory.

The Bush-Sharon meeting in Washington had been carefully orchestrated to buttress Sharon's standing among security-conscious Likudniks ahead of the May 2 party referendum on his unilateral disengagement plan. But Likud members, insufficiently impressed by Bush's assurances, decisively rejected disengagement (see below, pp. 217–18).

American Jewish organizations, which had geared up, on the eve of the referendum, to mobilize their political and public-relations resources on behalf of Sharon's policy, were dumbfounded at the rebuff rendered by his party. They were also fearful that the U.S. administration, having gone so far to accommodate Sharon's domestic political needs, would now back away from the Israeli prime minister, who had proved, in the end, unable to deliver. Groups never previously at a loss for public statements on Israel responded to reporters' questions with replies of "no comment at this time," or "we will wait and see." AIPAC (American Israel Public Affairs Committee), the premier pro-Israel lobby, put on hold an initiative it had conceived to draft and get congressional sponsors for legislation promulgating Bush's assurances to Sharon, and Sharon canceled plans he had made to come to the U.S. and address AIPAC's annual policy conference in Washington, scheduled to take place two weeks after the referendum. "Of course we're backing Sharon," one unidentified official of a Jewish organization told the *Forward* (May 7), "but this is an unbelievable fiasco." The only American Jews happy about the turn of events were the pro-settler elements, which had never disguised their opposition to disengagement.

Although Sharon was a no-show, President Bush addressed the AIPAC conference on May 18, and his words were carefully scrutinized by the

Jewish community. The president drew enthusiastic cheers and more than 20 standing ovations from the audience of 5,000 for his forceful defense of his policies in Iraq and for declaring that the U.S. and Israel were allies in the global war on terrorism. But while calling Sharon's disengagement plan "a bold and courageous step," Bush made no mention of the assurances on borders and refugees that he had given the Israeli prime minister in April. Israeli vice premier Ehud Olmert, undoubtedly delivering a message from Sharon, told the gathering that despite the result of the Likud referendum, the prime minister was determined to implement disengagement.

AIPAC's executive committee, however, did not officially endorse Sharon's plan nor did it request AIPAC members to lobby Congress for it, on the grounds that the initiative had not yet become Israeli government policy. The committee did, however, endorse Bush's April assurances to Sharon and supported congressional passage of a resolution to that affect. It pointedly voted down a proposed amendment that would have noted that those assurances had been given on the assumption of an Israeli pullout from some of the territories.

In the following weeks, mainstream American Jewish leaders sought to impress upon the Israeli government just how important it was — not only for securing congressional passage of the resolution, but also for the health of the U.S.-Israel relationship generally — to push disengagement forward. Most outspoken was editor and publisher Mortimer Zuckerman, immediate past president of the Conference of Presidents, who bluntly told the Israeli daily *Yediot Aharonot* that failure to carry out disengagement could induce the international community to put forward an "imposed solution that Israel won't be able to live with." Much of the organized American Jewish community heaved a collective sigh of relief when the Israeli cabinet voted to approve disengagement on June 6, even though Knesset passage, let alone actual implementation of the plan, was hardly assured.

AIPAC now lobbied feverishly to get Congress to approve its pro-Israel resolution. By the end of June both houses had done so, but the wording of the two statements that emerged differed significantly. The Senate version endorsed not only Bush's assurances to Israel but also the Israeli disengagement plan and the "road map," drawing praise from Americans for Peace Now for pointing out Israel's responsibilities. But the House of Representatives, largely upon the insistence of Majority Leader Tom DeLay (R., Tex.), required nothing from Israel, and simply endorsed Bush's guarantees that the "facts on the ground" would be taken into account in the final territorial settlement and that Israel need not accept the entry of Palestinian refugees. AIPAC, ignoring the Senate's more balanced language, announced its gratification that Congress recognized "the need for Israel to have defensible borders that reflect demographic realities." An unidentified insider told the *New York Jewish Week* (July 2), "It's all about how this is spun, now that Congress has acted. There's a lot of room for interpretation in these resolutions—and you can bet everybody with a position on peace is spinning like mad."

Seemingly uninterested in spinning was the Union for Reform Judaism, whose governing board approved a resolution endorsing Sharon's disengagement plan and U.S. support for it, but criticizing the administration and Congress for not insisting that Israel return to the bargaining table and ameliorate the "humanitarian conditions" of the Palestinians. These sentiments, conveyed in a letter to Secretary of State Colin Powell, were hailed by dovish American groups, which noted that Reform, claiming 900 congregations and 1.5 million members, was the largest Jewish denomination. But Abraham Foxman, national director of the Anti-Defamation League (ADL), wondered, in the absence of any sign of Palestinian moderation, "Who is America supposed to push Sharon to negotiate with?"

In July, American Jewish attention turned to the International Court of Justice (ICJ) in The Hague, which voted 14-1 (the U.S. judge being the lone dissenter) that Israel's security fence on the West Bank violated international law (see below, pp. 228–29). Since the beginning of the year, Jewish organizations that had international ties had been meeting with foreign diplomats to convince them to use their influence against the court's taking up the issue. Some 30 countries—including the U.S., Russia, and 14 European countries, as well as the European Union—submitted briefs urging the ICJ not to hear the case, and the American Jewish groups claimed some credit for this.

Once the ICJ put the case on its docket, however, the court's condemnation of the fence was assured, and it came on July 9. The American administration rejected the decision, and both houses of Congress passed resolutions denouncing it (see above, p. 140). Jewish concern now focused on UN headquarters in New York, where the Arab states proposed a resolution in the General Assembly endorsing the ICJ decision. It was sure to pass, but Jewish groups hoped to keep the majority for it down so as to head off possible action by the Security Council, the body with the authority to enforce ICJ rulings.

Differences emerged within the Jewish community over tactics. The

Conference of Presidents, reflecting a broad Jewish consensus as well as the preferences of the Israeli government, wanted to keep its diplomatic efforts at the UN low-key so as not to attract even more attention to the issue. Emphatically disagreeing was Foxman of the ADL, who considered the campaign against Israel's fence even more dangerous than the 1975 UN resolution equating Zionism with racism, and called for a public campaign to "delegitimize" the UN and the ICJ. The General Assembly vote, held July 20, disappointed pro-Israel activists. By a margin of 150-6, with 10 abstentions, that body endorsed the court ruling. All 25 European nations voted with the majority, even those that had originally counseled the court not to take up the matter. The Security Council, however, did not act.

In the fall, opposition to Sharon's disengagement policy on the part of the Jewish religious and political right became increasingly controversial. For one thing, inflammatory rhetoric emanating from Israeli national religious circles in opposition to uprooting settlers from their homes was coming to resemble that which preceded the assassination of Prime Minister Yitzhak Rabin in 1995. In addition, American Jewish groups sympathetic to the settlers prevented the Conference of Presidents from officially endorsing disengagement.

The leadership of American Orthodoxy had strong ties to an Israeli rabbinate that was overwhelmingly hostile to disengagement, some of whose most prominent figures declared territorial withdrawal a violation of Jewish law and urged their followers forcibly to resist government orders to evacuate settlements. American Orthodox groups, harboring some sympathy for this position but reluctant to countenance civil disobedience, sought refuge in ambiguity.

Thus the Rabbinical Council of America (RCA), the organization of Modern Orthodox rabbis, issued a statement on September 23 calling on all Jews "to engage in and foster respectful and reasonable debate and discussion of the undoubtedly important issues involved." One prominent member of the council, Rabbi Haskel Lookstein of New York, expressed his disappointment that the statement did not condemn hate speech, including death threats, directed against Prime Minister Sharon by religious extremists in Israel. The Union of Orthodox Jewish Congregations (OU), meeting in Israel in November, frankly acknowledged that "the debate in Israel . . . has evoked strongly held feelings within the Orthodox Union family," compounded by "profound identification" with the Jews living in the territories. Unable to reach a consensus on disengagement, the OU left the decision to "the citizens of Israel and the State of Israel's democratically elected institutions."

With no American Orthodox organization prepared to take on the hard-line Israeli rabbis, Rabbi Norman Lamm, chancellor of Yeshiva University, issued a joint statement with two prominent moderate Israeli rabbis condemning calls for resistance to disengagement orders. Lamm told the *Forward* (Dec. 3), "There's no room for encouraging or engaging in political or physical violence. It's not for rabbis to determine national military policy."

The ADL, frustrated that the Conference of Presidents would not officially endorse disengagement, approached other organizations to join with it in a pro-disengagement statement outside the conference framework. To head this off, the conference designated its October 14 meeting for discussion of the issue, once again raising an old sore point within the umbrella body. For years, left-leaning member organizations had felt that the conference, under the sway of its right-wing elements, had been reluctant to endorse Israeli peace initiatives espoused, the critics believed, by a majority of Israeli and American Jews. Malcolm Hoenlein, executive vice president of the conference, denied that there was any attempt to block an endorsement; rather, he said, the Jewish organizations had so far failed to develop a broad consensus on what such a document should say and whether its release should be postponed until the Israeli Knesset approved the policy.

The October 14 closed-door meeting yielded no consensus. A draft document circulated afterward noted that "a substantial majority" (some two-thirds, according to people who were there) of the organizations supported disengagement, but the conference as a body did not issue an endorsement. Conference chairman James Tisch explained, "We let the reader come to his own conclusion. By saying 'substantial majority,' which is what actuality there was, those who want to can say that there was. And, likewise, those who do not want to see it as a consensus don't have to see it as a consensus." In fact, neither side was happy, opponents of disengagement arguing that Tisch should not have given the impression of a consensus in favor of the policy when there was none, and proponents of the plan angry that a minority had been allowed to block the conference from issuing an official, full-throated endorsement.

Disappointed at the Conference of Presidents' equivocation, the left-leaning Israel Policy Forum, in November, collected the signatures of some 70 Jewish leaders on a letter to Condoleezza Rice, the president's national security adviser and secretary of state designate. It requested the Bush administration to encourage the development of a new, moderate post-Arafat Palestinian leadership, and to become actively involved in brokering an Israeli-Palestinian peace settlement, since such a show of evenhandedness would enhance America's image in the Arab world and aid the war on terrorism. It called for Israel to make its disengagement plan bilateral instead of unilateral, to freeze its West Bank settlements, and to ease restrictions on Palestinian movement in the West Bank. Among the signers were the heads of the United Synagogue of Conservative Judaism and the Union for Reform Judaism.

Rice met with representatives of Jewish organizations—both those of the mainstream and left-leaning bodies such as the Israel Policy Forum—on November 29, at the White House. This was the first such meeting since President Bush's reelection. Seeking to satisfy the expectations of all, Rice praised Sharon's disengagement initiative and talked of active U.S. involvement in the peace process, including an insistence that Israel live up to "its responsibilities" under the "road map." But she also assured her guests that nothing would be done to undermine Israel's security. The major thrust of her remarks, according to those who were present, was the need to democratize Palestinian society.

ISRAEL ON CAMPUS

The debate that broke out in 2003 over how best to present Israel's cause on American campuses continued on into 2004. With pro-Palestinian students organizing, and faculty anti-Israel bias charged at a number of universities (see above, pp. 167–70), was the appropriate Jewish response reflexively to defend Israeli policy, as Natan Sharansky had urged on a tour of college campuses in 2003? Some thought otherwise. A number of Hillel directors and others familiar with the campus situation believed that young Jews could not be mobilized in large numbers in support of "occupation" and "settlements," and that student doubts about the policies of the current Israeli government should not be viewed as hostility or indifference toward the Jewish state. Avraham Infeld, named president of Hillel in February, was an advocate of the more open approach.

On several campuses, however, some Jewish student organizations would not countenance dissenters. In a wide-ranging report about the situation, the *Forward* (Apr. 16) noted that "pro-Israel organizations at American universities are increasingly becoming inhospitable places for dialogue . . . as fears of anti-Semitism have risen along with the stakes in the Middle East." At the Spitzer Hillel Forum in February, numerous students complained about being tarred as anti-Israel for expressing any reservations about Israeli actions, some adding that such narrow-mindedness alienated many from participating in Jewish activities on campus.

A widely reported episode at the University of Richmond epitomized the problem. On February 12, Jilian Redford, the 20-year-old president of the campus Hillel, e-mailed the Israeli embassy to complain that e-mails she was receiving from the embassy contained "radical Zionist propaganda," and that Hillel's purpose was "fostering religious life on college campuses and not organizing marches, protests, or listening to speakers who encourage us to hate our Palestinian neighbors in Israel" (*Forward*, May 7). The next day, an official of the Richmond Jewish Community Center, which oversaw the Hillel chapter, asked Redford to resign as president, and when she refused, removed her. Wayne Firestone, director of national Hillel's Campus Coalition, explained that while her views were certainly welcome at Hillel, her position as president required a more respectful tone toward the embassy. Redford subsequently became something of a heroic figure for Jewish groups critical of Israeli policy.

Despite such tensions, there was an overall sense that pro-Israel advocacy on campus had improved substantially. There were now some 25 different organizations ready to help students with speakers, programming, and advice. The five-day Charles Schusterman International Student Leaders Assembly, sponsored by Hillel in August, drew 400 young people who shared their experiences in countering pro-Palestinian student activists. One clear message that emerged was that a positive strategy of disseminating narratives about personal connections to Israel was far more effective than a negative stance of simply defending Israel against the charges of its enemies.

Another important communal initiative for cultivating enthusiasm for Israel among young Jews was Birthright Israel. Since its founding in 2000 by a small group of philanthropists in cooperation with the Israeli government and Jewish federations, it had, by 2004, brought some 68,000 Jews between the ages of 18 and 26 to Israel for ten days, free of charge. Follow-up surveys of participants indicated that the Israel experience enhanced their sense of Jewish identity. But the original funding had only been for five years; Israel, its economy shaky, would not commit to renewing its share of the costs, and many of the federations were finding it difficult to set aside money for this purpose. In February, the Avi Chai

Foundation, which ordinarily funded only Jewish educational projects, donated $7 million, enough to pay for the summer Birthright program.

But Birthright was no more immune to controversy than Hillel. In 2004, as in 2003, a small number of American students who came to Israel through Birthright did so not with the intention of experiencing Israel, but to join up with the International Solidarity Movement (ISM) in active opposition to Israeli army actions against Palestinians and the construction of Israel's security fence on the West Bank.

AMERICAN JEWS, IRAQ, AND DARFUR

On May 11, Nicholas Berg, a 26-year-old American Jew working as a contractor in Iraq, was kidnapped and killed. His killers videotaped the execution and made it available on the Internet. It was unknown whether the fact that he was a Jew had anything to do with his fate.

The murder of Berg came at a time when the connection of American Jews to the Iraq war was a matter of controversy. One subject of discussion was the silence of most Jewish organizations—which had generally supported the war in Iraq—about the mounting evidence of the abuse of Iraqi prisoners. As of early May, only the ADL, the National Council of Jewish Women, and the Religious Action Center of Reform Judaism had publicly criticized the treatment of prisoners. The other Jewish groups had no comment, some explaining, off the record, that they did not want to appear partisan, especially in a presidential election year.

By late May, talk of an alleged Jewish role in masterminding and pursuing the Iraq war, which had surfaced when hostilities began in 2003 and then quieted down, resurfaced. Some but not all of the impetus came from political opponents of the administration seeking, in an election year, to discredit the war. On May 20, Sen. Ernest "Fritz" Hollings (D., S.C.), who had announced his retirement, said on the floor of the Senate that the war was being fought for Israel's benefit. Three days later, retired general Anthony Zinni, who had served as President Bush's emissary to the Middle East, expressed the same sentiment on the CBS television show "Sixty Minutes," adding that this was "the worst-kept secret in Washington." Rep. Nita Lowey (D., N.Y.), herself Jewish, placed a different spin on the theme, telling the *Forward* (May 28) that Bush's Middle East policies were causing a rise of anti-Semitism around the world, prompting Abraham Foxman of the ADL to accuse her of "something worse than blaming the victim, blaming someone who stands up for the victim."

Ironically, a report emanating from Israel, issued by the Jewish

Agency's Jewish People Policy Planning Institute (JPPPI), echoed Lowey. It urged Israel, when formulating policy, to take into consideration the effect of its actions on the Diaspora, especially since "The U.S.'s pro-Israel leanings antagonize other countries, including some in the West, thus generating hostility against Jewish communities."

At the same time, Jewish organizations had to fend off the charge that U.S. support for Israeli policies was endangering American interests in Iraq and throughout the Muslim world. Nicholas Kristof, in the *New York Times* (May 26), claimed that only pressure on Israel to make concessions to the Palestinians could ease Arab suspicions of U.S. intentions. And that very week, the eagerly anticipated report of the 9/11 Commission noted that resentment at American support for Israel was a central factor in motivating Muslim terrorists.

A crisis in another part of the world provided the Jewish community with a far less controversial kind of involvement. Over the course of the year, a number of national Jewish organizations and local federations held meetings and public events, some in conjunction with other religious and ethnic bodies, on the ethnic cleansing and widespread hunger in Darfur, in western Sudan, and raised large sums to help the victims. It was the U.S. Holocaust Memorial Museum, however, that brought the issue to prominence in the Jewish community by organizing a mission to the region in May, issuing reports on what it saw there, and, on one day in June, suspending all museum activities for half an hour, replacing them with a special program on Darfur. The museum's efforts might well have influenced the decision of the Bush administration, in September, finally to refer to the situation as genocide.

Religious Trends

Denominational developments during the year occurred under the shadow of the 2000–01 National Jewish Population Survey (NJPS). Its results were released in 2003 amid considerable controversy (see AJYB 2004, pp. 114–116), and its implications only began to be grasped in 2004. The NJPS indicated that, over the previous decade, Reform had replaced Conservative Judaism as the largest denomination, with 39 percent of synagogue-member households identifying as Reform and 33 percent as Conservative. Meanwhile, the Orthodox share of such households had risen from 16 to 21 percent, a figure that was likely to grow substantially over time since the Orthodox constituted a plurality of denominationally affiliated Jews under age 18. But the fastest growing group of American

Jews was the element that called itself nondenominational or secular; 13 percent of American Jewry in 1990, they now constituted 25 percent.

The gains made by Reform and Orthodoxy at the apparent expense of the middle-of-the-road Conservative movement evoked a prediction from the Reform rabbinical organization's top professional of Conservatism's demise. Rabbi Paul Menitoff, executive vice president of the Central Conference of American Rabbis (CCAR), declared in February that young Conservative Jews were leaving the movement, dissatisfied with its reluctance to accept the inevitability of intermarriage—and thus the Jewish identity of children of Jewish fathers and non-Jewish mothers—as well as its failure to recognize the validity of homosexual relationships. Menitoff declared that Conservative Judaism was doomed, over time, either to merge with Reform, or die. Conservative leaders reacted with outrage, and some of Menitoff's Reform colleagues expressed regret at his violation of the tacit rules of interdenominational politesse.

CONSERVATIVE JUDAISM

Menitoff's dire prediction was premature, to say the least, but his diagnosis of the malaise of the Conservative movement was essentially accurate. Not only were Conservative numbers down, but the two-edged issue of homosexuality—whether to ordain gay rabbis and whether to allow the performance of same-sex commitment ceremonies—was proving deeply divisive. Among the rabbinical students at the Jewish Theological Seminary (JTS), the Conservative rabbinical school, and among the younger rabbis, sentiment was strongly in favor of liberalization. And in July 2003, the president of the movement's congregational body, the United Synagogue of Conservative Judaism, had called for a review of Conservative policy. But more traditional forces, headed by the JTS chancellor, Dr. Ismar Schorsch, categorically opposed any change (see AJYB 2004, pp. 102–03). In February 2004, Schorsch declared fatly that there was no "Halakhic justification" for changing the ban on homosexuality, and besides, such a shift would split the movement and lead inevitably to a relaxation of the taboo on intermarriage. In March, he told a reporter, "This is an issue which has come from outside the movement and the seminary. It's a head-on collision between traditional Jewish values and American society" (*New York Jewish Week,* Mar. 21).

And there were other problems facing Conservative Judaism. The movement had begun ordaining women in 1985. In early August 2004, the Rabbinical Assembly of Conservative Judaism issued a 15-page report, "Gender Variation in the Careers of Conservative Rabbis: A Survey of Rabbis Ordained Since 1985," showing that male Conservative rabbis earned, on average, far more than their female colleagues. While part of the differential was due to the fact that the males tended to move on to senior positions and larger communities more quickly than the women, the study found a gender gap even among rabbis holding comparable pulpits. In response to the findings, the organization proposed the establishment of mentoring programs for female rabbis, greater public visibility for these rabbis, and monitoring of the procedures of rabbinic search committees.

As if the movement had not heard enough bad news during the year, there were indications of financial difficulties. In June, the United Synagogue, as a cost-cutting measure, let go its director of social action and did not appoint a replacement, all the while denying that this would diminish Conservative involvement in public affairs. And in December, JTS was reported to be $50 million in debt, its longtime comptroller having resigned on November 9. On December 17, Chancellor Schorsch, in an e-mail to faculty, students, and donors, stressed the institution's financial health, pointing out that what it owed was "less than half of our endowment."

REFORM JUDAISM

Reform Judaism, meanwhile, took pride in its newly acknowledged position as the largest denomination, in the full realization that many were drawn to affiliate because of Reform openness to intermarried families, gays, and other previously excluded groups. This outreach thrust co-existed with a greater interest, primarily among younger Reform Jews, in the practice of Jewish ritual.

Not only had there been a resurgence of such traditional practices as prayer in the Hebrew language and the wearing of head covering, prayer shawl, and tefillin during services, but also, the *Forward* reported (Mar. 5), there was now only one Reform temple in the country that held Sunday services, a phenomenon that had been widespread until the mid-twentieth century. And despite the movement's historical allegiance to the American public-school system and disdain for forms of education that set Jewish children apart from other Americans, there were, by 2004, more than 20 Reform day schools in operation, educating thousands of students.

The kosher laws became a focus of discussion in 2004. The Spring issue of *Reform Judaism,* the quarterly published by the CCAR, featured several articles on kashrut and announced the inauguration of a CCAR task force on the subject. Its chair, Rabbi Bennett Miller, explained, "It's no longer a movement perceived of as 'We don't do this or we don't do that.' All Jewish experience is available to us, and we have the opportunity to pick and choose which aspects would give meaning to our lives." Rabbi Eric Yoffie, president of the URJ, who maintained a kosher home, noted: "Many rituals we once saw as having no redeeming value in many instances in fact contribute to enriching Jewish lives." Some rabbis urged that synagogues and other communal institutions be kept kosher even if most members did not have kosher homes, so that no one would feel excluded from public events. One Reform summer camp, in Ontario, Canada, was already kosher. To be sure, skeptical views were also represented in the journal, some pointing out that whatever the interest of rabbis in the matter, rank-and-file Reform Jews were indifferent, and others arguing that non-ritual issues having to do with social action and public policy should get priority.

ORTHODOX JUDAISM

The self-confidence that had long been growing in Orthodox ranks, bolstered by the results of the NJPS, received another boost from the 2004 election, in which the Republican presidential campaign targeted the Orthodox vote, and with considerable success. While some two-thirds of the overall Jewish vote went to Democratic challenger John Kerry, around the same percentage backed George W. Bush, the Republican incumbent, among Orthodox voters.

While this divergence raised some concern in the Jewish community about a potentially damaging cleavage between the Orthodox and non-Orthodox sectors, Orthodox leaders viewed the numbers as a long overdue declaration of Orthodox independence from the liberal tendencies of the broader community: not only their strong support for Israel, the argument went, but also their traditional values were more in consonance with the Republican administration than with the Democrats.

An unprecedented assertion of Orthodox triumphalism came just a few weeks after Election Day, at the Thanksgiving-Day-weekend convention of the *haredi* (sectarian) Orthodox organization Agudath Israel. There, the executive vice president, Rabbi Shmuel Bloom, noted the declining numbers of non-Orthodox Jews and urged the Orthodox to prepare for the day when they would constitute the American Jewish majority. Agudath Israel, he suggested, would have to move beyond its current focus on religious matters and take the lead in such areas as anti-Semitism, support for Israel, and public policy. "The things we rely on secular Jews for—who's going to do that if the secular community whittles down?"

Another escalating Orthodox phenomenon was interest in novel religious stringencies. In May, a good number of Jewish women discarded or even burned their human-hair wigs, some of which had cost thousands of dollars. Orthodox law mandated hair covering for married women, and many who fulfilled this requirement with wigs rather than hats or scarves used hair originating in India. But rumor now had it that Indian women had this hair cut as a religious ritual at Hindu temples, which, if true, would render it idolatrous in Orthodox eyes, and therefore unfit for use. Then, in June, questions were raised about the kosher status of the New York City water supply. Copepods, tiny crustaceans that could not be seen with the naked eye, were found in the water, and these were not kosher. Some Orthodox Jews resorted to the use of bottled water, or installed filters on their water taps.

These cases illustrated some interesting aspects of contemporary Orthodoxy. First, the ubiquity of the Internet ensured that the issues would be instantly known and debated all over the Jewish world. This, in turn, brought on international consultations, as Israeli and American rabbis visited India to research the practices of Hindu temples, and bottles of New York water crossed the Atlantic for examination by Jerusalem rabbis. Also, the general media found these matters fascinating, the *New York Times* placing the wig story on page one (May 14), and the water story on page one of its metro section (Nov. 7). And finally, as might be expected in an age of short attention spans, both issues quickly vanished from public discussion, with few in the Orthodox community having any idea if or how they were finally resolved.

The blurring of lines between *haredi* and Modern Orthodoxy also continued apace, as the latter found itself pulled further to the religious right. Perhaps the best illustration was the virtual extinction of mixed-gender seating at Orthodox synagogues, a practice that had been widespread a generation earlier. In June, Agudas Achim, a synagogue in Columbus, Ohio, voted to switch its affiliation from Orthodox to Conservative rather than provide separate seating, leaving only one mixed-seating congregation (in Denver) within the OU.

Even as American Orthodoxy turned more inward, countervailing forces seemed to push it toward greater openness. Exhibit number one was the widespread feeling that the so-called *shidduch* system, whereby young men and women met only by prior arrangement through a matchmaker, and only after thoroughly "checking out" each other's credentials, was at least partly to blame for the growing population of unmarried Orthodox singles. Several Orthodox organizations—including one called "End the Madness," especially founded for the purpose—held conferences and issued publications to address the problem. The Rabbinical Council of America went so far as to issue an official endorsement of one of the numerous Orthodox Internet dating sites, SawYouAtSinai.com, calling it a "Halakhically permissible way for people to find their match."

The Jewish Orthodox Feminist Alliance (JOFA) held its fifth international conference in February, its theme, "Male and Female, God Created Them: Women and Men in Partnership," indicating a desire to draw more men to the sessions. About 1,000 people attended, about 21 percent of them male. Topics discussed included sexual abuse, ways of dealing with the plight of women refused Jewish divorces by their husbands, and the inclusion of women in Jewish ritual. There was also a report of a study documenting the attitudes of Orthodox Jewish women toward sexuality. Causing the biggest stir was the willingness of at least some of the Orthodox rabbis present to entertain the possibility of women rabbis.

The five-year-old Yeshiva Chovevei Torah, on the Upper West Side of Manhattan, embodied the aspiration of that element of the Orthodox community that deplored the perceived trend toward Orthodox sectarianism and believed that Yeshiva University, previously the sole Modern Orthodox rabbinical school, had allowed itself to be swept up by it. In 2004, Chovevei Torah graduated its first class of nine rabbis; all found rabbinic positions either with congregations, Jewish schools, or campus Hillels. At the seminary's first annual dinner, in late March, Rabbi Avi Weiss, the founder and dean, declared: "We can transform the fabric of the Jewish community" so that Orthodoxy is "nonjudgmental, persuasive but never coercive," and thus able to address Jews far beyond Orthodox precincts.

CHABAD-LUBAVITCH

The evening of June 21 marked the onset of the tenth yahrzeit (anniversary of date of death) of Rabbi Menachem Mendel Schneerson, the Lubavitcher Rebbe. Although he had died childless at the age of 92 without picking a successor, and the movement had divided over whether or not he would rise from the grave as the Messiah, Chabad was flourishing. It was clear, in retrospect, that the rebbe had set in place an effective, decentralized system of outreach in which Chabad emissaries, imbued with missionary fervor, saw themselves as fulfilling his direct instructions to bring Jews around the world closer to Judaism. Some 4,000 of these emissaries were active, double the number in 1994; a new Chabad house opened somewhere on the average of one every ten days.

One key to Chabad success was the emissaries' distancing themselves from messianic rhetoric, thus avoiding the taint of extremism and possible heresy. Another was its openness to nonobservant Jews who had no intention of adopting an Orthodox lifestyle, an approach that brought political and financial backing from members of Reform and Conservative congregations (the bulk of Chabad funds came from non-Orthodox donors), and opportunities to participate in and influence the programs of local Jewish federations. Chabad's growth earned it both respect and envy from non-Orthodox groups.

Local Chabad rabbis organized numerous events commemorating the *yahrzeit,* and many followers came to pray at the rebbe's grave in Queens, New York, to mark the occasion. The movement's annual convention for its emissaries, in November, had to be held at the 69th Regiment Armory in Manhattan, since no hotel ballroom could accommodate the more than 2,500 Chabad activists who came from as far away as China, Nepal, and Paraguay. That same night, the messianist faction of Chabad held a competing event at movement headquarters in Brooklyn.

Organizational Developments

UNITED JEWISH COMMUNITIES

Created in 1999 out of a merger between the Council of Jewish Federations, the United Jewish Appeal, and the United Israel Appeal, United Jewish Communities (UJC) coordinated the network of some 200 local Jewish federations in the U.S. and Canada. A study completed in late 2004 but not yet released documented widespread disappointment with the organization on the part of communal officials intimately involved in its operation. *From Chaos to Chaos? How Jewish Leaders Reinvented Their National Communal System,* by Gerald Bubis and Steven Windmueller, concluded that lack of proper planning for the merger and the absence of an overall "vision" for the new entity had led to "chaos."

Fully cognizant of the problem, Howard Rieger, previously the head of United Jewish Federations of Greater Pittsburgh, took over as UJC president on September 1. Rieger made it clear from the outset that UJC would have to narrow its focus and not duplicate work that could be done by other agencies. Specifically, he told reporters that managing the decennial National Jewish Population Survey (NJPS) might not be a UJC priority. The annual General Assembly of the UJC, held this year in Cleveland in November, reflected Rieger's perspective, emphasizing the "nuts and bolts" of fund-raising, strategic planning, provision of services, and advocacy, rather debates over "big ideas."

AIPAC

On August 27, the American Jewish community was shocked to learn, from a CBS report, that two AIPAC officials, Steven Rosen, its foreign policy director, and Keith Weissman, a specialist on Iran, were being questioned by the FBI. This was the result of a two-year investigation about the two men passing on information to the Israeli embassy that they received from Pentagon analyst Larry Franklin about Iran. Since such exchanges of information had been considered routine, Jewish leaders found themselves in the dark about the purpose of the investigation, one explaining to the *New York Jewish Week* (Sept. 3), "we are operating with almost no real information." AIPAC, for its part, emphatically denied any wrongdoing, said it would cooperate fully with federal authorities, and elicited statements of support from prominent political figures and all of the Jewish organizations.

As the FBI investigation intensified over the next few weeks, concern mounted in the Jewish community that a weakened AIPAC could seriously undermine Israel's standing in Washington, and that the scandal could once again resurrect the allegation that the primary loyalty of American Jews was to Israel, not the U.S. Two theories developed about what lay behind the challenge to AIPAC. One was anti-Semitism (see above, p. 171), a suspicion encouraged by the fact that David Szady, the FBI man in charge of the investigation, had been charged in the past with mistreating Jewish FBI employees, most notably in the Adam Ciralsky case in 1999 (see AJYB 2000, p. 168.) Another hypothesis, not necessarily incompatible with the first, was that the anti-AIPAC initiative was an attempt by elements in the government hostile to neoconservative policy makers to discredit AIPAC and Israel, and thereby change the administration's pro-Israel foreign policy in the Middle East.

On December 1, the FBI conducted a raid of AIPAC headquarters, and four of the organization's top officials, including Executive Director Howard Kohr, were issued subpoenas by a federal grand jury. In a December 10 conference call with Jewish organizations, Kohr urged patience and pledged that his organization would be vindicated. Two weeks later, reports surfaced that Franklin, the Defense Department analyst who had provided the information to the AIPAC figures, had done so as part of a "sting" operation orchestrated by the FBI.

WORLD JEWISH CONGRESS

At the end of August, a serious public dispute broke out at the World Jewish Congress (WJC), the high-profile group known for its aggressive work in the area of Holocaust restitution. The spark was a memo written by Isi Leibler, a senior vice president of the organization, an Australian Jew who now made his home in Israel. Leibler charged financial irregularities on the part of WJC chairman Israel Singer, pointing specifically to a $1.2-million account in a Swiss bank under Singer's control. Leibler called for the WJC to institute changes in its procedures to ensure transparency and accountability. Singer denied the allegation, claimed that the Swiss account had been set up to fund his pension, and suggested that Leibler was seeking to take over the organization.

The WJC leadership—most particularly its president, Edgar Bronfman—backed Singer. Leibler made his case at a meeting of the WJC steering committee on September 20, after which Bronfman relieved him of his position in the organization. After the meeting, Bronfman announced that, in light of the controversy, he would run for another term as WJC president.

But Leibler refused to give up his post. In November, Alfred Donath, president of the Swiss Federation of Jewish Communities, added his voice to the call for financial transparency, demanding an independent audit. When Donath refused to drop his request, he was "suspended" from the governing body of the European Jewish Congress, an affiliate of the WJC. But by year's end, pressure generated by negative publicity seemed likely to force the organization into opening its financial records for examination.

AMERICAN JEWISH CONGRESS

Rarely had any American Jewish organization so swiftly changed direction as the American Jewish Congress under the leadership of Jack Rosen, formerly its president and now its chairman. Known historically for its liberal domestic social agenda, AJCongress now championed aggressive opposition to international anti-Semitism and a hard-line pro-Israel stance, while Rosen's personal ties to President Bush smoothed relations with political conservatives.

But AJCongress got caught in an embarrassing situation during 2004. In August, it made headlines by announcing the appointment of Alon Pinkas, about to step down as Israeli consul general in New York, to the newly created position of CEO. This was the first time that a former Israeli diplomat was chosen for a high-level job at an American communal organization. Pinkas said that his experience in dealing with Israeli-American relations and his connections with American Jewish leaders would stand him in good stead in the new post. But the move was not looked upon kindly in Israel, which had a law on the books barring any diplomat from accepting employment in the country where he served until two years had passed after the end of his tenure there, and AJCongress put the appointment "on hold." In December, a panel of administrative judges in Israel ruled that Pinkas could not take the position.

Trends and Ideas

INTERMARRIAGE

The publication of *Double or Nothing: Jewish Families and Mixed Marriage,* by Brandeis University professor Sylvia Barack Fishman, brought a degree of scholarly rigor to the hotly contested issue of intermarriage. Rather than addressing the issue quantitatively, Fishman reported on over 250 interviews she conducted with families as part of a project commissioned by the American Jewish Committee. Among her conclusions was that the Jewish partner and his/her family are often reluctant to urge the non-Jewish partner to adopt Jewish practices; that homes providing children elements of two religions are far less likely to produce Jewishly identified children than homes that are unambiguously Jewish; and that Jewish education, a Jewishly active family, and a Jewish peer group were the key factors in determining the Jewish identity of children, whether intermarried or not.

The book was not welcomed by elements of the Jewish community that saw intermarriage as an inevitable trend in an open society; they resented what they saw as Fishman's negative portrayal of mixed-religion families. One Jewish leader who saw no point in maintaining the traditional Jewish aversion to intermarriage was Edgar Bronfman, president of the World Jewish Congress. Bronfman told the *Jewish Chronicle* (London) that such opposition was "racist" and "begins to sound a little like Nazism." For Bronfman, the choice was between "an attempt to double the amount of Jews that there are, or we can irritate everybody who's intermarried, and lose them all."

In October, the Jewish Outreach Institute, which advocated inclusion of such mixed-religion families in Jewish life, issued a study, "Rabbis and the Intermarried Family in the Jewish Community." It was the report of a survey of how 183 Conservative, Reform, and Reconstructionist rabbis dealt with officiation at interfaith marriages, the status of the children of mixed marriages, and the participation of non-Jewish parents in their children's Jewish life-cycle events. The most striking finding was that even Conservative rabbis, barred by their interpretation of Judaism from performing intermarriages, were often quite willing to allow non-Jewish family members to participate in some way at the bar/bat mitzvah of their Jewish relatives.

With much of the community eager to blur the lines between Jew and non-Jew (after all, Democratic presidential candidate John Kerry was something of both), the casting of a non-Jew, Alfred Molina, as Tevye in a new Broadway production of *Fiddler on the Roof* should not have raised many eyebrows. In fact, most Jewish critics treated the production harshly, charging that Molina's performance universalized what had been a Jewish play; "Sunset on a Jewish 'Fiddler'" was the headline in the *New York Jewish Week* (Feb. 27).

GAYS AND LESBIANS

Nowhere were the changing American attitudes toward homosexuality more evident than in the Jewish community. The *2004 Annual Survey of American Jewish Opinion,* commissioned by the American Jewish Committee, found that only 13 percent of American Jews opposed legal recognition of gay unions and just 24 percent favored President Bush's proposed constitutional amendment defining marriage as between a man and a woman. These were far lower figures than in the broader American population.

The organizations of Reform Judaism backed gay marriage as a civil right. The Conservative movement, in the midst of a jarring internal conflict over the matter (see above, p. 198), took no public position, although many of its rabbis argued against any discrimination on grounds of sexual orientation.

Only the Orthodox stood adamantly against the legitimization of homosexuality, but even in that sector there were signs of change. The release of a film in 2003, *Trembling Before God,* a moving portrayal of Orthodox homosexuals, evoked considerable empathy in Orthodox circles. And in 2004, Rabbi Steven Greenberg, the first openly gay Orthodox rabbi, caused something of a sensation with his book, *Wrestling With God and Men: Homosexuality in the Jewish Tradition,* in which Greenberg related how he came to terms with his homosexuality and sought to combine it with the Orthodox way of life. He told an interviewer (*New York Jewish Week,* Feb. 27) that he wanted "a 16-year-old in an Orthodox day school who discovers that he or she is gay to know there's a decent life inside the community that he or she can plan for."

Rabbi Sharon Kleinbaum of Congregation Beth Simchat Torah in Manhattan, the nation's largest gay synagogue, urged her fellow rabbis to officiate at gay marriages, even though they were illegal in New York, as an act of civil disobedience. More than 200 members of the New York clergy, most of them rabbis, signed a pledge to do just that, which was posted on the Web site of Kleinbaum's synagogue. Although she performed the wedding of two women on Long Island in late March, the district attorney declined to press charges.

SCHOLARSHIP, MYSTICISM, AND MADONNA

Of the many scholarly books on Jewish themes to appear during 2004, four publications were immediately recognized as masterpieces. Two were histories of the Jews in America, published to coincide with the celebration of the 350th anniversary of Jewish settlement in what would become the United States (a comprehensive review of the commemoration of this milestone will appear in AJYB 2006). Brandeis University historian Jonathan Sarna's *American Judaism: A History* was a comprehensive and provocative treatment of the religious development of American Jewry, while *The Jews of the United States,* by Hasia Diner of New York University, concentrated on social, economic, and cultural trends.

The Five Books of Moses: A Translation with Commentary, by the literary scholar Robert Alter, who taught at Berkeley, set a new standard for Bible translation. Alter's expertise in Hebrew and the Jewish interpretive tradition, combined with his command of English style, made this translation both faithful to the sound and rhythm of the original, and an elegant literary work in its own right.

The first two volumes of Daniel Matt's translation, with notes, of the *Zohar,* the basic text of the Kabbalah, appeared in 2004, with many more volumes in preparation. This monumental accomplishment, titled *The Zohar: Pritzker Edition,* had been years in preparation. It opened up to the modern reader an exceedingly dense and enigmatic book that was, in essence, a mystical commentary on the Torah. Matt's scholarly approach to Kabbalah, Jewish mysticism, was not widely shared. Kabbalah, to be sure, was extremely popular in the U.S., both in the Jewish community and outside it, but in a very watered-down version that appealed to the current vogue of spirituality and individual self-fulfillment. An organization called the Kabbalah Center, based in Los Angeles with branches in ten other American cities and several foreign countries, promoted Kabbalah as an "ancient spiritual wisdom" not confined just to Jews, and the books published by the group's leader, Yehuda Berg, undoubtedly sold many more copies than Matt's work. But the center's real star was one of its many celebrity recruits, the pop diva Madonna, who, though not Jewish, adopted the name Esther, and paid a highly publicized visit to Israel for the High Holy Days (which gleeful Israeli officials believed would help boost tourism).

LAWRENCE GROSSMAN

Review
of
the
Year

OTHER COUNTRIES

Israel

THE PALESTINIAN INTIFADA that began in late September 2000 petered out in the course of 2004, largely due to effective Israeli security measures. The most controversial of these, the barrier gradually being erected on the West Bank to keep out potential suicide bombers, was declared illegal by the International Court of Justice in a decision that many viewed as politically motivated, and that Israel ignored.

Convinced that the Palestinians were not prepared to negotiate a peace agreement, Israeli prime minister Ariel Sharon pushed through a controversial plan to disengage unilaterally from heavily Palestinian areas by pulling completely out of the Gaza Strip and giving up four settlements in the northern West Bank. It remained unclear whether Sharon intended any further territorial concessions beyond these.

The political cost of the initiative was high, as Sharon alienated his pro-settler constituency, including a significant portion of his own Likud Party. This necessitated reorganizing the government coalition and relying on the support of Labor to effect disengagement. Furthermore, the prospect of having to force unwilling settlers from their homes raised the possibility that religious soldiers, told by their rabbis that abandoning Israeli land was against the Torah, might refuse to carry out disengagement orders.

Domestically, a heightened sense of personal security due to the decline in terror attacks and the free-market policies put in place by Finance Minister Benjamin Netanyahu triggered a definite upturn in the economy. But some pointed out that the price paid—budget and benefit cuts that impacted on the most vulnerable strata of society—was dangerously widening the gap between rich and poor.

POLITICS AND DIPLOMACY

The Disengagement Initiative

Prime Minister Ariel Sharon dropped a political bombshell on December 15, 2003, when he announced a plan of unilateral withdrawal from some of the territories so as to secure "those parts of the Land of Israel that will be an inseparable part of the State of Israel in any future settlement" (see AJYB 2004, pp. 189–90).

Sharon gave the first detailed exposition of what he had in mind in a February 2, 2005 interview with the daily *Ha'aretz*. He said, "I have given an order to plan for the evacuation of 17 settlements in the Gaza Strip. It is my intention to carry out an evacuation—sorry, a relocation—of settlements that cause us problems and of places that we will not hold onto anyway in a final settlement, like the Gaza settlements." There were, at the time, only 17 settlements in Gaza, and Sharon proceeded to state the obvious: "I am working on the assumption that in the future there will be no Jews in Gaza." Also to be abandoned, he said, were "three problematic settlements in Samaria," the biblical term for the northern West Bank. (A fourth settlement there was subsequently added to Sharon's list.) The prime minister acknowledged the gravity of the move, which, he noted, "is not simple and cannot be done overnight. We are talking of a population of 7,500 people. It's not a simple matter. We are talking of thousands of square meters of hothouses, factories, and packing plants. There are people who are third generation there."

Dov Weisglass, a confidant of Prime Minister Sharon and his bureau chief, presented Sharon's disengagement plan to U.S. national security adviser Condoleezza Rice on January 23. Toward the end of February, Shin Bet head Avi Dichter was told by Egyptian officials during a visit to Cairo that Egypt did not object to Israel's plan to withdraw from the Gaza Strip, but that it expected Israel to coordinate the pullout both with Egypt and with the Palestinians.

Jewish settlers in the territories were quick to condemn the plan. Bentzi Lieberman, chairman of the Yesha Council, the organization of Jewish communities in Judea, Samaria, and Gaza, told Israel Radio the move "only gives a prize to terrorism," adding that he did not think Sharon's coalition, which included the right-wing National Union and the National Religious Party (NRP), could survive if it carried out the disengagement.

Signs of unrest in the coalition were not long in coming. Shortly after

Sharon's announcement, the NRP and the National Union both announced that they would quit the government immediately should the cabinet endorse the scheme. In fact, these parties were under pressure from settler groups to do even more: the Yesha Council was reportedly pressing them to leave the government if Sharon so much as went ahead with a planned meeting with President Bush to present his disengagement proposal. Another sign of the settlers' determination was a report that surfaced on February 15 to the effect that the Gaza settlers planned two new settlements in the southern part of the Gaza Strip and one at the northern end, and intended to welcome another 100 families into the existing Katif and Neve Dekalim settlements.

Sharon traveled to Washington for an April 14 meeting with President George Bush, the tenth between the two men. Through an exchange of letters, it accomplished what Sharon had hoped—an American endorsement of his disengagement plan. Bush's letter placed support for disengagement within the context of the "road map" plan accepted by both Israel and the Palestinians in 2003 (see AJYB 2004, pp. 159–160), which, the president insisted, remained the framework for peace. The American letter acknowledged Israel's need for a security fence on the West Bank, although considering it a temporary measure and not a marking of the future border between Israeli and Palestinian territory. While Bush reiterated the American commitment to "the establishment of a Palestinian state that is viable, continuous, sovereign, and independent," he made two key concessions to the Israeli position. On the issue of settlements, any final deal should take into account the then-current "demographic realities" on the West Bank. As for the Palestinian refugee problem, that should be solved by settling refugees in the territory of the proposed Palestinian state, not through wholesale recognition of a Palestinian "right of return" under which the refugees and their descendants could live in the State of Israel.

Sharon was quoted in *Yediot Aharonot* as saying the Palestinians had suffered "a lethal blow," and the Israeli media generally agreed that the Sharon-Bush meeting had been a triumph for the prime minister. Danny Rubinstein, for example, the Palestinian affairs commentator for *Ha'aretz,* called the Bush letter "one of the greatest political defeats in years" for the Palestinians. Rubinstein quoted Ziad Abu Amar, a member of the Palestinian parliament, as saying: "What is still left to negotiate between us and Israel if President Bush has already made a decision on two key issues, settlements and refugees?"

But Ze'ev Schiff, the well-connected defense analyst of *Ha'aretz,* suggested caution: "Whoever thinks of Bush's statements as the second Balfour Declaration in terms of their importance to Israel is getting carried away." True enough, he noted, the denial of the "right of return" was a significant victory for Israel. On the question of territory, however, Schiff called Sharon's achievement "only partial," since the U.S. leader had "again promised the Palestinians a viable state, and a state cannot be viable when it is made up of patches of territory. Palestine will be a state whose borders will be determined in negotiations between the sides and taking Security Council Resolution 242 into account, and not by a separation fence being built today to thwart terror attacks, and so must be temporary." Schiff pointed out that Bush's reference to "new realities on the ground" was double-edged. While it recognized, on the one hand, that Israeli settlement in the West Bank could not be ignored, it also implied, on the other, that the hundreds of thousands of Palestinians who had settled in the Jerusalem area constituted a permanent presence, making ongoing Israeli control over East Jerusalem problematic.

Palestinian Authority leader Yasir Arafat, who at first had condemned Sharon's disengagement plan as an Israeli trick to undermine a more comprehensive settlement, and then on March 11 welcomed "any simultaneous Israeli withdrawal from any part of our land," reacted to the Bush letter with indignation. "Our destiny is to defend our land and sacred places and our rights in freedom and independence—and the return of the refugees," he said in a speech on Palestinian TV. On April 15, Arafat wrote UN secretary general Kofi Annan to complain about the disengagement plan and President Bush's support for it. Annan responded, in a letter released to the press on April 30, that "effective measures to curb terrorism and violence" by the PA "would help the international community ensure that any withdrawal from Gaza is part of the implementation of the 'road map' and not a substitute for it." Annan also said that Israel remained obligated to carry out its existing obligations, including a freeze on settlement construction and the dismantling of existing illegal outposts.

The EU responded to the Bush-Sharon exchange of letters with an implicit rebuke of the American acceptance of "new realities on the ground," saying it would not recognize any unilateral borders changes; the agreement of both parties to the conflict was necessary. Speaking to reporters on April 16, during a meeting of EU foreign ministers in Ireland, EU foreign-policy chief Javier Solana said that the "road map," not the Bush statement, remained the basic guideline for reaching a final Israeli-Palestinian solution.

Sharon Fights for His Plan

The Prime Minister's Office released a general outline of the disengagement plan on April 18. It declared Israel's commitment to resolution of the conflict "on the basis of the principle of two states for two peoples, the State of Israel as the state of the Jewish people and a Palestinian state for the Palestinian people, as part of the implementation of President Bush's vision." There currently was, however, "no reliable Palestinian partner with which it can make progress in a bilateral peace process," and so "a plan of unilateral disengagement" was necessary. The "relocation" from Gaza and part of northern Samaria, the document continued, "will reduce friction with the Palestinian population, and carries with it the potential for improvement in the Palestinian economy and living conditions." This should induce the Palestinians to "take advantage of the opportunity created by the disengagement in order to break out of the cycle of violence and to reengage in a process of dialogue."

Hoping to achieve a clear mandate from his own party before carrying out this controversial policy, Prime Minister Sharon arranged for the Likud bloc to hold a referendum on disengagement. In the days leading up to May 2, the referendum date, opponents of the plan both within and outside Likud launched a well-organized and well-financed effort to convince Likudniks to vote against their leader, including arranging personal visits by Gaza settlers to the homes of party members. On April 27, Israel Independence Day, hundreds of thousands of right-wing Israelis jammed into Gush Katif, in Gaza, for a demonstration of solidarity with the settlers that was also a show of strength for the upcoming referendum. Some came in their own cars, others in chartered buses; many were stuck in traffic jams for hours.

On May 1, the day before the crucial Likud vote, Sharon knew that disengagement was in trouble and sought to sway wavering Likud members by suggesting that should the party reject his policy new elections might be necessary, an eventuality that jeopardized the parliamentary careers of Likud's 40 Knesset members. Sharon told Channel Two TV that defeat in the referendum would create "very, very difficult conditions" for him to continue as prime minister.

But the veiled threat was not enough to turn the tide. The next day, his disengagement plan went down to defeat overwhelmingly by 59.5 percent to 39.7 percent, with 51.7 percent of the 193,000 registered Likud members casting ballots. Sharon did not call for new elections, instead insisting that that he would carry on with disengagement despite the clear opposition of his party's rank and file. "One thing is clear to me," Sharon said. "The people of Israel did not elect me to sit on my hands for four years. I was elected to find a way to bring peace . . . ." He was seconded by Deputy Prime Minister Ehud Olmert, a strong ally, who called the plan "unstoppable." Acknowledging that the results of the referendum were negative, Olmert nevertheless asked, "Is that the end of the story? No. Is that the end of the process? No." "In the end," he continued, "there will be a disengagement in Gaza, because the alternative . . . is more murder, terrorism, and attacks, without our having an intelligent answer to the question of what 7,500 Jews have to do among 1.2 million Palestinians" in the Gaza Strip. U.S. secretary of state Colin Powell, clearly disappointed by the result of the referendum, noted: "The Likud Party didn't vote for it. But when we look at the Israeli public, there's an 80-percent approval rating for this kind of initiative."

An estimated 150,000 people jammed into Tel Aviv's Rabin Square on May 15, in a rally supporting Israeli withdrawal from the Gaza Strip sponsored by the opposition Labor Party and others. Organizers claimed that they represented the views of Israel's majority, pointing out that the turnout at the rally exceeded the 100,000 voters who had participated in the Likud referendum.

Sharon tried to get a revised disengagement plan through his cabinet on May 30, but it was defeated by 12 to 11. Among those voting in the negative were three senior Likud figures, Finance Minister Benjamin Netanyahu, Foreign Minister Silvan Shalom, and Education Minister Limor Livnat. But the prime minister was not about to give up, and on June 4, two days before the next scheduled cabinet meeting, Sharon changed the ministerial balance by firing two National Union ministers, party leader Avigdor Lieberman (minister of transport) and Benny Elon (minister of tourism), pushing the National Union out of his coalition.

Both men were informed by phone about their ouster, and the cabinet secretary summoned them to appear at 9 a.m. on June 4 to be handed their official letters of dismissal. But Elon went into hiding to avoid receipt of the letter, believing that in this way he remained in the cabinet even though absent, and thus would deny Sharon a majority. From his hiding place, Elon told Israel Radio that the dismissal could not be formalized until he received the letter, and, in any event, he could not verify that the phone call he had received was actually authorized by Sharon. Lieberman, for his part, challenged his dismissal as undemocratic. "I'm being fired for disagreeing with the prime minister," he told Israel Radio. But Ehud Olmert defended the shakeup, arguing that "the prime minister has the right to replace a coalition partner who is no longer suitable."

The June 6 cabinet meeting approved the disengagement plan in principle by 14 to 7, though the specific settlements to be evacuated would be determined later on. Olmert called the decision "a historical turning point in the Middle East. This is the first time that such a plan was adopted by the Israeli cabinet, namely that Israel will, unfortunately in the circumstances, dismantle settlements and pull out of the Gaza Strip." But NRP leader Effi Eitam, the minister of housing, signaled that he was on his way out of the cabinet, saying that the vote "is one of the most bitter, horrible decisions made by any government since the establishment of the State of Israel. It means that we are about to transfer thousand of Jews from their homes and to create a Hamas, Jihad, Hezballah state on the blood of innocent Jews." Two days later Eitam and former NRP leader Yitzhak Levy, deputy minister in the Prime Minister's Office, resigned from the cabinet without immediately joining the opposition (apparently on the advice of Rabbi Mordechai Eliyahu, a former Sephardi chief rabbi of Israel), but their four fellow NRP Knesset members, including Minister of Social Welfare Zevulun Orlev, remained in the government coalition.

Settlers and their backers continued to ratchet up the pressure against the disengagement plan. On July 25, they staged what was perhaps their most spectacular effort—a human chain extending from the settlement of Nissanit in the southern Gaza Strip to the Western Wall in Jerusalem. According to some estimates, as many as a quarter of a million people took part.

On an August 12 tour of the West Bank, Olmert sparked settler ire by saying that the disengagement plan was only a first step. It "will not be the last, but only the beginning of withdrawals from Judea and Samaria," *Ma'ariv* quoted him as saying. And the deputy prime minister also justified the fact that the pullout was unilateral, with nothing demanded of the other side. "If we cannot negotiate a settlement now, better to take our fate into our own hands and unilaterally do what we must to preserve and protect Israel's interests, keeping what we can and leaving what we cannot. Swallowing more than we can chew will not serve the national interest."

Hoping to convince his erstwhile supporters that he was indeed committed to "keeping what we can," Sharon moved to tighten Israel's grip on parts of the West Bank. This was extremely controversial in Israel. In May, State Comptroller Eliezer Goldberg had disclosed that the Housing Ministry, headed by Effi Eitam, had spent over $6 million on unauthorized construction in the settlements at the same time that other government bodies were trying to curtail settlement expansion. Attorney

General Menachem Mazuz ordered a freeze on all money for settlement construction. But on August 17, Sharon authorized construction of 1,000 housing units in four West Bank settlements, in addition to 600 previously announced units just outside Jerusalem.

An official in the Prime Minister's Office said that the new units did not violate any agreements with the U.S. because they were within the settlement blocs implicitly recognized as Israeli in President Bush's April 14 letter to Sharon. But a spokesman for the U.S. State Department said the next day that American recognition of the "facts on the ground" referred to a final peace agreement, not to interim steps, and the day after that, National Security Advisor Rice took the position that expansion of settlements was inconsistent with the "road map." But on August 20, the *New York Times* reported that the State Department had no objection to the "natural growth" of "at least some Israeli settlements in the occupied West Bank," although it would not say this publicly. On August 24 the State Department said it would send a team to Israel to determine, in practical terms, what constituted "settlement activity." PA prime minister Ahmed Qurei reacted with incredulity, saying, "I don't believe that America says now that settlements can be expanded. This thwarts and destroys the peace process."

But the promise of new construction in the settlements did not help Sharon within his party. He suffered another political defeat on August 19, when the Likud convention voted down his efforts to broaden the government coalition by bringing in the Labor Party, so as to ease passage of the disengagement plan. The convention, meeting in Tel Aviv's Mann Auditorium, voted by a 58-percent majority to bar Labor's entry, and then, by a margin of just five votes, defeated a proposal which would have allowed Sharon to negotiate with "all Zionist parties" on joining the government. Though Sharon said before the vote he would not consider the decision binding, the rebuff was stinging, since his supporters had invested a great deal of time and effort in trying to convince party members to back their position.

He called the convention decisions "irresponsible" and said he would push ahead with his coalition efforts. "I am determined to implement the disengagement plan, and to enlarge the government to include Labor," said a letter from the prime minister to Labor leader Shimon Peres, published in the daily *Yediot Aharonot* on August 22. Labor, for its part, said it was suspending negotiations in light of Likud's actions, and would work to bring about early elections.

If his efforts were being frustrated in his party, Sharon had more success with the "inner" security cabinet. On September 14, that body of top ministers approved, nine to one, an outline plan authorizing the government to begin making advance payments to families that obligated themselves to leave the Gaza settlements.

A Determined Opposition

The ferment against the withdrawal took a very serious turn in October, when former Ashkenazi chief rabbi and NRP spiritual leader Rabbi Avraham Shapira called on soldiers and border police to disobey all orders to evacuate settlements and to tell their commanders they intended to do so. His statement, which was supported by other rabbis both in the territories and within Israel proper, caused a considerable stir.

Both Defense Minister Shaul Mofaz and Chief of Staff Moshe (Bogie) Ya'alon lashed out at the suggestion of refusal. Ya'alon, speaking at an Ashdod ceremony for the navy's fallen, said: "The phenomenon of refusal is dangerous to us as an army, as a society and as a state. It is illegitimate and inappropriate." He said that soldiers and officers of the IDF would carry out the orders passed on to them by the political leadership "professionally, and with the understanding and sensitivity mandated by the complexity of these missions." Ya'alon called on rabbis not to put officers and soldiers "into impossible situations" by calling on them to refuse orders.

A large number of rabbis signed an open letter opposing refusal. Among them was Rabbi Shlomo Riskin, formerly of Lincoln Square Synagogue in New York and now the rabbi of Efrat, in the West Bank near Bethlehem. Riskin did not believe, in principle, that Jewish law prohibited ceding land, and cited several precedents to prove the point. Nevertheless, Riskin opposed Sharon's unilateral disengagement plan, and even so denounced refusal of orders to carry it out. "And despite the terrible pain [of withdrawal], refusal is many times worse, since it could lead us downhill to the end of the very existence of the State of Israel," he said.

Clearly intending to mollify the government's pro-settler critics, Dov Weisglass, Prime Minister Sharon's senior adviser and frequent emissary to Washington, stirred up a hornet's nest with statements he made early in October to *Ha'aretz*. The disengagement plan, Weisglass said, was a means of freezing the peace process by pulling out of Gaza and the northern West Bank, and then standing pat. "The disengagement is actually formaldehyde," he said. "It supplies the amount of formaldehyde that is necessary so there will not be a political process with the Palestinians." Weisglass continued: "And when you freeze that [peace] process you prevent the establishment of a Palestinian state, and you prevent a discussion of the refugees, the borders and Jerusalem. Effectively the whole package called the Palestinian state, with all that it entails, has been removed indefinitely from our agenda. And all this with authority and permission. All this with a presidential blessing and the ratification of both houses of Congress."

Deeply embarrassed by the Weisglass story, Sharon insisted that he supported the "road map" and its intended goal, the establishment of a Palestinian state. The disengagement plan, he said, was meant to serve "until the time at which a Palestinian partner could be found who would fulfill all the required commitments in the 'road map,' and with whom it would be possible to hold diplomatic negotiations and move forward toward peace." Weisglass himself protested that the statements attributed to him were taken out of context.

The Americans accepted Sharon's explanation at face value: Secretary of State Powell said that the administration had no doubts about Sharon's commitment to the "road map," and State Department spokesman Adam Ereli said that Weisglass's statements did not match Israel's official government position as presented to the Americans.

Tensions mounted in advance of a scheduled October 26 Knesset vote on the disengagement plan. Security services were on high alert, and the guard around Sharon was reinforced. According to one report, the prime minister was accompanied to the key Knesset session by no less than 18 bodyguards. Shimon Peres said the atmosphere reminded him of the autumn of 1995, just before the assassination of then prime minister Yitzhak Rabin. Political jockeying in advance of the Knesset vote was intense, with several key Likud figures holding out until the last minute before declaring their intentions. Pressure was particularly high on senior party ministers like Netanyahu, Shalom, and Livnat, who faced the tricky challenge of not seeming to defy those opposed to disengagement, on the one hand, or to defy the prime minister, who could take away their cherished cabinet portfolios, on the other.

Sharon won by what seemed a comfortable margin—67 for, 45 against, and seven abstentions. But 17 of the "nay" votes came from members of his own Likud, including Minister without Portfolio Uzi Landau, the leader of the Likud "rebels" against disengagement, and Michael Ratzon, the deputy minister of industry and trade. Sharon proceeded to fire both of them from their posts. The NRP, still technically a coalition member, voted against Sharon as well.

Immediately after the vote, Netanyahu, Shalom, and Livnat, together with Agriculture Minister Yisrael Katz, announced that they would resign from the government within two weeks if Sharon did not agree to hold a national referendum on the pullout plan. At the same time, the remaining NRP MKs, including Zevulun Orlev, who had stayed in the cabinet, announced their departure from the coalition. Livnat, Katz, and Shalom soon withdrew their threats, as they put it, for the good of the party. But Netanyahu held out until the last moment: only on November 9 did he announce that he would not resign. He continued to back the idea of a national referendum and claimed that a majority of Likud MKs agreed with him, but acknowledged that a bill to that effect could not pass the Knesset. Speaking just days before Yasir Arafat's death, Netanyahu said that the illness of the Palestinian leader also had to be taken into account. "The expected departure of Arafat from the Palestinian leadership creates a new situation," he said.

A few days later, after a Knesset vote on the budget had to be put off because the government could not muster a majority, Sharon aides accused Netanyahu of "new heights of sabotage" for allegedly continuing to undermine the disengagement plan even after withdrawing his resignation threat. The press quoted sources close to the prime minister as saying that Netanyahu had not tried hard enough to pass the budget. *Ha'aretz* reported Sharon's aides saying: "Instead of concentrating on passing the budget, as his job requires, Netanyahu is busy traveling to dinners overseas, being involved in failed putsch attempts and initiating political spin that is harmful to Israel." Netanyahu's people, naturally, denied the charges and expressed surprise at the vehemence of the attack against the finance minister.

Sharon faced another test of sorts on November 21, when the Likud held elections for three key party chairmanships—of its central committee, secretariat, and bureau. In each of the races, antidisengagement "rebels" went down to defeat, although none of the winners could be called avid Sharon supporters. In the race for the central committee post, Tzachi Hanegbi, a minister without portfolio, defeated "rebel" leader Uzi Landau. Agriculture Minister Yisrael Katz won the secretariat post over "rebel" MK Michael Ratzon and Sharon's choice, MK Avraham Hirschsohn. Health Minister Danny Naveh topped MK Gilad Erdan for the bureau position.

A legislative hurdle was cleared on November 30, when the Knesset passed a preliminary reading of the bill authorizing a compensation package for settlers. Once again, a seemingly convincing majority—this time 64-44—was deceptive, hardly boding well for the government. Fully 16 of the 40 Likud MKs voted against the bill, and it had the solid support of the opposition Labor Party. It still faced a tortuous path through Knesset committees before final passage. (On December 28, the Knesset Law Committee, responsible for preparing the bill for its second and third readings, would deadlock 8-8, delaying passage on this essential part of the withdrawal package.)

Coalition in Crisis

Sharon suffered another parliamentary defeat on December 1, when the first reading of the 2005 budget was defeated by 69 to 43. The 15 members representing Shinui, the anticlerical party, voted against the bill after Sharon had agreed to payments of about 400 million shekels to religious institutions in order to gain the votes of ultra-Orthodox MKs. Sharon himself brought the situation to a head, calling the first of three votes on the budget in the knowledge that it would fail, giving him a chance to reshuffle his shaky coalition. After the vote Sharon dismissed the five Shinui ministers, with the intention of inviting Labor and the Ashkenazi ultra-Orthodox party United Torah Judaism (UTJ) into the government. The entry of Labor (19 MKs) and UTJ (five MKs) would give Sharon 66 of the 120 seats in the Knesset.

While the Likud was engaged in internal battles over disengagement and possible coalition partners, Labor had plenty of infighting of its own. In late November, Ehud Barak—who, after losing the 2001 special prime ministerial election to Sharon, had said he was taking a break from politics—announced that he was returning to the fray and would seek the party leadership. During a debate at a Labor meeting on when to set the date for a leadership primary, Barak objected to delaying tactics by supporters of incumbent leader Shimon Peres, who wanted to wait until after coalition negotiations with the Likud had been resolved. Barak wanted an immediate decision.

At one point Barak rushed to the podium, snatched the microphone from the chairman of the meeting, and demanded a secret ballot on the issue, saying, "Anything else is an attempt to steal the party and we will not let this happen in the year 2004. Period." Barak came under sharp criticism for what was seen as unseemly conduct, and he tried to explain his action on Kol Yisrael Radio: "I am not happy about the way I was forced to act," he said. "But I was forced to do so because I want the party to have a real democracy." Barak's impulsiveness spurred a wave of hostility that seemed likely to dim the former prime minister's hopes of a political comeback. "The nerves of this man of cool temperament, who infiltrated the camp of terrorists in Lebanon disguised as a woman, didn't stand up to his attempt to infiltrate the camp of his own party," wrote *Yediot Aharonot* political commentator Sima Kadmon. Haim Ramon, a Labor rival and architect of the potential deal for Labor's entry into the Sharon government, reminded all those who needed to be reminded that Barak, after his crushing defeat in 2001, had fled politics. "For the past three-and-a-half years, we have tried to rise from the ruins to which Barak sent us," Ramon said. "He hasn't learned a thing."

Sharon, who had been denied the right to negotiate with Labor by the Likud Central Committee in August, returned to the same body in December to ask once again for authorization. In canvassing party members, he made it clear that there was only one alternative to a coalition with Labor — new elections, which would likely cost the Likud a large chunk of its 40 Knesset seats. Speaking to party MKs on December 6, he said that he, personally, was not afraid of elections. "The one who is likely to be hurt by early elections is the Likud itself," he said. This time, the party forum backed Sharon by 1,410 to 856, or 62 to 38 percent. Sharon then invited both Labor and United Torah Judaism to begin coalition talks.

Sharon broke off talks with Labor briefly on December 16, after Dalia Itzik, a former minister and Labor negotiator, bragged to a forum of her party that Sharon was "groveling" to get Labor into his government. "He's running after us, not we after him," she said. "After 30 years [the Likud] are seeing how right we were. They are contractors implementing our policy." Likud circles were furious, saying that Itzik's statements did not indicate a desire for genuine partnership. After Likud broke off the talks, these sources told *Ha'aretz,* "Let's see who grovels now."

But over the course of the next week, a coalition agreement was reached — almost. The only thing holding it up was Likud unwillingness to change the law allowing there to be only one deputy prime minister, a post held by Olmert, so as to allow Peres to hold the same title. (In the end, Labor would relent, Peres would be given a different title, and the new government would be formed in early January 2005.) On December 23, the Labor Central Committee provided a surprise by choosing two relatively young party men, Ophir Pines-Paz and Yitzhak Herzog, as the senior ministers for the eight cabinet posts allotted to the party (in addition to that to be held by Peres). The other ministers chosen, all of them former cabinet members, were, in order, Binyamin (Fuad) Ben-Eliezer,

Dalia Itzik, Shalom Simhon, Matan Vilna'i, and Haim Ramon. Pines-Paz later said he would take the Interior Ministry, the most influential post offered to Labor, while Herzog, son of the late president of Israel Chaim Herzog and grandson of an Ashkenazi chief rabbi, opted for the Ministry of Housing.

As the disengagement plan and the construction of a new coalition moved forward, the campaign against the pullout also intensified. On December 19, the Yesha Council urged its supporters to engage in nonviolent civil disobedience to block the evacuation of the Gaza and northern Samaria settlements. Council leader Pinhas Wallerstein said that Israelis should "violate the transfer law en mass and be ready to pay the price of mass imprisonment." Wallerstein said he was "not afraid to go to jail" in order to voice his opposition to "the immoral crime of forcibly uprooting Jews from their homes." "Sharon's dictatorship has pushed us into a corner," said council spokesman Yehoshua Mor-Yosef, maintaining that the prime minister had ridden roughshod over the settler movement's efforts to have the issue decided in a national referendum. Left-leaning MKs and leaders of Peace Now called on the attorney general to open a criminal investigation against Wallerstein.

Some settlers involved in the campaign to urge soldiers to refuse evacuation orders began wearing orange Stars of David, but the uproar this triggered among Holocaust survivors and others brought the practice to an end after a few days. The strongest comment came from Maj.-Gen Elazar Stern, head of the army's manpower division, who told Channel Two: "Settlers who wear an orange star are Holocaust deniers, because if what was done in the Holocaust resembles what we are doing to them, it means that the Holocaust was not so terrible or unique."

In a speech on December 20, Moshe Karadi, chief of the national police, said he worried that "public opposition" could prevent the disengagement from taking place. Karadi indicated he was assigning some 5,000 police officers—two for every adult Jewish settler in Gush Katif—to the operation, and that the army would supply at least the same number. "We believe that of all the burdens we have, the inability to fulfill a government decision is the worst of all," Karadi said to the annual conference of local government officials.

At the same time, Chief of Staff Ya'alon expressed concern over the refusal campaign, which boasted that it had enlisted "thousands" of adherents. Indeed, 34 reserve offices, including four battalion commanders, notified their brigade commanders that they intended to refuse orders to evacuate settlements. (It was later disclosed that these officers were all from settlements on the West Bank, and belonged to a regional defense unit that in any case was not going to be handling the evacuation.) There were allegations that Kach, the outlawed organization of followers of the late Rabbi Meir Kahane, was distributing the addresses of high-ranking Orthodox IDF officers, so that opponents of disengagement could demonstrate in front of their homes. *Ha'aretz* political commentator Akiva Eldar cited reports that Gaza settlers had mobilized both manpower and money from abroad to aid in their fight against disengagement. According to Eldar, the settlers claimed that they had thousands of inquiries from Christians, as well as Jews, who volunteered to come to Gush Katif and resist the evacuation. A group of a dozen right-wing Knesset members also pledged resistance. Effi Eitam, the former NRP leader, told Army Radio on December 24 that he and 11 others had signed a declaration to "prevent with our bodies the immoral and inhumane expulsion of thousands of heroic pioneer settlers."

But the settler front was far from solid. On December 26, Yonatan Bassi, the Orthodox kibbutz member chosen by Sharon to head the Disengagement Administration, announced that all the residents of the Gaza settlement of Pe'at Sadeh and five other settler families had agreed to move, as a group, to a moshav in the Negev. Speaking at a news conference, Bassi said he saw "the beginning of a great movement of settlers towards dialogue with us." Now that the political situation was becoming clearer, he continued, more and more individual settlers and "officials of settlements" were approaching the government to discuss relocation within Israel proper.

Even before the start of disengagement, there were mixed signals about what the government intended to do afterward. Deputy Prime Minister Olmert told the *Jerusalem Post* that a second disengagement plan, involving wider areas of the West Bank, was in the works. "There is no option of sitting and doing nothing," Olmert said. "Israel's interest requires a disengagement on a wider scale." But Prime Minister Sharon's bureau issued a statement denying there was any such plan. There would be no further disengagements, according to the statement, and the only peace program to which Israel would be a party was the "road map."

Marking a year since he unveiled his disengagement plan, Sharon presented a status report at the annual Herzliya Conference on National Security on December 16. "We stand before a window of unique opportunity," he said. "Who knows when we will have this opportunity in the future? We must not miss this opportunity to reach an agreement." The prime minister noted that whether the planned disengagement would lead to diplomatic progress depended on the PA's ability to move against terrorism, carry out internal reforms, and end anti-Israel incitement. Addressing the Palestinians, he declared: "We have no desire to rule over you, we have no desire to control your affairs." But Mahmoud Abbas, who had just replaced the deceased Arafat as the Palestinian leader (see below, p. 248), told the Associated Press that Sharon's insistence on retaining Israeli control over most of the West Bank settlements and all of Jerusalem made his plan "a disaster . . . closing all the doors to peace," and called on President Bush to withdraw his support for Israel's disengagement strategy.

DEFENSE AND SECURITY

The Fence

Construction of the controversial security fence on the West Bank continued in 2004, and was marked by intermittent confrontations between army and police guarding the construction and a smattering of Israeli and Palestinian demonstrators protesting it. The issue of the fence — overshadowed in the press and the public consciousness by the controversy over Prime Minister Sharon's disengagement plan — moved in and out of several courts over the course of the year.

On July 9, the International Court of Justice (ICJ) sitting in The Hague ruled that Israel's security fence violated international law and must be dismantled. The ruling, which surprised no one, was decided by 14 to 1, with only Thomas Buergenthal, an American judge, dissenting. The court said the fence (which it called a "wall," the term favored by the Palestinians) "cannot be justified by military exigencies or by the requirements of national security or public order." The majority of the judges was "not convinced that the specific course Israel has chosen for the wall was necessary to attain its security objectives," and "considers that the construction of the wall and its associate regime creates a 'fait accompli' on the ground that could well become permanent, in which case, and notwithstanding the formal characterization by Israel, it would be tantamount to de facto annexation." And therefore: "That construction, along with measures previously taken, thus severely impeded the exercise by the Palestinian people of its right to self-determination."

The ruling, requested by the UN General Assembly, was an "advisory opinion" and nonbinding. Even so, the tribunal's decisions carry moral and political weight, and some of its past rulings, such as the one in 1971 that declared South Africa's occupation of Namibia illegal, were used to pressure governments in the court of international public opinion.

The White House dismissed the ruling, reiterating its earlier position that the matter should never have been taken up by the court. "We do not believe that that's the appropriate forum to resolve what is a political issue. This is an issue that should be resolved through the process that has been put in place," presidential spokesman Scott McClellan said. On July 15, the U.S. House of Representatives passed HR713, deploring the General Assembly's misuse of the ICJ. The resolution, which passed 361-45, was introduced by Reps. Mike Pence (R., Ind.), Ileana Ros-Lehtinen (R., Fla.), and Shelley Berkley (D., Nev.). It charged that the ICJ ruling "seeks to infringe on Israel's right to self-defense" and condemned the PA for failing to engage in a sustained fight against terror. "By condemning the ruling of the International Court of Justice, Congress has given voice to the compassion and commitment that the American people feel toward our precious ally Israel," said Congressman Pence.

Yasir Arafat, in contrast, praised the decision. According to Reuters, he told reporters, "This is an excellent decision. We thank the court in The Hague. This is a victory for the Palestinian people and for all the free peoples of the world." PA prime minister Ahmed Qurei (Abu Ala) agreed, saying that the court had now made clear "that this racist wall is illegal to the root, and Israel should stop building it and take down what has already been built of this wall."

Sharon aide and spokesman Ra'anan Gissin belittled the court's action. "After all the rancor dies, this resolution will find its place in the garbage can of history. The court has made an unjust ruling denying Israel its right of self-defense," he said. Speaking before the July 11 cabinet meeting, Sharon himself drew a connection between the ICJ ruling and a terror attack in Tel Aviv that had just taken place. He said: "I want to make clear that Israel categorically rejects the advisory opinion . . . . It is one-sided, based on political considerations, and totally ignores the reason for building the fence, which is Palestinian terrorism." The court, he said, dealt only with the Israeli response, "which happens to be the most appropriate way to combat the terrorists." Noting the latest terror incident, the prime minister said that "it is not for nothing that the Palestinians opposed the building of the fence; they know full well that it will make it very difficult for them to continue their murderous attacks."

On July 20, the UN General Assembly voted 150-6, with 10 abstentions, to endorse the ICJ decision, and called on member states to comply with their obligations under it, including "not to recognize the illegal situation resulting from the construction of the wall in the occupied Palestinian territory, including in and around East Jerusalem," and "not to render aid or assistance in maintaining the situation created by such construction." The six states voting against the resolution were Australia, the Federated States of Micronesia, Israel, Marshall Islands, Tuvalu, and the U.S. Abstaining were Cameroon, Canada, El Salvador, Nauru, Papua New Guinea, the Solomon Islands, Tonga, Uganda, Uruguay, and Vanuatu. After the vote, Dan Gillerman, Israel's ambassador to the UN, wryly remarked, "Thank God the fate of Israel and of the Jewish people is not decided in this hall."

To be sure, the fence was a matter of some controversy in Israel. At the time of the court ruling, approximately one-third of the projected 425-mile-long barrier had been completed, made up of a combination of barbed wire, electronic fences, ditches, and, in some places, huge concrete slabs. There was virtual unanimity among Israelis about the legitimate security function served by the barrier, as shown by the dramatic drop in the number of suicide attacks since sections of it had gone up, but its precise route was another matter. In a series of rulings, the Israeli High Court of Justice had ordered the rerouting of certain portions that it believed caused undo hardships to Palestinians by cutting them off from farmland, schools, and hospitals.

The latest such decision came on June 30, not long before the ICJ ruling, when the Israeli court ordered the Defense Ministry to reroute a 30–40 km portion of the fence northwest of Jerusalem, finding that the route "established for the security fence, which separates the local inhabitants from their agricultural lands, injured the local [Palestinian] inhabitants in a severe and acute way, while violating their rights under humanitarian international law." An alternative route would have to be found "which will provide a fitting, if not an ideal, solution for the security considerations." At the same time, the court affirmed that Israel had a legal right to build the barrier. Ze'ev Boim, the deputy defense minister, commented that the court ruling would of course be honored, even though the delay involved meant that the fence would not be completed until 2006, putting the lives and welfare of tens of thousands of Jerusalemites at risk.

Visiting Israel on September 14, German interior minister Otto Schily rejected the comparison made by some in his country between Israel's fence and the Berlin Wall. "Those who draw comparisons with the Berlin Wall are wrong, because it does not shut people in and deprive them of their freedom," he told Deutschlandfunk Radio. "Its purpose is to protect Israel from terrorists."

At year's end Israel's Ministry of Defense estimated that at least 90 percent of planned terror attacks had been prevented largely by the fence. Ironically, the clearest indication of the barrier's utility came from the successful terrorist attacks. In almost all cases, the perpetrator crossed into Israel at a location where the fence was not yet built, or else was forced by the fence to take a circuitous route into Israel and thus not be able to reach the populated area originally targeted for terror.

Israelis and Palestinians

Although the intifada that broke out in late September 2000 (see AJYB 2001, pp. 494–502 and subsequent volumes) had clearly lost much of its steam, episodes of violence and Israeli measures to cope with them continued on into 2004.

On January 19, an Israeli soldier was killed by a Hezballah missile while clearing mines along the Lebanese border, and the next day Israeli jets hit Hezballah targets in the area. Clashes continued intermittently all along the Gaza Strip during the month. On January 28, 13 Palestinians were reported killed in a particularly fierce encounter near Netzarim, the Jewish settlement located virtually in the midst of Gaza City. Eleven Israelis were killed and over 50 wounded in a January 29 bomb attack on a No. 19 Egged bus near the corner of Gaza Road and Arlozorov Street in Jerusalem's Rehavia neighborhood.

The bodies of soldiers Benny Avraham, Avi Avitan, and Omar Sueid, killed by Hezballah in October 2000 at Har Dov on the Lebanese border (see AJYB 2001, p. 484), were laid to rest on January 30, a day after they were returned to Israel in a deal that involved the freeing of 436 Palestinian and Arab prisoners. The exchange took place in Germany, whose government facilitated it (for details see below, p. 416).

As part of the arrangement, reserve colonel Elhanan Tannenbaum was freed after over three years in Hezballah captivity. Following a brief reunion with his family, Tannenbaum began the lengthy process of interrogation by police and security officials. After first claiming that he had been seized while in Lebanon in search of information about missing airman Ron Arad, Tannenbaum told his interrogators that he actually had been kidnapped in Dubai where he had gone to close a drug deal.

That Israel had gone to such lengths to free a drug dealer triggered severe criticism. The daily *Ma'ariv* reported that during the 1970s Tannenbaum's father-in-law had managed the Sharon family ranch and had been part owner of a business together with Sharon's late wife. Sharon dismissed suggestions that these connections had anything to do with the deal, even though, according to *Ma'ariv,* the prime minister had met eight times with Tannenbaum's family, seeing them far more frequently than the kin of other missing Israelis. On March 30, after 70 days of interrogation by Israeli police and security agents, Tannenbaum was placed under house arrest at the home of his sister in Herzliyah. Although he was suspected of fraud, forgery, and planning to smuggle drugs into Israel—apparently as part of an attempt to cover his heavy debts—it was decided, in the end, not to press charges.

Aziz Mahmoud al-Shami, a member of the Islamic Jihad's military wing, was killed in an Israeli helicopter attack on his car, on a Gaza City street, on February 7. Shami, 37, had been involved in many terror attacks, Israeli sources said, including the double suicide bombing near a bus stop at the Beit Lid intersection, north of Tel Aviv, in 1995, in which 22 Israeli soldiers and civilians were killed.

The army, on February 16, informed the parents of three Lebanon war MIAs, Zechariah Baumel, Yehudah Katz, and Zvi Feldman, that the men had been formally designated as fallen soldiers whose place of burial is unknown, and therefore the search for them would end. They had been unaccounted for since their tanks were ambushed by Syrians in the Lebanese village of Sultan Yakub on June 12, 1982. But the families fought the decision, and in November, the army reversed itself and returned the missing soldiers to the MIA category.

In late February, the long-simmering crisis between PA leader Yasir Arafat and his prime minister, Ahmed Qurei (Abu Ala), intensified. In a February 14 meeting at Arafat's Mu'qata headquarters in Ramallah, Abu Ala reportedly threatened to resign if Arafat did not give in to European Union demands for transparency in the payment of salaries to security personnel. He said that the PA coffers were empty, and the EU would not provide funds to pay salaries unless its requests for transparency were met. In a related development, Israeli security forces confiscated over $8 million from Arab banks in Ramallah on February 25, claiming it came from accounts linked to Islamic Jihad, Hamas, and Hezballah. Israel said the confiscated money would be used on "projects that benefit Palestinian welfare."

Israeli contacts with the Palestinians continued on a low key. On February 26, Weisglass and Shalom Turgeman, a Sharon political adviser, met with Hassan Abu Libdeh, an aide to Abu Ala, in the hope of preparing for a meeting between Sharon and the PA prime minister. Weisglass called the meeting—which had been delayed because of the January 29 bombing in Jerusalem—"positive and effective."

Four Palestinian terrorists and two Palestinian policemen who tried to stop them were killed during an abortive March 6 bombing attack at the VIP crossing of the Erez checkpoint in Gaza. The following day, Israeli troops conducting a raid near Gaza's al-Burej refugee camp and killed 14 Palestinians in what the Associated Press called the "deadliest confrontation in Gaza in 17 months." The battle pitted hundreds of Palestinians armed with assault rifles against Israeli troops backed by helicopters and tanks. That afternoon, tens of thousands of Palestinians participated in the funeral services of those who were killed. Avi Pazner, speaking for Israel, said that "terrorism is pouring out of this refugee camp, and we have to stop it." Palestinian cabinet minister Sa'eb Erakat had a different view. "At a time when they are speaking about withdrawing from Gaza," he said, "they are destroying Gaza."

On March 14, four Palestinian men who had gone on trial in February for the bomb attack of October 15, 2003, that killed three U.S. embassy security men near Erez, were released by a Palestinian court because of lack of evidence. The U.S. had offered a $5-million reward for the arrest and conviction of the perpetrators, and its patience was running thin. On May 7, the U.S. announced that in light of PA's failure to find those responsible, it had stopped funding two water-development projects in the Gaza Strip. Speaking to a congressional hearing on the Middle East in July, Deputy Assistant Secretary of State David Satterfield said: "There has been no satisfactory resolution of this case. We can only conclude that there has been a political decision taken by the chairman [Arafat] to block further progress in the investigation."

Security forces apprehended a ten-year-old boy on March 15 who was transporting a bag with explosives. Apparently, the material was intended to be used by operatives of Fatah's Tanzim in a terror attack on Israelis. The boy had been given the bag to transfer across a roadblock near Nablus for a fee, and the Israelis freed him because he had been ignorant of its contents.

On March 19, residents of the peaceful French Hill neighborhood, on the slopes of Mt. Scopus in East Jerusalem and not far from the Hebrew University, were shocked when Elias Khoury, 20, a Hebrew University student and son of a prominent East Jerusalem attorney, was killed in a drive-by shooting while jogging. Al-Aqsa Martyrs Brigades apologized when it learned that the victim was not a Jew, but a Christian Arab. The killers were arrested on April 23, stopped by police while on their way to another attack in the French Hill area. The men, who belonged to no official terror organization, also confessed to the shooting of another Israeli in the Givat Hamivtar neighborhood between Ramat Eshkol and French Hill.

Targeting Terror

In mid-March, large numbers of Israeli troops deployed just outside the Gaza Strip amid reports that Sharon had ordered the IDF and the Shin Bet secret service to act against leaders of the terror groups. The IDF, in a report to the security cabinet, recommended "making the organizations pay a stiff price" in Gaza before implementation of disengagement, since it was vital to prevent these groups, particularly Hamas, from creating the sense that the Israeli move was actually flight under fire, and thus, in their view, a repetition of the pattern created by the Israeli withdrawal from southern Lebanon in 2000.

Action was not long in coming. In a sunrise helicopter attack on March 22, Israeli missiles killed Sheikh Ahmed Yassin, the founder and spiritual leader of Hamas, and seven others. Yassin, 66, had been confined to a wheelchair by an injury he suffered at the age of 12. He became affiliated with the Muslim Brotherhood in the 1950s, while studying at Cairo's Ein Shams University. Arrested in 1983 by Israel, he was sentenced to 13 years in prison on charges of weapons possession and forming an anti-Israel underground organization. He was released in 1985 as part of a prisoner exchange between Israel and the Popular Front for the Liberation of Palestine, and founded Hamas in 1987, just before the start of the first intifada. He was arrested again in 1989 and sentenced to life in prison on a variety of charges, including inciting the killing of Israeli soldiers. But in 1997, Yassin was released in a deal with Jordan for the freedom of two Israeli agents who were involved in a botched attempt on the life of Khaled Masha'al, a key Hamas leader then based in Amman. Yassin was virtually blind, had little hearing, and suffered from various respiratory diseases, but remained a charismatic figure with great influence as long as he lived. After the assassination, Dr. Abdel Aziz Rantisi, now the top Hamas leader in Gaza, pledged that Sharon and other Israeli leaders "will never feel security and safety," and called President Bush "an enemy of God and Islam." Six Israelis were hurt in two attacks in the Tel Aviv area hours after Yassin was killed: three were wounded by a Palestinian wielding an ax near an army installation in Ramat Gan, and the three others were stabbed on a Jaffa bus.

While the Israeli consensus was that the blind sheikh "had it coming to him," there were differences of opinion about the wisdom of the assassination. The left-leaning *Ha'aretz* called the move "wrongheaded" and expressed concern that it might trigger a wave of terror. The *Jerusalem Post,* which leaned to the right, said that "compared to Arab ruthlessness against Muslim fanatics, Israel uses kid gloves." Dr. Reuven Paz of the Interdisciplinary Center in Herzliya, an expert on Islamic terror, said he was "not one of those who uncorked a bottle of champagne upon hearing the news of Yassin's killing, though I assume some in the IDF did celebrate." Paz noted that, in some ways, Yassin was a moderate: he did not support Osama bin Laden, he opposed terror attacks outside Israel and the territories, and saw the struggle against the Jewish state as a fight against occupation. Far from considering the assassination as a death blow for Hamas, Paz felt that it would adversely affect the Palestinian Authority and weaken Gaza security chief Muhammad Dahlan, on whom the U.S. pinned high hopes.

In a statement issued on the day of the assassination, EU foreign ministers said that Hamas was guilty of "atrocities . . . which have resulted in the deaths of hundreds of Israelis" and that Israel had the right to protect itself against terrorism. But they also noted that "Israel is not, however, entitled to carry out extrajudicial killings" and said that Yassin's assassination "has inflamed the situation . . . . Violence is no substitute for the political negotiations which are necessary for a just and lasting settlement."

On March 25, the U.S. vetoed an Algerian-sponsored resolution condemning Israel for the Yassin assassination. Ambassador John Negroponte, the U.S. representative, called the resolution unbalanced since it failed to take into account the "terrorist atrocities" committed by Hamas. The American veto came after Algeria had refused to add language condemning Hamas or other terror groups. The vote was 11-1, with Great Britain, Germany, and Romania abstaining.

One indirect result of the Yassin killing was the collapse of the Arab League summit, which had been scheduled for Tunis at the end of March. Arab leaders had hoped to use the conference to relaunch the Saudi-crafted peace initiative of 2002 that offered peace to Israel in return for withdrawal from all lands overrun in the 1967 war (see AJYB 2003, pp. 195–98), and to submit their own proposals for political reforms in the PA. But widespread outrage in the Arab world made it politically risky for some of the Arab states to pursue a peace initiative

Hamas promised a stepped-up campaign of suicide bombings in revenge for the assassination. But the only incident over the next two week was a bombing at the Erez industrial zone at the northern edge of the Gaza Strip in which one Israeli was killed. Even so, security forces were on high alert over the Passover holiday, guarding synagogues, national parks, markets, and shopping malls, and, according to an Army Radio report, ten attempted suicide bomb attacks on Israeli targets were thwarted during that week. Two of these were to have been carried out by women, one was supposed to be a triple suicide bombing in a large Israeli city, and another was to have been carried out with a device containing AIDS-infected blood.

Immediately after Passover, on April 17, missiles fired from an Israeli helicopter killed Abdel Aziz Rantisi, who had replaced Sheikh Yassin at the head of Hamas. Rantisi was killed shortly before 9 p.m., together with one of his bodyguards and his driver. Ten other people, including Rantisi's wife, were injured in the attack, which occurred on a street in the Sheikh Radwan neighborhood of Gaza City and about 100 meters from Yassin's grave. At Rantisi's funeral, in which thousands participated, new Hamas leader Ahmed Baher pledged vengeance, at a time of Hamas's choosing. He said: "There is no doubt that the assassinations of Yassin and Rantisi are losses to the Hamas movement. But the response will come at a suitable time. Jihad will continue. All we need is patience." But Baher's bluster came as tighter Israeli security precautions, as well as offensive actions against key men in the resistance movement, made terror operations more difficult for Hamas.

Two Israeli Arabs were arrested on April 18 and accused of the July 2003 killing of Cpl. Oleg Shaichat, who was picked up while hitchhiking and murdered near his Upper Nazareth home (see AJYB 2004, p. 174). They were nabbed after a shooting attack in which Shaichat's M-16 rifle was used. A few weeks later, several residents of Kafr Kana who had been accused of the Shaichat killing and held by the authorities for ten months were released and the charges against them dropped.

Israeli troops killed four Palestinians on April 23. Three were militants from the Fatah movement in Qualqilya, in the northern West Bank, who were shot by a special unit of Israeli troops disguised as Arabs. The fourth fatality was Yasir Abu Leimun, who was killed in Taluza, north of Nablus. Abu Leimun's wife, Dalal, said that her late husband, who taught hospital management at the Arab-American University in Jenin, had no political affiliation. A week later, after an investigation by the IDF Central Command, the army apologized for the killing. It explained that Abu Leimun had wandered into an area where Israeli troops were chasing two wanted men, and that he was dressed like the suspects.

Pregnant mother Tali Hatuel, 34, and her four young daughters, all 11 or under, were killed by terrorists near the entrance to the Gush Katif settlement bloc in the southern Gaza Strip on May 2. Troops in the area rushed to the rescue after a joint Palestinian force, including members of Islamic Jihad and Al-Aqsa Martyrs Brigades, fired on Hatuel's car, disabling it, but they did not arrive in time to stop the execution-style killings. Later in the day, missiles fired by Israeli helicopters hit a 14-story building in the center of Gaza City. Earlier the same day, security personnel at the Karni crossing in the north-central Gaza Strip found an explosives belt in a truck filled with produce bound for Israel.

On May 4, the PA released funds it had frozen nine months earlier from bank accounts belonging to several charities affiliated to Dawa, the civilian arm of Hamas. The money was transferred to the Gaza bank accounts of the charities, including that of Al-Mujamma al-Islami, founded by Sheikh Yassin.

Rising Tensions

On May 11, six Israeli soldiers were killed in Gaza's Zeitoun neighborhood when the explosives-laden armored personnel carrier in which they were riding hit a booby-trapped mine during an incursion to blow up Qassam missile workshops. Hamas and Islamic Jihad displayed what they said were body parts of the six soldiers. "We possess the remains of your bodies that were thrown into the streets of Gaza," the two organizations said in a statement. Al-Jazeera, the Arabic-language satellite channel, broadcast a video showing what it said were two masked Islamic Jihad activists with what they claimed to be the head of an Israeli soldier on the table before them. Maj. Gen. Dan Harel, head of the IDF's Southern Command, told reporters his troops would remain in Zeitoun until the remains of their comrades were recovered. Those remains were subsequently handed over to Israel by representatives of the Palestinian Red Crescent Society.

The next day, five members of the IDF's anti-tunnel unit were killed when a rocket-propelled grenade (RPG) scored a direct hit on their armored personnel carrier, which was filled with explosives to blow up smuggling tunnels between Gaza and Egyptian Sinai, in the so-called Philadelphi Corridor at the southern end of the Gaza Strip. For most of the following day, Israeli troops scoured the sandy area searching for body parts of their fallen comrades. Over the ensuing days, 29 Palestinians were killed and more than 150 wounded in clashes with Israeli troops, PA sources said. Israeli troops began demolishing Palestinian homes in an effort to widen the narrow corridor, but on May 16 Israel's High Court of Justice issued a restraining order barring these demolitions.

On May 14, Syrian president Bashar al-Assad rejected an American demand that he expel Hamas and Islamic Jihad leaders—including Khaled Masha'al of Hamas and Ramadan Abdallah Shami of Jihad—from Damascus. The Syrian leader claimed that they "are not leaders, they are political spokesmen." In addition, he told visiting American editors, the men "can only return to their home country, and if they do that Israel will imprison them."

On May 15, Yasir Arafat delivered a televised speech marking the 56th anniversary of the Nakba (Disaster), as the Palestinians call Israel's successful battle for independence in 1948. The PA leader called on his people to "terrorize the enemy." Arafat said: "Acts of sacrifice, determination and revolution have sent a message to the world that Palestine is the homeland of the Palestinian nation and it has no other, and it will not accept an alternative to its homeland." But others in the Palestinian leadership were delivering different messages. Abu Ala, who met with Secretary of State Powell at Amman Airport, said that the two had "very, very constructive" talks. Other PA officials, including Foreign Minister Nabil Shaath, indicated they were ready for a cease-fire with Israel as a step towards implementing the "road map." From Damascus, however, Hamas leader Masha'al, on May 18, rejected any such idea, charging that Israel had launched a "war of annihilation" against the Palestinians. "The choice is between death and death," Masha'al told the Associated Press.

Israel launched a major operation into the Gaza Strip on May 17. At least ten Palestinians were killed two days later when an IDF tank fired a shell that passed through an abandoned building and hit a group of about 3,000 marchers demonstrating against house demolitions in the Tel Sultan neighborhood of Rafiah, at the southern end of the Gaza Strip. According to Palestinians, most of those killed—and most of the demonstrators—were schoolchildren. Military sources said the shell was fired as a warning, to prevent the demonstrators from getting too close to the Israeli forces. In the past, they noted, armed militants had used demonstrators, including children, as cover in order to attack Israelis.

President Bush declined to comment directly on the attack, but, speaking to reporters at the White House, he said: "I continue to urge restraint. It is essential that people respect innocent life in order for us to achieve peace." Russia denounced the Israeli action as a "disproportionate use of force," and British prime minister Tony Blair said it was "unacceptable and wrong."

At the Knesset, which was in session when news of the Rafiah mishap broke, MK Muhammad Barakeh of the largely Arab party Hadash called the incident a "massacre" and demanded an international inquiry. Likud MK Yuval Steinitz, chairman of the Foreign Affairs and Defense Committee, said the events were "tragic," but noted that the Palestinians frequently sent civilians into danger areas on purpose. MK Ran Cohen of Meretz said the army should get out of Rafiah immediately.

A Tel Aviv District Court convicted Marwan Barghouti of five counts of murder on May 20. Leader of the Fatah Tanzim in the West Bank and one of the most popular Palestinian leaders, Barghouti had been captured during Operation Defensive Shield in 2002. The court acquitted him of direct involvement in 21 other slayings, ruling that the prosecution had not demonstrated that Barghouti was involved in their planning. Bearded, manacled, and wearing a blue prison uniform, Barghouti reiterated what he had said many times during his trial, that he did not recognize the authority of the "court of occupation." He added: "So long as the occupation continues, the uprising will not stop. As long as Palestinian mothers are weeping, Israeli mothers will also weep." He said he was "against killing innocents on either side." Throughout the trial, Barghouti had insisted he was an elected politician, not a terrorist leader, and that "we want freedom and a state, just like the Israelis."

Sentencing came on June 6, when Barghouti was given five life terms plus 40 years in jail for the killings, which included the death of a Greek monk on the outskirts of Jerusalem in 2001.

A report by Amnesty International released on May 26 accused Israel of killing some 600 Palestinians, including 100 children, during the course of 2003. The organization criticized Israel for abuses that it claimed constituted war crimes, including the use of human shields, wanton destruction of property, obstruction of medical assistance, and targeting of medical personnel. (Israel claimed that Palestinian groups used ambulances to transport terrorists and their materiel.) At the same time, Amnesty condemned the "deliberate targeting of civilians by Palestinian armed groups," viewing that also as a "crime against humanity." In a separate document, Amnesty urged Israel to investigate the deaths of Asuma al-Mughayr, 16, and her brother Ahmad, 13, who, it alleged, were shot in the head on the roof of their Rafiah home while collecting laundry and feeding pigeons.

According to *Ha'aretz*, 111 Palestinians, including 31 noncombatant civilians, were killed by the army in the territories during May. This figure was double the 55 killed in April and the highest monthly figure since Operation Defensive Shield on the West Bank in 2002. Defense Minister

Mofaz said that 18 Palestinians planning to carry out suicide bombings were arrested in May. Six more were about to be smuggled from Gaza into Israel in early June, but security services foiled the plan.

Prime Minister Sharon told the cabinet on June 20 that Israel would not dig a water-filled trench to block access along the southern end of the Gaza Strip, in the Philadelphi Corridor, without Egypt's consent. The Defense Ministry had already called for bids on a 4-km long, 100–120-meter wide, 15–25-meter deep excavation to inhibit the digging of tunnels used to smuggle arms into Gaza from Egypt. The ministry said it was standard practice to invite bids prior to the political echelon reaching a decision on a project.

In late June, the IDF said it was looking into allegations of abuse raised in "Breaking the Silence: Soldiers Tell About Hebron," a display of photographs and videos collected by four ex-soldiers who did military service in that city. The exhibit painted an extremely unflattering portrait of the interaction between Israeli forces and the over 100,000 Palestinian residents of Hebron, causing considerable controversy and garnering much press attention while it was on display at the Gallery of Geographic Photography in the Yad Eliyahu section of Tel Aviv.

Yasir Arafat, in a rare interview with an Israeli newspaper, told *Ha'aretz,* in an article published June 18, that his recognition of Israel's right to remain a Jewish state logically implied an acceptance of the idea that the Palestinian "right of return" may be limited. Arafat said it is "clear and obvious" that the refugee problem needed to be addressed in a way that did not change the Jewish character of Israel.

A striking 63.7-percent majority of the Israeli Jewish public thought that the government should encourage the emigration of Israeli Arabs, according to a Haifa University poll released on June 21. Conducted by school's National Security Studies Center and supervised by Prof. Gavriel Ben-David, the poll found that 48.6 percent of Israeli Jews felt the government was overly sympathetic to Israeli Arabs, 55.3 percent considered Israeli Arabs a danger to national security, and 45.3 percent favored depriving them of the right to vote and hold national office. About a quarter of those polled said they would think about voting for an extremist party such as the outlawed Kach, if such a party were allowed on the ballot. The data also showed hostility towards foreign workers: 72.1 percent backed the imposition of entry restrictions on such laborers, and 54 percent said their presence burdened the Israeli economy. The survey was based on the responses of 1,016 Jewish Israelis.

A suicide bomber who had planned to attack Caffit, a café on busy

Emek Refa'im Street in Jerusalem's German Colony, on July 13, backed down at the last minute, security forces disclosed on July 18. Malek Nasser al-Din, 41, intended to shoot the guard at the entrance and then to blow himself up inside, but had second thoughts and returned to his home in Hebron. Two days later he was killed in a fight with security forces who came to arrest him. Another suicide-bomb attempt, in the Sharon region north of Tel Aviv, on July 14, was aborted when security officers arrested two men trying to smuggle an explosive device into Israel in the upholstery of an armchair. This was the fifth bomb attack prevented since the beginning of July and the 87th since the start of 2004.

A Long, Hot Summer

Heavy clashes among Palestinian factions forced Arafat, on July 19, to cancel the appointment of his nephew, Musa Arafat, as head of the PA's national security apparatus. Arafat had originally appointed the nephew—then head of military intelligence—to bring some order to Gaza, which was rapidly falling into chaos as elements demanding reforms in the PA conducted a series of kidnappings of Arafat loyalists. But the appointment angered supporters of Muhammad Dahlan, formerly the security affairs minister in Gaza and a major force behind the reform movement, and anti-Arafat demonstrations broke out. Adding to the tension was a report in *Ha'aretz* that Musa Arafat had close ties with an extensive smuggling network at the southern end of the Gaza Strip. The military wing of Fatah, Yasir Arafat's own party, came out against the new powers for Musa Arafat, and so the PA leader had to rescind the appointment.

If more evidence was needed that the Palestinian leadership needed to establish order, it came the next day, when former PA information minister Nabil Amir was wounded by unknown gunmen. Yasir Arafat ordered police to investigate, and cabinet minister Sa'eb Erakat emphasized the seriousness of the situation. "If we can't restore public order and law . . . this will bring the most damage to the Palestinian people and their cause," he said. "It's the whole social fabric that is collapsing now."

On July 22, four days after refusing an offer by Qurei to resign as prime minister, Arafat finally agreed to give him full authority over the various overlapping PA security forces. But the prime minister found it impossible to exert control over the bewilderingly complex organizational apparatus, much of which still owed allegiance to Arafat, and unrest continued. Protesters burned a police station in Gaza City on July 24, and briefly took over an administrative building in the southern part of the Strip. Secretary of State Powell, on a visit to Budapest on July 27, expressed exasperation. What was needed, he said, was "real action that transfers power to the prime minister of the Palestinian people and the PA, and the consolidation of security services, with those consolidated services under the direction of the prime minister."

Hassan Za'anun, 16, was killed by members of the Al-Aqsa Martyrs Brigades on July 23, in a clash over whether the militants could use the Za'anun family's property in Beit Hanun, at the northern edge of the Gaza Strip, for firing Qassam rockets in the direction of the Israeli town of Sderot. According to a *Ha'aretz* report, six members of Al-Aqsa arrived in a van at the Za'anun property and set up a Qassam launcher near the family's home. Members of the family—most likely fearing that their house would be destroyed by Israeli return fire—tried to drive the militants off with sticks and rocks, but the latter opened fire, killing Hassan.

On the morning of July 19, Ghaleb Awali, a Hezballah leader, was killed in a car-bombing in Beirut. Hezballah immediately blamed Israel and threatened revenge, inducing Israel to increase its army alert along the northern border. Brig. Gen. Yossi Kuperwasser, chief of army intelligence research, met with Knesset members that day and raised the possibility that Iran might arm Hezballah with chemical weapons.

A bombing at the Qalandiya checkpoint north of Jerusalem on August 11 killed two Palestinian bystanders and wounded six Israeli border policemen and 13 other Palestinians. Security forces said that terrorists from the Al-Aqsa Martrys Brigades had been trying to smuggle the bomb into Israel.

A senior U.N. official said on August 12 that both Israel and the PA were violating international obligations. Kieran Prendergast, undersecretary for political affairs, made the statement in what he called a "depressingly familiar" monthly briefing. Israel, he said, was not living up to its obligation "to protect Palestinian civilians and not to destroy their property unless this is rendered absolutely necessary by military operations," adding that the scale of destruction in IDF operations "raises concerns about collective punishment." At the same time, acknowledged Prendergast, the PA had failed to protect Israeli citizens from attack. Prendergast noted what he called a new pattern of Qassam and mortar attacks by the Palestinians on Israeli territory, followed by Israeli helicopter attacks into Gaza. "For each side, the actions of the other does not in any way excuse it from fulfilling its obligations,' he asserted.

On August 31, 16 Israelis were killed and about 100 wounded in a double bus bombing in Beersheba, the "capital of the Negev," which had, until then, been barely touched by terror attacks since the beginning of the intifada. The buses were traveling along Beersheba's main street, Rager Boulevard, near the city hall. Hamas in Hebron claimed responsibility for the attack.

Saying that many of their demands for improved conditions had been met, almost 4,000 Palestinian security prisoners in Israeli jails ended an 18-day hunger strike on September 2. Israel Prison Service sources denied that any demands had been agreed to. Five days later, on September 7, Israel released 188 of the prisoners, citing lack of space.

Focus on Gaza

Army units destroyed a tunnel ten meters deep under a house in Deir al-Balah, in the Gaza Strip, on September 2. It was dug in the direction of the Kfar Darom settlement, half a kilometer away. As intermittent violence in the Strip continued, at least 14 militants were killed in a September 7 attack by Israeli helicopters on a Hamas training camp there.

The army announced on September 19 that it had developed and installed a new kind of radar that would give residents of Sderot 15–20 seconds of warning that Palestinian Qassam rockets had been fired at the town. But Sderot, near the border with the Gaza Strip, was hit by a Qassam the very next day, and subsequently continued to endure intermittent attacks. In response, Israeli helicopters attacked a Hamas training area on a soccer field in Sajaiyeh, a neighborhood in eastern Gaza City near the border fence with Israel. Thirteen people were killed in the rocket raid on what Israel called a facility for training terrorists and Hamas called a summer camp for Palestinian youths.

Izz a-Din al-Sheikh Khalil, a senior Hamas leader, was killed by a car bomb in Damascus on September 26. According to a report in *Ha'aretz,* Israeli security sources acknowledged that Israel was involved in the killing of Khalil, 42, whose main "claim to fame" was his role in training Yehiya Ayyash, Hamas's legendary bomb-making engineer who was killed when his booby-trapped cell phone exploded in January 1996. Khalil, expelled from Gaza to Syria in 1992, was thought to be in charge of Hamas military activities outside the territories. A Hamas spokesman vowed revenge, saying: "All these assassinations will not deter Hamas or stop it from carrying out its policies and its program. It shows that there is no use for a political solution to this conflict." The killing came just days after *Al-Hayat,* a London-based Arabic-language newspaper, reported that the intelligence service of an unnamed Arab state had passed on detailed information about the movements and residences of Hamas leaders outside the territories to the Mossad.

On September 30, Israel responded to repeated mortar and Qassam rocket attacks on Gush Katif and the northern Negev town of Sderot with what it called Operation Days of Penitence, largely in and around the Jabalya refugee camp in Gaza. A proposed UN Security Council resolution to condemn the Israeli action was vetoed by the U.S., on the grounds that it did not also condemn terrorism against Israel. The operation, which lasted until October 15, claimed about 100 Palestinian lives. The IDF claimed that the action seriously weakened the Hamas infrastructure in Gaza, but the rocket attacks continued.

The operation also served as the backdrop to a confrontation between Israel and UNRWA, the United Nations Relief and Works Administration, which provided assistance to Palestinians living in refugee camps. Israel had long charged the agency with turning a blind eye to terrorist incitement in the camps. On October 3, Peter Hansen, the UNRWA commissioner-general, caused a furor in Israel when he told an interviewer for the Canadian station CBC: "I am sure that there are Hamas members on the UNRWA payroll, and I don't see that as a crime." He went on to note that since Hamas had a political wing and therefore not everyone associated with the group was a militant, "we do not do political vetting and exclude people from one persuasion as against another."

The next day, even as Hansen's office was issuing a clarification claiming that he had meant Hamas "sympathizers" and not "members," and while the Security Council was deliberating the resolution condemning Israel, Israel's UN delegation presented a videotape to Secretary General Kofi Annan allegedly showing a Palestinian loading a Qassam rocket into the back of a van clearly marked "UN." Dan Gillerman, Israel's UN ambassador, called for an investigation of the incident and the firing of Hansen. After viewing the video, Hansen insisted that the item placed in the van was not a weapon but a folded stretcher. The following day, October 5, the IDF removed the video from its Web site and issued a statement saying: "The IDF is reviewing the analysis of the footage in which UNRWA vehicles are seen involved in suspicious activity in the combat zone in Gaza." Israel did not retract its charge, however. In the course of its investigation, Israel arrested 13 Palestinian employees of various UN bodies on suspicion of involvement in terror, and collected testimony about UN staff members who allegedly aided terrorists. A UN team was set up to investigate the charges.

An Israeli helicopter strike hit the Subaru automobile of Bashir Jabash, a senior Islamic Jihad commander in the Gaza Strip, on October 5; he and three other occupants of the car were killed. Israel considered Jabash, 38, responsible for the deaths of at least eight Israelis.

Another killing of a Palestinian that same day created a furor. Iman al-Hams, a 13-year-old Palestinian girl, was shot to death when she wandered close to IDF positions while walking to school in the Rafiah refugee camp. After she was initially shot, the company commander "confirmed the kill" by pumping bullets into the girl's body at close range. That officer first claimed he had been acting according to regulations, but soldiers from the company told the press about the officer's conduct and reports appeared in the media, including a broadcast on "Fact," a popular Channel Two news show, of an audiotape of the incident that seemingly incriminated the commander. The army initiated legal proceedings against him on a number of grounds, including obstruction of justice for attempting to stop the soldiers under his command from talking about the incident.

On October 7, twin terror bombings at resort hotels in Egyptian Sinai killed 32 people, 12 of them Israelis, and wounded about 120. The attacks took place at the Taba Hilton and Ras a-Satan, both heavily frequented by Israelis. Though initial reports indicated the involvement of Al Qaeda-affiliated terrorists, the Egyptians arrested local people they said carried out the atrocities.

Imad Kawasma, the head of the Hamas military wing in Hebron, surrendered to Israelis who had surrounded the safe house where he was hiding on October 13. Kawasma had dispatched the two suicide bombers responsible for the double bomb attack in Beersheba on August 31, in which 16 people were killed (see above, pp. 242–43). Those two bombers were Ahmad Kawasma and Nisam Ja'abari, both members of prominent Palestinian clans in Hebron.

Musa Arafat, Yasir Arafat's nephew whose appointment as head of PA security in July had raised so much opposition that it had to be withdrawn, escaped unharmed when a car bomb exploded near his convoy in Gaza City on October 13. Palestinian sources acknowledged that the bomb was Palestinian, not Israeli.

Conflict continued about the Philadelphi Corridor at the southern end of the Gaza Strip, as Israeli forces fought a continuing battle against Palestinian smuggling tunnels. On October 21, Engineers Corps Sgt. Moshe Almaliah, 35, was killed by a bomb in the area. On the same day, Adnan al-Ghoul of Hamas, known as "the father of the Qassams," and his deputy were killed by Israeli missiles in the Gaza Strip.

According to numerous reports in late October, Israeli security forces assumed that Palestinians in the Gaza Strip had at least five shoulder-fired antiaircraft missiles. Known in military jargon as Man Portable Air Defense Systems (MANPADS), these would endanger the helicopters used in many of the IDF's antiterror operations, such as the targeted elimination of terrorist leaders. Previously, the Palestinians had had no real air defense system, and IDF helicopters had virtually unhindered freedom of movement over Gaza.

November started off on a grim note when three Israelis were killed and 40 others injured in a suicide bombing at Tel Aviv's Carmel market on the first day of the month. The bomber was a 16-year-old Palestinian boy from the Askar refugee camp, near Nablus.

Israel's border defenses were penetrated twice in the first half of November; though neither incursion was deemed particularly dangerous, both created alarmed headlines. On November 7, Hezballah sent an unmanned aerial vehicle over the northern coast, flying as far south as the city of Nahariya before returning to Lebanese territory. The flight, by an Iranian-made drone, followed threats by Hezballah's Sheikh Hassan Nasrallah that his organization would respond to Israeli incursions over southern Lebanon. Though the capability to launch one such vehicle over Israel did not constitute a strategic threat or raise any real danger of attacks by drones, the fact that it took military intelligence by surprise was considered a matter of concern.

And on November 9, Israeli naval coastal defenses detected a submerged object, later identified as a submarine, which had penetrated two miles into Israeli territorial waters. The navy followed the sub, but when it attempted to close on the vessel, it headed back into international waters. Aryeh O'Sullivan, reporting in the *Jerusalem Post,* quoted a senior navy officer as saying: "We assume that the submarine belonged to a Western navy" and was either on a spying mission or testing Israel's level of alertness. But others noted that neighboring countries also had submarines—Egypt, Iran, and Turkey had active subs, and Syria and Libya had inactive ones.

Arafat Departs, Tensions Continue

The death of Yasir Arafat on November 11 brought a major change in Israeli-Palestinian relations. Arafat first took ill in mid-October while living in his rooms at the Muq'ata, the Ramallah office compound where he had been under virtual house arrest since Israel's Operation Defensive Shield in the spring of 2002 (see AJYB 2003, pp. 198–203). According to some of his associates, who were quoted in the *Guardian* newspaper after his death, Arafat suddenly experienced an onset of what seemed to be flu, with vomiting, diarrhea, and a slight fever. He could not hold food down, and lost weight rapidly.

Alarmed aides summoned a team of doctors from Egypt, who arrived on October 17, followed by a second medical team from Tunisia. Although his condition continued to decline, on October 24 he managed to rise from his sickbed to meet with members of the PLO Executive Council. But those present noticed that he was hardly himself. "When we met with him, he hardly recognized who was speaking," one of them said.

As Arafat's condition deteriorated, his wife, Suha, was summoned from Paris, where she had lived apart from him for several years. Some top Arafat aides insisted that their leader be taken abroad for treatment, and, after Qurei received a telephoned assurance from Sharon that Arafat would be allowed to return if he went abroad for medical help, the Palestinian leader left by helicopter for Amman, where he was put aboard a French military aircraft on October 29. Arafat spent five days at the Percy military hospital on the southern edge of Paris taking tests. But French doctors, including specialists in toxicology, made little progress in determining the cause of his illness other than to rule out leukemia.

On November 3, Arafat slipped into a coma. Awaiting word on his condition, President Bush was incorrectly informed on November 4 that the PA leader had died. He said: "My first reaction is God bless his soul. And my second reaction is that we will continue to work for a free Palestinian state that's at peace with Israel."

On November 7 the coma deepened. That day Suha Arafat called his associates who had come to Paris "those who want to inherit," and accused them of "trying to bury Abu Ammar" (Arafat's nom de guerre). On November 9, Arafat suffered a cerebral hemorrhage, and he died on the morning of November 11.

In a report on Arafat's illness, French doctors said he suffered from disseminated intravascular coagulation (DIC), usually the result of malignancy and infection, in which the blood vessels are blocked and clotting factors needed to control bleeding are impaired. But the doctors never ventured an opinion as to what brought all this about, that is, the cause of death.

Arafat was flown to Cairo for a formal funeral, and then to Ramallah for burial in the Muq'ata complex, for which Israel gave permission. The burial itself was chaotic, as thousands of Palestinians milled around the complex and swarmed over a helicopter bearing the body. Mourners clambered for a chance to touch Arafat's casket, as security personnel fought to carry it to the gravesite. Finally, the casket arrived at the concrete and marble tomb, into which officials poured about four buckets of soil brought from Jerusalem — where Arafat had said he wished to be laid to rest.

The PA announced elections for January 9, 2005, after the traditional 60-day mourning period. Meanwhile, Mahmoud Abbas (Abu Mazen), a longtime Arafat aide and PA prime minister in 2003, was named interim leader, but his succession was far from assured. On November 14, a group of masked gunmen forced their way into the official mourning tent for Arafat in the Gaza Strip while Abbas was there. In the ensuing scuffle, two men were killed. Abbas later downplayed the incident, which, he said, "had no personal or political character." He claimed that the intruders, from the Fatah Al-Aqsa Martyrs Brigades, had merely been firing into the air.

Human rights activists from the Mahsom Watch organization, which monitored Israeli checkpoints, disclosed on November 26 that a few days earlier, Israeli soldiers had forced a Palestinian man to play his violin for about two minutes before allowing him to pass through the Beit Iba roadblock north of Nablus. The incident, filmed by Mahsom Watch volunteer Horit Herman-Peled, took place on November 9. The army said the soldiers made the man open the case and play the instrument to demonstrate that there were no explosives inside, but said that the incident was "insensitively dealt with by soldiers who are faced with a difficult and dangerous reality." Palestinians had long claimed that the roadblocks, which made moving from one place to another on the West Bank extremely difficult, were a form of collective punishment rather than the security measures Israel said they were. The soldiers were reprimanded after an investigation.

The Philadelphi Corridor and arms smuggling into PA territory were on the agenda of conversations between Prime Minister Sharon and Secretary of State Powell on November 27. Sharon told Powell that while Egypt was doing more to stop smuggling than it had in the past, it could do still more. "It is not enough to guard the 200-km border and deploy troops," he said. "The smuggling has to be stopped in the mainland." Solving the smuggling problem, Sharon told Powell, would enable Israel to pull back completely from the Gaza Strip and have "neither responsibility nor blame" there, and allow the reopening of the Dahaniya airport and, eventually, Gaza port as well.

The IDF suspended antiterror operations by Shayetet (Flotilla) 13, the elite naval commando unit, after the fatal shooting on December 3 of Islamic Jihad member Muhammad Kamil when he was unarmed and already injured. The incident took place in Rab'a, a village near Jenin in the northern West Bank. An investigation showed that Kamil had surrendered his pistol to Palestinian civilians before he was shot and killed at a distance of 40 meters. The commandos said they thought Kamil had another weapon. A week later the suspension of Shayetet 13 was lifted, the IDF spokesman explaining that there had been no ethical failure on the part of the commandos, and that Kamil had not been "executed," as charged by B'Tselem, the human-rights organization.

On December 3, Deputy Chief of Staff Maj.-Gen. Dan Halutz said that Israel would not have approved the assassination of Hamas Gaza leader Salah Shehadeh in July 2002 had it known that large numbers of innocent civilians would also die in the operation (see AJYB 2003, p. 218). Sixteen Palestinian civilians—including nine children—were killed and dozens more wounded when the air force, which Halutz commanded at the time, dropped a one-ton bomb on Shehadeh's home in a residential area of Gaza City. Halutz made the statement in a declaration to the High Court of Justice in response to a challenge against his appointment as chief of staff lodged by Yesh Gvul (There Is a Border/Limit) and other left-leaning groups. They cited comments he made immediately after the operation in an interview with *Ha'aretz* to the effect that he had told the air force crew to "sleep well at night, your operation was perfect," and added: "By the way, I sleep well at night." Halutz now denied that he had been indifferent to civilian deaths.

Warming Up to Egypt

Azzam Azzam, a 41-year-old Israeli Druze who spent eight years of a 15-year espionage sentence in an Egyptian jail, returned home on December 5 to a hero's welcome. Wrapped in an Israeli flag, Azzam returned to Mughar, his home village, to wild celebrations. Azzam had been running an Israeli textile factory in Egypt at the time of his arrest in 1997. Sharon, who spoke with Azzam shortly after his release, described their conversation as "emotional." "Immediately after I was elected," Sharon told the freed prisoner, "I met with your family and I promised them that during my tenure as prime minister we would release you. Since then, I have worked tirelessly in all my meetings with Egyptians and others to do so, and, as I promised your family, I delivered."

Ostensibly, Azzam's freedom was secured by Israel's release of six

Egyptian students who were captured in August trying to infiltrate Israel from the Sinai, allegedly on their way to kill soldiers, hijack a tank, and rob a bank. But there was much more to the deal than that: the Azzam case was just one element of intensive negotiations that had taken place between Israel and Egypt on a whole host of issues. Signs of improvement in relations between the two countries came in the days preceding Azzam's release. On December 1, the Egyptian foreign minister paid a rare visit to Israel, where he made surprisingly upbeat statements. The next day, President Mubarak told reporters that Sharon represented the Palestinans' best chance for peace.

After Azzam's release, Israel announced that it would free an unspecified number of Palestinian prisoners it was holding, though Foreign Minister Shalom insisted that this was not part of a package deal for Azzam, but an independent decision by Israel to promote cooperation with the Palestinians. This was followed, in mid-December, by an agreement between Israel, Egypt, and the U.S. to establish what are called Qualified Industrial Zones in Egypt. This meant that products manufactured in the zones that had an Israeli component of 11.7 percent would be eligible for duty-free entry into the U.S. under Israel's free-trade agreement with it, an arrangement that would mean hundreds of thousands of new jobs for the hard-pressed Egyptian economy (see below, pp. 271–72).

Another element in the Israel-Egypt rapprochement was an agreement to have 750 Egyptian border guards, equipped with armored personnel carriers and antitank rockets, stationed at the country's frontier with southern Gaza, to prevent the passage of terrorists and weapons into Gaza once Israel withdrew. Formally, this would have required a change in the 1979 peace treaty with Israel, which allowed Cairo to post only civilian police along the frontier, but Israel did not want to reopen the treaty, and so the deal was secured through an exchange of letters. Originally scheduled for January 2005, the date for deployment of the border guards was moved to April. Earlier, Egyptian intelligence minister Omar Suleiman and Israeli defense minister Mofaz reached an agreement for Cairo to train 40 Palestinian police officers, in advance of Israel's planned disengagement from Gaza.

The agreed-upon prisoner release occurred on December 27, when 159 Palestinians were let out of Israeli jails; about a third of them had been arrested for being in Israel without the necessary permit, and not for serious security violations. PA leader Mahmoud Abbas expressed disappointment, saying he had expected "a more serious prisoner release."

Portents

A bomb-tunnel dug by Palestinian terrorists blew up at an Israeli checkpoint near Rafiah, at the southern end of the Gaza Strip, on December 12, killing five soldiers, all members of the IDF's Bedouin Desert Battalion. Hamas claimed credit for what it called Operation Angry Volcano, and said it had dug the 800-meter tunnel over four months in order to reach the outpost. The next day Sharon complained that the new PA leadership had not done enough to fight terror. "As of now, we don't see any change," he said.

Chitladda Tab-Asa, a 20-year-old female farm worker from Thailand, was killed in a December 13 rocket attack on the hothouses of Ganei Tal, a moshav in Gush Katif, in the southern Gaza Strip. A few days later, Thai labor minister Uraiwan Thientthong and the country's ambassador to Israel, Kasivat Paruggamanont, met with 150 of the estimated 300 Thais working in the Strip and advised them to leave the vicinity immediately. The Thai embassy, in fact, had been urging its nationals not to work in the area for some time.

On December 18, the British Foreign Office said that no final decision had been made on holding an international conference in London on Israeli-Palestinian issues early in 2005. Israel said it wanted the conference to concentrate on ending violence, while the PA wanted it to take up broader issues. Prime Minister Tony Blair discussed the proposed conference with both sides while on a visit to the region in late December. Blair made it clear that the Palestinians would get no political support from Britain if they did not crack down on terror. "There has to be a complete and total end to terrorism" for peace talks to succeed, he said in Jerusalem, adding that only when there are actions, "not just declarations," would it be possible to get back to the "road map."

Hamas scored heavily in the elections for 26 local governments on the West Bank that were held December 22. Hamas won seven races, compared to 12 for the ruling Fatah movement; in the seven other localities results were inconclusive, and coalition negotiations would decide the governing authorities. The Hamas victories, however, were mostly in smaller towns, while Fatah won in Abu Dis (Bethany) and Al-Azariyah, just east of Jerusalem, in Halhul near Hebron, and in Jericho. In all, Fatah won nearly 65 percent of the 306 seats up for election. Danny Rubinstein, the veteran Palestinian affairs expert who wrote for *Ha'aretz,* suggested that the significance of the elections was less the actual results than the fact that Hamas had adopted the character of an organized political party within the PA, and raised the possibility that Hamas would similarly participate in the PA parliamentary elections, due in the spring. Of more immediate interest was the PA presidential election scheduled for January 9, 2005. Mahmoud Abbas (Abu Mazen), the interim leader, evoked a positive reaction from the U.S. on December 14, when he told *Asharq al-Awsat,* a London-based Arabic-language newspaper, that the use of weapons in the intifada had been an error. "Using the weapons was a mistake and has got to stop," he said, adding that it was important "to separate the uprising from the arms, because the uprising is a legitimate right of the people to express their rejection of the occupation by popular and social means." White House spokesman Scott McClellan welcomed these words and saw them as a necessary step toward fighting terror, a prerequisite "for a viable state to emerge." In fact, Abbas had opposed the armed intifada since it was launched in late September 2000, and said so in closed-door meetings. In public, he had only hinted at that position so as not to come into open conflict with Arafat, the uncontested leader of the Palestinians during his lifetime. Prime Minister Sharon and his closest aides avoided any show of support for Abbas so as not to damage his standing on the Palestinian "street" or his prospects in the upcoming election, and declined comment on his statement.

Abbas's election as head of the PA had actually been assured the day before his remarks, on December 13, when Marwan Barghouti, the jailed leader of Fatah Tanzim, dropped out of the race. Barghouti had originally supported Abbas, the official Fatah candidate, but then decided to run himself as an independent candidate. But now, in a press conference in Ramallah, Barghouti's wife Fadwa and two allies, Ziad Abu Ein and Ahmed Ghanem, read out a letter in which Barghouti withdrew the candidacy he had presented only ten days earlier. Ghanem explained Barghouti's move as expressing his "desire to underscore that the charade of a democratic Palestinian election under international sponsorship cannot hide the fact that the election is taking place under occupation and violations of international law." Ghanem stressed that the decision was not based on personal motives, but from the ex-candidate's "understanding and vision of the general Palestinian interest."

If Israeli expectations for Abbas as a moderate figure willing to make a deal were high, the candidate did something to dash them on December 26. Speaking in Al-Bireh, near Ramallah, he demanded the removal of the separation fence and an end to settlements, even those that, in the Israeli consensus, would have to remain if a peace deal was ever struck. "We will not accept settlements," Abu Mazen said, "and that includes

Ma'ale Adumim, Gush Etzion, and Ariel." At the same time, however, the PA was apparently taking some steps to tone down media incitement against Israel. The London-based *A-shark al-Awsat* reported in late December that PA officials had met with TV stations to review films and song videos that encouraged attacks against Israel.

Terror Toll

The number of Israelis killed in terror attacks during 2004 was 117, down 45 percent from 2003, when 214 were killed. There was a parallel decline of 41 percent in the number of seriously injured, from 1,004 in 2003 to 589 in 2004.

Security forces attributed the trend—and the corresponding drop in the number of attacks—to more effective security measures rather than to any decline in the motivation of potential attackers. Indeed, a large number of Palestinian would-be terrorists were stopped inside the West Bank, before they could reach Israeli population centers.

Nevertheless, there were 16 "successful" suicide attacks in 2004 causing 55 deaths, as compared to 26 suicide attacks causing 144 deaths in 2003. At the same time, the number of recorded attacks on the Gaza border town of Sderot and on Israeli settlements in the southern Gaza Strip increased significantly.

A key factor in the apparent decline in terror in the northern West Bank, from the area Israelis call Samaria, was the security fence (see above, pp. 228–31). In 2003, before the fence was erected in the area, the terror infrastructure in Samaria was responsible for 12 large-scale attacks, wounding 374 people and killing 74. In 2004, with the fence in place there, two major attacks occurred, killing 14 and injuring 106.

According to the security forces' year-end report, the existence of the fence closing off most of the northern West Bank border with Israel forced terrorists to find other routes into Israel. In fact, the perpetrators of two major attacks—at French Hill in Jerusalem on September 22 and at the Tel Aviv Carmel Market on November 1—entered Israel via Jerusalem's northern neighborhoods. In the case of the Carmel Market attack, the perpetrator, a boy of 16, had gone from his home area of Nablus on a circuitous route through Jerusalem, rather than taking the more direct route that the fence now denied him.

The youth of the Carmel Market attacker, in which three Israelis died, was not atypical. The year 2004, according to the report of the security forces, saw a 64-percent increase in the number of minors involved in terror attacks. Women were also increasingly being enlisted to carry out "missions," even by the Islamic Jihad and Hamas fundamentalist Muslim groups.

The role of Hamas in terrorist activities increased dramatically during the year. Israeli authorities said that Hamas was responsible for 555 attacks in 2004, up sharply from 218 in 2003. Much of this increase took the form of attacks by mortar and homemade Qassam rockets in the south of the country, on Gush Katif settlements and the town of Sderot. For the year, mortar fire rose by 500 percent and the number of Qassam attacks by 40 percent. The number of attacks carried out by Fatah Tanzim (including the Al-Aqsa Martyrs Brigades) declined from 117 in 2003 to 97 in 2004. Islamic Jihad was responsible for 106 attacks in 2004, up from 71 in the previous year—but did not succeed in carrying out even one "successful" suicide-bomb attack.

Another report linked Hezballah to 20 percent of the terror attacks on Israeli targets in the West Bank and Gaza. Speaking on Israel Radio, unnamed officials confirmed reports of a growing role for the Iranian-backed group, saying that it had given $9 million directly to Fatah Tanzim and the Al-Aqsa Martyrs Brigades. According to the officials, Hezballah directed no less than 51 separate terror cells, and was actively attempting to recruit Israeli Arabs.

According to figures published by the Palestinian Red Crescent Society, 881 Palestinians died and 4,009 were injured by Israeli action during the course of 2004. October was the bloodiest month, the Red Crescent reporting 142 deaths and 343 injuries, followed by May, when 128 were killed and 545 injured.

Israeli Victims of Terror Attacks, 2004

January 13—Ro'i Arbel, 29, of Talmon, is killed in a shooting ambush on a vehicle near his home in the northern West Bank. Three other passengers are wounded.

January 14—Cpl. Andrei Kegeles, 19, of Nahariya; Sgt. Tzur Or, 20, of Rishon Lezion; security guard Gal Shapira, 29, of Ashkelon; and Border Policeman St.-Sgt. Vladimir Trostinsky, 22, of Rehovot, are killed and ten others wounded when a female suicide bomber detonates a bomb at the Erez Crossing in the Gaza Strip. .

January 29—Eleven people are killed and over 50 wounded, 13 of them seriously, in a suicide bombing of an Egged bus No. 19 at the corner of Gaza and Arlozorov streets in Jerusalem. Both the Fatah-related Al-Aqsa Martyrs Brigades and Hamas claim responsibility. The bomber: Ali Yusuf Jaara, a 24-year-old Palestinian policeman from Bethlehem. The victims: Avraham (Albert) Balhasan, 28, Rose Boneh, 39, Hava Hannah (Anya) Bonder, 38, Viorel Octavian Florescu, 42, Natalia Gamril, 53, Baruch (Roman) Hondiashvili, 38, Dana Itach, 24, and Eli Zfira, 48, all of Jerusalem; Anat Darom, 23, of Netanya; Yechezkel Isser Goldberg, 41, of Betar Illit; and Mehbere Kifile, 35, of Ethiopia.

February 22—Eight people are killed and over 60 wounded, 11 of them schoolchildren, in a suicide bombing on Jerusalem bus No. 14A near the Liberty Bell Park. The bomber is from the Bethlehem area. The victims: Israel Ilan Avisidris, 41, Lior Azulai, 18, Yaffa Ben-Shimol, 57, Yuval Ozana, 32, and Benaya Yehonatan Zuckerman, 18, all of Jerusalem; Rahamim Doga, 38, of Mevasseret Zion; and Yehuda Haim, 48, of Givat Ze'ev.

February 26—Sgt.-Maj. (res.) Amir Zimmerman, 25, of Kfar Monash is killed and two other soldiers wounded when two Palestinian terrorists open fire near the Erez Crossing between the Gaza Strip and Israel. The terrorists are killed by IDF forces.

February 27—Eitan Kukoi, 30, and his wife, Rima Novikov Kukoi, 25, are killed in a terrorist shooting attack on the Lahav-Ashkelon Road, along the Green Line with the West Bank.

March 14—Ten people are killed and 16 wounded in a double suicide bombing at Ashdod Port. Hamas and Fatah claim responsibility. The victims: Gil Abutbul, 38, Danny Assulin, 51, Avraham Avraham, 34, Zion Dahan, 30, Maurice Tubul, 30, and Mazal Marciano, 30, all of Ashdod; Ophir Damari, 31, and Moshe Hendler, 29, of Rehovot; Avi Suissa, 56, of Kiryat Malakhi; and Pinhas Avraham Zilberman, 45, of Tel Aviv.

March 19—George Khoury, 20, a Christian Arab and the son of well-known attorney Elias Khoury of Beit Hanina, is shot to death from a vehicle while jogging in the north Jerusalem neighborhood of French Hill. The Fatah Al-Aqsa Martyrs Brigades, which claimed responsibility for the attack, later publishes an apology.

April 3—Ya'akov (Kobi) Zagha, 40, of Avnei Hefetz, is shot dead by a terrorist outside his home after his daughter Hani, 14, is shot and wounded. Hamas claims responsibility.

April 17—Border Policeman Kfir Ohayon, 20, of Eilat, is killed and three others wounded by a Palestinian suicide bomber at the Erez Crossing.

April 25—Border Policeman Yaniv Mashiah, 20, of Jaffa, is killed and three others are lightly wounded just an hour after the beginning of Memorial Day for Israel's fallen soldiers when shots are fired at their vehicle near Hebron.

May 2—Pregnant mother Tali Hatuel, 34, and her daughters Hila, 11, Hadar, 9, Roni, 7, and Merav, 2, of Katif in the Gaza Strip, are killed, and another civilian and two soldiers wounded when two Palestinian terrorists fire on an Israeli car at the entrance to the Gaza Strip settlement bloc of Gush Katif. Fatah and Islamic Jihad claim joint responsibility for the attack.

May 11—Six IDF soldiers are killed during an IDF operation to target Qassam workshops in Gaza City, when an armored personnel carrier hits a large explosive charge planted by Palestinian terrorists. Hamas and the Islamic Jihad claim responsibility. The soldiers: Sgt. Adaron Amar, 20, of Eilat; Sgt. Aviad Deri, 21, of Ma'ale Adumim; Sgt. Ofer Jerbi, 21, of Moshav Ben-Zakai; Sgt. Ya'akov (Zelco) Marviza, 25, of Kibbutz Hama'apil; Sgt. Kobi Mizrahi, 20, of Moshav Mata; and Sgt. Eitan Newman, 21, of Jerusalem.

May 12—Five soldiers are killed and three are lightly injured while preparing to detonate a weapon-smuggling tunnel on the Philadelphi Route near the Israeli-Egyptian border in the vicinity of Rafiah. Their armored personnel carrier exploded, apparently after being hit by an antitank rocket. Islamic Jihad claimed responsibility for the attack. Those killed: Cpl. Elad Cohen, 20, of Jerusalem; Sgt.-Maj. Aiman Ghadir, 24, of Bir Makhsur; Capt. Aviv Hakani, 23, of Ashdod; Sgt. Za'ur (Zohar) Smelev, 19, of Ofakim; and Sgt. Lior Vishinski, 20, of Ramat Gan.

May 14—Sgt. Rotem Adam, 21, of Rishon Lezion, and Sgt. Alexei Hayat, 21, of Beersheba, are killed and two other soldiers wounded by Palestinian sniper fire in the Rafiah refugee camp in the southern Gaza Strip.

May 29—Maj. Shahar Ben-Yishai, 25, of Menahemia, is killed by

Palestinian gunfire following a search in the Balata camp near Nablus.

June 21—Thai worker Weerachai Wongput, 37, dies of shrapnel wounds from a mortar shell fired into greenhouses in Kfar Darom in the Gaza Strip. The mortar was fired by Palestinians trying to divert attention from an attempt to infiltrate the settlement.

June 27—Sgt. Ro'i Nissim, 20, of Rishon Lezion, is killed and five other soldiers wounded when their outpost in the Gaza Strip is blown up by Hamas terrorists who tunnel under the position and detonate a massive explosive charge.

June 28—Mordechai Yosepov, 49, and Afik Zahavi, 4, are killed when a Qassam rocket fired by Hamas terrorists in the Gaza Strip lands near a nursery school in the northern Negev town of Sderot.

June 29—Moshe Yohai, 63, of Ashdod, is found shot to death in Beit Rima, a Palestinian Authority-controlled village near Ramallah, where he had apparently gone on business.

July 4—Victor Kreiderman, 49, of Mevo Dotan, is shot to death by Aqsa-Martyrs Brigades terrorists as he and his wife drive near the West Bank village of Yabad. His wife, Emma, is lightly wounded.

July 6—Capt. Moran Vardi, 25, of Binyamina, of the Navy Shayetet 13 (Flotilla 13) commando unit, is killed, and three others wounded in an exchange of fire between IDF forces and Palestinians while attempting to arrest terrorists in Nablus.

July 11—Sgt. Ma'ayan Na'im, 19, of Bat Yam, dies and 33 are wounded when a bomb explodes at a bus stop not far from the old Central Bus Station in downtown Tel Aviv at about 7 a.m.

August 13—Shlomo Miller, 50, of Itamar in Samaria, is killed by a Palestinian terrorist who opens fire outside the settlement gate. The Al-Aqsa Martyrs Brigades claims responsibility.

August 31—Sixteen people are killed and 100 wounded in two suicide bombings within minutes of each other on two Beersheba city buses, on route nos. 6 and 12. The buses were traveling along Beersheba's main street, Rager Blvd., near the city hall. Hamas in Hebron claimed responsibility for the attack. The victims, all residents of Beersheba: Shoshana Amos, 64; Aviel Atash, 3; Vitaly Brodsky, 52; Tamara

Dibrashvilli, 70; Raisa Forer, 55; Larisa Gomanenko, 48; Denise Hadad, 50; Tatiana Kortchenko, 49; Rosita Lehman, 45; Karine Malka, 23; Nargiz Ostrovsky, 54; Maria Sokolov, 57; Roman Sokolovsky, 53; Tiroayent Takala, 33; Eliyahu Uzan, 58; and Emmanuel Yosef (Yosefov), 28.

September 22—Two Border Policemen, Lance Cpl. Menashe Komemi, 19, of Moshav Aminadav, and Lance Cpl. Mamoya Tahio, 20, of Rehovot, are killed and 17 Israelis wounded in a suicide bombing carried out by a female terrorist at the French Hill junction hitchhiking post in northern Jerusalem. The Fatah Al-Aqsa Martyrs Brigades claims responsibility. The victims prevented a much larger toll by preventing the bomber from getting close to the bus-stop area.

September 23—Capt. Tal Bardugo, 21, and St.-Sgt. Nir Sami, 21, both of Jerusalem, and St.-Sgt. Israel Lutati, 20, of Neve Dekalim, are killed by several Palestinian terrorists armed with AK-47 assault riffles and hand grenades, who infiltrated the military post near the community of Morag in the southern Gaza Strip. Another soldier and a journalist were also wounded in the exchange of fire in which the terrorists were killed. Two Fatah-related terror groups and Islamic Jihad claimed responsibility for the attack.

September 24—Tiferet Tratner, 24, of Jerusalem, is killed in her home in Neveh Dekalim by a mortar strike on the Gush Katif settlement bloc in the Gaza Strip.

September 29—Dorit Aniso, 2, and Yuval Abebeh, 4, children of Ethiopian immigrants living in Sderot, are killed while playing in the street by a Qassam rocket fired from Gaza. Some 20 people are wounded. Hamas claims responsibility.

September 30—St.-Sgt. Gilad Fisher, 22, of Mitzpeh Hoshaya, is killed before dawn when Hamas terrorists, under cover of heavy fog, attack an IDF lookout post east of Beit Hanoun in the Gaza Strip. Two other soldiers are wounded. The terrorists are killed.

September 30—Shlomit Batito, 36, of Nissanit, is shot and killed by Hamas terrorists while jogging on the road. Sgt. Victor Ariel, 20, of Kadima, a medic, is killed by a grenade thrown by one of the terrorists as he runs to aid Batito. Soldiers kill the terrorists.

October 6—Pratheep Nanongkham, 24, a greenhouse worker

from Maha Sarakham province in Thailand, is killed when armed terrorists infiltrate the hothouse area of Kfar Darom in the central Gaza Strip. Hamas claims responsibility for the attack.

October 7—A total of 32 people are killed in terror bombings at two Sinai holiday resorts frequented by Israelis, 29 at the Taba Hilton and three at Ras a-Satan. Among the dead were 12 Israelis; over 120 were wounded. The Israeli victims at Taba: Assaf Greenwald, 27, of Ramat Gan; Hafez al-Hafi, 39, of Lod; Rotem Moriah, 27, of Tel Aviv; Tzila Niv, 43, and her two sons, Gilad, 11, and Lior, 3, of Rakefet; Oleg Paizakov, 32, and his wife Ludmilla, 30, of Bat Yam; and Khalil Zeitounya, 10, of Jaffa. The Israeli victims at Ras a-Satan: Michal Alexander, 27, of Ganei Tikva; Roy Avisaf, 28, of Kfar Sava; and Einat Naor, 27, of Kibbutz Zikim.

October 19—Sgt. Yair Nisim Turgemann, 22, of Kiryat Arba, is killed at an IDF base near Mevo Dotan in the northern West Bank when Palestinian gunmen open fire from Palestinian territory west of the community. Al-Aqsa Martyrs Brigades claims responsibility.

October 21—Sgt.-Maj. Moshe Almaliah, 35, of Dimona, a career NCO in the IDF Engineering Corps, is killed by a Hamas bomb explosion during construction work on the Philadelphi Corridor at the southern end of the Gaza Strip.

October 28—Sgt. Michael Chizhik, 21, of Tiberias, is killed and six other soldiers wounded in a mortar shell attack on an IDF outpost at Morag in the southern Gaza Strip.

November 1—Three people are killed and over 30 wounded in a suicide bombing at the Carmel Market in central Tel Aviv. The Popular Front for the Liberation of Palestine in Nablus claims responsibility for the attack, carried out by Amar Alfar, 18, from Askar refugee camp in Nablus. The victims: Tatiana Ackerman, 32, of Tel Aviv; Leah Levine, 64, of Givatayim; and Shmuel Levy, 65, of Jaffa.

December 7—St.-Sgt. Nadav Kudinski, 20, of Kiryat Gat, of the Oketz canine unit, is killed by a bomb, along with his dog, when a booby-trapped chicken coop explodes northwest of the Karni Crossing in the Gaza Strip. Four soldiers are wounded in the exchange of fire while evacuating him.

December 12—Five soldiers are killed and another five wounded when a tunnel filled with 1.5 tons of explosives is detonated under an IDF post at the Rafah crossing, followed by the infiltration of the post by two terrorists who open fire and activate another explosive device. The dead, all from the army's Bedouin Desert Patrol unit: Sgts. Araf Azbarga, 19, of Kseifeh; Sa'id Jahaja, 19, of Arara; Hussein Abu Leil, 23, of Ein Mahal; Cpl. Adham Shehada, 19, of Turan; and Sgt. Tarek al-Ziadne, 20, of Rahat.

December 14—Chitladda Tap-arsa, 19, a female agricultural worker from Udon Thani's Nong Han in northeastern Thailand, is killed and two other foreign workers, from Thailand and Nepal, are wounded by mortar shells fired at Ganei Tal in the Gush Katif settlement bloc.

December 21—Ariella Fahima, 39, of Moshav Nehusha south of Beit Shemesh, is stabbed to death at the door to her house, apparently by a terrorist who infiltrated the perimeter fence.

December 22—Salem (Sami) al-Kimlat, 28, a Bedouin from the town of Rahat employed as a security guard at the construction site of the security fence west of Hebron, is shot and killed by Palestinian terrorists.

Other Security Matters

WEAPONS EXPORTS

Israeli defense exports approached $4 billion in 2004, about 10 percent of the world market, according to Defense Ministry figures. Perhaps the most significant deal was struck on March 4 in New Delhi, when Moshe Keret, president of the government-owned Israel Aircraft Industries (IAI) signed a $1.1-billion contract to supply India with three Phalcon airborne warning and control systems. This was the largest single sale ever made by Israel's defense and aerospace industries, and part of a growing trade relationship with India (see below, p. 269). Israel had also tried to sell Phalcons, considered the best system in the world by many military experts, to Australia and Turkey, but they preferred U.S. systems.

Aeronautics Defense Systems, located in Yavne, near Ben-Gurion International Airport, registered the first Israeli sale of defense products to Russia. Irkut, the developer of the Sukhoi-30 advanced fighter, purchased the Israeli company's Aerostar unmanned aerial vehicle to help defend oil installations and other facilities. Aerostar had also been sold to several African countries, including Angola and the Ivory Coast, and, under a recent cooperation agreement with General Dynamics, several Aerostars were slated to be sold to the U.S. Navy. Another deal by an Israeli company with the American military was secured by Plasan Sasa Composite Materials, a small firm based in and owned by Kibbutz Sasa on the Lebanese border, which won one of the biggest non-high-tech contracts ever signed by an Israeli firm, a $144-million deal to provide truck protection systems for the U.S. Marine Corps.

Israeli exports to China, however, had created concern in Washington since the early 1990s, the Americans suspecting that made-in-the-U.S.A. technology was being transferred to the Chinese. In the summer of 2000, American pressure forced Israel to rescind the sale to China of Phalcon airborne early-warning systems even though they contained no U.S. technology and were mounted on a Russian-made Ilyushin airframe, on the grounds that possession of the advanced command-and-control aircraft would upset the military balance in the China Straits (see AJYB 2001, pp. 505–06). At the time, Israeli sources suggested that the real question involved Israeli competition with U.S. firms in the world arms market.

In 2004 a dispute arose over the resupply and repair of parts for Harpy unmanned aerial vehicles Israel had already sold and delivered to China. The question came up during a routine conversation, sometime in the fall, between Undersecretary of Defense Douglas Feith (known as a strong supporter of Israel), Amos Yaron, director general of the Israeli Defense Ministry, and Yekutiel Mor, the chief Israeli weapons-procurement official in the U.S. The Israelis mentioned the Harpy, which Israel had sold to China for $55 million long before the Phalcon dispute had even started. Feith was angered, believing (or seeming to believe) that Israel had broken its promise to stop selling strategic weapons to China. Yaron, according to press reports, was surprised that the Americans did not know of the Harpy deal, and upon checking Defense Ministry records found that the sale had been reported to the Americans "on a professional level" in the 1990s.

According to a report by *Ha'aretz* defense specialist Ze'ev Schiff, the Americans, themselves under pressure from the pro-Taiwan lobby, demanded that Israel not return the Harpy UAVs to China, even though they were clearly Chinese property. Such a move would certainly anger China, which still had bad memories of the 2000 Phalcon cancellation. State Councilor Tang Jiaxuan, China's deputy prime minister, was said to have discussed the Harpy case on a December 25 visit to Israel that included talks with the Palestinians. The Chinese official also invited Sharon to visit Beijing.

Feith, meanwhile, had broken off relations with Yaron, but on December 15, both Israel and the U.S. denied reports that the Americans had called on Israel to dismiss him. Yaron, for his part, refused to discuss the case or provide details at a December 29 meeting of the Knesset's Foreign Affairs and Defense Committee. All he would say was that "the problem will be solved because it has to be solved."

SECOND-GUESSING ON IRAQ

On March 28, a Knesset subcommittee headed by Foreign Affairs and Defense Committee chairman Yuval Steinitz (Likud) released an 81-page preliminary report on Israel's failure to provide accurate intelligence about Iraq's weapons capabilities before the Iraq war. It was the product of an eight-month investigation that questioned intelligence officials, military officers, and cabinet members. A much longer and detailed version of the report remained classified.

The subcommittee found that Israeli intelligence agencies suffered from a closed "information loop" so that information from foreign intelligence services was used as if it were fresh data when in fact the other states had obtained the material from Israel in the first place. Speculation was passed around in intelligence circles "without any substantiation from the field," resulting in an overestimation of Iraq's stock of missiles and its ability to strike directly at Israel. In a further criticism of Israeli intelligence, the subcommittee noted that the Israeli agencies had failed to develop sources of hard data within Iraq. But the report strongly rejected suggestions that the Israeli agencies had intentionally misled the U.S. and others in the hope of encouraging them to go to war against Iraq, a longtime enemy of Israel.

By August, classified copies of the longer document had been distributed to key figures in the political and defense establishment. Ze'ev Schiff of *Ha'aretz,* who was well-connected with the kind of people who got the report, said that it showed no "serious black holes" in the intelligence apparatus, despite the shortcomings in the Iraqi assessment process.

Prime Minister Sharon's bureau, on July 3, denied that any Israelis were involved in the interrogation of prisoners at the Abu Ghraib prison in Iraq. The charge was made by Brig. Gen. Janis Karpinski, the U.S. Military Police officer suspended after photos showed abuse of prisoners at the jail.

October also saw the publication of a report criticizing the effectiveness of the U.S. conquest of Iraq as part of its war against terror. The Jaffee Center for Strategic Studies at Tel Aviv University said, in its annual "Middle East Strategic Balance," that the actions in Iraq had diverted energies away from steps against other terror centers. If the goal in the war against terror is "not just to kill the mosquitoes but to dry the swamp," it was now clear "that Iraq is not the swamp," said one of the report's authors, retired general Shlomo Brom. "On a strategic as well as an operational level," Brom concluded, "the war in Iraq is hurting the war on international terrorism."

PROBLEMS DOWN UNDER

On July 15, a New Zealand court sentenced Israelis Eli Kara and Uriel Kelman to six months in jail for seeking to obtain a New Zealand passport fraudulently. The two men, suspected of being agents of the Israeli Mossad, had been arrested in March as they went to pick up the passport, and pleaded guilty to using the identity of a cerebral palsy victim to secure it. According to press reports, Kara, who claimed to be a travel agent based in Australia, had entered New Zealand 24 times, and Kelman, who traveled to New Zealand on a Canadian passport, was employed by YTS Stems, a firm specializing in high-tech surveillance. Two other suspects left New Zealand before they could be arrested. They were ex-diplomat Ze'ev Barkan and Anthony (Tony) David Resnick, a New Zealand native who had lived in Israel for 13 years.

Soon after the sentences were handed down, Prime Minister Helen Clark said the incident had "demeaned the integrity" of her nation's passport and constituted a severe breach of New Zealand's sovereignty. She suspended high-level contacts with Israel and said that an anticipated request by Israeli president Moshe Katzav to visit her country would be declined. Additional sanctions were imposed requiring official Israeli visitors to apply for visas and delaying approval of a new Israeli ambassador. Kara and Kelman were released from jail in late September and deported, after serving the required half of their sentences.

In July, shortly after the two suspects were convicted, a Jewish cemetery in Wellington was defaced, with 14 gravestones uprooted and Nazi slogans placed near the graves. David Zwartz, a leader of the Jewish community, said the attack had taken place in an atmosphere of "government-sanctioned anti-Israelism." He blamed Prime Minister Clark, declaring, "The strength with which she made that allegation and her comments about Israel led directly to what happened, to my mind."

SYRIAN RELATIONS

Late in the year, Prime Minister Sharon turned back overtures by Syrian president Bashar al-Assad for a renewal of peace talks, but the Syrian leader kept on trying. Assad sent out peace feelers in a meeting with UN special envoy Terje Larsen, who visited Damascus on November 25. "President Assad has reiterated to me today that he has an outstretched hand to his Israeli counterparts and that he is willing to go to the table without conditions," Larson said after they met. The message was nearly identical to that Assad dispatched earlier through others—U.S. Rep. Gary Ackerman (D., N.Y.), European diplomats, and Martin Indyk, the former U.S. ambassador to Israel.

The Syrians, however, made it clear that what they had in mind was an arrangement building upon what had been agreed to in over a decade of talks between various Israeli administrations and Assad's late father, Hafez al-Assad—Israeli withdrawal from the Golan Heights, almost all the way to the water line on the eastern shore of Lake Kinneret. Israel, for its part, officially maintained that if Assad wanted peace he should stop supporting terrorism and, in particular, shut down the offices that terror groups maintained in his capital, and rein in Hezballah, the Lebanese Shi'ite organization headed by Sheikh Hassan Nasrallah, that operated with Iranian sponsorship and express Syrian consent. Assad, hard-pressed by the U.S. as a supporter of terror, claimed that these offices in his capital engaged in public relations, not operations.

The Americans were skeptical about Assad's professed interest in a deal with Israel, since had he been serious, they argued, he would have used diplomatic back channels rather than sending his peace message via political figures and having them appear in the newspapers. But according to several reports, the IDF took Assad quite seriously and believed that the Syrian leader might be ready for peace if Israel withdrew to the 1967 borders. Lt. Gen. Moshe (Bogie) Ya'alon said in a mid-August interview with the daily *Yediot Aharonot* that withdrawal from the Golan Heights did not pose a serious military problem for Israel. "The army is able to defend any border," he declared. Sharon aides, however, said that Assad knew very well that Israel could not even consider a Golan Heights pullback at the same time it was disengaging from the Palestinians in the Gaza Strip and West Bank, and that Assad was taking a "free shot" to win himself public-relations points.

After the dramatic improvement in its relations with Israel in December, Egypt pushed for Syrian-Israeli talks. President Mubarak, on a December 7 visit to Kuwait, urged Prince Jabber Ahmed Sabah, the Kuwaiti ruler, to negotiate diplomatic ties with Israel and to push Syria into making dramatic political moves that could open a peace front with Israel. And Tareq el-Kouny, Egypt's chargé d'affaires in Israel (Egypt withdrew its ambassador shortly after the start of the intifada) said on December 9 that Cairo was "certain that the Syrians are serious in their intention to renew negotiations and we believe that Israel should consider this favorably." A comprehensive regional peace was in Egypt's interest, he explained, because it would lead to stability, attracting badly needed foreign investment.

DOMESTIC DEVELOPMENTS

Israel by the Numbers

The population of Israel at the end of 2004 reached 6.86 million people, according to Central Bureau of Statistics estimates published on December 30. That figure included 5.235 million Jews (76 percent of the total), constituting 39 percent of world Jewry; 1.337 million Arabs (20 percent); and 290,000 others (mostly immigrants and their families not listed as Jews by the Interior Ministry). In addition, the CBS said that the country had about 189,000 "foreigners," defined as people who have stayed in the country for less than a year. There were 1.7 million Muslims in the country, 16 percent of the total population; 450,000 Muslims were under the age of 14, fully one-quarter of all Israelis in that age group.

The nation's Christian population was 144,000, which was 2.1 percent of the total. Most of them (81 percent) were Christian Arabs, but there were also some 27,000 Christians who immigrated to Israel under the Law of Return, qualifying as Jews because of their first-degree relationship to Jews or because they had one Jewish grandparent. Most of this group had come to Israel since the early 1990s, in the waves of mass immigration from the former Soviet Union and Ethiopia, but another 5,000 had arrived in the 1970s and 1980s, mainly from Romania and Poland. While the country's Christian population had grown 420 percent since the founding of the state in 1948, its percentage of the total population dropped from 2.9 percent to 2.1 percent because the general population was growing faster. In the early years of the state, Christians amounted to over 20 percent of the Israeli Arab population, but that ratio fell to about 15 percent in 1972 and less than 9 percent in 2004.

Israel's population grew by 114,000 during 2004. The rate of growth compared to the previous year, 1.7 percent, was the lowest since 1990, at the beginning of the mass immigration from the former Soviet Union that saw more than a million people come to Israel.

Immigration in 2004 was 20,000, compared to 23,000 in 2003 and much higher figures during the previous decade. About 9,700 immigrants came from the former Soviet Union, 2,000 from France, and 3,700 from Ethiopia—mostly Falash Mura, descendants of Jews who had been converted to Christianity but still had close Jewish relatives. Immigration from the U.S. reached about 2,000 with the arrival, at year's end, of a flight of 300 new immigrants sponsored by the Jewish Agency and the Nefesh B'Nefesh immigration organization.

Average life expectancy was 81.2 years for females and 77.3 for males. The average for all Israelis, 79.2, tied Australia for seventh place among the world's countries (Japan topped the list at 81.6). On October 1, International Senior Citizens Day, the CBS published data about Israel's older residents as of the end of 2003. About 670,000 Israelis—some 10 percent of the population—were over age 65. The figure was lower than in Europe, where about 15 percent of the population was 65 or over. But it was higher than in Asia (6 percent) and Africa (3.2 percent). Among Israeli Jews, 12 percent of the population was 65 and over, quadruple the 3 percent figure for Israeli Arabs. Women were disproportionately represented among older Israelis, constituting 57 percent of those 65 and over, and 60 percent of those over 80.

Many of Israel's older people were in financial difficulty. In the 2003 CBS survey, 13 percent of those 65 and over said that they had refrained from buying food at least once during the preceding year due to lack of money; 44 percent said they had shut off heat in their homes to save money; 39 percent said they had no supplementary health insurance beyond the free national health membership in an HMO; and 5 percent said they had had their phones or electricity disconnected due to nonpayment of bills. While 91 percent of those 65 and over required prescription drugs, 15 percent said they did not purchase all of the drugs, which are sold to HMO members at a fifth or less of their list prices, because of lack of money.

Only 328,000 Israelis, 8 percent of the adult population, lived alone, the CBS reported. In the U.S., the figure was 26 percent, and in Sweden 42 percent. Israel also stood out in the possession of cell phones: its 955 phones per 1,000 people ranked second in the world behind Luxembourg.

The annual Health Ministry survey on smoking showed that 23.8 percent of Israelis were smokers, the lowest figure in the 32 years that the ministry had collected statistics. Most indicated that they picked up the habit in the army. But stopping smoking might have been a factor in a rise of 2 kg (4.4 pounds) in the weight of the average Israeli between 1998 and 2002. During that same period, the number of underweight women doubled to 16 percent. An even more alarming statistic, released by the Israel Cancer Association, was that 950–1,000 Israelis are diagnosed with skin cancer each year, second in the world to Australia.

Israel dropped from 21st to 26th on the 2004 Transparency International Corruption Perceptions Index, which measures the extent to which a country is seen as free of corruption. On a scale in which 10 is the perfect score, Israel's rating declined from 7.3 two years earlier to 6.4. The PA, with a score of 2.5, ranked 108th.

The Economic Picture

POSITIVE TRENDS

Interviewed in Washington in late September, where he had gone to attend the annual meeting of the International Monetary Fund, Finance Minister Benjamin Netanyahu justified the free-market economic reforms he had instituted, saying that they followed a tested formula. "Everything that we are doing now has already been done over the past 20 years in other countries that have surged forward, from New Zealand to Chile," he said. "In the past, Israel was a 'bad' country for business— the Histadrut, taxes, welfare—and things cannot go this way. On the other hand, we have the advantage of being a technological country, and if we combine this with a pro-business climate, our economy will also surge forward . . . . I speak with businessmen who tell me the only reason they come to Israel to invest and to do business is that they understand the economy is changing. Who would come to a country of high taxes, insane bureaucracy, and bloated unions?"

According to data provided in the Central Bureau of Statistics (CBS) annual report, 2004 was a year of substantial economic success, clearly attributable to the Netanyahu policies. But for those concerned with the social implications, the results were far less satisfying.

The GDP (Gross Domestic Product) rose during the year by a healthy rate of 4.3 percent, after rising only 1.3 percent in 2003 and falling by 0.7 percent in 2002. Total GDP, according to the estimates, amounted to about NIS 525.4 billion, or around $120 billion. With population rising by 1.7 percent, the increase meant that per capita GDP, a key figure, rose by 2.5 percent to $17,200, bringing Israel back to about where it had been five years earlier. Even so, this growth in per capita GDP lagged behind the 2.9 average for Western countries, where population was generally not rising.

This impressive growth was spurred by the business sector. It grew by 6 percent, driven by a 14.2-percent rise in the export of goods and services, reflecting both an improved world economy and a weakening U.S. dollar, which provided substantial price advantages for Israel's exports to Europe. Another major plus was the 30-percent increase in tourism, although it was far too early to speak of a boom in this vital industry, since revenues were still less than half of what they had been in 2000, when a record 2.5-million tourists visited Israel, the bulk of them before the start of the intifada in late September.

One major factor in the improved economic figures was a 19.6-percent rise in industrial exports, which added up to about $30 billion, a rise of nearly $6.7 billion. On a year-to-year basis, exports had risen by only 6.2 percent in 2003, and had actually fallen by 2.5 percent in 2002.

The export figure was somewhat misleading since it included $6.4 billion worth of polished diamonds, which had little added value. Diamonds were second only to high-tech products, which rose a healthy 21.7 percent to almost $11 billion. The technology figures included communications equipment, up 20.3 percent to $2.87 billion, and electronic components, which rose 12.7 percent to $1.7 billion. Also on the rise were chemicals (+24.4 percent, including fertilizers and pesticides); plastics and rubber (+17.2 percent); textiles and clothing (+10.2 percent to almost $1.1 million); and food exports, which were up 17.1 percent, reaching $600 million in the sector's fourth consecutive year of growth.

About 31 percent of the increase in exports, amounting to $2.1 billion, was to the U.S., 27 percent to the European Union, and 22 percent to Asia. Israel's exports to Europe rose by 18 percent since 2003. Ireland was up 62 percent; Switzerland 55 percent; Croatia 126 percent; Turkey 82 percent; Uzbekistan 51 percent; Russia 44 percent; Taiwan 95 percent; and Hong Kong 28 percent. During the same period, exports to the U.S. rose by about $1.1 billion to $7.5 billion, a 17-percent increase.

At the same time, total imports grew by 20 percent to $6.9 billion. Israel's trade deficit was therefore $200 million wider in 2004 than in 2003, standing at $6.7 billion. The EU accounted for 36 percent of imports of goods in 2004, and also 36 percent of the rise in imports. Imports from Asia contributed 25 percent to the total rise in imports.

Of particular significance was the steadily rising bilateral trade with India. In 2002 it had increased by $200 million, to $1.2 billion, almost equally divided between imports and exports, reached $1.46 billion in 2003, and $1.95 billion in 2004, a 36-percent increase. In 2004, Indian exports to Israel increased 25 percent to $1.3 billion, while Israel's exports to India rose 43 percent to $918 million.

Consumer confidence in Israel was up, spurred by an apparent decrease in the level and frequency of terror attacks, at least inside Israel proper. For the year, private consumption rose by 5.3 percent, spurred by a surge of 16.3 percent in the consumption of durable goods, including automobiles and household appliances. But while the consumption surge benefited some merchants, it had a lesser effect on the entire economy because durables were usually imported. The increase in nondurable goods, mostly local in origin, was much smaller, 4.2 percent.

Government consumption, on the other hand, declined by 2.3 percent as a result of budget-cutting. This helped free up resources for the private sector, an essential element for continued economic growth. At the same time, cuts in government payrolls increased pressure on the job market.

The deficit in the government's current account, according to the year-end estimate, amounted to NIS 20.6 billion, or about $4.7 billion based on the year-end dollar-exchange rate. That was NIS 8.5 billion higher than the 2003 deficit, but because of the sharp increase in GDP, represented a lower percentage of GDP (3.9 percent) than the 2003 deficit (5.8 percent of GDP). That 3.9 percent figure was below the government's planned deficit, as enshrined in the 2004 budget, of 4 percent.

In fact, according to an analysis in the *Globes* business daily, the government deficit was even lower if two major, non-operating deductions were taken into account—an allocation of NIS 1.9 billion to Israel Railroads for development, and NIS 5.3 billion in tax cuts. The two changes, the paper said, added up to 1.4 percent of GDP, and excluding them would make the government deficit for the year only 2.5 percent of GDP.

The major reason for the improved deficit performance was not the reduction in some government expenditures (as exemplified by a 3.2-percent cut in the social welfare allowances paid out by the National Insurance Institute, Israel's equivalent of social security, and by various state welfare agencies), but rather a significant 4.5-percent increase in government revenues. Most of that came from much higher tax receipts, up 4.4 percent compared to 2003, while total government expenditure remained constant.

HIGH INVESTMENT, LOW INFLATION

The improved economic climate was also reflected in the rate of investment. Total foreign investment in Israel in 2004, according to a Bank of Israel report, amounted to $6.08 billion, about 10 percent higher than the $5.53 billion invested in 2003. Net foreign investment in the Tel Aviv Stock Exchange was $566 million, up 52 percent over 2003, and foreign portfolio investment, at $5.3 billion, was a huge 230 percent higher than the 2003 figure. At the same time, there was more Israeli investment abroad, including investment by high-tech companies and in income-producing real estate. Total Israeli investment overseas stood at $8.6 billion, 17 percent more than in 2003.

Investment in the high-tech sector was seen as the main economic "engine" for future growth. Over the year, the IVC Research Center reported, 428 Israeli technology companies raised a total of $1.46 billion from local and foreign venture investors, as compared to $1.01 billion in 2003. Ze'ev Holtzman of Giza Venture Capital, who also chaired the IVC Research Center, said he expected the trend to continue into 2005. Confidence seemed particularly high in the second half of the year. In the third quarter, 113 companies raised $438 million, and in the fourth quarter, the same number of companies raised $366. The average size of investment, too, was substantial—$3.2 million, compared to only $2.6 million in the fourth quarter of 2003. In all, Israeli venture-capital investment totaled $665 million, up 58 percent from the $421 million invested in 2003.

Investment in life sciences, including biotechnology and medical devices, continued to show the strength it had exhibited over a four-year period; its share of total venture-capital investment was 22 percent, almost triple the 8 percent of 2000. Indeed, the new ISLI (Israel Life Sciences Industry) organization said that Israel had become the world leader in per-capita patents for medical devices, and fourth in the world, per capita, in biotech patents, behind Japan, Germany, and Great Britain. According to an ISLI study, Israel had 466 life-science companies, half of which had been founded in the past five years. Forty-one percent already generated some revenue, and one-fifth of the companies were engaged in clinical trials for their products or devices. The Israeli focus was on major diseases for which existing therapies were largely ineffective—67 companies were working on treatments for cardiovascular and peripheral vascular disease, 35 on oncology, 25 on neurodegenerative disease, and 15 on ophthalmic, orthopedic, and other age-related conditions.

Inflation for the year, reflecting continued weakness in the economy despite the positive signs, was 1.2 percent, toward the bottom of the government's target range of 1–3 percent. One reason for recent low inflation in Israel, where high levels of inflation had previously been the rule, was the rapid increase in low-price imports from Asia, which somewhat offset rising world energy prices. Other factors were the decline of labor costs achieved partly through increased productivity, and the depressed job market where employees tended to accept lower wages. If in past years the Bank of Israel's insistence on keeping interest rates high to control inflation was seen by some as bordering on obsession, the central bank at the end of 2004 was talking about taking measures to induce inflation, at least slightly.

TOURISM

The number of tourist visitors to Israel totaled 1.5 million in 2004, an increase of 41 percent over 2003. While this was impressive jump, it must be recalled that 2003, with the Iraq war in the news, was an especially bad year for tourism generally, and especially in the Middle East. The U.S. accounted for the largest number of tourists, 368,000, an increase of 39 percent. Next came France (268,000, up 47 percent); Great Britain (146,000, up 40 percent); and Germany (75,000, up 54 percent). Overnights in tourist hotels reached a total of 17 million in 2004, an increase of 12.5 percent over 2003. Only 3 million of these were foreign tourists, but that number was up 45 percent over 2003, while the figure for Israelis staying at the hotels, though much larger, increased by only 3.4 percent.

The improving incoming tourist figures, however, did not come close to the number of Israelis traveling abroad. No less that 3.6 million Israelis left the country on trips in 2004, an increase of 10 percent over 2003.

TRADE AGREEMENTS

Israel, Egypt, and the U.S. signed a landmark free-trade agreement in Cairo on December 14 (see above, p. 250). The deal created seven Qualified Industrial Zones, or QIZ (four in Cairo, two in Alexandria, and one in Port Said), with duty-free access to the U.S. so long as the goods produced had an Israeli component of at least 11.7 percent. Israeli-Egyptian cooperation in the zones was expected to be principally in textiles, but could expand to include leather products, ceramics, luggage, housewares, and even some food products. The agreement was modeled on a similar one with Jordan, concluded in the late 1990s, which resulted in Jordanian exports to the U.S. rising from $52 million in 2000 to $583 million in 2003. According to the *Jerusalem Report* magazine, Israel had originally offered the QIZ plan to Egypt at that time, but was turned down because of political considerations.

According to a report published in Beirut's *Daily Star* newspaper, much of the impetus for Egypt signing the deal came from the fact that the abolition of global export quotas for textiles, due in January 2005, would have allowed South Asian countries, particularly China and India, to push smaller producers like Egypt out of the market. Therefore, the article suggested, Egypt needed the advantage of duty-free entry into the U.S. in order to compete. Textile industry publications suggested that without the QIZ agreement, Egypt would have lost as much as $500 million of its annual trade with the U.S., which, in 2003, amounted to $1.13 billion. With the deal, Egypt expected to increase its exports of woven and knitted goods to the U.S. to about $2 billion by 2007.

Israel, for its part, expected it exports to Egypt—which had fallen from over $63 million before the intifada to about $25 million—to increase by some $50 million in the first year after the QIZ came into effect. Israeli manufacturers did not believe that the zones would take away business from Israeli firms. According to Dov Lautman of Delta Galil Industries, a major exporter of underwear and the operator of the largest Israeli textile plant in Egypt, most of the work carried out in Egypt would be simple sewing, which barely existed in Israel anymore. The most important benefit the deal would have for Israel was political—strengthening relations with Egypt.

Israel and the European Union agreed in early November on a method of marking Israeli goods originating in the territories for customs purposes, indicating whether they were produced in Israel proper or in the area under occupation. The agreement, based on a proposal by Ehud Olmert, deputy prime minister and minister of trade, industry, and labor, stipulated that products be labeled not only with the word "Israel," but with the city or town of origin as well. Signed in January 2005, it would go into effect in February.

The EU did not recognize settlements over the Green Line as part of Israel, and therefore exports from plants in the territories—amounting to an estimated $150 million annually—would be liable to customs duties estimated at $7–$10 million per year. This dispute between Israel and the EU, which had simmered for several years, was exacerbated in 2004 when EU customs inspectors began holding up shipments from Israel proper, including those of major exporters not linked to the territories, in order to check on the origin of the goods in the shipment. In many cases, the importer of the goods in Europe had to pay a deposit equivalent to the customs duty that would be due on the goods, in order to clear them from customs.

EMPLOYMENT, POVERTY, LABOR RELATIONS

There was slight improvement in the jobs picture for the year, but the situation remained grim for many Israelis. Unemployment declined from about 11 percent at the end of 2003 to 10 percent in late 2004. (Joblessness crossed the unenviable 10-percent threshold in October 2001, and had never dropped under it since.) Even the decline in unemployment was not due to a flood of new jobs, but to a tightening of the criteria under which unemployment compensation was awarded. Also, a good number of the 80,000–90,000 new jobs created during the year were part-time positions, often at minimum wage, and without the social benefits accruing to permanent, full-time employees. Indeed, as in the U.S., the trend in Israel was away from tenured employment to part-time or temporary jobs. Furthermore, Oded Tyrah, the outgoing president of the Israel Manufacturers Association, charged that 40 percent of employers disobeyed the law and paid workers less than the minimum wage.

The National Insurance Institute's poverty report for 2003 was released in late November of 2004. The number of Israelis living below the poverty line rose by 100,000, reaching 1.4 million, including 680,000 children. There were 190,000 families with an average gross income of NIS 3,750 or less a month, less than a third of the average national income. Worse yet, 611,000 wage earners, mostly in the part-time or temporary category and including service workers and security guards, earned less than NIS 2,000 a month. This figure included 80,000 of the 90,000 or so people lucky enough to find a job at all in 2003.

According to Prof. Zvi Sussman, former deputy governor of the Bank of Israel, the erosion of salaries and the consequent expansion of poverty among the lowest paid workers was a particularly Israeli problem. Israel, he said, was one of the few developed economies where the wage gap between unskilled and skilled labor had widened greatly in the last few decades. Sussman, who advocated a "negative income tax" for low-wage workers, placed some of the blame on the use of labor contractors by various employers, including the government. And inevitably, the situation of the poor was due to get worse, with additional cuts planned in some social allowances and in government payments to older Israelis.

Setting aside the quality of the work or the compensation for it, there was clearly more work to be had in 2004. There was an increase of 2 percent in the number of all work hours recorded by the CBS, including employed Israelis, legal foreign workers, and Palestinians legally permitted into Israel; in 2003 that increase in work hours was only 0.3 percent. Productivity—the net product per work hour—rose by 4.5 percent in the business sector after rising only 1.1 percent in 2003. This rise in productivity is typical of a recovering economy, where employers tend to increase the workload of the employees on their payrolls as orders pick up, before they commit to hiring new employees.

At the same time, the State Employment Service, an arm of the Ministry of Trade, Industry and Labor, reported a drop in the average number of jobseekers registering at its offices every month. For the year, the number of new jobseekers (including those who never had a job before) fell 12.5 percent to an average of 22,300 a month, from 25,400 in 2003. And the numbers dropped toward the end of the year: 227,200 jobseekers contacted the service in December, 1 percent fewer than in November. The number of jobseekers fell by a cumulative 6.4 percent in the last four months of 2004.

The job situation for municipal workers in many small local governments became something of a public scandal. Burdened by heavy debts and, in many cases, fiscal incompetence by elected political leaders, many municipalities did not pay their workers for extended periods, some for as much as two years. Local authorities argued that some of the burdens placed on them, including making welfare payments and running schools, were tasks delegated to them by the central government in Jerusalem with no regard for their ability to finance them. And some mayors claimed that cuts in allocations in the middle of the year by the central government, which provided the budget of some of the poorer towns and villages, had exacerbated the problem. In any event, a Dun & Bradstreet report indicated that the debts of local authorities increased by NIS 1.3 billion (about $400 million) over the course of the year.

Israel continued its policy of seeking out and expelling illegal foreign workers. Since the institution of the Immigration Police in 2002, about 116,000 foreign workers were expelled. Human-rights activists objected to the way that the workers—from the Far East, Africa, and Eastern

Europe—were picked up and detained before expulsion. Tens of thousands of foreign workers with legal permits remained in the country, most of them employed in agriculture, construction, or home health care. Intermittent friction continued between the Histadrut, Israel's trade-union federation, and the Finance Ministry—in particular, Finance Minister Netanyahu, whose preference for free-market policies threatened the position of organized labor (see AJYB 2004, pp. 201–04). But there were at least some signs of a meeting of the minds. In July and August, port workers staged a 23-day strike in protest against Netanyahu's plan to privatize the government-run ports, and to separate the ports of Ashdod, Haifa, and Eilat into three separate companies. The workers came under intense public pressure to go back to work, since the strike did damage to the economy as a whole by holding up exports and endangering agreements between Israeli exporters and their overseas customers. The strike ended with the workers withdrawing their demand for an indefinite postponement of the reform, a lien on the ports' assets in their favor, and the perpetuation, for now, of the Israel Ports Authority's monopoly over the ports.

The Histadrut called off a national strike on September 22, just hours after it had started, when an agreement was reached that would allow many local governments to pay workers, some of whom had not received salaries for long periods (see above, p. 274). The National Labor Court achieved a settlement by calling simultaneously for the payments and for the Histadrut to cooperate with the localities in working out recovery plans. And on December 11, the Finance Ministry and the Histadrut reached an agreement that averted a walkout of all public-sector workers by agreeing to cancel plans for the imposition of new taxes on "advanced training funds" that were part of government workers' wage package, on severance pay, and on shift work. In exchange, the Histadrut agreed to postpone a cost-of-living increment for public-sector employees to 2006, and not to go on strike.

Religion and State

CONVERSION

Israel's Law of Return granting automatic Israeli citizenship to Jews immigrating to Israel had been construed, over the years, to include people converted to Judaism abroad before their aliyah, whatever the denominational affiliation of the rabbi performing the conversion. But conversions in Israel were recognized only if the officiating rabbi was Orthodox, a situation that Reform and Conservative Jews decried as discriminatory. And Orthodox insistence on converting only those willing to maintain a basic level of Jewish religious observance created a situation in which large numbers of newcomers to Israel, many of them from the former Soviet Union, were not recognized by the rabbinate as Jews. An attempt to hammer out a compromise, based on the so-called Ne'eman Committee recommendations of 1998, whereby rabbis of all streams could teach conversion candidates in Israel but the ceremony itself would be done by an Orthodox religious court, was never accepted by the Orthodox establishment.

On May 31, 2004, Israel's High Court of Justice ruled on petitions brought by 15 foreigners who had studied for Reform or Conservative conversion while in Israel and then returned home for the actual ceremony, so that Israel would recognize them as Jews when they came back. In a 7-4 decision, the court sided with the converts. "It is hard to understand why a person who visited legally and even studied for a conversion in Israel and then converted abroad would not be seen as an immigrant under the Law of Return after he converted and asked to live in Israel permanently," a summary of the ruling said. Interior Minister Avraham Poraz, in a letter to the attorney general, announced his intention of granting immediate citizenship to 11 of the petitioners in the case. And, he continued, since the Israeli Reform and Conservative movements had promised to accept in their conversion programs only people who were already legal residents of Israel, and so the procedure would not enable non-Israelis to obtain "quickie" Israeli citizenship, Poraz would accept these conversions from now on.

Reform and Conservative leaders called the decision a breakthrough. "There are no longer any excuses to limit Conservative and Reform conversions in Israel, and if the Ministry of Interior tries to do so, they won't have legal ground, only political ground," said Nicole Maor, director of legal aid for new immigrants at the Israel Religious Action Center. But the court, in fact, had not ruled on the recognition of non-Orthodox conversions performed in Israel. Instead, it gave the government 45 days (the deadline would later be postponed) to present arguments about whether to maintain the status quo or to break the Orthodox monopoly on conversions in Israel. Minister Poraz said that he wanted to deal with the question in a way that "allows a large population in Israel to convert to Judaism."

But Prime Minister Sharon had other ideas. He ordered the government to respond to the court that, for the purpose of citizenship under the Law of Return, conversions performed in Israel were only valid if they were Orthodox. However the prime minister would not, as requested by the Orthodox parties, seek to amend the Law of Return so as to block those converted abroad by Reform or Conservative rabbis from Israeli citizenship. Sharon instructed Attorney General Mazuz to suggest to the court once again the solution proposed by the Ne'eman Committee, leaving the actual conversion in Orthodox hands but creating an interdenominational body to prepare the candidates. At the cabinet meeting where this was discussed, Poraz objected, saying it would "give no solution to tens of thousands of immigrants from the former Soviet Union, who came to Israel by virtue of the Law of Return but are not considered Jews by Halakhah."

The position of the government in support of the status quo was presented to the court in late November. While representatives of the Conservative and Reform movements expressed chagrin, other observers noted that Sharon had no other choice, since he was, at the time, seeking to push the anticlerical party Shinui (of which Poraz was a member) out of the coalition and to replace it not only with Labor, but also United Torah Judaism, and perhaps the Sephardi Orthodox party Shas as well (see above, p. 224).

CHIEF RABBI PROBE

In October, Channel Two TV carried a report that Rabbi Yonah Metzger, the Ashkenazi chief rabbi, had spent the previous Passover at the David Citadel Hotel in Jerusalem without paying for rooms or food, free services worth tens of thousands of shekels. On December 15, Attorney General Mazuz ordered a preliminary police investigation. Since Metzger was a technically a public employee, receipt of such benefits from private parties could well be construed as unlawful. However a spokesman for the rabbi said that Metzger "acted according to the conventions established long ago."

In the past, Metzger's name had come up in relation to other scandals, including alleged sexual harassment, threatening another rabbi, and charges of forging signatures on a marriage contract. When he was named chief rabbi in 2003, there were calls for him to turn the job down because he was not a trained rabbinical judge. But the appointment went through when Elyakim Rubinstein, the attorney general at the time, declined to intervene (see AJYB 2004, pp. 210–11).

Other Domestic Matters

CRIME

Concern about a rise in violent crime, especially organized crime, continued to plague the country in 2004. The most shocking incident occurred on the night of July 19, when Judge Adi Azar of the Tel Aviv District Court was shot dead at point-blank range outside his Ramat Hasharon home, the first murder of a judge in Israeli history. Four months later, police announced they had cracked the case and had arrested five suspects. Underworld figure Yitzhak Zuziashvili was accused of ordering the assassination from his jail cell. Imprisoned since 1996 for the murder of his former business partner, Zuziashvili had over the years repeatedly petitioned the courts for a retrial, to no avail. Police suspected that after making no progress in cutting short his sentence, Zuziashvili decided to order the murder of a randomly chosen judge to shake up the judicial system and possibly get his sentence shortened. Apparently he and a confederate compiled a hit list of eight judges, including Azar, whom they had never met nor heard of before.

Zuziashvilli's lawyer, David Weiner, 46, a deputy public defender, shot himself in the head on December 31, leaving behind a suicide note linking his action to his representation of Zuziashvilli. Authorities said that Weiner, who died on January 1, 2005, did not know of Zuziashvilli's involvement in the Azar murder until shortly before the case against his client was made public.

Four Israelis and four men from Belarus were charged on April 6 with attempting to murder three gangland figures, brothers Nissim and Yaakov Alperon, and businessman-restaurateur Ezra (Shuni) Gavrieli, father of Likud MK Inbal Gavrieli, who admitted to police that he ran an Internet gambling operation. The Belarus men were allegedly setting up a bomb-making factory in their Kfar Saba apartment where they were arrested. Police said they had a video showing that a bomb found in the underground parking lot of the Azrieli Towers shopping and office complex in central Tel Aviv had fallen off the car of Gavrieli.

After an investigation that lasted three years and spanned several countries, police arrested reputed underworld boss Ze'ev Rosenstein on November 6, on an international warrant for smuggling drugs from the EU to the U.S. The arrest warrant called for his extradition to the U.S., a process that could take months. U.S. federal documents released in Miami accused Rosenstein of trying to export 700,000 Ecstasy tablets to New

York. "I imagine he will sit behind bars for many years and we are very happy to have him do so in America," said a spokesman for the Israeli police. "The main thing is that he will be in prison." Rosenstein, 50, had long been accused of being one of Israel's top mob leaders, but, aside from a brief stint in prison for armed robbery in the 1970s, he had no prior convictions.

ADOPTION CASE

A complicated legal dispute over the custody of a baby dragged on through most of the year and drew considerable media attention. A mother who had given up her baby for adoption when it was ten days old without telling the father about its birth later changed her mind, informed the father, and sought to get her baby back. However, the six-month probationary period for adoptions had already passed.

A three-judge panel of the Tel Aviv District Court finally resolved the case on December 28, when the baby was 19 months old. The two-judge majority ruled for the natural parents, arguing that since the adoptive father suffered from a terminal kidney disease that could end his life within seven years, it would be best for the child to be raised by his biological parents. But presiding judge Saviona Roth-Levy favored the adoptive parents (she called them the "psychological parents"), who had developed a strong bond with the baby. The majority decision came despite a strong recommendation in favor of the adoptive parents by two court-appointed psychologists, who said that separating the child from people who had raised him would result in a sense of loss that might be irreparable, and that the biological parents were not sufficiently mature to meet the "well above average parental conditions" that the baby would require under the circumstances.

POLLUTION

The second annual "Environmental Poverty Report," issued on December 19 by Adam Teva V'Din, the Union for Environmental Defense, charged that polluters were punished infrequently and not very harshly. In fact, according to the report, several serial polluters got public money from the Industry and Trade Ministry's Investment Promotion Center, and from the government's Office of the Chief Scientist.

The government did take steps to deal with a particularly blatant pollution problem at the Ramat Hovav dump for hazardous wastes in the

Negev. But it did so only after the local government there petitioned the High Court of Justice, and the court, in turn, ordered the government to present it with a clean-up plan. On November 28, the cabinet decided that factories in the Ramat Hovav industrial zone would be required to curb excessive emissions and to treat the sewage they created rather than dumping it. A deadline of 2010 was set for a total clean-up, with air pollution targeted for elimination by 2007.

JEWISH EXTREMISTS

Brothers-in-law Yitzhak Pas of Hebron and Matityahu Shvu of the Ma'on outpost were sentenced to 15 months in prison for weapons-related offenses by a Jerusalem District Court on January 29, after a plea-bargain deal. Pas's infant daughter, Shalhevet, was killed by a Palestinian sniper in Hebron in March 2001.

Four men suspected of membership in a Jewish terror cell were arrested in early March. They were Eliran Golan, 22, his father Meir, 54, and Alex Rabinovitch, 20, all of Haifa, and Yevgeny Grossman, 22, of Ashdod. Eliran Golan was suspected of nine attacks against Arabs and left-wing Jews over the previous three years. Weapons and explosive devices were found in the Golan home. On March 22, Eliran Golan was charged with the attempted murder of Arab MK Issam Makhoul and at least three other people in the Haifa area.

On April 4, Tzuriel Amior, from the Adei Ad outpost in the West Bank, was acquitted by a Jerusalem District Court of charges that he belonged to the Bat Ayin Jewish terror cell. The court ruled that Amior's fingerprints, found on a bomb planted at a Palestinian girls' school in the East Jerusalem A-Tur neighborhood in April 2000, were not sufficient evidence to warrant convicting him. Three other members of the cell were convicted in September 2003 of planting the bomb.

Yigal Amir, the imprisoned assassin of Yitzhak Rabin, and a woman, Larissa Trimbobler, sought to marry, raising the question of whether a criminal guilty of such an act had the "right" to be married. In early September, members of the Amir family said that the marriage had taken place over the telephone in mid-August, claimed that it was valid under Jewish law, and demanded the convict's right to have conjugal visits.

LAND DECISION

The Israel Lands Authority in early May acceded to a 2000 High Court of Justice decision granting an Israeli Arab, Adel Ka'adan, 49, a surgical nurse in Hadera's Hillel Yaffe Hospital, the right to purchase property in the Jewish community of Katzir, in northern Israel. The Ka'adans had applied to live there in 1995, and after being rejected, they petitioned the court, which ruled that the state could not discriminate in the allocation of state lands. The Katzir admissions committee then rejected them on grounds of social incompatibility, and the Ka'adans again petitioned the High Court in September 2003. Katzir residents still had the option of appealing.

SPORTS

Israel won the first Olympic gold medal in the country's 56-year history in August, when 29-year-old Gal Fridman took first place in the Mistral windsurfing competition at the Athens games. As Israel had spent considerable time, effort, and money to send its 36-member delegation to Athens, Fridman's medal took on great significance, and Limor Livnat, the minister for education, culture, and sport, flew specially to the Greek capital to attend the prize ceremony. But, as *Ha'aretz* sports columnist Ron Koffman pointed out, the glitter of the gold was something of an illusion. Other countries with similar sized populations, including Norway, Slovakia, the Czech Republic, Kazakhstan, Estonia, and Slovenia, all garnered larger medal hauls.

There were a few other notable Israeli achievements in Athens. The nation won another medal when Arik Zeevi captured the bronze in the men's judo competition. Haile Satayiin, a 49-year-old immigrant from Ethiopia, took 20th place in the marathon, and gymnast Pavel Gofman provided a major surprise when he reached the finals in the men's all-around competition. And Marina Kravchenko reached the third round of the women's table tennis tourney, a notable achievement in a sport that has little following in Israel. There were also some major disappointments. Michael Kolganov, a medalist at the 2000 Sydney Games, failed to place in the kayak competition in Athens, and Gotcha Tsitsiashvili, the world champion in the 84 kg Graeco-Roman wrestling class, failed to make it past the first round, and announced his retirement. Another failure of sorts came from Alexander Averbukh, one of the favorites in the pole vault and the 2002 European gold medalist in the event, who reached the Athens finals but failed to win a medal, finishing eighth. Four other highly regarded Israeli entrants, in the 470-class sailing competitions, did not do even that well—both the women's pair of Vered Buskila and Nika Kornitzky, and the men's pair, Udi Gal and Gidi Klieger, ended up out of the top ten in their respective events.

Another important sports story was the effort by Livnat, Foreign Minister Shalom, and Finance Minister Netanyahu to prevent a decision to move the Euroleague's Final Four, Europe's premier basketball event, away from Tel Aviv on April 29–May 1 due to fears of terrorist retaliation after Sheikh Yassin's assassination. Citing similar concerns, the Spanish club Valencia forfeited a March 25 qualifying game with Maccabi Tel Aviv. In the end, Maccabi won the title by routing Skipper Bologna 118-74 before a packed audience in Tel Aviv's Nokia hall, formerly called Yad Eliyahu.

On May 6, Maccabi trounced Hapoel Jerusalem 108-85 to take the State Cup competition for the 34th time, and Maccabi made it a triple by sweeping crosstown rival Hapoel Tel Aviv in the Premier League playoff final. Hapoel Jerusalem won Europe's second most prestigious baskeball title, the ULEB Cup, on March 13, defeating favored Real Madrid of Spain 83-72 before 6,500 fans in Charleroi, Belgium.

Like basketball, Israeli soccer was dogged by the fear of terrorism. In March 2002, after an attack on a restaurant frequented by Tel Aviv Hapoel soccer players left three dead, UEFA, European soccer's governing body, issued a ban on international matches being played in Israel. But the ban was lifted on April 22, 2004, reflecting the return of relative security in the country.

Personalia

AWARDS AND HONORS

The 2004 Nobel Prize in Chemistry went to two professors at the Technion, Avraham Hershko, 66, and Aharon Ciechanover, 56, together with Irwin Rose of the University of California at Irvine, for their discovery of a method by which cells destroy unwanted proteins, which may aid the development of anticancer drugs.

The Israel Prizes, awarded on Independence Day, went to Prof. Sara Japhet, Hebrew University, biblical research; Prof. Zvia Amishai-Maisels, Hebrew University, art history; Prof. Esther Samuel-Cahn, Hebrew University, statistics; Prof. Abraham Doron, Hebrew University, social work; Russian-born Prof. Yosef Bernstein, Tel Aviv University, mathematics; Romanian-born Lia Van Leer, founder of the Jerusalem Cinemathèque, cinema; actress Gila Almagor; composer Gil Aldema; singer-actor Yehoram Gaon; sculptor Yigael Tumarkin; Prof. Aharon Razin, Hebrew University, biochemistry; Rabbi Yitzchak Dovid Grossman, founder of the Migdal Ohr school network for underprivileged children and new immigrants; Profs. Menachem Brinker and Dov Noy, Hebrew University, Hebrew and general literature; British-born Dr. David Harel, Weizmann Institute of Science and cofounder of I-Logic, a leading software firm, computer science (Harel's father won the Israel Prize for literature in 2002); and Moshe Schnitzer, founder of the Israel Diamond Exchange and its longtime president, lifetime achievement.

The Wolf Prizes, established by the German-born, Cuban-naturalized, Israeli resident Dr. Bernardo Wolf, who died in 1981: medicine — Robert Weinberg, MIT, for his discovery of the behavior of mutant genes in cancer cells, and Roger Tsien, University of California, San Diego, for work with fluorescent photolabile molecules; chemistry — Harry Gray, Cal-Tech, for pioneering work in inorganic chemistry; arts — cellist-conductor Mstislav Rostropovich and pianist-conductor Daniel Barenboim; agriculture — Yuan Longping, Hunan Province, China, and Steven Tanksely, Cornell University, for innovative development of hybrid rice; physics — Robert Brout and François Englert, Université Libre de Bruxelles, and Peter Highs, Edinburgh.

APPOINTMENTS

Former attorney general Elyakim Rubinstein, former state attorney Edna Arbel, Salim Jubran, and Esther Hayut were sworn in as justices of the High Court of Justice, Israel's supreme court, on May 24. Jubran, a former district court judge, became the first Israeli Arab member of the tribunal.

Moshe Karadi, who had been serving as police commander of the Southern District, took over as national police chief on August 1, succeeding Shlomo Aharonishki. Karadi, 44, a surprise choice, was given the position over more experienced candidates.

Zvi Hefetz was confirmed as Israel's new ambassador to the United Kingdom on January 18. Some British Jews who had objected to the political appointment of the Russian-born lawyer-businessman, who represented Russian media magnate Vladimir Gusinsky as vice chairman of the *Ma'ariv* newspaper board, claimed that he did not speak English (see below, p. 320).

Brig. Gen. Eliezer Shkedy, 47, took over as commander of the Air Force on April 4, succeeding Maj. Gen. Dan Halutz, who became deputy chief of staff.

DEATHS

Nissim Ezekiel, 79, the leading Indian poet writing in English and one-time representative of the JDC in Bombay, on January 9; Yossi Ginossar, 58, businessman, Israeli-Palestinian go-between, and former senior Shin Bet official, on January 12; philanthropist Gita Sherover, 87, whose projects included the Center for the Performing Arts and the Sherover Promenade in Jerusalem, and Beit Gabi at Lake Kinneret, on June 11; singer-actor Arik Lavi, 77, on June 29; author and political activist Moshe Shamir, 83, on August 20; Shaul Amor, 64, three-term Knesset member, minister without portfolio in Benjamin Netanyahu's cabinet, for 20 years mayor of the town of Migdal Haemek, and former ambassador to Belgium, on October 2; singer-songwriter Uzi Hitman, 52, on October 16; Arab-affairs expert Victor Nahmias, 71, a journalist who also served as a diplomat in Israel's embassy in Jordan, on October 29; national women's basketball star Nili Natho, 23, a Circassian from Kafr Kana, together with her sister Diana, 19, and Raja Talash, 24, a cousin, in a traffic accident, on November 6; Yitzhak Hershkowitz, 58, Public Works Department engineer, by his own hand, on November 20, after a TV broadcast of an investigative report on alleged department negligence in maintenance that led to several road accidents, including a 1999 bus crash near Golani junction in the North in which 17 people died; Rafael (Raful) Eitan, 75, IDF chief of staff during the 1982 Lebanese war, cabinet minister, and founder of the right-wing Tsomet party, drowned at Ashdod port on November 23; Yehudit Naot, 60, who stepped down as environment minister earlier in the year due to throat cancer, on December 16.

HANAN SHER

Canada

National Affairs

$\mathbf{P}$AUL MARTIN, chosen in November 2003 as the new Liberal Party leader and prime minister (see AJYB 2004, p. 231), sought his own mandate by calling an election for late June 2004. His principal opponent was Stephen Harper, leader of the Conservative Party.

During the five-week spring campaign, the Conservatives appeared to be on the verge of a breakthrough, but when the votes were counted they fell far short. The Liberals did lose their majority, but held onto enough seats to remain the leading party. They formed a minority government that was dependent primarily on the support of the New Democratic Party (NDP). Both the NDP and the Bloc Quebecois increased their presence in the House of Commons, with the Conservatives becoming the official opposition. Although in principle a minority government could finish the normal four-year term, another election was considered likely by 2006.

On election day, constituencies with substantial Jewish populations generally voted for Liberal candidates, especially in the Toronto and Montreal areas. Jews elected to the House of Commons included Susan Kadis in Ontario, Irwin Cotler, Jacques Saada, and Raymonde Falco in Quebec, and Anita Neville in Manitoba. A number of non-Jewish supporters of Israel were returned to their seats, while Yvon Charbonneau, an MP who was very hostile to Israel, did not seek reelection. The campaign was marred by the defacing of Saada posters with swastikas in his riding (district) south of Montreal. Election posters of Conservative candidate Jordan Katz in Windsor were similarly defaced. Earlier in the year Saada reported receiving a number of hostile letters and phone calls that attacked him as a Jew.

Prime Minister Martin retained the three Jews he had appointed to top positions upon taking office: Irwin Cotler as minister of justice and attorney general, Jack Austin as government leader in the Senate, and

Jacques Saada, previously government leader in the House, who became minister of economic development for Quebec and minister responsible for the Francophonie. Rosalie Silberman Abella was appointed to the Supreme Court of Canada, the third Jew to sit on the court.

In an interview with the *Canadian Jewish News,* Cotler described the extent to which his public life was grounded in Jewish values, mentioning his commitment to the biblical injunction, "Justice, justice shall you pursue." He elaborated in a November speech at York University, where he cited such Jewish principles as remembrance, guarding one's tongue, not being a bystander to evil, liberating captives, supporting women's rights, and protecting the most vulnerable.

Canada's economy prospered during 2004 despite the uncertainty introduced by the emergence of a minority government after the election. Economic expansion continued at a moderate pace, inflation was low, and unemployment dropped. The Canadian dollar appreciated significantly against its American counterpart, putting pressure on manufacturers and exporters to remain competitive.

The public prominence achieved by some Canadian Jews became a matter of controversy during the year. Leon Mugesera, accused of hate crimes in Rwanda, requested that the Supreme Court decline to hear a federal government appeal of a lower court decision that he should not be deported because the allegations had not been proved. His lawyer, Guy Bertrand, charged that the Supreme Court could not be impartial. Bertrand argued that not only had Justice Minister Cotler conspired with the Canadian Jewish Congress (CJC) and other intervenors in the case, but that Cotler was also a close friend of newly appointed Supreme Court Justice Rosalie Abella, whose husband, Irving Abella, and Cotler were both past presidents of CJC. (Justice Abella had previously recused herself from the case.) Mugesera stated in an affidavit that "I live in anguish, not knowing everything that awaits me and my family as a result of pressures by intervenors such as the powerful Canadian Jewish Congress in collaboration with the justice minister and attorney general." The Justice Department responded that the charges were "absurd, even shocking." In December, the Supreme Court rejected Bertrand's motion and proceeded to consider the government's appeal.

TERRORISM

In his new book, *Cold Terror: How Canada Nurtures and Exports Terrorism Around the World,* journalist Stewart Bell argued that even though the country had not yet experienced an attack, "Canada is itself a terror target," and quoted one of Osama bin Laden's taped messages to that effect. Bell also chronicled a series of Canadian actions that he saw as contradicting the government's tough official stance against terrorism. Other countries, he wrote, were "frustrated with Canada's inability to stop terrorist support and fund-raising, recruitment, passport forgery and plotting." Bell claimed that political influence exerted by certain ethnic communities inhibited necessary counterterrorism measures, and that "the Jewish community is almost alone in lobbying the Canadian government to take a tougher stand." Bell was not alone in his pessimistic assessment. In May, at a panel discussion in Toronto, John Thompson, president of the Mackenzie Institute, predicted an eventual attack in Canada, and Alan Baker, the new Israeli ambassador, noted that Canada's openness and ethnic diversity made it a prime target.

Rabbi Abraham Cooper, associate dean of the Simon Wiesenthal Center, visited Ottawa in January and urged government officials to take the lead in having suicide bombing declared a crime against humanity. Justice Minister Cotler later stated that existing legislation was sufficient to cover the offense.

In February, the *Globe and Mail,* citing a report by the U.S. Library of Congress, claimed that in 1999 Al Qaeda and Hezballah had planned simultaneous attacks on Jewish targets in Ottawa, Buenos Aires, and Paraguay, but that South American police foiled the plot.

Accused Canadian Hezballah agent Fauzi Mohammed Mustafa Ayub was released by Israel in January as part of a prisoner exchange that led to freedom for kidnapped Israeli businessman Elchanan Tannenbaum. It was not clear whether Ayub, who also held Lebanese citizenship, planned to return to Canada. Conservative Party foreign-affairs critic Stockwell Day expressed the hope that he would not be welcomed given the fact that he was "a known member of one of the most vicious terrorist groups in the world." In another case, Jamal Akkal, a Palestinian Canadian, pleaded guilty in an Israeli military court to conspiracy to commit manslaughter by attacking Israelis or Jewish community targets in North America. He was sentenced to four years in prison and fined 2,000 shekels.

The government banned the entry of the senior cleric at Saudi Arabia's Grand Mosque in Mecca because of his virulent anti-Semitic preaching. Sheik Abd al-Rahman al-Sudais, who had labeled the Jews "the scum of the earth" and urged his followers to eliminate them, had planned to attend a conference in Toronto in May.

Naji Antoine Abi Khalil, a citizen of both Canada and Lebanon who headed a shipping company in Montreal, and Tomer Grinberg, an Israeli living in New York, were indicted in June by a U.S. federal grand jury for planning to ship up-to-date night-vision equipment to Hezballah in Lebanon.

The Canadian Coalition for Democracies charged in November that a charity going by the name of the International Relief Fund for the Afflicted and Needy (IRFAN) was actually a Hamas front, noting that it had the same address and fax number as the defunct Jerusalem Fund for Human Services, previously the fund-raising arm of Hamas in Canada. The Israel-based Center for the Study of Intelligence and Terror issued a detailed report outlining the links between Hamas and IRFAN.

Efforts to deport convicted Palestinian terrorist Mahmoud Mohammad Issa Mohammad had been going on since 1988. As a member of the Popular Front for the Liberation of Palestine, he participated in an attack on an El Al plane in Athens in 1968. Convicted and jailed in Greece, he was freed after a year as part of a deal to obtain the release of another hijacked plane. Since coming to Canada, Mohammad had managed to string out his deportation proceedings interminably, his lawyer contending that deportation to his home country of Lebanon would endanger his life, that he was no longer a threat, that he had close family ties in Canada, and that Israel might get hold of him. Government lawyers in Federal Court insisted that he continued "to pose a risk to Canadian society." But in October the government conceded that it had made procedural errors in the case and agreed to a delay while a new risk assessment was conducted. This prompted lawyer David Matas to observe that "Canada is a haven for terrorists."

An official of BBC (B'nai Brith Canada) was forced to resign over remarks he made on television in October. Adam Aptowitzer, Ontario chair of B'nai Brith's Institute of International Affairs, said that Israel used terror and that this was acceptable. He explained that "terror is an option to be used by states in order to prevent deaths of their own citizens and of others . . . . when that is being done to prevent deaths, are we going to say that that is wrong?" Muslim and Arab groups quickly called on BBC to repudiate the statement, which it did, dismissing Aptowitzer and saying that he did "not reflect the position of B'nai Brith Canada."

Israel and the Middle East

In March, Israeli political scientist Gerald Steinberg criticized Canada's Middle East policy in his *Canadian Jewish News* column.

Canada tilted away from Israel, he claimed, largely out of a desire to show independence from the U.S. Australia, in contrast, which previously charted a similar course, had more recently drawn closer to Washington and farther from the Europeans in recognition of the terrorist threat and also to further the goals of democracy, security, and national defense. Canada, he concluded, should do the same. In August, Steinberg called on the new Canadian government to rethink its approach to the Arab-Israeli dispute, to stop confusing the symptoms (Israeli actions) with the disease (Palestinian rejectionism), and to begin distinguishing between terrorism and the response to terrorism.

Israel's government, however, saw things differently. Nimrod Barkan, an Israeli Foreign Ministry official who visited Canada in September, argued that precisely because Canada did not march in lockstep with the U.S., it had credibility in Europe to promote pro-Israel initiatives. Acknowledging that Canada's voting record in the UN left something to be desired, he nevertheless saw Canada as a supportive ally. Similarly, Israeli ambassador Alan Baker looked to Canada to play "a central role in helping to push forward the peace process" and "stressed the desire of Israel for Canada to become a more centrally involved player in the process . . . ." Israel welcomed Canada's offer to help oversee the Palestinian elections scheduled for early 2005.

A number of MPs expressed themselves on Middle East issues during the year. In January, Liberal Marlene Jennings called on the government to be more supportive of Israel, claiming that Canada's stance had become less sympathetic over the past decade. However, another Liberal MP, Pat O'Brien, termed Israel's security fence an "atrocity." Speaking in the House of Commons in February, he contended that "this wall denies basic human rights to the Palestinian people and further reduces the West Bank and the Gaza Strip to the status of concentration camps." Another Liberal MP refuted him from the floor the next day and Jewish groups met with him to question the analogy, but O'Brien stood by his words, though he did claim that he was using the term "concentration camps" generically, not in the Nazi context.

Two MPs representing the NDP went on a mission to Israel in August sponsored by the Canada-Israel Committee (CIC), but ran into hostility within their own party after their return. Twenty-seven party members, many of them Muslim, sent an open letter to NDP leader Jack Layton mentioning the trip, charging that it was a Jewish attempt to influence NDP policy, and complaining that the party, which had not been notably supportive of Israel in recent years, was now tilting toward the Jewish state. Layton's response to the letter was noncommittal and did not rule out the petitioners' suggestion that NDP MPs might have to obtain some form of party approval for such trips to Israel in the future.

Echoes of past episodes were heard when two Israeli men were arrested on passport fraud charges in New Zealand in April. One of the men had entered the country using a Canadian passport, but it turned out that he was indeed a Canadian national. In 1997, two Mossad agents posing as Canadian tourists had been picked up in Jordan, leading to some tense moments in Canadian-Israeli relations that were resolved when Israel promised not to use Canadian passports in covert operations. There was speculation that the two men apprehended in New Zealand were Mossad agents, and reports that a third man involved in the operation, who left New Zealand, may have been traveling on a stolen Canadian passport.

During Canada's election campaign, the leaders of the two major parties were interviewed by the *Canadian Jewish News*. Paul Martin denied that past Liberal governments had exhibited lack of support for Israel. He asserted a commitment to Israel's legitimacy and rejected any moral equivalence between terrorism and defending against it. With regard to Canada's position on future UN resolutions, he said that each one would be evaluated on its merits. Conservative leader Stephen Harper declared Israel's survival and security paramount and nonnegotiable, and criticized the government for a lax approach to terrorism and its Canadian infrastructure. Harper did not believe that Canada should be neutral on Arab-Israeli matters, asserting that "Israel is part of the democratic family of nations."

Despite revelations that Hamas members were on the payroll of the UN Relief and Works Agency (UNRWA) that aided Palestinian refugees, Canada maintained its annual $10-million funding of the agency. Peter Hansen, the UNRWA head, actually admitted employing Hamas personnel in a CBC interview in October, but later explained that he had meant to refer to "political sympathies, not membership." Jewish organizations such as the CIC and BBC called upon Ottawa to reconsider its funding of UNRWA, as did Stockwell Day, the opposition foreign-affairs critic.

Day, in fact, emerged during the year as perhaps the most consistently pro-Israel public figure in the country. When Canadian-Israeli Yechezkel Goldberg was killed in a January suicide bombing of a Jerusalem bus, the Canadian embassy in Israel declined to send anyone to express condolences to his mourning family, presumably because their home was beyond the Green Line. Stockwell Day issued a press release declaring the lack of a visit an "outrage" and "an insult to all victims of terror." Day

CANADA / 291

also joined the Jewish community in protesting the appointment of former MP Yvon Charbonneau, a man with a strongly anti-Israel past, as ambassador to UNESCO. (In correspondence with CJC president Ed Morgan, Charbonneau promised that he would only express views at UNESCO that reflected the positions of the government.) In addition, Day pointed out that over the previous ten years, Canada had voted in favor of 75 UN resolutions denouncing Israeli actions, abstained on 38, and never opposed any.

In July, there was a hint that Canada was shifting its voting policy in the UN when it was one of ten nations that abstained on a General Assembly vote demanding that Israel comply with the decision of the International Court of Justice (ICJ) on its security fence (see above, pp. 229–30). Supporting the resolution were 150 countries, including all 25 members of the European Union, with whom Canada usually voted. Only six nations voted against the resolution. Shimon Fogel, CEO of the CIC, found it significant that Canada had broken with the EU, but expressed disappointment that it had not voted against the resolution. A spokesperson for the Department of Foreign Affairs said that there had been no change in policy, as Canada had always been dubious about taking the case to the ICJ. In an official statement, the department tried to balance its doubts about the fence with Israeli security concerns.

On November 30, Alan Rock, Canada's ambassador to the UN, publicly stated that the country would henceforth reject "redundant, divisive" resolutions that "lack balance" and would support only those that were "reality-driven." In December, the Canadian UN delegation indeed appeared to be taking a new line. In the General Assembly it voted against two resolutions critical of Israel, one dealing with human-rights practices in the territories and the other regarding the special UN committee on the inalienable rights of the Palestinians. However, Canada did vote in favor of other resolutions opposed by Israel, including one on the risk of nuclear proliferation that singled out the Jewish state, on which it had abstained in previous years. At year's end, B'nai Brith Canada issued a report critical of Canada's performance in the General Assembly session, noting that its delegation voted for or abstained on 17 of the 19 resolutions B'nai Brith deemed to be tinged with anti-Semitism. But David Goldberg of the CIC observed that "we never anticipated Canadian voting behavior to change overnight. It's gradual. It's slow, but we are happy with the start."

The new Canadian Council for Israel and Jewish Advocacy, or CIJA (see below, p. 304) held its first parliamentary dinner in Ottawa in November. Prime Minister Martin declared that "Canada will not, nor will we ever, waver in our support for Israel," adding that "we believe strongly, incontrovertibly, in Israel's right to defend itself against those who would destroy it." In his keynote address, CBC commentator Rex Murphy condemned international hostility toward Israel. He lamented that decades after the Holocaust there were "intimations of hostility toward Jews again . . . ." Murphy denounced "the degree, the intensity, and the frequency of opprobrium directed by world bodies at Israel."

The refugee claim of Rabbi Erez Shlomo Elbarnes worked its way through the courts. Elbarnes—an Israeli who had spent time in a U.S. prison for kidnapping and was thus ineligible for permanent resident status in Canada—came to Quebec in 2001 on a temporary visa, and set up a small community of his fervently anti-Zionist followers in the town of Ste. Agathe. The federal government moved to deport him, but, in 2003, an Immigration and Refugee Board arbitrator ruled for Elbarnes based on his assertion that his anti-Zionist views would endanger him in Israel. Elbarnes's attorney reiterated that argument at a Federal Court hearing in December 2004, while a government lawyer responded that Israel was a democratic country and had numerous protections against persecution. The decision was pending as the year ended.

The number of Canadian Jews who relocated to Israel during 2004 was 312, a significant increase over the 228 who immigrated in 2003.

THE MEDIA AND PUBLIC OPINION

The CIC surveyed the attitudes of some 1,500 people across the country about the Middle East, and the results displayed widespread ignorance about Israel. Only 42 percent knew that Israel was a democracy, and 89 percent assigned equal responsibility for violence to Israel and the Palestinians. The predominant view among respondents was that Canada should remain neutral and that the media were biased against the Palestinians. Hershell Ezrin, CEO of the Canadian Council for Israel and Jewish Advocacy (CIJA), commented that "unfortunately, Canada is much closer to Europe in this regard" than to the U.S.

In its report on the survey, *Shared Values, Communicating to Canadians: Building Support for Israel,* the CIC concluded that "many of the time-tested approaches used by the Jewish community to communicate with Canadians are not working" and announced a new focus on the values shared by the two countries, the development of a consistent message, providing information about the real impact of violence on Israeli families, and highlighting Israel's desire for peace and social development. The findings also triggered a major effort to bring key people from influential sectors of Canadian society to Israel, and the number of such visitors more than doubled in 2004.

The reluctance to utilize the word "terrorist" when writing about Palestinian attacks on Israelis continued to be a matter of dispute in the media. CanWest Global Communications, publisher of 13 daily newspapers, announced in September that it would continue a policy announced earlier in the year to insert the word "terrorist" into Reuters dispatches to describe the perpetrators of such attacks despite complaints from the news agency, which preferred words like "insurgents," "militants," or "rebels." CIC communications director Paul Michaels pointed out a similar problem at the CBC, Canada's national public broadcaster. With no formal policy in place on the matter, the CBC identified "terrorism" in a number of contexts, but never when Israelis were victims.

Adbusters, a magazine based in Vancouver, ran a story in March about U.S. neoconservatives and the war in Iraq. The story listed some 50 neocons who reportedly had influence over U.S. policy, and the names of the 26 Jews on the list were checked off to distinguish them. The editor of the magazine and author of the article, Kalle Lasn, said he felt compelled to write this piece because "the mainstream and alternative media are somehow scared of talking about the Jewishness of the neocons and the Zionism there . . . and the influence this has on American foreign policy in the Middle East."

CBC television reporter Neil Macdonald continued to be a source of controversy even after he was transferred, in 2003, from Jerusalem to Washington (see AJYB 2004, p. 240). For example, in a story about Prime Minister Sharon's April meeting with President George Bush in Washington, Macdonald gave his own interpretation of Israel's Gaza disengagement plan: "It's the West Bank that Israel really wants, and Sharon, now with Bush's approval, intends to annex a large chunk of it," adding that Bush in effect had "sanctioned . . . Israel's designs on Palestinian territory." In December, both CIC and HonestReporting Canada charged that Macdonald had repeatedly injected his personal views into his news reporting, contravening CBC guidelines. B'nai Brith, for its part, urged the CBC "to uphold basic journalistic standards by immediately reviewing Macdonald's conduct and acting on their findings . . . . Failure to ensure his adherence to core journalistic principles would make the broadcaster complicit in a process through which double standards, demonization, and delegitimization of Israel have become the order of the day." Paul Michaels of the CIC found a silver lining in the cloud, observing that CBC coverage of the Middle East had become much more balanced since Macdonald left Jerusalem.

MediaNet Canada, owner of several radio stations and of Tamil TV in Toronto, was granted a license to operate Jewish Television (JTV) and distribute the channel through digital cable systems. Guidelines set by the Canadian Radio-television and Telecommunications Commission (CRTC) required that at least 55 percent of the programming be in Hebrew or Yiddish. JTV was to provide extensive coverage of Israel in addition to other Jewish-themed programming. Another new outlet for news and features about Israel and the Jewish community was begun by Montreal journalist David Ouellette, who launched a Web magazine, *Judeoscope—le magazine d'actualités à l'oeil nu.*

In the face of considerable opposition from Jewish groups, the CRTC granted a license to Al-Jazeera. However, cable operators wishing to offer the Arabic-language channel would have to comply with regulations—similar to those suggested by some Jewish groups—that were so stringent as to possibly deter the operators from getting involved, especially the requirement that cable and satellite providers "alter or delete" programming to insure that no abusive content was broadcast. CJC president Ed Morgan issued a statement on the decision: "Because of the history of anti-Semitic comment on Al-Jazeera, our first choice was not to have this broadcaster distributed in Canada. However, we are pleased that the alternatives CJC recommended to the CRTC to protect minority communities in Canada from vilification while still protecting free speech have been accepted." In contrast, B'nai Brith remained totally opposed to allowing Al-Jazeera into Canada.

In a March decision, the Quebec Press Council rejected David Ouellette's complaint about an article that appeared in 2003 in a small-town paper, *La Voix de l'Est,* which drew parallels between current Israeli policies and the crucifixion of Jesus. According to the council, it was not anti-Semitic. In another decision that same month, the council rejected a complaint against Global TV and filmmaker Martin Himel for his documentary *Confrontation at Concordia.* The accusation raised against the film, that it gave the impression that activists opposed to the war in Iraq were anti-Semitic, was unfounded, according to the decision. But the council chided Himel for not identifying the film as a work of opinion and for "gratuitously associating" the antiwar movement with Nazis.

In December CanWest Global Communications Corp., with headquarters in Winnipeg, acquired half ownership of the *Jerusalem Post* in a partnership with Mirkaei Tikshoret Group Ltd. The *Post* was one of the media properties sold by Hollinger International.

THE CAMPUSES

Since the outbreak of the current wave of Israeli-Palestinian violence in late 2000, some of the most significant struggles between Canadian supporters of Israel and their opponents took place on university campuses. Concordia University in Montreal achieved the greatest notoriety because of the confrontation that prevented former Israeli prime minister Benjamin Netanyahu from speaking there in 2002 (see AJYB 2003, pp. 310–12); York University in Toronto was another hotbed of anti-Israel activity.

In late 2003, the student government election at York resulted in the victory of a slate opposed to the anti-Israel incumbents, but the outgoing student council refused to ratify the result, preventing the victors from assuming their posts. In January 2004, the university administration responded by suspending funding for the student council, a step that finally induced the losing side to hand over control to the newly elected officers. But in the next election, held in November 2004, the pro-Palestinian element won 15 of the 19 council seats, and one of the new vice presidents was a spokesperson for Solidarity for Palestinian Human Rights (SPHR), the most aggressive anti-Israel group on Canadian campuses. The victorious slate called for "reinvigorated activism," and a former Hillel president said that "the atmosphere on campus has definitely taken a turn for the worse."

Earlier, in February, a local of the Canadian Union of Public Employees (CUPE)—which represented teaching and research assistants as well as contract faculty, and had a long anti-Israel record—sponsored a talk, "From Occupied Palestine," by a journalist and activist who had spent the previous summer in Jenin and Rafah. When some students challenged the one-sided nature of the presentation and expressed doubts as to whether their teaching assistants could be objective and fair-minded about the issue in the classroom, a union official observed that his members "believe the Israeli government acts in an oppressive fashion which needs highlighting and don't believe there is any need to present any evidence or justification for what is being done by the Israelis."

The next month, pro- and anti-Israel students clashed at York when SPHR and several other leftist and union groups sponsored a "street-theater" type event depicting the Israeli "occupation" in a grossly unfavorable manner, with mock "checkpoints" at which passing students were harassed. Jewish students responded by trying to block the installation of the checkpoints and the theatrical presentations. Afterward, the university suspended the activities of SPHR, Hillel, and another pro-Israel group for violating a ban on events in a particular building. A few days later, Hillel held a Jewish Unity Rally. MP Art Eggleton addressed the gathering, telling the students that "hatred of Israel is the new and clever guise of anti-Jewish prejudice." The suspensions of the groups were lifted after a week.

In November, York history professor David Noble (himself Jewish) handed out literature after a SPHR film presentation alleging that the York University Foundation "is biased by the presence and influence of staunch pro-Israel lobbyists, activities, and fund-raising agencies." He also listed the names of some board members and their links to Jewish community groups. York president Lorna Marsden condemned Noble's "highly offensive" material, and the CUPE local responded with a rally to protest restrictions on speech and assembly, support Noble, and demand that Marsden apologize to him. In addition to his anti-Israel activities, Noble sought to prevent the university from canceling classes on religious holidays such as Rosh Hashanah, Yom Kippur, and Good Friday, claiming violation of provincial law.

Two years after the fiasco of the Netanyahu visit, Concordia University was again embroiled in controversy. Hillel proposed inviting another former Israeli prime minister, Ehud Barak, to give a campus lecture. The administration turned this down on the grounds that it could not ensure security, but offered to cosponsor an off-campus talk. The Jewish students, backed by leaders of the Jewish community, insisted on a campus venue in order to demonstrate that threats of violence emanating from pro-Palestinian groups could not keep Israeli speakers away, but the university would not budge. Federation CJA president Sylvain Abitbol complained that "for the sake of not disturbing things, the Jews are being sacrificed," Israeli consul-general Marc Attali asked whether this meant that "an Israeli cannot speak there ever," and the *Canadian Jewish News* editorialized that "the university has effectively given a veto to the extremists and the abhorrers of tolerance on the question of who is a permissible campus guest." Concordia's rector, Frederick Lowy, published an article in three newspapers in October explaining the steps the university was taking to ensure proper security for controversial speakers. A month later, Lowy announced that Concordia was prepared to invite Barak to speak on campus during the first half of 2005, once security measures were in place.

In February, the National Film Board documentary about the university's 2002 Netanyahu incident, *Discordia,* premiered on campus. The directors were Ben Addelman and Samir Mallal. The film followed three of the main student protagonists in the conflict—a Palestinian-Canadian student activist, a Jewish supporter of the Palestinians, and a Hillel leader. Student elections were scheduled for March, and Hillel mounted a campaign to get out the vote, fearing that apathy might play into the hands of the most radical student politicians. In the end, a moderate slate prevailed and a number of candidates backed by Hillel won seats on the student council.

In addition to developments at York and Concordia, a number of other campuses witnessed varying degrees of tension over Israel-related matters. The SPHR chapter at McMaster University in Hamilton was put on probation in March for including a placard on its Web site denouncing Zionism as racism. SPHR at the University of Western Ontario in London joined a rally against anti-Semitism in April, and nevertheless, a few months later, erected a mock wall in the university's community center to protest Israel's security fence. SPHR also erected symbolic "apartheid walls" at the University of Ottawa and Carleton University, spurring the Jewish Students Association to increase its advocacy activities. Serge Elbaz, president of Center Hillel, described the Université du Québec à Montréal and the Université de Montréal as "bastions of pro-Palestinian militance." Due to declining Jewish enrollment at these institutions, he said, Hillel was at a disadvantage, but nevertheless brought Israeli speakers to the campuses. Hillel protested a series of three lectures at the Université de Montréal in November on "Israel and Palestine" that featured two anti-Zionist speakers (one of whom was Jewish) but no one favorable to Israel. In response, the university agreed to hold additional lectures in the series in 2005 with a pro-Israel academic.

In October, Mohamed Elmasry, a University of Waterloo professor who was also an advisor in the university's Middle East studies program and president of the Canadian Islamic Congress, stated on a Toronto television show that attacks on any Israeli adult were legitimate because all Israelis serve in the military. Waterloo's president, David Johnston, said he found that view abhorrent, and numerous other public figures also expressed outrage. After Elmasry backtracked and granted that his earlier comments were "totally unacceptable," the university decided not to pursue disciplinary measures demanded by CJC and BBC.

The selection of Mary Robinson to receive an honorary law degree at McGill University in June set off a major contretemps. History professor Gil Troy and others protested that her record as UN commissioner of human rights and chair of the infamous World Conference against Racism in Durban in 2001, which was tinged with anti-Semitism, should disqualify her from the honor. Eventually Robinson agreed to meet with her critics after receiving the degree. There were also protests against the honorary degree that Osgoode Hall Law School of York University conferred on Richard Falk. A number of students protested because Falk defended Palestinian "resistance to occupation," but Dean Patrick Monahan assured them that Falk opposed deliberate violence against civilians.

The Jewish community supported a number of nationwide campus initiatives. CIJA announced the establishment of a Canadian Federation of Jewish Students, which would contend with Muslim and Arab campus organizations that had a national focus. The first president of the federation, Alex Kemeny, sought to develop a strategic concept of Jewish advocacy. During its first year, the federation established a network of collaboration with a variety of bodies and helped students at several universities cope with anti-Israel activism. The Jewish community federations, meanwhile, funded National Jewish Campus Life, which hired seven Israel advocacy specialists to work on campuses in 2003–04, funded outreach initiatives, and ran programs to train student leaders.

In March, the Wolfond Center for Jewish Campus Life opened at the University of Toronto. Funded by UJA Federation of Greater Toronto, the facility soon became a focal point for Jewish activity on campus.

Anti-Semitism and Racism

Anti-Semitic incidents rose by nearly 50 percent in 2004, according to B'nai Brith Canada's annual audit. The 857 incidents, three times the number recorded in 2000, was the highest yearly total in the audit's 22-year history. BBC categorized 457 cases as harassment, 369 as vandalism, and 31 as violence. The province of Ontario was the site of 530 incidents, 405 of them occurring in the greater Toronto area. There were 257 incidents in Quebec, 187 of them in Montreal.

The accelerated pace of anti-Jewish activity was evident early in the year. Anti-Semitic graffiti were found in the Vancouver suburb of Richmond in February. In Vaughan, outside Toronto, two homes and 11 cars were smeared with anti-Semitic graffiti in March, one Holocaust survivor finding a swastika on her door. (Later that month, swastikas were spray-painted on the walls of a Muslim-owned business in Vaughan.) There was major anti-Semitic vandalism in Toronto toward the end of March: cemetery headstones were overturned; windows were broken and swastikas spray-painted on a synagogue; windows were broken at a day school; and UJA fund-raising signs were defaced.

The events in Toronto aroused the Jewish community, which organized a rally in protest against anti-Semitism that drew some 3,000 people, including elected officials and leaders of several ethnic and religious groups. Ontario prime minister Dalton McGuinty told the crowd that "this hate is the stuff of cowards," adding that "an attack on any of us is an attack on us all." After the rally, representatives of the national Jewish organizations met with McGuinty to express their concern about the attacks and to thank him and his colleagues for publicly condemning the incidents. On the day of the rally, Libby Davis, an MP for the NDP, introduced a resolution in the House of Commons condemning the recent attacks, which passed unanimously. In April, three teenagers, one 18 and the others 15, were arrested in connection with the vandalism in Toronto and charged with various counts of mischief. Police Chief Julian Fantino declared that "any hate crime . . . is absolutely unacceptable." In June, the Ontario attorney general consented to the filing of charges of willful promotion of hatred against the three.

An international conference on anti-Semitism was held in Montreal in March, cosponsored by the Canadian Institute for Jewish Research and the Quebec-Israel Committee. The keynote speaker was Israeli cabinet minister Natan Sharansky, who argued that the current wave of attacks on Jews around the world should not be shrugged off simply as fallout from the Middle East conflict, but in fact constituted the strongest manifestation of global anti-Semitism since the Holocaust.

The most significant anti-Semitic incident of the year came in April—the firebombing of the library of the United Talmud Torahs school in the St. Laurent area of Montreal just before Passover. Anti-Semitic flyers left at the scene blaming Israel for crimes against the Palestinians and warning "this is just the beginning" were signed "the brigades of Sheik Ahmed Yassin." The visual image of the library's smoldering ruins made a profound impact on the Jewish community, and the significance of the event reverberated across the country. Prime Minister Martin said that "it is against the values espoused by all Canadians" and an "unspeakable crime." Justice Minister Cotler, himself a graduate of the targeted school, promised to pursue the perpetrators with the full force of the law. The Quebec premier, Jean Charest, called on all Quebecers to denounce the bombing. He later toured the site and tried to reassure the students.

In May, three people—a mother, her son, and another young man, all reported to be of Lebanese origin—were charged with the crime, and all pleaded not guilty. Later in the year, charges against one of the young men were dropped because of insufficient evidence. In December, 19-year-old Sleiman Elmerhebi pleaded guilty to one charge of arson; the additional charge of conspiracy was dropped, much to the displeasure of Jewish leaders. At year's end, Elmerhebi's mother, Rouba Fahd-Elmerhebi, still faced the charge of being an accessory after the fact for trying to help her son escape from Canada. The library, meanwhile, was rebuilt with the help of donations from many sources. Over $400,000 was raised and more than 13,000 books were received to restock the library, which reopened in December. Education Minister Pierre Reid and Revenue Minister Lawrence Bergman attended the ceremony.

The pace of anti-Semitic incidents did not slow down. In April, 12 monuments were overturned at a Jewish cemetery in Kitchener, and, in Oshawa, a synagogue was defaced and a swastika painted on a Holocaust memorial plaque. Graves were desecrated in May at two more cemeteries, one in Montreal, where graffiti were written on gravestones, and the other in Quebec City, where 20 headstones were overturned. In June, a synagogue in Ottawa was desecrated with racist graffiti and swastikas. In the town of Markham, outside Toronto, more than 25 anti-Semitic messages and symbols were spray-painted in various locations in June. Calgary was the scene of two incidents of anti-Semitic graffiti in August, one a message of "Jews, go home" found near the Calgary Jewish Center, and the other a caricature of Prime Minister Sharon depicted as a Nazi.

A particularly nasty example of hate speech came from the leader of a Vancouver mosque, Sheik Younus Kathrada, in October. He denounced Jews as "the brothers of monkeys and swine," and stressed that the Koran depicts Jews as treacherous.

There were a number of legal developments related to anti-Semitism. After a preliminary hearing in January, Christopher Steven McBride was ordered tried for first-degree murder in the 2002 stabbing of David Rosenzweig in Toronto (see AJYB 2003, p, 313). A young man was acquitted in an Ontario court in July on charges of promoting hatred through the sale of 15 CDs at a party in 2003. Although their content was "horrific," in the judge's words, there was no proof that the man had sold them. In October, Kevin Haas, 21, was charged with seven counts of mischief and two of death threats for actions allegedly taken during the summer at Ryerson University in Toronto that were directed at both Jews and Muslims. (There were over a dozen incidents at Ryerson during the period.)

A Muslim newspaper in British Columbia, *The Miracle,* published an anti-Semitic article at the end of 2003. Nusrat Hussain, the editor, defended publication on the grounds of free expression, even though he said he did not agree with the content. But CJC, Pacific Region, demanded a criminal investigation, and the government of the province announced it would increase funding and support for its Hate Crimes Unit, which would look into the charges. Along similar lines, BBC asked the Alberta attorney general to investigate the possibility that *Alberta Arab News,* published in Edmonton, had violated the hate-crimes statute by running a series of articles that included Holocaust denial and charges of Zionist control over the media and government.

Despite the widespread concern in the Jewish community, Canadians did not generally see anti-Semitism as a serious threat to the nation, at least early in the year. An Environics poll in April showed that only about one-sixth of the Canadian population believed that anti-Semitism was on the increase. The figure for Quebec was somewhat higher, around one-fourth. Respondents, both nationally and in Quebec, were nearly evenly split over whether the cases of anti-Semitic vandalism that had occurred up to that time were random acts or part of a trend.

Holocaust-Related Matters

Legal proceedings against accused Nazi war criminals continued to grind along at a slow pace. From 1995, when the government began dealing with such cases through denaturalization proceedings followed by deportation, until the end of 2003, 1,684 files were opened and 19 cases initiated: six of them resulted in deportation and two others were not contested, the accused leaving the country voluntarily; in three cases the accused war criminal prevailed; four of the accused died before their cases were concluded; and four cases were still pending.

Two new cases were initiated in March 2004. Jura Skomatchuk of St. Catharines was alleged to have been an SS guard at the Trawniki training camp, later serving at the Poniatowa forced labor camp and the Sachsenhausen and Mauthausen concentration camps. Josef Furman of Edmonton was accused of taking part in the liquidation of the Warsaw Ghetto. According to the government, Furman, who came from Ukraine, was trained as an SS guard at Trawniki, and then helped clear the Warsaw Ghetto and the Bialystok Ghetto in 1943. Later he served at the Flossenburg concentration camp. Had these men told the truth about their wartime service when applying to immigrate to Canada, they would have been barred, and this was grounds for denaturalization and deportation. Both accused men denied the allegations.

There was a strange twist in the Helmut Oberlander case. In 2001, the cabinet ordered the denaturalization of Oberlander, who had worked as an interpreter for an infamous Nazi death squad responsible for thousands of murders in Ukraine during World War II. But a series of appeals delayed enforcement of the order and, in late 2003, a judge on the Ontario Superior Court of Justice ruled that the cabinet had acted improperly. In June 2004, the Federal Court of Appeals restored Oberlander's citizenship, an action that David Matas of BBC charged "basically guts the process of war criminal citizenship revocation." According to Matas, the decision not only in effect denied the criminal nature of the Nazi Einsatzgruppen, but also ignored the fact that Oberlander had lied about his past when entering Canada. The government was expected to appeal to the Supreme Court.

Ernst Zundel, the Holocaust denier and anti-Semite who entered Canada from Germany in 1958, continued his long legal battle with the authorities (see AJYB 2004, p. 248). In April 2003, the government began proceedings to deport him as a security threat. His challenge to his detention, pending court proceedings, was denied in January 2004 by Judge Pierre Blais of the Federal Court. In May, the Ontario Court of Appeal found that it did not have jurisdiction to hear his challenge to the government's security certificate declaring him a danger to Canada. In June, Judge Blais quashed subpoenas through which Zundel was trying to compel the testimony of leaders of CJC and B'nai Brith Canada (BBC) as well as that of a journalist and a judge who was once Zundel's attorney, to prove undue Jewish influence on his case. Judge Blais found that the Jewish organizations' involvement was open and legitimate. An appeal to the Supreme Court by Zundel's lawyers to deny the deportation order was denied in October.

Canada's first official Holocaust Memorial Day was observed on April 18, Yom Hashoah. Observances were held on Parliament Hill and at the Ottawa Conference Center. Justice Minister Cotler was the main speaker and Israeli Ambassador Haim Divon also addressed a crowd estimated at more than 1,000 that included members of both houses of Parliament and foreign diplomats.

When the National Gallery of Canada discovered that one of the paintings in its collection had been stolen from its Jewish owners by the Nazis, it endeavored to find the descendants of those owners and return the painting to them. CJC president Keith Landy praised the National Gallery for its persistence. In another controversy over the disposition of artwork, a lawyer in Hamilton, Andrew Orkin, and three of his South African relatives filed suit against actress Elizabeth Taylor over possession of a painting that Taylor purchased some 40 years earlier. Orkin claimed it belonged to his great-grandmother in Berlin, who had been forced to give it up due to "Nazi economic and political coercion" in 1939 before her departure for South Africa.

JEWISH COMMUNITY

Demography

An assessment by the Jewish People Policy Planning Institute (JPPPI), the first of an annual series, recognized that "Canada rates among the most successful of Diaspora communities." Not only was it one of the few that was growing, but the report also noted "an overall maintenance and even intensification of Jewish identity in Canada," attributing this at least partly to a strong day-school system.

Prof. Leo Davids of York University analyzed those who identified themselves as Jews by religion in the 2001 Census. He found 330,000 people, up from 318,075 in 1991. Of these, 18.5 percent were aged 14 or younger and 17.7 percent 65 or older. The number of Jewish immigrants during the previous decade was 22,365. The population was heavily concentrated geographically, 77 percent of Canadian Jews living in the Toronto and Montreal metropolitan areas and another 5 percent in Vancouver. (As the census included separate questions on religion and ethnicity, Davids's findings excluded Canadians who identified as Jews ethnically but did not profess the Jewish religion.) In Greater Toronto, by far the largest Canadian Jewish community — over 180,000 in 2001 — there were now three distinct areas of Jewish concentration: downtown (about 21,000); the York Region north of the city (about 60,000); and the Bathurst corridor (over 90,000). Explosive growth in the York Region led community planners to focus significant resources for the development of appropriate infrastructure there.

The rather modest 3.75-percent growth of the Canadian Jewish population over the decade 1991–2001 was infinitesimal compared to the increase in Muslim population, which grew nearly 129 percent, to reach 579,650 in 2001.

The rapid aging of the Canadian Jewish population made it likely that the over-65 age group would grow by about 50 percent by 2021 and place a strain on communal resources. The problem was especially dire in Montreal, where the proportion of senior citizens was increasing at the same time that the overall Jewish population was shrinking. The corresponding decline in the economically productive age groups "has implications for the economic viability of the Montreal Jewish community and its long-term ability to provide services and programs to its more vulnerable members," according to Charles Shahar, the Federation CJA demographer.

According to the census, nearly 50,000 Jews, about one-eighth of Canadian Jewry, lived below the poverty line, as did some 20 percent of its senior citizens. The highest proportion of poor Jews were found in Montreal, which had a relatively large percentage of ultra-Orthodox and elderly Jews.

Communal Affairs

The new Jewish umbrella organization, the Canadian Council for Israel and Jewish Advocacy (CIJA), began operations early in the year and named Hershell Ezrin, a man with considerable political and diplomatic experience, as CEO. Funded nationally through UIA Federations Canada, CIJA was designed to provide overall coordination for community work in support of Israel and the domestic Jewish agenda. It grew out of a perception among senior lay leaders that the work being done in these areas was inadequate. The surge of anti-Semitism and the emergence of university campuses as key battlegrounds gave further impetus to the initiative (see AJYB 2004, pp. 251–52).

CIJA had a national board with wide geographic representation, and a larger community council representing its member organizations. CIJA had oversight responsibility for the policies and resource allocations of the CJC, CIC, and the National Committee for Jewish Campus Life. Ezrin expressed optimism that CIJA's work would raise the community's profile among policymakers and the media, facilitate outreach to other minority communities and the creation of political alliances, and mobilize members at the grassroots level through political action committees. In an evaluation of CIJA's first year as 2004 drew to a close, cochairs Steven Cummings and Brent Belzberg pointed to a near doubling of community financial allocations for advocacy activities.

The Canadian Jewish Congress (CJC) switched the planned venue for its triennial plenary in June from Montreal to Ottawa, ostensibly so as to facilitate meetings with government officials. In fact, Ottawa was a compromise choice, as those seeking to move the conference actually wanted its relocation to Toronto, which had become the country's dominant Jewish community by far. This was only the second time that the meeting was held outside the two major centers. Much of the discussion at the plenary focused on dealing with anti-Semitism and providing security for the community.

The expansion of the Toronto community was felt not only in numbers but also in the range and scope of its programs. Annual fund-raising for UJA Federation of Greater Toronto grew from $34 million in 1995 to about $60 million in 2004, and foundation assets now exceeded $120 million. The federation launched an ambitious, multiyear $250-million project called Jewish Toronto Tomorrow, an effort to build the facilities needed for the coming decades. Already completed were a redeveloped Jewish center and new center for campus life, both in the downtown area. Other projects in the planning stage were the modernization and expansion of another existing Jewish center in the heart of Jewish Toronto and the construction of a major new multipurpose campus in rapidly growing Vaughan (in the York Region).

The increase in anti-Semitic incidents induced synagogues, schools, and other Jewish institutions to beef up security by hiring private guards or off-duty police officers to patrol their premises, and this, in turn, imposed additional costs on the organizations and stretched their budgets. Some synagogues levied special security fees on top of membership dues to offset the increased costs. Federation CJA in Montreal allocated $3 million to upgrade security at day schools and day-care centers. In April, representatives of UJA Federation and CJC met with top Ontario officials seeking government aid for security. Attorney General Michael Bryant said after the meeting that "this government firmly believes that no one deserves to live in fear. We will do everything we can to end this campaign of hate . . . ."

Montreal's Jewish General Hospital undertook a major expansion expected to cost over $53 million. In July, the Quebec government announced it would pay $24 million toward the project, the balance coming from private fund-raising. The two focal points of the expansion were the hospital's comprehensive cancer center and its cardiovascular sciences center.

A major reform of Quebec's health-care system threatened the autonomy of three Jewish institutions in Montreal, all dependent on public funds, which now might have to merge into larger institutions and lose their Jewish character and lay direction. The government sought to ease Jewish concerns by proposing a merger of the three Jewish facilities, the Jewish Eldercare Center, Mount Sinai Hospital, and Maimonides Geriatric Center, so that they would not be subject to more general consolidation. But even that was troubling for Jewish community leaders, who worried about the vitality of institutions that might lose their identity under a unified administration.

Two new Jewish projects with military themes were announced for Toronto. The city donated land in Earl Bales Park for a memorial to Jewish war veterans from all countries that would include a 350-seat amphitheater. Designed by the noted architect Daniel Libeskind and slated to open in 2005 close to a Holocaust memorial and a bust of Raoul Wallenberg, the memorial would be managed by the Jewish War Veterans of Canada. A second, independent undertaking was the creation of a Canadian Jewish military museum.

Religion

In December, the Supreme Court of Canada handed down a ruling on same-sex marriage in response to a reference from the government. It held that the government's proposed law to allow for same-sex marriage was constitutional, but that religious groups could decline to perform such rites. The issue had been brought to the court in the wake of several decisions by provincial courts throwing out laws that allowed only heterosexual unions. The federal government planned to introduce its new legislation in 2005. In its opinion, the court noted that "several centuries ago, it would have been understood that marriage be available only to opposite-sex couples. The recognition of same-sex marriage in several Canadian jurisdictions as well as two European countries belies the assertion that the same is true today."

The 25-member Canadian Coalition of Liberal Rabbis for Same-Sex Marriage welcomed the ruling "as a matter of social justice and religious conviction," and expressed pleasure at "the Court's recognition of the need to balance same-sex equality rights with protections for religious freedom." The coalition had filed a brief with the court while the case was under consideration, arguing that "many kinds of families, including those with same-sex partners, are capable of fulfilling Jewish family values," and that Jewish law is "not immutable." In contrast, Rabbi David Novak, professor of Jewish studies at the University of Toronto, opposed the ruling and said he worried that it might eventually threaten the integrity of religious traditions. Novak also criticized Justice Minister Cotler, who was responsible for shepherding the legislation through Parliament, for not in the least being influenced "by his Jewish tradition . . . ."

Rabbi Reuven Bulka of Ottawa said he would decline to wed a same-sex couple just as he would refuse to marry a Jew and a non-Jew, as both unions would violate Jewish law.

The Central Conference of American Rabbis (CCAR) held its annual meeting in Toronto in June. It featured a study session on the *Zohar*, the classic work of Jewish mysticism; an address by American Christian theologian Martin Marty; a discussion of congregational programs for adolescents; and affirmation of a commitment to the legitimacy of same-sex unions.

Rabbi Dow Marmur of Toronto wrote in the *Canadian Jewish News* in December about the emergence of what he called "post-Halakhic Judaism": rabbis and cantors of various persuasions were ministering to Jews for whom Halakhah, Jewish law, had "ceased to be normative, but for whom tradition matters." He found such trends in all the Jewish movements aside from the ultra-Orthodox, and expressed the hope that "parallel dynamics across denominational divides could reduce tensions and make for unity."

But leaders of the Conservative movement did not necessarily agree. After participating in a Conservative forum on intermarriage, Rabbi Baruch Frydman-Kohl of Toronto emphasized that his movement rejected two of Reform's innovations: the acceptance of children of non-Jewish mothers and Jewish fathers as Jewish, and allowing non-Jews to be synagogue members. Nevertheless, he affirmed the importance of drawing intermarried couples closer to the community.

At a meeting of the Canadian Region of the United Synagogue of Conservative Judaism, there were animated debates about issues of Jewish law. Rabbi Howard Morrison vigorously defended the movement as Halakhic, speaking of a long history of what he called Halakhic pluralism dating back to the ancient rabbis. But Rabbi Steven Saltzman raised the possibility that egalitarian synagogues, which provided equal roles for men and women, stretched acceptable limits and played "a risky game with the future." Saltzman added that ordination of homosexual rabbis or permitting consecration ceremonies for same-sex couples would constitute "the last nail in the coffin of any façade that this movement is Halakhic."

In February, Montreal's Vaad Ha'ir, which provided kashrut certification for the community, announced that it would not allow kosher food manufacturers and caterers under its supervision to use machine-made matzo or matzo products from the U.S. for Passover. (The ruling did not affect products sold at the retail level.) This meant that products certified by the Orthodox Union (OU) would be barred, reflecting a trend in the Vaad to defer to the strictest interpretations of Halakhah in the community, a position that drew criticism from some observant Jews. In the fall, a strike at Marvid, Montreal's sole supplier of kosher chickens, resulted in a shortage that led the Vaad Ha'ir to relax its normal prohibition of the importation of kosher meat that has not been slaughtered under its supervision.

Education

In December, Quebec Education Minister Pierre Reid announced that Jewish day schools in Montreal would be able to achieve associate status with public school boards, and thus receive an increase in public funding for their general-studies programs from 60 percent to 100 percent. The change would add about $10.5 million per year to the existing government grants. Federation CJA and its agencies negotiated the agreement with the government, which included a requirement that the Jewish schools develop intercultural-exchange programs.

After a long and acrimonious bargaining process that included a work-to-rule protest in 2002, the Federation of Teachers of Jewish Schools agreed to a five-year contract with the three large Montreal day schools.

Day-school parents in Toronto continued to be squeezed by steadily increasing tuitions and the government's refusal to provide any relief. Despite federation aid to needy families, enrollments began to drop, with some attributing the decline to the tuition situation. One advocate for affordable day schools, Jerrold Landau, called for a combination of political and communal action to address the crisis.

Construction began in the spring for a Jewish community high school in Vancouver, scheduled to open in 2005. In the fall, York University began to offer courses in Yiddish. York hosted the first Limmud Festival of Jewish Learning in November.

Community and Intergroup Relations

In a case that divided the Jewish community, the Supreme Court ruled 5-4 in June that Orthodox Jews living in a condominium building in Montreal had a right to erect their own sukkot on their balconies during the holiday, despite condominium rules governing the use of balconies. The court, declaring that sincerely held religious belief must be respected, overturned a Quebec Court of Appeal affirmation of a trial court ruling that was based on conflicting rabbinic testimony as to whether a religious

Jew was obliged to set up his or her own sukkah. B'nai Brith's League for Human Rights lauded the decision as "a landmark ruling that upholds the right of all Canadians to follow their religious practices without interference by the courts."

BBC and CJC both praised the Assembly of First Nations for rejecting the candidacy of David Ahenakew for a committee studying democratic reform of the AFN. Ahenakew, a former aboriginal leader, made headlines with an anti-Semitic diatribe in 2002 (see AJYB 2003, pp. 314–15).

The Ontario provincial government took up the question of amending its Arbitration Act to allow Islamic tribunals to use sharia (Islamic law) to decide cases when the parties voluntarily submitted to its jurisdiction. Jewish organizations were invited to submit their views to former attorney general Marion Boyd, who was assigned to review the use of religious courts. Such Jewish courts, battei din, had functioned under the act in the past. BBC president Harold Davis, stressing that point, advocated recognition of the Islamic religious courts as well.

Marc Attali, Israel's consul-general in Montreal, and CJC regional executive director David Birnbaum walked out of an interfaith ceremony honoring Dr. Martin Luther King, Jr., in January after a Muslim journalist used his speaking opportunity to condemn Israel. Attali said that Yahya Abdul Rahman took political advantage of the situation in a way that was inconsistent with the spirit of the occasion.

Religious leaders from several faiths convened in the Montreal Holocaust Memorial Center in July to pray for the victims of genocide in Sudan. Rev. Darryl Grey said that "as a community of faith we have a responsibility to be the conscience to government," while Rabbi Reuben Poupko denounced an apathy reflecting "a double-edged racism" that is indifferent to victims while not demanding enough of perpetrators.

The Lausanne Consultation on Jewish Evangelism, in cooperation with Jews for Jesus, sponsored a conference in April in Toronto on new strategies to convert Jews. Leaders of so-called messianic Jewish movements from throughout the Americas attended. Andrew Barron of Jews for Jesus told the conference that the operation in Canada "is small, but we're getting the gospel heard more than ever."

A complaint by a Jewish high-school student in the fall led the Toronto District School Board to reconsider its guidelines for teachers so as to ensure that sensitive material would be handled in a fair and balanced way. The student reported that a school presentation had ended with a poem about oppression of Palestinians by Israelis.

People for the Ethical Treatment of Animals (PETA) ran an outdoor exhibit, "Holocaust on Your Plate," in Montreal and Ottawa, and later tried to display it in Toronto, but officials turned down the request. The exhibition compared the treatment of abused livestock to the suffering of Jews in Nazi death camps. Jewish groups found the display offensive because it blurred the uniqueness of the Holocaust and trivialized the experience of European Jews. Furthermore, the utilization of photographic images from the U.S. Holocaust Memorial Museum violated the museum's rules.

Culture

Daniel Goldfarb's new play, *Modern Orthodox,* opened in New York in December. *Comment devenir une mère juive en 10 leçons* (How to Become a Jewish Mother in Ten Easy Lessons) by Paul Fuks had its Canadian premiere in June as one of the highlights of the biennial Quinzaine Sépharade de Montréal cultural festival. In Toronto, there was a Sabbath-observant theater company, Pushover Productions, making it possible for observant Jews to participate in theatrical performances.

Rosalind Rabbatz's and Iris Wagner's film, *Inspiring Figure: The Louis Rubenstein Story,* about a Montrealer who was a world-class figure-skating champion, premiered in Montreal in May. *Mr. Mergler's Gift,* directed by Beverly Shaffer, telling the story of a dying Jewish piano teacher and his last student, premiered in Montreal in September. John L'Ecuyer produced a television film about a Holocaust survivor in Montreal who became the country's most famous advocate for abortion rights and spent time in prison for it. Titled *Choice: The Henry Morgentaler Story,* it first aired in December.

Among the films at Hot Docs, the documentary film festival held in Toronto in April and May, were several submissions from Israel, including *Checkpoint* by Yoav Shamir, *No. 17* by David Ofek, and *My Family's Pizza* by Ronen Amar.

Canadian entries at the Toronto Jewish Film Festival in May included *Nobody Swings on Sunday* by Harry Rasky; *My Father's Camera* and *My Grandparents Had a Hotel* by Karen Shopsowitz; *Montreal Jewish Memories: Stories of the War Years 1939–45* by Dov Okouneff; *Impact of Terror* by Tim Wolochatiuk; *The Bund* by Andrea Feder and Carolina May; and *The Chosen People* by Igal Hecht. Numerous Israeli films were shown at both the Toronto and Montreal Jewish Film Festivals. *Behind Enemy Lines* by Dov Gil-Har had its world premiere in Toronto.

CANADA / 311

An Israeli film, *The Syrian Bride,* by Eran Riklis and Suha Arraf, won the top prize at the Montreal World Film Festival in September. The Canadian-Israeli-German film *Metallic Blues* by Danny Verete was also screened in Montreal. Anita Doron's *Elliot Smelliot* was shown at the Toronto International Film Festival in September.

Two new dramas about the Holocaust were produced in March, both in Toronto: Jonathan Garfinkel's play *The Trials of John Demjanjuk: A Holocaust Cabaret* and Robert Majzels's *This Night.*

Martin Himel's documentary *Jenin: Massacring Truth,* airing on Global TV in April, refuted war-crimes accusations against Israel. Tim Southam's *A Spy's Life: Kitty Harris,* shown on History Television in October, told about a Jewish woman from Winnipeg who worked as a spy in Europe for the Soviet Union during the Stalin era. *The Other Zionists* by Eric Scott was screened at the National Film Board in October and then shown on television. Its depiction of Israeli checkpoints in the West Bank created some controversy. While Scott believed that he was trying to get Israel to live up to its ideals, Université du Québec political scientist Julien Bauer saw the film as "a remarkable propaganda weapon against Israel."

A Jewish museum was to be built in downtown Montreal on land donated by the city. The expected opening was set for 2007. The museum would relate the Jewish experience in Canada, chronicling the contributions that Jews made to society. A cochair of the museum committee, Herschel Segal, said that "we have an uplifting story to tell about struggle, adaptation, and success."

The late Max Stern was an influential patron of contemporary Canadian art. Paintings from his collection were exhibited at the Montreal Museum of Fine Arts and at Concordia University beginning in September. The university established a visual arts building with its bequest from his estate; other beneficiaries were the Hebrew University of Jerusalem and McGill University.

McGill hosted an academic symposium in March on Mordecai Richler's literary legacy. Among the questions addressed was why Richler's work was not generally included in courses on Canadian literature, which Prof. Neil Besner of the University of Winnipeg thought had to with Richler being "too raw, too apt to jangle sensitivities." In March, Concordia University held a symposium on "New Readings of Yiddish Montreal" that featured an appearance by the acclaimed Yiddish writer Chava Rosenfarb and a tribute to her life's work. She also participated in a panel discussion in April at Concordia and expressed doubts about whether Holocaust literature could adequately convey what happened, saying: "Even for a person like myself . . . what I write is only an echo of the reality."

The Miles Nadal Jewish Community Center in Toronto hosted its first annual Yiddish seminar in August, which included intensive introductory language instruction as well as more advanced literary analysis. York University opened a Web museum, Mosaica, in June, devoted to contemporary Jewish art and culture.

Publications

Michael Greenstein published *Contemporary Jewish Writing in Canada: An Anthology*. It offered readers access to many different types of literature, including translations from French and Yiddish, short stories, and excerpts from novels. Greenstein's introductory essay gave added coherence to a valuable collection.

One of the country's best-known writers, Peter Newman, produced his memoir, *Here Be Dragons: Telling Tales of People, Passion and Power.* Newman's journalistic career gave him access to most of the movers and shakers who shaped Canada over the previous half century.

Chava Rosenfarb's *Survivors: Seven Short Stories* was translated by her daughter, Goldie Morgentaler. The stories all involved the struggle to adapt and adjust after the Holocaust.

Nonfiction books that dealt with aspects of Canadian Jewish life included the autobiographical *Six Lives: A Memoir* by Dow Marmur, who was born in Poland and later distinguished himself in rabbinical posts in England and Canada; *The Journals of Yaacov Zipper, 1950–1982: The Struggle for Yiddishkeit,* translated and edited by Mervin Butovsky and Ode Garfinkle, about the noted educator; *Identités mosaïques: entretiens sur l'identité culturelle des Québecois juifs* by Julie Chateauvert and Francis Dupuis-Deri; a collection of the essays of Yiddish journalist Israel Medres, *Between the Wars: Canadian Jews in Transition,* translated and edited by Vivian Felsen; Michael Posner's *The Last Honest Man, Mordecai Richler: An Oral Biography;* Muriel Gold's *Tell Me Why Nights Are Lonesome,* the story of the life and death of her father, a prominent Jewish civil servant in Montreal; *The Canadian Jewish War Memorial Book of Remembrance* by Oscar Adler; and James Laxer's memoir of his childhood, *Red Diaper Baby.*

Paul Charles Merkley stressed the positive role of evangelicals and expressed skepticism about the mainstream denominations in *Christian Attitudes towards the State of Israel.* Other nonfiction works included a memoir of the Lodz Ghetto, *Light at the End of the Tunnel* by Isadore Light; Ruth Mandel's *How to Tell Your Children about the Holocaust;* Judy Gordon's *400 Brothers and Sisters: Their Story Continues; Jewish Renaissance in Fifteenth Century Spain* by Mark Meyerson; Raphael Afilalo's translation and commentary on a work of the eighteenth-century Rabbi Moshe Chayim Luzzatto, *La Kabbalah du Ari Z'al selon le Ramhal;* David Frum's profile of *The Right Man: The Surprise Presidency of George W. Bush* and his coauthored *An End to Evil: How to Win the War on Terror* with Richard Perle; Jasmin Habib's articulation of a post-Zionist position favoring a binational state in *Israel, Diaspora, and the Routes of National Belonging;* Miriam Beckerman's translation of *Nightmares: Memoirs of the Years of Horror Under Nazi Rule in Europe, 1939–1945* by Konrad Charmatz; and *Dark Age Ahead* by Jane Jacobs.

Works of fiction included David Bezmozgis's *Natasha and Other Stories; The Master* by Colin Toibin; *The Singing Fire* by Lillian Nattel; *The Mermaid of Paris* by Cary Fagan; *The Last Light of the Sun* by Guy Gavriel Kay; *Gotz and Meyer* by David Albahari; *The Innocent Traitor* by Eric Rill; *Les contes des mille et une ères* by Oro Anahory-Librowicz; and *Look for Me* by Edeet Ravel. Books of poetry included *Borrowed Light* by Merle Nudelman; *Mask* by Elana Wolff; *At the Moonbeam Café* by Malca Litowitz; *A Day's Grace: Poems 1997–2002* by Robyn Sarah, *In the Worshipful Company of Skinners* by Endre Farkas; and *Foreplay* by Seymour Mayne and Christal Steck.

In December, noted Montreal writer Naim Kattan was awarded the Prix Athanase-David, the Quebec government's highest distinction for achievement in the arts.

Winners of the Canadian Jewish Book Awards were Kate Taylor, Lillian Boraks-Nemetz and Irene N. Watts, Loren Lerner, Henry G. Schogt, Aubrey Davis, Ruth Mandel, Merle Nudelman, Simcha Simchovitch, and Joel Yanofsky. David Bezmozgis won the Reform Judaism prize for Jewish fiction. J.I. Segal awards went to David Homel, Heather Laskey, Musia Landau, Simcha Simchovitch, Vivian Felsen, Haim Genizi, Neil Caplan, and Malcolm Clarke. David Solway won the Grand Prix du Livre de Montréal. Edeet Ravel and Joel Yanofsky won Quebec Writers Federation prizes.

Personalia

The following were appointed to the Order of Canada: companions — Avie Bennett and Martin Friedland; officers — David Bercuson, Irving Schwartz, William Weintraub, and Royden Rabinowitch; members —

Manuel Batshaw, Jonathan Wener, Abraham Arnold, Arthur Drache, Rabbi Lawrence Englander, Sidney Averson Katz, Harry Rosen, and Morton Brownstein. Bernard Shapiro, Samuel O. Freedman, and Jean-Charles Chebat were named to the Ordre National du Québec. Shapiro was also named ethics commissioner for the federal government. Sam Katz was elected mayor of Winnipeg and Stephen Mandel mayor of Edmonton. Alan Baker succeeded Haim Divon as ambassador of Israel to Canada. Jack Silverstone left his position as CJC executive vice president to become chief of staff to a federal minister. Michael Goldbloom became publisher of Canada's largest daily newspaper, the *Toronto Star.* Prof. Jim Torczyner of McGill University won two prizes for his work toward building peace in Middle East, the award for innovation in international education from the Canadian Bureau for International Education, and the Jordanian Red Crescent's gold medal for outstanding achievement in the humanitarian field. Adam Sol won Ontario's Trillium Prize for his poetry.

Ed Morgan and Victor Goldbloom were named, respectively, president and chair of the national executive of CJC. Marc Gold became national chair of CIC. Others who assumed leadership positions included Neil Duboff, president of the Jewish Federation of Winnipeg; Rose Lax, president of Herut-Likud Canada; Mark Rosen, president of the Atlantic Jewish Council; Ronald Appleby, president of Canadian Friends of the Hebrew University; David Bensoussan, president of the Communauté Sépharade du Québec; Arthur Silber, president of ORT Canada; Jay Brodbar, president of the New Israel Fund; Jack Silverstein, director of the UJA in Ottawa; and Jeffrey Boro and Joel Richler, presidents of CJC, Quebec Region and Ontario Region, respectively.

Members of the community who died this year included Bernie Offstein, in January, aged 64, an official of Maccabi Canada; noted Yiddishist and cultural pioneer Sara Rosenfeld, in January, aged 83; distinguished writer and poet Miriam Waddington, in March, aged 86; innovative film executive Nat Taylor, in March, aged 98; environmentalist Tooker Gomberg, in March, aged 48; writer Sheldon Oberman, in March, aged 54; Harry Mayerovitch, architect and illustrator, in April, aged 94; Benjamin Schneider, former federation executive, in April, aged 92; journalist Jerry Gladman, in June, aged 61; philanthropist Alexander Dworkin, in June, aged 94; lawyer and organizational leader David Litner, in June, aged 96; community activist and lay leader Anne Romoff Gross, in July, aged 89; Hungarian community leader Rabbi Miklos Schnurmacher, in July, aged 87; renowned classics scholar Paolo Vivante, in July, aged 81; community leader Hyman Soloway, in July, aged 90; former MP and senator Jack Marshall, in August, aged 84; chiropractor Michael Brickman, in August, aged 39; federation executive Gerry Koffman, in September, aged 54; philanthropist and community leader Lily Silver, in September, aged 85; health care fund-raiser Gloria Shapiro, in September, aged 49; retired cantor Joseph Cooper, in October, aged 81; psychiatrist and Holocaust chronicler Mina Deutsch, in October, aged 92; entrepreneur and community leader John Fienberg, in October, aged 87; community activist Thelma Steinman, in November, aged 92; developer and philanthropist Harold Green, in November, aged 78; retired camp director John Bernstein, in November, aged 86; pediatric neurosurgeon Harold Hoffman, in November, aged 72; restaurant owner Jerry Silverberg, in November, aged 58; builder, philanthropist, and community leader Max Sharp, in December, aged 102; and baseball book collector and mathematician Morris Liebovitz, in December, aged 69.

HAROLD M. WALLER

Western Europe

Great Britain

National Affairs

IN LOCAL ELECTIONS held in June 2004, Tony Blair's governing Labour Party came in third behind the Conservatives and the Liberal Democrats. The result was widely dismissed at the time as the product of a protest vote that would quickly evaporate, and this indeed proved to be the case. Nevertheless, the government, and Prime Minister Blair in particular, had clearly forfeited credibility. The primary reason was the war in Iraq: no weapons of mass destruction had been found, and the government had obviously relied on defective intelligence to justify its involvement. Furthermore, David Blunkett, the popular home secretary, had been forced to resign when his office was found to be involved in fast-tracking a visa for the Filipino nanny of Blunkett's lover. Blunkett brought more discredit on the government when a newly published biography revealed his outspokenly negative views on the competence of his colleagues. Recurring reports of rivalry between Blair and Chancellor of the Exchequer Gordon Brown added to public distrust of the government.

But none of this seriously shook its authority, either with the electorate or the government's own backbenchers. Even at the height of the Blunkett affair, polls showed Labour at 40 percent, the Tories at 31 percent, and the Liberal Democrats at 21 percent, not significantly different from the pattern of polls taken throughout the year. The dissatisfaction of backbenchers with the Iraq war, increased university tuition fees, and the ban on fox-hunting was easily absorbed, and Labour was almost universally expected to retain power at the forthcoming general election.

This did not necessarily suggest enthusiasm for Labour, but rather apathy. In the last general election, in 2001, turnout was 59 percent, meaning that more people did not vote than voted for the winning party. The Conservatives failed to benefit from Labour's difficulties. The impetus imparted by Michael Howard's accession to the party leadership in November 2003 (see AJYB 2004, p. 279) faded amidst confused Tory policies, repeated reshuffling of personnel, and internal policy divisions, especially over relations with Europe. Moreover, Tory support for the war in Iraq abandoned the antiwar weapon to the Liberal Democrats, who benefited accordingly. In the elections to the European Parliament, also in June, the Tory vote of 27 percent was its worst result in a national election for more than a century.

Israel and the Middle East

Britain's bid for an active role in a resumed Middle East peace process seemed to be succeeding in December 2004, when plans were announced for an international conference in London in early 2005. Participating would be foreign ministers and senior officials from the Quartet (the UN, EU, U.S., and Russia) and other countries ready to donate funds to build a viable Palestinian state with a stable democracy and transparent finances. Israel, by agreement with Prime Minister Blair, would not attend. The conference, Blair explained, would not substitute for the "road map," but be a bridge to return to it.

British enthusiasm for peacemaking had been invigorated by two events in November, the U.S. presidential election and the death of Palestinian leader Yasir Arafat. The need to revitalize the peace process was "the single most pressing challenge in our world today," said Blair, urging President George W. Bush, beginning his second term, to launch a fresh Israeli-Palestinian peace initiative. And in her speech opening Parliament, Queen Elizabeth promised, "My government will continue to support efforts to build peace in the Middle East, to promote democratic reform, and reduce conflict and extremism."

To this end, November saw Foreign Secretary Jack Straw on the West Bank assuring Palestinian leaders that the UK, as a key member of the EU and the UN Security Council, would help the Palestinians conduct their elections. The following month Blair was in Ramallah telling the new Palestinian prime minister, Mahmoud Abbas, that there could not be "successful negotiations or peace without an end to terrorism."

Britain's positive attitude toward Israeli prime minister Ariel Sharon's proposed unilateral pullout from Gaza was an integral element of her policy. To be sure, Blair met criticism in March when he joined Bush in welcoming the plan as a "potentially positive development." Some 50 former British diplomats signed an open letter to the prime minister, published in the newspapers, calling his endorsement "a backward step." But Blair noted, in June, that the planned disengagement could be the start of a process toward peace, and not just a "de facto final settlement." A new British initiative building on the withdrawal to jump-start Middle East peace moves, he revealed, had emerged at the G8 summit, where Britain took the lead in urging participants to address the need for peace in the region. The keys, Blair said, were security for Israel and proof, for the Palestinians, that Israeli disengagement could lead to a viable and democratic state. In October, Downing Street welcomed the Knesset's vote of approval for Sharon's plan, and Foreign Secretary Straw declared that Britain was ready to work with the Palestinian Authority "to ensure that Israeli disengagement from Gaza is successful for the Palestinians."

The UK was the Jewish state's "closest friend in the European Union," Israeli foreign minister Silvan Shalom told the *Jewish Chronicle* in February. "Britain will be a true and constant friend," agreed Chancellor Gordon Brown. Notwithstanding such professions of friendship, sections of British public opinion remained opposed to aspects of Israeli policy. In February, July, and again in December, a growing number of MPs (210 by December) signed parliamentary motions calling on Britain to urge Israel to halt construction of the West Bank security barrier. Israel's security measures were destroying the Palestinian economy and creating widespread poverty, according to the House of Commons Select Committee on International Development, which published a report, *Development Assistance and the Occupied Palestinian Territories,* in February. The proposed fence, the report stated, would destroy "the viability of a future Palestinian state," and furthermore, "the despair and anger felt by ordinary Palestinians at being denied the semblance of ordinary life were likely to further increase the supply of militants and suicide bombers."

Great Britain joined with the U.S., Israel, and other states in opposing the hearings before the International Court of Justice (ICJ) on the legality of the fence, but it did so on jurisdictional rather than substantive grounds, arguing that submission of the case to the ICJ politicized the international judicial tribunal. In fact, Britain supported a UN General Assembly nonbinding resolution calling on Israel to dismantle the barrier, a move that induced Israel's Ministry of Foreign Affairs to call in the British ambassador for an explanation, and the Board of Deputies of British Jews to write Foreign Secretary Straw in protest. "We have no objection to the construction of the barrier," responded Straw, "on condition it is built on internationally acknowledged borders or within Israeli territory." But to build it on occupied land, he said, was "unlawful."

In March, Straw, in Brussels for EU talks on tackling terrorism, acknowledged Israel's right to self-defense, but called its assassination of Sheik Ahmed Yassin "unacceptable, unjustified, and very unlikely to achieve its aims." Britain abstained on the UN Security Council vote condemning the assassination (a position denounced at a pro-Palestinian rally in London), but Middle East minister Baroness Symons summoned Israeli ambassador Zvi Shtauber to the Foreign Office, arousing protest from Jewish communal organizations.

In May, more than 70 MPs tabled a Commons motion condemning the destruction of Palestinian homes and the "wide-scale devastation" caused by the Israeli army's incursion into the Rafah refugee camp in Gaza, claiming it breached international law and could not be justified by Israel's claim of "urgent military need." After further Israeli incursions into Gaza in October, Straw voiced deep concern at "the level of violence and the number of deaths, including children . . . . While Israel has the right to defend itself against terrorism, it must act within international law." The same month, Straw criticized Israel's "disproportionate" response to the Qassam rocket attacks on Sderot in the Negev.

Individual cases sustained the unease about Israeli policy. In January, Israel arrested one of its soldiers for shooting British photography student and peace activist Tim Hurndall in Gaza in April 2003; a Scotland Yard team had launched an inquiry into the incident after the Westminster coroner requested the Metropolitan police to establish the facts about Hurndall's death in a London hospital. Hurndall's death had other repercussions as well: in June, Israeli officials investigated claims that Israeli troops fired at two British MPs and a peer visiting the site of Hurndall's shooting. In May, the widow of British filmmaker James Miller, killed by Israeli gunfire in May 2003, urged Straw to press Israel to prosecute those responsible (see AJYB 2004, pp. 158, 281).

Nor did Britain's Jewish community unanimously approve Israeli policy. A survey conducted in June by the United Jewish Israel Appeal (UJIA) among moderately identifying Jews revealed that fewer than a quarter of respondents supported Israel's current policies, though 78 percent "cared deeply about Israel." The same month, 340 British Jews signed an open letter calling on the Board of Deputies to represent the views of those critical of Israel's policies toward the Palestinians. "The Board is not and should not be the voice of the Israeli government," they argued. Earlier, in February, Scotland Yard was called in to investigate hate mail received by several Jewish opponents of Israel's treatment of the Palestinians.

In June, millionaire businessman Zvi Hefetz arrived in London as the new Israeli ambassador after intensive scrutiny, both in Great Britain and Israel, of his experience and command of spoken English.

Terrorism and Anti-Zionism

Jewish students faced threats on a regular basis, a Union of Jewish Students (UJS) delegation told a Home Affairs select committee of the House of Commons in December. The committee, gathering evidence on racism and terrorism, heard that university authorities were often slow to respond. The 1982 Education Act protecting freedom of speech could be interpreted to justify tolerating the activities of groups opposed to democratic values, said UJS campaigns organizer Danny Stone, and he called for a review of that legislation.

The situation at London University's School of African and Oriental Studies (SOAS), where a motion equating Zionism with racism had been carried, was of particular concern. SOAS was the venue, in December, of a conference on the Middle East that spawned a new organization, the British Committee for Universities in Palestine, whose manifesto called on British academicians to boycott Israeli educational institutions, but to support Israeli professors working with Palestinian colleagues in their demand for self-determination and academic freedom.

Other campuses could report more positive news. In March, a group at York University called Student Action for Palestine withdrew its earlier invitation to Dr. Azzam Tamimi, head of the Muslim Association of Britain, who was accused of supporting Hamas and calling for the destruction of the State of Israel. And in April, a motion to twin Liverpool University with Bir Zeit University, a Palestinian institution on the West Bank, did not pass.

In January, Liberal Democratic MP Jenny Tonge was sacked from her party's front bench for saying that she might consider becoming a suicide bomber were she forced to live like the Palestinians. The BBC came in for criticism the next month for arranging a visit for Tonge to Israel and the Palestinian territories.

Muslim clerics who preached death to unbelievers remained in the news (see AJYB 2004, p. 283). In February, three appellate judges cut two years off the nine-year jail sentence that had been passed on Jamaica-born Sheikh Abdul El Faisal at the Old Bailey in March 2003. Abu Hamza, a Muslim preacher linked to terrorist groups, had been stripped of his citizenship and ordered deported in 2003. In April 2004 the Special Immigration Appeals Committee postponed the hearing of his appeal against deportation until January 2005, giving him at least nine more months to stay in the country. In May, however, he was arrested in London on an extradition warrant issued by the American government for alleged hostage-taking in Yemen and support for terrorism, and in October was charged with 16 offenses at the Belmarsh maximum-security prison magistrates' court.

In March, Hamas claimed responsibility for the suicide bombing by two Britons of Mike's Place in Tel Aviv in April 2003 (see AJYB 204, p. 282) and showed a video of them wearing military uniforms, reciting Koranic verses, and brandishing assault rifles. The attack, said Hamas, was Islamic retaliation for Israel's killing of a senior Hamas official. The brother and sister of Omar Sharif, one of the two bombers, faced retrial in July after an Old Bailey jury could not reach a verdict on charges that included failure to disclose information that might have prevented an act of terrorism.

Britain remained the country most active in freezing the assets of terrorists. In March, Chancellor Gordon Brown froze funds held in Britain by five senior Hamas figures, including Abdel Aziz Rantisi, the new Hamas leader. According to the Treasury, there were "reasonable grounds" to suspect that these men had facilitated or participated in acts of terrorism.

In May, the Trades Union Congress rejected a call by pro-Palestinian MPs and lobbyists to back a campaign for economic sanctions against Israel. In August, the National Union of Journalists protested when an Israeli judge ordered British reporter Ewa Jasiewicz, said to have links to the pro-Palestinian International Solidarity Movement, to leave Israel. Jasiewicz did not pose a direct threat, the Israeli judge explained, but terrorists might take advantage of her gullibility. Israel deported Jasiewicz in November on the grounds that she had reentered the country in September under a false identity, having been refused entry under her real name. Ironically, Britain's ambassador to Israel, Simon McDonald, had written to the Israeli foreign ministry in September to register concern at the difficulties facing some British journalists entering Israel.

In June, Sir Sigmund Sternberg, who had announced an award of £2,000 to Iqbal Sacranie, secretary general of the Muslim Council of Britain, for her contributions to interfaith understanding, withdrew it after Sacranie accused Israel of "ethnic cleansing." Instead, the money went to a Gaza hospital.

London's left-wing mayor Ken Livingstone, entering his second term in office, aroused an outcry in the Jewish community in July when he ignored a plea from the Board of Deputies and welcomed a conference in London's City Hall organized by the Muslim Association of Britain. Among the attendees was Sheikh Yusuf al-Qaradawi, a reputed defender of suicide bombings who had urged Muslims to kill Jews and gays. A letter to Livingstone signed by all members of the United Synagogue (US) council denounced his "effusive welcome" to al-Qaradawi. But Livingstone replied that he would never share a platform with an anti-Semite, and that al-Qaradawi was actually "a leading voice of moderation" who was "totally opposed to anti-Semitism." In September, 13 national Jewish organizations, including the Board of Deputies, "appalled" by the mayor's invitation to al-Qaradawi to return to London for yet another visit and "horrified" by the lack of consultation with them, requested a meeting with Livingstone. The Board of Deputies again protested to Livingstone in October, this time about a reference he made to "Israel's illegal occupation of the West Bank and Gaza" in an article in his newsletter promoting a Palestinian trade fair.

One pro-Palestinian MP, George Galloway, founded a new party, which he called "Respect." In August it won a seat on the local council of Tower Hamlets' St. Dunstan and Stepney Green ward, East London.

In 2003, the Palestinian charity Interpal had launched a suit for defamation against the Board of Deputies after the latter was unsuccessful in convincing the Charity Commission that Interpal was a terrorist organization linked to Hamas and should have its assets frozen (see AJYB 2004, p. 283). In December 2004, the board successfully fought off an attempt to throw out its defense in the case. Also in December, ten pro-Palestinian demonstrators outside the Marks and Spencer store in Manchester, site of regular anti-Israel demonstrations, were arrested for violating conditions set by the police.

Controversy over the BBC's coverage of the Middle East continued during the year. In April, the new BBC chairman, Michael Grade, pledged that complaints of anti-Israel bias would receive a fair hearing. The very next month a BBC spokesman denied an accusation by Gideon Meir, deputy director general of the Israeli foreign ministry, that the network had paid for and obtained an interview with Mordechai Vanunu, recently released from an Israeli jail after serving 18 years for passing secret information about the country's nuclear capability to the *Sunday Times*, "in a cynical and unethical attempt to bypass Israeli security restrictions." "The BBC," said the spokesman, "was fulfilling its duty to report world events fairly and impartially." Ken Livingstone invited Vanunu to London, and 45 MPs signed a Commons motion urging the government to make representations to Israel to permit the visit. Israel opted not to extend the work visa of the deputy head of Jerusalem's BBC bureau, Simon Wilson, who had conducted the Vanunu interview. More complaints of pro-Palestinian bias came in November, when a BBC reporter described her tears when Yasir Arafat, old and ill, left his Ramallah stronghold for a hospital in Paris.

BBC's senior editorial adviser, Malcolm Balen, presented the results of a year-long analysis of the network's treatment of Middle East issues to the BBC's Journalism Board in November. His major conclusion was that reports needed to be placed in broader context. BBC director-general Mark Thompson accepted the suggestion and announced that changes would be made, including "enhanced" Middle East news coverage. But London lawyer Trevor Asserson, in a report he prepared entitled "The Documentary Campaign, 2000–04," asserted that the BBC's flaws ran far deeper. Studying the documentary output since the onset of the current intifada in the fall of 2000, Asserson charged the BBC with persistently breaching its duties of fairness and impartiality. In BBC programs about the Israel-Palestine conflict, the report found an "overwhelming bias," with 15 to 17 of the 19 programs examined portraying a "negative view of Israel."

Anti-Semitism

The Community Security Trust (CST) recorded an unprecedented 532 anti-Semitic incidents in 2004, up 31 percent from the 375 reported in 2003. Over half the incidents in 2004 consisted of "abusive behavior," there were four acts of extreme violence, and 28 involving Jewish schools and/or schoolchildren. Among the 17 synagogue desecrations were arson attacks on North London's South Tottenham Synagogue, and the outreach organization Aish in Hendon, North London, both in June. Five cemeteries suffered damage, Middlesborough in June, for example, and Birmingham's Witton Cemetery in August.

Although some suggested that the rise in the total number of incidents was at least partially due to more efficient record-keeping, CST spokesman Mike Whine described the figures as "appalling." He pointed especially to the disproportionate rise in attacks on Jews in the street, which reflected "a deteriorating situation" that would have been unthinkable a few years before. The near-record 100 incidents reported just in the month of March, following the assassination in Israel of Hamas leader Sheikh Yassin, proved, according to Whine, "a direct link between events in the Middle East and an increase in anti-Semitic incidents here."

Speaking before a meeting of Labour Friends of Israel in June, Prime Minister Blair said his government would not tolerate anti-Semitism or any threat to Britain's Jewish community. The Jews themselves signaled a more assertive stance toward the problem in August when they formed an Anti-Semitism Coordinating Unit supported by the Board of Deputies, the Union of Jewish Students (UJS), and the Conservative, Labour, and Liberal Democratic Friends of Israel. It was aimed at maintaining liaison with existing communal organizations, coordinating policy, and enhancing collective capacity.

The Crown Prosecution Service promised a "robust response" to crimes motivated by racial and religious hatred, and in some cases fulfilled this pledge. In July, for example, a man who assaulted two bar mitzvah boys outside a synagogue in Clapham, North London, was ordered jailed for two years and nine months by the Southwark crown court, and two teenagers who attacked Jews were given eight-year prison sentences at the Old Bailey. In December, however, United Synagogue burial chief Melvyn Hartog was "disappointed" when youths found guilty of extensive damage to Plashet Grove Cemetery, East Ham (East London), got off with 12 months of community service.

The apparent growth of the far-right British National Party (BNP) gave cause for concern. The party made a concerted effort to win votes in the spring elections for local councils, the European Parliament, and the post of lord mayor of London. Anticipating the BNP push, the Jewish community joined in campaigns that crossed lines of party and religion in seeking to thwart BNP ambitions. Speaking in Burnley in February, Tory leader Michael Howard called the BNP "a stain on British democracy." In March, Trades Union president Roger Lyons, returning from a visit to Auschwitz, promised a vigorous campaign against BNP influence. The Board of Deputies masterminded a Manchester-based campaign for Jewish representatives to meet their Muslim, Christian, Sikh, and Hindu counterparts to coordinate plans to combat the BNP, whose base of support was in the northwestern part of England. The board also launched a national drive to encourage Jews to overcome possible apathy and vote for other parties in order to defeat the BNP. On election day the Union of Jewish Students rented "battle buses" to transport voters to the polls.

Buoyed by an appearance by French far-right leader Jean-Marie Le Pen as guest of honor at a BNP fund-raising dinner in April, the party fielded 313 candidates for local council seats, 12 for the London Assembly, and

75 for the European Parliament. The BNP polled 800,000 votes in the European Parliament elections; 58,000 in the London mayoral poll; 90,000 for the London Assembly; and thousands more in other local elections. Its number of local councilors increased by five to 21, including one Jewish BNP member, Patricia Richardson, who won her Epping Forest, East London, seat with the claim that she aimed to set Britain "back on track."

The BNP continued to make small gains later in the year. A Yorkshire Tory councilor defected to its ranks in August, and in September a BNP candidate won a seat by a large majority in an East London by-election. On the other hand, a BBC broadcast in July, "The Secret Agent," reporting on an undercover investigation of the BNP, convinced Barclay's Bank to cancel the party's account there and led to 12 arrests, including that of BNP founder John Tyndall and its current leader, Nick Griffin, in December, on suspicion of incitement to racial hatred.

The Commission for Racial Equality, having already appointed a Muslim, named Julia Chain as its first (part-time) Jewish commissioner in January. Placing representatives of the two minority religions on the commission, said Chain, "reflects the fact that the rise of both anti-Semitism and Islamophobia are of concern to the whole community."

JEWISH COMMUNITY

Demography

There were 2,665 Jewish births in 2002, a rise from 2,640 in 2001 and 2,647 in 2000, but the Board of Deputies community research unit discerned a continuing long-term downward trend. Despite the slight rises in the most recent years, the number of annual births had been consistently below 3,000 since 1993, whereas it had fluctuated between 3,100 and 3,600 in the period 1986–92. A total of 932 synagogue marriages were recorded in 2003, up from 921 in 2002, while 284 gittin (religious divorces) were completed in 2003, as compared to 250 the previous year. Burials and cremations under Jewish religious auspices fell to 3,592 in 2003 from 3,670 in 2002. The bet din (religious court) of the Reform Synagogues of Great Britain accepted 111 proselytes in 2004, 15 more than it had in 2003.

Statistics derived from analyses of the 2001 national census—the first to ask a voluntary question about religious affiliation—were published intermittently throughout the year. The data confirmed "the statistics that we have been establishing from a whole range of data from synagogues and communities in the last 20 years," said Marlena Schmool, who retired as director of the Board of Deputies community issues department in 2003. The census, she said, gave "the largest sample of self-identifying Jews ever available. It was invaluable data."

In February, Barry Kosmin, director of the Institute for Jewish Policy Research (IJPR), said that the census indicated that almost one in 30 British Jews was nonwhite; furthermore, nearly 2,000 Asian Jews lived in Britain, 705 of them defining themselves as black and 105 as Chinese.

In July, more released statistics demonstrated the trend for Jews to quit central London and the inner suburbs and head northward, particularly to South Hertfordshire. Radlett, located in that area, was the English town with the highest percentage of Jews, 24.6 percent of a total population of 8,034. In neighboring Bushey, Jews constituted 19.28 percent of the 17,000 residents, and in Boreham Wood 11.38 percent of 31,172. Also in July, the Ashton Business School released an analysis of social and economic trends in Manchester Jewry, suggesting that the census figure of 21,307 be adjusted upward to between 23,000 and 27,000. The Jews, under this formula, formed just 1 percent of the Manchester population, but comprised 8.2 percent of British Jewry.

In October, the Office of National Statistics issued a publication, *Focus on Religion,* which contained data on the ethnicity, employment, health, and marriage patterns of religious minorities, based on the census. One of its findings was that 22 percent of the 267,000 persons who declared themselves Jewish were over 65 years of age.

Communal Affairs

The role of the Jewish Communal Leadership Council (JCLC), set up in October 2003, had to be clarified in February 2004 after a meeting of all 17 council members with Prime Minister Blair aroused the resentment of the Board of Deputies, which had traditionally spoken on behalf of British Jewry. Henry Grunwald, who was both the JCLC chairman and president of the board, explained that the latter "remained the central representative body for the Jewish community." The JCLC was not intended to supplant it, but rather to enhance its work and that of other organizations, strengthen British Jewry's voice in the wider society, and set internal priorities for the community. The JCLC was made up of the lay leaders of major Jewish organizations, plus seven members-at-large chosen on the basis of their individual expertise for a three-year renewable period. By November two more organizations had joined, raising the membership to 19.

The steering committee for a new cross-denominational Jewish community center in London, modeled on New York's Manhattan JCC, held its first meeting in February. The center aimed to offer diverse educational, cultural, social, and recreational activities to bring Jews who had dropped out of synagogue life back into the Jewish orbit and provide a forum for Jews of all persuasions. The committee emphasized that the center would not replace synagogues or other existing social venues, but would work in partnership or in a coordinating role to benefit the whole community.

Norwood, the community's leading family and children's welfare organization, received an unprecedented £2m donation from newspaper proprietor Richard Desmond in May toward the costs of relocating its Annie Lawson School from Ravenswood, Berkshire, to Bushey, more easily accessible to the North London community. Later in the year, Norwood lost its bid to continue running the national adoption register, ending what Minister of State Margaret Hodge called "an extremely productive three-year working relationship" with the Department for Education and Skills.

In July, the Otto Schiff Housing Association sold Heinrich Stahl House, North London, a former care home for German Jewish refugees, for £16.25m, two-thirds to go toward a new, state-of-the-art Jewish Care home, and the rest to World Jewish Relief (WJR).

In October, the Agudas Israel Housing Association, which was strictly Orthodox, revealed that it was negotiating with government-backed landowner English Partnerships to build an initial 300 homes in Milton Keynes to help ease the overcrowded in its prolific North London communities. The next month, the manager of the Poundbury, Dorset, community, created by Prince Charles, invited the association to come and "see what we are doing here." In December, Jewish Care launched an integrated long-term partnership with the Stamford Hill community, North London, which was affiliated with the Union of Orthodox Hebrew Congregations, whose traditional, less Orthodox, client base was "rapidly diminishing."

Religion

The United Synagogue (US), which represented moderate Orthodoxy and constituted Britain's largest synagogue grouping, was entering "a phase of substantial change," said US director of development Leonie Lewis in March. Its future guiding principle would be "community first, buildings second." Since many US buildings were aging and required major work, and pending legislation would require the construction of special facilities for the disabled, it was better to knock them down and start over again, she said. In addition, the single "cathedral" service was outdated, as current thinking favored smaller, more intimate prayer groups.

Finsbury Park Synagogue, North London, for example, defaced in 2002 and needing repair, was scheduled to close within the year, and a complex of flats and a new synagogue built on its site. The 106-year-old West Ham and Upton Park Synagogue, East London, one of US's oldest congregations, closed in May because of falling membership. In September it was announced that Clapton Federation Synagogue, South London, where a demographic shift had left a reduced and elderly congregation, was to be sold.

The Charity Commission ended a two-year inquiry into US affairs in April; it had originally been launched after a US lawsuit against cemetery employees collapsed (see AJYB 2002, p. 314). The commission declared itself satisfied with the improvements the US had made in its management practices. The inquiry's findings, US chief executive Rabbi Saul Zneimer said, drew "a line under the past."

In June, the US set up a Center for Rabbinic Development at the London School of Jewish Studies, formerly Jews' College, Hendon, North London, to train and support rabbis, and the next month the US community development group published a handbook for synagogue boards of management entitled *Working Together*. But US's relations with its clergy soured in October when the rabbi and cantor at the synagogue in Ilford, Essex, were informed of "potential redundancy." US officials, backed by the synagogue's honorary officers, felt that Essex's "dire financial position" (it had run up a deficit of more than £300,000 in five years) and decreasing male membership (down from 1,650 in 1988 to 855 in 2004) indicated it could not afford two full-time ministers. US president Peter Sheldon asserted nonetheless, in November, that that body was not deserting Essex but investing in it. In December, US leaders met with the organization's rabbis to repair relationships, although the discussion of pensions, housing, and the introduction of new disciplinary procedures to deal with congregants' complaints against ministers did not dispel the mood of unease. Rumor had it that the US planned to issue guidelines for dealing with "poor performance" by rabbis.

Even so, British Jews thought highly of their rabbis, according to a United Jewish Israel Appeal report published in September, based on a survey of Jewish identity in Britain. Conducted by an Israeli professor, Steven M. Cohen, and a Briton, Keith Kahn-Harris, the findings were based on interviews and questionnaires concentrating on "moderately engaged" Jews, the predominant group in the community.

The longest slander trial in British history, which generated enormous publicity in the press and considerable embarrassment in Jewish quarters, finally ended in June when a high-court jury cleared Yisrael Lichtenstein, *dayan* (religious judge) of the Federation Bet Din, of slandering Jewish businessman Brian Maccaba. The lawsuit had been initiated three-and-a-half years earlier, and the trial took 41 days.

In April, Chief Rabbi Jonathan Sacks, in conjunction with the Board of Deputies and the US, issued a statement distancing his office from the Kabbalah Center, the international network that sought to popularize Jewish mysticism by its association with celebrities such as Madonna. "The organization does not fall within the remit of the Chief Rabbinate or any other authority in the UK," the statement said. That same month the chief rabbi appointed an adviser on Jewish-Muslim relations to his cabinet. Rabbi Sacks explained this unprecedented move as an indication of the priority he gave the subject. It was announced in June that the chief rabbi would not move to the London suburbs, as previously announced (see AJYB 2002, p. 289), but would remain in St. John's Wood.

Safeguarding the Future, a strategic review commissioned by the Spanish and Portuguese Jews' Congregation, was released in April. Among its proposals was a name-change to Sephardi Jews' Congregation, as only 12 percent of the 1,000 members had Spanish or Portuguese origins. The review also suggested that Wembley Synagogue, North London, where membership was decreasing, consider relocating to Hampstead Garden Suburb or Elstree; that religious and cultural activity at Bevis Marks Synagogue in the City of London be revived; that Lauderdale Road Synagogue, North London, hold talks aimed at "constructive collaboration" with its breakaway Anshe Shalom congregation; and that the operation of the Sephardi bet din be reviewed to prevent it becoming a financial burden.

In July, the Oxford Center for Hebrew and Jewish Studies paid the Montefiore Endowment £450,000 for books and pamphlets from the college founded by Sir Moses Montefiore. The endowment raised another £4m in November at a bumper New York auction of rare books and manuscripts from the college, assigning the proceeds to a new "community kollel" at Lauderdale Road to train rabbis and educators.

In December, the council of Barnet, North London, approved a planning application for an *eruv* (the symbolic boundary enabling carrying on the Sabbath) in Edgware, on the model of the Northwest London *eruv* which became operative in March.

The Reform Synagogues of Great Britain (RSGB) issued *Our 2020 Vision,* a plan for the next two decades, in April. The document declared that RSGB would seek to become the "mainstream" of British Jewry by 2020 through a two-pronged strategy of supporting the work of individual synagogues and overseeing external representation and national projects. In a departure from previous policy, it gave formal recognition to the role of rabbis as part of a tripartite leadership, together with lay leaders and professionals.

In September, a new congregation in Manchester, the Metropolitan Liberal Jewish Congregation of Greater Manchester, considered applying for associate membership in Liberal Judaism, while an independent Edinburgh congregation, Sukkat Shalom, became Scotland's first Liberal congregation when it affiliated as the Edinburgh Liberal Jewish Community.

September also saw the launch of Jewish Heritage UK, an initiative to preserve British Jewry's synagogue treasures and historic sites.

Education

The projected Hertsmere Jewish High School, an Orthodox institution in Hertfordshire, finally received the go-ahead in December when it obtained a grant of £16m from the Department for Education and Skills after an earlier bid for government funding failed in February. There had previously been some controversy over the need for the school since there were already three Jewish secondary schools in London and little apparent need for another (see AJYB 2004, pp. 290–91). In January one of the existing schools, the Jewish Free School, North London, agreed to help Hertsmere during its initial phase. The new school was expected to open in 2006. The lingering fear that Jewish schools might end up undersubscribed caused the US's Agency for Jewish Education, in conjunction with the London Bet Din, to issue guidelines in February allowing US schools with openings to admit students who were not Jewish according to Halakhah (that is, did not have a Jewish mother).

Akiva, a primary school in Finchley, North London, that was under the auspices of the Reform movement, won capital funding from the government in February as a first step in its planned change from private to state status. In December it was announced that Menorah Girls' High School would come under the "voluntary aided" category in 2005.

In January, the Agency for Jewish Education organized Britain's first

Jewish Early Years Conference. Held in London, it attracted 250 educators and aimed at identifying the crucial components in Jewish primary-school education. The same month, the Board of Deputies inspection service, Pikuach, found that the quality of Jewish studies in Jewish schools had "improved greatly" over the previous four years.

In November it was announced that Pollak's boarding house for Jewish boys at Clifton College, Bristol—the only Jewish house at a British private school—would close in July 2005, since there were no longer enough boarders to justify the 127-year-old house.

At the beginning of the year, UJIA launched a survey to guide its spending on Jewish education and youth, which, according to its annual review, had increased from £4.2m in 2002 to £4.6m in 2003. Ben Leon, the UJIA chief executive, emphasized the organization's support for teacher training, but reported in June that "there were now no vacancies in Jewish schools for Jewish studies teachers." In November, the US launched an unprecedented plan to allow Jewish studies teachers to receive the government-backed postgraduate certificate of education.

In April, for the third consecutive year, UJIA refused funding for Betar, the Zionist youth group affiliated with the Israeli Likud movement. UJIA renewal director Michael Wegier explained, "We don't fund demonstrations outside Marks and Spencer. We don't fund political activities." In August, the government's Charity Commission struck Betar off its list of registered charities for engaging in "political" activity.

The London School of Jewish Studies, formerly Jews' College, announced plans in October to launch an M.A. degree program in Jewish ethics in conjunction with King's College, London, in September 2005.

Foreign Aid

In May, the heirs of menswear magnate Montague Burton rededicated the Galitsky Synagogue in Kiev, Ukraine, built in 1909 and now reopened as a Jewish Agency-run center for Jewish and Zionist learning. Girls' Action Project, an independent Jewish youth club in Golders Green, North London, collected 80 boxes of good-as-new clothing in July for poverty-stricken Jews in Ukraine. In September, the West London Synagogue announced it would fund the purchase of premises for a new Reform community in St. Petersburg, Russia, thanks to a million-dollar donation from a congregant.

World Jewish Relief (WJR) announced its support, in October, for several schemes: British bar mitzvah boys and bat mitzvah girls would twin with counterparts in four children's homes in the Ukraine and Moscow, the money raised going to the child in the FSU; pupils at Jewish Free School, Kenton, North London, would collect clothing, toys, and toiletries for two Jewish schools in Pinsk, Belarus; and US and Reform congregations in Radlett, Hertfordshire, would work together to collect clothing for Jews in Grodno, Belarus.

The Board of Deputies launched a campaign in September for the release of 11 Jews imprisoned in Iran. The next month, Reform young people in Brighton and Hove raised funds for a Jewish hospital in Tehran, in collaboration with WJR.

Publications

Two Israeli writers captured the 2004 Jewish Quarterly-Wingate Literary awards. The prize for fiction went to David Grossman for *Someone to Run With,* while Amos Elon won in the nonfiction category for *The Pity of It All: A Portrait of Jews in Germany, 1743–1933.* The TLS-Porjes Translation Prize for Hebrew into English was shared by Barbara Harshav for *The Labour of Life: Selected Plays by Hanoch Lvin* and Nicholas de Lange for *The Same Sea* by Amos Oz, whose autobiographical *A Tale of Love and Darkness* also appeared, again translated by de Lange.

Books by rabbis on religious subjects included *A Rabbi Reads the Bible* and *A Rabbi Reads the Psalms,* both by Jonathan Magonet; *Jewish Preaching: Homilies and Sermons* and *Their Heads in Heaven — Unfamiliar Aspects of Hasidism,* both by Louis Jacobs; *Reform Judaism and Modernity: A Reader,* an anthology edited by Jonathan Romain; *Judaism and Homosexuality* by Chaim Rapoport; *Moses, Book 1: Moses, Man of God* and *Moses, Book 2: The Law of Moses, Exodus, Leviticus, Numbers, and Deuteronomy,* newly translated and edited by Sidney Brichto, who also published *Apocalypse: A Revolutionary Interpretative Translation of the Writings of St. John;* and *The Treasure Within* by Jonathan Shooter. Other religious studies were *Liberal Judaism: The First Hundred Years* by Lawrence Rigal and Rosita Rosenberg; *Meshal Haqadmoni: Fables from the Distant Past by Isaac Ibn Sahula,* edited and translated by Raphael Loewe; *The Limits of Orthodox Theology: Maimonides' Thirteen Principles Reappraised* by Marc B. Shapiro; and *Bound by the Bible: Jews, Christians and the Sacrifice of Isaac* by Edward Kessler.

Historical works ranged from *The Temple of Jerusalem* by classical scholar Simon Goldhill, to *Our Hidden Lives: The Everyday Diaries of a Forgotten Britain,* which Simon Garfield based on diaries kept by ordinary people in the years following World War II. In between came *The*

Making of Western Jewry 1600–1819 by Lionel Kochan; *Pride Versus Prejudice: Jewish Doctors and Lawyers in England, 1890–1990* by John Cooper; *Jewish London: An Illustrated History* by Gerry Black; *The Jewish Victorian: Genealogical Information from the Jewish Newspapers, 1861–1870* by Doreen Berger; *Jewish Memories of the Twentieth Century,* edited by David Stebbing; and *Shalom Ireland: A Social History of the Jews in Modern Ireland* by Ray Rivlin.

Holocaust studies of all types abounded, including *The Origins of the Final Solution* by Christopher Browning; *Kerry's Children* by Ellen Davies; *The Unwritten Order: Hitler's Role in the Final Solution* by Peter Longerich; *Bloody Foreigners: The Story of Immigration to Britain* by Robert Winder; *My Wounded Heart: The Life of Lilli Jahn, 1900–1944* by Martin Doerry; *Nazi Looting* by Gerard Aalder; *Survival,* edited by Wendy Whitworth; *The Children's House of Belsen* by Hetty Verolme; *After Such Knowledge,* a meditation on the aftermath of the Holocaust by Eva Hoffman; *Eichmann: His Life and Crimes* by David Cesarani; and *Holocaust and Rescue: Impotent or Indifferent? Anglo-Jewry 1938–1945* by Pamela Shatzkes. Books concentrating on the survivors were *From the Edge of the World: The Jewish Refugee Experience through Letters and Stories* by Anne Joseph; *After the Holocaust: Jewish Survivors in Germany after 1945* by Eva Kolinsky; and *Generation Exodus: The Fate of Young German Refugees from Nazi Germany* by Walter Laqueur.

Autobiographies included *Winner Takes All,* a collection of anecdotes and musings on the movie business by Michael Winner; *Hitchhiking to Heaven: An Autobiography* by Lionel Blue; *Jew Made in England* by Anthony Blond; *All About Harry, the True Story of a Child Growing Up in London's 1920s East End* by Harry Laughton; and *The River of Angry Dogs* by Mira Hamermesh. Biographies were *Anthony Caro: Quest for the New Sculpture* by Ian Barker; and *Moshe Dayan* by Martin van Creveld. *Gaza Blues* was a composite work of fiction by Etgar Keret, an Israeli, and Samir El-Youssef, a Palestinian.

Works of fiction published in 2004 were *The Apologist* by Jay Rayner; *The Secret Purposes* by David Baddiel; *The Making of Henry* by Howard Jacobson; *Sarah* by Marek Halter; *Facing the Light* by Adèle Geras; *Hunting Midnight* by Richard Zimler; *My Nine Lives,* a fictionalized autobiography by Ruth Prawer Jhabvala; *Mordecai's First Brush with Love: New Stories by Jewish Women in Britain,* edited by Laura Phillips and Marion Baraitser; *After These Things* by Jenny Diski; *Young Turk* by Moris Farhi; and *The Killing Joke* by Anthony Horowitz.

The Israel-Arab conflict remained a popular subject. Publications included *The Birth of the Palestinian Refugee Problem Revisited* by Benny Morris; *Crossing the River Jordan: The Journeys of an Israeli Diplomat* by Jacob Rosen; *The Other Side of Despair: Jews and Arabs in the Promised Land* by Daniel Gavron; and *Refusenik! Israel's Soldiers of Conscience* by Peretz Kidron.

Poetry included two collections of Isaac Rosenberg's work: *Isaac Rosenberg: Selected Poems and Letters,* edited by Jean Liddiard, and *The Selected Poems of Isaac Rosenberg,* edited by Jean Moorcroft Wilson. Other works of poetry were *This Is Not My Nose* by Michael Rosen; *Burning Wire* by Ruth Fainlight; *Where Do People Go?* by Bernard Kops; *The Last Hour of Sleep* by Naomi Jaffa; *Flood Warning* by Berta Freistadt; and *Flight into Egypt* by Ian Blake.

Personalia

Honors accorded British Jews during the year included peerages awarded to Sir Stanley Kalms, former Conservative Party treasurer and leading retailer; Leonard Steinberg, founder of Stanley Leisure, the largest casino operator in the country, and president of the Manchester Jewish Federation, for services to charity and education; Iranian-born Sir David Alliance, founder of the textile group Coats Viyella and chair of one of the UK's largest mail-order companies, whose charitable works included the Alliance Foundation for the relief of poverty and the advancement of religion, education, and medical knowledge; historian Dr. Ruth Henig, chair of the Association of Police Authorities and a member of the National Criminal Justice Board; and Rabbi Julia Neuberger, also created a Dame earlier in the year, for services to several public bodies. Other newly created Dames were Gail Ronson, in recognition of her charitable work, and Fanny Waterman for services to music. Knighthoods went to senior civil servant Peter Gershon, chief executive of the Office of Government Commerce; and Clive Bourne for services to charity and education.

Notable British Jews who died in 2004 included Dayan Michael Fisher, emeritus senior rabbi of the Federation of Synagogues, in London, in January, aged 95; Peter Gellhorn, musician, in London, in February, aged 91; Leslie Levens, industrialist and philanthropist, in London, in February, aged 93; David Carrington, *Jewish Chronicle* journalist, in London, in February, aged 88; Lili Preiskel, patroness of the arts, in London, in February, aged 94; Jack Temple, alternative healer, in Surrey, in February, aged 86; Hymie Binder, weight-lifting champion, in London, in

March, aged 86; Sir Horace Phillips, the nation's first Jewish career diplomat, in London, in March, aged 86; Vilem Tausky, musician and conductor, in London, in March, aged 93; Bernard Mendelovitch, star of the Yiddish theater, in Bournemouth, in March, aged 79; John, Lord Diamond, Labor politician, first secretary to the treasury, 1964–70, in April, in Chalfont St. Giles, Buckinghamshire, aged 96; Paul Hamburger, musician, in Yeovil, Somerset, in April, aged 83; Harry Kleeman, chairman of the Central British Fund for World Jewish Relief, 1991–96, in Barbados, in April, aged 76; Hyam Maccoby, theological historian, in Leeds, in May, aged 80; Alex Rosenzweig, financial adviser active in communal cultural affairs, in London, in May, aged 65; Milton Shulman, drama critic, in London, in May, aged 90; Adèle Leigh, opera singer, in London, in May, aged 75; Sulamith Messerer, ballerina, in London, in June, aged 95; Jack Rosenthal, playwright, in London, in June, aged 73; Mike Woodin, academic and Green Party activist, in Oxford, in July, aged 38; Ellis Birk, influential communal leader, in London, in July, aged 88; Albert Friedlander, leading Reform rabbi and interfaith activist, in London, in July, aged 77; Arnold Ziff, philanthropist, in Leeds, in July, aged 77; Michael Hyam, barrister and judge, in London, in July, aged 66; Maurice Sumray, figurative painter, in St Ives, Cornwall, in July, aged 83; Peter Barnes, playwright, in London, in July, aged 73; Ethel de Keyser, antiapartheid activist, in London, in July, aged 77; Bernard Levin, controversial journalist, in London, in August, aged 75; Albi Rosenthal, antiquarian bookseller, in Oxford, in August, aged 89; Karl Brozik, leading figure in negotiating reparations for Holocaust survivors, in London, in August, aged 83; Jack Rosenberg, choirmaster and composer of Jewish liturgical music, in London, in August, aged 83; Basil, Lord Wigoder, chairman of the Liberal Party, 1963–65, chief whip, 1977–84, in London, in August, aged 83; Samuel Cohen, psychiatrist, in London, in September, aged 78; Harry Seltzer, comedian, in London, in September, aged 95; Bernice Rubens, prize-winning novelist, in London, in October, aged 81; Paul Shrank, chairman of the Masorti Assembly of Synagogues, 1998–2002, in London, in October, aged 57; and Alicia Markova, ballerina, in Bath, in December, aged 94.

MIRIAM & LIONEL KOCHAN

France

National Affairs

In the political sphere, the year 2004 in France began with impressive electoral victories by the left. In regional elections held March 21 and 28, the left, under the leadership of the Socialist Party, received 50 percent of the vote, with 37 percent going to the mainstream right and 12 percent to the far-right National Front. Twenty of the 22 regions making up metropolitan France elected left-leaning administrations. The result was interpreted primarily as a reaction against the domestic policies of the government of Prime Minister Jean-Pierre Raffarin, appointed by President Jacques Chirac. Nevertheless, the National Assembly continued to be dominated by Chirac's party, the UMP (initially the Union for a Presidential Majority, later renamed the Union for a Popular Movement with the same acronym). Thus, the punishment administered by the voters in late March was more an alarm bell than the beginning of real political change. To be sure, the powers of the regional presidents, almost all of whom were now Socialists, were far from negligible. But France was a very centralized country, the key authority remaining in Paris, in the hands of the president and his parliamentary majority.

These regional elections were closely followed by elections for the European Parliament on June 13. Once again, the stakes were limited in terms of power, since the real responsibilities in the European Union were essentially divided between the European Council, representing the member states, and the European Commission, a kind of government appointed by those states. Thus the major significance of the parliamentary elections was as a gauge of public opinion. The election was marked by low turnout and political fragmentation, a situation encouraged by the system of voting for party lists. Even so, it was impossible not to notice that the Socialists, with 29 percent of the vote, were the leading political party in France. The right was divided between the UMP with 17 percent and the Union for French Democracy (UDF) with 12 percent, while the National Front remained stagnant at a little under 10 percent.

As already noted, however, political power remained concentrated in the Elysée Palace, the residence of President Chirac, reelected in 2002 for a five-year term, and the Palais Bourbon, seat of the National Assembly, where the UMP had maintained a solid majority since 2002. With the next national elections scheduled for 2007, attention focused on the internal politics of the UMP, in which Nicolas Sarkozy had become an increasingly powerful figure. After the March elections, Sarkozy, who had gained prominence as minister of the interior, was shifted to economy minister in a government whose leader, Raffarin, had been politically weakened by the right's losses.

It was no secret that Sarkozy wanted to become president in 2007. His plan shocked no one, even in a country that frowns on personal ambition. Sarkozy had succeeded in establishing a public image as an "American-style" politician who engaged in "plain speaking" and placed a higher priority on action than ideology. He emerged personally unscathed from the right's recent election losses, which were attributed to President Chirac and Prime Minister Raffarin. Sarkozy's next step was to take control of the UMP.

This meant a confrontation with Chirac, who had never ruled out the possibility of running for a third term in 2007, and, even if he had no further presidential aspirations, could hardly be thrilled with the idea of his own party being led by a declared presidential candidate. But the dynamic that Sarkozy set in motion carried the day, thanks to the efforts of a large group of party officials who saw in him the promise of political renewal on the right. Chirac had to accept Sarkozy as UMP president, and the only condition he was able to extract was that Sarkozy would resign from the government upon his election to the party position. On November 28, Sarkozy was triumphantly elected president of the UMP with 85 percent of the vote.

Paradoxically, just as the right, after its punishment by the voters, appeared to be pulling itself together for the elections that loomed ahead, the big winner in the recent votes, the Socialist Party, was suffering from division and malaise. The "war of the leaders," which for years had pitted Lionel Jospin against Laurent Fabius, did not end with Jospin's retirement after his defeat in the 2002 presidential election. Instead, it continued as intensely as ever after Jospin was replaced by François Hollande.

The hostility between Fabius and Hollande crystallized around the question of the European constitutional treaty, whose text was to be released to French voters early in 2004. Some commentators suggested that Chirac's decision to submit the treaty to a referendum, when, technically speaking, a parliamentary vote would have been enough (some other European countries took this path), was made with the intent of provoking internal conflict among his Socialist adversaries. If so, the results exceeded expectations: the Socialists split between supporters of the proposed treaty, led by Hollande, and opponents, led by Fabius. This crisis would have a lasting effect on the party and prevent it from taking advantage of the electoral gains it achieved in 2004.

2004 was also the year in which the wearing of signs or clothing "conspicuously" (*ostensiblement*) indicating a religious affiliation in public primary, middle, and secondary schools was banned, in application of the principle of *"laïcité"* (the French form of secularism). The law giving effect to the ban was promulgated on March 15, after a near-unanimous vote in Parliament. Interpretation of the term *ostensiblement* was to be left to school principals and, if necessary, to the courts. While the law encompassed signs representing all religions, it was generally regarded as being directed at the Islamic veil.

Before it was passed, the law was the target of vigorous protests from extreme Muslim groups. It was also attacked by some far-left activists on grounds that it could potentially isolate Muslim girls from public education, since the only option consistent with their religious convictions would be to quit school. The reality proved far less dramatic. When students returned to school in September and October 2004, the vast majority of girls accepted the new rule, and only a few isolated cases of refusal to comply were reported.

Israel and the Middle East

How did French people regard Israel? A poll conducted among a representative sample of the French population by the French polling firm Sofres (part of the global TNS group) on behalf of the Institut Français in Tel Aviv gave a partial answer. The results were presented in the form of a "sympathy index," calculated as the percentage of those polled who expressed "sympathy" for a country minus the percentage who did not express sympathy. In the case of Israel, the sympathy index was negative (–10): that is, those who expressed sympathy (38 percent) represented a smaller percentage than those who did not express sympathy (48 percent). By comparison, Russia registered a strongly positive index (+20), "Palestine" a positive index (+7), and the U.S. a negative index (–6).

The same poll indicated that French people considered Israelis aggressive (68 percent agreed and 21 percent disagreed), powerful (68 percent agreed, 22 percent disagreed), courageous (60 percent agreed, 23 percent disagreed), not respectful of human rights (56 percent agreed, 29 percent disagreed), undemocratic (52 percent agreed, 29 percent disagreed), and not sincerely interested in peace (62 percent agreed, 25 percent disagreed). But despite all that, 46 percent of French people expressed the opinion that what united France and Israel was more important than what divided them, while only 30 percent expressed the contrary view. And 54 percent regarded relations between France and Israel as good, only 29 percent regarding them as bad. Finally, when people were asked who was primarily responsible for the current problems between Israel and the Palestinians, 23 percent blamed Israel as compared with 14 percent who blamed the Palestinians, while 40 percent answered "both," and 23 percent had no opinion.

Another poll, conducted among a representative sample of Israel's Jewish population on May 5, 2004, by the Israeli firm Market Watch on behalf of the country's Ministry of Foreign Affairs, completed the picture. (Both polls were aimed to coincide with a conference on Franco-Israeli relations in Tel Aviv, part of an initiative undertaken by the two governments to improve relations.) While 91 percent of respondents in the Israeli sample said they felt "great sympathy" or "some sympathy" for the U.S. (the highest score), followed by 79 percent for Britain and 64 percent for the Netherlands, France lagged way behind with 21 percent, just ahead of Germany's 17 percent.

The Israeli respondents considered the French "pro-Arab" (80 percent) and "hypocritical" (64 percent), but also "democratic" (62 percent) and "civilized" (62 percent). Only 14 percent of those surveyed believed that the French government was "energetically" fighting anti-Semitism, while 49 percent believed that it was doing "very little" or even "nothing at all." The response to another question helps cast light on this clearly incorrect perception of the situation in France. When people were asked what proportion of France's Jewish community, in their view, was annihilated in the Holocaust, only a small percentage (23 percent) gave the correct answer: the majority of Jews survived.

Thus, the dominant impression given by the polls was that Franco-Israeli relations were characterized more by mutual ignorance than by real hostility. However, an important gesture on the French side could not help but improve things. On June 7, the Paris City Council unanimously passed a resolution to name a street in the city after Theodor Herzl, the founder of Zionism, who died on that date a century earlier. The city's Socialist mayor, Bertrand Delanoë, supported the resolution, even praising the "excellent initiative" of the two councilors from the right-wing opposition who introduced it.

A little over a month before the June 13 European elections, with most of the lists of candidates already in place, a new list was announced. It was called Euro-Palestine, and its platform was consistent with the most radical anti-Israel positions. The leader was a surgeon named Christophe Oberlin, who had previously belonged to the Socialist Party and was a longtime pro-Palestinian activist, but the real force behind the initiative was in fourth place on the list. Her name was Olivia Zemor, and early in 2002 she and Nicolas Shahshahani had founded a pro-Palestinian organization called CAPJPO, the Coordination of Efforts for a Just Peace in the Middle East (Coordination des Appels pour une Paix Juste au Proche-Orient). These two founders of CAPJPO, both former Trotskyist activists, were anti-Zionist Jews, as were many of its other members. The Euro-Palestine list represented an attempted "opening" to activists who had no contact with Jewish groups, especially to the Arab-Muslim community, which was regarded as receptive to pro-Palestinian rhetoric.

The list was supported by Islamist groups and some far-left anti-Zionists, but attacked by the Communists and the Greens who worried that it would siphon off some of their votes. On June 8 it was repudiated by the official representative of the Palestine Liberation Organization in France, Leila Shahid, who argued that "a proliferation of lists can only help weaken solidarity with Palestine, not strengthen it." In the end, Euro-Palestine, whose presence was limited to the Paris region, was only a marginal force in the elections, with 1.83 percent of the vote in the region as a whole. There were, however, some neighborhoods with large Muslim populations where it received more than 5 percent and even a few where it exceeded 10 percent. Euro-Palestine continued to exist after the elections, but became increasingly indistinguishable from CAPJPO, serving as its public face.

On October 29, the head of the Palestinian Authority, Yasir Arafat, was transferred to a French military hospital in the Paris suburb of Clamart. A long period of uncertainty began, with contradictory declarations coming from various sources about his state of health. (The French military doctors maintained an almost total silence, broken only by a few press releases.) During this time, pro-Palestinian activists organized a vigil near the hospital, and were joined by some "anti-Zionist Jews" from outside France. The official announcement of Arafat's death came on November 11. Late that afternoon, his body left the Villacoublay military base on an air force airbus bound for Cairo, after an official ceremony on the tarmac attended by Prime Minister Raffarin.

This episode left many French people, especially French Jews, uneasy. Few questioned President Chirac's decision to welcome a gravely ill man to France, and the discretion of the French military doctors was understood and appreciated. However, questions were raised about the way Arafat's long agony was managed on the political and communications levels. Behind the parade of dignitaries to the Palestinian president's bedside, there appeared to be power struggles and financial intrigues (in February 2004, French judicial authorities had opened an investigation into major transfers of funds that benefited Arafat's wife, Suha, who was separated from her husband and divided her time between Paris and Tunis). Questions were raised about the conditions under which some people and not others were allowed access to Arafat's sickbed, about who determined the legal date of death, and about the source of rumors that Arafat may have been poisoned. Faced with these questions and others along the same lines, the hospital administration invariably replied that Arafat's family had legal privileges that it could not discuss.

Criticism focused particularly on the official acts that followed Arafat's death. First of all, the honors given Arafat at the Villacoublay military base far exceeded the minimum due the head of the PA: the French authorities evidently wished to make a dramatic "gesture." In addition, the official death certificate drawn up at the Clamart town hall gave Arafat's birthplace as "Al Qods/Jerusalem," although almost all biographies of Arafat agreed that he was born in Cairo, and that the Jerusalem birthplace was a fiction maintained for political reasons. The mayor of Clamart insisted that he was not making any judgement in signing this document. He said he was obliged to copy the information recorded in the *livret de famille* of Arafat and his wife, issued by the Ministry of Foreign Affairs (all French married couples and parents have a *livret de famille* or family booklet, which serves as the source for other legal notices concerning them). "It was in this *livret,* an official document," the mayor continued, "that his birthplace was given as 'Al Qods/Jerusalem.'"

A Ministry of Foreign Affairs spokesperson, Hervé Ladsous, was questioned about this matter on November 16. He explained that Yasir Arafat did indeed have a French *livret de famille,* because his wife Suha had acquired French nationality. In this *livret,* drawn up in 1996, the French authorities had carried over the information recorded in the supporting documents supplied by the applicants. Since Yasir Arafat had submitted a document according to which he had been born in Jerusalem, the authorities had no choice but to copy this information as it was. That is how Arafat, through French administrative procedures, gained recognition for the birthplace that he had chosen for himself, and how this choice accompanied him even in death.

Anti-Semitism and Racism

The main source of information on racism and anti-Semitism in France is the voluminous report published annually by the National Consultative Commission of Human Rights (CNCDH), an agency attached to the prime minister's office but comprised of representatives of religious bodies, trade unions, and antiracist groups, as well as independent figures. The statistics contained in this report are provided to the CNCDH by the Ministry of the Interior on the basis of information from the national and local police. The official statistics distinguish between "actions," defined as "acts against individuals and property presenting a certain degree of seriousness," and "threats," which are "threatening words or gestures, graffiti, tracts, hateful demonstrations, and other acts of intimidation." The data also specify the victims of the "actions" and "threats," the most significant distinction being that between anti-Semitism and other forms of racism and xenophobia.

The report for 2004, released on March 21, 2005, showed that Jews were the main victims of racist violence in France. In 2004, in the "Hexagon," or metropolitan France (not including Corsica, where nationalist agitation is tied up with racism and xenophobia), 200 "anti-Semitic actions" and 88 "racist actions" other than anti-Semitic were recorded. The disparity here is flagrant: Jews represent less than 10 percent of the population potentially threatened by racism (people with origins in northern and sub-Saharan Africa constitute the vast majority of this population), but they are by far the leading victims of violence.

This is a recent phenomenon, and its origin can be pinpointed to the beginning of the Palestinian intifada in the fall of 2000. In the five years preceding the intifada, 1995–99, public authorities recorded a total of 16 anti-Semitic "actions" in the Hexagon. In the next five years, 2000–04, their number increased to 672, while in the same period there were 205 racist "actions" directed at people who were not Jews. In 2004 alone, 36 of the 56 people injured in racist attacks were Jews. In the years since the intifada began, the percentage of all racist acts of violence that were directed at Jews ranged, depending on the year, between 65 and 80 percent. Put another way, statistically speaking a Jew is 20 to 30 times more likely to be the victim of a racist attack than an Arab or an African.

To be sure, Jews were hardly the only victims of racism in France. Discrimination in employment and housing, based on physical appearance or surname, was rarely directed against Jews and was much more likely to affect members of other minority groups. Clearly, two distinct processes were at work. On the one hand, social discrimination based on race, now rarely felt by Jews, had continued and even grown in relation to other minorities. On the other hand, there had emerged a pattern of anti-Jewish violence without parallel since World War II, caused by "fall-out" from the Middle East conflict.

No more than partial information was available about the perpetrators of anti-Semitic actions, as only about one in five had been apprehended by the police (a proportion that also held for those guilty of non-anti-Semitic racist acts). The CNCDH report indicated that of the 970 manifestations of anti-Semitism recorded in 2004 (200 "actions" and 770 "threats"), 27 percent were the work of "Arab-Muslim circles," 17 percent of "far-right circles," and 56 percent involved "individuals who were unknown in all respects." Restricting the analysis to violent "actions" changed the proportions somewhat, with 33 percent attributed to "Arab-Muslim circles," 7 percent to the far right, and 60 percent to unknowns. Either way, most incidents were not attributed to specific groups, and thus there was no basis for treating the acts, whether violent or not, as necessarily cases of political or ideological anti-Semitism. Rather, there was a cultural climate that allowed isolated individuals to act out anti-Jewish ideas. Beyond the actual violence—which remained limited, even if it had a traumatic effect on a significant part of the Jewish population—there was a kind of symbolic violence embodied both in images coming from the Middle East and commentary in France on these images.

This problem was highlighted by Jean-Christophe Rufin, who was commissioned by Interior Minister Dominique de Villepin to prepare a report on "the struggle against racism and anti-Semitism." Rufin—a doctor, president of a nongovernmental organization that focused on fighting world hunger, and a successful novelist—submitted the report on October 19, 2004. It distinguished among "three levels of responsibility" for French anti-Semitism: that of the perpetrators of violence; that of the "manipulators," for whom anti-Semitism was a "strategy"; and "that of the facilitators, who, through their opinions—or their silence—legitimize the *passages à l'acte* while being very careful not to commit such acts themselves." Rufin termed this third category "anti-Semitism by proxy," adding, "Of all the subtle forms of anti-Semitism by proxy, one in particular needs to be singled out, because it has emerged as a dominant form of discourse in the last few years: radical anti-Zionism . . . . In legitimizing the Palestinians' armed struggle, whatever form it takes, even when it is directed against innocent civilians, anti-Zionism proposes a radical reading of reality that serves to legitimize violent actions committed in France itself."

Around the time that Rufin submitted his report, an illustration of his argument—that criticism of Israel can easily be used to legitimize anti-Semitism—appeared in the form of Alain Ménargues. A journalist who had spent much of this career in the Middle East (he was the Beirut correspondent for Radio France, the public radio station, for many years), Ménargues was named news director of Radio France Internationale (RFI) on July 28, with the title of assistant executive director responsible for broadcasting and information. Radio France Internationale, a distinct entity from Radio France, is "the voice of France around the world," falling directly under the authority of the Ministry of Foreign Affairs.

In September, Ménargues published a book, *Le Mur de Sharon* (Sharon's Wall). In the course of promoting the book, Ménargues, speaking on the far-right station Radio Courtoisie on October 12, said: "I was shocked by the wall. I went to see various people about it—rabbis, politicians. If you read Leviticus in the Torah, what is this? It's the separation of the pure and the impure. To be able to pray, a Jew must be pure; everything that is contrary to this purity must be separated. . . . Read Leviticus. It's there in plain language. Which was the first ghetto in the world? It was in Venice. Who created it? It was the Jews themselves, to keep themselves separate from everyone else. Later, Europe put them in ghettos." He further explained that "from the beginning and wherever Jews have lived, they have constructed an 'eruv,' a symbolic wall to separate them from the others, the non-Jews, the goyim." According to Ménargues, "Sharon's wall" was therefore designed to separate the pure Jews from the Palestinian goyim, the "dangerous impure ones."

A spokesperson for the Foreign Ministry told reporters that he considered the comments of Ménargues "unacceptable." Jewish commentators (notably in the monthly *L'Arche,* which devoted a special issue to the affair) highlighted the factual inaccuracy of each of his points: the laws outlined in Leviticus regarding pure and impure related to the Temple service, not to relations between Jews and non-Jews; an *eruv* does not separate Jews from non-Jews but marks how far an observant Jew can carry an object on the Sabbath; and, as for the ghetto in Venice, it was built in 1516 on the orders of the Council of Nobles, over protests by the Jews.

It was the mobilization of the RFI journalists that broke the scandal. The fact that Ménargues's comments about "the separation of the pure and the impure" were made on a far-right station provoked a strong reaction among the editorial staff. The journalists declared in a press release that their response to "his remarks concerning the Jews and the State of Israel" was "indignation and rejection." This, added to the disclaimer already issued by the Ministry of Foreign Affairs, made the situation untenable. On October 18, it was announced that Ménargues had resigned from his position as news director of RFI, and that he would take on other responsibilities for the station. But Ménargues then publicly accused the RFI journalists' unions of being manipulated by "the associations for the protection or the defense of Israel," and presented himself (according to an October 19 article in the daily *Libération*) as a victim of "manipulation" by a "clique of clannish Jews." That same day, at a staff meeting, all RFI personnel denounced Ménargues's "insulting statements" that "apparently have nothing to do with reality," and rejected "all incitement of racial hatred." Later in the day, the RFI fired Ménargues.

When this affair began, there was a wave of solidarity for Ménargues in far-left and pro-Palestinian circles; they saw him as a "courageous man" who had done nothing more than "condemn Israeli policies." But when it became clear that Ménargues was a blatant anti-Semite, only those opponents of Israel who were least sensitive to charges of anti-Semitism—or, put simply, those most prone to anti-Semitism—remained loyal to his cause.

Another public figure who continued to fan the flames of controversy was Dieudonné M'Bala M'Bala, whose stage name was Dieudonné. A comedian born of a Cameroonian father and a white French mother, he had shocked viewers during a live television show broadcast on December 1, 2003, on the public channel France 3. Dressed as an Orthodox Jew, he had called on people to join "the American-Zionist axis," finishing up with a Nazi salute accompanied by a cry that many viewers heard as "Isra-Heil," which Dieudonné later claimed was simply the word "Israel." The reaction was strong: amid protests and some threats, theater owners in Paris and elsewhere canceled Dieudonné's show, and the probability of his appearing again on television was slim. In response, he declared that he was being persecuted by "the Zionists" (see AJYB 2004, pp. 319–20).

On February 28, 2004, in an interview with an Internet publication, he added another weapon to his arsenal of complaints against Jews, presenting himself as the spokesperson for blacks. He stated that before the incident in late 2003, he had submitted a proposal to the Centre National de la Cinématographie (CNC, the National Film Center), a public agency that granted loans for the production and distribution of French films, for a project involving a fictional film about the Code Noir that had regulated slavery in the French colonies. The request was turned down. Dieudonné concluded that this was because "the Zionists" controlled French cinema (the executive director of the CNC at the time, David Kessler, was a French civil servant from a Jewish family) and wanted to block the expression of black history. In April, in an interview with another Internet publication, Dieudonné said, "There is a very powerful lobby that thinks it has a monopoly on human suffering and that absolutely refuses to recognize us. . . . I really think that the Jewish lobby hates Blacks! . . . A Jew can just roll up his sleeve and show his number to have an automatic right of recognition. For me, my number is written all over my face! But they don't want to share that with us."

These and similar comments evoked protests in the media not only by Jews, but also by many French blacks. A major show was produced in Paris on March 15, "Laugh Against Racism," sponsored jointly by the Union of French Jewish Students and the SOS-Racisme, an antiracist organization with close ties to the Socialist Party. The show brought together many comedians from a variety of backgrounds, including Jews, Africans, and Arabs, who shared a dislike for Dieudonné's behavior. In May, Dieudonné, in turn, presented a new show at his own small Paris theater, ironically called "My Apologies." It consisted not of apologies but of further provocations.

A Paris court, on May 27, ruled in his favor in a case brought against him for the original 2003 television sketch. The judges rejected the accusation of anti-Semitism, holding that "the character personified by the accused did not represent Jews as a whole but rather a certain group of people identified by their political views." Dieudonné then threw himself into politics, most prominently as a candidate for the European Parliament on the Euro-Palestine list. After the European elections, however, he felt the need to distance himself from the originators of the list so as to avoid the taint of anti-Semitism. If anything, however, he became even more politically active. He and some associates, some of whom had associations with Holocaust denial, set up a Web site containing extensive material about "pro-slavery Jews," directly translated from the anti-Semitic literature put out by the Nation of Islam, the American movement led by Louis Farrakhan.

On November 11, at his theater, Dieudonné received a delegation of "anti-Zionist rabbis" who had come to France to pay homage to the deceased Yasir Arafat. After one rabbi, Yisroel Dovid Weiss, declared that "Israel will crumble because it is a nation based on lies, usurpation and blasphemy," Dieudonné responded, "I am very happy to hear you speak. I didn't realize that people like you existed. Where have you been all these years? No one ever hears about you! Is this because of a conspiracy?"

Holocaust-Related Matters

On July 11, the Court of Appeals, the highest court in France, rejected the final motion filed by the lawyers for former cabinet minister Maurice Papon. He had been sentenced to ten years in prison in 1998 for "complicity in crimes against humanity," specifically, arresting Jews in the Bordeaux region and handing them over to the Germans. On October 14, Papon was fined 2,500 euros for "illegally wearing the Legion of Honor," following the publication of a photo in a daily newspaper showing the medal on his jacket lapel. The medal had been officially withdrawn by a presidential decree in 1999.

JEWISH COMMUNITY

Communal Affairs

France's first Jewish-Muslim friendship association, Amitié Judéo-Musulmane de France, was established on November 21. The initiator was Rabbi Michel Serfaty, an Orthodox rabbi who, in addition to his role as professor of Hebrew at the University of Nancy and rabbi in the town of Ris-Orangis outside Paris, had for years organized trips for young Jews and Muslims from his area to Holocaust-related sites in Poland. Serfaty, who had himself been the object of an anti-Semitic attack by two young Arabs while on his way to the synagogue, wished to strengthen contact between the two communities so that Muslims could rediscover the true face of Judaism, as Christians had a generation earlier.

A Jewish-Christian friendship organization, Amitié Judéo-Chrétienne de France, had existed in France for years, as well as a movement bringing together all three religions, Alliance d'Abraham. But there had previously been no specific mechanism for Jewish-Muslim dialogue. On the Jewish side, Rabbi Serfaty obtained support from all the major organizations. But on the Muslim side, the only participant was the "moderate" movement whose leading figure was the spiritual leader of the Paris mosque, Dalil Boubakeur. In the end, the success of the group would depend on convincing the Muslim militants to participate.

348 / AMERICAN JEWISH YEAR BOOK, 2005

Publications

A number of original works of Jewish interest were published in France in 2004. In the realm of ideas: Henri Meschonnic's *Les Noms* (The Names), a translation of the Book of Exodus, and *Un coup de Bible dans la philosophie* (Biblical Dimensions in Philosophy); *Chemins de la Cabale* (Paths of the Kabbalah) by Charles Mopsik (who died in 2003); Nathan Weinstock's *Le Yiddish tel qu'on l'oublie* (The Yiddish We Have Forgotten); Benjamin Gross's *L'aventure du langage* (The Adventure of Language); and Catherine Chalier's *La langue de la vérité* (The Language of Truth), a translation with commentary of texts by the rebbe of Gur.

Current affairs: Jean Mouttapa's *Un Arabe face à Auschwitz* (An Arab Facing Auschwitz); Albert Memmi's *Le portrait du décolonisé* (Portrait of the Decolonized); Pierre-André Taguieff's *Prêcheurs des haine — traversée de la judéophobie planétaire* (Preachers of Hate: The Path of Worldwide Anti-Semitism); and Lisa Anteby-Yemini's *Les Juifs éthiopiens en Israël* (Ethiopian Jews in Israel).

Historical works: Dominique Bourel's *Mendelssohn, la naissance du judaïsme moderne* (Mendelssohn: The Birth of Modern Judaism); Florent Brayard's *La "solution finale de la question juive"* (The "Final Solution to the Jewish Problem"); Pierre Birnbaum's *Géographie de l'espoir — l'exil, les Lumières, la désassimilation* (Geography of Hope: Exile, the Enlightenment, De-assimilation); Jean-Marc Dreyfus and Sarah Gensburger's *Des camps dans Paris, juillet 1943 – août 1944* (The Paris Camps, July 1943 – August 1944); Léon Blum's *Lettres de Buchenwald* (Letters from Buchenwald), edited by Ilan Greilsammer; Myriam Anissimov's *Romain Gary;* Olivier Mannoni's *Manès Sperber;* and Michel Winock's *La France et les Juifs* (France and the Jews).

Finally, 2004 saw the publication of an autobiographical account by the great novelist Patrick Modiano, *Un pedigree* (A Pedigree).

Personalia

On May 7, medical professor Alexandre Minkowski died at the age of 88. Born in Paris, he became a specialist in treating newborns. His relationship with Judaism was ambivalent. Describing himself as a "not very Catholic Jew," he was actively involved in a number of "Third-World" causes, among them that of the Palestinians.

On May 23, Maxime Rodinson, a specialist in Oriental studies, died at the age of 89. Born in Paris to a Russian Jewish family, he was a longtime member of the Communist Party and remained a strong opponent of Zionism all his life. Although his specialty was Ethiopian literary language, he was more widely known for his books on Islam and the Arab world. He eventually accepted the existence of the State of Israel, but his sympathies remained with the Palestinians.

On August 31, André Caquot, an academician, died at the age of 81. This Protestant Christian was an eminent specialist in Semitic languages and biblical research. Professor at the Collège de France (the most prestigious of French universities), he had a vast knowledge of Jewish culture: he regularly attended Yom Kippur services at Paris's main synagogue and knew contemporary Israeli writers personally.

On September 5, historian Paul Sebag died at the age of 85. Born in Tunisia to a Jewish "bourgeois" family, he became an active Communist at a young age. A journalist and teacher, he actively participated in the movement for Tunisian independence. Unlike most Jews, he did not leave Tunisia after it separated from France in 1956. But he came to feel isolated in the new Tunisian society, and, in 1977, left for France where, after teaching for two years at the University of Rouen, he devoted his retirement to writing books on Tunisian history and Tunisian Jews.

On October 9, philosopher Jacques Derrida died at the age of 74. Born in Algeria to a Jewish family, he was barred, at age 12, from attending school by the Vichy collaborationist government; this event seems to have marked him for life. After difficult beginnings, he became one of France's great contemporary thinkers. His theory of "deconstruction" earned him international recognition. Derrida's relationship to Judaism remained complex: he was loath to identify himself with a particular community and maintained a very critical attitude toward Israel, but he asserted that he would never deny his Jewishness.

On October 12, Lazare Pytkowicz died at the age of 76. Born in Paris, he was only 14 when he joined the resistance against the German occupiers who had just deported his parents. Acting as liaison among resistance groups, he was arrested several times but always managed to escape. He was the youngest person in France to receive the title of Compagnon de la Libération (Companion of the Liberation), reserved for elite resistance fighters, during his lifetime. Later, he became a businessman, all the while remaining active in the Communist Party.

On November 11, filmmaker Richard Dembo died at the age of 56. Following the release of his first film, *La Diagonale du fou* (Diagonal of the Crazy) in 1984, he made relatively few movies. An observant Jew, he refused to film scenes that went against the rules of modesty specified in the Torah. He left a posthumous film, *La Maison de Nina* (Nina's House), about the treatment of Jewish children who survived the Holocaust.

On December 9, Marcel Suarès died at the age of 90. Born in Bayonne to a Portuguese Jewish family that had lived in the area since the sixteenth century, he joined the anti-German resistance early on and distinguished himself by carrying out many acts of sabotage in arms factories. His exploits earned him the title of Compagnon de la Libération. Suarès served as a bodyguard to General de Gaulle, and then returned to his hometown of Bayonne where he opened an electrical appliance store. For 42 years he served as a city councilor, and was an active member of the Bayonne Jewish community.

MEIR WAINTRATER

Belgium

National Affairs

The Belgian federal government is a loose confederation of three "regions"—the Flemish Region in the north, predominantly Dutch-speaking; the Walloon Region in the south, predominantly French-speaking; and the Brussels-Capital Region, with a mixed population—each enjoying a significant degree of autonomy. Dutch, French, and German (spoken primarily in Eupen and Malmédy) are all official languages. Federal legislative power is in the hands of a bicameral Parliament, and the cabinet, officially answerable to King Albert II, a constitutional monarch, is required by law to contain an equal number of French- and Dutch-speakers. A coalition of neoliberals and socialists controlled the federal government in 2004, each element composed of two parties, one Flemish and the other Walloon. Guy Verhofstadt of the Flemish Liberals and Democrats (VLD) was prime minister.

Elections were held in June for the regional governments. Once again, the big news was a significant gain for the far-right separatist Vlaams Blok (Flemish Bloc) in the Flemish Region. The party increased its share of the vote from 24.1 to 32 percent and gained ten seats in the regional parliament. Although this made it the second largest party, the other factions continued their policy of refusing to enter into a coalition with it, effectively keeping the Vlaams Blok out of the government. It was already the largest party on the Antwerp City Council and the fifth largest in the Federal Parliament. Although outlawed later in the year, it would reconstitute itself under a different name (see below, p. 355). The far-right party in French-speaking Belgium, the Front National Belge (FNB), won 5.4 percent of the vote in Brussels to secure four seats, a gain of two, and 8.1 percent in the Walloon Region, a gain of three seats for a total of four. The neoliberal parties and the Greens lost ground in all three regions, while the socialists made gains. The elections resulted in a reshuffling of cabinet positions on the federal level, the most important change being the replacement of Foreign Minister Louis Michel by Karel De Gucht.

In the 2004 election, Mrs. Monique Langbord-Faynsztein became the first Jewish alderman in Forest, one of Brussels's 19 boroughs. This came on the heels of another first, the election of Claude Marinower, an

Antwerp Jew, to the Federal Parliament in 2003, representing the VLD. Two Islamist parties ran in the Brussels regional election. Neither came near to winning parliamentary representation, as the great bulk of Muslim voters cast their ballots for the mainstream French-speaking parties. Of the 72 francophone members of the new Brussels parliament, 15 were of North African origin and two of Turkish descent, while one of the Flemish members was of Arab background.

The European Union, headquartered in Brussels, welcomed ten new members in May—Cyprus, Malta, Estonia, Hungary, Latvia, Lithuania, Poland, the Czech Republic, Slovakia, and Slovenia. The issue of Turkey's accession to the EU remained controversial. Other candidates for membership were Bulgaria, Romania, and Croatia.

The Nihoul-Dutroux affair that transfixed and horrified Belgium for eight years ended after a 17-week trial in Arlon that ran from March 1 to June 22, under a heavy media spotlight. This case involved the kidnapping, drugging, raping, and killing of six young girls in 1995 and 1996 (see AJYB 2004, pp. 327–28). Marc Dutroux was given a life sentence, and his confederates received shorter prison terms: Michelle Martin, 30 years; Michel Lelièvre, 25 years; and Michel Nihoul, 5 years.

Yet another murder of a young Belgian girl was solved during the year when the body of Elisabeth Brichet, missing since 1990, was found on July 3, buried ten feet underground near a building on the grounds of Le Sautou Château, at Donchery, near Sedan, in France. The murderers were Michel Fourniret and his wife, Monique. The pair had convinced the girl to come with them, and then abused and strangled her. Michel Fourniret, under questioning, admitted to committing eight other murders as well, and was suspected of a ninth. Since several of the victims were French nationals, once the Belgian examining magistrate completes his work on the Brichet case, it would be the turn of the the French justice system to investigate this serial killer.

On a far happier note, 2004 began with a blessed event in the royal family, the birth of a baby girl—Princess Louise—to Prince Laurent, the younger son of King Albert II and Queen Paola, and Princess Claire.

Israel and the Middle East

Belgium's official position, like that of the EU, was that there should be a negotiated two-state solution to the Israeli-Palestinian conflict. And like the great majority of the other EU states, Belgium's voting record in the UN was predictably pro-Palestinian.

While Belgium had balanced this stance with good bilateral ties with Israel for some time, the years 2002 and 2003 had been catastrophic for Belgian-Israeli relations. The reason was the ongoing legal struggle to have Ariel Sharon and other Israeli nationals tried for alleged war crimes under Belgium's so-called law of universal jurisdiction that made possible prosecutions in Belgium for acts done anywhere in the world. It was not until August 5, 2003, that the law was changed to require some link of the accused or of the crime to Belgium in order for universal jurisdiction to apply, thus putting an end to the Sharon prosecution (see AJYB 2004, pp. 329–30).

Foreign Minister Michel sought to mend fences with a visit to Israel in February 2004. After holding talks with Israeli leaders, Michel issued a public statement regretting the legal steps against Sharon. He called the universal-jurisdiction law "the cause of misunderstandings that have been most prejudicial to the relations between our countries." Apologizing, Michel declared that "we have turned the page, and I return to my country firmly convinced that we can now resume a fruitful and constructive dialogue with our Israeli friends." Israeli foreign minister Silvan Shalom paid a return visit to Belgium in December, and met with Prime Minister Verhofstadt and the new foreign minister, Karel De Gucht. The two ministers agreed on a new bilateral customs agreement.

Trade between Belgium and Israel continued to grow. In 2004, Israeli exports to Belgium were worth almost $3 billion, and Belgian exports to Israel a little over $4 billion, both higher than in 2003. By far the largest single item of trade on both sides was diamonds. Israel was the 15th most important supplier of goods and services to Israel, and the 13th biggest customer for Belgian goods and services. The Flemish Region, far more highly industrialized than the Walloon Region, accounted for over 94 percent of Belgian exports to Israel.

Anti-Semitism and Extremism

Brussels hosted an EU seminar on February 18 about the resurgence of anti-Semitism. Among the speakers were German foreign minister Joschka Fischer, World Jewish Congress president Edgar Bronfman, Nobel laureate Elie Wiesel, and European Commission president Romano Prodi.

The choice of a Belgian site for the meeting was ironically on target: 2004 was studded with a host of anti-Semitic incidents in the country. Most took the form of anti-Semitic graffiti, but several were far more serious. The first to receive national publicity occurred on January 28, at a qualifying match for the European soccer championship between Belgium and Israel that took place indoors in Hasselt. About a dozen people in the bleachers, some painted in Hamas colors and carrying Hamas and other terrorist organizations' banners, hurled insults and abuse at the Israeli players throughout the match, shouting (in Dutch) "Let's slit the Jews throats," "Hamas, Hamas," and "Gas all the Jews." The city brought charges against these individuals, and one Muslim member of the Belgian soccer team was suspended.

On February 15, a Jew from Antwerp was riding on the Antwerp-Charleroi train. When it stopped in Brussels South Station, he took the opportunity to pray. A man who looked about 20 years old came up, placed a knife under his throat, and asked if he was Jewish. Getting no reply, the assailant called him a "dirty Jew" and threatened: "The next time I see you on the train, I'll have your hide and I'll kill you." None of the other passengers interfered, and the assailant got off the train.

On April 1, the prime minister's office and several newspapers received e-mail messages allegedly from Hamas, threatening attacks on Jews, shops, and buses in Antwerp, in retaliation for Israeli actions against Palestinians. One paper reported that a name on the e-mail it got was that of a man suspected of involvement in the Madrid train bombing of March 11. That same month, in a decision that spoke volumes about the toleration for anti-Semitism among political progressives, the Jewish Secular Community Center (CCLJ), a left-wing Jewish group that sought reconciliation between Jews and Muslims, announced that it would not participate in a demonstration organized by a left-wing umbrella organization because the Jews would not be allowed to carry placards denouncing anti-Semitism.

On June 24, around 8:30 p.m., five youths apparently of foreign origin stood in front of a yeshiva in Wilrijk and hurled anti-Semitic insults at the students inside. A dozen of the latter, exasperated by the situation, came out of the yeshiva and headed for the youths, who ran away. About 10:30 p.m. two of the yeshiva students came out on the street and began talking with two other friends. Suddenly, they found themselves face to face with about 15 North African youths who had been hiding up the street. The gang was armed with iron bars, tennis racquets, and blades. They chased the four students, setting upon them out of the blue without any provocation or exchange of words. In the course of the chase the assailants managed to grab one of the boys, 16-year-old Noach Schmahl, the son of a Dutch rabbi, beat him about the head with the iron bars, and stab him in the back. The victim was hospitalized with a punctured lung; the assailants got away. This incident seems to have set off a series of copycat crimes. Until the end of October, Jewish youths were periodically threatened and assaulted without provocation in downtown Antwerp and Wilrijk.

Alarm bells went off in government circles. On June 26, two days after the Wilrijk stabbing, Belgian officials and representatives of all the political parties attended a meeting denouncing such acts, held at the Jewish Martyrs' Monument in Brussels. Two days later, the mayor of Antwerp attended a rally to combat anti-Semitism in his city and pledged that the police would give the problem top priority. Prime Minister Verhofstadt met with Jewish leaders on June 30, and the next day told Parliament: "Every anti-Semitic aggression is not only directed against the physical persons but also against the fundamental values of our country." In his annual address on National Day, July 21, King Albert II concluded his remarks as follows: "Let us take an uncompromising stance on all acts of racism, anti-Semitism, and xenophobia, wherever they come from. It is in that spirit that the Queen and I hope to continue serving you for many years to come."

That month, the federal government adopted ten measures to counter hate crimes, including provisions for preventive detention, directions to prosecutors to follow through aggressively on all suspected cases, and steps to upgrade security at synagogues and other Jewish institutions. In addition, two federal ministries took action. The Ministry of Foreign Affairs delegated Ambassador Jan Deboutte, one of its senior diplomats, to coordinate measures to fight anti-Semitism, and the Ministry for Social Integration announced the creation of a "watchdog unit" to monitor trends.

The national revulsion against group hatred seemed to carry over to the Belgian judicial system. On April 21, the Court of Appeal in Ghent ruled that the Vlaams Blok—the xenophobic but not overtly anti-Semitic Flemish far-right party—was in violation of the antiracism laws because of its "permanent incitement to segregation and racism." Many observers, and not just on the extreme right, suspected that the government's prosecution of the case at least partly reflected a concerted effort to remove the political threat posed by the antiestablishment party. The Supreme Court upheld the decision on November 9. Five days later the Vlaams Blok officially disbanded and its leaders created a new party, Vlaams Belang (Flemish Interest). At the inaugural event for the new entity, one leader uttered veiled threats against the prosecutors and judges involved in banning its predecessor party.

Holocaust-Related Issues

In 2003, the government called upon the Center for Historical Research and Documentation on War and Contemporary Society, a major Belgian archive on the World War II era, to establish "the facts and possible responsibilities of the Belgian authorities in the persecution and deportation of the Jews of Belgium . . . ." The center organized a research team in 2004, which, in September, began its investigations.

A royal decree on July 31, drafted and approved by the government, extended by one year from September 9, 2004, the life of Belgium's National Commission for Restitution. Originally set up in December 2001, the commission was charged with arranging reparations for members of Belgium's Jewish community whose property was stolen or left behind during World War II, and their heirs. Almost 6,000 individual claims, twice the original estimate, had been made by the original filing deadline of September 9, 2003, and in the 12 months since, 1,013 dossiers were settled, 79.3 percent of them in favor of the claimant. The extension would provide more time to wrap up the processing of claims. Priority was to go to the roughly 3,000 claimants over age 70. Once all the valid claims are satisfied, the remaining money allocated for restitution would be transferred to a newly created Belgian Judaism Foundation, administered by representatives of Belgian Jewry, for distribution to Jewish social and cultural programs and to combat racism and bigotry.

The primary Holocaust archive in Belgium was the Jewish Museum of Deportation and Resistance, located in Mechelen/Malines, on the site of what had been Dossin Barracks, where Belgian Jews and Gypsies were taken to await deportation. In March 2004, the museum completed processing the Register of Antwerp's Jewish Citizens, a mammoth task that involved indexing 10,012 names and 20,024 pictures, and then began work on the 217 binders of the Register of Jewish Residents of Belgium, which contained 40,000 forms. Another project was inventorying and digitizing 4,441 envelopes of personal documents taken from detainees at Dossin Barracks, which had been transferred to the museum by the War Victims Department in 2003. Meanwhile, the Finance Ministry deposited with the museum the unclaimed contents of bank vaults that had belonged to Jewish families, and the Interior Ministry gave the museum permission to digitize the Immigration Police's files on Jews and Gypsies who were deported from Belgium.

The museum's holdings were further enriched in the course of the year by gifts of many personal documents and mementos from survivors. Some 900 documents from private individuals were catalogued, digitized, and processed for preservation in 2004. Also, the museum was given permission to make digital copies of the large Brachfeld collection, containing copies of files submitted to the State of Israel for awarding the title of "Righteous Gentile." They contained invaluable information about Belgians who helped to hide Jews from the Nazis, including 400 videotapes of interviews with them.

The chairman of the Forum of Jewish Organizations, which represented many Jewish groups in the Flemish Region, accompanied King Albert II and Prime Minister Verhofstadt to Poland on January 27 for the ceremony marking the 60th anniversary of the liberation of the Nazi camps and the end of World War II that the Polish government hosted at Auschwitz-Birkenau. For those who were not there, the Forum later organized a short gathering at the Jewish Monument in Antwerp.

On September 5, the Jewish Museum of Deportation and Resistance and the Forum of Jewish Organizations commemorated 60 years since the liberation of Dossin Barracks by gathering as many former inmates as possible, along with their families, for a special ceremony. A large number of Dutch-speaking political authorities attended, as well as an impressive audience. Another 60-year commemoration occurred earlier, on June 1, when Prof. Georges Schneck, a former member of the resistance and honorary president of the Central Consistory of Belgium, participated in the ecumenical ceremony at the Mardasson Memorial in Bastogne, held to recall the famous Battle of the Bulge. Although the battle actually took place in December 1944, the ceremony was held in June so that many American veterans, in Europe to mark 60 years since D-Day, might attend. Yet another 60th was commemorated in September, that of the liberation of Brussels. The first liberators were members of the Piron Brigade, which included a number of Jews.

JEWISH COMMUNITY

Communal Affairs

The Central Consistory of Belgium was the officially recognized body representing Belgian Jewry, acting for the community in contacts with the government, foreign Jewish communities, and other religious and ethnic groups. In 2004 much of its time was devoted to discussions with government officials at various levels on the need to provide security from anti-Semitic violence, and to intergroup dialogue that might calm tensions. The president of the Consistory gave presentations at a number of meetings of international Jewish bodies.

The CCOJB (Coordinating Committee of Jewish Organizations of Belgium) was the umbrella group for 40 Jewish organizations in Belgium, primarily in the francophone parts of the country. It was a member of the World Jewish Congress and the European Jewish Congress. Like the Consistory, it combated anti-Semitism and maintained regular contact with the relevant authorities, organized events commemorating the Holocaust, and maintained relations with other religious bodies in the hope of promoting tolerance and mutual respect.

A roughly equivalent function in the Antwerp area was provided by the Forum of Jewish Organizations (Forum der Joodse Organisaties), whose involvement in various aspects of Holocaust commemoration is detailed above. Since a disproportionate number of anti-Semitic incidents took place in or near Antwerp, the Forum was heavily involved in fighting racism and anti-Semitism throughout the year. Its members participated in TV debates and gave newspaper interviews, took part in public discussions, and participated in interreligious meetings.

Coordinating social welfare services in the Jewish community was the Brussels-based Central Administration of Jewish Welfare Organizations (Centrale des Ouevres social juives), which provided funds for the various Jewish institutions that dealt with the needy. In the light of the deteriorating economic situation in Belgium and in Europe as a whole, applications for aid were becoming more numerous. The primary recipient of its funding was the Jewish Social Service Office, which marked its 60th anniversary in 2004 (its original beneficiaries had been Holocaust survivors). The office maintained an old-age home, Jewish schools and cultural centers, athletic facilities, a summer camp, and an educational loan fund. Its personnel also paid visits to people living alone and helped the incapacitated with household chores.

Radio Judaica, the only Jewish radio station in Belgium, had been the first to operate in Europe, beginning in 1980. It could be heard in Antwerp, Brussels, and Liège. The station's impact was significant, as it provided a positive image of the Jewish community to the many non-Jewish listeners, served as source of information about developments in Israel, alerted people to anti-Semitic incidents, and functioned as the voice of the Belgian Jewish community. The station was a project of the Ben-Gurion Circle, founded in 1977 to counteract anti-

Israel propaganda. Among its 2004 activities were programs on anti-Semitism, Israeli business opportunities, and Jewish refugees from Arab countries. There were also other pro-Israel groups in Belgium. The Center for Information and Documentation (CID), for example, sent out about ten e-mail bulletins a week about Israel and the Middle East to more than 1,000 subscribers. It also sponsored lectures and exhibits about Israel, and concerts by visiting Israeli musicians. WIZO (Women's International Zionist Organization) performed the dual roles of uniting Jewish women through the bonds of friendship, and raising money to support its institutions in Israel.

Taking a rather different tack was the Jewish Secular Community Center (CCLJ), which, as part of its humanistic rather than theistic understanding of Jewish culture, promoted the views of the Israeli peace camp and criticized Israeli actions it deemed unjust. The organization ran non-religious celebrations of Jewish holidays and rites of passage, provided Jewish education in secular form, and sought to combat the influence of the extreme right on Belgian life.

Education

There were three Jewish schools in Brussels, all accredited by the state. The largest, Ganenou Athenaeum, with both primary and secondary programs, was modeled on Israeli secular schools, and its degree was recognized by Israel's Education Ministry. Its students were required to master both the official Belgian state curriculum and a program of Jewish studies that, while not Orthodox, stressed the celebration of Jewish holidays, Zionism, and a positive Jewish identity in a spirit of tolerance.

Maimonides Athenaeum, the next largest, was Orthodox and maintained programs from infant daycare through the end of secondary school. It was founded in 1947 to service the educational needs of children of Holocaust survivors. Although most of the students now did not come from Orthodox homes, the curriculum of Jewish studies was highly traditional as well as Zionistic. Beth Aviv, the smallest and most ideologically liberal school, had only a kindergarten and primary school.

The three institutions differed in their admission standards. Maimonides would not accept children from mixed-faith marriages where the mother was not Jewish, or those with a mother converted by a non-Orthodox rabbi; Ganenou would accept the latter but not the former. Beth Aviv accepted both categories, but if graduates with a non-Jewish mother wanted to continue at the Ganenou secondary school, they would first have to convert to Judaism.

Antwerp, with its large Orthodox presence, had a quite different educational profile. Fully 90 percent of Jewish children in the city attended Jewish schools, all of which were Orthodox. The two largest were Tachkemoni, run by the Shomre Hadass community, and Yesode Hatorah, under the auspices of the stricter Machsike Hadass, which maintained separate sections for boys and girls. Tachkemoni was known for its advanced training in Hebrew language that enabled its graduates to proceed directly to higher educational institutions in Israel with no need for special language instruction. A smaller school, Yavne, was Modern Orthodox and Zionist. All three of these schools were accredited by the government. In addition, several Hasidic communities had their own small private schools, none of which was accredited and some of which offered only religious studies.

Adult Jewish education was provided by the Jewish Studies Institute, which operated as part of Brussels Free University. In addition to maintaining a two-year academic program leading to a degree, the institute sponsored popular classes and lectures open to the general public. The 2004 lecture topics included a comparison of the views of Martin Buber and Emmanuel Lévinas about Judaism; love, sexuality and procreation in the Jewish tradition; the "founding myths" of anti-Semitism; the first-century confrontation between the Jewish philosopher Philo and Emperor Caligula; and the contemporary resurgence of Hasidism. The other Belgian universities also offered programs in Jewish studies.

Intergroup Relations

On January 14, the Consistory paid tribute to the late Abbot Jean-Marie Schoefs in a special ceremony. Abbot Schoefs spearheaded the Jewish-Christian dialogue in Belgium following the proclamation of the Nostra Aetate encyclical by Pope John XXIII in 1965. Sister Marie-Hélène Fournier, of Notre Dame de Sion, passed away on March 9. Well known for her commitment to Jewish-Christian rapprochement, she, together with Abbot Schoefs, Dean Omer Hamels, and Father Georges Passelecq (all three now deceased), were the Christian founders of the Organe de Concertation entre Juifs et Chrétiens (OCJB), which regularly brought together Jewish, Roman Catholic, and Protestant leaders for consultations on common concerns.

Mel Gibson's controversial film, *The Passion of the Christ,* was released in Belgium on April 7, in the middle of Passover and a few days before Easter Sunday. The movie had already been previewed by journalists and religious leaders. The Jewish community was virtually unanimous in condemning it as violently anti-Semitic. At least one leading Catholic cleric, Msgr. Joseph De Kesel, the auxiliary bishop of Brussels, agreed; he found the violence "absurd." There were several lively public debates about the film, including one sponsored by the Institute of Jewish Audiovisual Memory on September 21 between Msgr. André Leonard, bishop of Namur, and Prof. Thomas Gergely, director of the Jewish Studies Institute. The controversy was surely one factor in making the movie a great commercial success in Belgium.

An important interfaith conference took place on April 14 at the German embassy in Brussels under the aegis of the embassy, the Consistory's Commission for Pluralist Relations, the Catholic National Commission for Relations with Judaism, and the Flemish Working Group for Relations with Judaism (VKPB). The featured speaker was Sir Sigmund Sternberg, who discussed how to promote dialogue between religions and combat anti-Semitism in Belgium.

The Sisters of Zion, a tiny Catholic group dedicated to developing good relations with the Jewish people, continued its work, even though membership fell from three to two in 2004. The sisters met with parishes, priests, parents, and catechists eager to understand the Jewish roots of their Christian faith, and wrote articles about Judaism for various magazines. The group maintained membership in several Jewish-sponsored organizations, one sister participated in the Catholic National Commission for Relations with Jewry, and another served on the CID board of directors.

Also involved in intergoup work was the European Jewish Information Center (CEJI), headquartered in Brussels. It sought to adapt the Classroom of Difference program, initiated in the U.S. by the Anti-Defamation League, to the Belgian educational system. The program trained student "leaders" in individual schools to help create an atmosphere of tolerance and mutual understanding between students of different religious and ethnic backgrounds. Work was begun in 2004 on a new manual for coordinators, and inquiries were made to government officials about the possible involvement of the Ministry of Education and the Ministry of Social Integration in the program.

Another CEJI initiative was the development of new teaching tools about anti-Semitism. With support from the Belgian Foreign Ministry, a roundtable for educators on the subject took place in December, conducted both in Dutch and French. Another roundtable was scheduled for January 2005, followed by a projected trip to Yad Vashem in April 2005.

Culture

In April, the Jewish Museum of Belgium finally moved into its impressive new home at the heart of the Sablon neighborhood, with its museums, art galleries, and antique shops. The first exhibition there, "Déballage" (Taking off the Wraps), by the Liège artist Jacques Charlier, opened officially on May 4. The museum's holdings primarily reflected the lives and history of Belgium's Jews since the eighteenth century. It held works by some 250 Jewish artists, and a photograph and slide library with some 20,000 items that depicted scenes from Jewish life in Belgium and Israel. The museum also organized educational activities including interactive guided tours of its exhibitions, story hours, workshops, talks, and walks around town on specific themes. Four specialized libraries—general and reference, Yiddish, Jewish art, and Judaism in Belgium—with total holdings of close to 25,000 publications, were open to the public. Other libraries were for the time being open only to researchers.

Another important cultural institution, the Contemporary Memory Foundation, was created in 1994 to make the Jews' contributions to the Belgian nation during the twentieth century better known. It did this through the collection of documents and recorded interviews, sponsorship of research, and dissemination of the research findings to the public through an annual bulletin, *Les Cahiers de la Mémoire contemporaine.* It was also in the process of constructing a Web site.

The foundation set up a traveling exhibition in late 2003 that continued to be presented around the country in 2004, called "Places of Memory." It depicted the lives of young Belgian Jews in several communities during the twentieth century, covering such topics as school, work, youth movements, summer camps, and hiding out during the Holocaust. The foundation published several books in 2004, including *Les curateurs du ghetto: L'Association des Juifs en Belgique sous l'occupation nazie,* a collection of essays about the Association of Jews in Belgium under the Nazi occupation, and *Orientalisme et études juives à la fin du XIXe siècle: Le manuscrit d'Emile Ouverleaux* by Jean-Philippe Schreiber and Philippe Pierret, on late-nineteenth-century Orientalism and Jewish studies. Among the research projects underway were a study of Jewish children's schooling during the war, especially the effects of the occupying force's order of December 1941 banning Jewish children from public schools, and the clandestine migration of Belgian Jewish Holocaust survivors to Palestine between the end of World War II and the proclamation of the State of Israel in 1948.

The Institute of Jewish Audiovisual Memory (IJAM) began 2004 in major financial difficulty, and two full-time staff members had to be let go on April 30. But the efforts of volunteers and the appointment of a new board of directors enabled the institute to maintain its programs. It held a series of lectures and discussions running from January through March on cultural relations between Belgium and Europe's German-speaking countries, organized in cooperation with the Goethe Institute, the French-speaking Catholic University of Louvain, the Dutch-speaking Catholic University of Leuven, and Debelux (Germany-Belgium-Luxembourg Chamber of Commerce).

The IJAM screened Jewish-themed films throughout the year. It also chose the Israeli films to be shown the Mediterranean Film Festival held at the Botanique Cultural Center on December 2–11, and decided which one of them would be the topic of a special discussion — *Tehora* (Purity) by Anat Zuria, which dealt with the ritual immersion of women in Jewish tradition. Professor Liliane Vana of the Sorbonne, an expert on women and Jewish law, conducted the session.

GEORGES SCHNEK

The Netherlands

National Affairs

MURDER

For the Netherlands, 2004 was "the year of terror and fear," according to *NRC Handelsblad,* the country's least sensationalist daily. On November 2, on a quiet street in Amsterdam, a 26-year-old man identified by the police only as "Mohammed B." (the surname was later determined to be Bouyeri) fired several shots at moviemaker and publicist Theo van Gogh. He then stabbed the victim and used the knife to pin a letter to the dead body. The letter's contents tied the murder to van Gogh's views on Islam, and threatened the lives of several politicians. In addition — though this received scant mention in the media and the political arena — it threatened Jews.

Van Gogh had written a regular column in which he insulted many groups (including Jews), often in coarse language. On August 29, about two months before the murder, Dutch television broadcast van Gogh's film *Submission-I,* an attack on Islamic repression of women that seemed calculated to offend, featuring nude women with texts from the Koran written on their bodies. Van Gogh produced the film along with a member of parliament from the liberal VVD party, Ayaan Hirsi Ali — a Somali-born woman who was waging her own personal crusade against Islamic fundamentalism. Hirsi Ali was one of those threatened in the murder letter.

This was the second recent politically motivated murder, coming just two and a half years after right-wing populist politician Pim Fortuyn was assassinated by a left-wing environmental activist (see AJYB 2003, p. 426), the first political assassination in the country since 1672. The Dutch people's image of their nation as a place of tolerance and freedom of speech, cultivated for centuries and rattled by the Fortuyn murder, was replaced, after van Gogh's killing, by a state of panic and identity crisis. But the fact that this time the deed was done by a Muslim fundamentalist led many to say, in hindsight, that they had seen it coming.

IMMIGRATION AND DEMOGRAPHY

For centuries, small immigrant groups had been absorbed rather easily by simply ignoring cultural differences in the hope that they would disappear—which, generally, they did. Until well into the twentieth century, Jews constituted the only distinguishable minority group—and a small, highly integrated one, at that. But since the 1970s, the number of non-Western immigrants rose some 1,000 percent to 1.6 million, constituting 10 percent of the total population. Most were men who had been recruited for menial labor, from poor rural areas in Turkey and Morocco. Both Dutch society and the immigrants themselves assumed their stay to be a "work-and-go" arrangement, and neither made any attempt at absorption.

Roughly one million of the immigrants were Muslims; instead of going back home, most imported wives from their home countries. Many perceived Holland's permissive society as a moral threat to their families. By 2004, the majority lived in poor inner-city neighborhoods, and a relatively high percentage was unemployed. While children were better educated than their parents, they tended to fall behind in the Dutch school system. Those from traditional homes with authoritarian fathers had difficulty adjusting to an environment that did not appear to have any rules—and yet did. The policy of ignoring cultural differences, or dubbing them "an enrichment" regardless of how some of these youngsters behaved, became increasingly difficult to sustain.

When, particularly after 9/11, the realization finally struck that these Muslims were here to stay, tensions rose, and in 2002 Pim Fortuyn seemed poised to achieve a political landslide by, in the words of his followers, "saying what we think." Fortuyn argued that the country was "full up," called Islam a "retarded culture," and sought a complete halt to immigration. Public opinion swung radically to making no allowances at all for immigrants and to demand total assimilation. When Fortuyn was assassinated, the Dutch were greatly relieved that the murderer was a left-wing activist born and bred in the Netherlands, rather than a Muslim. But in 2004, the "pressure cooker" (a term that figured with great regularity in the media) finally burst with the murder of van Gogh.

The rate of Dutch population growth had been declining since 2000, and in 2004 was down to a rise of "only" 34,000, the lowest growth rate since 1920 and half that of 2003. But the Netherlands was still the most densely populated European country, with some 16.3 million inhabitants sharing 13,000 square miles. (As a basis for comparison, Maryland, the

42nd largest American state, is only about 690 square miles smaller, but has a population of only 5.5 million.)

For the first time in 20 years, the number of people leaving the country (a record 112,000) was greater than the number of immigrants (90,000, 14 percent less than the year before). This was due partly to a slowing economy, but also to stricter immigration laws. Roughly 3,900 arrived from Turkey, 2,800 less than in 2003, and Moroccan immigration, estimated at 2,900, was down by about 2,000 from the previous year. Family reunion and the "importation" of spouses remained the main motives for immigration. Despite the immigration decline, a much higher birthrate (eight times the overall rate) ensured the continuing growth of the percentage of non-Western inhabitants.

POLITICS AND SOCIETY

Politically, the atmosphere was grim, the tensions over immigration heightened by political and financial scandal, as well as budget cuts that triggered strikes and social unrest. Two years after the murder of their leader, Pim Fortuyn's followers were still rudderless, with LPF (List Pim Fortuyn) members of parliament berating each other in their late leader's hyperbolic language, one discredited parliamentarian sending fake Islamic death threats to himself and another party member. By the end of 2004, the LPF's following had dwindled to zero, but Fortuyn's ideas were very much alive.

The up-and-coming man of 2004 was Geert Wilders. A member of parliament for the ruling liberal VVD, Wilders took up the right-wing banner and, in opposition to his party's declared policy, rabidly opposed Turkey's entry into the European Union on the grounds that this would "increase integration problems." Wilders proposed stricter immigration laws and a five-year moratorium on allowing entry for the purpose of family reunification. In September, his party expelled him because of his dissident views. Wilders, keeping his parliamentary seat, founded his own one-man party, Group Wilders. Two weeks later, he proposed a law allowing the government to close down mosques suspected of inciting hatred. By the end of the year, opinion polls showed that if elections were held then, Group Wilders would win 28 seats in the 150-member chamber—more than the number held by the VVD, the government party that expelled him. Even before the murder of van Gogh, Wilders received death threats because of his anti-Islamic statements. And he was not the only one.

The general atmosphere was grim, with widespread public loss of confidence in the local and national authorities. A review of the year's events gives a sense of the situation.

On January 9, the minister of immigration announced that unsuccessful asylum seekers would be "housed in departure centers." On January 13, a 16-year-old Turkish student shot and killed the deputy head of his school in The Hague, prompting Prime Minister Jan Pieter Balkenende to warn of "a spiral of increasing violence." Three days later, (Jewish) Labor alderman Rob Oudkerk resigned from the Amsterdam City Council after the daily *Parool* reported that he admitted to using cocaine, surfing pornographic Web sites, and visiting heroin-addicted prostitutes. That same day, the nation's Temporary Committee on Research for Integration Policy reported its finding that the absorption of many immigrants had "succeeded or partially succeeded"; but this assertion was greeted with wall-to-wall skepticism. On January 23, a confused former student stabbed a teacher at a school for children with hearing, speech, and language difficulties. The teacher barely survived.

Violence and threats continued. In February, Koos Plooy, the public prosecutor of Amsterdam responsible for fighting organized crime, requested a transfer after months of living under constant police protection because of repeated death threats. In March, after terror attacks in Spain and elsewhere, the government announced a national warning system for terror threats and a change in the law to allow the introduction of evidence from the national intelligence service in court cases. In April, a female lawyer spotted VVD leader Jozias Van Aartsen near the government buildings in The Hague and ran him down in her car, as she later said, "on an impulse." Later that month the cabinet announced compulsory exams for immigrants to demonstrate their integration into Dutch society, tough measures against illegal immigrants, and restrictions on renting out apartments in the poor neighborhoods of the four big cities to deprived immigrants. The head of the national intelligence service warned against a "considerable and conceivable" threat of Islamic terrorism in the country.

In July, three rappers were arrested for lyrics threatening Ayaan Hirsi Ali, the Somali-born VVD member of parliament, but the court released them. Later that month, police in Nijmegen arrested two men, one Lebanese and the other Syrian, suspected of planning an attack on the yearly national four-day hike. They were released due to lack of evidence. In August, the controversial film by van Gogh and Hirsi Ali, *Submission-I,* was broadcast.

In September, police raided the home of a Moroccan family in Utrecht, looking for explosives. Two men and a woman were arrested but later released, and the raid was widely criticized. On September 30, a 34-year-old Moroccan translator working for the national intelligence service was arrested for leaking state secrets. Investigators found that he was part of a group possibly linked to the terrorist attacks in Spain. The group included Mohammed B., who would later murder van Gogh, but at the time authorities considered him a minor player and released him.

In October, the Amsterdam prosecutor, Joost Tonino, resigned after a taxi driver picked up a (crashed) computer containing confidential information that Tonino had put out with the garbage, and handed it over to a well-known crime reporter. Later that month, for the first time in Dutch history, a premier league soccer match was aborted after fans chanted hate slogans. Also in October, a couple fled from its home in the Amsterdam Diamant neighborhood after months of abuse from Moroccan-born youngsters. After some procrastination, Mayor Job Cohen imposed an order on the troublemaking boys restricting their movements.

On November 2, Theo van Gogh was murdered and, after a shoot-out in a nearby park, police arrested Mohammed B. Two days later, the letter pinned to the body was made public, and Ayaan Hirsi Ali, threatened in the letter, went into hiding. On November 8, an Islamic primary school in Eindhoven was severely damaged in a bomb attack, and arson was attempted on two mosques in Rotterdam and two churches, one in Utrecht and the other in Amersfoort. Within the next few days an Islamic primary school in the village of Uden was burned down, a church in Boxmeer was torched, and slogans with anti-Muslim content as well as others extolling the murder of van Gogh were found on walls.

National television carried live coverage of what could only be described as war scenes in the streets of The Hague on November 10, as an apartment was taken by storm. Tanks were ordered in after two suspected terrorists threw a hand grenade at the police, wounding three. They were eventually arrested, one in his underwear, on suspicion of plotting to murder members of parliament. A few days later a mosque in Helden was destroyed by fire.

There was considerable fallout from the van Gogh assassination. A parliamentary debate on November 12 was the scene of highly critical remarks about the effectiveness of the national intelligence service. Four days later a committee set up to evaluate the service concluded that it lacked sufficient funds and manpower to ensure security. The cabinet pledged extra funds (almost $170 million) to fight terrorism, plus 500 additional employees for the national intelligence service. On November 29, Ayaan Hirsi Ali announced from her hiding place that she was at work on a follow-up to *Submission-I.*

In December, the national police arrested a Dutch businessman, "Frans van A.," for supplying Saddam Hussein with raw materials for chemical weapons and thus being an accomplice in genocide. But the man later turned out to be an informer on the payroll of the national intelligence service.

Despite these stresses, most of the Dutch people, while concerned, did not seem to feel that their daily lives were affected (except possibly when watching the news). One opinion poll found that the Dutch were greatly worried about criminality, health, norms and values, foreigners, security in general, and terrorism in particular. Asked to grade the quality of their society on a scale of one to ten, they collectively rated it a five. (Five years earlier, when the last such poll was taken, it had been graded a seven.) Yet most were satisfied with their lives—50 percent were "satisfied," 28 percent "very satisfied," and 3 percent "exceptionally satisfied."

Other news that kept the country occupied included the deaths of Queen Beatrix's elderly parents—Juliana, born in 1909, in March, and Bernhard, born in 1911, in December. There was the controversial marriage in April of Prince Johan Friso to a woman previously associated with assassinated drug lord Klaas Bruinsma. Since the government refused permission for the marriage, Johan Friso lost all rights to the throne. The royal family remained quite popular in the Netherlands, and equally so within the Jewish community.

The Dutch involvement in Iraq made headlines with the trial, in January, of "Erik O.," a sergeant-major who had shot an Iraqi citizen, and his subsequent acquittal. In May came the first Dutch casualty in Iraq, and the second followed in August. The government decided, in November, to go along with the widespread international opposition to the war and to withdraw the 1,350 Dutch troops stationed in southern Iraq.

Arjan Erkel, a member of Doctors Without Borders, was released by his Chechen kidnappers in April after 20 months of captivity, in return for a ransom of a million euros. Controversy erupted in June when the minister of foreign affairs, who put up the ransom money, claimed it was a loan that had to be paid back, while Doctors Without Borders considered it a gift.

In June, 39.1 percent of the Dutch people voted in elections for the European Parliament, lower that the 44.2 percent overall figure for the 25 EU member states.

IMPLICATIONS FOR JEWS

Ironically, Jews, some of whom had been targets of hooliganism on the part of young Moroccans (see below, p. 373), were affected by the anti-immigrant backlash. This was due partly to oversight and partly to a "political correctness" that did not want to appear to be discriminating against Muslims.

A complicated system requiring people from non-Western countries (the "M" word was not mentioned), even those born in the Netherlands and possessing Dutch nationality, to take obligatory (and expensive) integration tests was applied indiscriminately to include Israelis. Indeed, ordinary Dutch Jews with one foreign parent or grandparent were categorized as "second generation immigrants." Furthermore, observant Dutch Jews unable to find suitable marriage partners in Holland's small community were hindered by strict rules against importing foreign spouses. Calls to close down fundamentalist Islamic schools, which were thought to hinder integration, also threatened the two Jewish day schools. Teachers of Jewish studies who failed a Dutch language test were banned from teaching, along with Arab teachers of Islam. Government funding for "education in non-Western living languages" was stopped, including not only Arabic, but also modern Hebrew.

Ayaan Hirsi Ali campaigned against the circumcision of boys, having in mind her own Muslim community, which accounted for the vast majority of the 15,000 boys circumcised yearly in the country. Yet the Jewish practice of circumcision was also threatened. "Hirsi Ali has taken her anti-religious crusade a step too far," said Ronny Naftaniel, an official of the Netherlands Central Jewish Organization. After considerable negotiation, Hirsi Ali, in an interview with the *Nieuw Israelitische Weekblad,* withdrew her initiative, explaining that she did not want to drive male circumcision underground. Meanwhile, hospital circumcisions had been removed from the nation health insurance package.

In addition, popular antagonism toward groups seen as "different" created a dangerous climate for Jews, and the community, almost exclusively Holocaust survivors and their descendants, felt less secure. In the words of Ruben Vis, secretary of the Central Jewish Organization: "The secret of good democracy is not just that the majority decides; it should allow minorities to enjoy life as well. One minority that has been living here for four centuries is finding life increasingly less enjoyable here."

Israel and the Middle East

Dutch relations with Israel continued much as before, apart from the case against the Israeli security fence (or "wall," depending on who was reporting) before the International Court of Justice (ICJ) in The Hague. The UN General Assembly had requested the court's opinion in December 2003; strictly speaking, the decision was advisory and not legally binding. Hearings before the ICJ started on February 23, 2004, and lasted two weeks. The media were out in full force throughout, and public discussion raged. The Dutch generally opposed the fence, and particularly its route, which, in many places, ran outside the 1967 Green Line. The ICJ verdict, reached in July, was that those parts of the fence running outside the Green Line were illegal and should be dismantled.

Jewish organizations in the country largely agreed with the position of the Israeli government that this was not a matter for the ICJ and that the court was being misused for political purposes. Even those who disagreed with the fence or with its route saw politics behind the absence of any discussion of the Palestinian terror campaign that led to the construction of the fence in the first place. Ruben Vis noted: "Like most other lawyers, I think this case should not be heard in The Hague. I also fear the 'Durban effect': if you target Israel alone in human rights matters, the effect is anti-Semitic."

Neither Israel nor the U.S. sent representatives to the proceedings. Richard Heidemann, an American lawyer and honorary president of B'nai B'rith International, held "shadow" hearings elsewhere in the city, attracting many spectators, including two members of the European Parliament, Charles Kinnock of Great Britain and Anne André-Léonard of Belgium. The Heidemann "court" heard testimony from 18 Israelis who had lost family members in terror attacks. Zaka, the Israeli organization of volunteers who recover dead bodies after terror attacks, exhibited the wreckage of a Jerusalem number 19 bus in front of the ICJ courtroom. A suicide bomber had killed 11 Israelis in this bus in January, and it became the focus for pro-Israel and anti-ICJ demonstrators from Poland, Russia, Italy, France, the UK, Germany, and the U.S.—including two congressmen, Robert Wexler (D., Fla.) and Steve Chabot (R., Ohio). The municipality of The Hague took steps to separate demonstrators for and against the ICJ hearings.

Very few Dutch Jews demonstrated. Greatly outnumbering them were about 1,000 members of Christians for Israel, bused in from remote parts of the country and brandishing photos of Israeli terror victims, despite a ban by the mayor of The Hague, who considered it a "provocation." The Dutch Jews who did demonstrate were members of Jewish youth organizations, Orthodox rabbis and officials, and some Liberal rabbis.

Anti-Semitism and Extremism

Two reports on anti-Semitism in Europe, including the Netherlands, were published during the same week in 2004, both based on data gathered in 2003. Their conclusions were rather different, since one sought to measure manifestations of anti-Semitism, and the other tried to get at anti-Semitic attitudes.

In 2004, the Organization for Security and Cooperation in Europe (OSCE) held its annual International Conference on Anti-Semitism in Berlin. At the conference, in April, the European Monitoring Center on Racism and Xenophobia released its annual report on racism and xenophobia in the European Union, which noted a sharp rise in anti-Semitic incidents in most European countries, listing the Netherlands, France, Germany, the UK, and Belgium as particularly problematic. (Twenty countries sent government ministers to the conference, but not the Netherlands, whose term as chair had just expired.)

Just days earlier, the Anti-Defamation League (ADL) reported the results of its survey of anti-Semitic attitudes in the EU, and concluded that they had declined slightly as compared to 2002. Germany had the highest level of anti-Semitism and the Netherlands the lowest—despite being one of only two countries where anti-Semitic feelings had increased, from 7 to 9 percent. The ADL report was received with considerable skepticism, especially since its claim of declining anti-Semitic sentiment in Belgium and France was seemingly belied by the actual experiences of the Jews living there. (To cite but one example, 16-year-old Noach Schmahl, the son of a Dutch rabbi, and three friends were attacked outside their yeshiva in Antwerp, Belgium, by "about 15 boys of North African descent" with knives and iron bars. Noach, stabbed in the back, had to be hospitalized.)

In the Netherlands, where the government did not keep track of anti-Semitic incidents, the only reliable source of information was the yearly report of CIDI, the Center of Information and Documentation on Israel. It noted 334 incidents for 2003, a decline from the 359 reported the year before, but that 2002 figure had marked a huge 140-percent increase from 2001. The number of incidents reported to CIDI in the first four months of 2004 appeared to confirm the downward tendency, reported the organization's second-in-command, Hadassah Hirschfeld. Serious incidents (physical violence, threats, and desecrations) had declined by 40 percent as compared to the same time period in 2003, and were of a less violent nature. In one example, a recognizably Jewish man in Amsterdam was pelted with stones and insults. "Though this kind of attack is totally unacceptable, it is as nothing compared to the situation in France, the UK, and Belgium, and particularly in Paris and Antwerp, where some incidents were life-threatening," Hirschfeld wrote.

As had been the case for several years, many anti-Semitic incidents appeared connected to violence in the Middle East, as Israeli government actions were used as pretexts to accuse Jews in general of serious crimes. In addition, Arab satellite broadcasts, widely received in immigrant homes, suggested all sorts of conspiracy theories tying American policies in Iraq to American Jews and to Israel. Somewhat artificially, the CIDI report considered purely anti-Israel manifestations as "political opinions" and did not include them, so that the cry "Sharon murderer" would not count as anti-Semitism, but "Adolf Sharon" would, by equating actions of the Israeli prime minister with those of the Nazis against the Jews.

Despite the statistically positive picture, CIDI noted three negative trends. First, there was a rise in the number verbal or written insults aimed at Jews. Second, the perpetrators were increasingly from the Moroccan sector: 43.5 percent of victims who thought they recognized the attackers said they were "of predominantly North Africa descent" (a euphemism for Moroccans), an increase of 2.5 percent since the previous year. Third, anti-Jewish incidents in and near schools continued to rise steadily, and particularly for schools with many Islamic pupils. Since high birthrates were sure to drive up the percentage of school-age children from Islamic homes, this phenomenon was most worrisome.

Anti-Semitic incidents connected to schools received considerable attention in the Dutch media. One daily quoted the Amsterdam alderman in charge of education to the effect that teachers had complained to him that if they mentioned the Holocaust, "the class gets out of hand. Pupils become extremely noisy, chanting all sorts of things, and the classroom atmosphere becomes threatening. Occasionally, the car tires of the 'offending' teacher were punctured. Teachers also reported very real phone threats, such as, "you'd better watch out, we know where your kid goes to school." In one incident in March, reported to CIDI, two 18-year-old girls of North African descent told another pupil of a school in Dordrecht, "Jews are dangerous, it says so in the Koran," and "America is a very dangerous country because many Jews live there and the American government consists solely of Jews."

Slogans like "Hamas, Hamas, all the Jews to the gas" or "Joduh, Joduh" (Je-ews, Je-ews), common at soccer matches (see below), had become so common that the word "Jew" took on a new meaning as a general term of abuse among the young. A survey of 11,000 secondary school teachers commissioned by the Ministry of Education and released in May 2004 found that half the teachers had heard insults about Jews over the previous 12 months (it was statistically unlikely that these were all directed at Jewish pupils), and half also reported that they knew pupils who denied the Holocaust. To be sure, group hatred was even more common against Muslim youngsters: 70 percent of the teachers heard insults directed at Islam.

In early May, several projects were launched to sensitize young Muslims to Jewish sensibilities. In a project funded by the Amsterdam municipality, university students of Moroccan descent taught a series of lessons about World War II and the Holocaust in schools with a high percentage of Islamic pupils. Similarly, Moroccan organizations such as Islam and Citizenship developed programs to highlight the fate of Moroccan soldiers who fought for the Allies in World War II. In one Amsterdam neighborhood during the 2004 commemoration of the war's end, young people read out the names of Moroccans who lost their lives in battle. The year before, Moroccan boys in this neighborhood had disturbed the traditional two minutes of silence for the dead by chanting *"Joden, die moeten we doden"* (we have to kill Jews).

Some of the more popular Dutch soccer teams—notably the Amsterdam team Ajax—had been dubbed "Jewish" by fans and opponents alike (though Ajax had only one Jewish player in 2003, and none at all thereafter). Fans of opposing teams would shout anti-Jewish slogans ("Hamas, Hamas, all the Jews to the gas") or make hissing (gas) noises, just as racist insults would be hurled at black players. This had become such a frequent occurrence that a new term, "speech choir," was invented for groups of fans shouting discriminatory insults in unison. The Dutch Soccer Union reported two specific "speech choir" incidents to the CIDI in 2004, and these were passed on to the public prosecutor. The Center for Reporting Football Vandalism provided statistics of the number of arrests made during soccer matches and the charges leveled, without specifying the ethnic groups that were targeted. In the season that ended in 2003, 25 people were arrested for "deliberate racial insults," two for "inciting hatred," one for "participating in discriminating activities," and ten for "discrimination."

The police had to be called in to restore order during soccer matches a few times during 2004. In August, fans of FC Utrecht refused to leave the center of Amsterdam and go to the match against Ajax that they had come for. When they start chanting about Hamas and gas, riot police arrested a large number and removed 68 of them from the city. In October, Belgian Club Brugge fans went around Amsterdam shouting that they were going "Jew hunting" with the help of ADO The Hague fans. A battle broke out in the stadium between these fans and Ajax supporters. A total of 100 arrests were made on the Leidsche Plein and in the stadium. Also in October, for the first time in Dutch soccer history, a referee stopped a match. This happened in Enschede, at a contest between FC Twente and Young Ajax, when Twente fans started chanting the same Hamas line. The public prosecutor fined Twente the equivalent of nearly $4,000, which the team paid.

JEWISH COMMUNITY

Demography

The most recent demographic survey of the Jews in the Netherlands, published in 2001, was the first to be conducted in 35 years. It estimated the Jewish population at 44,000, or 0.275 of the total Dutch population, which was 16 million in 2001. In 2004, the country's population had grown to 16.3 million, but the Jewish community, if it was growing at all, was doing so at a much lower rate, and thus constituted a steadily declining percentage of the population. There were no evident changes in Jewish demographic behavior. Dutch Jews tended to postpone marriage longer than the general population; young Jews were highly likely to marry non-Jews (in 2001, the figure was 76 percent of men and 68 percent of women); more Jewish women than other Dutch women remained childless; and Jewish families had an average of 1.5 children (in 2001) as compared to the national average of 1.9. The vast majority of Dutch Jews did not associate with any Jewish organization, and many who identified as Jews described themselves as nonreligious.

In 2004, sociologist Marlene de Vries followed up on the 2001 survey by investigating nonreligious Jews in greater depth. Her book, *Een bli-jvende band? Niet-religieuze joden en hun binding aan het jodendom* (A Lasting Bond? Nonreligious Jews and Their Ties to Judaism), was based on interviews with 30 such Jews, all born after World War II. They related memories of a warm yet restrictive Jewish atmosphere when they were growing up; the role of the Holocaust and the State of Israel in their Jewish identification; and their wish simultaneously to participate in the non-Jewish world, to hold on to as much as possible of Jewish tradition, and prepare their children to do the same. They were strongly critical of Orthodox Judaism, and noted how a growing concern with anti-Semitism affected their sense of Jewishness.

Jewish organizations reacted with dismay. Doubting that such loosely affiliated Jews could possibly maintain the Jewish continuity of their families, community leaders made the involvement of nonreligious Jews a priority, and allocated for this purpose a large part of the Holocaust restitution money that was set aside for communal projects.

Communal Affairs

Fearing for the future of the community, Jewish bodies launched outreach programs to attract new members. The Orthodox umbrella organization, NIK, claimed success in expanding its membership to 4,875, a net growth of 31 over the previous year. The largest community within NIK, that of Amsterdam, gained 112 new members, many of them young, which, computed together with deaths and resignations, amounted to a net gain of five persons. The year 2003 had ended with a net loss of 72.

The "Portuguese" Sephardic Congregation, reduced to about 400 members in the whole of the Netherlands, still struggled under the enormous cost of maintaining its historical heritage — most notably the monumental seventeenth-century Esnoga structure in Amsterdam and the Ets Haim Library. The library, housing 30,000 printed works and 500 manuscripts — many of them unique — was placed on UNESCO's "Memory of the World" list of protected libraries.

As for the non-Orthodox groups, the Liberal Jewish Community of Amsterdam remained stable with 1,633 members. A new player on the religious scene was the Masorti (Conservative) community, launched in the town of Almere in October 2004, with plans to branch out into other Dutch cities. Masorti Netherlands, which joined the World Council of Conservative/Masorti Synagogues and received help from Masorti London, was yet too small to employ its own rabbi.

The survival of the Jewish Organization for Social Work (JMW), which provided help for the poor and disadvantaged, was threatened during 2004. In July, the city of Amsterdam announced, as part of budget cuts for 2005, an end to all funding for JMW since, it claimed, nonsectarian institutions could take over the work. (This was part of the broader effort to stop financial support for "ethnic" services—including Islamic ones—in the city.) Roughly half of all Dutch Jews lived in greater Amsterdam, and about 15 percent of these appealed for help to JMW in the course of a year. The disproportionately aged nature of the Jewish population—some 80 percent of JMW clients were Holocaust survivors—meant that Jews needed such aid at about five times the rate of the general population. In August, the city council relented; it would not cut JMW's funds for 2005, but would review the budget for 2006.

Then, toward the end of the year, two separate lawsuits were initiated against JMW over its planned merger with a number of foundations for the care of Jewish orphans that had ceased functioning years before but still existed legally. Since 1986, JMW had taken over most of their responsibilities, and managed their capital and interest. In 2004 it sought a formal merger, but the two suits, launched by other Jewish organizations and individuals, meant that no steps could be taken until the courts rendered verdicts, which would not take place before 2005.

The youth movement Ijar organized an international "Meet Market" weekend in Amsterdam; it attracted 200 young Jews from the Netherlands, France, Switzerland, Ireland, Italy, the UK, Canada, and the U.S. On a sadder note, the Jewish Youth Center in Amsterdam closed its doors. The center, with its many facilities, had been conceived as a lively meeting place and a focus of activities for young Jews. But the youth organizations involved were unable to organize enough events and attract enough visitors, and the center had been operating at a huge loss for some years.

In other communal news, the Jewish community of Rotterdam celebrated the 50th anniversary of the local Orthodox synagogue, built to replace two synagogues that were destroyed in the bombing of Rotterdam in May 1940. The Jewish cemetery in Geervliet, south of Rotterdam, was restored. Earlier, a complete inventory (entitled *Matsewa*) was published listing and showing every gravestone, and providing information about the person buried there. In the city of Venlo, a medieval *mikveh* (ritual bath) was discovered during road construction. Dating from before 1350, it is the oldest known *mikveh* in the Netherlands.

Many old synagogue buildings were restored in 2004. One was the beautiful synagogue of Enschede, dating from 1928, now restored to its former glory and rededicated. Enschede welcomed its own rabbi again, opened an institute for Jewish learning, and scheduled regular concerts in the building. For months after the rededication, visitors flocked to the synagogue in such numbers that there were not enough volunteers to provide guided tours.

On the initiative of B'nai Brith, the Netherlands participated in the European Jewish Heritage Day for the first time in 2004, joining 25 other European countries that had been involved since 1999. Ten synagogues opened their doors to the public, together drawing about 1,300 visitors. In Groningen, a temporary exhibition on twentieth-century Jewish life in the Folkingestraat opened in the synagogue on that street.

2004 was the year of Jewish reunions. These included a reunion of the youth movement Habonim, for which some 300 former members came from within the Netherlands but also from Israel, the U.S., Germany, Belgium, Spain, and the UK. The oldest participant, 90-year-old Seraphina Boas, told of her years in the prewar precursor of Habonim, Joodsche Jeugd Federatie, founded in 1919. Another reunion was of 254 former pupils of Jewish children's homes (for children who lost one or both parents, or whose families had been disrupted by the Holocaust), which met in April. Some participants flew in from as far away as Canada.

Jom Havoetbal, the annual Jewish soccer tournament, celebrated its 25th anniversary in 2004. It was one of very few events that appealed to the entire community, from the secular to the Orthodox. So popular had the tournament become that a limit had to be placed on teams from other European countries, as well as on new Dutch teams. Some 2,300 spectators watched 55 teams (and the other spectators, of course). Mover and shaker Philippe Rubens was awarded royal honors for his part in coordinating this event.

Intergroup Relations

Dialogues and joint cultural programs with the Muslim community were stepped up in an attempt to improve relations. Several synagogues, including the Amsterdam Liberal Synagogue, exchanged visits with local mosques, and Jewish youth movements with Muslim counterparts. An unusual example of intergroup activity was the Moroccan-Jewish soccer tournament organized in De Baarsjes, an Amsterdam neighborhood where tensions ran high and anti-Semitic incidents were frequent.

Individual Jews and Moroccans organized the competition. Players—including the chairman of the NIK national Orthodox umbrella organization, a goalkeeper—and fans alike considered it a huge success, and the day passed without incident. The only criticism came from other ethnic groups, as local boys originating from Turkey and Suriname complained about being excluded, and said they wanted to participate with teams of their own next year.

Despite such activities, tensions were still very real. Apart from actual anti-Semitic incidents (see above), there were other problems. For example, the chairman of the youth movement run by Milli Gorus, the organization of Turks in the Netherlands, told an interviewer that he "did not believe in the European murder of six million Jews." But it was Milli Gorus that insisted that he resign, indicating that Holocaust denial was not part of its official ideology.

Holocaust Restitution

In 2000, the Dutch government, banks, insurance companies, and the stock exchange had contributed to a restitution fund. Most of the money had been divided among the survivors and their heirs. Twenty percent of the total, the so-called "Maror" money, had been earmarked for communal purposes, and this continued to be allocated in subsequent years. In 2004, scores of new projects were funded in two rounds. Some $4.4 million was divided among 27 projects for Dutch Jews living in Israel, many of them involving old age homes. Despite the allocations, there were complaints that payments were too slow.

Several claims for the restitution of artworks were resolved and the works were turned over to the original owners or their heirs.

Publications

More than 200 years after the death of Sha'oel Halevi Hager (1712–85), chief rabbi of The Hague, his manuscripts were published as a book, *Binyan Sha'oel,* by one of his successors, Rabbi P.A. Meijers, now living in Antwerp. The book, in Hebrew, included Torah commentaries, answers to questions of Jewish law, and letters, as well as supplementary material on the history of Ashkenazi communities in the Netherlands—particularly Amsterdam and The Hague—from the beginning of the eighteenth century until the Hololcaust.

A new Dutch translation of Theodor Herzl's *De Jodenstaat* (The Jewish State, originally written in German in 1896) was published by the Federation of Dutch Zionists on the centennial of Herzl's death. The existence of *NIW (Nieuw Israelitische Weekblad)*, the Dutch Jewish weekly, was threatened by financial difficulties. It raised subscription fees (which had been kept artificially low for a long time) and many subscribers rallied with additional voluntary contributions. "The paper you are holding now is the only binding factor that keeps Dutch Jewry together. There is nothing else," wrote popular novelist Leon de Winter. "The *NIW* is vital for the continuity of Dutch Jewry." The paper, founded in 1865 and now the oldest opinion weekly in the country, had come out regularly for 138 years, ceasing publication only during World War II; two weeks after the liberation of the Netherlands, it rolled off the press again. In September, *Orange Juice,* a new magazine for Jews aged between 18 and 35, was launched, funded with Holocaust restitution money.

A dissertation analyzing by region the survival rate of Dutch Jews during the Holocaust was published, *Een onderzoek naar de overlevingskansen van joden in de Nederlandse gemeenten, 1940–1945,* by Marnix Croes and Peter Tammes. It showed that Jews in the southern provinces of the country had a better chance of survival than those in the north, and estimated the national rate of Jewish survival at 29.6 percent. While previous scholars suggested that some 8,000 Jews who went into hiding were caught, Croes and Tammes set the figure higher, at 12,000.

In *Niet voor de school, niet voor het leven* (Not for the School, Not for Life), Peter Hermans chronicled the lives (and, in half the cases, deaths) of 65 Jewish pupils of the Barlaeus Gymnasium in Amsterdam after the Nazis forced them to move to segregated Jewish schools in May 1940.

Eene zeer twistzieke natie. Aspecten van de geschiedenis van de joodse gemeenschap in Winschoten 1686–1943 (A Very Quarrelsome Nation. Aspects of the History of the Jewish Community in Winschoten 1686–1943), by P. Brood and E. Schut, was a fascinating and beautifully illustrated account of conflicts in the Jewish community of Winschoten and the role played by a band of Jewish robbers who operated in the area.

Personalia

Several Dutch Jews received awards and honors during the year. Rabbi Jacob David Schmahl was awarded the Torah and Halakhah Prize of Jerusalem for his book, *Kisa'ot lebeth David,* on financial and business disputes in Jewish law. Poet Nachoem M. Wijnberg received the Paul

Snoek Poetry Award from the Belgian town Sint-Niklaas for his 2001 book *Vogels* (Birds). Author Helga Ruebsamen was awarded the prestigious Anna Bijns Award for her complete works. Her stories center on the polarities of fantasy/reality, intoxication/clarity, and world citizenship/Jewish identity.

Veteran Israeli diplomat Shabtai Rosenne was awarded The Hague Prize for International Law. This was a new award, which the city intended to make the "Nobel Prize for international law." Jews who received royal honors were Deborah Maarsen, the driving force of the Zichron Menachem organization that sponsored annual trips to the Netherlands for Israeli children suffering from cancer; and Gerard Klein and Fiep Maas, chairman and secretary, respectively, of the Jewish community of Hilversum, which they helped rebuild after the Holocaust. Yad Vashem, Israel's Holocaust memorial, honored the popular Majoor Bosschardt of the Dutch Salvation Army for saving 70 orphans, including many Jews, during World War II.

Prominent Jews who died in 2004 included I.B. van Creveld, historian of the Jewish community in The Hague, aged 83; film director and television presenter Ralph Inbar, aged 65; Sal Zanten, active in the Jewish community of Den Bosch and the NIK national Orthodox umbrella organization, aged 83; Jacques Furth, oldest member and one of the founding fathers of the Nederlands Auschwitz Comité, aged 93; Louisa (Wiesje) Aldewereld, managing director of the Joodse Invalide (old age and rehabilitation home) in Amsterdam for 20 years, aged 97; Saul Smit, who helped rebuild the Jewish community in Zaandam and held many Jewish communal offices there, aged 92; and Aron Spijer, businessman, and member of the board and the burial society of the Jewish community in The Hague, aged 79.

ELISE FRIEDMANN

Italy and the Vatican

National Affairs

T HE ITALIAN GOVERNMENT of Prime Minister Silvio Berlusconi remained one of President George W. Bush's staunchest allies in Europe even though most Italians opposed U.S. policy in Iraq. Italy also maintained exceptionally good relations with Israel. In a meeting in July with a delegation from the Anti-Defamation League, Berlusconi said: "Italy is the closest friend of the United States and Israel. We shall continue along the road we started out on together."

U.S. vice president Dick Cheney visited Italy in January and thanked the government for its help in Iraq. Bush visited in June to mark the 60th anniversary of the liberation from the Nazis. On his itinerary was a visit to the Ardeatine Caves, site of Italy's worst Nazi atrocity, the March 1944 murder of 335 Roman men and boys; some 75 of the victims were Jews. Berlusconi, in turn, visited Washington in December, and one of the topics discussed during a White House meeting with the president was the Israeli-Palestinian peace negotiations.

In November, Gianfranco Fini became the country's new foreign minister, replacing Franco Frattini, who became justice commissioner of the European Union (Fini also retained his previous post as deputy prime minister). The move capped Fini's political and personal journey from neofascist to leader of the mainstream conservative right. Fini, 52, began a decade earlier to win respectability for his National Alliance party. In the process, he mended fences with Jews, paid homage at Auschwitz and other Holocaust sites, and visited Israel. Fini received a warm welcome on another official visit to Israel a few days before being named foreign minister (see below, p. 384).

In October, after tough negotiations, European leaders signed the new European Constitution at a ceremony in a palace on Rome's Capitoline Hill. Over the objections of the Vatican and several other countries, the document did not include any reference to the role of Christianity (or Judaism) in shaping European history and civilization.

Despite widespread popular opposition, Italy maintained 3,000 troops in Iraq, the third largest national contingent. A number of protests against the war took place during the year, including a demonstration by as many as a million people in Rome in March. In September, Italians were shocked by the murder in Iraq of an Italian journalist, Enzo Baldoni, who had been held hostage by terrorists, but the government insisted it would not withdraw its forces. Two Italian women aid workers who were held by terrorists were released.

In February, a report by Italy's secret services said that the country had become a "base of departure for aspiring members of Islamic Jihad and suicide bombers." According to the report, cells of Islamic militants in Milan, Cremona, Parma, and Reggio Emilia recruited suicide bombers to carry out attacks in Iraq. In May, antiterrorist police arrested five people belonging to one of these groups.

Israel and the Middle East

ITALY

Rome's Jewish monthly, *Shalom,* described the warm ties between Italy and Israel as "a model of international relations." Participating in an international tourism convention in Milan in February, Israeli officials noted that about 26,000 Italians visited Israel in 2003, an increase of 53 percent over 2002. (In October, Jessica and Sabrina Rinaudo, two vacationing Italian sisters, were killed in the terrorist bombing of the Hilton Hotel in Taba. It was announced that a forest of 500 trees would be planted in Israel in their honor.) In April, numerous politicians and other dignitaries attended a reception in Rome for Israel Independence Day, hosted by Israeli ambassador Ehud Gol. Separately, Oded Ben Hur, Israel's ambassador to the Vatican, hosted a reception for senior Vatican officials. Another reception marking the day drew more than 1,000 people in Milan.

The large number of visits back and forth between Italian and Israeli officials also demonstrated the friendly bilateral relations. Foreign Minister Frattini came to Israel and met with senior government officials early in the year. In August, Israeli foreign minister Silvan Shalom attended the annual convention of the Italian Catholic group Communion and Liberation, where he had a heated face-to-face public debate with his Palestinian counterpart, Nabil Shaath. Both men expressed the desire for renewed peace negotiations, but clashed so sharply on almost every other issue that one reporter termed it a "dialogue of the deaf." Reuven Rivlin, speaker of the Israeli Knesset, visited Italy in November.

When Deputy Prime Minister Gianfranco Fini arrived in Israel in November just before being named foreign minister, he was greeted with enthusiasm. Fini attended a conference on international cooperation in Tel Aviv and met with senior Israeli officials, including Prime Minister Ariel Sharon, President Moshe Katzav, and Foreign Minister Shalom. He also had a session with "Italkim," Israelis of Italian origin. While in the country Fini said, "We must act in a way that Israel and Italy create an economic relationship that is increasingly intense and innovative, that will be an example for the whole region, and that will help create the conditions for a stable and lasting peace."

Italy also maintained good relations with Arab states, and there were many exchanges with Arab leaders. In February, Palestinian Authority prime minister Ahmed Qurei met Berlusconi and other Italian officials during a two-day visit to Rome that was part of a tour of European Union countries, and he also received an award from Rome's mayor. In April, the Italian Foreign Ministry hosted a conference on the country's aid programs to the Palestinians, both those carried out by the ministry and others run by Italian regional and local institutions.

In the eyes of many Italian Jews, some leftist politicians, journalists, nongovernmental groups, students, and street protesters crossed—by a wide margin—the line between legitimate criticism of Israeli actions and anti-Semitism. Italy's left-wing opposition and the leftist media generally supported the Palestinian cause and sharply criticized Israeli policy in a manner that those sympathetic to Israel considered heavily one-sided. For example, in a move that triggered considerable controversy, Oliviero Diliberto, secretary of the Italian Communist Party, met in Beirut with Hezballah leader Sheik Nasrallah.

Already Libya's biggest trading partner, Italy boosted its ties with the North African state. Berlusconi visited Libya and met several times with Col. Muammar Qaddafi. In February, in fact, Berlusconi became the first Western leader to visit Libya since it declared, in December 2003, that it would end development of weapons of mass destruction. During another visit by Berlusconi, in October, Qaddafi said that the 20,000 Italians expelled from Libya in 1970 were now free to visit. That same month, a group of exiled Libyan Jews living in Italy made a four-day visit to Tripoli (see below, p. 393).

The Federation of Italy-Israel Associations held its congress toward the end of October. Founded in 1988, the federation had more than 50 branches around the country, and the members were mainly non-Jews. About 400 people attended the congress, which opened in Rome, and 60 of them then flew on to Jerusalem to conclude the proceedings there, becoming part of the largest-ever Italian solidarity mission to Israel. Some 230 people took part in the mission, sponsored by the federation, WIZO, Keren Hayesod, and Keren Kayemet.

Throughout the year there were conferences, roundtables, seminars, and debates (some broadcast on radio or television) on the subject of the Middle East. Discussion was often heated, with American and Israeli policy frequently coming under sharp criticism. In November, the city of Milan hosted a conference about Jewish refugees who fled Arab countries beginning in 1945. Many new books were published on the Middle East, Iraq, Islam, and the threat of global Islamist terrorism. In April, journalist Oriana Fallaci published a new book, *La Forza della Ragione* (The Force of Reason). In her trademark polemical style, she accused Europe of having given in to what she described as an "Islamic invasion," and condemned the Roman Catholic Church for showing weakness in the face of militant Islam.

Jews expressed concern over a song, "Marika," by pop star Roberto Vecchioni, which appeared to show sympathy for a young terrorist. In response, Vecchioni said that he would no longer perform the song at his concerts.

Jews critical of Israeli policy toward the Palestinians also made their voices heard. In January, a group of young Jews who regarded themselves as Zionists but opposed the Israeli occupation of the territories and supported the Israeli peace movement screened the documentary *Don't Say You Didn't Know — Israeli Voices Against the Occupation,* by Italian-American director Joseph Rochlitz, at Rome's Jewish Community Center. In the summer, an Italian Jewish group calling itself Martin Buber-Jews for Peace spearheaded a statement signed by nearly 600 Diaspora Jews criticizing the policies of the Sharon government. Published as a full-page ad in the Israeli dailies *Ma'ariv* and *Ha'aretz,* the statement said that the policies pursued by the Israeli leadership had not provided Israel with security. The ad backed alternative initiatives such as the so-called "Geneva Accord."

THE VATICAN

Negotiations between the Vatican and Israel aimed at finding solutions to several unresolved bilateral issues, suspended in 2003, resumed during the summer of 2004. The key matters under discussion were the safeguarding of church property and holy sites in Israel, the tax status of

Catholic religious institutions, visa regulations for priests and members of Catholic religious orders in Israel, and the participation of Israel in certain church-run educational initiatives.

Earlier, in April, church officials said that the visa applications of 138 Catholic clergy, many of them Arabs, had been held up by Israel's Interior Ministry, a 60-percent increase over the previous year. Further talks on the visas were held in September, and in December the Israeli ambassador to the Holy See announced that a solution was near.

The pope, who had strongly opposed the U.S.-led war in Iraq, told visiting President Bush in June that he hoped for a speedy return of Iraq's sovereignty, and also expressed to Bush his concern about "grave unrest" in the Middle East. Addressing the UN General Assembly in September, the Vatican foreign minister, Archbishop Giovanni Lajolo, asserted that "everyone can see" that the Iraq war "did not lead to a safer world, either inside or outside Iraq." He went on: "The Holy See believes it is now imperative to support the present government in its efforts to bring the country to normality and to a political system that is substantially democratic and in harmony with the values of its historic traditions."

As he had done often in recent years, the pope issued repeated calls for a halt to Israeli-Palestinian violence, which he termed "an endless conflict that is fed by reciprocal hate and desire for vengeance." On several occasions he urged the international community to help bring the sides back to the negotiating table.

In February, the pope met with Palestinian prime minister Ahmed Qurei and repeated criticism he had first made in 2003 of the security barrier Israel was building in the West Bank. After the death of Yasir Arafat in November, the Vatican issued a statement of sympathy that called him "a leader of great charisma who loved his people and tried to guide them towards national independence." The pope, who had met with Arafat several times, sent a message to the Palestinian people saying that he prayed that the "star of harmony" would soon bring peace to the Holy Land and that both Israelis and Palestinians could live "reconciled among themselves as two independent and sovereign states."

Anti-Semitism and Racism

Visiting Italy in January, Natan Sharansky, the Israeli minister for Diaspora affairs, gave a formal address to the Italian Senate in which he warned about the rise of a "vicious" new form of anti-Semitism in Europe. What was new, he explained, was the transfer of "classical" Jew-hatred to an equally irrational hatred of the Jewish state. Sharansky reiterated his thesis in a talk at the Rome Jewish Community Center.

That same month, Prime Minister Berlusconi announced the formation of a committee composed of representatives of several government ministries to investigate and fight anti-Semitism and racism. Citing "profound concern about the rise of episodes of intolerance and anti-Semitism in Europe," he said the committee would track such episodes, seek ways to educate people against the attitudes that lead to them, and punish acts of bias. In February, the Chamber of Deputies passed three motions charging the government to combat anti-Semitism by systematically monitoring the situation and taking concrete measures—including educational programs in the schools—to "accentuate the struggle against this execrable phenomenon."

Italy, in fact, experienced little of the anti-Semitic violence witnessed in several other European countries. Even so, public-opinion polls indicated lingering anti-Semitic stereotypes as well as sharp opposition to Israeli policy toward the Palestinians that at times crossed the line into anti-Semitic expressions.

A poll conducted in 2003 that received considerable publicity in early 2004 was carried out in Italy and eight other West European countries on behalf of Milan's *Corrière della Sera* newspaper. It identified 15 percent of respondents as "strongly" anti-Semitic and found that some 40 percent believed that Jews "have a special relationship with money." Over one-third felt that Jews "should stop playing the victims because of the Holocaust and the persecutions of 50 years ago." Fewer than 60 percent found Israel "sympathetic." Sociologist Renato Mannheimer, who directed the survey, wrote that "it is sure that, in all nine countries, anti-Semitic attitudes are closely correlated with anti-Israel attitudes."

Another poll focusing specifically on Italy was released in January, "Italian Public Opinion on the Israel-Palestinian Conflict and the Middle East Question." Based on interviews with 1,500 people and conducted by the Eurispes Research Institute, it found that even though most were not anti-Semitic, more than one-third of the sample believed that Jews "secretly control economic and financial power and the media." More than 90 percent supported Israel's right to exist, but over half were critical of current Israeli policy toward the Palestinians and nearly 36 percent agreed with the statement that the Sharon government was carrying out "a real, true genocide, and behaves toward the Palestinians the way the Nazis behaved toward the Jews."

In August, the Rome city government assured Israeli ambassador Ehud

Gol of its commitment to fighting anti-Semitism, asserting in a letter to the ambassador that Mayor Walter Veltroni's "attention and resolve" in confronting any expression of anti-Semitism, racism or xenophobia "goes without saying." This was in response to a personal letter that Gol had written to Veltroni expressing dismay at anti-Semitic and anti-Israel slogans found scrawled in a Rome park, which, Gol feared, could signal an emerging new manifestation of anti-Semitism. The graffiti, removed by city workers the day they were discovered, included swastikas and slogans such as *"Juden Raus"* and "Death to Zion." Several similar incidents occurred elsewhere in Italy. In Genoa, the street sign marking a square named after the city's wartime rabbi, Riccardo Pacifici, who was killed in Auschwitz, was plastered over with a sign "renaming" the square "Piazza Yassin" after Palestinian Sheikh Ahmed Yassin, who was killed by Israeli forces. It said that Sheikh Yassin had "fallen in the name of freedom." In April, a Milan court convicted Pietro Aligi Schiavi for sending anti-Semitic hate mail to Milan Jewish community president Roberto Jarach and fined him 5,000 euros.

In October, Israeli diplomat Shai Cohen was heckled by a group of 20 students at the University of Pisa who prevented him from giving a scheduled talk on "Israel, the Only Democracy in the Middle East." The hecklers, some wearing the Palestinian kaffiyeh around their necks, shouted such slogans as "Sharon assassin," "Israel is a death dealer," and "Zionism is a crime against humanity." There were students present who sought to calm the situation and defended Cohen's right to speak, but to no avail. Italian Jews were angered by the incident, but even more by the general lack of condemnation of it by leftist politicians and media.

There were several conferences, symposia and other meetings on anti-Semitism and how to combat it. Psychologist David Meghnaghi, a professor at Rome's University Tre, organized a committee of professors from around the country to fight anti-Semitism, particularly in the academic setting. Rome was the site of a conference in February on the image of Jews in the Arab media. In November, Prof. Meghnaghi, in collaboration with the Union of Italian Jewish Communities (UCEI) and University Tre, organized a session titled "Between Old and New Anti-Semitism." In December, the Italian government, in association with the ADL and the Italian newspaper *Il Foglio,* conducted a two-day conference on the topic "Anti-Semitism—A Threat to Democracy" that included as speakers high-ranking political figures and leading journalists from Italy, the U.S., and Israel.

The Rome municipality carried out a number of projects aimed at promoting religious and ethnic tolerance and combating racism and anti-Semitism. These were coordinated by Franca Eckert Coen, a former director of Rome's Jewish Community Center who now worked as counselor for multiethnic policy for the city.

Holocaust-Related Developments

Italy marked Holocaust Remembrance Day, January 27, with dozens of high-profile events ranging from solemn commemorations attended by top government officials to exhibitions, lectures, films, broadcasts, concerts and performances, and the so-called Match of Memory, a celebrity soccer game held to raise funds for a planned Holocaust museum in Rome. Organizers sold 20,000 tickets for the match, but only 3,000 people braved the cold rainy weather to attend. Among them were Mayor Veltroni and other dignitaries, including guest of honor Elie Wiesel, who was also honored in a ceremony at Rome's Campidoglio city hall. Schools held classes about the Holocaust, radio and television broadcast special programs, and magazines and newspapers published a wide range of articles on the subject. Nevertheless, public-opinion polls released on the eve of the observances showing that many Italians and other Europeans still maintained anti-Semitic stereotypes (see above, p. 387) indicated that much educational work remained to be done.

Beginning in February, Italy assumed the year-long presidency of the Task Force for International Cooperation on Holocaust Education, Remembrance and Research. The 16-member task force had been set up by the Swedish, British, and U.S. governments in 1998 to raise global consciousness about the Shoah.

The city of Rome hosted a series of events throughout the year to promote memory, awareness, and understanding of World War II, the Holocaust, and Jewish history aimed specifically at high school students. Called "Rome 1944–2004: Memory, Resistance, and Liberation," it included exhibits, conferences, commemorations, and projects. Special commemorations marked the 60th anniversary of the Nazi slaughter of 335 Romans at the Ardeatine Caves in March 1944, as well as the liberation of Rome by American troops in June 1944. And in October, for the second consecutive year, more than two dozen Rome high schools took their students on an educational trip to Auschwitz as part of a project called "We Remember." Also in October, on the 61st anniversary of the deportation of Jews from Rome, an exhibition on the persecution of Italian Jews opened in the Vittoriano, a gallery in Rome's "Altar of the Homeland" monument.

In April, Mayor Veltroni announced that Villa Torlonia, the former residence of fascist dictator Benito Mussolini, would open in 2006 as a Holocaust museum. (A series of Jewish catacombs dating to ancient times lies beneath the villa and its extensive grounds.) In April, Catania, in Sicily, hosted a conference on Italy's fascist-era anti-Semitic laws. A book on the effects those laws had on the economic activity of Rome's Jews was published in the fall.

There were a number of seminars and conferences on Holocaust themes, and several books were published as well. An international conference on Primo Levi took place in Rome. In April, a new International Museum of Memory was inaugurated at the site of the World War II concentration camp of Ferramonti in Calabria. In October, the Hungarian Academy in Rome sponsored a conference and exhibition marking 60 years since the deportation of the Hungarian Jews. The Jewish community, Rome authorities, a university, and several organizations jointly produced a documentary film, *Born Twice, the Story of Settima, a Roman Jew,* for use in schools. It was based on interviews with Settima Spizzichino, the only Roman woman to survive Auschwitz out of the 600 who were deported in October 1943.

In February, an olive tree from Jerusalem was planted in the courtyard of Italy's oldest police training facility in honor of Giovanni Palatucci, an Italian police chief who saved thousands of Jews from deportation during the Holocaust and later died at Dachau. A scholarship was also announced in Palatucci's memory, to be awarded for the best university thesis by an Italian police officer dealing with the Shoah, racism or multiethnic society. Palatucci served as the commissioner of Rijeka, today in Croatia but during World War II under Italian jurisdiction and known as Fiume. Between 1937 and 1944 he saved more than 5,000 Jews by providing them with false documents and safe-conduct permits. In May, a new school in Rome was named in Palatucci's honor. At the same time, another new school was named in honor of the Di Consiglio family of Rome that was wiped out in the Holocaust: 22 members were deported and murdered at Auschwitz, and seven were killed in the Ardeatine Caves massacre. In June, a commemorative mass was held in Rome to honor Portuguese diplomat Aristides Sousa Mendes, who helped save thousands during World War II by granting false documents.

In January, an Italian court charged seven former SS members with the

August 1944 killing of 560 people in the Tuscan village of Sant'Anna di Stazzema. German interior minister Otto Schily visited Sant'Anna in August on the 60th anniversary of the massacre and said it marked "a day of shame" in German history. In March, Rome officials banned rival demonstrations for and against a pardon for convicted Nazi war criminal Erich Priebke that had been planned for the same time on the same day in the same part of the city. Prefect Achille Serra cited the "climate of tension" in banning the rallies. Priebke, 90, was serving a life sentence for his role in the Ardeatine Caves massacre. Karl Hass, a former SS major serving a life sentence under house arrest in Switzerland for his role in the Ardeatine Caves massacre, died in April at the age of 92. In December, a military court in La Spezia acquitted former SS officer Hermann Langer, 85, of having commanded the September 1944 massacre of about 60 people at a monastery in Farneta, Tuscany, that sheltered Jews during World War II.

JEWISH COMMUNITY

Communal Affairs

About 35,000 Jews were believed to live in Italy, although only some two-thirds were formally affiliated with Jewish communities. Rome, with about 15,000 Jews (12,000 formally affiliated), and Milan, with about 10,000, were the largest communities. The rest of the country's Jews were scattered in a score of other towns and cities, mostly in northern and central Italy, in communities ranging from a handful of people to a thousand or so. All were linked under an umbrella organization, the Union of Italian Jewish Communities (UCEI), whose leadership, under president Amos Luzzatto, served as the political representative of Italian Jewry.

A small Jewish community was reorganized this year in Trani, in southern Italy's Puglia region, through the joint efforts of the culture and education department of the UCEI and Chabad. For the first time in 500 years, Yom Kippur services were held in the town, one of Rome's seven congregations "lending" a rabbi and a cantor for the occasion. About 30 people participated. Trani's mayor made the former Colona Monastery available as a house of worship until the medieval Scolanova Synagogue, long used as a church, is restored. Trani had a thriving Jewish community in medieval times, until Jews were expelled in the sixteenth century.

Orthodoxy was still the only officially recognized form of Judaism in Italy, a point reiterated during the year by Chief Rabbi Riccardo Di Segni of Rome, who stated that his community "is and must remain Orthodox." Italian Orthodoxy encompassed three ritual traditions: Sephardi, Ashkenazi, and Italian, the latter a local rite that evolved from the Jewish community that lived in the country during the Roman Empire. Chabad-Lubavitch maintained a strong presence in Rome, Milan, Venice, Florence, Bologna, and elsewhere. Rome was home to the Italian Rabbinical College. Under the direction of Rabbi Di Segni, it trained rabbis as well as teachers for Jewish schools, coordinated a university degree course in Jewish studies open to any member of a Jewish community, and offered various other courses in Jewish culture. In Milan, a new yeshiva program directed by the chief rabbi, Giuseppe Laras, was conducted at the main synagogue.

In December, however, Laras shocked the community by announcing plans to step down as chief rabbi after 25 years in the post. Noting divisions in the community, he asserted that these were less serious than in the past, but acknowledged that there had been a drop in the number of people formally affiliated. However, he added, the community now was "richer in activities, initiatives and interests, both religious and cultural, even if there still remains a wide sector of 'invisible' people who, because they are 'invisible,' we are not able to reach or involve."

Not only were Reform and Conservative streams not recognized by the UCEI, but there were also complaints in some communities by less observant Jews that local rabbis had become more rigid in their practice. Several small Reform congregations operated independently, including Lev Chadash and Beth Shalom in Milan, which employed rabbis from abroad to conduct services and hold classes for members and potential converts. Both of these Milan congregations were affiliated with the World Union for Progressive Judaism (WUPJ). Similar small groups existed in Rome and Florence, and as the Italian Reform communities expanded they began to form an embryonic alternative to the Orthodox establishment. Lev Chadash was especially active, hosting young liberal Jews from elsewhere in Europe for a Purim celebration. For the High Holy Days in the fall, an American, Barbara Aiello, took up her post at Lev Chadash as Italy's first woman rabbi.

The Rome Jewish community held elections for its board in April and the results bore witness to the political and ideological splits within the membership. A group considered conservative that ran under the slogan "For Israel" won 15 seats on the board, edging out a left-leaning group called "For the Young People, Together," which won 13 seats. In June, the board unanimously reelected 65-year-old Leone Paserman, from the "For Israel" faction, president of the community.

Results of a survey of elderly Jews in Milan were released in the spring, based on telephone interviews with a representative sample of 200 of the 1,243 Jews over age 70 registered as members of the local Jewish community. Only 40 percent had been born in Italy; of the rest most came from Egypt and Turkey, and others from Greece, Romania, Iran, Syria, Lebanon, and Libya. Even though more than 60 percent had children living in Milan, 40 percent lived alone, 63 percent speaking on the phone with their children or grandchildren at least once a day. These older Jews were much better educated than their non-Jewish Italian counterparts, 22 percent having completed university studies. Almost all those questioned were in regular contact with the Jewish community in one way or another: some 77 percent said they read the community monthly, *Il Bollettino,* and another 19 percent said they just leafed through it.

Rome's Jewish community had a different ethnic makeup: between one-third and one-half of Rome's Jews were members of families that had been forced to leave Libya following the Six-Day War of 1967. In October 2004, after Libyan leader Col. Muammar Qaddafi told President Berlusconi that the 20,000 Italians expelled from Libya in 1970 were now free to visit (see above, p. 384), a group of Italian Jews of Libyan origin made a four-day visit to Tripoli. Warmly welcomed, they met with senior officials who raised the possibility that they might regain Libyan passports and have dual Italian-Libyan citizenship. During their talks, the Jews raised the issue of compensation for property left behind, and the Libyans advised them to draw up and submit lists of such property. The group had expected to meet with Qaddafi but did not, in the end, do so. In December, Libyan Jews now living in Italy, Britain, the U.S., France, and Israel formed an international committee to seek compensation.

The major Jewish communities in Italy offered a full infrastructure serving varied needs: religious institutions, Jewish schools and other educational facilities, health and welfare services, and Jewish cultural and community centers. The women's organization ADEI-WIZO was especially active, as were various support and solidarity groups for Israel. There were kosher facilities, including public restaurants, in some cities. In May, some 1,000 people filled Milan's main synagogue for the annual joint bat mitzvah ceremony at which, this year, 16 girls took part.

The Rome Jewish community inaugurated new premises for its old age home and was in the process of restoring buildings for a modern new school complex in the heart of the old ghetto. In the fall, a new step was taken with an agreement between the Rome municipality and the Jewish community to construct an *eruv* (symbolic enclosure enabling observant Jews to carry on Shabbat) in the city, to be in place by June 2005. In the spring, hundreds of people attended the UCEI's annual cultural and educational weekend in a resort hotel on the Adriatic Sea. This year's theme was Torah, symbols, and idolatry.

A range of Jewish youth groups were active, sponsoring educational, social, and recreational activities. In June, for example, more than 450 young people, including many from other countries, took part in the so-called "Zooish" Shabbaton (youth weekend) in Milan. At the end of October, the annual fall Moked youth meeting was held at Montecatini spa in Tuscany, its theme being a century of the Jewish youth movement in Italy. That same weekend Rome hosted "Ring," an educational and social gathering of Jewish students from all over Europe. And during the summer, Jewish institutions and organizations hosted a group of 50 Israeli children, victims of terrorism, for a vacation in Tuscany.

Jewish-Catholic Relations

January 17 marked the Catholic Church's annual "Day of Judaism." In Milan, a public meeting between Jews and Catholics, Protestants, Orthodox, and other Christians took place in the main synagogue. The event came soon after the Council of Christian Churches in Milan issued an expression of solidarity with the Jewish community in the face of anti-Semitism. In Rome, a gala Vatican concert aimed at promoting reconciliation among Catholics, Jews, and Muslims took place. Pope John Paul II presided, flanked by a rabbi and an imam. The concert was held before 7,000 people, including dignitaries of the three religions from around the world, among them Israel's two chief rabbis. The venue was the Pope Paul VI Auditorium, and the music was performed by the Pittsburgh Symphony Orchestra conducted by Gilbert Levine, an American Jew, son-in-law of a Holocaust survivor, and a Papal knight. The Israeli chief rabbis, Yonah Metzger and Shlomo Amar, also had a private audience with the pope, the first such Vatican audience for Israeli chief rabbis. (The pope had met Israel's previous chief rabbis when he visited Israel in 2000.) Metzger and Amar urged the pope to continue speaking out against anti-Semitism, and the pope assured them that he remained committed to improving Catholic-Jewish relations.

Mel Gibson's controversial movie *The Passion of the Christ* opened on nearly 700 screens across Italy just two days before Good Friday. Tickets sold out at many cinemas, and the film posted a record opening-day take of more than 1.2 million euros ($1.5 million), more than 60 percent of the total money earned by all movies shown around the country that day. Response to the film was mixed. Furio Colombo, editor of the leftist daily *L'Unità,* called it a sadistic, pornographic, and blasphemous horror show, "the most anti-Semitic film in the history of the cinema." Many Catholic clergy, though, including some senior Vatican officials, responded with enthusiasm and encouraged the faithful to see it. They praised *The Passion* for its unflinching depiction of Jesus's torment and argued that the violence could be redemptive. In February, before the movie's release, Jewish leaders, including Israeli chief rabbi Metzger and Rome chief rabbi Di Segni, had called on the Vatican to condemn the film as anti-Semitic, but got no response. The actor who played Jesus, Jim Caviezel, a devout Catholic, had an audience in March with Pope John Paul II, who had seen the film the previous December.

The pope met several times during the year with Jewish leaders. At an audience in February with a delegation from the American Jewish Committee, he told the group, "There is regrettably a great need to repeat our utter condemnation of racism and anti-Semitism" and reiterated that "violence in the name of religion is always a desecration to religion." He also lamented that the Holy Land "continues to be afflicted by violence and suffering" and said he prayed that "a just solution will be found which respects the rights and security of both Israelis and Palestinians." In March, the pope expressed similar sentiments in a meeting with a delegation from the American Jewish Joint Distribution Committee (JDC). In November, Muslim, Orthodox Christian, and Jewish religious leaders from Azerbaijan had an audience with the pope. The Anti-Defamation League met with him in December. An earlier ADL delegation had met in July with other Vatican officials to discuss the opening of the Vatican's World War II-era archives, anti-Semitism, and the broadening of Catholic-Jewish relations.

The pope sent two senior cardinals to represent him at celebrations marking the 100th anniversary of Rome's Great Synagogue in May (see below, p. 398). The pontiff also issued a message on the occasion reiterating his condemnation of anti-Semitism and calling for further cooperation. "The dutiful deploring and condemnation of hostilities against the Jewish people, which often characterized history, is not enough," he wrote. "We need to also develop friendship, esteem and brotherly relations" with Jews.

There were a number of interreligious meetings and conferences throughout the year in Italy and elsewhere. A dozen cardinals, six chief rabbis, and other representatives from Europe, North America, and Israel participated in what was called a World Symposium of Catholic Cardinals and Jewish Leaders, in New York in January. In July, the 18th meeting of the International Liaison Committee of Jewish and Catholic leaders took place in Buenos Aires. It released a statement expressing "total rejection of anti-Semitism in all its forms, including anti-Zionism as a more recent manifestation of anti-Semitism." In September, Chief Rabbi Metzger of Israel attended a weeklong interreligious conference organized by the Milan archdiocese and the St. Egidio community, a Catholic social action group, where he called for a Jerusalem-based "religious United Nations" to promote dialogue.

In October, delegations from Israel's Chief Rabbinate and the Vatican's Commission for Religious Relations with Jews met for three days near Rome. They issued an appeal to respect the "sacred character" of Jerusalem and condemned all "actions of disrespect" toward religious sites, symbols, and people. The participants declared that they "were not enemies, but unequivocal partners in articulating the essential moral values for the survival and welfare of human society."

During the encounter, the rabbis and priests also attended lectures by Cardinal Walter Kasper and Rome chief rabbi Di Segni marking the opening of a new program at Gregorian University on the Catholic Church's teachings about Judaism and the Jewish people. Di Segni acknowledged progress in Catholic-Jewish relations but complained that the Church "engaged in the dialogue using its own language, its own mentality, its own culture, its own vision of the world, its own needs," leading to an "asymmetry" in the discussion. He singled out several recent Vatican actions of concern to Jews: the canonization of Edith Stein, a Jewish convert to Catholicism killed in Auschwitz; preliminary steps to the beatification of Eugenio Zolli, the World War II chief rabbi of Rome who converted to Catholicism under the influence of Pope Pius XII; and the enthusiasm among Vatican officials for *The Passion of the Christ.* Kasper gave a much more optimistic account of the state of Catholic-Jewish relations, saying that they had progressed "remarkably."

Another development that dismayed some Jews was the beatification in October of Anna Katharina Emmerich, a nineteenth-century German nun whose graphic visions, published after her death, inspired Mel Gibson's grisly depiction of the crucifixion in his film. The Vatican said that

Emmerich was honored for her virtuous life, not her visions. In December, the Vatican set Cardinal Clemens August von Galen, an anti-Nazi German bishop who denounced Hitler and died in 1946, on the path to beatification.

There were a number of historical revelations during the year based on material found in the Vatican's secret archives recently opened to scholars. In March, for example, documents surfaced indicating that soon after Adolf Hitler came to power in 1933, Italy's fascist dictator, Benito Mussolini, may have secretly attempted to persuade him not to persecute the Jews. Other newly released documents fed both sides of the controversy over the role of Pope Pius XII during the Holocaust, critics feeling that Pius failed to do enough to save Jews, defenders arguing that he did all he could. In the summer, the Vatican said it planned to release more than two million files about prisoners of war and other missing persons from the World War II period. According to the Vatican, the documentation was "testimony to the ample charitable and social work inspired by principles of universality and impartiality" during the pontificate of Pius XII.

At the end of December, the *Corrière della Sera* newspaper published a letter dated October 20, 1946, suggesting that the Vatican, with the approval of Pius XII, had ordered church authorities in France not to return Jewish children who had been baptized to save them during the Holocaust. The letter, sent by the Holy Office, the Vatican department responsible for church discipline, to the future Pope John XXIII, Angelo Roncalli, then the Holy See's envoy in Paris, stated: "Children who have been baptized may not be entrusted to institutions that are not in a position to guarantee them a Christian upbringing." The letter, unearthed by a historian editing Roncalli's diaries, ended with the words, "Please note that this decision has been approved by the Holy Father."

During the year, the pope and other Vatican officials expressed continuing concern at what they saw as a secularist, "anti-Christian" movement in the European Union. Some even attempted to have "Christophobia" recognized as a form of prejudice equal to anti-Semitism or hatred of Muslims. The Vatican—and the pope personally—had pressed hard but unsuccessfully for an explicit reference to Europe's "Christian roots" in the new European Constitution that was signed in Rome in October (see above, p. 382). Furthermore, the Vatican expressed outrage when the European Parliament Committee on Civil Liberties rejected the candidacy of a devout Catholic, Rocco Buttiglione, the Italian nominee for the post of EU commissioner of justice. Buttiglione had expressed traditional conservative Catholic views on the subjects of homosexuality and women.

Culture

There were numerous Jewish and Jewish-themed cultural events organized by Jewish communities and institutions, private organizations and promoters, civic and state bodies, or a combination of these.

In April, a new Jewish museum opened on the top floor of the synagogue in Genoa with an exhibition of works by Marc Chagall that depicted biblical scenes. A series of events marked the 100th anniversary of the Tempio Maggiore, or Great Synagogue, in Rome. The first, in May, was an exhibition tracing the history of the synagogue that was displayed in the expanded new premises for Rome's Jewish Museum on the lower floor of the synagogue complex. Senior government and other officials attended the main centennial ceremony, held in the ornate sanctuary on May 23. The Jewish community had invited Pope John Paul II to the event but he declined, saying he did not want to detract from the impact of his first historic visit to the synagogue in 1986. Instead, Cardinal Camillo Ruini, president of the Italian Bishops Conference, and Cardinal Walter Kasper, head of the Vatican's office for relations with Jews, represented him. Celebrations, which ran into October, included cultural events and an international academic conference on Roman Jewish history. Both Italy and Israel issued commemorative postage stamps.

There were efforts to conserve, preserve and protect other sites of Jewish heritage in Italy. During the year a member of the Italian Senate, Loredanna De Petris, spearheaded legislation to fund the restoration of the Jewish catacombs under Villa Torlonia in order to open them to the public. Parliament also examined other proposed legislation that would provide funds to finance the maintenance and restoration of Italian synagogues over the next few years. A conference in May was devoted to a 40-million-euro project to develop the area where the ancient Jewish cemetery of Ancona is located, possibly add a small museum there, and make it into a park. In August, regional authorities in Calabria announced plans to conserve the ruins of the ancient synagogue at Bova Marina, near Reggio Calabria, discovered in 1983, so that they might be visited by the public. The Veneto Region allocated 700,000 euros for the restoration and care of seven Jewish cemeteries in the region.

Italy was an enthusiastic participant in the fifth annual European Day of Jewish Culture, held on September 5 in 25 countries; the theme for 2004 was Judaism and education. After the keynote opening ceremony in Pisa, some 37,000 people visited numerous Jewish sites in 45 localities around the country.

The Israeli embassy sponsored a number of performances, exhibits, and appearances by Israeli cultural figures. In Milan, the Mario Negri Medical Research Institute and Israel's Weizmann Institute collaborated on a series of symphonic concerts to raise funds for their work, under the title "Music and Research Together for Health."

Rome's Jewish community center hosted the city's second Jewish film festival in February, including screenings of Jewish and Israeli films as well as roundtable discussions and lectures. French director Claude Lanzmann, who produced the Holocaust documentary *Shoah,* was one of the speakers. The seventh annual Pitifest Festival of Jewish Cinema and Culture, held December 5–8 in the Tuscan hill town of Pitigliano, featured several films and exhibitions about Anne Frank, and also hosted the premiere of *Binario 21* (Track 21), a video about the deportation of Italian Jews to Auschwitz, and a series of Israeli films. The Venice Film Festival in September screened two Israeli films, *Hotel Promised Land,* Israeli filmmaker Amos Gitai's docudrama about sex slavery in Israel, and *Take a Wife* by Ronit and Shlomi Elkabetz, about Israelis of Moroccan origin in Haifa in 1979. Director Michael Radford's film version of *The Merchant of Venice,* starring Al Pacino as Shylock, had its world premiere at the festival.

There were many Jewish-themed concerts, plays, and theatrical performances during 2004. Among them, Jewish actress and playwright Laura Forti staged *Dimmi* (Tell Me), a play based on her family's history, and Hasidic pop star Avraham Fried sang in Rome's prestigious new Auditorium concert hall in a performance organized by Chabad. Rome's Ha Kol Jewish choir performed at the Summer Festival of Two Worlds in Spoleto. In September, Israeli dancer and choreographer Yasmeen Godder performed at the Enzimi dance festival in Rome. A new adaptation for the stage of *If This Is a Man,* by Primo Levi, opened in Rome in October. The writings of Etty Hillesum, the Dutch intellectual and diarist killed at Auschwitz, formed the basis of a play staged at Rome's Theater Sala Uno in the fall. Moni Ovadia, Italy's foremost Jewish stage performer, continued touring with his production of *Fiddler on the Roof,* bringing it for the first time to Rome. Israel's Habima acting troupe performed in Milan at the end of the year.

Pianist and musicologist Francesco Lortoro continued work on a series of recordings he called Musica Judaica, a collection of all music composed by Jews in concentration camps between 1933 and 1945. Among the many Jewish-themed exhibitions was "The People of the Dream," 50 graphics by Vittorio Pavoncello inspired by the Torah, which opened at Rome's Vittoriano museum in October. A month-long one-man show by Israeli designer Ron Arad, who had collaborated with many Italian design companies, opened in Vicenza in September.

Numerous books by Jewish authors and other books of Jewish interest were published, and so there were plenty of book launches, readings, roundtables, and other literary happenings. Rome's Jewish monthly, Shalom, routinely reviewed more than a dozen books per issue. Italy's main Jewish publishing house, the Florence-based Giuntina, initiated a new series of translations of works by contemporary Israeli authors. The first books to appear were The Rosendorf Quartet by Nathan Shaham and The Salted Biscuits of Grandma Sultana by Dan Benaya-Seri.

One of the most important Italian books of Jewish interest was Mitzva, a personal evocation of his Jewish identity by Alain Elkann, a leading writer, socialite, and adviser to the Italian government whose son was vice chairman of the Fiat motor industry and heir to the Agnelli dynasty. Another notable book was Roma delle religioni (Rome of the Religions), a book of text and photographs about the various faiths held by Rome's inhabitants. My Father, Il Duce, a memoir of Italy's fascist dictator Benito Mussolini by his son, Roman Mussolini, sold well and made headlines by presenting a positive view of Mussolini's private life. Ritrovare se stessi: Gli ebrei nell'Italia postfascista (Finding Themselves Again: The Jews of Postfascist Italy) by Guri Schwarz told the story of Italian Jewry's postwar development. Other books included Attese (Waits), a novel by Elena Loewenthal, and Gli Antisemiti Progressisti (Liberal Anti-Semites) by Fiamma Nirenstein, about left-wing anti-Semitism.

In February, a conference of Jewish archivists took place in Florence. Two significant conferences took place in Milan in March, one on the subject of Jews and politics, the other on the contribution of religions to the construction of a united Europe. In December, Italy's first national conference of Yiddish studies was held in Rome, marking the 100th anniversary of the birth of Isaac Bashevis Singer.

At the end of the year, Israeli writer Amos Elon left Israel and moved permanently to Tuscany, where he had had a home for years.

Personalia

In January, the Italian government awarded Leone Paserman, president of the Rome Jewish community, the Gold Medal for Civic Values. In April, it gave the Grand Cross of the Republic to director Steven Spielberg, who also received a David of Donatello Award—Italy's equivalent of the Oscar—for his lifetime achievement in cinema. In October, the Federation of Italy-Israel Associations awarded the 2004 Correct Information Award to journalist Fiamma Nirenstein and to the newspaper *Il Foglio*. At a ceremony in Rome, the Swedish prime minister presented a new award, the Per Anger Prize, to 97-year-old Monsignor Gennaro Verolino, who, during World War II, saved thousands of Jews in the Budapest ghetto by granting them false papers.

In May, Polish-born filmmaker Roman Polanski, the Academy Award-winning director of *The Pianist,* was awarded an honorary doctorate by the Department of Literature and Philosophy of Rome's Sapienza University in recognition of "the fundamental relationship of a Polish Jewish intellectual and artist to the entirety of European culture." (Polanski survived the Kraków ghetto during the Shoah.) Angelica Edna Livi Calo, a Roman Jew living in Israel, and a Palestinian Christian, Samar Shahar, were awarded the first Women's Peace Prize by Catholic officials in Assisi during ceremonies marking the 750th anniversary of the Basilica of Saint Francis. The Italo-Israeli writer Manuela Dviri and the Palestinian writer Suad Amiry received the international Viareggio-Versilia Prize, recognizing them as "two people who have spent their lives for culture, understanding among peoples, social progress, and peace."

In June, the Rome Jewish community presented a commemorative scroll to Brown University professor David Kertzer in honor of Kertzer's late father, Rabbi Morris Kertzer, who, as a U.S. Army chaplain in 1944, led the first Shabbat service in Rome's Great Synagogue after liberation. The next month the Rome chapter of B'nai Brith awarded its first Golden Menorah Award—honoring persons who demonstrate support of or solidarity with Israel—to writer Massimo Teodori, who organized a pro-Israel march in Rome in 2002. In December, Italy named ADL national director Abraham Foxman a Commendatore of the Italian Republic, one of the country's highest civilian honors.

In February, Andrea Jarach was elected president of the Federation of Italy-Israel Associations. Rome Jewish community member Angelo Pavoncello was elected the new president of the council of Rome's 15th municipal district. In July, Giorgio Sacerdoti was elected president of the

Contemporary Jewish Documentation Center (CDEC), Italy's leading institute for research on anti-Semitism and the Holocaust. Leone Kalon took up the post of chief rabbi of Livorno in September. In May, Cobi Benatoff, an Italian Jew who was president of the European Jewish Congress, ended his tenure as president of the European Council of Jewish Communities, and in the summer assumed the presidency of the Milan Jewish community's school foundation. In December, the Anti-Defamation League named Rome lawyer Alessandro Ruben as its chairman in Italy.

Writer Alberto Lecco died in May at the age of 83. In October, Oscar Mires, a past president of B'nai Brith in Milan, died. Stefano Madia, an actor and journalist who was also a leading member of the Rome Jewish community, died in December, aged 49. Other deaths included author Elisa Springer, a survivor of Auschwitz, Bergen Belsen, and Terezin, and artist Aldo Di Castro.

RUTH ELLEN GRUBER

Switzerland

National Affairs

THE PARLIAMENTARY ELECTIONS of October 19, 2003, marked a sharp shift to the right in the country's politics as the Swiss People's Party (SPP) finished first with 26.6 percent of the vote, and party leader Christoph Blocher was named justice minister. In a departure from the Swiss tradition of devising government policy by consensus of the multiparty seven-member executive, Blocher and his party fought aggressively for toughening Switzerland's laws regarding foreigners, whether asylum seekers or children of immigrants.

The SPP opposed passage of two referenda aimed at easing the naturalization process for Switzerland-born children and grandchildren of immigrants. In 2004, as voters debated the proposals, the party ran a campaign with blatantly racist messages—advertisements depicting black and brown hands greedy for Swiss passports; misleading statistics on the Muslim population; and pejorative slogans against immigrants from the former Yugoslavia and other countries. In the end, the strategy worked, as both referenda went down to defeat, a great political coup for Blocher. The party also succeeded in making it more difficult for asylum-seekers to enter Switzerland. Its next announced goal was forcing 500,000 Swiss citizens with dual nationality to choose between their Swiss and their foreign citizenships.

Blocher and his followers also had an impact on the country's justice system. A popular referendum requiring life sentences for certain designated "dangerous" crimes passed overwhelmingly even though it was opposed by all parties except the SPP, which wholeheartedly endorsed it. In fact, the only referendum during 2004 that could not be described as an SPP victory was that held on stem-cell research, which, surprisingly, was approved by a large margin.

Switzerland continued to watch the expansion and development of the European Union from the sidelines. As more Eastern European countries joined, Switzerland, at the center of Europe, stood out as one of the very few nonmembers on the continent, leading to speculation that it might ultimately become the only outsider.

This political climate of extreme conservatism, isolationism, and xenophobia alienated people with other perspectives. One was Swiss artist Thomas Hirschhorn, who announced that he would not exhibit his works in Switzerland so long as Blocher was in the government. From his home in Paris, Hirschhorn infuriated many politicians by ridiculing Swiss democracy, and launched an artistic attack on Blocher with an installation at the Swiss Cultural Center in Paris titled "Swiss-Swiss Democracy." The center was funded by the taxpayers of Switzerland, and the nation's parliament, the Federal Assembly, retaliated by slashing over a million dollars from the annual budget of the national cultural foundation that administered it.

Israel and the Middle East

On December 1, 2003, the "Geneva initiative" was signed in Switzerland. It called for a comprehensive resolution of the Israeli-Palestinian conflict through a two-state solution based on the negotiations brokered by the U.S. at Camp David and Taba in 2000–01. An unofficial proposal drawn up by a number of prominent Israeli and Palestinian individuals, it was sponsored by the Swiss Ministry of Foreign Affairs under the leadership of Foreign Minister Micheline Calmy-Rey (see AJYB 2004, pp. 360–61). Although the Swiss government responded favorably to Israeli prime minister Ariel Sharon's unilateral Gaza disengagement plan as a sign of progress, it remained committed to the Geneva initiative because of its multilateral approach. Throughout 2004, Switzerland continued to speak out on behalf of the initiative and sought to expand its network of supporters. But since the plan lay dormant, superseded by Sharon's unexpected proposal, Switzerland was in no position to take a leadership role in the resolution of the conflict.

There was growing sentiment in Switzerland—though not in official circles—for a binational Israeli-Palestinian state. This proposal meant the end of Israel as an independent entity, its Jewish population eventually turning into a minority governed by an Arab majority. Some of its anti-Zionist supporters dubbed it the Lausanne initiative, after the Swiss city on Lake Geneva where they held a conference to promote binationalism. This created some confusion with the government-supported Geneva initiative, named for the city only 40 miles away on the same lake.

During 2004, Switzerland ratcheted up its pro-Palestinian activities. Positioning itself at the forefront of respect for international law, the government repeatedly criticized Israeli policies, and received a mandate from the UN General Assembly to report on legal and humanitarian consequences of the security fence that Israel was building in the West Bank. In September, Calmy-Rey led a Swiss delegation that paid a visit to PLO chairman Yasir Arafat, toured a number of Palestinian cities, and reported that an international conference was necessary under the provisions of the Fourth Geneva Convention to discuss Israel's treatment of civilians in the territories.

Jean Ziegler, a former Socialist member of the Swiss parliament and now UN special rapporteur on the right to food, urged the European Union to suspend ties with Israel, which he accused of creating a "humanitarian food crisis." Ziegler also suggested a boycott of the Caterpillar company for selling armored bulldozers to Israel, which, he said, were then used to destroy Palestinian houses, in Ziegler's view a violation of human rights. Israel rejected his report on the grounds that the recommendations were politically motivated, and called on the UN to replace Ziegler as rapporteur for abusing his mandate. Ziegler had a long record of involvement with the Swiss anti-Israel group Collectif Urgence Palestine and other similar organizations.

Pro-Palestinian activists continued to attract media attention and address public forums; pro-Israel voices, in contrast, were rarely heard. It was quite common to see advertisements for film documentaries, lectures, and radio or TV shows reflecting the hard-line Palestinian point of view, sometimes with an anti-Semitism tinge. Editorials and letters to the editor were virtually unanimous in condemning U.S. and Israeli actions in the Middle East throughout the year. Some pieces in the mainstream papers even went so far as to express admiration for suicide bombers, and came up with arguments to blame Israel for the deaths of Israelis in the terrorist attacks against hotels in Taba, Egypt (see above, p. 245).

Switzerland's reputation was tarnished during the year when allegations surfaced that Saddam Hussein's regime had deposited billions of dollars of illegal payments from the UN's "oil for food" program in Swiss bank accounts between 1990 and 2003. The scandal also implicated a Swiss company that had been supposed to monitor the program, but instead allegedly helped Iraq evade the international embargo by arranging to sell Iraqi oil to private companies (at a profit), and then paid off the Iraqi regime with generous bribes sent to those Swiss bank accounts.

Anti-Semitism and Extremism

The federal police issued a report indicating that no extremist group—whether of the right or the left—seriously threatened national security.

Nevertheless, it showed a dramatic increase in violent incidents perpetrated by far-left groups, which now had a combined membership estimated at 2,000. They were bolstered by support from antiglobalization activists, who organized demonstrations against meetings of the WTO (World Trade Organization), WEF (World Economic Forum), and G8 that took place in Switzerland.

The far right, for its part, consisted of skinheads, fascists, nationalists, neo-Nazis, and simple hooligans. They had no recognized leader, but operated through independent cells that law enforcement found difficult to infiltrate. Imitating American racist fringe groups, they called for "white power," criticized democracy as a threat to civilization, and maintained ties with Holocaust deniers, who acted as their "intellectual" arm by organizing lectures, publishing newsletters, and building international networks. A number of the most notorious deniers had been tried and convicted under the antiracism laws in recent years, two of them fleeing the country to avoid prison—Jürgen Graf to Iran and René-Louis Berclaz to Serbia. Negotiations with the Serbian ambassador about extraditing Berclaz were fruitful, and the convicted man turned himself in at the end of December 2004, a year after his escape.

For some time, the far right had sought heightened visibility through media stunts such as parades and public displays of Nazi symbols in the streets, at stadiums, and in schools. Over the course of several years, skinheads had sought to disrupt the Swiss president's annual address to the nation, delivered on the Grütli hill to mark the national holiday. This year, authorities limited access to the Grütli hill to ticket holders in order to prevent the skinheads from displaying armbands, flags, and other Nazi paraphernalia as they had in the past. Two weeks after this event, the Federal Court interpreted the Swiss law against racism so as to place severe limits on extremist activities. Previously, only "public" racist meetings were illegal, whereas "private" events, that is, those by invitation only, were not covered by the law—a loophole that skinheads and others used to rally hundreds of sympathizers in secret locations, by invitation only. The new court ruling, however, defined any gathering of 40 or more people who did not know each other before as a "public" meeting whether or not it was publicly advertised, and therefore made it subject to the antiracism law.

Some extremists were willing to use violence even to the point of murdering one of their own whom they suspected of disclosing inside information. In 2004, four skinheads belonging to the Chevaliers of the Aryan Order were tried for killing a 19-year-old member of the group. The leader was sentenced to life imprisonment, two accomplices received 16-year prison terms, and the fourth person involved was sent to an institution for delinquent minors.

While the Swiss People's Party, now the most important political faction in Switzerland, had clearly shifted in a sharply rightward direction, there were groups even further to the right. Some tried, with minimal success, to enter mainstream politics. Partei National Orientierter Schweizer (PNOS), founded by skinheads, and the National Swiss Party both brought forward candidates for local elections, but they went down to defeat. The far-right Freedom Party had representatives on the city council in Biel, one of whom, Jürg Scherrer, was reelected in spite of his repeated racist and anti-Semitic statements that bordered on illegal incitement to group hatred, but the party remained of marginal significance.

More than a century ago, in 1893, Switzerland had outlawed the ritual slaughter of animals in the hope of discouraging Jews from settling in the country. An attempt to lift the ban in 2001 triggered a backlash led by the powerful Swiss Society for the Protection of Animals, which urged an amendment to the 1893 law ending even the importation of kosher and halal slaughtered meat from abroad. That this would make it impossible for observant Jews and Muslims to eat meat in Switzerland was acknowledged by the initiative's backers, some of whom had no hesitation in urging those affected to "become vegetarian or leave the country." The Society for the Protection of Animals launched an advertising campaign in Zurich early in 2004 that juxtaposed images of badly treated animals with pictures of inmates of Nazi concentration camps. The language of the initiative, however, seemed likely to alienate others outside the Jewish and Muslim communities since it would also ban the consumption of frog legs, battery farming, and other common techniques or practices.

Anti-Semitism continued to be expressed publicly in newspaper op-eds, letters to the editor, public lectures, and cultural events. Verbal abuse, insults, and graffiti were frequent. Fewer physical attacks were reported, but, for the first time in Switzerland, a Jewish day school and a Jewish sports club in Geneva were broken into, computers stolen, and anti-Semitic slogans scribbled.

Dieudonné, a French-Cameroonian stand-up comic, was scheduled to perform in Geneva, having already made a name for himself in France for racist and anti-Semitic statements, glorification of Osama bin Laden, accusations that Israel financed apartheid and genocide, and impersonations of a Nazi "rabbi" representing the "American-Zionist axis" (see AJYB 2004, pp. 319–20). The Geneva Department of Cultural Affairs banned his show, but this only triggered a vast campaign in defense of the humorist, who was portrayed as a victim of political correctness, censorship, and the "very powerful Jewish lobby." Dieudonné did issue a public apology to people of "Jewish religion that he may have hurt," but his letter continued, "Ariel Sharon's policies are those of a criminal and have to be denounced without being accused of anti-Semitism." His show, rescheduled, sold out quickly, and six months later he returned to perform again. In an interview with a major daily, Dieudonné declared that he knew "who the real fascists are, now that I need bodyguards because of the Zionist campaign against me . . . . I wish that the Arabs get the atom bomb as soon as possible, it is the only way to install a real democracy."

Islamic fundamentalism was fast becoming a major force in Switzerland as the country became a center for laundering money, training radical imams, and building fundamentalist networks. In 2004, Swiss police arrested Mohamed Achraf, a Moroccan terrorist who operated between Zurich and Madrid and was involved in the planning of major burglaries in Switzerland to finance the terror attack that took place in Spain.

Two of the most important Islamic figures in Europe were the Geneva-based brothers Hani and Tariq Ramadan. Both were frequently in the public eye. In 2003, Hani wrote an op-ed in the French daily *Le Monde* defending the stoning of adulterous women and describing AIDS as a deserved "punishment" for homosexuals. He was immediately fired from his teaching position in a Geneva public school, but a few months later, in 2004, an administrative court ruled that he had to be reinstated. Local authorities in Geneva refused and appealed the decision. As if to demonstrate that his views had not changed, Hani Ramadan subsequently published a book on Islamic law in which he described stoning as a compassionate punishment.

Even more controversial was Tariq Ramadan, who taught philosophy in a Geneva public high school and Islamic thought at the University of Fribourg. While cultivating the image of a moderate Muslim intellectual, some of his published work clearly indicated an affinity with the teachings of his grandfather, Hassan el-Banna, founder of the radical Muslim Brotherhood in Egypt (see AJYB 2004, pp. 317–19). Early in 2004, he announced he was leaving Switzerland to accept a tenured position in Islamic studies at the University of Notre Dame in the U.S. Some European commentators discretely expressed relief to see this controversial figure depart the continent. But weeks before he was due to leave Switzerland, Ramadan's American visa was revoked without explanation, and the academic year began at South Bend without him. Toward the end of 2004, still not having received any explanation from the U.S. State Department for the visa denial, Ramadan resigned his position at Notre Dame.

Mel Gibson's film *The Passion of the Christ* was a commercial success in Switzerland, thanks especially to massive attendance by Christian groups. Only one area of the country, the Neuchâtel region, did not get to see it, and this was because the major manager of movie theaters there, a Jew, refused to distribute what he called an "anti-Semitic film."

Holocaust-Related Matters

La Suisse et les Nazis: le Rapport Bergier pour tous (Switzerland and the Nazis: The Bergier Report for Everyone), which appeared in 2004, was a summary version of the massive 25-volume report of the special Swiss historical commission that was published in 2002 detailing Switzerland's role during the Holocaust, focusing on such issues as refugee policy and financial dealings with Nazi Germany. The shorter publication, designed for the general public, was prepared by journalist Pietro Boschetti. This French edition was privately sponsored, and there was as yet no funding for the issuance of a German edition.

Legislation was passed during the year granting pardons to those who had been punished for breaking the law to help save refugees in Switzerland during World War II. The first pardon went to Aimée Stitelmann, a Jewish citizen of Switzerland who was arrested and briefly jailed for feeding and hiding Jewish children. Her name was cleared by an ad hoc commission 60 years after the event. Twenty-six more cases, some of them posthumous, were submitted for review but had not been acted on at year's end.

Despite the new law, the Swiss ambassador to Israel, Ernst Iten, refused to attend the unveiling of a street sign renamed after Paul Grüninger, a Swiss police officer who was dismissed from his job and disgraced for forging documents to save 3,600 Jewish refugees. The ambassador explained that the new street was located in the Pisgat Ze'ev neighborhood of Jerusalem, located beyond the Green Line and thus outside the internationally recognized border. The Israeli press commented sarcastically about Switzerland's adjustable neutrality and its perhaps deliberate confusion between Holocaust memory and Israeli politics.

In the six years that had elapsed since the 1998 "global settlement" between Swiss banks and lawyers representing Holocaust survivors or their heirs, only a fraction of the $1.25 billion settlement had been distributed to those entitled to compensation. Judah Gribetz, the "special master" in the case, proposed that 75 percent of the unclaimed funds (amounting to many millions of dollars) should go to needy Holocaust survivors in the former Soviet Union, an idea that many survivors in the U.S. and Israel believed shortchanged them. U.S. District Court Judge Edward Korman had not yet made a final decision at the end of 2004.

A Swiss appeals court granted a group of Roma (Gypsies) the right to sue IBM over its alleged role in the Holocaust, the first such case against the U.S. computer maker. The court ruled that IBM, by providing the use of its technology, may have helped the Nazi regime pursue its policy of mass murder more quickly and efficiently than would otherwise have been possible.

JEWISH COMMUNITY

Switzerland's 2000 national census showed the Jewish population stable at around 17,800, some 0.25 percent of the country's total of seven million people. The number of Muslims was close to 300,000, or 4.26 percent, a significant jump from 0.26 percent in 1970. The number of Jewish communities declined by one, with the merger of the small congregation in Vevey-Montreux into the larger Lausanne congregation, after the Jewish old-age home in Montreux, where the synagogue was located, was sold to the city.

Although Jews were completely integrated into Swiss life, two religious issues remained problematic: the ban on ritual slaughter (see above) and the shortage of space in Jewish cemeteries that could provide perpetual plots. In some Swiss cities, such as Geneva, old Jewish cemeteries were almost full, and the creation of new private cemeteries was forbidden. Rather than having to conduct burials in secular cemeteries without perpetual plots, Jewish communities sought to negotiate arrangements with local authorities whereby both Jewish and municipal burial laws would be respected.

The umbrella organization for Swiss Jewry, the Swiss Federation of Jewish Communities, celebrated its centennial anniversary in a solemn commemoration attended by political and religious officials. A bilingual book (in French and German) was published for the occasion, *Vie et culture juives en Suisse—Jüdische Lebenswelt Schweiz.* Founded in 1904 to protect the rights of Swiss Jews in the wake of the national ban on ritual slaughter, the federation expanded its role by establishing ties with leaders of other religious groups, politicians, intellectuals, social workers, and others. It developed a welfare network for Jewish refugees in Switzerland during World War II, voiced its concerns to the government regarding restitution of Holocaust victims' assets, and, while maintaining an attitude of Swiss patriotism and political neutrality, opposed anti-Semitism. To be sure, the organization had been subject to criticism from those who considered it too timid and conciliatory on issues of anti-Semitism, or inconsistent in regard to Israeli policies. Even so, its prominent role in the debate over Switzerland's role during World War II raised the federation's profile in the community. Run by volunteers and a tiny professional staff, it maintained relations with other Jewish communities in Europe and beyond.

Alfred Donath, president of the federation, took sides in a controversy involving the World Jewish Congress (WJC). During the year, the WJC abruptly closed a Swiss bank account containing $1.2 million, transferring the sum to an undisclosed beneficiary. A few months later, the WJC made an apparently unrelated decision to shut down its Geneva office, angering the employees and the local Jewish community. When the bank withdrawal was disclosed, Donath insisted on a "prompt accounting of this matter" and on an independent audit of the WJC, for which he was suspended from the European Jewish Congress, the WJC's regional affiliate. Another critic, WJC vice president Isi Leibler, an Australian Jew now living in Israel, was stripped of his membership on the group's steering committee. The Swiss media had a field day with the story since the WJC had been at the forefront of the battle with Swiss banks over the Holocaust-era bank accounts, and now the Jewish organization had to explain about its own Swiss bank account. After weeks of heated exchanges gleefully reported in the media, the WJC apparently agreed to an independent audit, but Donath had not yet been rehabilitated within the European Jewish Congress.

Sigi Feigel, a prominent lawyer who presided over the largest Jewish community of Switzerland, the Israelitische Cultusgemeinde Zurich, died at the age of 83, having devoted his life to fighting racism, bigotry, and anti-Semitism. In his last years, Feigel was often in disagreement with the leadership of the Federation of Jewish Communities and with the Israeli government.

BRIGITTE SION
(WITH THE ASSISTANCE OF JOSEPH ALPERN)

Central and Eastern Europe

Germany

National Affairs

THE GERMAN-AMERICAN relationship, which soured over the U.S. decision to go to war with Iraq in 2003, improved slightly after President George Bush's reelection to a second term, when, partially out of necessity, he and German chancellor Gerhard Schröder established a cordial working relationship. The two countries cooperated on several issues, including combating terrorism, fighting anti-Semitism, and promoting democracy, particularly in the Middle East.

President Bush publicly thanked Germany for playing a major role in the UN-mandated International Security Assistance Force in Afghanistan, which was under German command from February 9 through August 10. While Germany maintained its policy of not sending troops to serve in Iraq, it continued to provide security for the U.S. bases on German soil and cooperated in providing intelligence on Iraq and the surrounding countries. As investigations in Great Britain and the U.S. revealed that the evidence for weapons of mass destruction in Iraq was even weaker than first thought, German cynicism about the war grew, compounded by revelations of abuse of prisoners in the Abu Ghraib prison in Iraq.

Both Schröder and Foreign Minister Joschka Fischer stressed that the transatlantic partnership was essential to the security of Europe and the world. There was, however, some disappointment in Germany that the U.S. would not express clear support for the country's bid for permanent-member status on the UN Security Council.

A major issue of transatlantic concern was Iran's nuclear policy. The foreign ministers of Germany, England, and France negotiated intensively in 2004 with the Iranian government to prevent it from developing nuclear weapons. Both the U.S. and Israel questioned the efficacy of these negotiations. In June, the International Atomic Energy Agency said it had found traces of enriched uranium—necessary to produce nuclear weapons—in Iran, as well as evidence that Iran was importing parts to build centrifuges.

The primary domestic issue in German national politics during 2004 was the slow economy. Reforms, scheduled to take effect in January 2005, designed to restructure the tax base, improve health care, and streamline welfare and unemployment payments—initiated by the center-left Social Democratic-Green government and supported by the conservative opposition parties—encountered growing resistance. Arousing particular anger was the reduction, in some cases, of government benefits, and a provision requiring recipients of welfare payments to accept low-paying temporary jobs. Groups from all across the political spectrum opposed to the reform program carried out protests. Paul Spiegel, head of the Central Council of Jews in Germany (CCJG), warned that extremist groups on the right or left could use these demonstrations to radicalize voters. Opposition to the reforms was strongest in eastern Germany, the formerly communist German Democratic Republic. Though the standard of living had risen there in the 15 years since unification, the area remained economically disadvantaged, with unemployment ranging from 20 to 40 percent.

The economic situation caused Schröder's Social Democratic Party (SPD) to lose much popular support in 2004, and some of its left-leaning activists considered forming their own faction to challenge the prime minister in the next federal election. The Green Party gained strength, partly because of the personal popularity of its government ministers. The Free Democratic Party regained some of the popularity it lost in the 2003 election, and the reconstituted Communist Party, which had no seats in the Bundestag, also seemed to be on the upswing.

German-Jewish relations continued to play an important role in the transatlantic picture, as illustrated by a conference held in May in Washington, D.C. Hosted by the German Historical Institute, this "First International Dialogue Between Young Germans and Young American-Jewish Leaders" was the brainchild of Simon Nauerz, a young German volunteer associated with Action Reconciliation Service for Peace who was working with the American Jewish Committee in Washington. Other bodies beside the institute and the AJC involved in the planning were the German embassy, the U.S. Holocaust Memorial Museum, the Jewish Youth Philanthropy Institute, the German School, and the Goethe Institute. The 20 young adults who participated began with a reception at the German embassy followed by a roundtable discussion on the topic, "Beyond Anti-Semitism and Philo-Semitism: Searching for Normality in German-Jewish Relations."

In May, CCJG head Paul Spiegel lauded Germany's outgoing president, Johannes Rau, as a friend to Jews and to Israel, and thanked him for his commitment to building relations between Jews and non-Jews. Rau's successor was Horst Köhler, 61, former head of the International Monetary Fund (IMF), who assumed the presidency on July 2. The role of president was nonpartisan and largely symbolic. Köhler, nominated by the conservative Christian Democratic Union (CDU), narrowly defeated Gesine Schwan, president of Viadrina University in Frankfurt/Oder, gaining the support of 604 of the 1,205 delegates, half of whom were members of parliament and the other half chosen by the 16 states.

In the days before the election, controversy erupted over the Nazi past of one CDU electoral delegate. The Vienna-based Simon Wiesenthal Center pushed for the removal of Hans Filbinger, 90, a military judge during the Nazi era, who had handed down death sentences to deserters. Filbinger had resigned as governor of the state of Baden-Württemberg in 1978 after his past was revealed. According to the Wiesenthal Center, after World War II, Filbiger headed the Weikersheim Study Center, a controversial institute that had reportedly invited Holocaust revisionists and deniers to speak.

Immigration remained a live issue in Germany. There were some 7.3 million noncitizens living in the country—nearly 9 percent out of a population of 82 million. Most of the noncitizens, nearly six million, were from other European countries, mostly Turkey, Italy, Greece, and former Yugoslavia. The next largest groups, in descending order, were Asians, Africans, North and South Americans, and Australians. An estimated 200,000 foreigners were arriving in Germany each year.

A major debate developed during the summer, when a ship run by the private German humanitarian organization Cap Anmur docked illegally off the coast of Italy with Africans aboard. The organization claimed that these were Sudanese refugees escaping the brutal civil war in their country, and were therefore entitled to asylum. But the Italian government insisted that they were not from Sudan, and deported most of the passengers back to Africa. In the wake of this incident, German interior minister Otto Schily proposed that Europe set up refugee camps in North Africa to process applications for those seeking to immigrate to Europe, in order to deter people from taking the risk of going to sea to escape poverty and discrimination. Some critics considered his approach a pretext to prevent refugees from crossing into Germany.

WAR ON TERROR

A report released in May by the Federal Department for Protection of the Constitution indicated that Islamic extremism remained Germany's greatest domestic security threat. According to the report, there were 24 radical Islamic groups in the country in 2003 with a combined membership of 30,900, essentially unchanged from 2002. The vast majority of these people, 26,500, were of Turkish background, while 3,300 were Arabs. Interior Minister Schily, commenting on the findings, said that Germany was not only a staging ground for terror attacks elsewhere, but was also a potential target itself, "because Germany, in the eyes of Islamists, belongs in the camp of the so-called crusaders, the helpers of the U.S.A. and Israel."

In August, it was learned that a September 11 terror suspect on trial in Hamburg reportedly approved of the Nazi genocide against Jews. In the retrial of Mounir El Motassadeq, a 30-year-old Moroccan, on charges of involvement in an Al Qaeda terror cell, Ralf G., 34, who had shared an apartment with the defendant in 1996 and 1997, testified that Motassadeq once said, "what the Germans did back then, that was really not so bad, with the Jews and so on." According to the witness, he then told his roommate that he did not want to hear such statements, and ended the conversation. He described Motassadeq's relationship with the leader of the September 11 attack, Mohammed Atta, as very close. The retrial followed the March 2004 decision of an appeals court to overturn Motassadeq's 2003 conviction on the grounds that the U.S. had denied his lawyers access to testimony from a key member of the Al Qaeda Hamburg cell who was on trial in the U.S. After the Americans granted access to the testimony, Motassadeq's retrial began on August 10.

In related news, Germany, in November, agreed to cooperate with the U.S. in the trial of French national Zacarias Moussaoui, charged in the September 11 attacks. The arrangement was predicated on American assurances that evidence obtained from Germany would not be used to obtain the death penalty.

In September, the Interior Ministry banned a planned "First Arab and Islamic Congress in Europe" scheduled for October 1–3 in Berlin. Conference organizer Fadi Mahdi—who, on his Web site, had condemned "American and Zionist Nazism" and called for the "final slaughter"—was deported to his previous country of residence, Lebanon. German law allowed the banning of organizations whose activities were deemed illegal or anti-democratic. In response to the German decision, Fadi Mahdi told *Der Spiegel* that the congress might take place in Vienna, whereupon calls came for the mayor of that city to prohibit it.

Interestingly, an interfaith pro-democracy group with many members of Arab and Muslim background pushed for the German ban. It declared, in an open letter to Berlin mayor Klaus Wowereit, that "the extremists who want to meet here in October are declared enemies of the freedom for which we, and our city, stand. Their declared goal is to export extremism and violence."

In December, a bid to lift Germany's ban on an Islamist group failed. The Federal Administrative Court of Leipzig turned down a request by the Al-Aqsa charitable organization to be allowed to gather funds again, since the group supported terrorist organizations based in the Middle East, including Hamas, and thus "attacks the concept of understanding between peoples." Interior Minister Schily had banned the group in 2002, but it had won a brief reprieve while the courts considered the case. Schily described the 2004 decision as a "clear signal that Germany will not tolerate organizations that collect donations to support violence and terror abroad. No one can hide under the cover of supposedly pure humanitarianism."

Israel and the Middle East

GERMANY AND ISRAEL

In a dramatic story early in the year, Germany brokered a historic prisoner exchange between Israel and Hezballah. On January 29, under tight security, two jets landed at the Cologne-Bonn airport before dawn, within minutes of each other. One, from Beirut, carried kidnapped Israeli businessman and reserve soldier Elhanan Tannenbaum along with the bodies of three Israeli soldiers. The other, from Tel Aviv, had 36 Arab prisoners and a German Hezballah member, Steven Smyrek, who had been in Israeli custody. The exchange took place smoothly, unaffected by news of a suicide bombing on a bus in Jerusalem that killed ten. Smyrek promised police that he would not attack Israeli institutions in Germany, but later said he would ask for permission to live in Lebanon, where he would continue his fight against Israel.

Germany remained Israel's strongest supporter within the EU in 2004, and its second biggest economic partner after the U.S. Nevertheless, there were signs of strain in the relationship as the route of Israel's security fence, its expansion of settlements, and the continuing policy of "targeted assassinations" came under criticism.

In April, Foreign Minister Fischer condemned Israel's killing of Hamas leader Abdel Aziz Rantisi. "We consider this [targeted assassination] a means that must not be used," Fischer said.

In August, after the International Court of Justice ruled against Israel's security barrier, Germany joined the rest of Europe in issuing a joint statement approving the decision and urging both parties to abide by the "road map" plan. Pressure for such a statement came from France, and Germany agreed to it only after securing language that emphasized Israel's right to self-defense in accordance with international law. Even so, supporters of Israel in the U.S. feared that, in the name of European unity, Germany was abandoning its usual policy of abstaining or voting against such anti-Israel measures.

Germany's particular sensitivity to the issue of the security fence was underscored in February, when Ludger Volmer, a Green Party member of the Bundestag, made a comparison that drew considerable attention. Volmer, his party's foreign policy spokesman, said he welcomed Prime Minister Ariel Sharon's proposal to remove Jewish settlements from Gaza, but criticized what he called a policy of "strict separation" between Israelis and Palestinians in the form of "this monstrous barrier that is being built there and that bears a fatal resemblance to the Berlin Wall." To be sure, he went on to say, the Palestinians "must find the power to finally bring terrorism by Palestinian groups to an end, and they must discontinue their inflammatory anti-Israel and anti-Jewish propaganda." Critics were quick to point out the fundamental difference between the two barriers: the Berlin Wall was designed to stem a mass exodus of skilled workers and professionals from East Germany, while the one Israel was erecting, as Volmer acknowledged, was to block acts of terror

In June, during the election campaign for delegates to the European Parliament, the Green Party distributed about 5,000 posters featuring a photograph of a peace march in London, where a banner could be seen that said "Victory to the Intifada." The problem was not discovered until three weeks after the posters' release, and though instructions were given to destroy them, some were still visible in four cities on the day of the election. The Greens reportedly also scrapped flyers that included photos of another banner supporting a boycott of Israel. The party's director, Steffi

Lemke, apologized to Israeli ambassador Shimon Stein. Campaign posters expressing love and support for Israel were put up by a conservative fringe party, the Bible-True Christians.

This was not the only indication during 2004 that German fundamentalist Christians were fascinated by Israel: they also set up an "Institute for Israelology" at the Free Theological Academy in Giessen. Billed as "the first of its kind in the 2,000-year history of Christianity," it was designed to disseminate information about Israel from a fundamentalist standpoint, based on a belief that Israel should not give up any territory and that Jews should convert to Christianity. The initial seed money for the institute was close to $1 million.

In August, Foreign Minister Fischer made his second visit of the year to Israel as part of a larger Middle East trip that also took him to Lebanon, Syria, and Egypt. He avoided meeting with Yasir Arafat, his office saying that scheduling difficulties prevented him from visiting the Palestinian territories. Instead, he met Palestinian prime minister Ahmed Qurei and Egyptian president Hosni Mubarak in Cairo. In Israel, Fischer praised Prime Minister Sharon's plans to dismantle the settlements in Gaza, telling his Israeli counterpart, Foreign Minister Silvan Shalom, that the move was a step toward restarting the peace process. Fischer raised with Shalom European concerns about the route of the security fence, plans for expanding some settlements, and the Iranian nuclear program, a subject that also worried Shalom.

At a November discussion on Mideast policy hosted by the Bundeswehr in Berlin, Israeli ambassador Stein said he found it "unbelievable that the European Union had not yet put Hezballah on the list of terror organizations. Germany has tried to do this," he said, adding that "there should be a clear signal" from Europe on this matter.

In an effort to gauge what young Germans knew about Israel, the German-American Society of Hamburg conducted a survey of 1,500 people aged 15–24 living in the city. The results indicated considerable ignorance about the Jewish state. While 71 percent knew that Israel was founded in 1948, 59 percent thought Israel was a military state or a monarchy, only 28 percent knew that almost one-third of Israel's citizens were not Jewish, and just 39 percent were aware that Germany was Israel's second most important economic partner.

PA CORRUPTION

An EU investigative team reported in February that it had evidence that Yasir Arafat channeled Palestinian Authority money to politicians and diplomats for their personal use, and to the terrorist Al-Aqsa Brigades, a group connected with his Fatah movement that had claimed responsibility for suicide bombings since the start of the second intifada. To make matters worse, German media carried reports that PA funds were also siphoned off to Arafat's private accounts in Cairo and Switzerland.

In June, Uzrad Lew, an Israeli banker and Arafat's former financial adviser, told the ARD TV news magazine "Report München" that the PA was building the "world's largest terror financing network" with EU money. ARD cited documents showing the transfer of about $65 million from an account in Geneva via a London bank to the PA in Ramallah. The funds landed in the same account to which the EU made its contributions. ARD said it also had proof that Fatah activists — including Marwan Barghouti, then serving five life terms in an Israeli prison for his role in terrorist attacks — had access to these funds. And ARD reported the existence of money orders signed by Arafat for terrorists who had committed murder in Israel and Jordan.

The issue was brought up in July at the EU Parliament, where German members condemned European foreign ministers for failing to address the problem. No action was taken, however, and further discussion was postponed until September. "This is a mistake, because even the Palestinians are talking about Arafat, and there are demonstrations for reform in the PA," said Armin Laschet, CDU representative to the EU body, and one of several German politicians who pressed the matter. Laschet charged that the PA apparently had "enough money to buy Challenger airplanes in the Caribbean or to give millions of euros to Mrs. Arafat in Paris," while average Palestinians lived in substandard conditions. Abdallah Frangi, the PA representative in Germany, denied the allegations, suggesting that they were part of a campaign by supporters of Israel to "manipulate German public opinion against the Palestinians and their striving for their own state." The complaints of Germans and others did lead to a change in the disbursement of funds to the PA. Through the end of 2003, the EU contributed ten million euros per month with virtually no controls on how it would be spent. But it tightened oversight procedures beginning in 2004, so that money could go only to specific, authorized projects.

Germany viewed the death of Yasir Arafat in November as an opportunity to build a new Palestinian leadership that not only would be more committed to peace with Israel, but also more transparent in its financial operations.

Anti-Semitism and Extremism

GOOD AND BAD NEWS

Two significant events in Germany called attention to anti-Semitism in 2004. On the positive side, Germany hosted a historic conference on anti-Semitism in Europe. But on the negative side stood the alarming electoral success, in the eastern part of the country, of two extreme right-wing parties.

The conference took place on April 28–29 in Berlin under the auspices of the Organization for Security and Cooperation in Europe (OSCE). It was hosted by German foreign minister Joschka Fischer and chaired by Bulgarian foreign minister Solomon Passy. To a large extent, it was the result of a German-American effort to raise awareness, on the eve of EU enlargement, of the spread of anti-Semitism in Europe, especially the extent to which it was triggered by anti-Israel sentiment. The conference featured addresses by U.S. secretary of state Colin Powell, German president Johannes Rau, and Holocaust survivors Simone Veil and Elie Wiesel. Several hundred participants, ranging from politicians to religious leaders to OSCE personnel, attended. Also present were representatives of Egypt, Israel, Jordan and Tunisia, countries with the status of "Mediterranean Partners for Cooperation" in the OSCE.

A resolution was originally proposed—initiated by Jewish organizations (including the American Jewish Committee) and reflecting input from the U.S. State Department and the German Foreign Ministry—that condemned Muslim anti-Semitism tied to criticism of Israel, but this was opposed by Arab countries and some OSCE members. The final language of the resolution, released April 29, only hinted at this connection, stating "unambiguously that international developments or political issues, including those in Israel or elsewhere in the Middle East, never justify anti-Semitism."

Several concrete recommendations emerged from the conference, including the appointment of a coordinator for monitoring anti-Semitic crimes in Europe. Wolfgang Benz, head of the Center for Research on Anti-Semitism of the Technical University of Berlin, said the conference showed "that anti-Semitism is not a legitimate political instrument, and it sends a signal to the Eastern European states that have not always seen it that way."

There were a number of important preconference events. The AJC and CCJG hosted a gathering of nongovernmental organizations. This was an outgrowth of work by the AJC Task Force on Anti-Semitism and Education, which had received a German government grant for a European Workshop on Anti-Semitism and Education, April 18–20, for educators from six countries. The World Jewish Congress hosted a meeting featuring presentations by German politicians, and cosponsored, together with the World Union of Jewish Students, a gathering at the Berlin Jewish Museum of some 50 young Jews from 23 countries. Also prior to the conference, the Anti-Defamation League released a poll that showed declining anti-Semitism in Europe at the same time that anti-Israel sentiment was rising there.

In June, less than two months later, far-right parties surprised the country by taking nearly 7 percent of the vote in local elections in the state of Saxony. The largest of these groups, the National Democratic Party (NPD), attracted enough votes to qualify for about one million euros in campaign costs. For the June elections to the European Parliament, the NPD fielded a joint "National Alliance" list together with two other extremist parties, the German People's Union (DVU) and the Republikaners, and it managed to win 10.3 percent of the vote in the town of Chemnitz, in what had been East Germany.

With state elections in the former East German states of Saxony and Brandenberg scheduled for September 19, the right-wing groups campaigned for support by blaming foreigners for crime and unemployment, expressed resentment at reminders of the Holocaust, and propounded vehemently racist, anti-Semitic, and anti-American views. The NPD and DVU reached an agreement whereby the former would not run in Brandenburg and the latter would sit out the Saxony election, so as to maximize the chances that each party would garner the 5-percent threshold vote necessary for parliamentary representation in one of the states.

The strategy worked, as the extremists made significant gains. For the first time since 1968, the NPD crossed the 5-percent threshold to place representatives in Saxony's parliament, gaining 9.2 percent of the vote. The DVU, which was already represented in the Brandenburg parliament, won 6.1 percent of the vote there.

The results were greeted with alarm within the German mainstream. Sociologist Richard Stöss and political scientist Jürgen Falter of Mainz suggested that as many as half of those who voted for these fringe parties were not ideological supporters but rather protest voters, and predicted that "if there is no kind of economic miracle" in the former East Germany, the extremist right wing could soon get as many as 15 percent of the vote. The pro-democracy Antonio Amadeu Foundation, founded by Annette Kahane, a member of the Berlin Jewish community, called on the moderate parties to make funds available for a long-term fight against right-wing extremism.

Paul Spiegel, the CCJG president, told the *Tagesspiegel* newspaper that the election results were due to two factors, the economic situation and the failure of the political mainstream to educate the voters in Saxony and Brandenburg about the nature of democratic reforms. Spiegel also pointed out that the election results could make things even worse for the economy by discouraging foreign investment, and criticized Interior Minister Schily for having dropped attempts to ban the NPD in 2003 (see AJYB 2004, p. 373).

Not long after the election, in late September, charges were filed against Udo Voigt, president of the NPD, for remarks he made in an interview with the extreme right-wing newspaper *Junge Freiheit*. Voigt called Hitler a "great statesman" and the current government of Germany an "illegitimate system" requiring "revolutionary change."

SURVEYS AND STRATEGIES

In all, Germany registered 869 anti-Semitic incidents in 2004, according to the annual report prepared by the postcommunist Party of Democratic Socialism. Most were committed by right-wing extremists; only 11 were attributed to "foreigners." The bulk of the anti-Semitic incidents relating to Israel, however, were the work of left-wing extremists, the report said.

In December, the Berlin Senate's Department on Constitutional Protection issued a study reporting that there had been nine violent anti-Semitic attacks in the city during the first nine months of the year; in 2003, there were 12 such incidents, representing about 3 percent of all violent crimes in the capital. The anti-Semitic attacks were being committed by younger people; according to the study, the average age of known perpetrators in 2003 was 16, and the youngest arrested was 12. Claudia Schmid, head of the department that prepared the report, said it was unlikely that right-wingers would join forces with the 3,700 estimated Islamic extremists in Berlin, as neo-Nazis tended not to cross cultural boundaries.

Another study was issued in December, the annual "German Situation 2004," third in a series by sociologist Wilhelm Heitmeyer of the University of Bielefeld. It indicated that racism and xenophobia were on the rise, finding that 60 percent of Germans agreed that there were too many "foreigners" in Germany, up from 55 percent in 2003. Of the 2,600 people interviewed, almost 70 percent agreed that Muslim culture did not fit with Western mores; in 2003, 66 percent held this view. The study also found increased animosity toward homeless people, homosexuals, and the handicapped, and a growing number of respondents said they were worried about their economic situation.

Combating anti-Semitism remained a central theme in 2004, on both the European and national levels. The Amerian Jewish Committee in Berlin teamed up with the Heinrich Böll Foundation, associated with the Green Party, to host a series of roundtable discussions on anti-Semitism. In November, the Kreuzberg Museum in Berlin held a daylong symposium titled "United Against Anti-Semitism," featuring lectures and discussions. Also in November, at a meeting in Berlin, the European Jewish Congress pledged to continue its fight against anti-Semitism. Cobi Benatoff of Italy, EJC president, said the group would meet with EU education ministers to "find ways of introducing into the curricula in Europe subjects that will act as a vaccine against prejudice in our younger generations."

ISLAMIC EXTREMISM

Muslim anti-Semitism continued to be a problem, though for the most part it was nonviolent. In August, however, police arrested a 19-year-old man of Arab background in connection with an attack on an Israeli tourist near the Berlin Jewish Museum (the victim was not seriously injured). The alleged perpetrator was accused of coming up to three members of a tour group who were wearing *kippot,* identifying himself as a Palestinian, saying "Jews must be killed," and proceeding to kick the victim in the stomach. The suspect had a previous record of violent crimes.

In November, some 1,000 people demonstrated in Berlin, in one of several Shiite Islamist parades held around the world marking the end of the Ramadan month. The annual event was initiated in 1979 by Ayatollah Ruholla Khomeini of Iran, with the goal of condemning Israel's existence. Marchers held posters condemning "all forms of terrorism" and proclaiming the equal value of the three major faiths, which would one day live together in a "liberated Palestine." A pro-Israel counterdemonstration organized by the Berlin Alliance Against Anti-Semitism included many Iranian exiles who protested human rights abuses in their former country.

On December 1, *Vakit,* a Turkish-language newspaper, ran an article in which author Hasan Karakaya wrote, "The truth is: There was no Holocaust. And the so-called gas chambers also are a lie." Holocaust denial was illegal in Germany, and the state prosecutor in Hessen filed suit against the paper. Kristina Köhler, a CDU representative in the Bundestag, described the article's contents as "the most crass smear campaign," and Berlin's Department for Constitutional Protection noted that the paper was already notorious for earlier Islamist and anti-Semitic statements.

A Turkish national identified as Yakup T., imam of the Mevlana Mosque in Berlin, was ordered to leave Germany in December because of sermons he delivered expressing sympathy for suicide bombers, fomenting hatred toward Americans and Jews, and predicting "hellfire" for Germans. Senator for the Interior Ehrhart Körting (SPD) said the religious leader was preparing "fertile ground for terror acts," since, as an imam, he might be "a role model for many." Körting added that most Muslims living in Germany were opposed to violence.

RIGHT-WING EXTREMISM

Right-wing extremist organizations continued to try to evade the laws banning publication and distribution of neo-Nazi and racist literature and paraphernalia. In 2004, some of these groups claimed success in distributing a new CD in front of schools. Experts who examined the CD reported that it contained racist and nationalist ideology in a form designed to appeal to youth, and suggested that the coordinated effort represented a growing tendency of such groups across Germany to work together.

On January 30, an estimated 1,200 neo-Nazis and 3,500 counter-demonstrators came to blows over the controversial exhibit "Crimes of the Wehrmacht," which opened the day before in Hamburg, its last scheduled public display. A police contingent of 3,250 proved unable to keep the opposing groups apart. The exhibit, a project of the Hamburg Institute for Social Research, documented war crimes committed by the Nazi army during World War II. Protests against the traveling exhibit had been mounted since its first appearance in 1995, as critics claimed it wrongly criminalized German soldiers.

In March, the Münster Higher Regional Court, basing itself in part on the party's record of anti-Semitism, confirmed a ban by local authorities on planned demonstrations by the NPD against the construction of a synagogue in Bochum. The NPD formally protested the decision in Germany's highest court, in Karlsruhe. In June, after local police banned yet another NPD demonstration against the synagogue, the party obtained a temporary injunction from the court in Karlsruhe, and held its demonstration on June 28.

In April, the country's chief federal prosecutor charged four members and one supporter of the extremist Kameradschaft Süd of terrorism. They had been among those arrested in September 2003 for allegedly planning to explode a bomb at the cornerstone-laying ceremony of Munich's new Jewish community center (see AJYB 2004, p. 372). The leader of the group, Martin Wiese, was a well-known neo-Nazi who had led a right-wing demonstration against the Iraq war. Their defense attorney, however, argued that the only one who had expressed "clear criminal intentions" was a government informant who had infiltrated the cell.

On May 13, Martin Hohmann, a CDU member of the Bundestag, learned he would not face court charges connected to a speech he delivered on German Unity Day in 2003 (see AJYB 2004, pp. 375–76). The state prosecutor in Fulda announced that Hohmann, despite his reference to Jews as a "nation of perpetrators," had committed no statutory offence. The court rejected protests against its decision from the CCJG and the Jewish association in Hessen. Hohmann had kept his parliamentary seat after the incident but was dismissed from his party's caucus. Meanwhile, Defense Minister Peter Struck, who had reportedly received numerous death threats after firing Brigadier General Reinhard Guenzel for expressing support for Hohmann's anti-Semitic ideas, was under the highest security protection.

In June, swastikas and SS symbols were found scrawled across 45 stones in a Jewish cemetery in the western German city of Düsseldorf. Police said that the vandals probably climbed over the wall surrounding the cemetery. "It was very shocking," said Herbert Rubinstein, director of the State Association of Jewish Communities of North Rhine, who discovered the damage. The incident was barely reported in the German press, in conformity with the policy of the Jewish community to avoid sparking copycat crimes.

In August, nearly 4,000 neo-Nazis from across Europe marched into Wunsiedel, a town of 10,000. They had been doing this every year since 2001 in honor of Rudolf Hess, Adolf Hitler's deputy, who killed himself in the Spandau prison on August 17, 1987. The Bavarian administrative court turned down a request from city officials to ban the march. Instead, citizens of this small town responded with a festival promoting democracy and diversity, and hundreds of people—including the mayor, local legislators, priests, and church elders—sat down on the town's main street to block the path of the neo-Nazis. According to the U.S. State Department's annual report on human rights, police arrested 105 individuals for carrying guns and illegal symbols at the event.

Jewish visitors to Berlin in August discovered swastikas painted on a Holocaust memorial at Levetzowstrasse in Tiergarten, where one of Berlin's largest synagogues once stood. The design of the memorial represented the boxcars used to deport Jews from the synagogue, which the Nazis turned into a detention point for nearly 40,000 Jews.

In November, more than 1,000 right-wing extremists from around Germany demonstrated at a World War II military cemetery in Halbe, a city outside Berlin in the former East German state of Brandenburg. The demonstration, which the state high court had barred until 2003, was intended to mark Germany's national day of mourning for fallen soldiers. Some right-wingers had adopted the day as a time to celebrate their heroes, members of the SS and the Wehrmacht. Their theme was "Glory and Honor to the German Frontline Soldiers," and although photographers were kept away, eyewitnesses described participants marching in formation around a memorial stone where 24,000 SS men and German soldiers were buried, and a wreath-laying at the site. A roughly similar number of counterdemonstrators were there, saying they wanted to memorialize the victims of the Nazis as well as the Soviet soldiers who fell trying to defeat the German army. Some 1,800 police kept the two sides apart.

Holocaust-Related Matters

REMEMBRANCE

Nearly 60 years after the end of World War II, with the EU preparing for enlargement, the president of the Bundestag called for a European-wide Holocaust memorial day. Wolfgang Thierse (SPD) made the statement on Germany's annual remembrance day, January 27, the anniversary of the liberation of Auschwitz by Soviet troops in 1945. Calling the Holocaust "the largest, most terrible crime in world history," he argued that a common day of commemoration would promote the cultural integration of European member states.

In June, French president Jacques Chirac took an historic step, inviting German chancellor Schröder to participate in ceremonies in Caen,

France, marking the 60th anniversary of D-Day, one of many commemorations held in 2004 recalling the downfall of the Nazi regime. This was the first time that a representative of the German government was invited to attend this annual ceremony, and the invitation was widely praised in Europe as proof of German-French reconciliation. Schröder used the occasion to stress Germany's special obligation to ensure that the crimes of Nazi Germany not be repeated.

A few weeks later, Schröder visited the grave of his father, a German soldier killed fighting in Romania, and was greeted warmly by the local population. He also visited Poland on the 60th anniversary of the beginning of the Warsaw uprising, where he said that Germans had no claim against Poland for expelling millions of ethnic Germans after the war. This angered organizations in Germany that represented the expellees, since their constituents felt that both Poland and the Czech Republic should compensate Germans for lost property and for the death of family members who perished as a result of the expulsion.

The chancellor found himself in hot water with these groups again when, agreeing with former president Johannes Rau, he rejected a proposal for a memorial to ethnic German expellees to be placed near the central Holocaust memorial, which was to open in 2005. Eastern European leaders also strongly opposed this private German initiative on the grounds that it could have the effect of minimizing German responsibility for World War II.

Indeed, funding for sites of memory in Germany became a controversial issue in 2004, as public opinion came increasingly to resent the alleged neglect of the suffering of German civilians and those persecuted by the postwar communist regime in East Germany. Politicians from the conservative CDU pushed for creation of a national foundation to oversee all memorial sites in the country, but critics said that the wording of their proposed legislation—including as "victims" those mistreated by the communists as well as civilians who suffered during the war—paved the way for the relativization of history. Avner Shalev, chairman of Yad Vashem, Israel's Holocaust memorial, wrote an open letter to CDU leader Angela Merkel urging her to reconsider the proposal. As the year ended, the proposed legislation was to be revised by the Bundestag's Cultural Commission. Earlier, in January, the CCJG, together with Holocaust memorial directors across the country, announced their withdrawal from the memorial foundation in the state of Saxony, in protest against what they called the relativization of history.

Germany marked two milestones in 2004 in the construction of its national Holocaust memorial, due to open in May 2005 near Berlin's Brandenburg Gate. In July, Bundestag president Thierse presided at ceremonies marking the completion of the roof on the memorial's cavernous underground "documentation center." And in December, another public event marked the placement of the last cement stele in the memorial, which was to have a total of 2,751 of the gray cement pillars on the 204,440-square-foot site. Architect Peter Eisenman, who had designed the memorial with artist Richard Serra, said he hoped the structure would "bring a new sense of the relationship of history to the present, so that the history is not clouded over."

The question of whether demonstrations should be banned near the memorial arose when NPD leaders applied for permission to rally at the Brandenburg Gate on May 8, 2005, the 60th anniversary of the end of World War II. Among those favoring a ban were CCJG head Paul Spiegel and Minister of the Interior Schily, but Eisenman, the architect, opposed attempts to curb demonstrations. Bundestag president Thierse agreed with Eisenman. Acknowledging there was no way to protect the memorial from all vandalism, he said he had faith in the goodwill and decency of the public. There would be a 24-hour-a-day watch, but no fence and no constant police presence.

Another major topic of discussion in Germany in 2004 was whether the vast art collection of Friedrich Christian ("Mick") Flick, grandson of convicted Nazi war criminal and industrialist Friedrich Flick, should open at Berlin's Hamburger Bahnhof Museum. Critics said Flick's collection of works by such artists as Marcel Duchamp, Marc Chagall, Piet Mondrian, Gerhard Richter, Sigmar Polke, Richard Serra, and Cindy Sherman was bought with profits inherited from his grandfather's huge wartime armaments factory, which used slave labor. Furthermore, Flick had not contributed to the German fund for slave laborers. Flick, for his part, complained about being held liable for the crimes of an ancestor. In an open letter, he wrote, "the family name Flick comes with a special responsibility," adding that he did not intend to "relativize or make people forget" his grandfather's crimes. The exhibit opened in September, but not before a special program in Berlin, organized by the Fritz-Bauer Institute of Franfurt, where several women described what it was like to work as slave laborers in the Flick explosives factory. Afterward, the Institute of Contemporary History in Munich said it would initiate a research project on the wartime history of the Flick family.

In June, the Anne Frank Center in Berlin marked the 75th anniversary of Anne Frank's birth with an exhibit of 40 photos by her father, Otto Frank, including images never before seen by the public. Similar exhibits also opened at the Kraushaar Gallery in New York and the Anne Frank House in Amsterdam. Included in the Berlin showing were pictures of Anne and her sister Margot as children, school photos, and street scenes. The family was arrested and deported in August 1944. There were no photos taken of the family in hiding.

Also in June, the American journalist Varian Fry, who helped more than 1,500 people escape Nazi-occupied France, was posthumously honored with an "information" bus shelter in Berlin, including a photo of Fry in Berlin and an accompanying text in German and English. It was located at the crossroads of a street named for Fry in Berlin's newly redeveloped Potsdamer Platz. The project was supported in part by the AJC office in Berlin and by Wall AG, a bus-shelter manufacturer.

Construction of a permanent home for Topography of Terror, Berlin's archive and exhibit about the Nazi secret police, began in June. The center's temporary building, located over the unearthed basement of an annex to Gestapo headquarters and open to visitors and researchers, contained documents and photographs related to the history of the Gestapo and the SS. The new documentation center was expected to open in 2007.

Due to the advanced age of the defendants, neither of two cases involving alleged Nazi war criminals resulted in any jail time. The state court in Hagen announced in February that the 88-year-old Dutch-born Herbitus Bikker, a former SS man accused of murdering a member of the Dutch resistance in 1944, was unable to follow the proceedings, and therefore the case had to be dropped. Bikker had been convicted of murder and sentenced to death in Holland in 1949; the sentence was later commuted to life in prison, but he escaped the Breda jail in 1952 and found a haven in Germany. As a former soldier in the German army, he was safe from extradition.

In June, Germany's highest court announced that 95-year-old Friedrich Engel, the former SS chief in Genoa, would not have to serve his seven-year sentence for shooting 59 Italian prisoners in 1944, because of his physical condition. Engel had organized the shootings as revenge after Italian partisans attacked a cinema for German soldiers, killing five of them. In a book about Engel's case published in Germany in May, *History on Trial—The Case of Engel,* a former Hamburg deputy mayor and international law specialist, Ingo von Münch, called Engel's actions morally reprehensible but not murder according to German law.

There was a great deal of interest in Nazi memorabilia, both authentic and fake, during the year. In January, the yacht that belonged to Hermann Göring went on sale in Egypt. German boat dealer Christopher

Brunner-Schwer said he hoped to make a fortune selling the boat, put up for sale by the American widow of an Egyptian oil agent. "Arabs like the boat's history," he said, "and that is raising the price." The forged Hitler "diaries" resurfaced in 2004, as well. In April, the second part of the scandalous fake went on the auction block in Berlin. Written by the late con artist Konrad Kujau and passed off as the real thing to *Stern* magazine in 1983, it was expected to bring in some 7,000 euros. Reportedly, Kujau wrote this last volume, which covered the period April 15–30, 1945, well after the *Stern* scandal broke.

In October, 13 pages from the authentic diary of the notorious Nazi doctor Josef Mengele surfaced in the possession of the Federal Police of Brazil, in São Paulo. In these papers, Mengele defended his views on racial superiority. They were originally taken in 1985 from the home of a friend of Mengele. After the war, the Nazi doctor hid out with a farmer's family in Upper Bavaria, and fled to Argentina in 1948. Ten years later, he went to Paraguay and finally to Brazil, where he died in 1979 at the age of about 67, in a swimming accident.

In December, Walter Gaudnek, a 71-year-old German-American art professor who taught at the University of Central Florida, caused a stir with an exhibit featuring caricatures of Hitler that went on display for two weeks in a town 25 kilometers from Dachau, the former Nazi concentration camp. Gaudnek's cartoon-like works depicted Hitler as a "pop icon," and included swastikas and other Nazi symbols. Charlotte Knobloch, a vice president of the CCJG, commented that it was "extremely dangerous" to depict Hitler in such a light "because these presentations can be completely misunderstood; the perpetrator can appear to be a victim." The local mayor, Konrad Wagner, agreed, saying that the exhibit gave a "disagreeable" impression, adding, "if the artist had asked me in advance, I would have advised him against presenting it."

COMPENSATION

In 2004, the Conference on Jewish Material Claims Against Germany distributed approximately $820 million in direct compensation payments to Jewish victims of Nazi persecution and their heirs in more than 60 countries. This was the largest single-year distribution of compensation payments in the history of the organization. The funds came from eight different compensation and restitution programs that the organization administered (see "Fifty Years of Holocaust Compensation," AJYB 2002, pp. 3–84).

The largest source of money was the Program for Former Slave and Forced Laborers, which concluded three years of payments in August 2004 with a second payment to 131,000 survivors totaling $401 million. Between June 2001 and July 2004, a total of $703 million was paid as a first installment. In 2004, each former slave laborer received approximately $3,000, and former forced laborers a smaller amount.

In addition, the Claims Conference made slave labor payments from the Swiss Banks Settlement, as compensation for Nazi profits transacted through Swiss banks. Under this portion of the program, the Claims Conference paid more than $217 million to 150,140 survivors. Including the new payments, the Claims Conference had distributed more than $1.3 billion in compensation payments to Jewish former slave and forced laborers since 2001. Also under the Swiss Banks settlement, the Claims Conference paid those who were turned back at the border, expelled from the country, or mistreated while there.

In February, the German government and industry's Foundation for Remembrance, Responsibility and the Future said it wanted unclaimed funds returned to it over the next 30 months so that they might be distributed to other survivors. Some organizations in eastern and central Europe entrusted with the task of distributing funds to survivors had been overwhelmed with claims, and some funds reportedly were squandered. Most claimants in the slave and forced labor category were not Jewish.

Other programs from which payments were made in 2004 included the Article 2 and Central and Eastern European Fund (CEEF) pension programs, the Hardship Fund, and the Fund for Victims of Medical Experiments and Other Injuries. The Claims Conference negotiated these programs and tried to expand eligibility for additional survivors. In 2004, for example, the German government agreed to include in the Article 2 and CEEF programs survivors of Bulgarian labor battalions, and liberalized criteria for survivors who had lived illegally under a false identity or with false papers, provided they met the other eligibility requirements of the programs.

Payments in 2004 of approximately 27 million euros were made from the Claims Conference Goodwill Fund to heirs to Jewish property in the former East Germany. These were for properties claimed by the Claims Conference under German law, and for which heirs came forward with a valid claim after the German deadline. The conference negotiated the law establishing the right of owners and heirs to claim properties in former East Germany.

The Claims Conference also provided technical assistance in processing claims and payments to the International Commission on Holocaust Era Insurance Claims and the Claims Resolution Tribunal responsible for dormant accounts under the Swiss Banks Settlement. These two programs paid a total of about $54 million in 2004, an amount not included in the Claims Conference compensation total. Gideon Taylor, executive vice president of the conference, said that ongoing needs would be discussed with the German government.

The conference in 2004 identified and issued a symbolic payment of 8,300 marks (approximately $5,400, or 4,240 euros) to an additional 704 living Jewish victims of Nazi medical experiments, bringing to 2,482 the number of survivors in this category receiving compensation. And the organization uncovered new information about gruesome experiments that had never before been recorded, enabling many victims to be declared eligible for payment. Testimonies of survivors were turned over to the United States Holocaust Memorial Museum in Washington, D.C., and to Yad Vashem in Israel. Some were posted on the Claims Conference Web site, www.claimscon.org. Survivors could collect from a 50-million-mark fund for Jewish and non-Jewish victims of Nazi experimentation and for children of forced laborers who were in special homes.

In May, Germany committed funds for homecare for Nazi victims, in a move that the Claims Conference saw as a breakthrough. Following negotiations, the government agreed to allocate an initial sum of $7.2 million in 2004. The Claims Conference said that the funds would be distributed by social service agencies worldwide.

Following the death of Karl Brozik on August 18 at the age of 78 (see below, p. 441), the Claims Conference named Moshe Jahoda to succeed him as head of its office in Germany. Born in 1926 in Vienna, Jahoda had been serving as associate executive vice president of the conference and head of its Austrian office.

JEWISH COMMUNITY

Demography and Immigration

According to the Central Welfare Council of Jews in Germany, the official Jewish population in Germany rose from 102,000 in 2003 to roughly 105,600 in 2004. About 4,700 new immigrants arrived in 2004, mostly from the former Soviet Union. But newly enacted legislation was likely to diminish this flow.

Jewish immigration from the FSU began in earnest in 1990, when Germany, eager to rebuild its shattered Jewish community, applied to these Jews the "contingency refugee" regulations initially created in response to the Vietnamese "boat people." Up to 5,000 Soviet Jews per year were allowed to enter Germany, where they would enjoy residency rights and the full package of social benefits, but not immediate citizenship. This influx tripled the size of the Jewish community over the next 14 years.

However, new rules announced in December 2004, to go into effect the next month, imposed certain restrictions: the newcomers would have to demonstrate that they would be self-supporting, that they could speak German, and that there was no impediment to their acceptance into a Jewish congregation. Federal Interior Minister Schily insisted that these regulations in no way signaled a departure from the policy of welcoming Jewish immigrants. The Conference of Interior Ministers of the German states was charged with overseeing implementation of the new system.

It was no secret that the Israeli government had a hand in designing the new rules. Beginning in 2002, the number of Soviet Jews opting for Germany had exceeded the number choosing Israel as their destination, not only siphoning off badly needed Jewish immigrants from the Jewish state, but also calling into question Zionism's central contention, that Israel was the haven for the world's Jewish refugees. Jewish leaders in Germany, however, were not pleased, CCJG vice president Charlotte Knobloch reporting that the new law left her with a "bitter taste." Of special concern was the possibility that 27,000 Soviet Jews who had already submitted applications for admittance to Germany might have to begin the process from scratch. Interior Minister Schily reassured the CCJG that such decisions would be made only after consultation with the Jewish umbrella organization.

Judith Kessler, a sociologist who had written about FSU Jewish immigration to Germany, and who also served as editor of *Juedisches Berlin,* the Jewish community's monthly, calculated that implementation of the law in its present form would mean that "only 30 people will come for every 100 that used to come." Kessler believed that the government's action was "a trial balloon" to gauge public reaction, and might be followed by further restrictions.

Communal Affairs

In July, the Reform movement, which originated in nineteenth-century Germany, took the first step toward regaining an official place in the landscape of German Jewry when the CCJG for the first time welcomed congregations of the Union for Progressive Judaism under its umbrella. This meant that the 15 UPJ congregations, which had a combined membership of about 3,000, could now proceed to seek legal corporate status, and each congregation that did so would become eligible to apply for a share of the approximately $4 million in federal funding that the CCJG distributed to member congregations.

Leaders of German Reform saw the move as a milestone in the history of the movement. The announcement followed years of intensive lobbying by the UPJ, with help from the American Reform movement and the World Union for Progressive Judaism (WUPJ). Originally, the CCJG had fought such recognition on the grounds that the UPJ threatened to split German Jewry and that its congregations recognized non-Jews as Jews. In fact, Germany's Reform movement required that members have a Jewish mother, or else convert to Judaism. But it did open its doors, without offering membership, to non-Jewish spouses and children, and its conversions were not necessarily recognized by the Orthodox.

As the opposition to Reform had gradually subsided over the previous decade, the CCJG had slowly increased support for nontraditional forms of Judaism. Once the UPJ congregations received full funding from the CCJG, they were expected to use the money for projects aimed at integrating new immigrants and for youth programming. There were those who argued that Reform, which did not make stringent demands on its followers, was the Jewish sector that was most likely to attract the Russian-speaking immigrants.

Albert Meyer, the new president of the 12,000-member Berlin Jewish Community, insisted in January that the Claims Conference ante up more money to help his financially strapped community. Meyer, a 56-year-old attorney, said that the conference was legally bound to support German Jewry through a share of its profits from unclaimed Jewish property, but that so far it had contributed only "peanuts."

In March, Israel's Ashkenazi chief rabbi, Yonah Metzger, visited Berlin for the cornersone-laying ceremony of the new Chabad-Lubavitch Albam Jewish Education and Family Center. The following month, Daniel Coats, the U.S. ambassador to Germany, and former New York City mayor Ed Koch—who was in town to chair the American delegation to the OSCE conference on anti-Semitism—were among those to attach the first mezuzah on the building. The center, "a meeting place for hundreds of women and men of different ethnic origins," was to include a day-care center and school, library, youth lounge, multimedia center, café, lecture hall, synagogue, visitor center, and playground.

Berlin's Rykestrasse Synagogue, one of the few in Germany to survive the Kristallnacht pogroms of November 9–10, 1938, marked its centennial in April. The celebration featured cantorial performances, addresses by Berlin public officials, and a benediction by Rabbi Ernst M. Stein. Hermann Simon, a historian and director of the Foundation for the New Synagogue-Centrum Judaicum, the central archive of Germany's Jewish community, wrote a small volume on the synagogue's history to mark the occasion. Five hundred copies were to be given to Berlin schools to raise awareness of local Jewish history. On November 9, 1938, when Nazis burned and looted synagogues across the country, the fire department protected this magnificent structure because of the danger that any fire might spread to neighboring non-Jewish property.

Israeli president Moshe Katzav was in Berlin for Israel Independence Day, and joined Ambassador Stein at the annual concert and reception at the Berlin Philharmonic on April 29. In May, on the secular date of Israel's 56th birthday, some 75 Berlin Jewish students held the city's first European "Israel Day" celebration. The first such event, in 2003, had been held in Munich, and sites scheduled for upcoming years included London and Bologna.

That Germany desperately needed more rabbis and Jewish educators was the conclusion of a high-level U.S. rabbinic delegation that visited Germany in May. The 12 rabbis, members of the United Jewish Communities Rabbinic Cabinet, spent several days in Berlin meeting with leaders of the Jewish community. The delegation issued a statement urging American Jews to be more supportive of Jews in Germany, and suggesting that American rabbinic groups encourage young rabbis to spend time working in Germany.

Also in May, "Sarah-Hagar," an interfaith group of Jewish, Muslim, and Christian women, held its first conference, in Berlin. A culmination of several smaller gatherings, the event was supported by the Federal Ministry of Family, Seniors, Women and Youth, and included an ecumenical service. The participants said they would petition the German government to fund an ongoing women's educational center to promote dialogue and conflict resolution.

In July, three well-known Jewish musicians—klezmer clarinetist Giora Feidman, pianist Uri Cain, and Alan Bern of the Brave New World klezmer group—took the stage at Munich's Staatsoper International

Theater to raise money for Munich's new Jewish community center, under construction at Jakobsplatz. A portion of the sold-out concert's proceeds went toward the building fund; costs for the land and the complex were covered by the Jewish community, the state of Bavaria and the semi-private Bavarian State Trust, the city of Munich, and private donations. Construction was expected to be complete by the end of 2006.

Julius Schoeps, director of the Moses Mendelssohn Center at the University of Potsdam, announced the establishment of the Moses Mendelssohn Foundation in September. Its stated goal was to uphold the values of Mendelssohn, the eighteenth-century Jewish philosopher who lived in Berlin: enlightenment and tolerance in education, science, and society. The foundation would support programs dealing with the history of Jews in Europe and specifically in Germany, as well as the building and administration of senior homes and student dormitories.

In November, the AJC in Berlin marked ten years of close cooperation with the German army on educational matters. AJC executive director David Harris received the Golden Cross, the army's highest honor, from Defense Minister Peter Struck, in recognition of "ten years of fruitful cooperation."

Education

In January, Touro College Berlin, which opened in the fall of 2003, was feted as an affirmation of the rebirth of Jewish life in Germany and of the enduring U.S.-German relationship. Present at the event was Bernard Lander, founder and president of Touro College in New York, who was in his late 80s. The 18 original students in the Berlin college had grown to 70 in 2004. The school, which prepared students for an American business degree, also had a required course on the Holocaust.

The Network of Jewish Women, cofounded in 2002 by Gabriel Noa Lerner and Ewa Alfred, held its second national congress in May in Munich, focusing on the self-image of Jewish women. The event was supported by the Jewish Community of Munich and Upper Bavaria, and the Federal Ministry of Family, Seniors, Women and Youth.

A new textbook for Russian-speaking Jewish immigrants in Germany appeared in July 2004 that combined instruction in the German language with lessons about Judaism. *Pluspunkt Deutsch fuer juedische Einwanderer* (Extra Credit German for Jewish Immigrants), published by the Berlin-based Cornelsen Publishing Company, was the brainchild of Rabbi Gesa Ederberg, who had led the small Jewish congregation in Weiden on a part-time basis since 2001, and the project received funding from the CCJG and the School for Adult Education in Weiden. Designed to ease the integration process into German life and to forestall the influence of Christian missionary groups, the text did not favor any particular interpretation of Judaism.

Rabbi Ederberg also organized a day of workshops in Weiden for the Conservative movement in Germany on how to organize and lead synagogue services, with funding from the CCJG. And in August, he opened a kindergarten in Berlin for children aged two to five.

The Association of Jewish Students in Germany, representing some 15,000 Jews between the ages of 18 and 25, held several significant programs in 2004, including a seminar marking the centennial of the death of Theodor Herzl. Held in Hohenems, Austria, in July, it focused on Herzl's life and the meaning of Zionism in the twenty-first century.

For the fourth year, four Berlin universities and the University of Potsdam presented a joint summer semester program in Jewish studies. Courses covered such diverse topics as Jewish texts and liturgy, the role of women in rabbinic literature, German-Jewish literature of the twentieth century, introduction to Midrash, and Yiddish for historians.

In 2004, the AJC marked the completion of the first of a projected three-year tolerance and pro-democracy training program in three Berlin high schools. The program was based on AJC's model American program "Hands Across the Campus," started in 1981.

Culture

With more than 700,000 visitors in 2004, the Berlin Jewish Museum continued to break records. The two-millionth visitor crossed the threshold of the three-year-old museum in August. (That total included 18,691 visitors to the museum annex in the Mitte section of Berlin, the former Otto Weidt Workshop for the Blind, where several Jews were hidden from the Nazis.) Of the many exhibits mounted in 2004, one that drew particular attention was "10+5=God: The Power of Numbers and Signs," which focused on the power of symbols in Judaism and the tension between religious tradition and modern conventions. It revealed subtle connections between science, religion, and the everyday within the context of the last 200 years of German Jewish history.

A highlight at Berlin's New Synagogue-Centrum Judaicum Foundation was an exhibit on "Pioneers in Celluloid," Jews in the early years of filmmaking. Accompanied by a showing of films, the exhibit delved into the early years of the industry in Germany, including the impact of anti-Semitism.

Marking 50 years since the end of the Auschwitz trials in Frankfurt, the Fritz-Bauer Institute of Frankfurt curated a traveling exhibit on the trials. In all, 20 defendants—19 SS men and one former prisoner—stood trial, and there was testimony from 211 eyewitnesses. The proceedings, widely covered by the press, opened the eyes of many Germans to the crimes committed in their name.

The Fritz-Bauer Institute also teamed up with the Hessian Ministry for Science and Art to mount an exhibit on "Legalized Robbery," about how Nazi Germany robbed Jews of their property before allowing them to emigrate, or deporting them to concentration camps or death camps. The exhibit included several lectures, films, and a walking tour of Wiesbaden. As a complement to the exhibit, the Museum for German Jewish History in Wiesbaden, Aktives Museum Spiegelgasse, opened an exhibit in November on "Jewish Neighbors in Wiesbaden and Mainz," about the fate of several local Jewish families during the Nazi period.

"Medicine and Crime," exhibited at the Memorial and Museum at Sachsenhausen, near Berlin, dealt with the misdeeds committed at this former concentration camp in the name of science. It included material donated by the University of Tübingen about Nazi anthropologist Robert Ritter, who did "Gypsy research."

The Jewish Museum of Franken mounted an exhibit about kashrut that was both educational and entertaining. Museum director Daniela Eisenstein said that the aim was to show both how simple the Jewish dietary laws were, and also how difficult it could be to keep kosher in Germany. Included was a "supermarket" that challenged visitors to check if the items for "sale" were kosher. The museum also presented an exhibit on "The First Family Archive of the Rothschilds," showing for the first time objects gathered for the 70th birthday of Salomon von Rothschild in 1844 in Frankfurt. The material, stolen by the SS in 1938, was brought by Soviet troops to Moscow in 1945, and returned to the Rothschild Archive in London in 2001.

The Jewish Film Festival in Berlin celebrated its tenth anniversary in June with a varied program of new and classic films. In all, there were 23 films from Israel, Great Britain, the U.S., Australia, Sweden, Portugal, Russia, Argentina, and France. A retrospective book about the festival was published.

Two books published in 2004 focused on Jews and Jewish issues in postwar Germany for an English-speaking readership. The Humanities Laboratory published *A Jew in the New Germany,* a collection of essays by the witty and acerbic German Jewish columnist Henryk Broder, edited by Sander L. Gilman and Lilian M. Friedberg. Y. Michal Bodemann's *A Jewish Family in Germany Today: An Intimate Portrait,* which came out toward the end of the year, was published by Duke University Press. Bodemann, a sociologist, traced the history of one family with origins in Eastern Europe through the generations, illuminating postwar trends in German Jewish identity.

The "Jewish Miniatures" series—short books on important Jewish figures and institutions—added six titles in 2004: biographies of prewar German department store magnate Oscar Tietz, former head of the German Jewish community Heinz Galinski, film director Billy Wilder, and TV personality Hans Rosenthal; a book on the historic Rykestrasse Synagogue; and a guide to Jewish holidays in Russian.

Deutscher Taschenbuch Verlag published several notable titles of Jewish interest in 2004: *Marcel Reich-Ranicki,* a portrait of the German Jewish literary critic, by Thomas Ainz; *Isaac Bashevis Singer* by Stephen Tree, the first German biography of the great Yiddish writer, marking the centennial of his birth; and a German edition of Eli Barnavi's *Universal History of the Jews, from Their Beginnings to Today,* edited by Israeli historian Frank Stern.

Personalia

Michel Friedman was elected president of the German board of Keren Hayesod, the fund-raising umbrella for Israel of non-American Diaspora Jewish communities. Friedman, 48, was a longtime communal activist and outspoken supporter of Israel. An editor and TV journalist as well as an attorney, Friedman had served as vice president of the CCJG and president of the European Jewish Congress, but had to resign these positions in 2003 following charges of cocaine possession. At that time he pledged to mend his ways and return to public life (see AJBY 2004, pp. 385–86).

In another communal appointment, CCJG vice president Charlotte Knobloch, who headed both the Jewish Community of Munich and that of Upper Bavaria, became vice president of the World Jewish Congress.

American Jewish businessman Arthur Obermayer presented the fourth Obermayer German Jewish History Awards in Berlin on January 27, 2004, Germany's Holocaust Remembrance Day. These honored non-Jewish Germans who contributed toward recording or preserving the Jewish history of their communities. The honorees were Lothar Bembenek, a teacher from Wiesbaden who helped create the Aktives Museum Spiegelgasse for German Jewish History in Wiesbaden; Dorothee Lottmann-Kaeseler, who, as curator of the museum in Wiesbaden since 1998, pushed to preserve the city's oldest Jewish building; Klaus-Dieter Ehmke, a medical doctor from Berlin who restored a Jewish cemetery in Niederhof; Cordula Kappner, a librarian from Hassfurt, Bavaria, who spent 20 years researching local Jewish history in the Franconia region and mounted 34 separate exhibits in villages that once had Jewish communities; Jürgen Sielemann, an archivist and historian from Hamburg who initiated a project to post on the Internet the names of 5 million emigrants who came through the port of Hamburg, and who founded Germany's only society for Jewish genealogy; and Christiane Walesch-Schneller, a medical doctor from Breisach, Baden-Wuerttemberg, who saved the site of the former headquarters of the Jewish community in that town from demolition, and converted it into a Jewish research and educational center.

Daniel Barenboim, conductor of the Staatskapelle and the Staatsoper Berlin, received the year's Buber-Rosenzweig medal in Münster from the German Coordinating Council of the Societies for Christian-Jewish Cooperation. Named for the philosophers Martin Buber and Franz Rosenzweig, the annual prize was initiated in 1968.

The CCJG presented its annual Leo Baeck Prize to historian Fritz Stern, professor emeritus at Columbia University, in November in New York City. Foreign Minister Fischer, who spoke, said that Stern, whose family fled Nazi Germany in 1938, was largely responsible for the "excellent and balanced research being conducted on Germany and German history" in America. Stern's best known book, a study of Otto von Bismarck and his Jewish banker, Gerson von Bleichröder, was *Gold and Iron: Bismarck, Bleichröder and the Building of the German Empire.*

In November, the Berlin Jewish Community gave its 16th annual Heinz Galinski Prize to Ernst Cramer, 91, who escaped Nazi Germany and returned after the war to build a distinguished career in journalism with the Axel Springer Company. Since 1981, he headed the late publisher's philanthropic foundation in Berlin. The 5,000-euro prize was named for the former leader of Berlin's Jewish community, who died in 1992. Cramer said he would donate the 5,000-euro award to the Women's International Zionist Organization (WIZO).

On September 6, Hilde Schramm, 68, the eldest daughter of Nazi armaments minister Albert Speer, received Berlin's Moses Mendelssohn Award for her work promoting tolerance and reconciliation. In 1994, she started a foundation called Zurückgeben (Giving Back), using her inheritance to promote Jewish women in the arts and academia. She said she would donate part of the 10,000-euro prize to her foundation, and the rest to another foundation, Kontakt, which helped Nazi victims in Eastern Europe not covered by the German government fund for former slave laborers, and the Berlin-based Center for Victims of Terror.

Karl Brozik, who championed the rights of Holocaust survivors, died at the age of 78 on August 18. A survivor of Auschwitz, he led the Frankfurt office of the Conference for Jewish Material Claims Against Germany since 1987. His funeral in Frankfurt was attended by German Jewish leaders as well as representatives of the worlds of politics, social work, and the arts. Born in what is now the Czech Republic, Brozik was the only member of a family of 26 to survive the Holocaust. Over the years, Brozik's work helped make about $8.7 billion in restitution funds available to Holocaust survivors and institutions that support them around the world. He received the Wilhelm Leuschner Medal of the State of Hessen in 1997, and the Medal for Resistance Against Fascism from the Czech Republic in 1999. The city of Frankfurt honored him with a plaque in 2002.

TOBY AXELROD

Austria

National Affiliation

National Affairs

AUSTRIAN PRESIDENT Thomas Klestil died on July 6, two days before his the end of his term, at the age of 71. One of his chief accomplishments was helping Austria shed the taint of its Nazi past by acknowledging it honestly on numerous occasions. In a state visit to Israel early in his presidency, he expressed sympathy for the victims of the Holocaust and noted, with sadness, the role that many Austrians played in carrying it out. President Klestil appeared in his official capacity at numerous commemorative ceremonies for Austrian Holocaust victims and at Jewish religious and cultural events, the last one being an address at the Theodor Herzl Symposium on June 14 (see below, p. 445). Critics occasionally complained that Klestil overstepped the ceremonial bounds of his office, as when he unsuccessfully opposed the decision of his own conservative People's Party (ÖVP) to form a coalition with the far-right Freedom Party (FPÖ) in 2000. Front-page photos of a stone-faced Klestil swearing in members of the Freedom Party to government posts spoke volumes about his opposition to letting those linked to anti-foreigner and past anti-Jewish sentiments into the government.

Klestil's successor was Heinz Fischer, 65, of the opposition Social Democrats, who was elected in April, defeating Foreign Minister Benita Ferrero-Waldner of the ruling People's Party by 52.4 to 47.6 percent. Fischer, Austria's first head of state from a leftist party in 31 years, won on a platform of defending the welfare state and Austria's neutrality (Austria was one of four neutral EU nations, along with Finland, Ireland, and Sweden). Following his election, the new president announced he had suspended his membership in the Social Democratic Party so that he could be seen as representing all Austrians. His acceptance speech was interrupted by applause when he described how happy he was that his 95-year-old father-in-law, who survived a Nazi concentration camp, was at the ceremony.

Most political analysts felt that the presidential contest would have little impact on national parliamentary elections, due by 2006, or on the current balance of power between the center-right ÖVP-FPÖ coalition

442

headed by Chancellor Wolfgang Schüssel, and the opposition, made up of Social Democrats and Greens. The governing coalition continued in office despite threats from the FPÖ to resign if Chancellor Schüssel supported EU entry talks with Turkey. Even the already completed enlargement of the EU, which accepted ten new countries in April, caused unease among Austrians, many of whom feared a loss of jobs to cheap labor pouring in from the neighboring Czech Republic, Slovakia, and Hungary. On the traditional May 1 holiday, an estimated 100,000 people marched through the streets of Vienna in protest against the government, charging that it had done little to protect Austrian workers in the enlarged Europe.

After suffering a string of electoral defeats since 2000, the far-right Freedom Party scored a surprise victory in March in the Carinthia provincial elections, receiving 42.5 percent of the vote, slightly up from the 42.0 percent it won in 1999, insuring that Jörg Haider, the former leader of the FPÖ and still its best known figure, would remain governor of the province. But few expected a return to Haider's heyday of 2000, when he stunned Europe by taking his anti-immigration party into the national government (see AJYB 2001, pp. 397–98).

Analysts were quick to point out that the Carinthia vote did not portend a national trend, as that same day, in the regional election in Salzburg, the Freedom Party vote fell by more than half, to 8.7 percent. In elections for the European Parliament in June, the party lost over 17 percentage points from its previous showing, taking just 6.3 percent of the vote. The party confirmed its dramatic slide in popularity in September, when, in the small alpine province of Voralberg's election, the FPÖ lost more than half its support, declining from 27.5 percent in 1999 to 13 percent. In contrast, the front-running People's Party gained 11 percent, and the Social Democrats and Greens about 4 percent each. By year's end, Haider's home turf, Carinthia, was the only one of the nine Austrian provinces where the FPÖ had not suffered a sharp defeat in regional elections since 2000.

Israel and the Middle East

Israel had withdrawn its ambassador from Vienna when the Freedom Party entered the coalition government in 2000, and only in July 2003 did it announce that it was prepared to normalize relations, even though the party was still in the coalition. On February 5, 2004, Ambassador

Avraham Toledo, previously the Israeli chargé d'affaires, presented his ambassadorial credentials to President Klestil. Austria had kept its ambassador in Tel Aviv the entire time. In December, Ambassador Toledo completed his tour of duty and returned to Israel. A new ambassador had not yet been named.

Austria continued to cast its vote in the UN together with the bulk of the EU countries, generally against Israel and in favor of the Palestinians. Thus on July 20, Austria was part of the large General Assembly majority that supported a resolution calling on Israel to dismantle its West Bank security barrier, in conformity with the decision by the International Court of Justice.

Even so, bilateral relations between Israel and Austria received a boost with the visit in October of Israeli president Moshe Katzav, the first time an Israeli head of state had set foot in the country. During his four days in Vienna, Katzav held talks with President Fischer, Chancellor Schüssel, and the new foreign minister, Ursula Plassnik, who had been sworn in only a few hours before the meeting. Katzav's message was that Israel preferred to look to the future rather than dwell on past tensions between the two countries. Fischer characterized the Israeli president's visit as "very, very significant," and Ariel Musicant, head of the Israelitische Kultusgemeinde (IKG), Austrian Jewry's communal organization, said it was a "step towards normalcy" in Israeli-Austrian relations. Katzav ended his stay in Austria by laying a wreath at a memorial for the country's Holocaust victims.

There was also an exchange of visits between the respective presidents of the two countries' parliaments. Reuven Rivlin, president of the Knesset, arrived in Austria in September. Characterizing his visit as a "gesture of friendship," he called Austria an "honest broker" in Israel's relationship with the European Union, and spoke positively of Austria's dealing with its dark Nazi past. In a meeting with Austrian parliamentarians, Rivlin discussed his country's policy toward the Palestinians and defended the West Bank security barrier as a justifiable means of protecting Israeli citizens from terrorist attacks. The president of Austria's parliament, Andreas Khol, came to Israel in December, and met with government and political leaders. While in Tel Aviv, he spoke with a group of Israelis of Austrian origin about programs to provide compensation to victims of National Socialism.

The 100th anniversary of the death of Theodor Herzl—both the founder of modern Zionism and a notable Viennese cultural figure—provided occasion for interaction between Austrians and Israelis. In the first diplomatic exchange to follow the reestablishment of Austrian-Israeli relations, Austria's interior minister, Ernst Strasser, represented his country at an international conference on Herzl and Zionism held in Jerusalem in June. Strasser told the participants that he fully understood Austrian Jewish survivors of the Holocaust who had made new lives for themselves in Israel, but also had great respect for those who chose to return to Austria. Strasser held consultations with Israeli experts on the subject of international terrorism and visited the Yad Vashem Holocaust Memorial in Jerusalem, which cooperated closely with Austria's Holocaust Memorial in Mauthausen, the site of Austria's notorious death camp. Strasser, whose office was responsible for that memorial, announced an "intensification" of exchanges between the two institutions.

On June 14, Vienna hosted the Theodor Herzl Symposium at its city hall. President Klestil delivered the opening address, praising Herzl's vision that led to the establishment of the Jewish state, pointing out the contributions Jews had made to Austrian culture, and warning of a new form of anti-Semitism endangering Europe. This was the fifth and last Herzl Symposium, a series that began in 1986 to mark the centenary of the publication of his landmark *Der Judenstaat* (The Jewish State), with successive symposia dedicated to the centenaries of other milestones in Herzl's career.

In a festive ceremony on July 3, the actual date of Herzl's death, Vienna renamed a city square Theodor Herzl Platz. Addressing the large crowd, Israeli ambassador Toledo said that the location was chosen, in part, because it was situated near the offices of the daily newspaper *Die Presse,* whose predecessor, *Die Neue Freie Presse,* had employed Herzl as a correspondent. The decision to rename the square after the Zionist leader was not without its detractors. About 20 Orthodox Jews protested at the dedication, chanting "Zionism is Atheism." Complaints also came from the Arab League, which urged the city to reconsider the move for the sake of continued "good relations" with the Arab world, and from a spokesperson for Vienna's Muslim population, which numbered about 120,000.

In another event marking the Herzl anniversary, the postal services of Austria, Hungary (where Herzl was born in 1860), and Israel issued a commemorative stamp. The stamp was identical in all three countries except for the denomination and country name. On the left side it depicted the head of Herzl with a full beard, and on the right was the title of his famous book in Hungarian, German, and Hebrew.

Holocaust-Related Matters

RESTITUTION

The Nationalfond, responsible for handling claims for restitution by Austrian survivors of the National Socialist era, announced that it would make an additional payment of 1,000 euros to each victim. In 2002, the fund was authorized to distribute $150 million dollars to be paid out as partial compensation for the loss of property of various kinds, setting a deadline for applications of June 2004. An estimated 20,000 claimants had each received $7,000 dollars, and the new 1,000-euro disbursement per person came from the 21-million-euro balance that remained in the fund. Hannah Lessing, secretary general of the Nationalfond, announced that the money would be distributed in 2005, in order of the age of the claimant.

In addition to payments to individuals, the Nationalfond provided financial support to medical, cultural, and social-service organizations catering to the needs of survivors. For example, it distributed money to the Amcha association in Israel, which provided psychological services to survivors suffering emotional problems, to Yad Vashem for archival purposes, to the U.S. Holocaust Memorial Museum for digitalizing archival material of the Austrian Jewish community, and to a Jewish social center in Buenos Aires, Argentina, for purchasing a computer and engaging the services of instructors to teach Austrian survivors how to use the Internet to contact relatives and friends in far-off countries.

Another major activity of the Nationalfond was related to the General Settlement Fund (GSF), established by the Austrian government under terms of an agreement signed in Washington, D.C., on January 17, 2001. Through voluntary payments from the GSF, Austria acknowledged its moral responsibility for losses and damages inflicted upon Jewish citizens and other victims of National Socialism. Monies for the fund were to come from the Republic of Austria and Austrian companies, which had pledged $210 million. Persons or associations persecuted by the Nazi regime or forced to leave the country to escape such persecution, and who/which suffered property losses or damages, were eligible to apply. By the filing deadline of May 28, 2003, 19,100 claims had been submitted (see AJYB 2004, pp. 399–400). A condition of the agreement setting up the GSF was that no money would be paid out until all class-action suits against Austria and/or Austrian companies relating to the Holocaust were dismissed. At year's end, two such suits were still pending in U.S. federal courts, in New York and Los Angeles. Even when they were settled or dismissed, the fund could not make any payments until all claims were processed. In anticipation, the Nationalfond enlarged its administrative staff so as to complete the research on the claims already submitted.

The Holocaust Victims' Information and Support Center (HVISC, or Anlaufstelle), established by the IKG in July 1999, continued its work of promoting and protecting the interests of Jewish Holocaust victims and their heirs in and from Austria. In seeking to identify and quantify real-estate assets owned by the Jewish community before 1938, the Anlauf-stelle had a team of historians conducting research in January 2004 into 2,722 properties now owned by the Austrian government, and, in December, into 1,964 properties in the hands of the city of Vienna. Both investigations turned up flaws in the initial restitution process. In the first group, there were 15 cases of "extreme injustice," and in the second, 33. Meantime, the deadline for filing claims, extended to December 31, 2004, could possibly be pushed back even further. As part of its work, the Anlaufstelle prepared applications on behalf of these heirs for submission to the GSF.

The HVISC was also preparing a detailed report, to be released in 2005, on the properties owned by the 34 prewar Jewish communities of Austria, along with those that had belonged to Jewish associations and foundations. The successor organizations of these bodies were now in Vienna, Linz, Innsbruck, and Graz. Once this work was completed, the IKG would use the report as the basis for seeking compensation. Another activity of the HVISC was reconstructing and reorganizing the archives of the Vienna Jewish community to have them available on line by 2005. Once inventoried, this mass of documentation will be microfilmed by the U.S. Holocaust Memorial Museum and the Genealogical Society of Utah.

The Versohnungsfund (Reconciliation Fund) continued to make payments to former slave and forced laborers. Drawing on contributions from the Austrian government and Austrian businesses, the fund disbursed 350 million euros to more than 130,000 people since beginning operation in 2001. In 2004, the fund paid out 50 million euros to approximately 17,000 applicants. Payments ranged from 1,500 to 7,600 euros, with those forced to labor in factories receiving 2,500 euros. The fund was slated to wind up its work by the end of 2005.

Representatives of the Anlaufstelle sat on two governmental bodies dealing with the restitution of looted artwork, the Austrian Commission for the Investigation of the Provenance of Art Objects, and the Viennese Restitution Commission. The Anlaufstelle assisted both bodies in formulating criteria for research and restitution. In that capacity it located and arranged the return of an Egon Schiele painting that was hanging in the Austrian Gallery to the estate of Heinrich Rigger, as well as six paintings from the former collection of Gottlieb and Mathilde Kraus that were in the possession of the Austrian Gallery, the Albertina, and the Joanneum Museum in Graz.

The U.S. Supreme Court ruled in 2004 that Austria and its national museum could be sued by an 88-year-old Los Angeles woman seeking to recover six paintings that belonged to her family before the Nazi takeover of Austria. By a 6-to-3 vote, the court upheld an appeals court ruling in 2002 that rejected a request by Austria and its government-run museum to dismiss the case. The original suit had been filed in federal court by Maria Altmann, alleging the theft of six Gustave Klimt paintings from her uncle, Ferdinand Bloch. Valued at $135 million, the paintings had been housed in the Austrian Gallery. In a unanimous ruling, the appeals court held that if Altmann's allegation of wrongful taking were proven, the paintings were indeed appropriated in violation of international law, and she therefore could sue the Austrian government in U.S. courts (see AJYB 2004, pp. 401–02). The issue before the Supreme Court was jurisdictional—whether the Foreign Sovereign Immunities Act, adopted in 1976 to open the federal courts to specific categories of cases against foreign governments, applied to cases that predated the law's enactment. Speaking for the majority, Justice John Paul Stevens answered that question in the affirmative.

Lawyer Edward Fagan, on behalf of the Association of Holocaust Victims for Restitution of Artwork and Masterpieces, filed an $18-billion lawsuit in July against the Austrian government, alleging the country profited from, or wrongly kept, artworks stolen by the Nazis. The suit was filed in New York federal district court. Fagan, best known for landing a $1.25-billion settlement in 1998 from Swiss banks on behalf of Holocaust victims, filed an identical suit against Germany the previous month.

REMEMBRANCE

President Fischer, in October, unveiled a plaque at an army barracks in the town of Enns honoring Robert Bernardis, the highest ranking Austrian officer executed by the Nazis for involvement in the unsuccessful plot to kill Adolf Hitler on July 20, 1944. His family had been punished as well: his wife and mother were sent to concentration camps, and his two children to "reeducation" camps. At the ceremony—attended by Bernardis' 95-year-old widow—Fischer said the honor came "late, but not too late."

The president was alluding to the great reluctance of conservative military officers to commemorate the heroism of Bernardis and the anti-Nazi resistance, which they viewed as treason against the state, a view that was shared by many older Austrians. Not only did their opposition delay creation of the memorial for 60 years, but it also induced Defense Minister Günther Platter to reject suggestions by Austrian political figures to rename an actual barracks after Bernardis, and to dedicate just the plaque.

Even so, the marked change that had occurred over the years in Austrian public opinion about the Nazi era became evident when a spokesman of the far-right Freedom Party used the occasion to praise Bernardis. A Green Party representative urged the government to go even further and rehabilitate the reputations of the "simple soldiers" who had been court-martialed and executed for refusing to obey orders in Hitler's army, and who still were considered criminals under Austrian law.

Vienna's head of municipal planning, Rudolf Schicker, announced plans, in cooperation with the IKG, to erect a memorial to the 65,000 Austrian Jews deported by the Nazi regime. It would be built on part of the grounds of the former Aspang railway station in the Landstrasse, presently a huge abandoned area. The first step in the process was an international architectural competition to take place in 2005. Elsewhere on the grounds a school would be built dedicated to the memory of Aron Menczer, an important Zionist educator. In September 1942, Menczer was deported to the Theresienstadt ghetto, where he continued his educational work. A year later, in October 1943, he accompanied a group of children to Auschwitz, where he met his death. Also planned on another part of the site was a residential project called "Eurogate" that would house 13,000 people and have at its entrance a memorial commemorating the 40,000 Jews who were deported from the Aspang station. The original railroad tracks were to be integrated into the memorial.

The National Library staged an exhibition of books, manuscripts, and photos that were looted from Jews between 1938 and 1945. The library was then headed by a high-ranking Nazi, Paul Heigl, who, along with members of his staff, ordered the ransacking of Jewish books and manuscript collections in Germany and the occupied countries. In recent years researchers had been working to identify looted books and manuscripts and determine their provenance and, following approval by the Ministry of Education, then seek the assistance of the IKG and the Nationalfond in tracing the owners or heirs. The library published a volume of articles, *Looted Books: The Austrian National Library Confronts its National Socialist Past.*

Two Austrian historians writing in the German weekly *Der Spiegel* in October reported that SS chief Heinrich Himmler gave orders in the fall of 1944, when German troops were retreating before the Russian army, to dismantle the gas chambers and crematoria at Auschwitz so as to erase evidence of Nazi crimes, and send some of the equipment to the Mauthausen concentration camp, in Austria, for reuse. The historians, Bertrand Perz and Florian Freund, found a letter, dated February 10, 1945, to Mauthausen officials from J.A. Topf and Sons, a German company that made many of the incinerators for the Nazi death camps, that talked about sharply expanding the Austrian camp's gas chamber on the assumption that "all the parts of the Auschwitz Concentration Camp be used again." Accounts by Mauthausen survivors indicated that some equipment from the Auschwitz camp did arrive, but there was not enough time to redeploy the gas chambers at Mauthausen before Germany surrendered.

JEWISH COMMUNITY

Demography

The number of Jews registered with the IKG stood at 6,890, an increase of 98 from 2003. The rise was attributed not to an actual growth in numbers—immigration was virtually frozen—but rather the registration of people who had not previously affiliated. Knowledgeable observers placed the actual number of Jews in the country, as defined by Jewish law, at about 12,000. As had been true for generations, the overwhelming majority lived in Vienna. Only 300–400 made their homes elsewhere, primarily in the large provincial cities of Graz, Salzburg, Innsbruck, and Linz.

An estimated 40 percent of the Vienna Jewish community was now Sephardi, as was a majority of the Jewish population under age 25. This was believed to reflect their relatively large families. To address this demographic reality, a second Sephardi center was opened during 2004 in Vienna's 20th district.

Communal Affairs

The IKG, the community's official organization, completed a much-needed revision of its statutes, which were first promulgated in 1890. The new rules would go into effect following approval by the government. While the IKG's financial situation had stabilized, the various programs it conducted continued to suffer from a budgetary shortfall due, according to its president, Ariel Muzicant, to the failure of the federal government to provide money to which the IKG was entitled. Upon the conclusion of the Washington agreement of January 2001 dealing with Holocaust compensation, he had demanded a separate agreement with the Austrian government to help underwrite IKG expenses (see AJYB 2003, p. 501). Muzicant refused to take money from the GSF, since those funds were earmarked for victims of the National Socialist regime.

The government responded in 2003 by offering the community interim financial aid in the form of interest-free loans amounting to 772,000 euros annually for 2003, 2004, and 2005, which the IKG accepted. The government had already made good on the first and second of the annual payments, and supplemental subsidies in the amount of 200,000 euros were paid out to the IKG to cover the rising cost of its social programs. In addition, the Austrian provinces paid half the 18 million euros they had pledged to the Federation of Jewish Communities of Austria under an agreement signed in May 2002. The balance would not be forthcoming until the class-action suits against Austria and Austrian companies were withdrawn or settled.

Approximately 100 leading Orthodox rabbis from Europe, the U.S., and Israel met in Vienna in February to discuss means of stimulating a revival of Judaism in Eastern Europe, where Jewish life had been seriously diminished by the devastation of World War II and the Holocaust, and then repressed over more than four decades of communist rule. Participants in the three-day conference, sponsored by the Brussels-based Rabbinical Center of Europe (RCE), were welcomed by President Klestil, who asserted "that Jews from all parts of the world are welcomed in Austria." Klestil paid special tribute to the role Jews had played in the intellectual, cultural, and scientific life of Austria, and said that Austrians must not forget "that our country also took part in unforgettable crimes directed at the Jewish people."

The rabbinic conference made a symbolic gesture of reconciliation with the European Union, presenting European Commission (EC) president Romano Prodi an award for humanitarian achievement. It came as

Prodi and Jewish leaders sought to patch up differences following recent disputes. One involved an EU-commissioned survey in 2003 that listed Israel at the top of the list of nations seen by Europeans as threats to world peace, which several Jewish groups condemned as methodologically flawed and inflammatory. Another was the charge that the EC, the executive body of the EU, had sought to bury evidence that Arab and Muslim minorities were disproportionately involved in anti-Semitic attacks against Jews and Jewish institutions in Europe.

At the conference came the announcement of the pending inauguration of the first Jewish teachers academy in Vienna since World War II. The prewar school was burned down in 1938 on Kristallnacht, when synagogues and Jewish-owned businesses were destroyed throughout Germany and Austria. The new institution, financed by the Austrian government and the Ronald S. Lauder Foundation, would send its graduates to the former communist countries to help rebuild Jewish life there.

In February, Austria's state secretary for the arts, Franz Morak, presided over the opening of Or Chadash, the new synagogue of Vienna's liberal Jewish community, in Leopoldstadt, in the city's second district. The city of Vienna contributed 125,000 euros to meet the costs of design and construction.

The projected Wiesenthal Institute for Holocaust Studies (see AJYB 2003, p. 507) had still not opened, as its supporters had not yet raised the requisite funds. Meantime, a board of directors was appointed and a search was underway for a chairman. Once established, the institute would be endowed with the combined resources of the IKG's communal archives, the archives of the Austrian anti-Nazi resistance, and the Wiesenthal Documentation Center.

The Lauder Business School-Vienna International College, which opened in October 2003, completed its first year in 2004. The school offered a four-year program in international marketing and management, leading to a master's degree. Students came from many different countries, and although the business courses were taught in English, there was also instruction in German, Russian, and Hebrew, and a program of Jewish studies was also available. The college maintained a kosher dining facility for students and faculty, and no classes were held on Saturdays or Jewish holidays. The city of Vienna donated the four buildings that housed the school, and the Lauder Foundation financed the renovation of the facility. As a publicly accredited educational institution, it qualified for funding from the federal government.

The Lauder Chabad Campus, which opened its doors in September

2000, had an enrolment of 400 students in classes ranging from kindergarten through elementary and high school. The high school's first 14
graduates received their diplomas in June 2004.

Among the exhibits mounted by the Vienna Jewish Museum was one
on the musical works of Hans Gal and Egon Wellesz, two prominent Jewish composers who made a mark in Vienna's musical world during the interwar period. Both men fled in 1938 to Great Britain, and neither
returned after the war, although Gal turned down an attractive offer. The
exhibit, which ran from February 25 to May 2, featured musical scores,
scripts, personal documents, and photographs.

The museum also had an exhibit titled "Children — Kinder — Kinder-
lach," of photographs of Jewish children taken by Roy Mittelman. It ran
from June 9 to September 12. For more than 20 years, Mittelman had
taken photographs of Jewish children in Buenos Aires, Casablanca,
Tallinn, Budapest, and other locations he had visited on behalf of humanitarian organizations. Silently and unobtrusively, he observed them
learning, praying, playing, or napping. "A photographer," Mittelman explained, "has to be a good listener, he has to listen with his eyes."

Another exhibition presented by the museum was "The Liebens — 150-
Year History of a Viennese Family," which ran from November 11 to
April 3, 2005. The Liebens were a prominent Viennese Jewish bourgeois
family that included merchants, bankers, grand dames, scientists, inven-
tors, and artists who left their mark on the life of the city. Ignaz L. Lieben
was appointed professor of chemistry at the University of Vienna, and
from 1863 to 1937 the prize given in his name was considered one of the
most prestigious awards in Austrian science. Ignaz's grandson, Robert von
Lieben, was a pioneer in the early development of the radio. Marie-
Louise von Motesiczky, a great-granddaughter of Ignaz L. Lieben, distinguished herself as a painter. The family's storied progress came to an
abrupt end with the annexation of Austria by Nazi Germany in March
1938, leading to persecution, flight, and exile even for those members of
the family who had long been baptized. The Lieben Prize was restored in
2004 through the generous support of the American chemist and entrepreneur Alfred Bader, who was also driven out of Austria in 1938.

Personalia

Great Britain awarded an honorary knighthood to Nazi-hunter Simon
Wiesenthal in recognition of a "lifetime of service to humanity." Wiesenthal, 95, survived imprisonment in German concentration camps during

World War II, and since then dedicated his life to bringing Nazi war criminals to justice. The knighthood also recognized the work done by the Los Angeles-based Simon Wiesenthal Center, founded in 1977 to promote Holocaust remembrance and the defense of human rights.

Franz Cardinal König, who served as archbishop of Vienna from 1956 until his retirement in 1985, died in March at the age of 98. He was a skilled diplomat who helped break down barriers between the Catholic Church and Eastern European governments during the Cold War, and was instrumental in bringing about the nomination of Cardinal Karol Wojtila, who was to become John Paul II. During the Second Vatican Council of 1962–65, Cardinal König was at the forefront of those who pushed for improved ties with Jews and Eastern Orthodox Christians.

MURRAY GORDON SILBERMAN

East-Central Europe and the Balkans

Throughout the region, countries had to deal with struggling economies, endemic corruption, political bickering, and organized crime. Most governments remained allies of the United States, although some reevaluated their involvement in Iraq.

On May 1, less than 15 years after the fall of the Iron Curtain, the former communist states of Poland, Hungary, the Czech Republic, Slovakia, Slovenia, Lithuania, Latvia, and Estonia become full-fledged members of the European Union, along with the island nations of Cyprus and Malta. Little more than a month earlier, at the end of March, Bulgaria, Romania, Slovakia, Lithuania, Slovenia, Estonia, and Latvia entered NATO.

Altogether, fewer than 150,000 Jews lived in the ten new EU states. Like their non-Jewish fellow citizens, Jews in these countries had to adjust to new political and economic realities and therefore viewed EU enlargement with emotions ranging from eagerness to anxiety. Many hoped to take advantage of enhanced business, educational, and other opportunities, and others believed that enlargement might facilitate contact among Jewish communities. But some Jews feared the prospect of inflation and other negative economic consequences. And there were those who worried that "new" forms of anti-Semitism couched in anti-Zionism might find their way from Western Europe into countries that, until now, had maintained policies supportive of Israel.

Albania

In May, *Archaeology* magazine reported that the ruins of an ancient synagogue had been unearthed in Albania by a joint team of Albanian and Israeli archaeologists. Dating from the fifth or sixth century CE, the synagogue was located in the coastal town of Saranda. The ruins included mosaic pavements depicting, among other images, a menorah, a citron tree, and a ram's horn, as well as a structure that may be an ark.

In September, the Albanian parliament adopted a law establishing a Holocaust Memorial Day. Official promulgation of the law took place in the capital, Tirana, in November.

Bosnia and Herzegovina

Bosnia and Herzegovina continued to recover slowly from the war that ended in 1995. By September, according to the UN, a million refugees had returned to the country. A major symbolic milestone was the completed restoration of the historic Old Bridge in Mostar, which had been destroyed by Bosnian Croat fire in 1993. Britain's Prince Charles, leaders from other Balkan states, the French and Italian foreign ministers, and European Union external affairs commissioner Chris Patten attended a gala rededication ceremony in July.

Still, the jobless rate was over 40 percent, salaries were low, and thousands of foreign soldiers remained stationed in the country to keep the peace. There were reports of radicalization among some segments of the local Muslim population, particularly elements linked to two Saudi-financed mosques. In October, Bosnia's Regional Museum in Sarajevo—which has a special room devoted to the historic Sarajevo Haggadah—had to close its doors to the public because of lack of funds to pay for salaries and winter heating.

In April, Sarajevo hosted a Balkan summit of leaders from Albania, Bosnia, Bulgaria, Croatia, Greece, Macedonia, Romania, Serbia and Montenegro, and Turkey. The participants, who included heads of state and of government, issued a declaration calling for increased regional cooperation.

Fewer than 1,000 Jews lived in Bosnia and Herzegovina. About 700 lived in Sarajevo, of whom 180 were Holocaust survivors. There were also a few very small provincial communities such as Banja Luka (about 70 members), Doboj and Mostar (about 40 each), Zenica, and Tuzla. Bosnia had no resident rabbi, but Sarajevo-born Eliezar Papo, director of the Center for Sephardic Studies at Ben Gurion University in Israel, came twice a year to officiate, on the High Holy Days and Passover.

High Holy Day services this year had special significance. On the eve of Rosh Hashanah, Sarajevo's sixteenth-century Old Synagogue, which had been turned into a Jewish museum after World War II, was reconsecrated as a house of worship, and services were held there for the first time in more than 60 years. During the Bosnian War, the museum had been closed to visitors and the space used as a storage place for collections from other museums in the city. In the summer of 2004, the museum in the synagogue reopened under new management that included representatives of the Jewish community as well as city officials.

There were plans to update and convert the Old Synagogue and its museum into a facility that would serve as a cultural and educational center, with a new museum section detailing the operation of the Jewish community during the recent war, when the community's social welfare organization, La Benevolencija, acted as a key conduit for nonsectarian humanitarian aid. For the time being, most Jewish communal activities in Sarajevo took place in the 100-year-old Ashkenazic synagogue complex, which, after the war, was converted to include offices and function rooms as well as a sanctuary.

There were Jewish-themed cultural and educational events during the year. In November, the King David Theater, a young-persons' drama group from Belgrade, presented a play in Ladino by Laura Bohoreta Papo. Bohoreta, who died before World War II, was regarded as Sarajevo's premiere female playwright in the Ladino dialect. This performance, Sarajevo's first in Ladino in about 70 years, was funded by the American Jewish Joint Distribution Committee (JDC).

Also aided by the JDC and other international bodies, La Benevolencija continued to oversee programs that helped needy Bosnians, Jews and non-Jews alike. It distributed items ranging from used clothing to toiletries to reading glasses. A home-care program provided assistance to 670 elderly Serbs, Croats, Muslims, and Jews in Sarajevo and five provincial cities. There was also a countrywide breast cancer support and awareness initiative, and a training program to help local people set up small businesses. The World Bank helped support a "micro" credit institution to provide small loans to new enterprises.

A key source of funds for a number of projects was Dr. Alfred Bader, a successful chemist and art collector and dealer based in Milwaukee, who disbursed funds through the JDC for targeted programs that were overseen by local Jewish communities. Several of these helped disabled people in Sarajevo, Mostar, and Banja Luka (also see "Czech Republic," below).

Throughout the year, Jewish community leader Jacob Finci continued to press for the establishment of a "Truth and Reconciliation Commission," modeled on that of South Africa, to investigate the causes of the Bosnian war.

Bulgaria

Although Bulgaria remained the poorest EU candidate state, a jump in tourism improved its economic performance somewhat: GDP grew by 5.7 percent in the first nine months of the year as compared to 4.2 percent in 2003. Despite the growth, average monthly wages remained around $150 and gross domestic product per person was less than a third of EU levels. Annual inflation for 2004 was 4 percent. The country was plagued by rampant corruption and organized crime, which EU officials said could slow its accession, which was scheduled for 2007. A poll showed that 96 percent of Bulgarians believed their country was corrupt. Gangland-style killings and other bloody street violence sparked protests against the government of Prime Minister Simeon Saxe-Coburg, whose approval rating late in the year plummeted to 10 percent, according to opinion polls.

Bulgaria remained a firm ally of the U.S. in Iraq. In May, Foreign Minister Solomon Passy said that Bulgaria would maintain its 500 troops in Iraq despite threats from Osama bin Laden against coalition forces. In November, a court in Pazardzhik convicted a radical Muslim prayer leader, Ahmed Moussa Ahmed, an ethnic Roma, of inciting religious intolerance and ethnic hatred and trying to convert the country into an Islamic state. He was fined and given a three-year suspended sentence.

This year, Bulgaria chaired the 55-member Organization of Security and Cooperation in Europe (OSCE). In April, Foreign Minister Passy chaired a high-level international meeting on combating anti-Semitism that was sponsored by the OSCE and held in Berlin. There, he helped forge a "Berlin Declaration," adopted unanimously by the OSCE governments, that pledged to fight "new forms" of anti-Semitism and rejected any use of the Middle East conflict to justify hate crimes against Jews. In a brief ceremony at the end of the conference, Passy presented the yellow star his grandfather had worn as a Jew in Bulgaria during the Holocaust to German foreign minister Joschka Fischer.

A major issue throughout the year was the case of five Bulgarian nurses and a Bulgarian doctor who were placed on trial in Libya on the charge of intentionally infecting more than 400 children with the AIDS virus as part of an experiment to find a cure. In May, a Libyan court sentenced the nurses and a Palestinian doctor to death on the charges, and jailed the Bulgarian doctor for changing money on the black market.

About 5,000 Jews were officially registered as living in Bulgaria, although Jewish communal officials estimated that the actual number of Jews could be as many as 8,000. At least half of the Jews lived in the capital of Sofia, nearly 1,500 in Plovdiv, and nearly 500 in Varna.

Supported in part by the JDC, Sofia boasted a full infrastructure for Jewish communal life, including a magnificent, recently restored synagogue; a Jewish community center, Beit Ha'am (which had a kosher restaurant); a Jewish newspaper; an extensive social welfare network (including an old-age home); social and educational programs for young people, seniors, and the middle generation; and many other activities. About 350 Jewish children made up nearly half the student body of a state-run school in Sofia that included Hebrew language and Jewish subjects in the curriculum and received support from the Lauder Foundation. The community ran cultural activities throughout the year and maintained a Jewish camp near Sofia that had both summer and winter activities.

Jewish communities around Bulgaria were linked through the Shalom organization, which had 19 branches and ran cultural, educational, and social programs, including Sunday schools in Sofia, Plovdiv, Burgas, Ruse, and Varna for about 300 children aged 6–16. Chabad ran a center in Sofia that had been in operation since 2001, as well as a Website, www.-chabad-bulgaria.org.

Bulgarian Jews maintained contacts with Jewish communities outside the country, including a partnership arrangement with the Jewish Federation of Greater Kansas City. Bulgarian Jews took part in international conferences, seminars, and other events. In May, a Bulgarian Jewish singing group entertained delegates to the General Assembly of the European Council of Jewish Communities in Budapest.

There were efforts to preserve the Ladino language, culture, and traditions. The Shalom organization in Sofia, for example, had a weekly Ladino club for mostly elderly Ladino speakers to teach the language to younger people. Archivists at the State Archives in Sofia received a grant from a British source to go through a rich trove of Ladino material long kept in boxes in the basement. Also, Bulgarian artists and experts took part in the Esperansa festival of Sephardic culture that was held in Belgrade (see below, p. 494).

In July, Germany agreed to compensate Jews who had been forced to work in Bulgarian labor camps during World War II. Jews placed in any of the 112 Bulgarian camps were now eligible for monthly pensions and a one-time compensation payment. The extent of forced Jewish labor in Bulgarian camps only came to light when previously classified documents were released after the fall of communism. Bulgaria had long prided itself on the fact that it did not permit its 50,000 Jews to be deported to Nazi death camps, although it did allow 14,000 Jews in Bulgarian-occupied Greece and Macedonia to be deported. According to research conducted by the Claims Conference, however, tens of thousands of Jews were forced to work in labor camps under conditions of "malnourishment, exploitation, and brutal labor." The work they were forced to do "consisted primarily of road and railway construction, often in difficult marshy locations, involving long workdays, heavy work norms, and exposure to extreme temperatures." The prisoners "faced frequent beatings by superiors, subsisted on an inadequate diet, and lacked the clothing or boots needed for working in the cold, rugged terrain."

Throughout the year, an America woman, Sally Hindman, sought to raise funds to restore the synagogue in the seaport city of Varna and to create a monument there to the more than 200 Jews who died when the ship *Salvador,* which left Varna for Palestine on December 4, 1940, sank in the Sea of Marmara off the Turkish coast. Varna was a main point of departure for European Jews fleeing Nazi persecution who sought to reach Palestine.

Croatia

In January, at a ceremony in Zagreb attended by President Stipe Mesic, six Croats were honored as Righteous Gentiles for saving Jews during the Holocaust. In March, moving away from the hard-line nationalist approach his party had held in the past, Prime Minister Ivo Sanader condemned crimes committed by the Nazi-allied Ustashe regime during World War II. He did this on his first official visit to the site of the Jasenovac concentration camp where, between 1941 and 1945, the Ustashe brutalized or killed tens of thousands of Jews, Serbs, Gypsies, and antifascist Croats. "Croatia's history had only too much suffering and Jasenovac was one of the worst. We have to speak up so that the Ustashe crimes are not forgotten," Sanader said. His HDZ party was founded by the late President Franjo Tudjman, whose government was often accused of whitewashing Ustashe crimes and reinstalling some symbols of their rule.

Croatia and Israel maintained close relations, and tens of thousands of Israeli tourists visited Croatia. In October, the Israeli foreign ministry announced it would send a full-time resident ambassador to Zagreb. The two countries established full diplomatic links only in 1998, after Tudjman apologized for comments considered anti-Semitic. Since then, Israel had been represented in Croatia by its ambassador in Vienna.

In June, Efraim Zuroff, director of the Simon Wiesenthal Center's Jerusalem office, launched Operation Last Chance, a public Nazi-hunting campaign, in Croatia (see also "Hungary," below). It offered a $10,000 reward to anyone who helped uncover, prosecute, and punish Nazis or Nazi collaborators still at large. It did not take long for Zuroff to receive death threats from Croatian extremists, and there were also threats against Croatian Jews. A letter signed "Anti-Jewish Movement" read: "[We] are looking for a sword which will cut off your head. Jew-boy Zuroff what you are asking for is what you will get. If a single Croat is arrested, detained or maltreated in any way because of your sick Jewish ideas, we warn you: We will start to kill your Jewish compatriots in Croatia! We know your names and addresses." The letter was marked with a "U" to indicate sympathy for the Ustashe. Copies were also sent to the justice minister, the head of the country's Helsinki committee, and Croatia's Civic Center for Human Rights. A Croatian Web site went so far as to offer a reward to anyone who would kill Zuroff and blow up the offices of the Civic Center.

But his campaign brought results. Zuroff said that within three weeks of launching the appeal, the Wiesenthal Center had been able to make a fully documented war-crimes case against 91-year-old Milivoj Asner, who was still living in Croatia. And Zuroff said that President Mesic had pledged to help bring Asner, who was a Croatian police chief during World War II, to justice.

At the end of August, Sanader's government ordered the removal of plaques put up to honor two Ustashe officials. One, set up in 2002 in the town of Slunj, honored military commander Jure Francetic. The other, erected earlier in August on a wall surrounding a church in the town of Lovinac by a group funded by nationalist emigrés, honored the writer Mile Budak. He served as religion and education minister in the Ustashe government and signed the racist laws that led to the murder of Jews, Roma, and Serbs. Budak was executed in 1945 as a war criminal. The government said the plaques went "against Croatia's constitution and [harmed] Croatia's reputation and interests." The cabinet also requested the Justice Ministry to draft amendments to the penal code that would ban the promotion of all totalitarian ideologies, including communism and fascism.

According to the left-wing newspaper *Novi list,* 17 towns and villages in Croatia had streets named after Budak. This continuing positive evaluation of his career was further reinforced in August, at the very time that the government was removing the plaque honoring his name, when some 120 Croatian intellectuals signed a petition to reopen the 1945 case against Budak on the grounds that the proceedings had amounted to a communist show trial and did not meet standards of justice.

About 2,000 Jews lived in Croatia, most of them in Zagreb, which had a Jewish community center and prayer room, under the leadership of

Rabbi Kotel Dadon. The Zagreb community, almost self-sufficient financially, received some aid from the JDC to operate an old-age home accommodating up to 80 residents, including elderly Jews who fled Bosnia during the war there. In the summer, also with JDC help, the Jewish community reinstituted, for the first time since the disintegration of the former Yugoslavia, a children's camp along the Dalmation coast that brought together some 60 youngsters for two weeks of activities. During the year, the community worked on plans for a new complex of buildings to house its activities, on the site of the Main Synagogue, torn down by the Nazis. The principal smaller Jewish communities in the country were those of Split, Dubrovnik, and Osijek.

There were a number of Jewish cultural and educational initiatives throughout the year. The community's Israeli dance troupe performed regularly at Jewish functions and also for the general public. In January, an exhibition of photographs taken secretly by a German soldier in the Warsaw Ghetto in 1941 took place in Zagreb at the Jewish community center. President Mesic, Prime Minister Sanader, and the German ambassador to Croatia attended the opening. In August, the fifth biennial Conference on the Social and Cultural History of the Jews on the Eastern Adriatic Coast took place in Dubrovnik, sponsored by the University of Zagreb's Center for Advanced Academic Studies. On Sukkot, the Croatian Jewish community hosted the annual Beyahad Jewish culture week, a gathering of more than 200 Jews from all over the former Yugoslavia as well as foreign guests, held on the island of Hvar. As usual, the program included a mix of social events, lectures, performances, and exhibits.

Czech Republic

The Czech Republic, which joined the European Union on May 1, marked the 15th anniversary of its "velvet revolution" that ousted the communist regime in November. The economy was shaky as unemployment soared throughout the year, reaching a post-World-War-II record of 10.8 percent in January 2005. The average monthly wage was about $700—five times what it was in 1989—but consumer prices were about ten times higher. Prime Minister Vladimire Spidla resigned at the beginning of June, touching off a government crisis that was only resolved in late August when a new prime minister, Stanislav Gross, was approved by Parliament.

The country enjoyed excellent relations with Israel, and Jewish observers said that media coverage of the Middle East situation was generally balanced, if not pro-Israel. In February, the Evangelical Church of the Bohemian Brethren, the country's largest Protestant church body, issued a statement backing the construction of Israel's West Bank security barrier. It called Israel's move "in the interest of the protection of its citizens against the monstrous aggression of Palestinian terrorism," and declared, "Every appeal against the separating barrier should also be accompanied with the same appeal for the destruction of terrorist organizations in Palestinian territories and in Arab countries." In March, however, President Vaclav Klaus called Israel's assassination of Hamas leader Sheik Ahmed Yassin a "terrorist act." Speaking in Lisbon, Klaus and Portuguese president Jorge Sampaio declared that such acts should not be repeated.

There were many visits by Czech officials to Israel and other countries in the Middle East, and by representatives of those nations to the Czech Republic. By July, Czech diplomats had traveled to the region at least 15 times and had received more than a dozen high-level visitors, including Israel's foreign minister and deputy prime minister Silvan Shalom, King Abdullah II of Jordan, and Nabil Shaath, foreign minister of the Palestinian Authority. During Shalom's visit in June, his first to one of the new EU members since accession, he said the Czech Republic "could play a positive role in shaping Europe's approach toward the Arab-Israeli conflict." In December, Czech foreign minister Cyril Svoboda spent three days in Israel, where he met with Shalom and discussed bilateral relations as well as relations between the EU and Israel. Svoboda urged greater EU and NATO participation in the Middle East peace process.

The Czech Republic marked its first official Holocaust Memorial Day on January 27. As part of the observances, the Prague Jewish community and the Mauthausen International Committee, an organization of Mauthausen camp survivors based in Austria, sponsored a performance at the Prague State Opera of *The Song of Terezin* by American composer Franz Waxman, a German Jew who fled to the U.S. to escape the Shoah. Written in 1962, the piece was inspired by poems composed by children held in Terezin. In June, the Mauthausen Committee awarded medals to Prague Jewish community chairman Tomas Jelinek and Austrian lawmaker Maria Berger for their role in organizing the concert.

JEWISH COMMUNITY

About 3,000–4,000 Jews were known to live in the Czech Republic, although community leaders said the number was probably higher. About half the Jews lived in Prague. In addition, about 2,000 Israelis were believed to live in the Czech Republic. The first baby in at least 30 years underwent *brit milah* (ritual circumcision) at Prague's Jubilee synagogue in April; he was the son of the synagogue's Orthodox rabbi.

Prague's Jewish community, which controlled large real-estate holdings that had been returned by the state after 1989, was embroiled in bitter factional conflict throughout the year. Although mainly involving the lay leadership, it spilled over into the religious sphere as well. At the heart of the problem was an intense power struggle between supporters and opponents of Tomas Jelinek, an economic advisor to former president Vaclav Havel, who was elected to a second term as chairman of the Prague community in April. Jelinek took office promising to bring a new era of transparency and openness, and to reach out to non-Orthodox Jews. But the bruising electoral campaign exposed raw divisions in the community.

The victory of Jelinek's faction, Coalition for a Democratic Community, brought the ouster from the community board of two veteran Jewish leaders, Leo Pavlat, director of the Jewish Museum, and Jiri Danicek, editor of the community monthly, *Rosh Chodesh*. Jelinek said their responsibilities as heads of institutions run, or partly run, by the community represented a conflict of interest with their board membership.

In June, the leadership fired Rabbi Karol Sidon as chief rabbi of Prague. "Rabbi Sidon has not been able to do his job as a chief rabbi properly, and he failed in all important aspects of what his office is expected to do," Jelinek said. "There was criticism from the left and the right. He was running the rabbinate in such a way that it would never have religious authority." There had been specific complaints that Sidon was too Orthodox for a community whose members were largely secular, and that he did not reach out to non-Orthodox Jews.

While Sidon retained his post as chief rabbi of the Czech Republic, with the support of the Federation of Czech Jewish Communities, the Prague community appointed the local Chabad rabbi, Manis Barash, as rabbi of the historic Old-New Synagogue, the symbol of Prague Jewry that had been in continuous use for more than 700 years. Sidon accused Chabad of trying to take over the Prague community, a charge Barash denied. But the replacement of Sidon with Barash upset the small number of Czech Jews who regularly attended the Old-New Synagogue. Eventually, Sidon began conducting services for them in the High Synagogue, located directly across the street from the Old-New Synagogue. The latter, by the end of the year, was mainly attended by Israelis and tourists.

The conflict rocked the Jewish community and also spilled over into the mainstream media, which ran articles and commentaries about it. The case went before a rabbinical court in Israel, which ruled that the post of Prague chief rabbi should be left vacant and that Sidon should become "president" of the rabbis in Prague and in the Czech Republic. Meanwhile, more strife shook the community. Seventeen teachers at the Lauder Jewish school quit following the resignation of the school's principal under pressure from the Jelinek leadership. The principal's ouster, in turn, was related to a scandal in 2003, when pornography was found on the school's Internet server (see AJYB 2004, p. 419). Another controversy flared when Jelinek gave a public-relations firm community members' addresses and e-mail contacts without their knowledge or approval. (Jelinek said he had signed a data-protection agreement with the firm and that the information would be used only within the community.) Yet another point of contention was one of Jelinek's key projects, a proposed old-age home for Holocaust survivors. He accused the previous community leadership of neglecting the needs of Holocaust survivors and spending too much of the community's assets on "stone"—that is, on the Jewish Museum and the restoration of historic cemeteries, synagogues, and Jewish heritage sites.

During the summer, opponents of Jelinek—many of them members or allies of the old leadership—formed an opposition group that they called the Platform for a Community for All. It accused the Jelinek administration of "dictatorial methods" that were "unbefitting the leadership of any Jewish community," and pressed for its ouster. In November, at the end of a nine-hour community assembly that, according to witnesses, was marked by name-calling, shouting, and insults, 173 out of the 190 people present voted to remove Jelinek and his three deputy chairpersons from office. But Jelinek refused to accept the decision. (That same month, results of an audit of the community ordered by Jelinek were released. Conducted by the firm Ernst and Young, it found that poor property management may have cost the community millions of dollars over the years and that community rules were violated.)

At year's end it was still not clear who was in charge. A new community assembly in December confirmed the November vote to oust Jelinek, but all the 230 members who attended the meeting were supporters of the Platform for a Community for All. Meanwhile, the Jelinek leadership organized a mail-in ballot, and 404 out of the 500 people who responded voted to keep Jelinek in charge. Platform supporters called the mail-in vote invalid, and Jelinek supporters called the community assembly vote invalid. The Czech government, for its part, recognized the rival community chairman chosen by the Platform, Frantisek Banyai, and registered him as the legitimate communal leader. Jelinek supporters protested, and Jelinek himself refused to vacate his office in the Jewish Town Hall. On December 17, there was a scuffle when private security guards hired by Jelinek prevented Banyai from entering community headquarters. Petr Halva, head of the community's election oversight committee, charged Banyai supporters with breaking Jelinek's door and cutting some phone lines.

Despite the turmoil, there were numerous Jewish-themed cultural and educational events throughout the year. In January, an exhibit on 85 years of JDC activity in Czech and Slovak lands opened at Prague's National Library. At the end of April, Prague hosted an international conference titled "The Future of European Jewish Heritage," which drew scholars, museum directors, activists, and others from across Europe as well as the U.S. and Israel. A number of efforts were under way to restore or preserve sites of Jewish heritage. In Libochovice, about 40 miles from Prague, volunteers from Germany, Italy, France, and Estonia joined young local volunteers to clean up and restore the historic Jewish cemetery, which was devastated during and after World War II. The project, financed by the Czech-German Future Fund, also included workshops about Judaism and Jewish culture, as well as trips to Terezin and Prague. During the summer, a group of Israeli students made a detailed documentation of Jewish heritage in several towns.

In the fall, the Jewish Museum of Prague marked ten years since the government transferred ownership to the Jewish community. The museum had originally been founded in 1906. During World War II, the Nazis used it to store items looted from more than 150 destroyed Jewish communities in Bohemia and Moravia. After the war, it was nationalized and run by the communist state. Visited by more than half a million people a year, it was now one of the Czech Republic's most popular museums. As part of the anniversary celebrations, museum director Leo Pavlat announced that the institution would expand its operations outside of Prague to help preserve and promote Jewish heritage in provincial towns and cities. Beginning in 2006, he said, hundreds of thousands of dollars from museum profits would be channeled to ten Jewish communities, and they, in turn, would decide how best to use the funds. The museum also completed a $2.2-million renovation and reconstruction of the synagogue in Prague's Smichov district, for use as a central archive of surviving documents from Jewish communities in Bohemia and Moravia dating back to the fifteenth century. In April, a book produced by the museum about synagogue textiles won an award from the Ministry for Culture.

In July, the town of Holesov hosted a six-day Jewish culture festival focusing on Jewish mysticism. Among those attending the festival were young people from South Korea, the U.S., Canada, Poland, Belgium, France, and other countries who had volunteered to clean up the Holesov Jewish cemetery. Another Jewish cultural festival during the summer took place in Trebic. In August, "Israel Uncensored," an exhibit of polemical posters created by Israeli designers and students, formed part of an exhibition mounted in the former barracks at Terezin to commemorate the anniversary of the 1968 Soviet-led invasion of Czechoslovakia. In November, a collection of rare Hebrew manuscripts and medieval texts known as the Saraval Legacy was exhibited at Prague's National Library.

There were also numerous educational programs on Judaism, Jewish culture, Jewish history, and the Holocaust. In November, some 60 teachers had to be turned away from "How to Teach the Holocaust," a Holocaust education program at Terezin, because there was no room for many of the applicants. The program, for elementary and high-school teachers, was initiated in 2000.

Still, anti-Semitic sentiments existed in the Czech Republic, and Jewish sources in Prague believed that the ugly turmoil in the Jewish community, widely reported in the local media, could only strengthen them.

To be sure, the government was responsive to Jewish concerns. In January, Michal Zitko, who published a Czech translation of Hitler's *Mein Kampf,* received a three-year suspended sentence on charges of promoting Nazism. In April, skinhead leader Jaroslav Broz was convicted of organizing the distribution of Nazi propaganda and songs with lyrics that incited hatred; he was sentenced to five years in jail, and four codefendants were put on probation for three years. Also in April, Jewish leaders protested the publication of *Bolshevism from Moses to Lenin,* a Czech translation of dialogues between Adolf Hitler and Dietrich Eckhart, editor-in-chief of the Nazi daily *Volkischer Beobachter.* Senator Daniel Kroupa called for a police investigation, saying the book was "quite simply a piece of overt anti-Semitism."

There were also acts of vandalism against Jewish targets. For example, thieves stole valuable tombstones from the historic Jewish cemetery in Mikulov, apparently to reuse them for new grave markers. In May, the synagogue in Krnov was defaced, and in September, for the second time in two years, a Holocaust monument in Ostrava was spray-painted with Nazi symbols and anti-Semitic slogans. These episodes led Jews to form a Czech Anti-Defamation Association in the summer.

In October, authorities charged seven fans of the Sparta soccer team with chanting anti-Semitic slogans at a rival team from Ostrava, Banik Ostrava. In December, a court in Jesenik sentenced 22-year-old Petr Blajze to seven months in prison for having used Nazi slogans and other threats while apparently trying to break into an asylum house for Roma (Gypsies); a second man was given a suspended sentence. Blajze had previously been accused of other violent incidents against Roma: in June, for example, he and two other men were charged with carrying out a racially motivated attack on a Roma couple in Jesenik.

In December, a Prague court reversed an earlier ruling that had acquitted Russian rock singer Denis Gerasimov of propagating racism and possessing Nazi propaganda. Gerasimov, whose group, Kolovrat, was popular with skinheads and other extremists, had been arrested at Prague airport in February. About to return to Russia after giving a concert in eastern Bohemia attended by skinheads from all over the region, Gerasimov was charged with possessing Nazi symbols and neo-Nazi music CDs, having neo-Nazi symbols on his clothes, and supporting a movement aimed at suppressing others' rights and freedoms. The court decision that acquitted him in October, subsequently reversed, said that neither his clothes nor the CDs could spread neo-Nazism, as "all the objects were shut in a suitcase."

In April, Yad Vashem recognized a Czech woman, Alice Horakova, as a Righteous Gentile for having saved a Jewish girl from being transported to the Terezin concentration camp in 1944. In the same ceremony, two other Czechs were posthumously recognized as Righteous Gentiles. Also in April, Jewish filmmaker Martin Smok was fined $1,500 by Czech authorities for obstructing an investigation into the death of Charles Jordan, a JDC official whose body was found floating in the Vltava River in Prague in 1967. Smok had approached the police to present a fresh lead in the case, based on the statement of a witness who came forward after a documentary by Smok on the murder was broadcast on Czech TV. The fine was ordered because police said Smok refused to reveal the identity of the alleged witness.

In September, the country's Via Bona Honorary Award for outstanding philanthropy was presented to Alfred Bader, an 80-year-old Vienna-born chemist and art collector and dealer who lived in Milwaukee. In 1938, when he was 14, Bader fled Vienna on a *kindertransport* train for London. He lost his family in the Holocaust. Bader's charitable efforts in the Czech Republic include annual awards to chemistry students, a chair at Masaryk University in Brno, a community-based project to help Roma, an art history grant, and the rebuilding of a Prague playground after the devastating floods of 2002.

Greece

Kostas Karamanlis of the conservative New Democracy Party was elected prime minister in March. In elections for the European Parliament in June, Georgos Karatzaferis of the extreme nationalist and xenophobic People's Party (LAOS) won a seat with 4.1 percent of the vote, the first electoral success for the far-right in 20 years. (The party failed to win any seats in the Greek parliamentary elections earlier in the year.) Greece marked its first National Day of Remembrance of Greek-Jewish Victims of the Holocaust on January 27.

Greece hosted the Olympic Games in August, where windsurfer Gal Fridman presented Israel with the country's first gold medal ever (he had won a bronze in 1996). For the Olympics, a kosher restaurant opened in Athens to serve Jewish athletes and tourists. In July, to mark the upcoming Olympics, a park named Athens 2004 was dedicated in Zur Moshe, a moshav (cooperative settlement) near the Israeli town of Netanya that had been founded by Greek Jews in the 1930s. The creation of the park, funded by the Greek Foreign Ministry and private donors in Greece and Israel, was initiated by Elias Messina, a Greek Jewish architect who divided his time between the two countries, and his wife.

In October, a delegation from the American Jewish Committee met with Foreign Minister Petros Molyviatis, Education and Religious Affairs Minister Marietta Yiannakou-Koutsikou, George Papandreou, leader of Greece's main opposition party, and Athens mayor Dora Bakoyannis. The AJC urged the government to deepen its contacts with Israel and stressed how important it was for Greece to continue to support its small Jewish community.

About 5,000 Jews lived in Greece. Most were well integrated into society and many were intermarried. There were nine organized Jewish communities—Athens (the largest), Thessaloniki (or Salonika), Larissa, Chalkis, Volos, Corfu, Trikala, Ioannina, and Rhodes—all of them grouped under the umbrella Central Board of Jewish Communities (KIS). The only synagogues to hold regular services were in Athens, Thessaloniki, and Larissa, and there were Jewish schools in Athens and Thessaloniki. The 1,000-member community in Thessaloniki was considered to be the most active in the country, with a Jewish choir, social welfare programs, an old-age home, and a Jewish community center that was a focal point for younger Jews. In January, Elie Wiesel spoke at a Holocaust memorial ceremony in the city, and the Jewish community made Wiesel and his wife honorary members. In July, Thessaloniki resident Hella Kounio, the oldest survivor of the Greek Holocaust, died at the age of 98. She had been 37 when she was deported to Auschwitz in 1943.

The Jewish Museum, founded in 1977 in Athens, mounted exhibitions and held events relating to the Greek Jewish heritage. During the year, Greece joined the Task Force for International Cooperation on Holocaust Education, Remembrance and Research. David Saltiel, president of the Jewish community of Thessaloniki, Moisis Konstantinis, president of KIS, and Zanet Battinou, director of the Jewish Museum, had worked with the Ministry of Education for several years on how to incorporate Holocaust education into the Greek school system.

Some observers raised concern about mounting anti-Semitism in the country. Anti-Semitic articles appeared in the extreme right-wing media, and even mainstream newspapers occasionally ran anti-Semitic political cartoons that were critical of Israeli policies and of Prime Minister Sharon. Some compared Israeli policy toward the Palestinians to Nazi treatment of the Jews. In October, for example, the financial newspaper *Epihiro* ran a photograph of ovens with a caption making that equation. Anti-Semitism and anti-Israeli sentiment were often linked with anti-Americanism. In August, after the Olympic Games, racist and anti-Semitic graffiti appeared along a 70-kilometer stretch of highway between Athens and Tripolis.

In October, when Israeli ambassador Ram Aviram paid a courtesy call on the prefect of the Cretan town of Chania, the latter, George Katsanievaki—well known for his hostility to Israel—unleashed a diatribe against the Jewish state, calling Sharon the "anti-Christ" and telling the ambassador that "the feelings of the people of Chania toward Israel are anything but friendly."

Mikis Theodorakis, the Greek composer best known for the score of the film *Zorba the Greek,* sought to mend his relations with Jews by arranging an interview with a reporter for the Israeli daily *Ha'aretz.* Theodorakis, however, who had outraged Jews around the world by allegedly calling them "the root of all evil" in November 2003 (see AJYB 2004, p. 421), only made matters worse in August 2004 by explaining that he actually said that Jews were *at* the root of all evil. He went on to allege that Jews controlled the world's banks, mass media, and symphony orchestras, and had manipulated the American government to go to war in Iraq. Even while professing himself a "true friend of the Jewish people," he condemned the Jewish religion for promoting "psychological masochism."

Hungary

Hungary joined the European Union on May 1. In September, 43-year-old multi-millionaire Ferenc Gyurcsany was named prime minister of the Socialist-led coalition. He replaced Peter Medgyessy, who resigned. Hungary had been part of the "coalition of the willing" in Iraq, but the deployment of its 300-member military contingent was unpopular among Hungarians. The government pulled its troops out of Iraq in December, after parliament refused to extend the unit's mission beyond 2004.

Relations between Hungary and Israel were close. Israeli investment in Hungary was particularly strong. According to Peter Kiss, an aide to the prime minister who visited Israel in July, Israelis had invested over $2 billion in Hungary over the past decade, an amount second only to investors from the U.S. Israeli investment focused on real estate, infrastructure, and industry, including pharmaceuticals. Israeli president Moshe Katzav visited Hungary in April for ceremonies marking 60 years since the Nazi deportations from Hungary (see below, p. 474). In June, Hungary resigned from the UN Committee on the Exercise of the Inalienable Rights of the Palestinian People. The Anti-Defamation League praised the move, calling the committee, "a body which promotes a one-sided and propagandistic perspective of Israel and the Israeli-Palestinian conflict."

In January, visiting former U.S. secretary of state Madeleine Albright told former Hungarian prime minister Viktor Orban that she was concerned about "some of the more extremist views" expressed by members of Orban's opposition FIDESZ party, and warned that it was counterproductive for FIDESZ to support "extremist nationalist views." Orban, however, defended his record and disagreed with her criticism. On February 12, FIDESZ stayed away from a wreath-laying ceremony honoring victims of World War II and those killed by Hungary's Nazi occupiers and the home-grown fascist Arrow Cross militia. The next day, FIDESZ also boycotted a ceremony marking the 59th anniversary of the liberation of Budapest by Soviet troops, saying that that event had not represented liberation, but rather the start of a brutal communist occupation. On the day after that, February 14, about 800 members and sympathizers of the neo-Nazi Blood and Honor Association held a "counter-commemoration" honoring the Germans and pro-Nazi Hungarians defeated by the Soviet troops.

At the beginning of the year, the radio station Tilos Radio was at the center of controversy. It stemmed from a live program aired on December 24, 2004, during which host Zoltan Bajtai, apparently intoxicated, said he would like to "exterminate all Christians." The remark drew widespread protest, Tilos Radio apologized, and Bajtai was fired. But the incident escalated into a broader scandal with overt anti-Semitic overtones. On January 11, several thousand people held a protest rally against Tilos Radio organized by right-wing groups, whose leaders whipped up the crowd. The writer Kornel Dobrentei stated: "It is good if one has the will and courage to protest the religion-cloaked war waged on us to eliminate our people; to protest the moral holocaust of the Hungarian nation directed by fake prophets dressed in camouflage and hiding their faces behind masks—only their beards are real!" He went on, "And they are waiting, ready to pounce, to censure our gripe as nationalism and anti-Semitism, to sully our reputation worldwide." The crowd chanted "dirty Jews," and far-right protesters burned an Israeli flag.

This drew sharp protest from mainstream political parties, the Israeli embassy, and the Hungarian Jewish community, which condemned both the flag-burning and the remark about eliminating Christians. Two men were arrested for burning the flag, and police seized right-wing nationalist material at the home of one of them. On January 21, the National Radio and Television Authority ordered Tilos Radio off the air for 30 days, but a court reversed the ban eight days later. The station got into more hot water when an announcer read out what was described as a text message from a listener that called former prime minister Orban a fascist. On February 11, police said they had concluded that Bajtai had not committed a crime with his remark about Christians, since it was not "incitement against a community." The affair had further fallout. Dobrentei was on the board of the Hungarian Writers Association, and, beginning in March, more than 160 writers quit that organization to protest its refusal to distance itself from Dobrentei's remarks. The association issued a statement explaining that it did not want to "play the role of the thought-police."

The U.S. State Department's annual *Country Report on Human Rights Practices* for 2003, released in February 2004, noted that the Hungarian Jewish community was concerned about anti-Semitism in the media, including some that were state-run. This assertion drew criticism from the Federation of Hungarian Electronic Journalists, which charged that the report tried to brand as "anti-Semitic" programs and editors that were simply "not to the liking" of a certain group.

There were various manifestations of right-wing extremism and racism. A neo-Nazi group called the Hungarian Future Group, believed to have only a few dozen members, placed posters around Budapest honoring World War II fascist leader Ferenc Szalasi; the government closed down its Web site in September. Also in September, widespread criticism in the media, from political parties, and from organizations—including the Alliance of Hungarian Jewish Communities—greeted a decision by the police to grant a permit to the Hungarian Future Group for a rally on October 15 marking the 60th anniversary of the coup that put the Arrow Cross, Hungary's pro-Nazi fascist militia, in power. Among other protests, about 1,000 people staged a demonstration against the planned rally outside Budapest's House of Terror museum.

Police, meanwhile, arrested the group's leader, 26-year-old Diana Bacsfi, who was sentenced to ten days in jail for disturbing the peace. The October 15 rally was canceled at the last minute on a technicality, after Budapest officials issued a permit allowing the youth wing of the Alliance of Free Democrats, a party that was in the government coalition, to stage its own counter-rally in the same place where the neo-Nazis wanted to demonstrate. In the end, about 25,000 people took part in an antifascist rally that day, organized by various groups, including the Jewish community, human-rights organizations, and parties of the center-left government. Culture Minister Istvan Hiller told the crowd, "We don't tolerate fascism in any of its forms."

A Holocaust memorial in Budapest was vandalized on January 27, the date marked as Holocaust Memorial Day in parts of Europe. In February, the Budapest Municipal Council rescinded permission it had granted earlier for the erection of a statue to Pal Teleki, prime minister in 1920–21 and 1939–41. (A statue of Teleki had already been erected in the town of Balatonboglar, despite Jewish protests.) Under Teleki's rule Hungary introduced anti-Semitic legislation, including a "numerus clausus" law limiting the admission of Jewish students to universities—the first such measure in Europe. The Ministry of Culture, the Alliance of Hungarian Religious Jewish Communities, and the Simon Wiesenthal Center had all protested erection of the statue.

In February, a government commission consisting of scholars, church dignitaries, and politicians that had been set up to examine and evaluate evidence on the Holocaust in Hungary held its first session, chaired by Prime Minister Medgyessy. Results of a survey on Holocaust awareness in Hungary released that same month indicated that only 2 percent of adult Hungarians were well informed about the Holocaust, and 16 percent knew nothing about it. The best-informed respondents were in the 26–45 age bracket. This poll of 1,000 people was commissioned by the Holocaust Documentation Center.

Various high-profile events marked the 60th anniversary of the deportation of Hungary's Jews to Auschwitz. Principal among them was the opening in April of a Holocaust memorial, museum, and documentation center in Budapest. The $8.5-million complex was built around an ornate synagogue on Pava Street, just outside the city center, which had been used as an internment camp in 1944–45 and then stood abandoned for many years. The new structures surrounding it featured broken contours, slanted walls, and narrowing corridors aimed at evoking a nightmare world.

Israeli president Moshe Katzav joined Hungarian Jewish and governmental leaders for the inauguration of the new facility on April 15. Security was very tight. On the day before the opening, Hungarian police detained three Arabs for allegedly plotting to blow up "a Jewish museum" in Budapest. Police denied a link between the terror plot and Katzav's three-day visit.

The new museum was only partially completed when it opened. A temporary exhibition was installed, as its planned permanent exhibition tracing the development of the Shoah in Hungary, including Hungarian complicity, was not yet ready. When fully functional, the complex would include archives and databases concerning the Holocaust in Hungary, as well as a memorial wall bearing the names of Holocaust victims—more than 40,000 had been inscribed so far. To be sure, this ambitious project drew criticism over its goals, concept, and location, as well as over the political maneuvers involved in setting it up. Critics included prominent members of Hungary's Jewish community, who faulted organizers for, among other things, going ahead too hastily without first thinking through many details.

The Simon Wiesenthal Center launched its Operation Last Chance campaign in Hungary in July, offering rewards of 10,000 euros for information leading to the capture of Nazi war criminals (see Croatia, above). Within two weeks, the campaign's local project manager resigned, after Hungary's data-privacy ombudsman said that the transmission of information about Hungarian individuals to the Wiesenthal Center headquarters in Israel could violate the nation's privacy laws. In October, the state-sponsored House of Terror museum launched a campaign to identify people who had helped rescue Jews during the Shoah. That same month a Socialist member of parliament, Janos Zuschlag, was forced to resign his seat after being caught on camera making a joke about Holocaust victims.

JEWISH COMMUNITY

Estimates of Hungary's Jewish population ran from 54,000 to 130,000, about 90 percent of whom lived in Budapest. The vast majority of Jews were nonpracticing and secular, and unaffiliated with Jewish institutions.

Hungarian Jewish communities were grouped under an umbrella body, the Alliance of Hungarian Jewish Communities. It was the official representative of Hungarian Jews to the state, which provided it $15 million in funding per year. Critics within the Jewish community had long called the alliance undemocratic and monopolistic, noting that it represented only about 5,000–6,000 dues-paying members, a tiny fraction of the total Jewish population, and had been managed by one executive director, Gusztav Zoltai, for 12 years.

In April, the alliance responded to the criticism by adopting a new constitution that promised to create a clearer and more transparent process for decision-making and financial management. It also transferred some powers from the executive director by delegating them to the elected leadership, and raised the possibility of involving Jewish organizations that were not members of the alliance, and thus "cautiously opening toward a wider segment of the Jewish community," explained Andras Heisler, president of the alliance.

Among the significant groups that operated outside the alliance were the Reform congregation Sim Shalom and Chabad, which, besides running its own synagogue and yeshiva, sponsored a variety of educational programs. In May, Chabad helped found a new Jewish community that, if its goals were met, would be able to mirror established Jewish communal structures and compete for public funding. It was called the Unified Hungarian Israelite Community (EMIH), and claimed to be the resurrected embodiment of the prewar "Status Quo Ante" community, one of Hungary's traditional Jewish streams. After obtaining the requisite 100 signatures, EMIH was registered with Hungarian authorities as an officially recognized religious body. This essentially put it on a juridical par with the Neolog and Orthodox communities. Its leader was Rabbi Shlomo Koves, a Hungarian-born adherent of Chabad.

The Pesti Shul, which was Modern Orthodox, functioned as a semiautonomous congregation, based in a small synagogue in central Budapest. Members paid nominal monthly dues. The congregation organized classes and monthly Shabbat gatherings, as well as a six-day camp around the Shavuot holiday. In December, the Pesti Shul had a joyous celebration to mark the accession of a Torah scroll from Lithuania, one of the 300 Torahs turned over to world Jewry several years earlier after languishing abandoned in storage since the Holocaust in Lithuania's National Library.

In May, Budapest hosted the third General Assembly of the European Council of Jewish Communities (ECJC). More that 1,000 representatives from over 40 countries attended the four-day event, whose theme was "Toward a New Era: Facing Together the Challenges of Being Jewish in an Enlarged Europe." This was just three weeks after ten new countries, including Hungary, joined the EU. "The significance of this, for Jews, cannot be overstated," said incoming ECJC president Jonathan Joseph. "We are looking at a politically united Europe for the first time ever. We are experiencing a reawakening of Jewish life and culture in Europe on a scale not seen for 100 years. How we respond over the next few years will be one of the most significant things we will do as a Jewish people, and particularly as a European Jewish people."

On the last day of the conference, police detained six members of a right-wing group called Conscience '88, who tried to stage an anti-Israel (verging on anti-Jewish) demonstration in a downtown square where Jewish organizations were marking the 56th anniversary of Israel. One woman burned a paper Israeli flag.

There were numerous conferences, exhibitions, concerts, seminars, and other Jewish-themed cultural and educational events throughout the year. In February, the Hungarian government awarded a grant to Centropa.org, an Internet-based oral-history project devoted to Central and Eastern European Jewry, to create a Hungarian-language Web site combining interviews of elderly Jews with their family photographs.

After a full-scale restoration, the historic Baroque synagogue in the northeastern village of Mád was dedicated at a ceremony in May that also commemorated the 60th anniversary of the deportation of local Jews to Auschwitz. According to the 2001 Hungarian Law on Cultural Heritage, the synagogue was on the list of the 263 most important monuments in the country, and therefore had to remain state property. The State Treasury Directorate sponsored the restoration, with additional funding from private donors through the Jewish Heritage Grant Program of the World Monuments Fund (WMF).

In the summer, a citizens' group called Ovas was formed to preserve Budapest's old Jewish neighborhood in the city's seventh district, where many buildings were threatened by the wrecker's ball of urban development. Ovas staged outdoor protests, meetings, and walking tours of the district, and sponsored a day-long conference on the issue in November. The group applied for a temporary preservation order for the whole neighborhood, which was granted in June. This designated the Jewish quarter as a cultural heritage area, so that only demolitions approved before June could be carried out, but not new ones.

In June, the 100th anniversary of the death of Theodor Herzl, father of Zionism, was marked with a ceremony at the Hungarian Academy of Sciences. Herzl was born in Budapest on May 2, 1860, next door to the city's main Dohany Street Synagogue, occupied today by the Jewish Museum. The seventh Jewish Summer Festival was held in Budapest at the end of August and beginning of September. Through the year, work progressed on a $15-million film version of Nobel Prize-winning author Imre Kertesz's book *Fateless*. Kertesz himself wrote the screenplay.

The Vienna-based Organization for Security and Cooperation in Europe (OSCE) named the Jewish Hungarian writer and political activist Miklos Haraszti as its representative on freedom of the media, charged with monitoring media developments in the OSCE participating states, and advocating and promoting full compliance with OSCE principles and commitments regarding freedom of expression. Haraszti, a former anti-communist dissident, was born in 1945 in Jerusalem. In the 1980s he edited the underground Hungarian periodical *Beszelo,* and after the fall of communism served in the Hungarian parliament. In May, Education Minister Balint Magyar wrote an article in Hungary's leading newspaper that for the first time openly discussed his Jewish roots.

In July, the minister of culture presented Israel's outgoing ambassador to Hungary, Judit Varnai-Shorer, with the prestigious Pro Cultura Hungarica Prize, honoring her role in the establishment of the Holocaust memorial and museum. Varnai-Shorer also received an award from Hungary's president. Also in July, the Jewish Agency awarded Hungarian Jewish educator Anna Szeszler, principal of the Lauder Yavne Jewish Community School in Budapest, the Max Fisher Prize for Jewish Education in the Diaspora. In December, Katalin Karady, one of the most popular Hungarian singers and actresses in the 1940s, was posthumously honored as a Righteous Gentile by Yad Vashem for helping to save Jews during World War II. Karady, who left Hungary in 1949, died in New York in 1990.

Following the death of Herman Fixler, 93, who had served as president for 35 years, Hungary's tiny Orthodox community elected Laszlo Herczog to succeed him.

Macedonia

President Boris Trajkovski, 47, was killed in a plane crash in Bosnia on February 26. Trajkovski, a strong advocate of European integration and friendship with the U.S., had had close ties with the Jewish community and attended Jewish holiday celebrations. In elections to replace him, Prime Minister Branko Crvenkovski won a decisive victory. In March, Macedonia applied to join the European Union. In November, the country held a referendum sponsored by Macedonian nationalists that would have reversed a law giving the Albanian minority more rights. Much of the country simply ignored it. Only 26 percent of Macedonia's 1.7 million eligible voters turned out, too few to make the result valid. EU officials believed that this result could only help Macedonia's chances of eventual EU membership.

About 200 Jews lived in Macedonia, almost all of them in the capital of Skopje and almost all of them intermarried. About 30 were young people. Thanks to far-reaching measures taken by the government to restitute Jewish communal property, the Jews of Macedonia were able to attain financial self-sufficiency in 2004. A special Holocaust Foundation set up by the government and the Jewish community—financed by revenues from property owned by Jews before World War II and left heirless afterward—made plans to build a $1-million Holocaust museum and education center in the old Jewish quarter of Skopje.

Poland

Prime Minister Leszek Miller resigned at the end of March after a group of lawmakers from his ex-communist Democratic Left Alliance split off and formed a rival social democratic party. Miller's government, plagued by corruption scandals and infighting, had been highly unpopular, with polls giving his coalition only a 4-percent approval rating. Miller's successor, former finance minister Marek Belka, was sworn in on May 2, the day after Poland joined the EU. He pledged sweeping reforms and described his foreign policy goals as "a successful fulfillment of our mission in Iraq" and overcoming obstacles to a new EU constitution. Belka lost a no-confidence vote less than two weeks after he was sworn in, but was confirmed in office several weeks later.

Poland was the largest of the ten new EU members, but it struggled with economic problems that included an unemployment rate of 20 percent. Warsaw was a staunch ally of the U.S. in the Iraq war, supplying a contingent of 2,400 Polish troops. Prime Minister Belka and Defense Minister Jerzy Szmajdzinski paid the troops a Christmas visit in December. At the beginning of April, Polish officials said there was a "clear" danger of a terrorist attack on Poland because of its Iraq role and close alignment with Washington.

Poland and Israel maintained strong links. During a visit to Poland in October, Israeli foreign minister Silvan Shalom said that Israel viewed Poland "as a true friend and close ally." He welcomed "the efforts made by Poland to address the past, and to educate the younger generation towards a future of tolerance, memory, cooperation, and understanding" and lauded "Poland's leading role in the global battle against anti-Semitism." Israeli investments in Poland amount to around $1 billion, but both Shalom and Polish president Aleksander Kwasniewski said that the level of trade between the two countries still fell short of its potential. Kwasniewski said he hoped that Poland's membership in the EU would attract more Israeli investment, especially in hi-tech, and increase trade. Defense ties between Poland and Israel were especially close.

Not only did the two countries share intelligence and counterterrorism information, but they were also engaged in a $255-million arms deal, under which Poland was purchasing 2,765 Israeli-made Spike LR anti-tank rockets over a ten-year period, part of a program to modernize its armed forces. At an official ceremony in Warsaw in November, Israeli defense minister Shaul Mofaz symbolically handed over to his Polish counterpart the first of the missiles. Mofaz signed a memorandum with Polish finance minister Jerzy Hausner to enhance industrial ties between the two nations.

With Poland now in the EU, a number of Israelis of Polish ancestry were reportedly attempting to gain Polish passports, both for business reasons and as a safety net should violence get worse in Israel. A staff member at the Polish embassy in Tel Aviv said the embassy was equipped to accept 100 applications a month, and about half of those received positive responses. In November, the town of Czestochowa, home of Poland's most sacred Catholic religious relic, the Black Madonna, signed a cooperation agreement with Nazareth and Bethlehem.

The U.S. State Department's report on global anti-Semitism, released in December, noted that surveys in Poland indicated a "continuing decline in anti-Semitic sentiment" over the past few years, and that "avowedly anti-Semitic candidates have won few elections." Nevertheless, it went on, "anti-Semitic feelings persisted among certain sectors of the population, occasionally resulting in acts of vandalism and physical or verbal abuse." There were persistent expressions of anti-Semitism, some contained in published pamphlets and others broadcast over the radical Catholic station Radio Maria. In April, the pastor of St. Brigid Church in Gdansk, Fr. Henryk Jankowski, told parishioners during services that "Jews killed Jesus and the prophets," and displayed posters asserting that only Christians could be true citizens. The archbishop of Gdansk subsequently removed Jankowski—already notorious for his previous anti-Semitic utterances—for this and other improprieties.

Aside from frequent graffiti found scrawled on walls around the country, the State Department report listed some specific instances of anti-Semitic actions. In June, for example, just a few days before the annual Festival of Jewish Culture, vandals defaced the Tempel Synagogue in Kraków with swastikas and a Star of David hanging from gallows. And in October, a young Jew from Sweden, wearing a *kippah,* was harassed by three Polish youths who shouted anti-Semitic slogans at him during a visit to Auschwitz-Birkenau.

During the year, the government provided grants to a number of organizations involved in anti-bias education, including the Jewish Historical Institute (ZIH) in Warsaw, which was a joint public/private venture, and such nongovernmental organizations (NGOs) as the Jewish Historical Association, which produced educational material on Jewish culture, the Holocaust, and religious tolerance. The public education office of the Institute of National Remembrance -Commission for the Prosecution of Crimes against the Polish Nation produced materials for use in schools, and sponsored a research and documentation project on "The Extermination of Jews in Poland."

During a meeting in November with a visiting delegation from the American Jewish Committee, the speaker of the Sejm (parliament), Jozef Oleksy, stressed that Poland condemned Europe's current wave of anti-Semitism as well as all attempts to rewrite the history of World War II. He suggested that the March of the Living, which brought young Jews to Poland and then to Israel, not just visit sites of Jewish martyrdom in Poland but also include meetings with Polish youth.

JEWISH COMMUNITY

Determining the number of Jews in Poland was no simple matter, with estimates ranging from a few thousand to as many as 20,000.

The Ronald S. Lauder Foundation, which, since the early 1990s, had run the country's most extensive Jewish educational programs, closed its administrative offices in Poland this year. It still, however, supported a number of activities, including the Jewish school in Warsaw, the monthly magazine *Midrasz,* the Lauder Genealogical Research Center, and the Moises Schorr Institute, an adult education facility in Warsaw. The JDC provided social welfare aid and also ran educational and leadership-training programs. The Polish Jewish community's Web site, www.jewish.org.pl, provided information about activities and programs. Other useful Web sites for Jewish developments in Poland were www.forumznak.org/pl, and a new site, http://fzp.jewish.org.pl/english/engind.html.

In January, Warsaw's Nozyk Synagogue was the scene of a joyous and moving ceremony, the bar mitzvah of Daniel Krajewski, son of Stanislaw Krajewski, the American Jewish Committee's Warsaw consultant, and his wife, Monika, an artist and teacher at Warsaw's Jewish school. Daniel was born with Down's syndrome, and a special format for the religious ceremony was worked out for him. Many members of the congregation were moved to tears, and the ceremony was the subject of a lengthy article in Poland's leading newspaper. This was believed to be the first bar mitzvah of a Down's syndrome boy in Polish history.

Officially recognized Jewish religious communities were grouped under an umbrella organization, the Union of Jewish Religious Communities in Poland. Though most Polish Jews were secular or not very observant, the religious orientation of the established Jewish communities was Orthodox. There were some complaints, even from religious Jews, that synagogue practices were "too orthodox" for many community members.

In Warsaw, the non-Orthodox group, Beit Warszawa, expanded its operations. Not a member of the union, it nevertheless cooperated with the Warsaw Jewish community on some initiatives. It had new premises in southern Warsaw, and was largely funded by a Polish-born American donor. Beit Warszawa had regular services, social events, concerts, and other programs. In June, singer and actor Theodore Bikel spent two weeks at Beit Warszawa. An American rabbinical student, Scott Perlo, served as a visiting rabbi there in the fall. The group also established "partner" arrangements with several Reform congregations in the U.S.

This year, for the first time, Chabad-Lubavitch sent full-time emissaries to Poland. On December 13, the deputy mayor of Warsaw, Andrzej Urbanski, together with Rabbi Yonah Metzger, Ashkenazi chief rabbi of Israel, participated in the first Chabad-sponsored public lighting of a Hanukkah menorah in the history of the Polish capital. Also taking part was Rabbi Michael Schudrich, who had just been named chief rabbi of Poland by the Union of Jewish Religious Communities. Schudrich, an Orthodox rabbi from the U.S., had a long history in Poland. He directed the Lauder Foundation in Poland in the 1990s, and for the past several years had served as rabbi of Warsaw and Lodz. The appointment as chief rabbi essentially formalized his role.

Several other Jewish groups operated in opposition to communities that were members of the union. Such bodies operated in Gdansk, Poznan, and Warsaw (where the breakaway community was founded by the former caretaker of the Jewish cemetery, after he was fired in 2002). In some cases these factions sharply criticized the established Orthodox communities and their leaders, including Rabbi Schudrich, and on occasion the rhetoric crossed the line of civility. It was often unclear to what extent religious differences, personality clashes, and/or financial motivations prompted the actions of the dissidents.

The Social-Cultural Association of Jews in Poland (TSKZ), a secular organization established in 1950 that had functioned throughout the communist era, also remained in existence, as did a number of other Jewish and pro-Jewish organizations around the country. Two of these, both in Kraków, were a small, independent Jewish student group called Cholent, and an association for Polish-Jewish dialogue, Gesher, made up of students from the Department of Jewish Studies of Kraków's Jagiellonian University.

Kraków, in fact, despite the small size of its Jewish community— about 200 members—hosted two important events in December. That month, the community marked the 700th anniversary of Jewish life in the city. A ceremony and concert in the restored Tempel Synagogue drew local and national dignitaries, including the city's archbishop, Cardinal Franciczek Macharski. Also, some 70 participants from 11 European countries, the U.S., and Israel came to Kraków on the occasion of the first pan-European conference for Jewish community volunteers, cosponsored by the JDC, the European Council of Jewish Communities, and the Polish Social Welfare Commission. Professionals and volunteers from each country presented information and conducted workshops about volunteer programs that helped the poor, the elderly, and children.

Numerous Jewish cultural, communal, and educational events took place around the country. In March, a Purim charity ball in Warsaw raised money for victims of terrorist attacks in Israel. It was hosted by the Israeli embassy and the Jewish Agency, and organized by local Jewish organizations with the assistance of the JDC and the Lauder Foundation. Several events took place that month to commemorate the forced emigration of 20,000 Jews from Poland during the "anti-Zionist" campaign by the communist government in 1968. In April, the first Warsaw International Jewish Motifs Film Festival took place, featuring more than 60 films from 20 countries. The Golden Phoenix grand prize went to Oren Rudavsky and Menachem Daum for *Hiding and Seeking*. Michal Nekanda-Trepka received the Warsaw Phoenix for the best Polish film, as well as an award from the Association of Playwrights and Composers, for his film, *The Last Witnesses*. A special award from the International Cultural Forum in Stockholm went to Vladimir Divinsky for *Once Upon a Time There Was Odessa*.

Also in April, the new Galicia Jewish Museum opened in Kraków. The museum was founded and run by British photographer Chris Schwarz and featured a permanent display of his photographs of Jewish sites in southern Poland. In June, a 200-page prospectus for the permanent exhibition of the planned Museum of the History of Polish Jews was issued in Warsaw. In addition, a major exhibition on local Jewish life and history opened in Czestochowa. Some 350 people who came from the city or traced their ancestry to it attended the opening events, which included the rededication of the restored Jewish cemetery and a three-day conference titled "Coexistence, Holocaust, Memory." The exhibition, cosponsored by the city of Czestochowa and the Jewish Historical Institute in Warsaw, moved to the Polish capital in October.

Several cities hosted festivals of Jewish culture during the year. In June, Wroclaw had its sixth SIMCHA Jewish culture festival; the Galicia Festival displayed images of formerly Jewish towns in the area; and the Jewish Historical Institute in Warsaw held an exhibition of photographs from the family of Zalman Kaplan, who was the photographer for the town of Szczeczyn before World War II. The annual Jewish Cultural Festival in Kraków featured some 150 lectures, concerts, exhibitions, book-launches and other events.

In October, in honor of the 100th anniversary of the birth of Isaac Bashevis Singer, Warsaw hosted a culture festival called "Singer's Warsaw." Organized by the Shalom American-Polish-Israeli Foundation, the program featured some 40 events, including plays, movie screenings, exhibitions, literary meetings, recitals, concerts, and large outdoor shows. That same month also witnessed the seventh Warsaw Jewish Book Fair, with readings, book-signings, and sale displays accompanied by meetings with authors, film screenings, and workshops in singing, calligraphy, and paper cutouts. There was significant Jewish participation in the annual Festival of Four Cultures in Lodz, honoring the four ethnic communities that historically coexisted in the city—Polish, Jewish, German, and Russian.

There were a number efforts aimed at conserving and repairing Jewish cemeteries and other Jewish heritage sites, with funding coming from a variety of private and public sources. In May, the U.S. and Poland signed an agreement, negotiated by the U.S. Commission for the Preservation of America's Heritage Abroad, to preserve Jewish cultural sites remaining from the Nazi occupation. The cemetery in the ski resort of Zakopane was refenced and cleaned up thanks to a donation from the U.S. ambassador to Slovakia, Ronald Weiser, and the efforts of the Foundation for Preservation of Jewish Heritage in Poland, established in 2001 by the World Jewish Restitution Organization and the Union of Jewish Communities in Poland. During the summer, about 45 American, Israeli, and Polish students spent three weeks cleaning up an overgrown Jewish cemetery and touring Jewish and other historic sites in Poland as part of Project Restore and Rebuild, a partnership between the Polish Union of Jewish Students (PUSZ), the Israeli branch of the World Union of Jewish Students, the Claims Conference, and the JDC.

There were several commemorative events related to the Holocaust. In January, low-key ceremonies at Auschwitz marked the 59th anniversary of the liberation of the notorious death camp, while plans went ahead for major ceremonies to be held in 2005 to mark the 60th anniversary. The Roman Catholic Church's annual Days of Judaism in January featured a commemorative event in Poznan, where artist Janusz Marciniak (who is not Jewish) shaped 600 burning memorial candles into a huge Star of David and set it floating on the surface of the swimming pool now located in what had been Poznan's synagogue. As the glowing Star of David floated on the water, some 600 people, most of them holding blue torch lights, crowded into the once-grandiose structure. Catholic officials and Warsaw's Rabbi Schudrich gave speeches, followed by a concert by the Poznan University Choir reflecting the themes of hope, reconciliation, and peace. At the end of the ceremony, Poznan's small Jewish community placed a commemorative plaque on the synagogue wall.

In April, President Kwasniewski attended the 60th anniversary of the Warsaw Ghetto Uprising and met with visiting officials representing the European Jewish Congress. Also in April, some 7,000 people, mostly teenagers from a score of countries, took part in the annual March of the Living commemoration at Auschwitz. In June, President Kwasniewski was at the dedication of a $4-million memorial at the long-neglected site of the Belzec death camp in southeastern Poland, where the Nazis murdered 500,000 Jews. The striking memorial was sponsored and financed jointly by the Polish government and the American Jewish Committee, exemplifying what was called a "model of cooperation between a government agency and Jews from abroad." That month it was announced that the ruins of gas chambers and crematoria at the former Auschwitz-Birkenau death camp complex would be preserved as a "warning" to future generations, and, at a government-sponsored international conference, Poland announced plans to open an international center for human-rights education in Oswieçim.

In July, Polish officials, the Israeli ambassador, and other dignitaries joined survivors to mark the 60th anniversary of the liberation of the former Nazi concentration camp at Majdanek. In August, Prime Minister Belka and other officials, along with hundreds of survivors and thousands of townspeople, participated in ceremonies in Lodz to mark the 60th anniversary of the liquidation of the Lodz Ghetto. A monument was inaugurated at the site of a former train station from which the Germans sent nearly 150,000 Jews to their deaths, plaques and markers were put up in the ghetto, and a guidebook to Jewish heritage and suffering in Lodz was published.

In September, the remains of 11 people believed to be Jews killed in the 1943 Warsaw Ghetto Uprising were buried at a ceremony in Warsaw's Jewish cemetery. The remains had been discovered during renovation of a building in the one-time ghetto area. The remains of about ten other Holocaust victims, recently discovered in the town of Nadarzyn, were buried at the same time. In early October, ceremonies in Warsaw marked the 60th anniversary of the suppression of the Warsaw Uprising, which began August 1, 1944, pitting 23,000 poorly equipped Polish fighters (including some survivors of the 1943 Warsaw Ghetto Uprising) against thousands of crack Nazi troops. The battle left 200,000 dead and the city almost totally destroyed.

There were a variety of educational initiatives in Poland centering on the Holocaust and Polish-Jewish relations. Prominent among them were the activities sponsored by the Borderland Foundation, in the northeast town of Sejny, and the Forum for Dialogue among Nations, based in the southern city of Gliwice. Two of the forum's initiatives were carried out jointly with the American Jewish Committee—a Polish-Jewish exchange program and a "next generation" program tied to the annual March of the Living—while others were the development of curricula on religious tolerance for Polish students; a program for Polish high school students to help maintain Jewish cemeteries; and a summer seminar for students of the Yiddish language. The forum also organized exchange programs between Polish and Israeli teachers and operated a Jewish Memory Project about the destroyed Jewish community of Gliwice.

In April, the Organization for Security and Cooperation in Europe

(OSCE) Office for Democratic Institutions and Human Rights, in cooperation with the Judaica Foundation in Kraków, published a book of essays on the importance of teaching about the Holocaust. In June, the Polish government sponsored an international conference where it proposed to open an international center for human-rights education in Oswięçim, the town near the site where the Auschwitz camp was built. And in July, experts from several Israeli institutes for Holocaust remembrance attended a seminar on Auschwitz in the Collective Memory in Poland and Abroad, held at, and organized by, the Auschwitz Museum Educational Center.

More than half a million people visited Auschwitz, including dignitaries, school and tour groups, and individuals. Some 6,000–7,000 people took part in the annual March of the Living in April. In addition to foreign teenagers, they included members of the Polish-Israeli Friendship Society, Polish survivors of Auschwitz, and members of the Polish Union of Jewish Students. In August, hundreds of Roma (Gypsies) from all over Europe gathered at Auschwitz to commemorate the 60th anniversary of the Roma Holocaust; at least 19,000 Roma were killed by the Nazis. In September, members of the English national soccer team, in Poland to play against the Polish team in nearby Katowice, visited Auschwitz after several team members requested that time be found in their schedule to do so.

In June, during an excavation of the foundations of the destroyed Great Synagogue in Oswięçim, archaeologists unearthed a trove of Jewish ritual objects buried since the Holocaust. And the Auschwitz Jewish Center, a place of prayer and study in the complex of a restored synagogue in Oswięçim, announced that the house next door to it, where the last Jew in town had lived until his death in 2000, would be turned into a museum of Jewish life.

The Simon Wiesenthal Center launched its Operation Last Chance initiative in Poland, as it did in other European countries (see above, pp. 460–61, 474), offering monetary rewards for people providing information leading to the capture of Nazi war criminals or collaborators. But the financial aspect of the initiative drew criticism from Jews and others, and one newspaper even refused to publish an ad for the campaign. In July, the Wiesenthal Center announced that it was launching inquiries into ten people as the result of calls received in response to the campaign.

Stanislaw Ryniak, the first person imprisoned at Auschwitz, died in February at the age of 88. Ryniak was not Jewish, but was arrested, accused of being a member of the Polish resistance, and sent to Auschwitz in June 1940. In March, the Rev. Stanislaw Musial, a Jesuit priest who was a Polish Catholic leader in interfaith dialogue, died in Kraków at the age of 65. Jacek Kuron, who led the struggle against Poland's communist leaders as a dissident in the 1970s and later became a popular government minister, died in June, aged 70. In August, the Nobel Prize-winning Polish poet Czeslaw Milosz died in Kraków at the age of 93. Milosz was close to Jews and Jewish causes from an early age, and some of his most eloquent and disturbing works dealt with Holocaust memory and the complex relations between Jewish and Catholic Poles. In November, Erna Rosenstein, a surrealist painter and poet whose works evoked her experience as a Jew in Nazi-occupied Poland, died in Warsaw at the age of 91.

In January, President Kwasniewski awarded outgoing Israeli ambassador Shevach Weiss the Great Cross of the Order of Merit, and named Joseph Malovany, the Israeli-born cantor of New York City's Fifth Avenue Synagogue, a commander of the Legion of Honor, Poland's equivalent of knighthood. In August, Prime Minister Belka awarded Eugene Ribakoff, president of the JDC, the Polish government's highest presidential honor, the Star Order of Merit of the Republic of Poland, both in honor of the JDC's 90th anniversary and in recognition of the organization's contribution to Polish Jewry since World War I. Also in August, President Kwasniewski posthumously conferred a Polonia Restituta Commander's Cross With a Star on Henryk Slawik, who, during the war, saved 5,000 Jews in Hungary when he headed a committee aiding Polish refugees in that country. Arrested by the Nazis in 1944, he died in the Mauthausen concentration camp. In October, Israeli ambassador David Peleg honored two Poznan families as Righteous Gentiles for saving Jews during the Holocaust.

Romania

Romania joined NATO in April. It hosted a meeting of NATO defense ministers in October, and had more than 700 troops stationed in Iraq.

Romania hoped to join the EU in 2007, but remained one of the poorest EU candidates, beset by widespread crime, abuse of power, and corruption. Transparency International, a watchdog agency, listed Romania as the most corrupt of the EU's new and candidate members. A report adopted by the European Parliament in March said Romania faced "serious difficulties" in fulfilling the requirements of EU membership and warned that accession by 2007 would be impossible in the absence of economic and political reforms. Specifically, it said, Romania had to fight corruption, end political interference in the judicial system, ensure freedom of the media, and curb police brutality. Mindful of the need to conform to criteria for EU membership, Romania sought to make amends for the 2003 row over President Ion Iliescu's apparent denial that his nation had been involved in the Holocaust. In June, the education minister announced plans to teach about the Holocaust in high schools, saying that about 500 teachers had been trained in Holocaust education with the help of experts from Yad Vashem. In October, Romania marked its first official Holocaust Remembrance Day. The official date was October 9, but the ceremonies were postponed three days to avoid conflict with Shabbat. The two houses of Parliament staged a joint session to mark the occasion, at which President Iliescu admitted Romania's role in the Shoah: "We must not forget or minimize the darkest chapter of Romania's recent history, when Jews were the victims of the Holocaust," he said, adding, "Taking the blame for the past means that we not only exercise our honesty but prove our democratic convictions." He acknowledged that death trains, mass deportations, and pogroms took place in Romania during World War II, and that state-sponsored anti-Semitism had existed in Romania before the war.

Other commemorative events were held in more than 30 towns and cities. In addition, there were lectures, symposia, exhibitions, film screenings, and other events dealing with the Holocaust in Romania. In August, government officials, including Romania's former king, participated in ceremonies marking the 60th anniversary of the palace coup that overthrew the pro-Nazi regime of Marshal Ion Antonescu and led to Romania joining the Allies in August 1944.

In November, a 33-member international committee that had been set up in 2003—in the wake of Iliescu's controversial remarks—to study the Holocaust in Romania presented Iliescu with a 400-page report on its findings. The panel, headed by Elie Wiesel, reported that Romanian authorities were responsible for the deaths of between 280,000 and 380,000 Jews and more than 11,000 Roma (Gypsies). In addition, some 132,000 Jews in Hungarian-occupied northern Transylvania were killed. The commission recommended establishing a Holocaust museum in Romania. Upon receiving the report, Iliescu repeated that Romania took responsibility for the actions of its wartime leaders and pledged to help educate Romanians about the findings "so that such tragedies will never happen again."

During 2004, Corneliu Vadim Tudor—chairman of the ultranationalist Greater Romania Party and a man with a history of outspoken anti-

Semitism, Holocaust denial, and promotion of the memory of Marshal Antonescu—sought to demonstrate that he was a changed man by associating himself with Israel and Jewish causes. In January, ignoring protests by Israel and the Jewish community, Tudor dedicated a statue to slain Israeli prime minister Yitzhak Rabin in the city of Brasov. "You cannot be a Christian and hate Jews," he told a crowd of about 1,000 people. "They gave us the Bible." But in Israel, Rabin's children issued a statement saying, "The whole issue is a false communication spin, and we fully protest Mr. Vadim Tudor's effort to use Yitzhak Rabin's memory for his own political profit."

In March, Tudor hired an Israeli company, Arad Communications, to run his campaign for the December presidential election. Company chief Eyal Arad, a former media adviser to Prime Minister Sharon, accepted the job despite protests in Israel and from Jewish groups. Arad said that Tudor had sincerely changed his views and that only Tudor had "the courage and the strength to change Romania." The ADL, however, issued a statement saying it was "appalled" that "a prominent Israeli" had agreed to run Tudor's campaign, "thereby giving credibility to Mr. Tudor and his party." In May, Tudor led a delegation of 100 members of his party on a visit to Auschwitz, where he was quoted as saying that the memory of the Holocaust should be preserved, as should the memory of "other crimes against humanity."

The new president elected in December to succeed Iliescu was not Tudor, but rather a centrist, Traian Basescu, who pledged to fight corruption and overhaul the government and the tax system. The parliamentary elections held the previous month brought to power a four-party centrist coalition headed by Prime Minister Calin Tariceanu and largely composed of young, Western-educated academics. The incoming foreign minister, Mihai Razvan Ungureanu, 36, a non-Jew, was a well-known scholar of Jewish studies and founder of the Center for Jewish Studies at A.I. Cuza University in Iasi, which he planned to continue to direct despite his new political post. Sworn in at the end of December, the new government pledged to implement tax reforms, fight corruption, and boost investment.

Just before leaving office, President Iliescu raised eyebrows when he awarded Tudor and another extreme nationalist politician, Gheorghe Buzatu, Romania's highest honor, the Star of Romania. Elie Wiesel, who had received the same honor from Iliescu in 2002, was so disgusted that he returned his award. "I hope you will understand that I cannot belong to any group of which Vadim Tudor is a member," Wiesel said.

Romania and Israel enjoyed close relations, partly due to the large number of Israelis of Romanian origin. There were also numerous Romanian guest workers in Israel. In March, President Iliescu postponed an official visit to Israel because of security fears following Israel's assassination of Hamas leader Sheikh Ahmed Yassin. In April, a gala concert at the Romanian Atheneum in Bucharest marked Israel Independence Day.

JEWISH COMMUNITY

About 12,000 Jews were believed to live in Romania, just under half of them in Bucharest and the others scattered in dozens of communities around the country. Only a handful of these had more than a hundred members. In August, Chabad celebrated five years of activity in Bucharest, and on September 1, a ceremony took place dedicating a new Torah at the Chabad synagogue, Yeshua Tova. Israel's former Sephardi chief rabbi, Mordechai Eliyahu, took part.

The Romanian Jewish community lost two of its most prominent personalities this year. Dr. Nicolae Cajal, the longtime president of the Federation of Romanian Jewish Communities (FEDROM) died in March at the age of 84. Cajal, FEDROM president since 1994, was also president of the Romanian Medical Sciences Academy and vice president of the Romanian Academy of Sciences. FEDROM director-general Iulian Sorin took over as interim president, serving in the role of community lay leader. Rabbi Ernest Neumann, who had served for many years as rabbi of Timisoara, died in April.

Supported by the JDC, FEDROM, and the Jewish Federation of Kansas City, a score of clubs for middle generation (aged 35–65) Jews operated around the country, part of a concerted policy to get members of this group more involved in communal life. In Iasi, there was a particularly well-attended program of lectures on Jewish topics, launches for books by Jewish authors, and communal celebrations of Jewish holidays. In Baia Mare, actress Maia Morgenstern, who played Mary in Mel Gibson's film *The Passion of the Christ,* drew a crowd when she discussed her career at an event for a middle-generation club. In June, middle-generation leaders from many communities took part in a seminar in Radauti. Eleven OTER clubs, for Jewish youth, were also active, organizing a number of activities and maintaining a Web site.

In October, about 40 Romanian Jewish communities staged the first "Mitzvah Days," part of an international project that emerged from a meeting of social welfare directors from European Jewish communities held earlier in the year in Budapest. Aimed at encouraging volunteerism, Mitzvah Days organized volunteers to visit elderly, sick, and lonely people at their homes, hospitals, old-age homes, seniors clubs, and day-care centers, and also to establish phone contact with welfare recipients who lived isolated in villages or in the countryside.

Many educational and cultural events took place throughout the year. At the end of March, a Romanian Cultural Institute was inaugurated in Tel Aviv. For the occasion, Romania's State Yiddish Theater troupe toured Israel for the first time. In May and June, Israel's Hacameri Theater troupe performed Hanoch Levin's *Requiem* at the International Theater Festival in Sibiu and at the National Theater in Bucharest (President Iliescu was in the audience). In May, a seminar on teaching the Holocaust in Romania was held at the Goren-Goldstein Center of the University of Bucharest. Participants came from Romania, Israel, the Czech Republic, and Hungary. In September, Romania took part in the European Day of Jewish Culture. Synagogues around the country opened their doors to visitors, as did the Jewish museums in Bucharest, Iasi, and Bacau. In October, the third Avram Goldfaden International Theater Festival took place in Iasi, featuring works by Jewish authors or dealing with Jewish topics. In December, the State Theater in Oradea hosted the premiere of *Shoah: Primo Levi's Version,* an adaptation of interviews with Levi, directed by Mihai Maniutiu.

In February, the Romanian-born Israeli scholar of Jewish mysticism Moshe Idel was awarded an honorary doctorate from the University of Bucharest. In March, President Iliescu awarded Rabbi Menachem Hacohen the Order of Cultural Merit of Officer Rank. Painter Alma Redlinger held a retrospective exhibition to mark her 80th birthday, and also was awarded a state medal. In September, Israeli author Amos Oz received the Ovidius Prize of the International Literature Days and Nights Festival, organized by the Romanian Writers' Union.

Serbia and Montenegro

Ten years after the Dayton Agreement that ended the war in Bosnia and five years after the NATO bombing campaign against Serbia proper, the country remained beset by a host of economic, social, and political woes. These included a low standard of living, unemployment, corruption, crime, and bitter political infighting. Throughout the year, former Serbian leader Slobodan Milosevic remained on trial at The Hague for war crimes.

The worst interethnic violence in several years flared in Kosovo in March, prompting NATO to send in troops. Clashes between Serbs and Albanians in more than ten towns left 22 dead and 500 injured, and a number of Serb homes and religious buildings were damaged or destroyed. In addition, the Hungarian minority in multiethnic Vojvodina province raised an alarm over Serb extremist violence against them. In July, the New York-based Hungarian Human Rights Foundation (HHRF) issued a report stating that assaults on non-Serbs, threats against ethnic Hungarian leaders, desecration of cemeteries, vandalism, and the proliferation of racist, xenophobic, and anti-Semitic graffiti were becoming "a near-daily occurrence" in Vojvodina.

That month, U.S. congressman Tom Lantos (D., Cal.) sent a letter to Serbian prime minister Vojislav Kostunica calling for "vigorous and substantive action to insure the safety and security" of the ethnic Hungarian community in Vojvodina and stating that he was "deeply troubled by the alarming escalation of anti-Hungarian, anti-Semitic, and anti-Roma violence." In September, Hungarian foreign minister Laszlo Kovacs called on EU foreign ministers to express concern over "atrocities against non-Serb communities in Vojvodina." He provided no examples, and Serbian officials said that the incidents had been exaggerated.

About 3,200 Jews lived in Serbia, about 2,000 of them in Belgrade and the rest in nine smaller communities. Few if any Jews lived in Montenegro. Serbian Jews were largely secular and the vast majority was intermarried, but the community's rabbi, Yitzhak Asiel, said there appeared to be a renewed interest in religious practice. Services were held at Belgrade's one synagogue on Friday nights, Saturdays, and holidays. Up to 300 people attended holiday services, and as many as 150 on Shabbat. Some 200 children attended Hebrew school, and according to Rabbi Asiel, who was also the community's ritual slaughterer, more people were attempting to keep kosher.

A high-level delegation from the World Jewish Congress visited Belgrade in October and met with Serbian political leaders as well as the Jewish community. As a result of the discussions, Serbia and Montenegro signed a World Jewish Congress petition for a UN resolution condemning anti-Semitism. Foreign Minister Vuk Draskovic pledged to fight anti-Semitism. He described it as "part of terrorism, and there must be no double standards in dealing with terrorists." The restitution of Jewish communal property seized during or after the Holocaust was also raised at the meetings.

Nonetheless, there were warnings during the year of increasing anti-

Semitism. In January, the editors of a Montenegrin literary periodical wrote to the public prosecutor of Montenegro charging that "a wave of anti-Semitism has spread over Montenegro" emanating from neo-Nazi, fascist, and extreme nationalist media. It noted two newspapers in particular, *Dan* and *Istok,* the latter having recently published a feature on the *Protocols of the Elders of Zion,* presenting that anti-Semitic forgery as factual. Also in January, a Holocaust monument in Novi Sad was vandalized. The Federation of Jewish Communities of Serbia and Montenegro, which had a commission that monitored anti-Semitic incidents, held a meeting in March to discuss the situation.

That month, Holocaust survivor Aca Singer was reelected president of the federation. The JDC, which provided substantial support for communal operations, sent a letter during the year to all Jewish communities in the country advocating greater transparency and democratic procedures. At Passover, the JDC sponsored a seder for the few Jews remaining in Kosovo as well as for Jewish soldiers stationed in the restive province.

In July, Mira Poljakovic, president of the Jewish community in Subotica—the country's third largest community with about 200 members— stepped down after receiving death threats. It was not clear who made these threats, but in 2001, Poljakovic, a well-known lawyer, had been attacked twice and beaten up, apparently for her activities in opposition to Milosevic. The Subotica community, in fact, was split between supporters and opponents of Poljakovic. The opposing faction organized its own association, called Shalom, which sponsored various activities, including a Passover seder held at Palic, a park outside of town, and a small Shabbat service in Sombor, gathering the first minyan there in years (fewer than 40 Jews live in Sombor). Organizers said they would hold similar Shabbat events in other tiny communities. At a meeting of the federation executive board in December, Shalom was granted subsidiary membership status.

Hanukkah was celebrated around the country with great enthusiasm. In an event initiated by the JDC, a torch was brought from one Jewish community to the next, from north to south throughout the country starting in Subotica, on the Hungarian border, to Novi Sad and Zrenjanin, and finally to Belgrade. At each stop, there was celebration with food, music, performances, and other events. A Jewish singing group from Bulgaria performed traditional Jewish songs.

There were many cultural activities throughout the year, as detailed in the federation's monthly newsletter, *Bilten.* In June, Belgrade, for the first time, hosted Esperansa, a major festival of Sephardi culture that takes place every two years. Events included exhibitions, concerts, performances, lectures, panel discussions, and workshops on Ladino and on Sephardi cuisine. More than 200 participants came from Jewish communities in Bosnia and Herzegovina, Bulgaria, Croatia, Greece, Macedonia, Romania, Slovenia, Serbia and Montenegro, and Turkey, as well as from Israel, Spain, France, Belgium, and the U.S. In September, events around the country marked the annual European Day of Jewish Culture. They included art exhibitions, bus tours of Jewish sites in Belgrade and Zemun, concerts, folk dancing, receptions, an exhibition of Purim masks, lectures on Jewish education and on Theodore Herzl, visits to synagogues, and klezmer music concerts. The Federation of Jewish Communities described the day as "remarkable," saying that nearly 2,700 visitors attended.

Through the year, work continued on a series of volumes called *We Survived,* which included the memoirs of dozens of Jews from all of the former Yugoslavia recounting how they survived the Shoah. In October, Serbia signed an agreement with the U.S. Commission for the Preservation of America's Heritage Abroad under which it committed itself to preserve and protect sites of Jewish cultural heritage.

In the summer and fall, a major clean-up operation took place at the historic Jewish cemetery in Nis, thus resolving a crisis that had attracted national and international media attention. The cemetery, abandoned after World War II, had become the site of a Roma (Gypsy) settlement. Some of the 120 homes used tombstones for building material, and much of the cemetery was used as a dump for rubbish and human waste. The summer clean-up took place in the open part of the cemetery, where the Roma did not live and where hundreds of tombstones still stood. It was organized by the JDC, funded by a donation of $18,000 from Dr. Alfred Bader of Milwaukee (see above, pp. 457, 468), who also funded other nonsectarian aid projects in Serbia. Paul Polansky, a Roma rights activist, was enlisted to oversee the project, employing workers from the Roma community living on the site. In September, Jasna Ciric, president of the tiny Jewish community in Nis, negotiated an agreement whereby the Serbian army sent 30 soldiers to work alongside the local Roma to clean up the area. In addition, the Nis municipality, the formal owner of the cemetery, agreed to carry out an extensive drainage project aimed at resolving serious sanitation problems surrounding the Roma settlement, and to provide a gate and fence. The synagogue in the town was also undergoing restoration.

Slovakia

In April, Ivan Gasparovic, leader of the Movement for Democracy (HZD), won election as Slovakia's new president, replacing Rudolf Schuster. He took office in June, just six weeks after Slovakia joined the EU. In order to bring its laws into conformity with EU standards, the parliament passed a law making it illegal to discriminate against anyone on the grounds of gender, sexual orientation, religion, nationality, ethnicity, or disability.

Concern over neo-Nazi, skinhead, and right-wing extremist activity was voiced throughout the year. The League Against Racism, which launched a nationwide antiracism campaign in January, estimated that there were about 5,000 active neo-Nazis in Slovakia and that they committed "hundreds" of attacks each year, most of them against Roma. Also in January, the European Commission against Racism and Intolerance issued a report saying that racial violence against Slovak Roma included "serious acts of police brutality." In late February, demonstrations by Roma in eastern Slovakia protesting cuts in welfare benefits escalated into civil unrest, looting, and clashes with police. The government deployed 1,000 troops to help police maintain order, and there were a number of arrests and injuries.

In May, Slovak public television canceled the broadcast of a documentary that dealt with an anti-Jewish pogrom that took place in the Slovak town of Topolcany in September 1945. It said that the cancellation was ordered because one of the people interviewed had made sharply anti-Semitic and anti-Roma statements. The Slovak Jewish community, however, protested the cancellation, suggesting that some political elements did not want the truth of the postwar pogrom to come out. After considerable controversy and debate, the documentary was broadcast a week later, along with a panel discussion of issues surrounding it.

In March, about 200 people gathered in Bratislava to mark the 65th anniversary of the establishment of the Nazi-allied independent Slovak Republic in 1939 and honor its leader, nationalist priest Father Jozef Tiso, who was executed after World War II as a war criminal. The group laid flowers and candles at Tiso's grave. In October, vandals painted swastikas on a World War II monument in northeastern Slovakia.

In January, President Schuster joined hundreds of other Slovaks at the annual commemoration of a Nazi massacre of 146 people in two Slovak villages. Just a few days earlier, 86-year-old Ladislav Niznansky was arrested in Munich and put under investigation for his role in that massacre and also in the firing-squad slaying of 18 Jews in another Slovak village. Formally charged with 164 counts of murder in March, he was accused of having headed the Slovak section of a Nazi unit code-named Edelweiss that hunted Slovak resistance fighters; a court in the former Czechoslovakia had tried him in absentia and sentenced him to death in 1962. Niznansky's trial started in Munich in September. The indictment stated that he "ordered that no living soul be allowed to escape and that anyone who tried to flee be shot," and that he personally shot at least 20 people. Niznansky pleaded innocent. In October, the court released him from custody, stating that witness testimony had not conclusively confirmed his participation in the massacres.

In June, a monument to Slovak Jews deported to Nazi death camps was erected in the town of Zilina. In March, a multimedia exhibition opened at the Slovak National Museum in Bratislava titled "Will We Leave?" Telling the stories of Jewish refugees trying to flee the Nazis, the exhibit was organized by the Jewish Museum of Vienna, the Culture Department of the city of Salzburg, the Austrian Culture Forum in Bratislava, and the Slovak Jewish Culture Museum. In August, impressive ceremonies marked the 60th anniversary of the Slovak national uprising against the Nazis. And in November, a monument honoring Raoul Wallenberg was unveiled in Bratislava.

There were a number of visits by government leaders to and from the Middle East. In January, President Schuster visited Egypt, where he and Egyptian president Hosni Mubarak agreed that a cessation of violence on all sides was a precondition for a renewed peace process between Israel and the Palestinians. In August, Defense Minister Juraj Liska visited the more than 100 Slovak troops stationed in Iraq, and also met with Iraq's defense minister. In September, the speaker of Israel's Knesset, Reuven Rivlin, visited Slovakia. Prime Minister Mikulas Dzurinda told him that Israel was entitled to protect its citizens by building its controversial security barrier. Rivlin also met with the new president, Gasparovic, and also participated in ceremonies honoring 12 Slovak families and individuals as Righteous Gentiles for having saved Jews during the Holocaust.

Slovakia's known Jews numbered about 3,000, about 750 of them registered with the community in the capital city of Bratislava. Baruch Myers, an American-born Chabad adherent, served as community rabbi, leading regular services. Chabad also ran a kindergarten that admitted only children who were Jewish according to Halakhah, traditional Jewish law. Much of the community was nonobservant, and some members were dissatisfied with what they saw as Myers's rigidity.

In April, the Bratislava Museum of Jewish Culture appeared to have won a reprieve from eviction when city authorities extended its lease until the end of 2004. The museum, a branch of the state-run Slovak National Museum, still faced possible eviction if the Bratislava city government went ahead with plans to sell the building in which it was housed. Museum directors and Jewish leaders launched a petition calling on the mayor to block the sale, saying eviction would "mean the end of the museum." In cooperation with the Ministry of Culture, the museum launched a Jewish Heritage Center to provide information about Jewish sites in Slovakia.

The government allocated substantial funding toward the restoration of synagogues in Levice, Malacky, Banska Stiavnica, and Spisske Podhradie. During the year, a new exhibition on the Holocaust was installed at the recently restored synagogue in Nitra. In September, an exhibition of photographs of Auschwitz opened at the former synagogue in Zilina. The journal *Architekura & Urbanizmus* (Architecture and Town-Planning Theory) devoted a double issue to Slovakian synagogue architecture, history, and preservation.

RUTH ELLEN GRUBER

Former Soviet Union

National Affairs

IN 2004, THE RUSSIAN FEDERATION continued to move in an authoritarian direction and away from democratization and integration with the West. Beset with a serious problem of terrorism, the Kremlin sought to create single-party hegemony and state-controlled capitalism, with little room for economic freedom. There were also indications that the government was testing out a more independent and assertive foreign policy not necessarily to the liking of the U.S.

The December 2003 parliamentary election was a huge victory for President Vladimir Putin, as his party, United Russia, won about 40 percent of the seats in the Duma (lower house of parliament), nationalist parties 20 percent, and the Communists 13 percent. The liberal, Western-oriented parties that criticized the government's rollback of post-Soviet democratic freedoms seemed unable to arouse the indignation of the public, and were left with virtually no representation.

Putin's reelection to a second four-year term as president in March 2004 was a foregone conclusion. While there was no question that his overwhelming victory in the first round testified to his genuine popularity, the fact remained that much of the media reporting the election campaign was government controlled, and leaders of the democratic opposition were too demoralized even to run against him. Having promised to build a "dictatorship of the law" when first elected in 2000, Putin took an increasingly authoritarian path after his reelection.

One manifestation of this was his reaction to the acts of terror committed, apparently, by Chechen separatists. Three of the year's deadliest terror acts took place over a period of ten days in late August and early September: the hostage-taking at a school in the southern town of Beslan left nearly 350 dead; explosions on board two civilian airplanes killed 93; and a bomb blast at a Moscow subway station left at least 12 dead. Showing no willingness to seek a peaceful solution to the seemingly intractable conflict in Chechnya, Putin used the terrorist threat to justify a sweeping constitutional reform, ending the direct election of provincial governors and turning them into Kremlin appointees.

The Kremlin tightened the screws on Yukos, the giant oil company, and on its founder and former head, Mikhail Khodorkovsky, of Jewish descent, who had been imprisoned since the fall of 2003 pending trial on Kremlin-orchestrated tax-fraud charges. Since the company's huge tax bill could not be paid, the government seized control of Yukos assets, and, in a scheme widely believed to have been designed by the Kremlin, its main production subsidiary was sold in the first days of 2005 at auction for half its estimated value to a previously unknown company. Within a few days, that firm transferred ownership to the state-owned oil company Rosneft.

This blatant expropriation of the country's largest oil company caused jitters among foreign investors at a time when Russia's phenomenal economic growth showed signs of sluggishness, despite record high oil prices. The Yukos affair and other high-profile cases of businesses being targeted by the tax authorities and prosecutors—which looked suspiciously like extortion attempts—soured the business climate. The flow of domestic capital out of the country during 2004 was the highest since Putin took office.

Russian courts continued to show a lack of independence, and the law-enforcement agencies remained targets for corruption charges. While some of the larger national print media retained a level of independence that enabled them to criticize the Kremlin, newspapers in the provinces and nearly all of the national television stations were controlled by the authorities, either directly or indirectly. Late in the year, Freedom House, in its "freedom index" ranking of countries, downgraded Russia to "not free," reflecting the continued erosion of political rights and civil liberties there.

Following his reelection, Putin named Mikhail Fradkov, a previously little known bureaucrat of Jewish descent, as prime minister. The appointment triggered ambivalent feelings within the Jewish community. While some feared that any failure by Fradkov could result in increased anti-Semitism, others believed that the appointment signaled that ethnic background was no longer an obstacle for appointment to high public office. Fradkov, who was afterwards found to have had longstanding ties to the KGB, seemed content to play a bureaucratic role, and maintained a low public profile. Weeks after his appointment, he appeared in public at a nationally televised Russian Orthodox religious celebration, holding a candle and crossing himself. Most probably Fradkov did this to dispel talk about his alleged earlier connection to the Jewish community, which some Jewish leaders claimed to know about.

Despite the economic warning signs, Russia continued to benefit from high oil prices. Salaries grew at an annual rate of 13 percent (after inflation) in the first three quarters of 2004. Consumer lending by Russian banks, which had risen by a multiple of 17 since 2000, doubled again in 2004. After years of stagnation, the number of small businesses in Russia rose by 10 percent this year, and direct foreign investment in the first half of 2004 grew by 35 percent. Russia continued to make the list of the most attractive countries for foreign investment, especially for retail expansion of Western businesses. In November, Fitch joined Moody's in raising Russia's credit rating to investment grade. Yet there had been no meaningful economic restructuring, and some analysts predicted that this would cost Russia dearly should oil prices drop.

As demonstrated by his landslide reelection, Putin remained very popular despite all the political, social, and economic problems. To some observers this fact demonstrated the weak democratic instincts of the Russian people, while others suggested that the nation quite reasonably admired his authoritarian approach as likely to maintain order, without reverting to the harsh repression of the past. In spite of the troubling trends, both the U.S. and the European Union remained fully engaged with the Putin government. For the Americans, Russia constituted an important ally in the global war on terror. As for the EU, access to Russian oil and gas made economic and political cooperation vital.

Late 2003 and 2004 brought drastic changes to a number of other FSU countries. In both Georgia and Ukraine, new leaders came to power after mass demonstrations protesting fraudulent elections. The new presidents pledged to address the difficult challenges of turning their nations into more transparent and predictable democracies with market economies, and developing respect for basic civil liberties such as freedom of speech and religion. In both cases, President Putin showed considerable irritation at the triumph of Western-oriented elements over political forces seen as closer to Russia.

In Georgia, the "rose revolution" of November and December 2003 forced the resignation of longtime president Eduard Shevardnadze, whose proclaimed reelection was clearly fixed, and his replacement by the U.S.-educated Mikhail Saakashvili. While most Georgian Jews had emigrated since the collapse of the Soviet Union, when the country had plunged into civil war and economic chaos, the small remaining Jewish community (estimated at less than 5,000) welcomed Saakashvili's victory and his subsequent efforts to democratize Georgia.

The presidential election in Ukraine, held in November 2004, was tightly contested. The candidate of the authorities in Kiev and the favorite of the Kremlin was Prime Minister Viktor Yanukovich, and he was backed largely by the Russian-speaking and highly industrialized east and south of the country. His opponent was Viktor Yushchenko, who, campaigning as both a Ukrainian nationalist and a European-style liberal, drew considerable support from voters in central and western Ukraine. The country's 95,000-strong Jewish community was also split, a majority apparently siding with the pro-Russian Yanukovich out of fear of the anti-Semitism associated with some radical nationalist figures backing Yushchenko, and the candidate's seeming reluctance early in the year to distance himself from them (see below, p. 507).

But Yushchenko proved sensitive to Jewish concerns, and made several statements in support of ethnic coexistence and freedom of religion. At the height of the election crisis in December, when masses of people gathered in Kiev to protest the tainted "election" of Yanukovich that had been announced by the authorities, Yushchenko attended a Hanukkah celebration in a Kiev synagogue, becoming the first important Ukrainian politician to visit a Jewish house of worship. By the time the country's "orange revolution" succeeded in installing Yushchenko in office in late December, Jewish fears were largely alleviated and his presidency was welcomed even by many Jewish leaders who had voted against him.

Belarus stood out as an exception to the democratizing tendency. President Alexander Lukashenko continued to exercise virtually complete authority, driving his country into further isolation from the rest of the region, including Russia. In October, deeply flawed parliamentary elections were followed by a national referendum that authorized Lukashenko, whose current term would expire in 2006, to serve an unlimited number of additional terms. Lukashenko was able to rule in this way because of the overall social tranquility in the country. While the press was strictly regulated, major religious faiths, including the Jewish minority, enjoyed considerable freedom so long as they avoided commenting on political matters.

Three of the former Soviet republics in Europe—Latvia, Lithuania, and Estonia—became members of the European Union on May 1. Jews living in the three countries were divided in their assessment of their new status. While many welcomed the enhanced ease of travel across Europe and the new possibilities for employment abroad, others feared that the changes in economic policy instituted in order to gain entry into the EU could hurt the large number of elderly Jews in the Baltic states, who relied almost entirely on government assistance.

Among the states of Central Asia, Uzbekistan showed signs of growing instability as President Islam Karimov found himself under fire from two directions. First, there was the ongoing campaign of terrorism conducted by militant Islamists. On March 29, bomb blasts near a crowded outdoor market in Tashkent's old city killed at least four people and injured 70. Then, on August 4, suicide bombers attacked the Tashkent embassies of the U.S. and Israel, killing several policemen. At the same time, the president's iron-fisted control over the country, which he justified as the only way to ensure stability, elicited increasing criticism and even indications of civic unrest, suggesting that the nation's surface placidity might be deceiving.

In Kazakhstan, meanwhile, President Nursultan Nazarbayev oversaw an oil-fueled economic upturn. He also arranged to have his supporters win a comfortable parliamentary majority in October elections that were widely criticized as fraudulent. Nazarbayev continued to play a visible role in the region as patron of a dialogue between moderate Islam and other faiths, including Judaism.

Israel and the Middle East

Russian-Israeli relations remained generally positive, although certain complications developed in the second half of the year.

In early 2004, Russia earned Israel's praise when it sided with the U.S., EU members, and dozens of other nations in opposing the hearings on the legality of Israel's West Bank security barrier that took place at the International Court of Justice in The Hague. Israel, for its part, on several occasions expressed understanding of Russia's fight against Chechen separatist guerrillas, apparently in the hope that, in return, Moscow might abandon its largely pro-Palestinian stance. Especially in the wake of the attack on the school in Beslan at the beginning of September (see above), there was considerable hope that Moscow would show greater understanding for Israel's situation.

Russian foreign minister Sergei Lavrov visited Israel days after the Beslan tragedy. He told reporters that contacts were already under way between the security forces of the two countries and thanked Israel for its help, but stopped short of agreeing with Israeli leaders that they shared a common antiterror agenda with the Russians. According to Lavrov, the Palestinians were legitimate resisters against Israeli occupation of the West Bank and Gaza Strip, while the Muslim separatist cause based in Chechnya was completely illegitimate.

Russia, a member of the diplomatic "Quartet" that was pushing the "road map" peace plan, was also at pains to make clear that it would not neglect the Arab world. As an apparent counterweight to U.S. influence in the Middle East, Russia—following the example of the old Soviet Union—worked to develop its own regional ties there, paying special attention to Syria, Turkey, and Iran. News of a projected billion-dollar arms sale to Syria, expected to include Iskandar-E (SS-26) surface-to-surface missiles and Igla (SA-18) antiaircraft rockets, was the latest sign of a major shift in Russia's Middle East policy that some experts feared might shake regional stability. Viewed in the context of Russia's nuclear cooperation with Tehran, already in place for a decade, there was cause for alarm in the U.S. and in Israel, which felt itself directly threatened. Some ascribed Moscow's new aggressiveness in the area to the war in Iraq, which had cost Russia its Middle East foothold, formerly provided by Saddam Hussein.

In Minsk, Belarus, the Israeli embassy was reopened in late 2004, a year after it was closed for budgetary reasons. The closure had troubled Belarusian Jews, whose leaders argued that it could damage diplomatic relations between the two countries.

Anti-Semitism and Extremism

RUSSIAN FEDERATION

Hate crimes caused mounting concern in Russia in 2004. Organizations that monitored the situation noted an increase in the number of ethnically and racially motivated attacks and in the number of hate groups. Although Jewish and human-rights organizations acknowledged some improvement in the response of government and law-enforcement agencies, and noted the helpful condemnations of such activities by President Putin, the general tendency of previous years persisted—to downplay or altogether deny the problem. In fact, Jewish organizations decided not to go public after several incidents, apparently for fear of alienating the authorities on whose goodwill they relied for the conduct of their day-to-day activities.

The strength of anti-Jewish feeling in the country made this reluctance to speak out understandable. According to surveys conducted by the Expertise Foundation in the first half of 2004, over 42 percent of Russians agreed that it was necessary "to limit the influence of Jews in governmental bodies, politics, business, judicial and educational systems and in the sphere of entertainment," while another 23 percent were unsure about the matter. Furthermore, 28 percent supported the idea of "limiting the area of Jewish residence on the territory of the Russian Federation." The Coordination Forum for Countering Anti-Semitism, a coalition of groups that monitor and combat anti-Semitism around the world, brought together by the Israeli government, listed two of the FSU republics, Russia and Ukraine, third and fourth on its list of countries with the largest number of anti-Semitic incidents in 2004. Combined, the two contributed almost one-third of all the incidents recorded worldwide, 99 out of 282—55 in Russia and 44 in Ukraine. Only rarely were the perpetrators apprehended.

While there were very few violent physical attacks on Jews in Russia in 2004, a large number were perpetrated against other minorities. According to human-rights activists, there were 44 racist murders committed in 2004 in Russia. Such attacks were especially frequent in Moscow, St. Petersburg, and the central Russian city of Voronezh, and in most cases the victims were natives of the southern parts of Russia and the FSU, or foreign nationals from African and Asian countries. Human-rights groups blamed most of these crimes on neo-Nazi skinhead gangs, whose collective membership was estimated at anywhere between 15,000 and 50,000 in all of Russia. Police, however, generally attributed the crimes to hooligans, and tended to deny the existence of racial motivations. A few attacks against Jewish targets in the south of Russia were blamed on radical Islamists.

A particularly heinous crime was the murder, in June, in St. Petersburg, of Nikolai Girenko, a researcher on extremist groups. Girenko, who was not Jewish, served as an expert witness in several cases involving neo-Nazis. The killers, never identified, were assumed to be extreme right-wing nationalists.

The most shocking killing of a Jew during the year was probably unrelated to anti-Semitism. On March 5, 29-year-old Zaur Gilalov, a successful businessman and philanthropist from the Caucasus, and head of the World Congress of Mountain Jews, was shot to death in Moscow while shopping for his upcoming wedding. Knowledgeable observers, pointing out that his father had also been gunned down, suspected that this was a contract murder related to the victim's business operations, or a family vendetta.

Two violent attacks on Jews occurred within the span of one week, both in or near Moscow's Marina Roscha, an area densely populated by Orthodox Jews and home to the city's largest Jewish facility, the Marina

Roscha synagogue and community center. On December 16, a Jew from southern Russia who was a member of Marina Roscha was stabbed on a tram and sustained a serious lung injury. And on December 23, an Orthodox Jew from Israel was beaten up by three young men not far from the synagogue. Marina Roscha had been the scene of earlier anti-Semitic attacks over the years, although most had not been reported. In yet another incident earlier that same month in the same neighborhood, a driver employed by the Jewish community, an Azeri Muslim, was stopped by a traffic policeman who pushed the driver and uttered anti-Semitic slurs, apparently after noticing a menorah display on top of the car. In light of these events, the Federation of Jewish Communities of Russia, which ran the Marina Roscha facility, considered the creation of a special security unit in the neighborhood.

A brief rundown of other anti-Semitic incidents during the year gives a sense of the situation. On January 6, a group of teenagers shattered the windows at the Or Hadash Synagogue in Omsk, Siberia. On March 5, a bomb exploded near the Mekor Haim Center in Moscow, also known as the Steinsaltz Institute; no one was injured. Also in March, windows were shattered in two separate incidents at a Jewish welfare center in Tula, in Central Russia, and at the only kosher restaurant in St. Petersburg. A gang of intoxicated neo-Nazi skinheads broke into the Jewish community center in Ulyanovsk, in the Volga region, on April 22, shattering several windows and tearing off Israeli flags that were on display. The attackers managed to escape before the police arrived. On May 19, vandals destroyed a menorah displayed in front of the Volgograd synagogue. Three days later, Molotov cocktails were thrown at a synagogue in Tyumen, Siberia. On June 30, an explosive device found near the entrance to the Choral Synagogue in St. Petersburg was defused before it went off. On August 10, attackers threw stones at a synagogue in Kostroma. Some 40 skinheads armed with iron rods and metal chains attempted to attack a synagogue in Penza in November, but were dispersed by police.

There were many desecrations of Jewish cemeteries. The most serious incident took place in St. Petersburg on December 17, when more than 100 tombstones were vandalized—about 50 of them badly damaged—in the Jewish section of a local cemetery. In the southern city of Astrakhan, four separate attacks on the Jewish cemetery were reported between January and March. In the wake of the St. Petersburg outrage, one of Russia's chief rabbis, Berel Lazar, urged authorities to set up a federal program to protect the cemeteries of the different faiths.

Human-rights investigators reported an increase in the number of anti-Semitic and neo-Nazi books, periodicals, and brochures published in Russia during the year. Dozens of newspapers, primarily outside the big cities, printed anti-Semitic articles, and many extreme nationalist Web sites continued to preach the hatred of Jews. In December, the Moscow Bureau on Human Rights called for a probe of two recently published books containing anti-Semitic propaganda that were freely sold in Russia, and were even available in a bookstore in the Russian parliament. The books, *Zionism as a Source of Fascism* and *The Time to Be a Russian,* violated Russian anti-hate legislation and propagated neo-Nazism, according to the bureau.

Since Putin became president in 2000, prosecutors opened a steadily increasing number of cases under Article 282 of the Russian Criminal Code prohibiting the incitement of ethnic and religious hatred. Putin reinforced the regime's commitment to fight such hatred in October 2004, with a call for society to unite with the government in a struggle against xenophobia. One major milestone in dealing with hate crimes was attained in March, the country's first-ever guilty verdict for a racially motivated murder: three skinheads were convicted of killing an Azerbaijani man. But this result was an exception—few of the cases that were initiated reached court, and, if they did, a suspended sentence was the usual outcome.

Some civil cases ended with closure of the offending media outlets. In Novosibirsk, a court shut down the anti-Semitic *Russkaya Sibir* newspaper for fomenting ethnic strife. A court in Ekaterinburg ordered the paper *Russkaya Obshchina Ekaterinburga* to cease publication since it had ignored multiple warnings from the Ministry of the Press to stop publishing anti-Semitic articles, including materials from the infamous *Protocols of the Elders of Zion.* In December, a court in Moscow annulled the mild one-year suspended sentence handed down a month earlier in the case of Viktor Korchagin, a publisher of anti-Semitic works, opening up the possibility of a new criminal case against him. Korchagin had gained particular notoriety for publishing a Russian edition of Hitler's *Mein Kampf.* But there were many similar cases that the courts dismissed, while leaving others to drag on for years with no resolution.

In a move that seemed to contradict at least the spirit of President Putin's publicly stated opposition to racism and anti-Semitism, the Russian government in June eliminated a program aimed at promoting ethnic and religious tolerance, "Forming Tolerant Consciousness and Preventing Extremism in Russian Society." Originally adopted in 2000 and scheduled to conclude in 2005, it was aborted a year early, ostensibly due to budgetary considerations.

As in previous years, there were cases of anti-Semitic remarks by high-level politicians, both Russian nationalists and leftists. Nikolai Kondratenko, a prominent Communist leader in the upper house of parliament known for his anti-Semitism, gave a speech in Beirut in June where he spoke of "Zionists" committing "genocide" against Russia, and called for Russians and Muslims to unite against a worldwide Jewish conspiracy. His remarks were widely reprinted. Vladimir Zhirinovsky, a member of the Duma, the lower house of parliament, and head of the nationalist Liberal Democratic Party of Russia, spoke on the floor of the Duma in August in opposition to a moment of silence in honor of Holocaust Remembrance Day, calling the commemoration "unacceptable."

UKRAINE

On January 28, a judge in Kiev ordered the closing of the opposition newspaper *Silski Visti* after finding it guilty of inciting ethnic strife with an article about Jews. The piece in question, "Jews in Ukraine Today: Reality without Myths," was laced with anti-Semitic slurs, describing Jews as a privileged minority in Ukraine that ran the country by controlling its media, finances, and economy. It even went so far as to accuse Jews of "organizing" the tragic 1932–33 famine in Ukraine to take "revenge" on millions of Ukrainians. The article claimed that the Soviet secret police had been almost entirely Jewish and run by "leaders of Zionism." Even more bizarre was the allegation that the Nazi invasion of Ukraine was assisted by a 400,000-strong "horde of Jewish SS men."

The court ruling became entangled in partisan Ukrainian politics, as many who opposed the government of President Leonid Kuchma—including liberals and moderate nationalists—accused Kuchma of masterminding the court decision with the intention of exploiting the offending article as an excuse to shut down the largest opposition paper, whose circulation of over 500,000 included many readers who resided in the provinces and rural communities. Opposition leader Viktor Yushchenko, who, later in the year, would be elected president of Ukraine, criticized the court verdict and said that the newspaper should only have been required to apologize. His stand worried some Jews, raising the fear that Yushchenko might side with extreme nationalists if elected president, a concern he later tried to address through friendly gestures toward the Jewish community (see above, p. 501).

There were several anti-Semitic incidents in Ukraine during the year, though few were reported by the media. In the capital city of Kiev, on May 23, more than 50 Jewish gravestones were vandalized at a cemetery. The Interior Ministry initially denied any vandalism, saying the graves were destroyed "all by themselves, because they were too old." But the local Jewish community described it as an organized anti-Semitic action. On July 11, a group of men approached Rabbi Chaim Pikovsky near Kiev's Brodsky Synagogue and started insulting him. One punched the rabbi in the face and the others struck him several times. Another rabbi was assaulted on a downtown Kiev street in September.

On three separate occasions, windows were shattered in the Chabad synagogue in Odessa, with no injuries reported. In the wake of these attacks, police set up security points around almost 30 Jewish sites throughout the city. On August 24, two rabbis were attacked on Odessa's busiest street by two intoxicated men, one of whom was arrested.

Gravestones in the Jewish section of the Don Sea cemetery in Donetsk, in the eastern part of the country, were vandalized on August 21; several were smashed beyond repair and others had swastikas daubed on them. That month there were also reports that yeshiva students had been beaten up in the city. Jews in Donetsk also became targets of harassment during the holiday of Sukkot, when a group of men disrupted a religious procession near a synagogue and threatened to kill the participants. On September 22, heavy stones were thrown through the front windows of the local Jewish orphanage in Donetsk, without injuring anyone. Four young men were apprehended and charged with the crime. In the last days of 2004, windows were shattered at a Jewish community center in the city of Simferopol.

OTHER STATES

In Belarus, Jewish activists and human-rights leaders complained that the government was not doing enough to counter anti-Semitism. Leonid Stonov, the U.S.-based director of the Bureau on Human Rights of the Union of Councils for Jews in the Former Soviet Union, even called for international sanctions against this former Soviet republic, citing frequent acts of vandalism against Jewish cemeteries and the open availability of anti-Semitic publications in stores selling Russian Orthodox literature. In July, Belarusian Jewish organizations announced the formation of an "antifascist" committee to stem rising anti-Semitism in the country.

The disrespect shown toward cemeteries in Belarus, some with graves dating back centuries, inflicted deep pain on the Jewish community. Local leaders in the Gomel region reported in January that the ancient Jewish cemetery in the town of Rogachev, which had not been used since the 1980s, had been turned into a soccer field. Another old and disused cemetery, in Chernikov in the Mogilev region, was used as a garbage dump and a place to graze cattle. Several years earlier, municipal authorities had removed the fence surrounding the 400-year-old cemetery, and the tiny Jewish community was unable to take care of its former burial ground. Despite repeated complaints to town officials and promises by the latter to protect the cemetery, nothing had been done.

In Moldova, several cases of vandalism against Jewish sites were reported in 2004. In March, 70 tombstones were damaged and defaced in the Jewish cemetery of Tiraspol, capital of the unrecognized Transdniestrian Republic, which split off from Moldova in the early 1990s. Jews there reported that the local authorities refused to help them clean off anti-Semitic graffiti and swastikas from the tombstones. In the same community of Tiraspol, arsonists attempted to set fire to a synagogue on May 5 by throwing Molotov cocktails at it and spilling flammable liquid near the front door. The fire was extinguished before it spread to the building.

In Uzbekistan, Jewish organizations in the capital, Tashkent, received warnings from the state security authority that they might become targets of militant Islamists who were becoming increasingly active in this Central Asian state, but no major incidents were reported.

Holocaust-Related Developments

Issues related to the crimes of the Holocaust era remained especially pressing in the Baltic countries, where the Nazi occupiers were often helped by local collaborators and where the postcommunist governments did not always display sensitivity to Jewish concerns. On July 6, for example, Estonian veterans of the Nazi Waffen-SS paraded through the capital city of Tallinn, attended a church service and a concert, and laid flowers at a war memorial. The celebration marked the 60th anniversary of battles fought by the Estonian SS against the Red Army. Many Estonians regarded the SS veterans as freedom fighters who fought alongside the Germans to liberate their country from Soviet occupation.

Russian Jewish groups—apparently acting on the advice of the Russian government, which complained about the treatment of ethnic Russians in the postcommunist Baltic states—several times accused Estonia and Latvia of fomenting anti-Semitism by allowing or endorsing such commemorations. In some cases, however, local Jewish leaders in these nations dismissed the accusations by Russian Jews and denied that their countries' leaders endorsed anti-Semitism or Holocaust revisionism. There were several other disturbing incidents in the FSU. In Lithuania, in August, vandals smeared paint on a Holocaust memorial in a forest near the town of Alytus, where thousands of Jews were murdered during World War II. In Belarus, both in the capital city of Minsk and in the town of Lida, about 110 miles west of Minsk, vandals defiled monuments to Jews killed in the Holocaust. In Ukraine, Oleg Tyagnybok, a member of Viktor Yushchenko's opposition parliamentary faction, Our Ukraine, made public anti-Semitic statements related to Ukraine's wartime history on July 17. But Yushchenko promptly issued a statement condemning Tyagnybok, and when the latter failed to apologize, expelled him from the party.

In Kharkov, Ukraine, a plan to build a gas station and stores on a highway near the location of a mass grave for thousands of Holocaust victims was scrapped following protests by local Jewish leaders.

JEWISH COMMUNITY

Demography

In October, Berel Lazar, the Chabad rabbi recognized as chief rabbi by the government, challenged the results of the first post-Soviet census in Russia that was taken in 2002, which found 259,000 Jews living in Russia out of a total population of 145 million. Lazar, like a number of other experts and religious authorities, believed that this figure represented only a fraction of all Russian Jews, since many hesitated to declare their nationality as Jewish. He called for the creation of a database of Jews living in the country using modern computer technology.

Meanwhile, the Jewish population of Russia and other FSU countries continued to decline due to unfavorable demographic trends—an aging Jewish population, high rates of intermarriage, and continuing, albeit slowed-down, emigration.

Jewish emigration to Israel continued to drop. In the calendar year 2004, 10,404 Jews from the FSU arrived in Israel, an 18-percent decrease from the 12,720 who left in 2003. Every FSU country except Moldova showed a significant decline in the number of emigrants to Israel as compared to the statistics of 2003, with the largest drop, 28 percent, coming in the Baltic states that joined the EU in 2004. The smallest decline, 3 percent, was in Moldova, the poorest FSU nation in Europe. Jews from the Russian Federation accounted for 36 percent of all FSU Jews resettling in Israel, and Jews from Ukraine made up 29 percent. Only 1,134 FSU Jews emigrated to the U.S. in 2004, the lowest number in decades.

For the third year in a row, the largest proportion of emigrating Jews went to Germany, about 20,000, up from 19,000 in both 2002 and 2003. The explanation often given for this was the contrast between the economic difficulties newcomers faced in Israel and the generous benefits available in Germany. The fact that almost twice as many Jewish emigrants were going to Germany than to Israel was the cause of some embarrassment to Jewish leaders in the FSU, testifying as it did to the low level of Jewish identification among those leaving. Toward the end of the year, new legislation was proposed in Germany aimed at limiting the entry of Jews from the FSU (see above, p. 433).

Organizational Life

There were a number of significant developments during 2004 in the communal organizations of Russian Jewry.

The Chabad-oriented Federation of Jewish Communities (FJC), led by Chief Rabbi Berel Lazar and largely financed by Israeli diamond merchant Lev Leviev, strengthened its position as the leading organization of Russian Jews through the great scope and variety of its activities and its close relations with the Kremlin. President Putin praised the activities of FJC on several occasions, and, in a meeting with Lazar in October, offered the group government assistance to help solve the problems of Jewish communities in the country's outlying regions.

The rise of FJC meant the continuing decline of its most important rival, the Russian Jewish Congress (RJC), linked, in the eyes of the authorities, to the now-exiled former media mogul Vladimir Gusinsky, once the most vocal critic of Putin. The RJC, now led by its president, Yevgeny Satanovsky, and chairman of the board, Mikhail Fridman — himself considered one of the Russian "oligarchs" stigmatized by the Kremlin — appeared incapable of challenging the power of the FJC. In late 2004, any remaining maverick proclivities of the RJC were stifled when Satanovsky was removed in an internal coup orchestrated by people close to Putin and to Moscow mayor Yuri Luzhkov. The new RJC president, Vladimir

Slutsker, was a financier and member of the parliament's upper house, as well as a leading Kabbalah enthusiast, but had no leadership experience in the Jewish community. Slutsker announced that with his ascension, the era of infighting within the Russian Jewish community was over, and that his priority was to establish good relations with the Kremlin and the FJC. The latter, for its part, welcomed the leadership change at the RJC.

Whereas the end of community schism was widely regarded as a positive development, some Jews voiced concern over the Kremlin's obvious manipulation of Jewish communal affairs, as the neutering of RJC removed the last vestige of independence in any national Jewish group. This was so despite the continued existence of a third body, the Congress of Jewish Religious Organizations and Communities (KEROOR), associated with another chief rabbi, Adolf Shayevich. Representing the interests of the country's non-Chabad Orthodox congregations, KEROOR lacked strong leaders, funding, and government favor, and its future was uncertain.

The Union of Religious Congregations of Modern Judaism in Russia (OROSIR), the central body of the Reform movement, kept a low public profile during 2004, concentrating on internal community building and training its own young leaders and rabbinic paraprofessionals. OROSIR was affiliated with the World Union for Progressive Judaism (WUPJ), and that umbrella body's global forum, scheduled to be held in Moscow in the summer of 2005, was expected to boost the local Reform group's profile, activities, and funding.

Other Jewish organizations active across the FSU were the American Jewish Joint Distribution Committee (JDC), which ran major welfare programs through its network of Hesed centers; the Jewish Agency for Israel, involved in facilitating aliyah and Jewish and Zionist education; and Hillel, a student group that operated dozens of off-campus clubs seeking to attract unaffiliated Jewish college youth and young professionals. All of these groups maintained ongoing operations in almost every republic of the FSU, relying on funds from overseas sources, most notably the North American Jewish federations, private donors, and, in the case of the JDC welfare programs, Holocaust compensation money.

Religion and Culture

The Chabad-run FJC and its affiliated structures not only wielded great authority in the Jewish community and enjoyed the favor of the government, but also dominated religious services, formal Jewish education, and culture. Most of the rabbis permanently working in FSU communities were foreign-born—mainly Israeli and American—emissaries of the Chabad Hasidic organization. At the third biannual FJC conference, held in Moscow in October, the organization announced that it ran 178 congregations in the Russian Federation, operated 35 synagogue buildings, maintained four yeshivahs, and employed 36 rabbis in 33 cities. Largely successful in getting across the message that its practices and lifestyle were virtually synonymous with traditional Judaism, Chabad was now the mainstream form of the Jewish religion throughout the region.

As for the other religious bodies, KEROOR claimed several dozen Orthodox non-Hasidic congregations and employed over a dozen rabbis, most of them Russian-born. OROSIR, affiliated with the Reform movement, had about 35 active congregations in Russia. There were also some 40 Reform congregations in Ukraine and another 20 in Belarus. Reform had six rabbis, all natives of the FSU and trained at the Leo Baeck College in London. They worked in congregations in Moscow, St. Petersburg, Kiev, and Minsk.

In Lithuania, the small Jewish community was rocked by a heated dispute over the post of chief rabbi that was extensively reported in the local and international press. The split was between indigenous Jewish activists and a U.S.-born Chabad rabbi, Sholom Ber Krinsky, who had long been the only resident rabbi in the capital city of Vilnius. The dispute erupted when Krinsky proclaimed himself Lithuania's chief rabbi without consulting community leaders. Many of them vigorously objected to a Hasidic rabbi exerting authority in Lithuania, which had a longstanding Mitnagdic (anti-Hasidic) tradition dating back more than two centuries. As accusations mounted between the two sides, the lay leaders went so far as to close the main Vilnius synagogue for a time. Raising the stakes of the battle was the matter of Holocaust restitution payments: whoever was considered the legitimate representative of the community would have the inside track on getting the money.

In Kazakhstan's capital city, Astana, a new synagogue, Beit Rachel Chabad Lyubavitch, was dedicated in September. President Nursultan Nazarbaev and Israel's Ashkenazi chief rabbi, Yonah Metzger, attended the opening ceremony for the new synagogue, which was built with funds provided by billionaire Alexander Mashkevich, leader of the Euro-Asian Jewish Congress, in memory of his mother. The event was widely covered in the media, and was used by the government to boost that country's international image as an island of tranquility and interethnic accord in an area that had lately seen a rise of Muslim fundamentalism.

There were about 100 Jewish day schools in the former Soviet republics, about two-thirds of them under the aegis of the Chabad-run Or Avner foundation, the movement's educational arm in the FSU. World ORT sponsored 15 schools in the region, focusing on computer training and technological education.

LEV KRICHEVSKY

Australia

National Affairs

AUSTRALIA ENTERED 2004 with Prime Minister John Howard facing an election later in the year, Australian military personnel in Iraq and Afghanistan, and the economy in vigorous health despite concerns over an overheating real estate market. The Federal Parliament approved a landmark free-trade agreement (FTA) with the U.S. during the year, which came into effect at the beginning of 2005.

Australia's involvement in Iraq, already controversial within the country, drew increasing criticism as the insurgency intensified and the search for weapons of mass destruction yielded inconclusive results. Fortunately, Australia suffered no military fatalities. In July, an independent report cleared the Howard government of the charge of pressuring Australia's intelligence agencies to support the case for war. But the report, by former diplomat and intelligence chief Philip Flood, found that intelligence on Iraq's suspected store of weapons had been inadequate.

The fight against terror closer to home continued, with enhanced security and intelligence cooperation between Australia and its Southeast Asian neighbors. An alarming reminder of the threat posed by the group Jemaah Islamiah came in September, when a car bomb exploded outside the Australian embassy in Jakarta, killing at least eight people and wounding more than 160. Australia secured its first conviction for terrorism when Jack Roche was sentenced to nine years in jail. Roche had conspired with Al Qaeda and Jemaah Islamiah to blow up the Israeli embassy in Canberra. Australian terror suspect David Hicks—captured in Afghanistan late in 2001 and held in detention at Guantanamo Bay since—was formally charged by U.S. authorities in June. Fellow Australian detainee Mamdouh Habib was later released without charge and returned to Australia in February 2005.

Although the Australian Labor Party's Mark Latham, recently installed as opposition leader, enjoyed a prolonged political honeymoon through early 2004, by midyear Prime Minister Howard had regained ascendancy in the Parliament. The national election on October 9 delivered a decisive victory to Howard's Liberal-National coalition, with an increased majority in the Parliament and control of its upper house, the Senate, for the first time in decades. The Labor Party was left in turmoil after its fourth consecutive defeat, with Latham facing criticism over his handling of the campaign. He abruptly quit politics altogether in January 2005, citing ill health. Paradoxically, Labor retained control of all eight state and territorial governments.

Among the minor parties, the Greens did not make the electoral gains that some had predicted. Right-wing populist Pauline Hanson mounted another unsuccessful campaign for the Senate, this time as an independent, but garnered more publicity for her appearances on a celebrity dancing show than for any discernible political platform.

Israel and the Middle East

The war in Iraq was the major focus of Australian political debate about the Middle East. In the lead-up to the October 9 election, Labor — which, in 2003, had opposed armed intervention in Iraq in the absence of a UN Security Council resolution mandating such action — pledged to remove the modest number of Australian troops in Iraq "by Christmas." The government criticized this as "cutting and running," and Labor leader Latham clarified that, should his party come to power, some Australian troops would remain in order to protect Australian diplomatic and aid officials.

At the end of 2004, Australia had 850 troops in and around Iraq. These consisted of 85 troops providing security to Australian civilians and the Australian representative office; a contingent of 150 Royal Australian Air Force Hercules personnel providing airlift support; 80 air-traffic controllers at Baghdad International Airport; 53 army officers training the new Iraqi army; 12 people in a Navy training team; 270 people on the *HMAS Melbourne* conducting maritime interception operations in the northern Gulf; and 160 air force personnel. There were also around 30 Australian civilian and military experts assisting the provisional authority in the country until the end of its tenure in July. Australia committed $125 million in reconstruction assistance for Iraq in 2003–04.

The Israeli-Palestinian conflict was not a prominent factor in the election campaign, as both major parties, in statements addressed to the Jewish community, pledged friendship with Israel and a commitment to peace. The reelected coalition government remained among Israel's closest diplomatic allies, while also continuing to support the establishment of a Palestinian state alongside Israel through President Bush's "road map" strategy. The Labor opposition followed a largely similar approach. There were fewer debates in the Parliament during 2004 on Israeli-Palestinian affairs than in 2003. The death of Yasir Arafat in November provided the occasion for one such debate. A prominent new Liberal MP, Malcolm Turnbull, spoke of fresh opportunities for peace opened up by the removal of Arafat from the scene, and Labor MP Michael Danby— the only Jewish member—remarked that "the greatest obstacle to achieving a peace settlement was the obstructionism of the late Yasir Arafat." But Julia Irwin, a backbench Labor MP, eulogized the Palestinian leader as a "remarkable man" who "represented more than anyone the hopes of the Palestinian people." Decrying those who described him as an obstacle to peace, she blamed Israel for the failure of the Oslo peace process, saying that "not a single one of the withdrawal agreements was honored by the Israeli government."

Parliament debated and unanimously passed a motion early in 2004 condemning the growth of international anti-Semitism in recent years, promising "to take all possible concrete actions at a national level to combat this threat to our peaceful and diverse nation," and calling on Australia to use its diplomatic efforts abroad to counter such manifestations. In the course of debate on the motion, representatives of both major parties noted a relationship between anti-Semitism and certain extreme criticisms of Israel. Beside the action by the Federal Parliament, the state parliaments in Victoria and New South Wales also unanimously condemned international anti-Semitism.

Foreign Minister Alexander Downer made a three-day official visit to Israel on January 25–27. Known to be a warm personal supporter of Israel, he declared at an Australia-Israel Chamber of Commerce dinner, "I am delighted to be here in Israel again to give my support as the foreign minister of Australia. Australia will always stand by you, through thick and thin, and in recent years, there's been more thin." While somewhat critical of the routing of Israel's West Bank antiterror fence, Downer opposed referral of the issue to the International Court of Justice in The Hague, saying, "political issues should not be referred to a judicial body. This current move sets a dangerous precedent."

Much of the foreign minister's stay was devoted to economic cooperation between the two countries. Downer urged that "mutual investments should be boosted in each other's economics and business partnerships formed, especially in the high-tech IT sector where Australia excels." Unfortunately, the visit was marred by controversy after the Israeli daily *Ma'ariv* incorrectly reported a remark by Downer about Australia's openness to tourism and immigration as an invitation for young Israelis to migrate to Australia, leading to public criticism of Downer by a number of Knesset members.

Downer issued repeated statements throughout the year condemning terror attacks on Israeli civilians and calling on the Palestinian leadership to take stronger action against them. He also issued a statement expressing "regret" in response to the International Court of Justice's advisory decision condemning Israel's security barrier, stating that Australia did not view the ICJ ruling as "appropriate, or helpful," adding, "As I have so often said before, Israel has a right to defend itself from acts of terrorism and the security barrier has been demonstrably successful in protecting innocent Israeli lives from suicide/homicide bombers."

A bipartisan Australian parliamentary delegation, led by Senator Sandy McDonald and Senator Kim Carr, which had visited Syria, Lebanon, and Israel in November 2003, issued a report in March 2004. After summarizing the opinions of the various parties with whom the group had contact during the visit, the report criticized Israel, stating, "It's hard to see any justification for the destruction of buildings, equipment and infrastructure, other than to punish and demoralize." Another parliamentary delegation consisting of six younger members went to Israel in February under the sponsorship of the Australia/Israel and Jewish Affairs Council's Rambam Fellowship: Senators Stephen Conroy, Linda Kirk, and Ursula Stephens, and MPs Steven Ciobo, Sophie Panopoulos, and Andrew Southcott.

Australia voted against a UN General Assembly "emergency special session" resolution on July 20 demanding that Israel dismantle its West Bank security barrier in response to the advisory decision of the International Court of Justice. The opposition (Labor) foreign affairs spokesperson Kevin Rudd stated that it would have been "more appropriate" had Australia abstained. At the regularly scheduled General Assembly session in December, Australia cast its vote against the Israeli positions on "Jerusalem," "the Golan," "peaceful settlement of the question of Palestine" (a resolution apparently endorsing the Palestinian "right of return"), and the "special information program on Palestine of the Department of Public Information of the Secretariat." But Australia once again voted against allocating funding to the "Committee on the Exercise of the Inalienable Rights of the Palestinian People," and for the first time opposed a resolution authorizing funding for the "Division of

Palestinian Rights" in the Political Affairs Department of the UN Secretariat.

Australia chaired the UN Human Rights Commission in 2004. It had pledged beforehand to continue its efforts, launched in 2000, to promote the reform of UN treaty bodies, including the UN Human Rights Commission. On March 24, Australia was one of the two countries to vote against the commission's condemnation of Israel for killing Hamas leader Sheikh Ahmed Yassin. While opposed to the killing, the Australian delegate said the resolution was one-sided.

In June, the American Jewish Committee awarded Prime Minister Howard its American Liberties Medallion at a ceremony in Washington. The award, the highest presented by the AJC, was bestowed "in recognition of [his] longstanding commitment, as a member of the Australian Parliament for more than 30 years, and as prime minister since 1996, to championing democracy and human rights, and his unequalled friendship toward the United States and support of Israel."

A controversy broke out in February over remarks made by Sheikh Taj-el-Din al-Hilaly, the imam of Sydney's Lakemba Mosque, during a visit to Lebanon. According to an Australian embassy translation of a published sermon he delivered during a meeting with Hezballah at al-Quds Mosque in Sidon, Hilaly called for jihad against Israel and said that "September 11 is God's work against oppressors." Prime Minister Howard told Parliament on February 19 that if the reported statements were accurate, "what Sheikh Hilaly said deserves to be condemned in the strongest possible terms. Incitement to a jihad against the State of Israel is utterly unacceptable coming from the leader of any community in this country."

In late December, Australia asked Amir Laty, a junior officer at the Israeli embassy in Canberra, to leave the country. The government attempted to keep the request private, but an Israeli source revealed it early in 2005, exciting media speculation about possible links to espionage. But the Australian government refused to explain, Israeli authorities claimed ignorance, and the reason for the decision remained unclear.

Elsewhere in the Middle East, Trade Minister Mark Vaile visited the United Arab Emirates in May 2003 and exploratory talks continued in 2004 on a free-trade agreement. Australia also continued its renormalization of relations with Libya, after diplomatic ties, severed for more than a decade, were renewed in 2002. Foreign Minister Downer visited Libya in May 2004, meeting with the prime minister, Dr. Shukri Ghanem, and Foreign Minister Avd al Rahman Shalgam. Downer pledged to establish an Australian diplomatic mission in Tripoli.

THE MEDIA

Australian media coverage of Israel remained unbalanced, but, overall, not as anti-Israel as in previous years. The worst of the mainstream newspapers was still the *Canberra Times,* the only daily in the nation's capital. It regularly ran columns by anti-Israel polemicists Gwynne Dyer and Robert Fisk, and reprinted pieces from Britain's most anti-Israel mainstream paper, the *Independent,* as well as occasional submissions from members of the International Solidarity Movement. Other problematic papers were the *Age* and the *Sydney Morning Herald,* both published by the Fairfax organization. Ed O'Laughlin, the Israel correspondent for the Fairfax papers, often offered an anti-Israel slant. Columns by Tony Parkinson, foreign editor of the *Age,* generally showed a more balanced understanding of the issues. Other informative and fair columnists were Greg Sheridan of the *Australian,* Andrew Bolt of the *Herald Sun,* and Piers Akerman of the *Daily Telegraph.*

In the electronic media, the public broadcasters—ABC and SBS—continued to present problems in their coverage of Israel. An ABC internal memo came to light instructing staff not to refer to Hamas, Islamic Jihad, or Hezballah as "terrorist" organizations because they were not so designated by the UN, ignoring the fact that these groups were deemed "terrorist" by the Australian government. Thus the ABC described attacks in Moscow, Beslan, Jakarta, and Iraq as "terrorist," but not similar actions against Israel. SBS, for its part, refrained from referring to any attackers as terrorists.

Both the print and electronic media tended to present Israeli actions in a negative light. For example, Australians were told that Ariel Sharon's intention to evacuate Gaza was not a step toward peace but evidence of an intention to keep the West Bank; that Israel's security barrier was a "wall"; and that the killings of Hamas leaders Sheikh Yassin and Abdel Aziz Rantissi would only lead to more bloodshed, with no mention of the two men's responsibility for terror attacks. Many of the obituaries of Yasir Arafat underplayed his terrorist record, some even lauding him.

Hostility toward Israeli policies, opposition to the war in Iraq, and exaggerated notions of Jewish influence sometimes led media commentators to credit classical anti-Semitic stereotypes. Thus Margo Kingston, editor of the *Sydney Morning Herald* Web site, wrote that "the fundamentalist Zionist lobby controls politics and the media in the U.S. and Australia," while *Sunday Age* columnist Terry Lane opined, "the Zionist lobby in this country is malicious, implacable, mendacious and dangerous." To be sure, such outbursts by mainstream journalists were rare.

Anti-Semitism and Extremism

There were 425 incidents of anti-Semitism reported in 2004, a decline in comparison to the two previous years, but still the third highest annual amount ever recorded. The pattern over a 15-year period indicated an alarming trend: 469 incidents in 1990–92; 679 in 1993–95; 899 in 1996–98; 953 in 1999–2001; and 1,553 in 2002–04.

Of the 2004 total, 25 were reports of assault and property damage; 47 of face-to-face harassment; 14 telephone threats; 33 examples of threatening and/or abusive hate-mail; 45 graffiti attacks; and 261 other incidents that included offensive e-mail, posters, leaflets, and stickers that qualified as "racist violence" under the definition of Australia's Human Rights and Equal Opportunity Commission.

Extremist groups in Australia varied greatly in their memberships, activities, and target audiences. Some of these organizations were not centrally focused on Jews, but rather appealed to populist and xenophobic emotions to propagandize against the rights of all "outsiders," primarily scapegoating indigenous Australians and immigrants. Examples were One Nation, the AUSI Freedom Scouts, the Australian National Socialist Movement, and the Australia First Movement.

The Adelaide Institute, a loose conglomeration of individuals around self-styled Holocaust revisionist Fredrick Toben, was surely the most malicious anti-Jewish Australian group. Its published materials and Web site promoted the fiction of a Jewish conspiracy that controlled governments around the world in the interests of Zionism, using the "hoax" of the Holocaust to displace the Palestinian people from their land.

The Australian League of Rights was once described by the Human Rights and Equal Opportunity Commission as "undoubtedly the most influential and effective, as well as the best organized and most substantially financed, racist organization in Australia." With a now elderly membership that still drew inspiration from the moribund Social Credit movement of the 1930s and 1940s, it held meetings, conducted action campaigns, and sought publicity for its anti-Semitic assessment of domestic and international affairs. Under its director, Betty Luks, the league published a weekly newsletter, a monthly magazine, and a quarterly journal, and maintained a Web site.

The Citizens Electoral Council (CEC) continued to distribute large quantities of literature reflecting the views of the American extremist Lyndon LaRouche, including charges of conspiratorial activity by Jewish and antiracist organizations in Australia. It spent hundreds of thousands of dollars on Australian electoral campaigns, much of it raised from donations of more than $1,500 each, but won very few votes, averaging 0.06 percent over the past decade. CEC ran ads in the press, radio, and on television, and was particularly active in handing out literature on college campuses and at outside venues hosting Jewish community functions. Its one partial success in 2004 was convincing a number of prominent Australians to join Islamic, Arab, and far-right extremists in signing a petition against Australia's antiterrorism legislation.

The deceptively named Australian Civil Liberties Union (ACLU) continued to advocate Holocaust denial, with most of the group's public announcements aimed at protecting the "rights" of Holocaust deniers and other extremists. John Bennett, the goup's motivating force, is on the editorial advisory committee of the *Journal of Historical Review* published by the notorious Institute for Historical Review in California.

In most cities, small groups of neo-Nazis, sometimes including violent skinheads, operated. They were suspected of racist violence against Asian students and harassment of members of left-wing groups. Many of these extremists were unaffiliated with any formal organization, but one group, Australian National Action, engaged in public activities of this sort. Its leader, Michael Brander, claimed on his Web site that he was being persecuted "because he states that he does not think that the plan to exterminate Europe's Jews in the Second World War is proven." Brander sued a journalist for defamation for calling him a racist, but the Adelaide magistrate ruled against him, noting that "denial of the Holocaust and failure to condemn the principles espoused by Adolf Hitler and the Nazi party" were proof of racism.

JEWISH COMMUNITY

Demography

As of 2001, the year of the most recent census, Australia's Jewish community numbered about 84,000, or 0.44 percent of the country's total population of 20 million. This was 4,000 higher than in 1996. The actual number of Jews was surely even more, as religion was an optional question on the census form. An estimated quarter of the population preferred not to answer the religion question (Jewish community leaders believed that many of the Jews not answering were Holocaust survivors fearful of "registering" as Jews). The actual number of Jews was thus probably 120,000.

Melbourne had the largest Jewish community in the country, followed by Sydney. The census showed that most Jewish newcomers to Australia were from South Africa, and that Hebrew was the primary language at home for 6,000 Australians.

Communal Affairs

Graeme Leonard succeeded Jeremy Jones in December as president of the Executive Council of Australian Jewry (ECAJ), the representative Jewish communal body, while Ron Weiser continued as president of the Zionist Federation of Australia. Mark Leibler remained national chairman of the Australia/Israel and Jewish Affairs Council (AIJAC), and Dr. Colin Rubenstein continued as its executive director. AIJAC maintained its close association with the American Jewish Committee. Stanley Roth continued as federal president of the United Israel Appeal, and Michael Naphtali as head of the Jewish National Fund.

Education

More than half of all Jewish children aged 4–18—including almost 70 percent of those aged 4–12—received full-time Jewish education in the 19 Jewish day schools in Australia. Spanning the religious spectrum, these schools continued to rank at the highest level for academic achievement, reflecting the community's major investment in the schools as a means of preserving Jewish continuity. Day-school enrollments continued to grow despite ongoing concerns over high costs and the challenge to the community to find new sources of funding.

There was an increased emphasis on adult education, largely under the influence of the Melton Program, which had nearly 500 students in Sydney and Melbourne. Short-term courses utilizing guest lecturers also proved popular. Top priorities for the future, according to Australian Jewish educators, were expanded Jewish studies on the university level and teacher education to provide quality faculty for the day schools.

On the university level, the Australasian Union of Jewish Students (AUJS) continued to play an active and effective role on campus, particularly in combating anti-Zionist and racist manifestations and promoting exchange programs for Australian Jewish students and their Israeli counterparts.

Interfaith Dialogue

Continuing cooperation between the different religious communities in Australia was evident in 2004 with a number of joint actions aimed at building interfaith harmony and cooperation. The Executive Council of Australian Jewry (ECAJ), the National Council of Churches in Australia, and the Australian Federation of Islamic Councils repeated their joint calls for tolerance, and together coordinated the groundbreaking "Journey of Promise," in which ten Jewish, Muslim, and Christian participants, aged 18–25, spent a week living and learning together. In Adelaide, the Jewish and Muslim communities initiated a "Children of Abraham" project of seminars, lectures, and dialogues. These activities received support from the Federal Government, which also co-hosted an international interfaith conference, together with the government of Indonesia, in December, at which a Hanukkah celebration was attended by representatives of ten Asian and Pacific governments, and prominent Christian, Muslim, Buddhist, and Hindu leaders. This took place in the Muslim nation of Indonesia.

Churches were also important proponents of diversity and tolerance, often in concert with the Jewish community. The Uniting Church in Australia continued to explore ways of taking joint action with the Jewish community to combat prejudice, the two groups holding their National Dialogue twice each year. The Catholic Church also was a partner of the Jewish community in promoting interreligious and multifaith understanding, as the ECAJ and the Catholic Bishops' Committee continued to hold their Annual Conversation. The mainstream Christian bodies maintained their policies of prohibiting the use of their premises by racist and anti-Jewish groups, and advising their representatives not to share platforms with known extremists. When Mel Gibson's controversial film, *The Passion of the Christ,* appeared in Australian theaters, a number of Christian leaders publicly warned against interpreting its message in an anti-Semitic fashion.

To be sure, not all Christian clergy were sympathetic to Jewish sensibilities. At a May 1 demonstration against Israel at that country's embassy in Canberra, Bishop George Browning of the Anglican Church accused the Jewish state of "systematic slaughter of the Palestinian people," claimed to understand suicide bombing as a natural reaction to Israeli oppression, and described Israel's erection of the security barrier as "spitting in the face of God." Relations with the organized Australian Muslim community were correct, if not cordial. Its leaders disassociated themselves from anti-Jewish acts that occurred during the year, such as the publication in *Salam,* the magazine of the Federation of Australian Muslim Students and Youth, of anti-Semitic remarks, the sale of the *Protocols of the Elders of Zion* at an Islamic bookstore in Sydney, and statements hostile to Jews expressed by extremist Muslims in Sydney and Melbourne as part of a fund-raising campaign for a new mosque.

Culture

Notable among the many Jewish cultural organizations operating in Australia were the Melbourne-based Jewish Museum of Australia and the Sydney Jewish Museum. Both were world-class institutions that maintained extensive permanent collections of Judaica and Holocaust memorabilia, and mounted special exhibitions from time to time. They also hosted numerous cultural events, including literary evenings, book launches, and musical and dramatic presentations. Adelaide's Jewish community maintained a virtual museum, the Adelaide Jewish Museum (www.adelaidejmuseum.org).

The annual Jewish film festival, which regularly attracted large and enthusiastic audiences, continued to be held in Sydney and Melbourne.

The Australia Israel Cultural Exchange (AICE), founded in 2002 and headed by Albert Dadon, made a significant contribution to the cultural life of both countries. Its activities in 2004 included an exhibition of Australian Aboriginal art and an Australian film festival in Israel, and Israeli film and documentary festivals in Australia.

Personalia

In January 2004, the Australian government conferred Australia Day honors on a number of prominent Jews. Former ECAJ president Nina Bassat was appointed a Member in the Order of Australia (AM) for her services to the Jewish community and her promotion of greater intergroup understanding. Rodney Rosenblum received an AM for his work with both Austcare and Jewish Care, while Raymond Joseph's AM was for services to the Jewish community of Victoria. In addition, Dr. Ernst

Ehrmann and Rysia Rozen both received medals in the General Division (OAM)—Dr. Ehrmann for his work in dentistry as well as in the Jewish community, and Ms. Rozen for her contribution to the Jewish community of Victoria, particularly the National Council of Jewish Women. The annual Queen's Birthday Honors awarded in June 2004 recognized the contributions of several members of the Jewish community. Rabbi Raymond Apple, Mrs. Eva Besen, and Prof. Fredrick Mendelsohn were made Officers of the Order of Australia (AO), while Brian Sherman and Marcus Schoenheimer received AMs. Rabbi Apple was honored for service to the community through promoting interfaith dialogue and harmony, and by raising awareness of social justice, ethical, and spiritual issues; Mrs. Besen for her contribution to the arts; Prof. Mendelsohn for his contribution to medicine, especially neuroscience and biomedical research; and Mr. Schoenheimer for service to manufacturing and industry, as well as to the Jewish community. Mr. Sherman, a board member of AIJAC and founding chairman of its Rambam Fellowship program, received his AM for services to the community as a philanthropist and benefactor to a wide range of arts, education, business, and commerce. Several members of the Jewish community received Medals in the Order of Australia (OAM). These included Eric Cohen, Dr. Hilton Immerman, Thomas Keleman, Henry Lippman, Mahla Pearlman, Phillip Samuell, and Harvey Teller.

The Australian Jewish community mourned the passing in 2004 of Tony Blashki, who played a role in the establishment of Mt. Scopus College; Judith Epstein, entertainer and author; and Isador Magid, cofounder of AIJAC and former chairman of the United Israel Appeal.

COLIN L. RUBENSTEIN

South Africa

T HE YEAR 2004 marked a decade since the emergence of a democratic South Africa, and the milestone triggered much reflection. Speaking for the Jewish community, Chief Rabbi Cyril Harris noted the nation's major achievements, political stability and a sound economy, although there still remained much to be done. Jews, he pointed out, were able to practice their religion freely, and, despite its diminishing size, the community was probably more "Jewishly vibrant" than ever before.

The general election, held April 14, saw the consolidation of power by the African National Congress (ANC), led by President Thabo Mbeki, and its allies, the Communist Party (SACP) and the Congress of South African Trade Unions (COSATU). Together, they won 69.69 percent of the national vote and control of all nine provinces. The Democratic Alliance (DA), led by Tony Leon, won 12.37 percent, and the Inkatha Freedom Party (IFP), led by Mangosuthu Buthelezi, garnered 6.97 percent, mainly from the KwaZulu-Natal Province. But the coalition's landslide victory was less than a resounding mandate. The number of voters was down, as nearly 7 million people who were registered stayed away from the polls and thus only 38 percent of registered voters chose the ANC. By virtue of heading the DA, the second largest party, Tony Leon, a Jew, was leader of the official opposition. Another Jew, Ronnie Kasrils, was appointed minister of intelligence in the new cabinet. There were two other Jewish members of Parliament, Ruth Rabinowitz (IFP) and Ben Turok (ANC).

The ANC-led government maintained its tight fiscal policies. Despite a substantially improved growth rate (approximately 3.5 percent) and the creation of new jobs, unemployment remained high. About 251,000 jobs were created between March and September, leaving unemployment at 4.1 million, which was 26.2 percent of the South African population. The strength of the South African currency, the rand, was of great concern to exporters.

South Africa championed multilateralism in the conduct of global affairs and supported the reform of international institutions such as the UN and the World Trade Organization (WTO). It devoted substantial attention to regional foreign policy, especially the consolidation of the New Partnership for Africa's Development (NEPAD) and initiatives to resolve regional conflicts. The crisis in Zimbabwe continued, however, despite President Mbeki's attempts to encourage that country's president, Robert Mugabe, to enter into negotiations with his political opponents. South Africa worked hard to keep Africa—and the southern hemisphere generally—on the global agenda, as formulated by the G8 industrialized nations.

Despite the governing coalition's strong parliamentary majority, tensions existed within it, especially over policy towards Zimbabwe. Another area of contention was the continuing wide disparity between whites and blacks in income, landholding, employment, education, and housing. There was a program called Black Economic Empowerment, a form of affirmative action, but its application and effectiveness remained unclear. The privatization of state-owned enterprises, to which the government was committed, proceeded slowly. Increasingly, President Mbeki tended to show impatience with his critics, including such antiapartheid veterans as Archbishop Emeritus Desmond Tutu.

HIV/AIDS remained a major problem. About 5 million South Africans—20 percent of the adult population—were HIV positive, and an estimated half million had developed AIDS. Following a major row between the Ministry of Health and the Treatment Action Campaign (TAC), a nongovernmental activist group that called for the use of antiretroviral drugs to combat AIDS, the government finally began to implement an antiretroviral program in 2004.

Even though a so-called National Crime Prevention program was in place, crime and lawlessness continued to plague the country. High-profile cases of corruption were increasingly featured in the newspapers, including the upcoming trial of Durban businessman Schabir Shaik, charged with fraud and with bribing the deputy president, Jacob Zuma. The case was scheduled for early 2005.

Warren Goldstein, the chief rabbi elect, delivered a prayer on behalf of the Jewish community at President Mbeki's inauguration. In an editorial entitled "Being Part of South Africa," the *SA Jewish Report* (Aug. 13) proclaimed that Jews "owe it to this country—and our own consciences—to give whatever we can to help all its peoples develop, and to participate fully in the building of a new South African nation in which we can be proud and feel at home." In November, a delegation of Jewish leaders led by SAJBOD (South African Board of Jewish Deputies) national chairman Michael Bagraim had a fruitful and productive meeting with an ANC delegation led by President Mbeki. Bagraim reported that he was "very optimistic regarding the future of our relationship with the government."

Israel and the Middle East

The South African government continued to pursue a pro-Palestinian line, although its official position was that Israel had a right to exist. The newly appointed ambassador to Israel, Major General Reverend Fumi Gqiba—a presidential appointee rather than a career diplomat—condemned suicide bombings at a luncheon in his honor organized by Jewish leaders, and said: "Israel is there to stay. Nobody will destroy it or wish it away. But the Palestinian state can also not be wished away." Yet there were disquieting suggestions that not everyone in the governing party agreed. A July posting on the ANC's Youth League Web site indicated fundamental hostility towards Israel, and stated that the very existence of the Jewish state was a "vexing question."

Alon Liel, an Israeli who had served as ambassador to South Africa from 1991 to 1994, visited in April and expressed alarm at the deterioration in relations. He told the *SA Jewish Report* that there was no country "outside the Arab world that has done more to harm its relations with Israel than South Africa. The government has emptied its relations with Israel of any content. The Israeli embassy is almost completely isolated here." Referring to South Africa's attempt to mediate the Israel-Palestine dispute in 2003 by bypassing the Israeli government and dealing with former Israeli officials (see AJYB 2004, p. 477), Liel acknowledged President Mbeki's good intentions. But he noted that the government's use of the South African paradigm in the Middle East was flawed. "The nature of the conflict," he said, "is completely different from the old conflict between black and white in South Africa, and the South African government doesn't seem to understand."

The next month, Daniel Pinhasi, the acting Israeli ambassador, denied that the decision to close Israel's South African trade office in Johannesburg was a sign that Israeli-South African links were being downgraded. Pinhasi explained the closure as a budgetary move, like a similar decision to close the trade office in Argentina. But he did consider the step regrettable, since it would add to the negative atmosphere between the two countries.

In June, South Africa hosted a meeting of the UN's Committee on the Exercise of the Inalienable Rights of the Palestinian People, in Cape Town. This committee had been established in 1975, the year the UN passed the "Zionism is racism" resolution, and this year's theme was "Achieving the Inalienable Rights of the Palestinian People: The Key to Peace in the Middle East." Recalling the way that the 2001 World Conference Against Racism, in Durban, had been hijacked by extreme anti-Israel and even anti-Semitic elements, the Jewish community sought to ensure against a repetition, and South African authorities acted to alleviate its fears.

Addressing the committee, President Mbeki argued there would be no solution to the Israeli-Palestinian conflict without the participation of the Palestinian Authority and President Arafat, and therefore it was wrong for Israel to prevent him from leaving his compound in Ramallah. Mbeki believed Arafat was sincere in seeking a solution to the conflict, and concluded, "We recognize the need for an independent sovereign state of Palestine with its capital in Jerusalem. None of us can feel secure while we see so many people dying all the time. It must be part of our principal African agenda to make sure that we engage this issue." An editorial in the *SA Jewish Report* (July 2) responded that a solution would "only be achieved when the Palestinians themselves stop trying to destroy Israel and focus their energies instead on building up their own society. This does not mean giving up their legitimate desire to be free of the harsh Israeli occupation over their lives and territory. This is achievable, even though the road is difficult."

Toward the end of the year, South Africa took steps to repair relations with Israel. In September, a senior delegation from Likud, Israel's ruling party, met for two days in Pretoria with a high-powered South African delegation headed by President Mbeki. South Africa's Department of Foreign Affairs described the sessions as "an integral part of ongoing efforts by South Africa to assist both Israelis and Palestinians to find common ground with a view to developing a just, lasting and comprehensive resolution to the current conflict." Pro-Palestinian groups condemned the meetings, the Palestinian Solidarity Committee describing them as an "outrage."

Ehud Olmert, the Israeli deputy prime minister and minister of trade and industry, visited South Africa in October both in order to discuss the Israeli-Palestinian conflict and to conclude an agreement on trade and investment between South Africa and Israel. Olmert told South African

Jews that the "political gesture" their government made in meeting with him should reassure them, and the *SA Jewish Report* (Oct. 29) welcomed the apparent warming of relations. This visit too attracted Palestinian protests. The Jewish community, meanwhile, maintained its close ties to the Jewish state. Jewish young people continued to attend programs in Israel, Zionist youth movements were strong, and the South Africa Israel Chamber of Commerce increased its presence. Dr. Efraim Zuroff, director of the Simon Wiesenthal Center in Israel, launched a very successful Israel United Appeal-United Communal Fund (IUA-UCF) campaign in March, and in June, the Women's Zionist Organization of South Africa sponsored a series of concerts in Cape Town and Johannesburg to demonstrate support for Israel.

Anti-Semitism

There was a marginal increase in reported anti-Semitic incidents during 2004. These came mostly in the form of verbal abuse and hate mail, threats, graffiti, and calls to talk shows, and there were reports of individual Jews being threatened. Swastikas were sometimes seen at sports matches involving Jewish day schools. The majority of these actions were attributed to members of the Muslim community. Hostility mounted particularly in the wake of Israel's killings of Ahmed Yassin and Abdel Aziz Rantisi (see above, p. 234–36). Sheikh Ebrahim Gabriels, president of the Muslim Judicial Council, was particularly vitriolic in his response to the death of Yassin, referring to Jews as "filthy people" who manipulated the gentiles through strategies spelled out in the *Protocols of the Elders of Zion*. In a case that drew great public outrage, a six-year-old child was dressed up as a suicide bomber at a Muslim rally in Pretoria.

In September, Voice of the Cape, a Muslim radio station, interviewed Sheikh Mogamat Colby, a South African studying at a *madrasa* (Islamic school) in Egypt. Colby claimed Jews murdered, raped, and killed mothers, children, and babies, and cited the *Protocols of the Elders of Zion* to show that Jews controlled "our land, all the means of the radio stations, the newspapers, the televisions—and this is how they have full control over the whole world." The SAJBOD lodged a complaint with the Independent Communications Authority of South Africa (ICASA). Voice of the Cape posted an apology, but this was not satisfactory to the SAJBOD, which resolved to pursue the matter further.

Holocaust-Related Matters

Holocaust denial continued to be peddled by diverse extremist types. Far-right newspapers such as *Die Afrikaner* often contained such material, as did the *Scribe,* an organ of the Pretoria-based Radio 584, a Muslim station.

The Jewish community fought Holocaust denial in the courts, as the SAJBOD's ongoing legal battle with Radio 786, a Muslim station run by the Islamic Unity Council (IUC), continued. This affair began in 1998, when the station aired an interview with Yaqub Zaki, a historian at the Muslim Institute in London, in which he denied that Jews had been gassed during the Holocaust and claimed that only about one million Jews had died then, from infectious diseases. The SAJBOD complained to ICASA that the interview violated the code of conduct for broadcasting services, which barred offensive material that was likely to harm relations between sections of the population. In April 2001, the Johannesburg High Court ruled against the SAJBOD on a technicality (see AJYB 2002, pp. 511–12). In November 2002, Advocate Roland Sutherland, chairman of the Broadcasting Complaints Commission, ruled in favor of the station and dismissed the SAJBOD complaint (see AJYB 2004, pp. 480–81).

In March 2004, the SAJBOD applied for a hearing to have Sutherland's decision overturned. Mervyn Smith, a past president of the SAJBOD and a member of the subcommittee handling the matter, told the *SA Jewish Report* (Mar. 5) that this was "a huge case for the country and one of the biggest in the history of South African Jewry in terms of freedom of speech. When judgment is eventually given it will be a definitive judgment both in this country and abroad on hate speech and what is permissible." This time the Johannesburg High Court upheld the SAJBOD application, directing ICASA to convene a formal hearing on the SAJBOD's complaint and the IUC to pay the SAJBOD's costs. The IUC's request for leave to appeal against the ruling for a formal hearing was dismissed.

Dr. Ze'ev Mankowitz delivered the fifth Ernest and Renee Samson Anniversary Lecture, "From Holocaust to Homeland: Between History and Memory," at the Cape Town Holocaust Center in September. The center also prepared curricular materials for high schools on the subject of the Holocaust. The project, called "The Holocaust: Lessons for Humanity," was sponsored by Archbishop Emeritus Tutu, a patron of the center.

JEWISH COMMUNITY

Demography

Further analysis of the 2001 national census indicated a Jewish population of about 72,000 amid a total of 44,819,777 South Africans. It showed that 95 percent of the country's Jews lived in Johannesburg, Cape Town, Durban, and Pretoria, and, within these cities, were highly concentrated in certain suburbs.

According to recent statistics drawn from the Israel United Appeal-United Communal Fund (IUA-UCF), Jewish emigration from South Africa had slowed significantly. Only 200 contributors to the fund emigrated in 2003, the lowest figure in years, and the Cape Town community's emigration rate dropped by half. Yehuda Kay, national executive director of the SAJBOD, told the *SA Jewish Report* (June 25) that the figures gave cause for optimism about the community's stability, but cautioned that it "was too soon to assess their long-term significance."

Norman Bernhard, rabbi emeritus of the Oxford Synagogue in Johannesburg, suggested the establishment of a Hebrew Immigrant Aid Society of South Africa, which would identify South African Jews who were having difficulties abroad and encourage them to return and replenish South African Jewry.

Communal Affairs

Fissures within the Jewish community came to the surface several times during the year. In March, Jewish Voices of South Africa, launched in 2002 by Jews who felt that the established communal structure was not committed to democratic values, held its annual general meeting. The chairman, Ivor Chipkin, spoke of a "fundamental shift" he thought was taking place within South African Jewry, as many Jews who did not feel represented by the dominant Orthodox leadership sought space for a more progressive approach. In an editorial comment under the title "Jewish Alternatives," the *SA Jewish Report* (Mar. 12) noted that the festival of Passover and the tenth anniversary of South Africa's democracy marked "a special opportunity to attempt to heal one of the saddest rifts in the community — between the mainstream Jewish community and left-wing Jews who became activists during the antiapartheid struggle."

The theme of the Cape Council centenary in August was "Living as Jews, South Africans, and Zionists." Speaker after speaker — most notably Ebrahim Rasool, the Cape premier—spoke out against fundamentalism, whether Christian, Jewish or Muslim. The keynote speaker, Rabbi David Rosen, director of international interreligious affairs for the American Jewish Committee, cautioned particularly against the fundamentalism of "Jewish insularity," often accompanied by what he called "delegitimization of those outside that group, in order to reinforce a sense of self-righteousness, thus leading to internal disunity and strife and doing more harm than good to the community at large." On the second day of the gathering, Jewish AIDS activist Nathan Geffen criticized the community's "unconditional support" for Israel and its failure to condemn Israel's "human rights abuses" against Palestinians. But Mervyn Smith, former national president of the SAJBOD, responded that the SAJBOD could not publicly criticize the government of Israel since that would be "highly destructive" to the fabric of Israel-Diaspora relations.

Following the conference, an important controversy about Jewish political behavior took place in the columns of the *SA Jewish Report* (Sept. 3, 10). Joel Pollak, a speechwriter for DA leader Tony Leon, took the Cape Council to task for praising Cape premier Rasool's remarks against fundamentalism while overlooking his words at a rally following Israel's assassination of Ahmed Yassin. "Rasool," Pollak noted, "described Yassin as 'one of the greatest inspirations' and prayed that Palestinians 'stand up to these enemies and never succumb, that they fight, and they fight under a flag of Islam.'" Furthermore, according to Pollak, Rasool did not distance himself from blatantly anti-Semitic statements made by others on that occasion, including some that cited the *Protocols of the Elders of Zion.* But the national chairman of the SAJBOD, Michael Bagraim, responded that the SAJBOD was not a political party but a "Jewish lobby organization whose purpose is to build relationships with government rather than to catch votes through point scoring or to indulge in publicity seeking."

South Africa's adoption of the Promotion of Equality and Prevention of Unfair Discrimination Act was acclaimed in the Jewish community for its protection of religious liberty and outlawing of hate speech. But Judge Ralph Zulman warned Jewish leaders that the law could have unexpected and uncomfortable implications for the country's Jews. It might, for example, interfere with existing admissions policies at Jewish institutions, since non-Jews seeking entrance to Jewish schools or old-age homes would be able to lodge complaints of discriminatory treatment if not admitted. Zulman suggested that Jewish institutions prepare a joint strategy on this matter.

A new coordinating council for the Jewish community of East London was launched in November. It comprised representatives of all East London's Jewish organizations, including the SAJBOD, *hevra kadishah* (burial society), Union of Jewish Women, Women's Zionist League, and the two congregations, one Orthodox and the other Progressive.

A number of communal celebrations punctuated the year. The United Institutions of Oudtshoorn celebrated its 120th anniversary. Oudtshoorn, referred to in the late nineteenth century as "the Jerusalem of Africa," was known for its ostrich feather industry, in which Jews were prominent. The Piketberg Jewish community, the Hebrew Order of David, and the Cape Council of the SAJBOD celebrated their centenaries.

South African Jewish leaders continued to build bridges to the wider population and to assist the disadvantaged. Habonim Dror provided financial aid and established a joint project with the Treatment Action Campaign (TAC) to supply antiretroviral treatment for HIV-positive persons. Tikkun ran a wide variety of programs promoting life skills, peer counseling, AIDS education, academic support for high-school students, alternatives to violence, and poverty relief. The Union of Jewish Women (UJW) joined up with a Jewish professional fund-raiser and a Muslim couple to initiate a program to fund foster care for abandoned children. The South African Union of Temple Sisterhoods continued its ongoing programs: feeding 3,000 children daily, and assisting the sick, aged, single mothers, and families in need of financial and moral support. The Jewish National Fund supported the Walter Sisulu Environmental Center in Mamelodi, near Pretoria. Herzlia-Weizmann Primary School provided books to Ntwasahlobo Primary School in Khayelitsha, located outside Cape Town.

Notwithstanding such charitable endeavors, Chief Rabbi Harris took the community to task for not sufficiently supporting them. He said, "There's an unfortunate reluctance, a sort of suspicion about interacting with the black majority—particularly on the part of the older generation—which is absurd. We're ten years down the line in democracy, our Board of Deputies has a very praiseworthy Proudly Jewish South African campaign and yet there's a kind of resentment." And Harris went on, "We're not saying that Jewish causes should take a back seat—but if you give 100 percent of your *tzedakah* to Jewish charities, you are doing something which is un-Jewish, because we have a reputation for always having cared for others outside our community."

A special Freedom Seder was held at Liliesleaf Farm, Rivonia, once the headquarters of Umkonto we Sizwe, the armed wing of the ANC.

Liliesleaf Farm was the site of the famous Rivonia raid that led to the imprisonment of Nelson Mandela and others, including prominent Jews. In December, Jewish community leaders took part in the National Consultative Conference of the Commission for the Promotion and Protection of the Rights of Cultural, Religious, and Linguistic Communities (CRL) in Durban. The CRL was launched in 2003 "to promote and develop peace, friendship, humanity, and national unity among cultural, religious, and linguistic communities."

Religion

Rabbi Warren Goldstein vacated his pulpit in Glenhazel, Johannesburg, to take up his position as chief rabbi elect in February. He was a fourth-generation South African with considerable experience in intergroup work, having coauthored, with Dumani Mandela, *Africa Soul Talk,* a dialogue on the values that should permeate the new South Africa. Goldstein's doctoral thesis, "Remoralizing Legal Systems: Insights from Jewish Law," dealt with the contemporary relevance of Jewish law. There was some criticism of the procedure through which his appointment was secured, but none about his qualifications. In an interview with David Saks, senior researcher at the SAJBOD (*SA Jewish Report,* Feb. 13), Goldstein said that it was important for Jews to be loyal South Africans and to take pride in South Africa's new democracy. Expressing optimism about the Jewish future in the country, he identified three priorities: to ensure the community's continuity and health; to make a positive impact on South Africa; and to benefit the State of Israel. Gala receptions were held in Johannesburg and Cape Town in honor of the outgoing chief rabbi, Cyril Harris. In Cape Town, communal leader Elliot Osrin paid tribute to Rabbi Harris, noting that he had "given our community a sense of dignity, a sense of pride and above all, a sense of direction."

The Johannesburg Bet Din (religious court) was involved in a major legal wrangle after it placed a Jewish man in *herem* (excommunication) for, among other things, refusing to comply with its ruling that he pay maintenance to his former wife. Although the man had originally agreed with the former wife to abide by the Bet Din decision, he subsequently applied to the High Court to set that ruling aside. The annual rabbinical conference, held in Durban, pledged full support to the Bet Din. Justice Frans Malan of the High Court found in favor of the Bet Din, describing *herem* as a legitimate "expression of communal disdain" directed at a person whose conduct was "not in full compliance with the ethical dictates of Jewish society." In light of the publicity that the case engendered, the Union of Orthodox Synagogues hosted a special breakfast for lawyers to apprise them of the role of the Bet Din.

Johannesburg continued to see a mushrooming of small Orthodox synagogues—six separate Chabad branches, four of Ohr Someach, and various religious Zionist congregations—and the debate on their possible impact accelerated. While some considered them a sign of religious vibrancy, others saw evidence of fragmentation. Most Johannesburg rabbis supported the phenomenon, as did Chief Rabbi Harris, who said he had no objection so long as these bodies were financially and spiritually viable. Harris suggested that the larger synagogues meet the demand for more intimate services by organizing such groups on their own premises to run parallel to the main service, but others felt that the motivation for the small synagogues had less to do with intimacy than with a desire to pray in the company of others with a similar level of observance.

In other religious news, the Green and Sea Point Hebrew Congregation celebrated its 70th anniversary, and bid farewell to Rabbi Dr. E. J. Steinhorn; the Claremont Hebrew Congregation, Cape Town, celebrated its centenary; Rabbi Daniel Sackstein was inducted as rabbi of the Cape Town Hebrew Congregation, the mother institution of South African Jewry; and Phina Hoberman was appointed to the Board of Directors of Women of Reform Judaism at its 44th assembly, held in Minneapolis.

Culture

Two noteworthy exhibitions at the South African Jewish Museum during 2004 were "Studio Encounter: Portraits by Irma Stern," and "Hidden Treasures of Japanese Art: The Isaac Kaplan Collection." An Israeli film festival was held in Cape Town, Johannesburg, and Pretoria.

The Arts and Cultural Trust gave its lifetime achievement award to Sylvia Glasser, the initiator of Moving Into Dance Mophatong, a multiracial dance group founded in 1978.

Publications of Jewish interest included *Judaism: A Growing Tradition* by Rabbi Dr. David Sherman; *Ali: The Life of Ali Bacher* an autobiography by the former national cricket captain and cricket administrator; *The Moon Can Wait,* a biography of the former Zimbabwe politician Abe Abrahamson, by Paul Clingman; *The Free Diary of Albie Sachs,* an autobiographical work by the human-rights activist and constitutional court judge; *Mulik the Zulik* by Holocaust survivor Shmuel Keren-Krol; *South African Jewish Board of Deputies (Cape Council, 1904–2004),* edited by

Gwynne Robins; *Namaqualand's Jewish Pioneers* by Phyllis Jowell and Adrienne Folb; *The First Hundred Years 1904–2004, 5664–5764: The Story of the Claremont Hebrew Congregation,* edited by Esther Surdut; and *An African Shopkeeper* by David Susman.

Personalia

Chief Rabbi Cyril Harris was given a special award by Keren Hayesod in Israel; veteran human-rights activist Helen Suzman was honored by the Jewish National Fund; Edna Freinkel received the Bronze Order of the Counselor of the Baobab from President Mbeki, for exceptional service to education; Alec Rogoff, doyen of the Durban Jewish community, was awarded an honorary doctorate by the University of Natal for his humanitarian contributions to it; and Mervyn Smith, past president of the SAJBOD, earned the Lexus Lifetime Achiever Award for his communal service. Marlene Bethlehem, past president of the SAJBOD, was appointed deputy chairperson of the Commission for the Protection of the Rights and Culture of Religious and Linguistic Communities.

Among prominent South African Jews who died in 2004 were Hal Shaper, lyricist and composer; Norman Sandler, educator; Louis Babrow, international rugby player; Lionel Abrahams, poet and writer; Ethel de Keyser, antiapartheid activist; Rolfe Futerman, pioneer of Israeli air power; Raymond Tucker, antiapartheid activist and human-rights lawyer; Franz Auerbach, educator, human-rights activist, and communal leader; Ray Alexander, antiapartheid activist and trade unionist; and Aaron "Okey" Geffin, international rugby player.

MILTON SHAIN

Directories
Lists
Obituaries

National Jewish Organizations*

UNITED STATES

COMMUNITY RELATIONS

AMERICAN COUNCIL FOR JUDAISM (1943). PO Box 9009, Alexandria, VA 22304. (703)836-2546. Pres. Stephen L. Naman; Exec. Dir. Allan C. Brownfeld. Seeks to advance the universal principles of a Judaism free of nationalism, and the national, civic, cultural, and social integration into American institutions of Americans of Jewish faith. *Issues of the American Council for Judaism; Special Interest Report.* (WWW.ACJNA.ORG)

AMERICAN JEWISH COMMITTEE (1906). The Jacob Blaustein Building, 165 E. 56 St., NYC 10022. (212)751-4000. FAX: (212) 750-0326. Pres. E. Robert Goodkind; Exec. Dir. David A. Harris. Protects the rights and freedoms of Jews the world over; combats bigotry and anti-Semitism and promotes democracy and human rights for all; works for the security of Israel and deepened understanding between Americans and Israelis; advocates public-policy positions rooted in American democratic values and the perspectives of

---

*The information in this directory is based on replies to questionnaires circulated by the editors. Web site addresses, where provided, appear at end of entries.

Jewish heritage; and enhances the creative vitality of the Jewish people. Includes Jacob and Hilda Blaustein Center for Human Relations, Project Interchange, William Petschek National Jewish Family Center, Jacob Blaustein Institute for the Advancement of Human Rights, Institute on American Jewish-Israeli Relations. *American Jewish Year Book; Commentary; AJC Journal.* (WWW.AJC.ORG)

AMERICAN JEWISH CONGRESS (1918). 825 Third Ave., Ste. 1800, NYC 10022. (212) 879-4500. FAX: (212)249-3672. E-mail: pr@ajcongress.org. Pres. Paul S. Miller; Exec. Dir. Neil B. Goldstein. Works to foster the creative survival of the Jewish people; to help Israel develop in peace, freedom, and security; to eliminate all forms of racial and religious bigotry; to advance civil rights, protect civil liberties, defend religious freedom, and safeguard the separation of church and state; "The Attorney General for the Jewish Community." *Congress Monthly; Judaism; Inside Israel; Radical Islamic Fundamentalism Update.* (WWW.AJCONGRESS. ORG)

AMERICAN JEWISH PUBLIC RELATIONS SOCIETY (1957). 575 Lexington Ave., Suite 600, NYC 10022. (212)644-2663. FAX: (212)644-3887. Pres. Diane J. Ehrlich; V-Pres., membership, Lauren R. Marcus. Advances professional status of public-relations practitioners employed by Jewish organizations and institutions or who represent Jewish-related clients, services, or products; upholds a professional code of ethics and standards; provides continuing education and networking opportunities at monthly meetings; serves as a clearinghouse for employment opportunities. *AJPRS Reporter; AJPRS Membership Directory.*

ANTI-DEFAMATION LEAGUE OF B'NAI B'RITH (1913). 823 United Nations Plaza, NYC 10017. (212)885-7700. FAX: (212)867-0779. E-mail: webmaster@adl.org. Natl. Chmn. Barbara B. Balser; Natl. Dir. Abraham H. Foxman. Seeks to combat anti-Semitism and to secure justice and fair treatment for all citizens through law, education, and community relations. *ADL on the Frontline; Law Enforcement Bulletin; Dimensions: A Journal of Holocaust Studies; Hidden Child Newsletter; International Reports; Civil Rights Reports.* (WWW.ADL.ORG)

ASSOCIATION OF JEWISH COMMUNITY RELATIONS WORKERS (1950). 7800 Northaven Road, Dallas, TX 75230. (214) 615-5229. FAX: (214)373-3186. Pres. Marlene Gorin. Aims to stimulate higher standards of professional practice in Jewish community relations; encourages research and training toward that end; conducts educational programs and seminars; aims to encourage cooperation between community-relations workers and those working in other areas of Jewish communal service.

CANFEI NESHARIM (2002). 111 Eighth Ave., 11th Floor, NYC 10011. (212)284-6745. E-mail: info@canfeinesharim.org. Exec. Dir. Evonne Marzouk. Educates about protecting the environment, from the perspective of Torah and Jewish law; encourages actions to protect the environment. *Compendium of Sources in Torah and Halacha* (biennial); *Newsletter* (monthly e-mail). (WWW.CANFEINESHARIM.ORG)

CENTER FOR JEWISH COMMUNITY STUDIES (1970). 1515 Locust St., Suite 703, Philadelphia, PA 19102. (215)772-0564. FAX: (215)772-0566. E-mail: jcpa@net vision.net.il or cjcs@worldnet.att.net. Jerusalem office: Jerusalem Center for Public Affairs. Pres. Amb. Dore Gold; Dir. Gen. Zvi Marom; Chmn. Bd. of Overseers Michael Rukin. Worldwide policy-studies institute devoted to the study of Jewish community organization, political thought, and public affairs, past and present, in Israel and throughout the world. Publishes original articles, essays, and monographs; maintains library, archives, and reprint series. *Jerusalem Letter/Viewpoints; Jewish Political Studies Review.* (WWW.JCPA.ORG)

CENTER FOR RUSSIAN JEWRY WITH STUDENT STRUGGLE FOR SOVIET JEWRY/SSSJ (1964). 240 Cabrini Blvd., #5B, NYC 10033. (212)928-7451. FAX: (212)795-8867. Dir./Founder Jacob Birnbaum. Chmn. Dr. Ernest Bloch. Campaigns for the human rights of the Jews of the former USSR, with emphasis on emigration and Jewish identity; supports programs for needy Jews there and for newcomers in Israel and USA, stressing employment and Jewish education. As the originator of the grassroots movement for Soviet Jewry in the early 1960s, possesses unique archives.

COALITION ON THE ENVIRONMENT & JEWISH LIFE (1993). 443 Park Ave. S., 11th fl., NYC 10016-7322. (212)684-6950, ext. 210. FAX: (212)686-1353. E-mail: info@coejl.org. Dir. Adam C. Stern. Promotes environmental education, advocacy, and action in the American Jewish community. Sponsored by a broad coalition of Jewish organizations; member of the National Religious Partnership for the Environment. *Bi-annual newsletter.* (www.coejl.org)

COMMISSION ON SOCIAL ACTION OF REFORM JUDAISM (1953, Joint Instrumentality of the Union for Reform Judaism and the Central Conference of American Rabbis). 633 Third Ave., 7th fl., NYC 10017. (212)650-4160. FAX: (212)650-4229. E-mail: csarj@urj.org. Wash. Office: 2027 Massachusetts Ave., NW, Washington, DC 20036. Chmn. Robert Heller; Dir. Rabbi Daniel Polish; Dir. Religious Action Center of Reform Judaism, Rabbi David Saperstein. Policy-making body that relates ethical and spiritual principles of Judaism to social-justice issues; implements resolutions through the Religious Action Center in Washington, DC, via advocacy, development of educational materials, and congregational programs. *Tzedek V'Shalom (social action newsletter); Chai Impact (legislative update).*

CONFERENCE OF PRESIDENTS OF MAJOR AMERICAN JEWISH ORGANIZATIONS (1955). 633 Third Ave., NYC 10017. (212) 318-6111. FAX: (212)644-4135. E-mail: info@prescon.org. Chmn. Harold Tanner; Exec. V.-Chmn. Malcolm Hoenlein. Seeks to strengthen the U.S.-Israel alliance and to protect and enhance the security and dignity of Jews abroad. Toward this end, the Conference of Presidents speaks and acts on the basis of consensus of its 54 member agencies on issues of national and international Jewish concern.

CONSULTATIVE COUNCIL OF JEWISH ORGANIZATIONS-CCJO (1946). 420 Lexington Ave., Suite 1731, NYC 10170. (212)808-5437. Chmn. Ady Steg & Clemens N. Nathan. A nongovernmental organization in consultative status with the UN, UNESCO, ILO, UNICEF, and the Council of Europe; cooperates and consults with, advises, and renders assistance to the Economic and Social Council of the UN on all problems relating to human rights and economic, social, cultural, educational, and related matters pertaining to Jews.

COORDINATING BOARD OF JEWISH ORGANIZATIONS (1947). 2020 K Street, NW, 7th Floor, Washington, D.C. 20006. (202)857-6540. FAX: (202)857-6689. Exec. V. Pres. Daniel S. Mariaschin. To promote the purposes and principles for which the UN was created.

COUNCIL OF JEWISH ORGANIZATIONS IN CIVIL SERVICE, INC. (1948). 45 E. 33 St., Rm. 601, NYC 10016. (212)689-2015. FAX: (212)447-1633. Pres. Louis Weiser; 1st V.-Pres. Melvyn Birnbaum. Supports merit system; encourages recruitment of Jewish youth to government service; member of Coalition to Free Soviet Jews, NY Jewish Community Relations Council, NY Metropolitan Coordinating Council on Jewish Poverty, Jewish Labor Committee, America-Israel Friendship League. *Council Digest.*

INSTITUTE FOR PUBLIC AFFAIRS (*see* Union of Orthodox Jewish Congregations of America)

INTERNATIONAL LEAGUE FOR THE REPATRIATION OF RUSSIAN JEWS, INC. (1963). 2 Fountain Lane, Suite 2J, Scarsdale, NY 10583. (914)683-3225. FAX: (914)683-3221. Pres. Morris Brafman; Chmn. James H. Rapp. Helped to bring the situation of Soviet Jews to world attention; catalyst for advocacy efforts, educational projects, and programs on behalf of Russian Jews in the former USSR, Israel, and U.S. Provides funds to help Russian Jewry in Israel and the former Soviet Union.

JEWISH COUNCIL FOR PUBLIC AFFAIRS (Formerly NATIONAL JEWISH COMMUNITY RELATIONS ADVISORY COUNCIL) (1944). 443 Park Ave. S., 11th fl., NYC 10016-7322. (212)684-6950. FAX: (212) 686-1353. E-mail: jcpainfo@thejcpa.org. Chmn. Marie Abrams; Exec. Dir. Rabbi Steve Gutow. National coordinating body for the field of Jewish community relations, comprising 13 national and 122 local Jewish community-relations agencies. Promotes understanding of Israel and the Middle East; supports Jewish communities around the world; advocates for equality and pluralism, and against discrimination, in American society. Through the Council's work, its constituent organizations seek agreement on policies, strategies, and programs for effective utilization of their resources for common ends. *Insider (Weekly).* (www.JEWISHPUBLICAFFAIRS.ORG)

JEWISH LABOR COMMITTEE (1934). Atran Center for Jewish Culture, 25 E. 21 St., NYC 10010. (212)477-0707. FAX: (212) 477-1918. Pres. Stuart Appelbaum; Exec. Dir. Avram B. Lyon. Serves as liaison between the Jewish community and the trade union movement; works with the U.S. and international labor movement to combat anti-Semitism, promote intergroup relations, and engender support for the State of Israel and Jews in and from the former Soviet Union; promotes teaching in public schools about the Holocaust and Jewish resistance; strengthens support within the Jewish community for the social goals and programs of the labor movement; supports Yiddish-language and cultural institutions. *Jewish Labor Committee Review; Issues Alert; Alumni Newsletter.*

———, NATIONAL TRADE UNION COUNCIL FOR HUMAN RIGHTS (1956). Atran Center for Jewish Culture, 25 E. 21 St., NYC 10010. (212)477-0707. FAX: (212)477-1918. Exec. Dir. Avram Lyon. Works with the American labor movement in advancing the struggle for social justice and equal opportunity, and assists unions in every issue affecting human rights. Fights discrimination on all levels and helps to promote labor's broad social and economic goals.

JEWISH PEACE FELLOWSHIP (1941). Box 271, Nyack, NY 10960. (914)358-4601. FAX: (914)358-4924. E-mail: jpf@forusa.org. Hon. Pres. Rabbi Philip Bentley; Ch. Murray Polner. Unites those who believe that Jewish ideals and experience provide inspiration for a nonviolent philosophy and way of life; offers draft counseling, especially for conscientious objection based on Jewish "religious training and belief"; encourages Jewish community to become more knowledgeable, concerned, and active in regard to the war/peace problem. *Shalom/Jewish Peace Letter.* (WWW.JEWISHPEACEFELLOWSHIP.ORG)

JEWISH WAR VETERANS OF THE UNITED STATES OF AMERICA (1896). 1811 R St., NW, Washington, DC 20009. (202)265-6280. FAX: (202)234-5662. E-mail: jwv@jwv.org. Natl. Exec. Dir. Herb Rosenbleeth; Natl. Commander Daniel Weiss.

Seeks to foster true allegiance to the United States; to combat bigotry and prevent defamation of Jews; to encourage the doctrine of universal liberty, equal rights, and full justice for all; to cooperate with and support existing educational institutions and establish new ones; to foster the education of ex-servicemen, ex-servicewomen, and members in the ideals and principles of Americanism. *Jewish Veteran.*

———, NATIONAL MUSEUM OF AMERICAN JEWISH MILITARY HISTORY (1958). 1811 R St., NW, Washington, DC 20009. E-mail: nmajmh@nmajmh.org. (202)265-6280. FAX: (202)234-5662. Pres. Edwin Goldwasser; Archivist Tom Wildenberg. Documents and preserves the contributions of Jewish Americans to the peace and freedom of the United States; educates the public concerning the courage, heroism, and sacrifices made by Jewish Americans who served in the armed forces; and works to combat anti-Semitism. *The Jewish War Veteran).*

NATIONAL ASSOCIATION OF JEWISH LEGISLATORS (1976). 65 Oakwood St., Albany, NY 12208. (518)527-3353. FAX: (518) 458-8512. E-mail: najl01@aol.com. Exec. Dir. Marc Hiller; Pres. Sen. Richard Cohen, Minn. state senator. A nonpartisan Jewish state legislative network focusing on domestic issues and publishing newsletters. Maintains close ties with the Knesset and Israeli leaders.

NCSJ: ADVOCATES ON BEHALF OF JEWS IN RUSSIA, UKRAINE, THE BALTIC STATES AND EURASIA (Formerly AMERICAN JEWISH CONFERENCE ON SOVIET JEWRY) (1964; Reorg. 1971). 1640 Rhode Island Ave., NW, Suite 501, Washington, DC 20036-3278. (202)898-2500. FAX: (202) 898-0822. E-mail: ncsj@ncsj.org. N.Y. office: 823 United Nations Plaza, NYC 10017. (212)808-0295. Chmn. Robert J. Moth, M.D.; Pres. Dr. Joel M. Schindler; Eexc. Dir. Mark B. Levin. Coordinating agency for major national Jewish organizations and local community groups in the U.S., acting on behalf of Jews in the former Soviet Union (FSU); provides information about Jews in the FSU through public education and social action; reports and special pamphlets, special programs and projects, public meetings and forums. *Newswatch; annual report; action and program kits; Tekuma.* (WWW.NCSJ.ORG)

———, SOVIET JEWRY RESEARCH BUREAU. Chmn. Denis C. Braham; Pres. Howard E. Sachs. Organized by NCSJ to monitor emigration trends. Primary task is the accumulation, evaluation, and processing of information regarding Jews in the FSU, especially those who apply for emigration.

NATIONAL JEWISH COMMUNITY RELATIONS ADVISORY COUNCIL (*see* Jewish Council for Public Affairs)

NATIONAL JEWISH DEMOCRATIC COUNCIL (1990). 777 N. Capital St., NE, Suite 305, Washington, DC 20002. (202)216-9060. FAX: (202)216-9061. E-mail: info@njdc. org. Chmn. Amb. Arthur Schechter; Founding Chmn. Morton Mandel; Exec. Dir. Ira N. Forman. An independent organization committed to strengthening Jewish participation in the Democratic party primarily through grassroots activism. The national voice of Jewish Democrats, NJDC is dedicated to fighting the radical right and promoting Jewish values and interests in the Democratic party. (WWW.NJDC.ORG)

REPUBLICAN JEWISH COALITION (1985). 50 F Street, NW Suite 100, Washington, DC 20001. (202) 638-6688. FAX: (202)638-6694. E-mail: rjc@rjchq.org. Natl. Chmn. Sam Fox; Hon. Chmn. Richard J. Fox, Lawrence Kadish, George Klein. Promotes involvement in Republican politics among its members; sensitizes Republican leaders to the concerns of the American Jewish community; promotes principles of free enterprise, a strong national defense, and an internationalist foreign policy. *RJC Bulletin.* (WWW.RJCHQ. ORG)

SHALEM CENTER (1994). 5505 Connecticut Avenue, NW, No. 1140, Washington, DC 20015. (877)298-7300. FAX: (888)766-1506. E-mail: shalem@shalem.org.il. Pres. Yoram Hazony (Israel); Academic Director, Daniel Polisar (Israel). The purposes and activities of the Shalem Center are to increase public understanding and conduct educational and research activities on the improvement of Jewish national public life, and to develop a community of intellectual leaders to shape the state of Israel into a secure, free, and prosperous society. *Azure.* (WWW.SHALEMCENTER.ORG)

SHALOM CENTER (1983). 6711 Lincoln Dr., Philadelphia, PA 19119. (215)844-8494. E-mail: shalomctr@aol.com. (Part of Aleph Alliance for Jewish Renewal.) Exec. Dir. Rabbi Arthur Waskow. National resource and organizing center for Jewish perspectives on dealing with overwork in American society, environmental dangers, unrestrained technology, militarism, and corporate irresponsibility. Initiated A.J. Heschel 25th Yahrzeit observance. Trains next generation of *tikkun olam* activists. Holds colloquia on issues like environmental causes of cancer. *New Menorah.* (WWW.SHALOMCTR.ORG)

STUDENT STRUGGLE FOR SOVIET JEWRY (*see* Center for Russian Jewry)

UN WATCH (1993). 1, rue de Varembé, PO Box 191, 1211 Geneva 20, Switzerland. (41-22)734.14.72. FAX: (41-22)734.16.13. E-mail: unwatch@unwatch.org. Exec. Dir. Hillel Neuer; Chm. Amb. Alfred H. Moses. An affiliate of the AJC, UN Watch measures UN performance by the yardstick of the UN's Charter; advocates the non-discriminatory application of the Charter; opposes the use of UN fora to attack Israel and promote anti-Semitism; and seeks to institutionalize at the UN the fight against worldwide anti-Semitism. *The Wednesday Watch(English and Spanish).* (WWW.UNWATCH.ORG)

UCSJ: UNION OF COUNCILS FOR JEWS IN THE FORMER SOVIET UNION (Formerly UNION OF COUNCILS FOR SOVIET JEWS) (1970). 1819 H St., NW, Suite 230, Washington, DC 20005. (202)775-9770. FAX: (202)775-9776. E-mail: ucsj@ucsj.com. Pres. Yosef I. Abramowitz; Natl. Dir. Micah H. Naftalin. Devoted to promoting religious liberty, freedom of emigration, and security for Jews in the FSU (former Soviet Union) through advocacy and monitoring of anti-Semitism, neo-facism, human rights, rule of law, and democracy. Offers educational, cultural, medical, and humanitarian aid through the Yad L'Yad partnership program pairing Jewish communities in the US and the FSU; advocates for refuseniks and political prisoner. (WWW.FSUMONITOR.COM)

WORLD CONGRESS OF GAY, LESBIAN, BISEXUAL & TRANSGENDER JEWS (1980). 8 Letitia St., Philadelphia, PA 19106-3050. (609)396-1972. FAX: (215)873-0108. E-mail: president@wcgljo.org. Pres. Scott R. Gansl (Philadelphia, PA); V.-Pres. Francois Spiero (Paris, France). Supports, strengthens, and represents over 67 Jewish gay and lesbian organizations across the globe and the needs of gay and lesbian Jews generally. Challenges homophobia and sexism within the Jewish community and responds to anti-Semitism at large. Sponsors regional and international conferences. *The Digest.* (www.WCGLJO.ORG/ WCGLJO/)

WORLD JEWISH CONGRESS (1936; org. in U.S. 1939). 501 Madison Ave., 17th fl., NYC 10022. (212) 755-5770. FAX: (212) 755-5883. Pres. Edgar M. Bronfman; Co-Chmn. N. Amer. Branch Prof. Irwin Cotler (Montreal) & Evelyn Sommer; Dr. Avi Beker, Secretary General. Seeks to intensify bonds of world Jewry with Israel; to strengthen solidarity among Jews everywhere and secure their rights, status, and interests as individuals and communities; to encourage Jewish social, religious, and cultural life throughout the world and coordinate efforts by Jewish communities and organizations to cope with any Jewish problem; to work for human rights generally. Represents its affiliated organizations-most representative bodies of Jewish communities in more than 80 countries and 35 national organizations in American section-at UN, OAS, UNESCO, Council of Europe, ILO, UNICEF, and other governmental, intergovernmental, and international authorities. *WJC Report; Boletin Informativo OJI; Dialogues; Dateline: World Jewry; Coloquio; Batfutsot; Gesher.*

CULTURAL

AMERICAN ACADEMY FOR JEWISH RESEARCH (1929). 420 Walnut Street, Philadelphia, PA 19106. (215)238-1290. FAX: (215)238-1540. Pres. Robert Chazan. Encourages Jewish learning and research; holds annual or semiannual meeting; awards grants for the publication of scholarly works. *Proceedings of the American Academy for Jewish Research; Texts and Studies; Monograph Series.*

AMERICAN GATHERING OF JEWISH HOLO-CAUST SURVIVORS. 122 W. 30 St., #205. NYC 10001. (212)239-4230. FAX: (212)279-2926. E-mail: mail@americangathering.org. Pres. Benjamin Meed. Dedicated to documenting the past and passing on a legacy of remembrance. Compiles the National Registry of Jewish Holocaust Survivors-to date, the records of more than 165,000 survivors and their families-housed at the U.S. Holocaust Memorial Museum in Washington, DC; holds an annual Yom Hashoah com-

memoration and occasional international gatherings; sponsors an intensive summer program for U.S. teachers in Poland and Israel to prepare them to teach about the Holocaust. *Together (newspaper).*

AMERICAN GUILD OF JUDAIC ART (1991). 15 Greenspring Valley Rd., Owings Mills, MD 21117. (410)902-0411. FAX: (410) 581-0108. E-mail: office@jewishart.org. Pres. David Klass; 1st V.-Pres. Richard McBee. A not-for-profit membership organization for those with interests in the Judaic arts, including artists, galleries, collectors & retailers of Judaica, writers, educators, appraisers, museum curators, conservators, lecturers, and others personally or professionally involved in the field. Helps to promote members' art. *Hiddur (quarterly); Update (members' networking newsletter).* (WWW.JEWISHART. ORG)

AMERICAN JEWISH HISTORICAL SOCIETY (1892). 15 W. 16 St., NYC 10011. (212) 294-6160. FAX: (212)294-6161. E-mail: ajhs@ajhs.cjh.org. Pres. Sidney Lapidus; Dir. Dr. Michael Feldberg. Collects, catalogues, publishes, and displays material on the history of the Jews in America; serves as an information center for inquiries on American Jewish history; maintains archives of original source material on American Jewish history; sponsors lectures and exhibitions; makes available audiovisual material. *American Jewish History; Heritage.* (WWW.AJHS. ORG)

AMERICAN JEWISH PRESS ASSOCIATION (1944). Natl. Admin. Off.: 1828 L St. NW, Suite 720, Washington, DC 20036. (202)785-2282. FAX: (202)785-2307. E-mail: toby@ajpa.org. Pres. Aaron Cohen; Exec. Dir. Toby Dershowitz. Seeks the advancement of Jewish journalism and the maintenance of a strong Jewish press in the U.S. and Canada; encourages the attainment of the highest editorial and business standards; sponsors workshops, services for members; sponsors annual competition for Simon Rockower Awards for excellence in Jewish journalism. *Membership bulletin newsletter.*

AMERICAN SEPHARDI FEDERATION (1973). 15 W. 16 St., 6th Floor, NYC 10011. (212)294-8350. FAX: (212)294-8348. E-mail: asf@cjh.org. Pres. David E.R. Dangoor; Exec. Dir. Vivienne Roumani-

Denn. The central voice of the American Sephardic community, representing a broad spectrum of Sephardic organizations, congregations, and educational institutions. Seeks to strengthen and unify the community through education, communication, advocacy, and leadership development, creating greater awareness and appreciation of its rich and unique history and culture. *Sephardic Today.* (WWW.ASFONLINE.ORG)

AMERICAN SOCIETY FOR JEWISH MUSIC (1974). c/o The Center for Jewish History, 15 W. 16 St., NYC 10011. (212)294-8328. FAX: (212)294-6161. Pres. Michael Leavitt; V.-Pres. Judith Tischler & Martha Novick; Sec. Fortuna Calvo Roth; Bd. Chmn. Rabbi Henry D. Michelman; Treas. Cantor Nathaniel Benjamin. Promotes the knowledge, appreciation, and development of Jewish music, past and present, for professional and lay audiences; seeks to raise the standards of composition and performance in Jewish music, to encourage research, and to sponsor performances of new and rarely heard works. *Musica Judaica Journal.*

ASSOCIATION OF JEWISH BOOK PUBLISHERS (1962). c/o Jewish Book Council, 15 East 26th Street, 10th Floor, New York, NY 10010. (212)532-4949. FAX: (212)481-4174. Email: arjhill@jewishbooks.com. Pres. Ellen Frankel. As a nonprofit group, provides a forum for discussion of mutual areas of interest among Jewish publishers, and promotes cooperative exhibits and promotional opportunities for members. Membership fee is $85 annually per publishing house.

ASSOCIATION OF JEWISH LIBRARIES (1965). 15 E. 26 St.,10th fl, NYC 10010. (212)725-5359. FAX: (212)481-4174. E-mail: ajl@jewishbooks.org. Pres. Pearl Berger; V.-Pres. Ronda Rose. Seeks to promote and improve services and professional standards in Jewish libraries; disseminates Jewish library information and guidance; promotes publication of literature in the field; encourages the establishment of Jewish libraries and collections of Judaica and the choice of Judaica librarianship as a profession; cocertifies Jewish libraries. *AJL Newsletter; Judaica Librarianship.*

B'NAI B'RITH KLUTZNICK NATIONAL JEWISH MUSEUM (1957). 1640 Rhode Island Ave., NW, Washington, DC 20036. (202)857-6583. FAX: (202)857-1099. A center of Jewish art and history in the nation's capital, maintains temporary and permanent exhibition galleries, permanent collection of Jewish ceremonial objects, folk art, and contemporary fine art, outdoor sculpture garden and museum shop, as well as the American Jewish Sports Hall of Fame. Provides exhibitions, tours, educational programs, research assistance, and tourist information.; *Permanent collection catalogue; temporary exhibit catalogues.*

CENTRAL YIDDISH CULTURE ORGANIZATION (CYCO), INC. (1943 incorporated) (1948-non profit status). 25 E. 21 St., 3rd fl., NYC 10010. (212) 505-8305. FAX: (212)505-8044. E-mail: cycobooks@earthlink.net. Pres. Dr. Barnett Zumoff; Exec. Officer Hy Wolfe. To promote the Yiddish word that is Cyco's purpose. We do this through the promotion, publication and distribution of Yiddish books, music books, CDs, tapes and albums. All in Yiddish!

CONFERENCE ON JEWISH SOCIAL STUDIES, INC. (formerly CONFERENCE ON JEWISH RELATIONS, INC.) (1939). Bldg. 240, Rm. 103. Program in Jewish Studies, Stanford University, Stanford, CA 94305-2190. (650)725-0829. FAX:(650)725-2920. E-mail: jss@leland.stanford.edu. Pres. Steven J. Zipperstein; V.-Pres. Aron Rodrigue. *Jewish Social Studies.*

CONGREGATION BINA (1981). 600 W. End Ave., Suite 1-C, NYC 10024. (212)873-4261. E-mail: samueldivekar@hotmail.com . Pres. Joseph Moses; Exec. V.-Pres. Moses Samson; Hon. Pres. Samuel M. Daniel; Sec. Gen. Elijah E. Jhirad. Serves the religious, cultural, charitable, and philanthropic needs of the Children of Israel who originated in India and now reside in the U.S. Works to foster and preserve the ancient traditions, customs, liturgy, music, and folklore of Indian Jewry and to maintain needed institutions. *Kol Bina.*

CONGRESS FOR JEWISH CULTURE (1948). 25 E. 21 St., NYC 10010. (212)505-8040. FAX: (212)505-8044. E-mail: kongres@earthlink.net. Exec. Dir. Shane Baker. Congress for Jewish Culture administers the book store CYCO and publishes the world's oldest Yiddish journal, *The*

Zukunft. Currently producing a two volume anthology of Yiddish literature in America. Activities include yearly memorials for the Warsaw ghetto uprising and the murdered Soviet Yiddish writers, also readings and literary afternoons. *The Zukunft; Bulletin: In the World of Yiddish.*

ELAINE KAUFMAN CULTURAL CENTER (1952). 129 W. 67 St., NYC 10023. (212) 501-3303. FAX: (212)874-7865. Email: lhard@ekcc.org. Hon. Chmn. Leonard Goodman; Chmn. Elaine Kaufman; Pres. Phyllis Feder; Exec. Dir. Lydia Kontos. Offers instruction in its Lucy Moses School for Music and Dance in music, dance, art, and theater to children and adults, in Western culture and Jewish traditions. Presents frequent performances of Jewish and general music by leading artists and ensembles in its Merkin Concert Hall and Ann Goodman Recital Hall. The Birnbaum Music Library houses Jewish music scores and reference books. *In Harmony (quarterly newsletter); EKCC Events (bimonthly calendar); Bimonthly concert calendars; catalogues and brochures.* (WWW.EKCC.ORG)

HOLOCAUST CENTER OF THE UNITED JEWISH FEDERATION OF GREATER PITTSBURGH (1980). 5738 Darlington Rd., Pittsburgh, PA 15217. (412)421-1500. FAX: (412) 422-1996. E-mail: lhurwitz@ujf.net. Pres. Holocaust Comm. Chair Dr. Barbara Burstin; UJF. Ch. James A. Rudolph; Dir. Linda F. Hurwitz. Develops programs and provides resources to further understanding of the Holocaust and its impact on civilization. Maintains a library, archive; provides speakers, educational materials; organizes community programs. Published collection of survivor and liberator stories. (WWW.UJFHC.NET)

HOLOCAUST MEMORIAL CENTER (1984). 28123 Orchard Lake Rd., Farmington Hills, MI 48334. (248)553-2400. FAX: (248)553-2433. E-mail: info@holocaustcenter.org. Founder & Dir. Rabbi Charles Rosenzveig. America's first free-standing Holocaust center comprising a museum, library-archive, oral history collection, garden of the righteous, research institute and academic advisory committee. Provides tours, lecture series, teacher training, Yom Hashoah commemorations, exhibits, educational outreach programs,

speakers' bureau, computer database on 1,200 destroyed Jewish communities, guided travel tours to concentration camps and Israel, and museum shop. Published *World Reacts to the Holocaust; Survey of U.S. Federal, U.S. State and Canadian Provincial Support forHolocaust Education, Newsletter.*

HOLOCAUST MEMORIAL RESOURCE & EDUCATION CENTER OF CENTRAL FLORIDA (1982). 851 N. Maitland Ave., Maitland, FL 32751. (407)628-0555. FAX: (407)628-1079. E-mail: execdir@holocaustedu.org. Pres. Stan Sujka, MD; Bd. Chmn. Tess Wise. An interfaith educational center devoted to teaching the lessons of the Holocaust. Houses permanent multimedia educational exhibit; maintains library of books, videotapes, films, and other visuals to serve the entire educational establishment; offers lectures, teacher training, and other activities. *Newsletter; Bibliography; "Holocaust-Lessons for Tomorrow"; elementary and middle school curriculum.*

HOLOCAUST MUSEUM AND LEARNING CENTER IN MEMORY OF GLORIA GOLDSTEIN (1995) (Formerly ST. LOUIS CENTER FOR HOLOCAUST STUDIES) (1977). 12 Millstone Campus Dr., St. Louis, MO 63146. (314)432-0020. FAX: (314)432-1277. E-mail: dreich@jfedstl.org. Chmn. Richard W. Stein; Curator/Dir. Of Ed. Dan A. Reich; Exec. Dir. Barbara Raznick; Dir. Of Admin. & Dev. Brian Bray. Develops programs and provides resources and educational materials to further an understanding of the Holocaust and its impact on civilization; has a 5,000 sq. ft. museum containing photographs, artifacts, and audiovisual displays. *Newsletter.*

INTERNATIONAL ASSOCIATION OF JEWISH GENEALOGICAL SOCIETIES (1988). 4430 Mt. Paran Pkwy NW, Atlanta, GA 30327-3747. (404)261-8662. Fax: (404) 228-7125. E-mail: homargol@aol.com. Pres. Howard Margol. Umbrella organization of more than 70 Jewish Genealogical Societies (JGS) worldwide. Represents organized Jewish genealogy, encourages Jews to research their family history, promotes new JGSs, supports existing societies, implements projects of interest to individuals researching their Jewish family histories. Holds annual conference where members learn and exchange ideas. (WWW.IAJGS.ORG)

INTERNATIONAL JEWISH MEDIA ASSOCIA-
TION (1987). U.S.: c/o St. Louis Jewish
Light, 12 Millstone Campus Dr., St.
Louis, MO 63146. (314)432-3353. FAX:
(314)432-0515. E-mail: stlouislgt@aol.
com and ajpamr@aol.com. Israel: PO
Box 92, Jerusalem 91920. 02-202-222.
FAX: 02-513-642. Pres. Robert A. Cohn
(c/o St. Louis Jewish Light); Exec. Dir.
Toby Dershowitz. 1828 L St. NW, Suite
402, Washington, DC 20036. (202)785-
2282. FAX: (202)785-2307. E-mail: toby@
dershowitz.com. Israel Liaisons Jacob
Gispan & Lifsha Ben-Shach, WZO Dept.
of Info. A worldwide network of Jewish
journalists, publications and other media
in the Jewish and general media, which
seeks to provide a forum for the exchange
of materials and ideas and to enhance the
status of Jewish media and journalists
throughout the world. *IJMA Newsletter;
Proceedings of the International Conference on Jewish Media.*

INTERNATIONAL NETWORK OF CHILDREN OF
JEWISH HOLOCAUST SURVIVORS, INC.
(1981). 13899 Biscayne Blvd. Suite 404, N.
Miami, FL 33181. (305)919-5690. FAX:
(305)919-5691. E-mail: info@hdec.org.
Pres. Rositta E. Kenigsberg; Founding
Chmn. Menachem Z. Rosensaft. Links
Second Generation groups and individuals throughout the world. Represents the
shared interests of children of Holocaust
survivors; aims to perpetuate the authentic memory of the Holocaust and prevent
its recurrence, to strengthen and preserve
the Jewish spiritual, ideological, and cultural heritage, to fight anti-Semitism and
all forms of discrimination, persecution,
and oppression anywhere in the world.

JACOB RADER MARCUS CENTER OF THE
AMERICAN JEWISH ARCHIVES (1947). 3101
Clifton Ave., Cincinnati, OH 45220.
(513)221-1875 ext. 403. FAX: (513)221-
7812. E-mail: aja@cn.huc.edu. Exec. Dir.
Dr. Gary P. Zola. Promotes the study and
preservation of the Western Hemisphere
Jewish experience through research, publications, collection of important source
materials, and a vigorous public-outreach
program. *American Jewish Archives Journal, Monographs, Pamphlets, booklets, educational materials and posters.*

JEWISH AMERICAN SOCIETY FOR HISTORIC
PRESERVATION (1997). 16405 Equestrian
Lane, Rockville, MD 20855. (301)977-3637.
FAX: (301)977-3888. E-mail: jashp1@

msn.com. Pres. Jerry Klinger. Identifies
and publicizes sites of American Jewish
historical interest; in cooperation with
local historical societies and houses of
worship, promotes programs to stress the
commonality of the American experience.
(WWW.JASHP.ORG)

JEWISH BOOK COUNCIL (1946; REORG.
1993). 15 E. 26 St., NYC 10010. (212)532-
4949, ext. 297. E-mail: jbc@jewishbooks.
org. Pres. Rabbi Maurice S. Corson; Bd.
Chmn. Henry Everett; Exec. Dir. Carolyn
Starman Hessel. Serves as literary arm of
the American Jewish community and
clearinghouse for Jewish-content literature; assists readers, writers, publishers,
and those who market and sell products.
Provides bibliographies, list of publishers, bookstores, book fairs. Sponsors National Jewish Book Awards, Jewish Book
Month, Jewish Book Fair Network. *Jewish Book Annual; Jewish Book World.*
(WWW.JEWISHBOOKCOUNCIL.ORG)

JEWISH FEDERATION'S LOS ANGELES MU-
SEUM OF THE HOLOCAUST (MARTYRS
MEMORIAL) (org. mid-1960s; opened
1978). 6006 Wilshire Blvd., Los Angeles,
CA 90036. (323)761-8170. FAX: (323)
761-8174. E-mail: museumiemp@
jewishla.org. Chmn. Gary John Schiller;
Director Rachel L. Jayoela. A photo-
narrative museum and resource center
dedicated to Holocaust history, issues of
genocide and prejudice, curriculum development, teacher training, research and
exhibitions. *PAGES, a newslettr; Those
Who Dared; Rescuers and Rescued; Guide
to Schindler's List; Anne Frank: A Teaching.*

JEWISH HERITAGE PROJECT (1981). 150
Franklin St., #1W, NYC 10013. (212)925-
9067. E-mail: jhpffh@jps.net. Exec. Dir.
Alan Adelson. Strives to bring to the
broadest possible audience authentic
works of literary and historical value relating to Jewish history and culture. With
funding from the National Endowment
of the Arts, Jewish Heritage runs the National Initiative in the Literature of the
Holocaust. Not a grant giving organization. Distributor of the film *Lodz Ghetto,*
which it developed, as well as its companion volume *Lodz Ghetto: Inside a
Community Under Siege; Better Than
Gold: An Immigrant Family's First Years
in Brooklyn.*

JEWISH MUSEUM (1904, UNDER AUSPICES OF JEWISH THEOLOGICAL SEMINARY). 1109 Fifth Ave., NYC 10128. (212)423-3200. FAX: (212)423-3232. Dir. Joan H. Rosenbaum; Bd. Chmn. Robert J. Hurst. Expanded museum features permanent exhibition on the Jewish experience. Repository of the largest collection of Jewish related paintings, prints, photographs, sculpture, coins, medals, antiquities, textiles, and other decorative arts-in the Western Hemisphere. Includes the National Jewish Archive of Broadcasting. Tours, lectures, film showings, and concerts; special programs for children; cafe; shop. *Special exhibition catalogues; annual report.* (WWW.THEJEWISH MUSEUM.ORG)

JEWISH PUBLICATION SOCIETY (1888). 2100 Arch St., 2nd fl., Philadelphia, PA 19103. (215)832-0600. FAX: (215)568-2017. E-mail: jewishbook@jewishpub.org. Pres. Allan R. Frank; CEO/Ed.-in-Chief Dr. Ellen Frankel. Publishes and disseminates books of Jewish interest for adults and children; titles include TANAKH, religious studies and practices, life cycle, folklore, classics, art, history. *Booklink JPS Catalogue.* (WWW.JEWISHPUB.ORG)

JUDAH L. MAGNES MUSEUM-JEWISH MUSEUM OF THE WEST (1962). 2911 Russell St., Berkeley, CA 94705. (510)549-6950. FAX: (510)849-3673. E-mail: pfpr@ magnesmuseum.org. Pres. Fred Weiss; Dir. Susan Morris. Collects, preserves, and makes available Jewish art, culture, history, and literature from throughout the world. Permanent collections of fine and ceremonial art; rare Judaica library, Western Jewish History Center (archives), Jewish-American Hall of Fame. Changing exhibits, traveling exhibits, docent tours, lectures, numismatics series, poetry and video awards, museum shop. *Magnes News; special exhibition catalogues; scholarly books.*

JUDAICA CAPTIONED FILM CENTER, INC. (1983). PO Box 21439, Baltimore, MD 21282-1439. Voice Relay Service (1-800)735-2258; TDD (410)655-6767. E-mail: lweiner@jhucep.org. Pres. Lois Lilienfeld Weiner. Developing a comprehensive library of captioned and subtitled films and tapes on Jewish subjects; distributes them to organizations serving the hearing-impaired, including mainstream classes and senior adult groups, on a free-loan, handling/shipping-charge-only basis. *Newsletter.*

LEAGUE FOR YIDDISH, INC. (1979). 200 W. 72 St., Suite 40, NYC 10023. (212)787-6675. E-mail: mschaecht@aol.com. Pres. Dr. Zuni Zelitch; Exec. Dir. Dr. Mordkhe Schaechter. Encourages the development and use of Yiddish as a living language; promotes its modernization and standardization; publisher of Yiddish textbooks and English-Yiddish dictionaries; most recent book *The Standardized Yiddish Orthography(New York,200); Afn Shvel (quarterly).* (WWW. METALAB.UNC.EDU/YIDDISH/YIDLEAGUE)

LEO BAECK INSTITUTE, INC. (1955). 15 W. 16 St., NYC 10011-6301. (212)744-6400. FAX: (212)988-1305. E-mail: lbi1@lbi. org. Pres. Ismar Schorsch; Exec. Dir. Carol Kahn Strauss. A research, study, and lecture center, museum, library, and archive relating to the history of German-speaking Jewry. Offers lectures, exhibits, faculty seminars; publishes a series of monographs, yearbooks, and journals. *LBI News; LBI Yearbook; LBI Memorial Lecture; occasional papers.*

LIVING TRADITIONS (1994), (c/o WORKMAN'S CIRCLE) 45 EAST 33RD STREET, NEW YORK, NY 10016. (212)532-8202. E-mail: henry@livingtraditions.org. Pres. Henry Sapoznik; V.-Pres. Sherry Mayrent. Nonprofit membership organization dedicated to the study, preservation, and innovative continuity of traditional folk and popular culture through workshops, concerts, recordings, radio and film documentaries; clearinghouse for research in klezmer and other traditional music; sponsors yearly weeklong international cultural event, "Yiddish Folk Arts Program/'KlezKamp.'" *Living Traditions (newsletter).* (WWW.LIVINGTRADITIONS. ORG)

MARTIN BUBER INSTITUTE (1990), 203 Rocking Stone ave., Larchmont, NY 10538. (914)833-7731. E-mail: HM64@columbia. edu. Hon. Chmn. Prof. Maurice Friedman; Pres. Dr. Hune Margulies. Sponsors seminars, workshops, conferences, and publications to encourage the exchange of ideas about the life and thought of Buber. *Martin Buber Review (annual).*

MEMORIAL FOUNDATION FOR JEWISH CULTURE, INC. (1964). 50 West Broadway, 34th Floor, NYC 10004. (212)425-6606. FAX:

(212)425-6602. Pres. Prof. Anita Shapira; Exec. V.-Pres. Jerry Hochbaum. Through the grants that it awards, encourages Jewish scholarship, culture, and education; supports communities that are struggling to maintain Jewish life; assists professional training for careers in communal service in Jewishly deprived communities; and stimulates the documentation, commemoration, and teaching of the Holocaust. (WWW.MFJC.ORG)

MUSEUM OF JEWISH HERITAGE—A LIVING MEMORIAL TO THE HOLOCAUST (1984). One Battery Park Plaza, NYC 10004-1484. (212)968-1800. FAX: (212)968-1368. Bd. Chmn. Robert M. Morgenthau; Museum Pres. Dr. Alfred Gottschalk; Museum Dir. David Marwell. New York tri-state's principal institution for educating people of all ages and backgrounds about 20th-century Jewish history and the Holocaust. Repository of Steven Spielberg's Survivors of the Shoah Visual History Foundation videotaped testimonies. Core and special exhibitions. *18 First Place (newsletter); Holocaust bibliography; educational materials.* (WWW.MJH-NYC.ORG)

MUSEUM OF TOLERANCE OF THE SIMON WIESENTHAL CENTER (1993). 9786 W. Pico Blvd., Los Angeles, CA 90035-4792. (310)553-8403. FAX: (310)553-4521. E-mail: avra@wiesenthal.com. Dean-Founder Rabbi Marvin Hier; Assoc. Dean Rabbi Abraham Cooper; Exec. Dir. Rabbi Meyer May. A unique experiential museum focusing on personal prejudice, group intolerance, struggle for civil rights, and 20th-century genocides, culminating in a major exhibition on the Holocaust. Archives, Multimedia Learning Center designed for individualized research, 6,700-square-foot temporary exhibit space, 324-seat theater, 150-seat auditorium, and outdoor memorial plaza. (WWW.WIESENTHAL.COM)

NATIONAL FOUNDATION FOR JEWISH CULTURE (1960). 330 Seventh Ave., 21st fl., NYC 10001. (212)629-0500. FAX: (212)629-0508. E-mail: nfjc@jewishculture.org. Pres. Carol B. Spinner; Exec. Dir. Richard A. Siegel. The leading Jewish organization devoted to promoting Jewish culture in the U.S. Manages the Jewish Endowment for the Arts and Humanities; administers the Council of American Jewish Museums and Council of Archives and Research Libraries in Jewish Studies; offers doctoral dissertation fellowships, new play commissions, and grants for documentary films, recording of Jewish music, contemporary choreography, fiction and non-fiction writing, and cultural preservation; coordinates community cultural residencies, local cultural councils, and national cultural consortia; sponsors conferences, symposia, and festivals in the arts and humanities. *Jewish Culture News; Culture Currents (electronic).*

NATIONAL MUSEUM OF AMERICAN JEWISH HISTORY (1976). Independence Mall E. 55 N. Fifth St. Philadelphia, PA 19106-2197. (215) 923-3811. FAX: (215) 923-0763. E-mail: nmajh@nmajh.org. Dir./CEO Gwen Goodman. The only museum in the nation to offer education, exhibits, and programs dedicated to preserving the history and culture of the Jewish people in America; located across from the Liberty Bell. (WWW.NMAJH.ORG)

NATIONAL MUSEUM OF AMERICAN JEWISH MILITARY HISTORY (*see* JEWISH WAR VETERANS OF THE U.S.A.)

NATIONAL YIDDISH BOOK CENTER (1980). 1021 West St., Amherst, MA 01002. (413) 256-4900. FAX: (413)256-4700. E-mail: yiddish@bikher.org. Pres. Aaron Lansky; V.-Pres. Nancy Sherman. Since 1980 the center has collected 1.5 million Yiddish books for distribution to readers and libraries worldwide; digitized more than 12,000 Yiddish titles, offered a range of educational programs in Yiddish and modern culture, and published *Pakn Treger,* an award-winning English-language magazine. (WWW.YIDDISHBOOKCENTER.ORG)

ORTHODOX JEWISH ARCHIVES (1978). 42 Broadway, New York, NY 10004. (212) 797-9000, ext. 73. FAX: (212)269-2843. Exec. V.-Pres. Rabbi Shmuel Bloom & Shlomo Gertzullin; Dir. Rabbi Moshe Kolodny. Founded by Agudath Israel of America; houses historical documents, photographs, periodicals, and other publications relating to the growth of Orthodox Jewry in the U.S. and related communities in Europe, Israel, and elsewhere. Particularly noteworthy are its holdings relating to rescue activities organized during the Holocaust and its traveling exhibits available to schools and other institutions.

RESEARCH FOUNDATION FOR JEWISH IMMI-GRATION, INC. (1971). 570 Seventh Ave., NYC 10018. (212)921-3871. FAX: (212) 575-1918. Sec./Coord. of Research Herbert A. Strauss; Archivist Dennis E. Rohrbaugh. Studies and records the history of the migration and acculturation of Central European German-speaking Jewish and non-Jewish Nazi persecutees in various resettlement countries worldwide, with special emphasis on the American experience. *International Biographical Dictionary of Central European Emigrés, 1933-1945; Jewish Immigrants of the Nazi Period in the USA.*

SEPHARDIC EDUCATIONAL CENTER (1979). 10808 Santa Monica Blvd., Los Angeles, CA 90025. (310)441-9361. FAX: (310) 441-9561. E-mail: secforever@aol.com. Founder & Chmn. Jose A. Nessim, M.D. Has chapters in the U.S., North, Central, and South America, Europe, and Asia, a spiritual and educational center in the Old City of Jerusalem, and executive office in Los Angeles. Serves as a meeting ground for Sephardim from many nations; sponsors the first worldwide movement for Sephardic youth and young adults. Disseminates information about Sephardic Jewry in the form of motion pictures, pamphlets, and books, which it produces. *Hamerkaz (quarterly bulletin in English).* (WWW.SECWORLDWIDE.ORG)

SEPHARDIC HOUSE-THE CULTURAL DIVISION OF ASF (1978). 15 West 16th Street, NYC 10011. (212)294-6170. FAX: (212) 294-6149. E-mail: sephardichouse@cjh.org. Pres. Morrie R.Yohai; Dir. Dr. Janice E. Ovadiah. A cultural organization dedicated to fostering Sephardic history and culture; sponsors a wide variety of classes and public programs, film festivals, publication program disseminates materials of Sephardic value; outreach program to communities outside of the New York area; program bureau provides program ideas, speakers, and entertainers; International Sephardic Film Festival every year. *Sephardic House Newsletter; Publication Catalogue.* (WWW. SEPHAR DICHOUSE.ORG)

SIMON WIESENTHAL CENTER (1977). 1399 South Roxbury Drive., Los Angeles, CA 90035-4701. (310)553-9036. FAX: (310) 553-4521. Email: avra@wiesenthal.com. Dean-Founder Rabbi Marvin Hier; Assoc. Dean Rabbi Abraham Cooper; Exec. Dir. Rabbi Meyer May. Regional offices in New York, Miami, Toronto, Paris, Jerusalem, Buenos Aires. The largest institution of its kind in N. America dedicated to the study of the Holocaust, its contemporary implications, and related human-rights issues through education and awareness. Incorporates 185,000-sq.-ft. Museum of Tolerance, library, media department, archives, "Testimony to the Truth" oral histories, educational outreach, research department, international social action. *Response Magazine.* (WWW.WIESENTHAL. COM)

SKIRBALL CULTURAL CENTER (1996), AN AFFILIATE OF HEBREW UNION COLLEGE. 2701 N. Sepulveda Blvd., Los Angeles, CA 90049. (310)440-4500. FAX: (310) 440-4595. Pres. & CEO Uri D. Herscher; Bd. Chmn. Howard Friedman. Dedicated to exploring the connections between four thousand years of Jewish heritage and the vitality of American democratic ideals. It welcomes and seeks to inspire people of every ethnic and cultural identity. Guided by our respective memories and experiences, together we aspire to build a society in which all of us can feel at home. Skirball Cultural Center achieves its mission through pubic programs that explore literary, visual, and performing arts from around the world; through the display and interpretation of its permanent collections and changing exhibitions; through scholarship in American Jewish history and related publications; and through outreach to the community. (WWW.SKIRBALL.ORG)

SOCIETY FOR THE HISTORY OF CZECHOSLO-VAK JEWS, INC. (1961). 760 Pompton Ave., Cedar Grove, NJ 07009. (973)239-2333. FAX: (973)239-7935. Pres. Rabbi Norman Patz; V.-Pres. Prof. Fred Hahn; Sec. Anita Grosz. Studies the history of Czechoslovak Jews; collects material and disseminates information through the publication of books and pamphlets; conducts annual memorial service for Czech Holocaust victims. *The Jews of Czechoslovakia (3 vols.); Review I-VI.*

THE SOCIETY OF FRIENDS OF TOURO SYNA-GOGUE NATIONAL HISTORIC SITE, INC. (1948). 85 Touro St., Newport, RI 02840. (401)847-4794. FAX: (401)845-6790. E-mail: info@tourosynagogue.org. Pres. M. Bernard Aidinoff; Exec. Dir. Michael L. Balaban. Helps maintain Touro Synagogue as a national historic site, opening and interpreting it for visitors; promotes public awareness of its preeminent role in the tradition of American religious liberty; annually commemorates George Washington's letter of 1790 to the Hebrew Congregation of Newport. *Society Update.*

———, TOURO NATIONAL HERITAGE TRUST (1984). 85 Touro St., Newport, RI 02840. (401)847-0810. FAX (401)847-8121. Pres. Bernard Bell; Chmn. Benjamin D. Holloway. Works to establish national education center within Touro compound; sponsors Touro Fellow through John Carter Brown Library; presents seminars and other educational programs; promotes knowledge of the early Jewish experience in this country.

SPERTUS MUSEUM, SPERTUS INSTITUTE OF JEWISH STUDIES (1968). 618 S. Michigan Ave., Chicago, IL 60605. (312)322-1747. FAX: (312)922-6406. Pres. Spertus Institute of Jewish Studies, Dr. Howard A. Sulkin. The largest, most comprehensive Judaic museum in the Midwest with 12,000 square feet of exhibit space and a permanent collection of some 10,000 works reflecting 5,000 years of Jewish history and culture. Also includes the redesigned Zell Holocaust Memorial, permanent collection, changing visual arts and special exhibits, and the children's ARTIFACT Center for a hands-on archaeological adventure. Plus, traveling exhibits for Jewish educators, life-cycle workshops, ADA accessible. *Exhibition catalogues; educational pamphlets.*

———, ASHER LIBRARY, SPERTUS INSTITUTE OF JEWISH STUDIES (APPROX. 1930), 618 S. Michigan Ave., Chicago, IL 60605. (312) 322-1749, FAX (312) 922-6406. Pres. Spertus Institute of Jewish Studeis, Dr. Howard A. Sulkin; Director, Asher Library, Glenn Ferdman. Asher Library is the largest public Jewish Library in the Midwest, with over 100,000 books and 550 periodicals; extensive collections of music, art, rare books, maps and electronic resources; nearly 1,000 feature and documentary films available on video cassette. Online catalogue access available. Also, the Chicago Jewish Archives

collects historical material of Chicago individuals, families, synagogues and organizations. *ADA accessible.*

SURVIVORS OF THE SHOAH VISUAL HISTORY FOUNDATION (1994). PO Box 3168, Los Angeles, CA 90078-3168. (818)777-7802. FAX: (818)866-0312.Exec. Dir. Ari C. Zev. A nonprofit organization, founded and chaired by Steven Spielberg, dedicated to videotaping and preserving interviews with Holocaust survivors throughout the world. The archive of testimonies will be used as a tool for global education about the Holocaust and to teach racial, ethnic, and cultural tolerance.

UNITED STATES HOLOCAUST MEMORIAL MUSEUM (1980; OPENED APR. 1993). 100 Raoul Wallenberg Place, SW, Washington, DC 20024. (202)488-0400. FAX: (202)488-2690. Chmn. Fred S. Zeidman; Dir. Sara J. Bloomfeld. Federally chartered and privately built, its mission is to teach about the Nazi persecution and murder of six million Jews and millions of others from 1933 to 1945 and to inspire visitors to contemplate their moral responsibilities as citizens of a democratic nation. Opened in April 1993 near the national Mall in Washington, DC, the museum's permanent exhibition tells the story of the Holocaust through authentic artifacts, videotaped oral testimonies, documentary film, and historical photographs. Offers educational programs for students and adults, an interactive computerized learning center, and special exhibitions and community programs. *United States Holocaust Memorial Museum Update (bimonthly); Directory of Holocaust Institutions; Journal of Holocaust and Genocide Studies (quarterly).* (WWW.USHMM.ORG)

THE WILSTEIN (SUSAN & DAVID) INSTITUTE OF JEWISH POLICY STUDIES (1998). 160 Herrick Road, Newton Centre, MA 02459. (617)559-8790. FAX: (617)559-8791. E-mail: wilstein@hebrewcollege.edu. Dir. Dr. David M. Gordis; Assoc. Dir. Rabbi Zachary I. Heller; Chmn. Howard I. Friedman. The Wilstein Institute's West Coast Center in Los Angeles and East Coast Center at Hebrew College in Boston provide a bridge between academics, community leaders, professionals, and the organizations and institutions of Jewish life. The institute serves as an international research and development resource for American Jewry. *Bulletins, various newsletters, monographs, research reports, and books.*

YESHIVA UNIVERSITY MUSEUM (1973). Center for Jewish History, 15 W. 16 St., NYC 10011-6301. (212)294-8335. E-mail: dgoldman@yum.cjh.org. Dir. Sylvia A. Herskowitz; Chmn. Erica Jesselson. Collects, preserves, and interprets Jewish life and culture through changing exhibitions of ceremonial objects, paintings, rare books and documents, synagogue architecture, textiles, contemporary art, and photographs. Oral history archive. Special events, holiday workshops, live performances, lectures, etc. for adults and children. Guided tours and workshops are offered. Exhibitions and children's art education programs also at branch galleries on Yeshiva University's Main Campus, 2520 Amsterdam Ave., NYC 10033-3201. *Seasonal calendars; special exhibition catalogues; newsletters.*

YIDDISHER KULTUR FARBAND-YKUF (1937). 1133 Broadway, Rm. 820, NYC 10010. (212)243-1304. FAX: (212)243-1305. E-mail: mahosu@amc.one. Pres./ Ed. Itche Goldberg. Publishes a bimonthly magazine and books by contemporary and classical Jewish writers; conducts cultural forums; exhibits works by contemporary Jewish artists and materials of Jewish historical value; organizes reading circles. *Yiddishe Kultur.*

YIVO INSTITUTE FOR JEWISH RESEARCH (1925). 15 W. 16 St., NYC 10011. (212) 246-6080. FAX: (212)292-1892. E-mail: yivomail@yivo.cjh.org. Chmn. Bruce Slovin; Exec. Dir. Dr. Carl J. Rheins. Engages in historical research and education pertaining to East European Jewish life; maintains library and archives which provide a major international, national and New York resource used by institutions, individual scholars, and the public; provides graduate fellowships in East European and American Jewish studies; offers Yiddish language classes at all levels, exhibits, conferences, public programs; publishes books. *Yedies-YIVO News; YIVO Bleter.*

———, MAX WEINREICH CENTER FOR ADVANCED JEWISH STUDIES/YIVO INSTITUTE (1968). 15 W. 16 St., NYC 10011.

(212)246-6080. FAX: (212)292-1892. E-mail: mweinreich@yivo.cjh.org. Provides advanced-level training in Yiddish language and literature, ethnography, folklore, linguistics, and history; offers guidance on dissertation or independent research; postdoctoral fellowships available.

YUGNTRUF-YOUTH FOR YIDDISH (1964). 200 W. 72 St., Suite 40, NYC 10023. (212) 787-6675. FAX: (212)799-1517. E-mail: ruvn@aol.com. Chmn. Dr. Paul Glasser; V.-Chmn. Marc Caplan; Coord. Brukhe Lang Caplan. A worldwide, nonpolitical organization for young people with a knowledge of, or interest in, Yiddish; fosters Yiddish as a living language and culture. Sponsors all activities in Yiddish: reading, conversation, and creative writing groups; annual weeklong retreat in Berkshires; children's Yiddish play group; sale of shirts. *Yugntruf Journal.*

ISRAEL-RELATED

THE ABRAHAM FUND (1989). 477 Madison Ave., 4th fl., NYC 10022. (212)303-9421. FAX: (212)935-1834. E-mail: info@ AbrahamFund.org. Chmn. Alan B. Slifka, Exec. V.P. Dan Pattir. The Abraham Fund Initiatives (TAFI) seeks to enhance relations between Israel's Jewish and Arab citizens by promoting increased dialogue, understanding, and democracy. Founded in 1989, TAFI has contributed more than $8 million to community-based coexistence projects. TAFI also develops regional and national coexistence programs in partnership with other major institutions in Israel and orchestrates public advocacy campaigns to implement change.

AMERICA-ISRAEL CULTURAL FOUNDATION, INC. (1939). 51 E. 42nd St., Suite 400, NYC 10017. (212)557-1600. FAX: (212)557-1611. E-mail: info@aicf.org. Chmn. Emer. Isaac Stern (in memoriam); Pres. Vera Stern. Supports and encourages the growth of cultural excellence in Israel through grants to cultural institutions; scholarships to gifted young artists and musicians. *Newsletter.* (WWW.AICF.ORG)

AMERICA-ISRAEL FRIENDSHIP LEAGUE, INC. (1971). 134 E. 39 St., NYC 10016. (212) 213-8630. FAX: (212)683-3475. E-mail: aifl@aifl.org. Pres. Mortimer B. Zuckerman, Chmn. Bd. Kenneth J. Bialkin, Exec. V. Pres. Ilana Artman. A non-sectarian, non-partisan, not-for-profit organization which seeks to broaden the base of support for Israel among Americans of all faiths and backgrounds. Activities include educational exchanges, missions to Israel for American leadership groups, symposia and public-education activities, and the dissemination of multi media information. *Newsletter.*

AMERICAN ASSOCIATES, BEN-GURION UNIVERSITY OF THE NEGEV (1972). 1430 Broadway, 8th Floor, New York, NY 10018. (212)687-7721, (800)-Aabgu. FAX: (212)302-6443. E-mail: info@ aabgu.org. Pres. Zvi Alov; Exec. V-Pres. Seth Moscovitz. Since 1972, the American Assoicates, Ben–Gurion University of the Negev has played a vital role in building a world-class center for research and education in the desert. A nonprofit cooperation with ten regional offices throughout the United States, AABGU prides itself on its efficiency and effectiveness in raising funds to help Ben-Gurion University bring knowledge to the Negev and to the world. AABGU plays a vital role in helping BGU fulfill its unique responsisbility to develop the Negev, the focus of the future of Israel.(WWW.AABGU.ORG)

AMERICAN COMMITTEE FOR SHAARE ZEDEK MEDICAL CENTER IN JERUSALEM (1949). 49 W. 45 St., Suite 1100, NYC 10036. (212)354-8801. FAX: (212)391-2674. E-mail: pr@szmc.org.il. Natl. Pres. & Chmn. Intl. Bd. of Gov. Menno Ratzker; Chair Erica Jesselson. Increases awareness and raises funds for the various needs of this 100-year old hospital, including new medical centers of excellence, equipment, medical supplies, school of nursing and research; supports exchange program between Shaare Zedek Jerusalem Medical Center and Albert Einstein College of Medicine, NY. *Heartbeat Magazine.*

AMERICAN COMMITTEE FOR SHENKAR COLLEGE IN ISRAEL, INC. (1971). 855 Ave. of the Americas, #531, NYC 10001. (212) 947-1597. FAX: (212)643-9887. E-mail: acfsc@worldnet.att.net. Pres. Nahum G. (Sonny) Shar; Exec. Dir. Charlotte A. Fainblatt. Raises funds and coordinates projects and research with Shenkar College of Engineering and Design, Israel. A unique government academic institute in Israel dedicated to education and reaseach in areas impacting Israel's industries and its artistic and scientific de-

velopment. Textile, Fashion, Interior and Product design courses are offered with Scientific courses: Plastics, Chemistry, Software and Industrial Management and Marketing. Certified by Israel's Council of Higher Education, it offers continuing education and complete testing facilities for the textile/apparel industry and plastics engineering. *Shenkar News.*

AMERICAN COMMITTEE FOR THE BEER-SHEVA FOUNDATION (1988). PO Box 179, NYC 10028. (212)534-3715. FAX: (973) 992-8651. Pres. Ronald Slevin; Sr. V.-Pres. Joanna Slevin; Bd. Chmn. Sidney Cooperman. U.S. fundraising arm of the Beer-Sheva Foundation, which funds vital projects to improve the quality of life in the city of Beer-Sheva: nursery schools for pre-K toddlers, residential and day centers for needy seniors, educational programs, facilities and scholarships (especially for new olim, the physically and mentally challenged), parks, playgrounds, and other important projects. Also offers special services for immigrants—such as heaters, blankets, clothing, school supplies, etc. *Brochures.*

AMERICAN COMMITTEE FOR THE WEIZMANN INSTITUTE OF SCIENCE (1944). 130 E. 59 St., NYC 10022. (212)895-7900. FAX: (212)895-7999. E-mail: info@acwis. org. Chmn. Robert Asher; Pres. Albert Willner, M.D.; Exec. V.-Pres. Martin Kraar. Through 13 regional offices in the U.S. raises funds, disseminates information, and does American purchasing for the Weizmann Institute in Rehovot, Israel, a world-renowned center of scientific research and graduate study. The institute conducts research in disease, energy, the environment, and other areas; runs an international summer science program for gifted high-school students. *Interface; Weizmann Now; annual report.* (WWW.WEIZMANN-USA.ORG)

AMERICAN FRIENDS OF ALYN HOSPITAL (1932). 51 East 42nd Street., Suite 3088, NYC 10017. (212)869-8085. FAX: (212)768-0979. E-mail: friends@alynus. org. Pres. Minette Halpern Brown; Exec. Dir. Cathy M. Lanyard. Supports the Alyn Hospital (Woldenberg Family Hospital/Pediatric and Adolescent Rehabilitation Center) in Jerusalem. Treats children suffering from birth defects (such as muscular dystrophy and spina bifida) and traumas (terrorism, car accidents, cancer, and fire), enables patients and their families to achieve independence and a better quality of life. (www. ALYNUSA.ORG)

AMERICAN FRIENDS OF ASSAF HAROFEH MEDICAL CENTER (1975). PO Box 21051, NYC 10129. (212)481-5653. FAX: (212) 481-5672. Chmn. Kenneth Kronen; Exec. Dir. Rhoda Levental; Treas. Robert Kastin. Support group for Assaf Harofeh, Israel's third-largest government hospital, serving a poor population of over 400,000 in the area between Tel Aviv and Jerusalem. Raises funds for medical equipment, medical training for immigrants, hospital expansion, school of nursing, and school of physiotherapy. *Newsletter.*

AMERICAN FRIENDS OF BAR-ILAN UNIVERSITY (1955). 235 Park Ave. So., NYC 10003. (212)673-3460. FAX: (212)673-4856. Email: nationaladmin@biuny.com, beverlyf@biuny.com. Chancellor Rabbi Emanuel Rackman; Chmn. Global Bd. Aharon Dahan; Pres. Amer. Bd. Melvin Stein; Exec. V.-Pres. Gen. Yehuda Halevy. Supports Bar-Ilan University, an institution that integrates the highest standards of contemporary scholarship in liberal arts and sciences with a Judaic studies program as a requirement. Located in Ramat-Gan, Israel, and chartered by the Board of Regents of the State of NY. *Bar-Ilan News; Bar-Ilan University Scholar; Heritage Newsletter . . .*

AMERICAN FRIENDS OF BETH HATEFUTSOTH (1976). 633 Third Ave., 21st fl., NYC 10017. (212)339-6034. FAX: (212)318-6176. E-mail: afbhusa@aol.com. Pres. Stephen Greenberg; Chmn. Sam E. Bloch; Exec. Dir. Gloria Golan. Supports the maintenance and development of Beth Hatefutsoth, the Nahum Goldmann Museum of the Jewish Diaspora in Tel Aviv, and its cultural and educational programs for youth and adults. Circulates its traveling exhibitions and provides various cultural programs to local Jewish communities. Includes Jewish genealogy center (DOROT), the center for Jewish music, and photodocumentation center. *Beth Hatefutsoth (quarterly newsletter).*

AMERICAN FRIENDS OF HAIFA UNIVERSITY (*see* American Society of the University of Haifa)

AMERICAN FRIENDS OF HERZOG HOSPITAL/ EZRATH NASHIM-JERUSALEM (1895). 800 Second Ave., 8th fl., NYC 10017. (212) 499-9092. FAX:(212)499-9085. E-mail: herzogpr@hotmail.com. Co-Pres. Dr. Joy Zagoren, Amir Sternhell; Exec. Dir. Stephen Schwartz. Herzog Hospital is the foremost geriatric and psychiatric health care facility in Israel, and a leading research center in genetics, Alzheimer's and schizophrenia, with expertise in neurogeriatrics, physical rehabilitation, and long-term respiratory care. Its Israel Center for the Treatment of Psychotrauma provides therapy and seminars to help Israelis cope with the ongoing violence. (www.HERZOG HOSPITAL.ORG)

AMERICAN FRIENDS OF LIKUD. P.O.Box 8711, JAF Station, NYC 10116. (212)308-5595. FAX: (212)688-1327. E-mail: Thelikud@aol.com. Natl. Chmn. J. Phillip Rosen, Esq; Pres. Julio Messer,M.D; Natl. V. Pres. Jacques Torczyner; Natl. Treasurer Milton S. Shapiro, Esq.; Exec. Dir. Salomon L. Vaz Dias. promotes public education on the situation in the Middle East, particularly in Israel, as well as advancing a general awareness of Zionism; provides a solid partnership of public support for the State of Israel, its citizens and its democratically-elected governments.

AMERICAN FRIENDS OF NEVE SHALOM/ WAHAT AL-SALAM (1988). 4201 Church Road, Suite 4, NYC 10013. (856) 235-3667. FAX: (856) 235-4674. E-mail: afnswas@oasisofpeace.com. Pres. Deborah First; V.-Pres. Adeeb Fadil; Exec. Dir. Deanna Armbruster. Supports and publicizes the projects of the community of Neve Shalom/Wahat Al-Salam, the "Oasis of Peace." For more than twenty years, Jewish and Palestinian citizens of Israel have lived and worked together as equals. The community teaches tolerance, understanding and mutual respect well beyond its own borders by being a model for peace and reaching out through its educational institutions. A bilingual, bicultural Primary School serves the village and the surrounding communities.

AMERICAN FRIENDS OF RABIN MEDICAL CENTER (1994). 220 Fifth Avenue, Suite 1301, NYC 10001-7708. (212) 279-2522. Fax: (212)279-0179. E-mail: afrmc826@aol. com. Bd. Chmn. Abraham E. "Barry" Cohen; Exec. Dir. Burton Lazarow. Supports the maintenance and development of this medical, research, and teaching institution in central Israel, which unites the Golda and Beilinson hospitals, providing 12% of all hospitalization in Israel. Department of Organ Transplantation performs 80% of all kidney and 60% of all liver transplants in Israel. Affiliated with Tel Aviv University's Sackler School of Medicine. *New Directions Quarterly.*

AMERICAN FRIENDS OF RAMBAM MEDICAL CENTER (1969). 226 West 26th Street, NYC 10001. (212)644-1049. FAX: (775)562-5399. E-mail: michaelstoler@princeton commercial.com. Pres/CEO. Michael R. Stoler. Represents and raises funds for Rambam Medical Center (Haifa), an 887-bed hospital serving approx. one-third of Israel's population, incl. the entire population of northern Israel (and south Lebanon), the U.S. Sixth Fleet, and the UN Peacekeeping Forces in the region. Rambam is the teaching hospital for the Technion's medical school.

AMERICAN FRIENDS OF THE HEBREW UNIVERSITY (1925; INC. 1931). 11 E. 69 St., NYC 10021. (212)472-9800. FAX: (212) 744-2324. E-mail: info@afhu.org. Pres. Ira Lee Sorkin; Bd. Chmn. Keith L. Sachs; Exec. V.-Pres. Peter Willner. Fosters the growth, development, and maintenance of the Hebrew University of Jerusalem; collects funds and conducts informational programs throughout the U.S., highlighting the university's achievements and its significance. *Wisdom; Scopus Magazine.* (WWW.AFHU.ORG)

AMERICAN FRIENDS OF THE ISRAEL MUSEUM (1972). 500 Fifth Ave., Suite 2540, NYC 10110. (212)997-5611. FAX: (212) 997-5536. Pres. Barbara Lane; Exec. Dir. Carolyn Cohen. Raises funds for special projects of the Israel Museum in Jerusalem; solicits works of art for permanent collection, exhibitions, and educational purposes. *Newsletter.*

AMERICAN FRIENDS OF THE ISRAEL PHILHARMONIC ORCHESTRA (AFIPO) (1972). 122 E. 42 St., Suite 4507, NYC 10168. (212)697-2949. FAX: (212)697-2943. Interim Pres. Lynn Syms; Exec. Dir. Suzanne K. Ponsot. Works to secure the financial future of the orchestra so that it may continue to travel throughout the world bringing its message of peace and cultural understanding through music. Supports the orchestra's international touring program, educational projects, and a wide array of musical activities in Israel. *Passport to Music (newsletter).*

AMERICAN FRIENDS OF THE OPEN UNIVERSITY OF ISRAEL. 180 W. 80 St., NYC 10024. (212)712-1800. FAX: (212)496-3296. E-mail: afoui@aol.com. Natl. Chmn. Irving M. Rosenbaum; Exec.V.-Pres. Eric G. Heffler. *Open Letter.*(www. OPENU.AC.IL)

AMERICAN FRIENDS OF THE SHALOM HARTMAN INSTITUTE (1976). One Penn Plaza, Suite 1606, New York, NY 10119. (212) 268-0300. FAX: (212)239-4550. E-mail: afshi@afshi.org. Pres. Richard F. Kaufman; Exec. Dir. Robbi Bensley. Supports the Shalom Hartman Institute in Jerusalem, an international center for pluralist Jewish education and research, serving Israel and world Jewry. Founded in 1976 by David Hartman, the Institute includes: the Institute for Advanced Judaic Studies, with research centers for contemporary halakha, religious pluralism, political thought and peace and reconciliation; the Institute for Teacher and Leadership Training, educating Israeli principals, teachers, graduate students and leaders; and the Institute for Diaspora Education, which offers seminars and sabbaticals to rabbis, educators and lay leaders of diverse ideological commitments. (www. HARTMANINSTITUTE.COM)

AMERICAN FRIENDS OF THE TEL AVIV MUSEUM OF ART (1974). 545 Madison Ave., 8th Floor (55 St.), NYC 10022. (212)319-0555. FAX: (212)754-2987. Email: dnaftam@aol.com. Chmn. Steven P. Schwartz; Exec. Dir. Dorey Neilinger. Raises funds for the Tel Aviv Museum of Art for special projects, art acquisitions, and exhibitions; seeks contributions of art to expand the museum's collection; encourages art loans and traveling exhibitions; creates an awareness of the museum in the USA; makes available exhibition catalogues, monthly calendars, and posters published by the museum.

AMERICAN-ISRAEL ENVIRONMENTAL COUNCIL (Formerly COUNCIL FOR A BEAUTIFUL ISRAEL ENVIRONMENTAL EDUCATION FOUNDATION) (1973). c/o Perry Davis Assoc., 25 W. 45 St., Suite 1405, NYC 10036. (212)840-1166. Fax: (212)840-

1514. Pres. Alan Silberstein. A support group for the Israeli body, whose activities include education, town planning, lobbying for legislation to protect and enhance the environment, preservation of historical sites, the improvement and beautification of industrial and commercial areas, and sponsoring the CBI Center for Environmental Studies located in Yarkon Park, Tel Aviv. *Yearly newsletter; yearly theme oriented calendars in color.*

AMERICAN ISRAEL PUBLIC AFFAIRS COMMITTEE (AIPAC) (1954). 440 First St., NW, Washington, DC 20001. (202)639-5200. FAX: (202)347-4889. Pres. Howard Friedman; Exec. Dir. Howard A. Kohr. Registered to lobby on behalf of legislation affecting U.S.-Israel relations; represents Americans who believe support for a secure Israel is in U.S. interest. Works for a strong U.S.-Israel relationship. *Near East Report.* (WWW.AIPAC.ORG)

AMERICAN-ISRAELI LIGHTHOUSE, INC. (1928; reorg. 1955). 276 Fifth Ave., Suite 713, NYC 10001. (212)686-7110. Pres. Mrs. Leonard F. Dank; Sec. Mrs. Ida Rhein. Provides a vast network for blind and physically handicapped persons throughout Israel, to effect their social and vocational integration into the mainstream of their communities. Center of Services for the blind; built and maintains Rehabilitation Center for blind and handicapped persons (Migdal Or) in Haifa.

AMERICAN JEWISH LEAGUE FOR ISRAEL (1957). 130 E. 59 St., 12th Floor, NYC 10022. (212)371-1583. FAX: (646)497-0093. E-mail: ajlims@aol.com. Pres. Dr. Martin L. Kalmanson; Exec. Dir. Jeffrey Scheckner. Seeks to unite all those who, notwithstanding differing philosophies of Jewish life, are committed to the historical ideals of Zionism; works independently of class, party, or religious affiliation for the welfare of Israel as a whole. Not identified with any political parties in Israel. Member of World Jewish Congress, World Zionist Organization. *Newsletter.* (WWW.AMERICANJEWISH LEAGUE.ORG)

AMERICAN PHYSICIANS FELLOWSHIP FOR MEDICINE IN ISRAEL (1950). 2001 Beacon St., Suite 210, Boston, MA 02135-7771. (617)232-5382. FAX: (617) 739-2616. E-mail: apf@apfmed.org. Pres. Sherwood L. Gorbach, M.D.; Exec. Dir. Ellen-Ann

Lacey. Supports projects that advance medical education, research, and care in Israel and builds links between the medical communities of Israel and N. Amer.; provides fellowships for Israeli physicians training in N. Amer. and arranges lectureships in Israel by prominent N. Amer. physicians; sponsors CME seminars in Israel and N. Amer.; coordinates U.S./ Canadian medical emergency volunteers for Israel. *APF News.*

AMERICAN RED MAGEN DAVID FOR ISRAEL, INC. (1940) (a/k/a ARMDI & Red Magen David). 888 Seventh Ave., Suite 403, NYC 10106. (212)757-1627. FAX: (212)757-4662. E-mail: armdi@att.net. Natl. Pres. Robert L. Sadoff, M.D.; Exec. V.-Pres. Benjamin Saxe. An authorized tax-exempt organization; the sole support arm in the U.S. of Magen David Adom (MDA), Israel's equivalent to a Red Cross Society; raises funds for the MDA emergency medical, ambulance, blood, and disaster services which help Israel's defense forces and civilian population. Helps to supply and equip ambulances, bloodmobiles, and cardiac rescue ambulances as well as 45 pre-hospital MDA Emergency Medical Clinics and the MDA National Blood Service Center and MDA Fractionation Institute in Ramat Gan, Israel. *Lifeline.*

AMERICAN SOCIETY FOR TECHNION-ISRAEL INSTITUTE OF TECHNOLOGY (1940). 810 Seventh Ave., 24th fl., NYC 10019. (212) 262-6200. FAX: (212)262-6155. Pres. Evelyn Berger; Chmn. Larry Jackier; Exec. V.-Pres. Melvyn H. Bloom. The American Technion Society (ATS) raises funds for the Technion-Israel Institute of Technology. Based in New York City, it is the leading American organization with more than 20,000 supporters and 197 satellite offices around the country, the ATS is driven by the belief that the economic future of Israel is in high technology and the future of high technology in Israel is at the Technion . . . *Technion USA.* (www.ATS.ORG.MAIL)

AMERICAN SOCIETY FOR THE PROTECTION OF NATURE IN ISRAEL, INC. (1986). 28 Arrandale Ave., Great Neck, NY 11024. (212) 398-6750. FAX: (212) 398-1665. E-mail: aspni@aol.com. Co-Chmn. Edward I. Geffner & Russell Rothman. A nonprofit organization supporting the work of SPNI, an Israeli organization devoted to environmental protection and nature education. SPNI runs 26 Field Study Centers and has 45 municipal offices throughout Israel; offers education programs, organized hikes, and other activities; seeks ways to address the needs of an expanding society while preserving precious natural resources. *SPNI News.*

AMERICAN SOCIETY FOR YAD VASHEM (1981). 500 Fifth Ave., 42nd Floor, NYC 10110-4299. (212)220-4304. FAX: (212) 220-4308. E-mail: info@yadvashemusa. org. Chmn. Eli Zborowski; Dev. Dir. Shraga Y. Mekel; Ed. Dir. Marlene Warshawski Yahalom, Ph.D. Development and educational arm of Yad Vashem, Jerusalem, the central international authority created by the Knesset in 1953 for the purposes of commemoration and education in connection with the Holocaust. *Martyrdom and Resistance (newsletter).* (WWW.YADVASHEM.ORG)

AMERICAN SOCIETY OF THE UNIVERSITY OF HAIFA (Formerly AMERICAN FRIENDS OF HAIFA UNIVERSITY) (1972). 220 Fifth Ave., Suite 1301, NYC 10001. (212) 685-7880. FAX: (212)685-7883. E-mail: asuhtr@att.net. Pres.Paul Amir; Sec./Treas. Robert Jay Benowitz. Promotes, encourages, and aids higher and secondary education, research, and training in all branches of knowledge in Israel and elsewhere; aids in the maintenance and development of University of Haifa; raises and allocates funds for the above purposes; provides scholarships; promotes exchanges of teachers and students.

AMERICAN ZIONIST MOVEMENT (Formerly AMERICAN ZIONIST FEDERATION) (1939; REORG. 1949, 1970, 1993). 110 E. 59 St., NYC 10022. (212)318-6100. FAX: (212) 935-3578. E-mail: info@azm.com. Pres. Melvin Salberg; Exec. Dir. Karen J. Rubinstein. Umbrella organization for 20 American Zionist organizations and the voice of unified Zionism in the U.S. Conducts advocacy for Israel; strengthens Jewish identity; promotes the Israel experience; prepares the next generation of Zionist leadership. Regional offices in Chicago and Dallas. Groups in Detroit, Pittsburgh, Washington, DC. *The Zionist Advocate.* (WWW.AZM.ORG)

AMERICANS FOR A SAFE ISRAEL (AFSI) (1971). 1623 Third Ave., Suite 205, NYC 10128. (212)828-2424. FAX: (212)828-

1717. E-mail: afsi@rcn.com. Chmn. Herbert Zweibon; Exec. Dir. Helen Freedman. Seeks to educate Americans in Congress, the media, and the public about Israel's role as a strategic asset for the West; through meetings with legislators and the media, in press releases and publications AFSI promotes Jewish rights to Judea and Samaria, the Golan, Gaza, an indivisible Jerusalem, and to all of Israel. AFSI believes in the concept of "peace for peace" and rejects the concept of "territory for peace." *The Outpost (monthly).* (WWW.AFSI.ORG.AFSI)

AMERICANS FOR PEACE NOW (1984). 1815 H St., NW, Suite 920, Washington, DC 20006. (202)728-1893. FAX: (202)728-1895. E-mail: apndc@peacenow.org. Pres. & CEO Debra DeLee; Chmn. Patricia Barr and Luis Lainer. Conducts educational programs and raises funds to support the Israeli peace movement, Shalom Achshav (Peace Now), and coordinates U.S. advocacy efforts through APN's Washington-based Center for Israeli Peace and Security. *Jerusalem Watch; Peace Now News; Settlement Watch; Fax Facts; Middle East Update (on-line); Benefits of Peace.* (WWW.PEACENOW.ORG)

AMIT (1925). 817 Broadway, NYC 10003. (212)477-4720. FAX: (212)353-2312. E-mail: info@amitchildren.org. Pres. Sondra Sokal; Exec. Dir. Marvin Leff. The State of Israel's official reshet (network) for religious secondary technological education; maintains innovative children's homes and youth villages in Israel in an environment of traditional Judaism; promotes cultural activities for the purpose of disseminating Zionist ideals and strengthening traditional Judaism in America. *AMIT Magazine.*

AMPAL-AMERICAN ISRAEL CORPORATION (1942). 1177 Avenue of the Americas, NYC 10036. (212)782-2100. FAX: (212) 782-2114. E-mail: ampal@aol.com. Bd. Chmn. Daniel Steinmetz; CEO Shuki Gleitman. Acquires interests in businesses located in the State of Israel or that are Israel-related. Interests include leisure-time, real estate, finance, energy distribution, basic industry, high technology, and communications. *Annual report; quarterly reports.*

ARZA/WORLD UNION, NORTH AMERICA (1977). 633 Third Ave., 6th fl., NYC

10017-6778. (212)650-4280. FAX: (212) 650-4289. E-mail: arza/wupjna@urj. org. Pres. Philip Meltzer; Exec. Dir. Rabbi Ammiel Hirsch. Membership organization dedicated to furthering the development of Progressive Judaism in Israel, the FSU, and throughout the world. Encourages Jewish solidarity, promoting religious pluralism and furthering Zionism. Works to strengthen the relationship of N. American Reform Jews with Progressive Jewish communities worldwide and to educate and inform them on relevant issues. *Quarterly newsletter.* (WWW.ARZA WUNA.ORG)

BETAR EDUCATIONAL YOUTH ORGANIZATION (1935). 4 East 34th Street, NYC, 10016. (646)742-9364. FAX: (646)742-9666. E-mail: newyork@betar.org. Pres. Dany Danon; Exec. Officer Itzik Simhon. Betar is a Zionist active college students' movement, which dedicates itself to promoting Israeli issues in the American media. Betar was founded in 1923 by Zeev Jabotinsky, among its' famous alumni are Nenachem Begin and Itzhak Shamir. Betar's goal is the gathering of all Jewish people in their ancient land.

BOYS TOWN JERUSALEM FOUNDATION OF AMERICA INC. (1948). 12 W. 31 St., Suite 300, NYC 10001. (212)244-2766. (800) 469-2697. FAX: (212)244-2052. E-mail: btjny@compuserve.com. Raphael Benaroya, Pres. Michael J. Scharf; Hon. Chmn. Josh S. Weston; Chmn. Raphael Benaroya; Exec. V.-Pres. Rabbi Ronald L. Gray. Raises funds for Boys Town Jerusalem, which was established in 1948 to offer a comprehensive academic, religious, and technological education to disadvantaged Israeli and immigrant boys from over 45 different countries, including Ethiopia, the former Soviet Union, and Iran. Enrollment: over 1,000 students in jr. high school, academic and technical high school, and a college of applied engineering. Boys Town was recently designated as the "CISCO Regional Academy," the first center in Jerusalem for the instruction of the CISCO Networking Management Program. *BTJ Newsbrief*

BRIT TZEDEK V'SHALOM—JEWISH ALLIANCE FOR JUSTICE AND PEACE (2002). 11 E. Adams St., Suite 707, Chicago, IL 60603. (312)341-1205. FAX: (312)341-1206. E-mail: info@btvshalom.org. Pres.

Marcia Freedman; Exec. Dir. Aliza Becker. Works for the achievement of a negotiated settlement of the Israeli-Palestinian conflict guided by the traditional Jewish obligation to pursue peace and justice, in the conviction that security for Israel can only be attained through the establishment of an economically and politicvally viable Palestinian state, necessitating an end to Israel's occupation of land acquired in the 1967 war and an end to Palestinian violence; its national office and 30 chapters around the country engage in grassroots political advocacy and public education. *Action Alerts.* (WWW. BTVSHALOM.ORG)

CAMERA-COMMITTEE FOR ACCURACY IN MIDDLE EAST REPORTING IN AMERICA (1983). PO Box 35040, Boston, MA 02135. (617)789-3672. FAX: (617)787-7853. E-mail: media@camera.org. Pres./ Exec. Dir. Andrea Levin; Chmn. Joshua Katzen. CAMERA monitors media coverage of Israel, responds to error, omissions, and distortion, promotes factual information and works to educate the media and public about key issues related to conflict in the Middle East. CAMERA encourages members to participate in fostering full and fair coverage through communication with the media. *CAMERA Media Report (quarterly); CAMERA on Campus;CAMERA Media Directory, CAMERA Monographs, Action Alerts, Backgrounders.* (WWW.CAMERA.ORG)

COUNCIL FOR A BEAUTIFUL ISRAEL ENVIRONMENTAL EDUCATION FOUNDATION (*see* American-Israel Environmental Council)

DEVELOPMENT CORPORATION FOR ISRAEL (Formerly STATE OF ISRAEL BONDS) (1951). 575 Lexington Ave., 11th Floor, NYC 10022. (212)644-2663. FAX: (212) 644-3887. E-mail: raphael.rothstein@israelbonds.com. Bd. Chmn. Burton P. Resnick; Pres./CEO Joshua Matza. An international organization offering securities issued by the government of Israel. Since its inception in 1951 has secured $25 billion in investment capital for the development of every aspect of Israel's economic infrastructure, including agriculture, commerce, and industry, and for absorption of immigrants. *Israel Hadashot-News.* (WWW.ISRAELBONDS.COM)

EMUNAH OF AMERICA (Formerly HAPOEL HAMIZRACHI WOMEN'S ORGANIZATION) (1948). 7 Penn Plaza, NYC 10001. (212) 564-9045, (800)368-6440. FAX:(212)643-9731. E-mail: info@emunah.org. Natl. Pres. Dr. Marcia Genuth; Exec. V.-Pres. Carol Sufian. Maintains and supports 200 educational and social-welfare institutions in Israel within a religious framework, including day-care centers, kindergartens, children's residential homes, vocational schools for the underprivileged, senior-citizen centers, a college complex, and Holocaust study center. Also involved in absorption of Soviet and Ethiopian immigrants (recognized by Israeli government as an official absorption agency). *Emunah Magazine; Lest We Forget.* (WWW.EMUNAH.ORG)

FEDERATED COUNCIL OF ISRAEL INSTITUTIONS—FCII (1940). 4702 15th Ave., Brooklyn, NY 11219. (718)972-5530. Bd. Chmn. Z. Shapiro; Exec. V.-Pres. Rabbi Julius Novack. Central fund-raising organization for over 100 affiliated institutions; handles and executes estates, wills, and bequests for the traditional institutions in Israel; clearinghouse for information on budget, size, functions, etc. of traditional educational, welfare, and philanthropic institutions in Israel, working cooperatively with the Israeli government and the overseas department of the Council of Jewish Federations. *Annual financial reports and statistics on affiliates.*

FRIENDS OF ISRAEL DISABLED VETERANS—BEIT HALOCHEM (1987). 1133 Broadway, Ste. 232, NYC 10010. (212)689-3220. FAX: (212)253-4143. E- mail: info@FIDV. org. Bd. Chmn. Richard L. Golden; Exec. Dir. Linda E. Frankel. Raises funds to assist disabled Israeli war victims, including civilian victims of terrorism; maintains four centers in Israel providing physical and emotional rehabilitation for them. (WWW.FIDV.ORG)

FRIENDS OF THE ISRAEL DEFENSE FORCES (1981). 298 5th Avenue, NYC 10001. (212) 244-3118. FAX: (212)244-3119. E-mail: fidf@fidf.com. Chmn. Marvin Josephson; Pres. Jay Zises; Natl. Dir. Brig. Gen. Eliezer Hemeli. Supports the Agudah Lema'an Hahayal, Israel's Assoc. for the Well-Being of Soldiers, founded in the early 1940s, which provides social, recreational, and educational programs for sol-

diers, special services for the sick and wounded, and summer programs for widows and children of fallen soldiers. (WWW.FIDF.COM)

GESHER FOUNDATION (1969). 25 W. 45 St. Suite 1405, NYC 10036. (212)840-1166. FAX: (212)840-1514. E-mail: gesherfoundation@aol.com. Pres./Founder Daniel Tropper; Chmn. Philip Schatten. Seeks to bridge the gap between Jews of various backgrounds in Israel by stressing the interdependence of all Jews. Runs encounter seminars for Israeli youth; distributes curricular materials in public schools; offers Jewish identity classes for Russian youth, and a video series in Russian and English on famous Jewish personalities.

GIVAT HAVIVA EDUCATIONAL FOUNDATION, INC. (1966). 114 W. 26 St., Suite 1001, NYC 10001. (212)989-9272. FAX: (212) 989-9840. E-mail: mail@givathaviva.org. Chmn. Yvonne Baum Silverman; Exec. Dir. Robert Levy. Supports programs at the Givat Haviva Institute, Israel's leading organization dedicated to promoting coexistence between Arabs and Jews, with 40,000 people participating each year in programs teaching conflict resolution, Middle East studies and languages, and Holocaust studies. Publishes research papers on Arab-Jewish relations, Holocaust studies, kibbutz life. In the U.S., GHEF sponsors public-education programs and lectures by Israeli speakers. *Givat Haviva News; special reports.* (WWW.DIALOGATE. ORG.IL)

HABONIM-DROR NORTH AMERICA (1935). 114 W. 26 St., Suite 1004, NYC 10001-6812. (212)255-1796. FAX: (212)929-3459. E-mail: programs@habonimdror. org. (Mazkir Tnua) Jamie Levin; Shliach Onri Welmer. Fosters identification with progressive, cooperative living in Israel; stimulates study of Jewish and Zionist culture, history, and contemporary society. Sponsors summer and year programs in Israel and on kibbutz, 7 summer camps in N. America modeled after kibbutzim, and *aliyah* frameworks. *B'Tnua (on-line and print newsletter).* (WWW.HABONIM DROR.ORG)

HADASSAH, THE WOMEN'S ZIONIST ORGANIZATION OF AMERICA, INC. (1912). 50 W. 58 St., NYC 10019. (212)355-7900. FAX:

(212)303-8282. Pres. June Walker; Exec. Dir. Morlie Hammer Levin. Largest women's, largest Jewish, and largest Zionist membership organization in U.S. In Israel: Founded and funds Hadassah Medical Organization, Hadassah College of Jerusalem, Hadassah Career Counseling Institute, Young Judaea summer and year-course programs, as well as providing support for Youth Aliyah and JNF. U.S. programs: Jewish and women's health education; advocacy on Israel, Zionism and women's issues; Young Judaea youth movement, including six camps; Hadassah Leadership Academy; Hadassah-Brandeis Institute for International Research on Jewish Women; Hadassah Foundation. *Hadassah Magazine; Update; Hadassah International Newsletter; Medical Update; American Scene.* (WWW.HADASSAH.ORG)

————, YOUNG JUDAEA (1909; REORG. 1967). 50 W. 58 St., NYC 10019. (212)303-8014. FAX: (212)303-4572. E-mail: info@youngjudaea.org. Natl. Dir. Doron Krakow. Religiously pluralistic, politically nonpartisan Zionist youth movement sponsored by Hadassah; seeks to educate Jewish youth aged 8-25 toward Jewish and Zionist values, active commitment to and participation in the American and Israeli Jewish communities; maintains six summer camps in the U.S.; runs both summer and year programs in Israel, and a jr. year program in connection with both Hebrew University in Jerusalem and Ben Gurion University of the Negev. College-age arm, Hamagshimim, supports Zionist activity on campuses. *Kol Hat'nua; The Young Judaean; Ad Kahn.* (WWW.YOUNGJUDAEA. ORG)

HASHOMER HATZAIR, SOCIALIST ZIONIST YOUTH MOVEMENT (1923). 114 W. 26 St., Suite 1001, NYC 10001. (212)627-2830. FAX: (212)989-9840. E-mail: mail@hashomerhatzair.org. Dir. Giora Salz; Natl. Sec. Moran Banai. Seeks to educate Jewish youth to an understanding of Zionism as the national liberation movement of the Jewish people. Promotes aliyah to kibbutzim. Affiliated with Kibbutz Artzi Federation. Espouses socialist-Zionist ideals of peace, justice, democracy, and intergroup harmony. *Young Guard.* (WWW.HASHOMERHAZAIR. ORG)

INTERNS FOR PEACE INTERNATIONAL (1976). 475 Riverside Dr., Room 240., NYC 10115. (212)870-2226. FAX: (914)686-8896. E-mail: ifpus@mindspring.com. Intl. Dir. Rabbi Bruce M. Cohen; Intl. Coord. Karen Wald Cohen. An independent, nonprofit, nonpolitical educational program training professional community peace workers. In Israel, initiated and operated jointly by Jews and Arabs; over 250 interns trained in 35 cities; over 80,000 Israeli citizens participating in joint programs in education, sports, culture, business, women's affairs, and community development; since the peace accord, Palestinians from West Bank and Gaza training as interns. Martin Luther King Project for Black/Jewish relations. *IFP Reports Quarterly; Guidebooks for Ethnic Conflict Resolution.* (WWW.INTERNSFOR PEACE.ORG)

ISRAEL CANCER RESEARCH FUND (1975). 1290 Avenue of the Americas, NYC 10104. (212)969-9800. FAX: (212)969-9822. E-mail: mail@icrfny.org. Pres. Yashar Hirshaut, M.D.; Chmn. Leah Susskind; Exec. V.P. Donald Adelman. The largest single source of private funds for cancer research in Israel. Has a threefold mission: To encourage innovative cancer research by Israeli scientists; to harness Israel's vast intellectual and creative resources to establish a world-class center for cancer study; to broaden research opportunities within Israel to stop the exodus of talented Israeli cancer researchers. *Annual Report; Research Awards; ICRF Brochure; Newsletter.*

ISRAEL HISTADRUT FOUNDATION (*see* Israel Humanitarian Foundation)

ISRAEL HUMANITARIAN FOUNDATION (IHF) (1960). 276 Fifth Ave., Suite 901, NYC 10001. (212)683-5676, (800)434-5IHF. FAX: (212)213-9233. E-mail: info@ihf. net. Pres. Marvin M. Sirota; Exec.V.-Pres. Stanley J. Abrams. Since 1960, Israel Humanitarian Foundation (IHF) has funded more than 130 social service projects in Israel that provide funds and programs in a diverse range of areas. IHF strives to improve the standard of living of the Israeli population through its support for education, youth in need, elder care, the disables, and medical care & research projects that directly benefit thousands of people in need.

ISRAEL POLICY FORUM (1993). 165 East 56th Street, 2nd Floor, NYC 10022. (212)245-4227. FAX: (212)245-0517. E-mail: ipf@ipforum.org. 1030 15 St., NW, Suite 850, Washington, DC 20005. (202)842-1700. FAX:(202)842-1722. E-mail: ipf@ipforum.org. Pres. Seymour Reich. An independent leadership institution whose mission is to encourage an active U.S. role in resolving the Arab-Israeli conflict. IPF generates this support by involving leaders from the business, political, entertainment, academic, and philanthropic communitites in the peace effort, and by fostering a deeper understanding of the peace process among the American public. *Forum Fax, Washington Bulletin, Security Watch.* (WWW.IPFORUM.ORG)

THE JERUSALEM FOUNDATION, INC. (1966). 60 E. 42 St., Suite 1936, NYC 10165. (212) 697-4188. FAX: (212) 697-4022. E-mail: info@jfoundation.com. Chmn. Kenneth J. Bialkin; Exec. Dir. Dorothy Kauffman. A nonprofit organization devoted to improving the quality of life for all Jerusalemites, regardless of ethnic, religious, or socioeconomic background; has initiated and implemented more than 1,500 projects that span education, culture, community services, beautification, and preservation of the city's historic heritage and religious sites.

JEWISH INSTITUTE FOR NATIONAL SECURITY AFFAIRS (JINSA) (1976). (202)667-3900. E-mail: info@jinsa.org. Pres. Norman Hascoe; Exec. Dir. Tom Neumann. A nonprofit, nonpartisan educational organization working within the American Jewish community to explain the link between American defense policy and the security of the State of Israel; and within the national security establishment to explain the key role Israel plays in bolstering American interests. (WWW.JINSA.ORG)

JEWISH INSTITUTE FOR THE BLIND-JERUSALEM, INC. (1902, Jerusalem). 15 E. 26 St., NYC 10010. (212) 532-4155. FAX: (212) 447-7683. Pres. Rabbi David E. Lapp; Admin. Eric L. Loeb. Supports a dormitory and school for the Israeli blind and handicapped in Jerusalem.*INsight.*

JEWISH NATIONAL FUND OF AMERICA (1901). 42 E. 69 St., NYC 10021. (212) 879-9300. (1-800-542-TREE). FAX: (212) 570-1673. E-mail: communications@jnf.org. Pres. Ronald S. Lauder; Exec. V.-

Pres. Russell F. Robinson. Jewish National Fund is the American fund-raising arm of Keren Kayemeth LeIsrael, the official land agency in Israel and is celebrating its 100th Anniversary this year. JNF works in the following areas: water resource development, afforestation and ecology, eduction, tourism and recreation, community development and research. (WWW.JNF.ORG)

JEWISH PEACE LOBBY (1989). 8604 Second Avnue, PMB 317, Silver Spring, MD 20910. (301)589-8764. FAX: (301)589-2722. Email: peacelobby@msn.com. Pres. Jerome M. Segal. A legally registered lobby promoting changes in U.S. policy vis-a-vis the Israeli-Palestinian conflict. Supports Israel's right to peace within secure borders; a political settlement based on mutual recognition of the right of self-determination of both peoples; a two-state solution as the most likely means to a stable peace. *Annual Report.*

KEREN OR, INC. Jerusalem Center for Multihandicapped Blind Children (1956). 350 Seventh Ave., Suite 200, NYC 10001. (212)279-4070. FAX: (212)279-4043. E-mail: kerenorinc@aol.com. Chmn. Dr. Edward L. Steinberg; Pres. Dr. Albert Hornblass; Exec. Dir. Rochelle B. Silberman. Funds the Keren-Or Center for Multi-Handicapped Blind Children at 3 Abba Hillel Silver St., Ramot, Jerusalem, housing and caring for over 70 resident and day students who in addition to blindness or very low vision suffer from other severe physical and/or mental disabilities. Students range in age from 1 1/2 through young adulthood. Provides training in daily living skills, as well as therapy, rehabilitation, and education to the optimum level of the individual. *Insights Newsletter.*

LABOR ZIONIST ALLIANCE (Formerly FARBAND LABOR ZIONIST ORDER) (1913). 275 Seventh Ave., NYC 10001. (212)366-1194. FAX: (212)675-7685. E-mail: labzionA@aol.com. Pres. Jeffry Mallow; Exec. Dir. Ari M. Chester. Seeks to enhance Jewish life, culture, and education in U.S.; aids in building State of Israel as a cooperative commonwealth and its Labor movement organized in the Histadrut; supports efforts toward a more democratic society throughout the world; furthers the democratization of the Jewish community in America and the welfare of Jews everywhere; works with labor and liberal forces in America; sponsors Habonim-Dror labor Zionist youth movement. *Jewish Frontier; Yiddisher Kempfer.* (WWW.JEWISH FRONTIER.ORG)

MACCABI USA/SPORTS FOR ISRAEL (Formerly UNITED STATES COMMITTEE SPORTS FOR ISRAEL) (1948). 1926 Arch St., 4R, Philadelphia, PA 19103. (215)561-6900. Fax: (215)561-5470. E-mail: maccabi@ maccabiusa.com. Pres. Toni Worhman. Sponsors U.S. team for World Maccabiah Games in Israel every four years; seeks to enrich the lives of Jewish youth in the U.S., Israel, and the Diaspora through athletic, cultural, and educational programs; develops, promotes, and supports international, national, and regional athletic-based activities and facilities. *Sportscene Newsletter; Commemorative Maccabiah Games Journal; financial report.* (WWW.MACCABIUSA.COM)

MERCAZ USA (1979). 155 Fifth Ave., NYC 10010. (212)533-7800, ext. 2016. FAX: (212) 533-2601. E-mail: info@mercazusa.org. Pres. Rabbi Vernon H. Kurtz; Exec. Dir. Rabbi Robert R. Golub. The U.S. Zionist organization for Conservative/Masorti Judaism; works for religious pluralism in Israel, defending and promoting Conservative/Masorti institutions and individuals; fosters Zionist education and *aliyah* and develops young leadership. *Mercaz USA Quarterly Newsletter.* (WWW.MERCAZ USA.ORG)

MERETZ USA FOR ISRAELI CIVIL RIGHTS AND PEACE (1991). 114 W. 26 St., Suite 1002, NYC 10001. (212)242-4500. FAX: (212)242-5718. E-mail: mail@meretzusa. org. Pres. Jeremiah S. Gutman; Exec. Dir. Charney V. Bromberg. A forum for addressing the issues of social justice and peace in Israel. Educates about issues related to democracy, human and civil rights, religious pluralism, and equality for women and ethnic minorities; promotes the resolution of Israel's conflict with the Palestinians on the basis of mutual recognition, self-determination, and peaceful coexistence. *Israel Horizons.* (WWW.MERETZUSA.ORG)

NA'AMAT USA, THE WOMEN'S LABOR ZIONIST ORGANIZATION OF AMERICA, INC. (1925). 350 Fifth Ave., Suite 4700, NYC 10118-4799. (212)563-5222. FAX: (212) 563-5710. E-mail: naamat@naamat.org. Natl. Pres. Lynn Wax. Part of the World

Movement of Na'amat (Movement of Working Women and Volunteers), the largest Jewish women's organization in the world, it helps provide social, educational, and legal services for women, teenagers, and children in Israel. It also advocates legislation for women's rights and child welfare in Israel and the U.S., furthers Jewish education, and supports Habonim Dror, the Labor Zionist youth movement. *Na'amat Woman magazine.* (WWW.NAAMAT.ORG)

NATIONAL COMMITTEE FOR LABOR ISRAEL (1923). 275 Seventh Ave., NYC 10001. (212)647-0300. FAX: (212)647-0308. E-mail: ncli@laborisrael.org. Pres. Jay Mazur; Exec. Dir. Jerry Goodman; Chmn. Trade Union Council Morton Bahr. Serves as a bridge among Israel's labor sector, including its General Federation of Labor, Histadrut, the American labor movement, the Jewish community and the general public. Brings together Jews and non-Jews to build support for Israel and advance closer Israel-Arab ties. Cooperates with Israels labor sector. National in scope, it conducts education in the Jewish community and among labor groups to promote better relations with labor Israel. Raises funds for youth, educational, health, social and cultural projects in Israel from a constituency which includes labor unions, foundations, government agencies and individual donors and supporters. *Occasional background papers* (WWW.LABORISRAEL.ORG)

NEW ISRAEL FUND (1979). 1101 14th St., NW, 6th fl., Washington, DC 20005-5639. (202)842-0900. FAX: (202)842-0991. E-mail: info@nif.org. New York office: 165 E. 56 St., NYC 10022. (212)750-2333. FAX: (212)750-8043. Pres. Yoram Peri; Exec. Dir. Norman S. Rosenberg. A partnership of Israelis and North Americans dedicated to promoting social justice, coexistence, and pluralism in Israel, the New Israel Fund helps strengthen Israeli democracy by providing grants and technical assistance to the public-interest sector, cultivating a new generation of social activists, and educating citizens in Israel and the Diaspora about the challenges to Israeli democracy. *Quarterly newsletter; annual report; other reports . . .* (WWW.NIF. ORG)

PEF ISRAEL ENDOWMENT FUNDS, INC. (1922). 317 Madison Ave., Suite 607, NYC 10017. (212)599-1260. Chmn. Sidney A. Luria; Pres. B. Harrison Frankel; Sec. Mark Bane. A totally volunteer organization that makes grants to educational, scientific, social, religious, health, and other philanthropic institutions in Israel. *Annual report.*

POALE AGUDATH ISRAEL OF AMERICA, INC. (1948). 2920 Avenue J, Brooklyn, NY 11210. (718)258-2228. FAX: (718)258-2288. Pres. Rabbi Fabian Schonfeld. Aims to educate American Jews to the values of Orthodoxy and aliyah; supports kibbutzim, trade schools, yeshivot, moshavim, kollelim, research centers, and children's homes in Israel. *PAI News; She'arim; Hamayan.*

———, WOMEN'S DIVISION OF (1948). Pres. Miriam Lubling; Presidium: Sarah Ivanisky, Tili Stark, Peppi Petzenbaum. Assists Poale Agudath Israel to build and support children's homes, kindergartens, and trade schools in Israel. *Yediot PAI.*

PRO ISRAEL (1990). 1328 Broadway, Suite 435, NYC. (212)594-8996. FAX: (212) 594-8986. E-mail: proisrael@aol.com. Pres. Dr. Ernest Bloch; Exec. Dir. Rabbi Julian M. White. Educates the public about Israel and the Middle East; provides support for community development throughout the Land of Israel, particularly in Judea, Samaria, Gaza, and the Golan Heights. Projects include the Ariel Center for Policy Research and Professors for a Strong Israel.

RELIGIOUS ZIONISTS OF AMERICA (1909). 7 Penn Plaza, Suite 205, NYC 10001. (212) 465-9234. FAX: (212)465-9246. Email: mizrachi@rza.org. Pres. Rabbi Yosef Blau; Exec. Dir. Alan Mond. Disseminates ideals of religious Zionism; conducts cultural work, educational program, public relations; raises funds for religious educational institutions in Israel, including yeshivot hesder and Bnei Akiva. *Voice of Religious Zionism.* (WWW. RZA.ORG)

———, BNEI AKIVA OF THE U.S. & CANADA (1934). 7 Penn Plaza, Suite 205, NYC 10001. (212)465-9536. FAX: (212)465-2155. Shaliah, Rabbi Shaul Feldman; Natl. Dir. Steve Frankel. The only religious Zionist Youth movement in North America, Educating thousands of youths from grade school throughout the US and Canada. We have five summer camps in North America and a summer pro-

gram in Israel. We educate towards the values of the Religious Zionist Movement which sees the place of all Jews, in Israel, involved in social action, and committed to Orthodox Torah values. *Akivon; Pinkas Lamadrich; Daf Rayonot; Me'Ohalai Torah; Zraim.*(WWW.BNEI AKIVA.ORG)

———, NATIONAL COUNCIL FOR TORAH EDUCATION (1939). 7 Penn Plaza, Suite 205, NYC 10001. (212)465-9234. FAX: (212)465-9246. E-mail: mizrachi@rza. org. Pres. Aaron S. Tirschwell; Chmn. Rabbi Mark Dratch. Organizes and supervises yeshivot and Talmud Torahs; prepares and trains teachers; publishes textbooks and educational materials; organizes summer seminars for Hebrew educators in cooperation with Torah Department of Jewish Agency; conducts ulpan. *Ohr HaMizrach, Torat Yisrael (weekly).* (WWW.RZA.ORG)

SCHNEIDER CHILDREN'S MEDICAL CENTER OF ISRAEL (1982). 130 E. 59 St., Suite 1203, NYC 10022. (212)759-3370. FAX: (212)759-0120. E-mail: mdiscmci@aol. com. Bd. Chmn. H. Irwin Levy; Exec. Dir. Shlomit Manson. Its primary goal is to provide the best medical care to children in the Middle East. *UPDATE Newsletter*

SOCIETY OF ISRAEL PHILATELISTS (1949). 24355 Tunbridge Lane, Beachwood, OH 44122. (216)292-3843. Pres. Robert B. Pildes. MD; Exec. Secry. Howard S. Chapman; Journal Ed. Dr. Oscar Stadtler. Promotes interest in, and knowledge of, all phases of Israel philately through sponsorship of chapters and research groups, maintenance of a philatelic library, and support of public and private exhibitions. *The Israel Philatelist; monographs; books.*

TEL AVIV UNIVERSITY: AMERICAN COUNCIL (Formerly AMERICAN FRIENDS OF TEL AVIV UNIVERSITY, INC.) (1955). 39 Broadway, 15th Floor., NYC 10006. (212)742-9070. FAX: (212)742-9071. Email: info@ tauac.org. Pres. Sam Witkin; Natl. Chmn. Joel Tauber. Promotes higher education at Tel Aviv University, Israel's largest and most comprehensive institution of higher learning. Included in its nine faculties are the Sackler School of Medicine with its fully accredited NY State English-language program, the Rubin Academy of Music, and 70 research institutes, including the Moshe Dayan Center for Middle East & African Studies and the Jaffe Center for Strategic Studies. *Tel Aviv University News; FAX Flash, Connections Newsletter (quarterly).*

THEODOR HERZL FOUNDATION (1954). 633 Third Ave., 21ˢᵗ fl., NYC 10017. (212)339-6040. FAX: (212)318-6176. Email: info@midstream.org. Chmn. Kalman Sultanik; Sec. Sam E. Bloch. Offers cultural activities, lectures, conferences, courses in modern Hebrew and Jewish subjects, Israel, Zionism, and Jewish history..

———, HERZL PRESS. Chmn. Kalman Sultanik; Dir. of Pub. Sam E. Bloch. Serves as "the Zionist Press of record," publishing books that are important for the light they shed on Zionist philosophy, Israeli history, contemporary Israel and the Diaspora and the relationship between them. They are important as contributions to Zionist letters and history. *Midstream . . .*

TO SAVE A LIFE (2003). 16405 Equestrian Lane, Rockville, MD 20855. (301)977-3637. FAX: (301)977-3888. E-mail: tosavealife@hotmail.com. Pres. Jerry Klinger. Provides an opportunity to give directly, efficiently, and personally to help needy Israelis; identifies small charities that are below the radar screen. (WWW.TSAL.ORG)

TSOMET-TECHIYA USA (1978). 185 Montague St., 3rd fl., Brooklyn, NY 11201. (718)596-2119. FAX: (718)858-4074. E-mail: eliahu@aol.com. Chmn. Howard B. Weber. Supports the activities of the Israeli Tsomet party, which advocates Israeli control over the entire Land of Israel.

UNITED CHARITY INSTITUTIONS OF JERUSALEM, INC. (1903). 1467 48 St., Brooklyn, NY 11219. (718)633-8469. FAX: (718) 633-8478. Chmn. Rabbi Charlop; Exec. Dir. Rabbi Pollak. Raises funds for the maintenance of schools, kitchens, clinics, and dispensaries in Israel; free loan foundations in Israel.

UNITED ISRAEL APPEAL, INC. (1925). 111 Eighth Ave., Suite 11E, NYC 10011. (212) 284-6900. FAX: (212)284-6988. Chmn. Bennett L. Aaron; Exec. V.-Chmn. Daniel R. Allen. Provides funds raised by UJA/Federation campaigns in the U.S. to aid the people of Israel through the programs of the Jewish Agency for Israel, UIA's operating agent. Serves as link between American Jewish community and Jewish Agency for Israel; assists in resettlement and absorption of refugees in Israel, and supervises flow and expenditure of funds for this purpose. *Annual report; newsletters; brochures.*

UNITED STATES COMMITTEE SPORTS FOR ISRAEL (*see* MACCABI USA/SPORTS FOR ISRAEL)

US/ISRAEL WOMEN TO WOMEN (1979). 45 West 36ᵗʰ Street, 10ᵗʰ Floor, NYC 10018. (917) 351-0920. FAX: (917) 351-0921. E-mail: info@usisraelwomen.org. Ch. Nina Kaufman, esq.; Exec. Dir. Joan Gordon. Provides critical seed money for grassroots efforts advocating equal status and fair treatment for women in all spheres of Israeli life; targets small, innovative, Israeli-run programs that seek to bring about social change in health, education, civil rights, domestic violence, family planning, and other spheres of Israeli life. *Newsletters. (WWW.USISRAEL WOMEN.ORG)*

VOLUNTEERS FOR ISRAEL (1982). 330 W. 42 St., Suite 1618, NYC 10036-6902. (212) 643-4848. FAX: (212)643-4855. E-mail: vol4israel@aol.com. Pres. Jeanne S. Schachter; Vice Pres. Carol Stein. Provides aid to Israel through volunteer work, building lasting relationships between Israelis and Americans. Affords persons aged 18 and over the opportunity to participate in various duties currently performed by overburdened Israelis on IDF bases and in other settings, enabling them to meet and work closely with Israelis and to gain an inside view of Israeli life and culture.

WOMEN'S LEAGUE FOR ISRAEL, INC. (1928). 160 E. 56 St., NYC 10022. (212)838-1997. FAX: (212)888-5972. E-mail: wliny@aol.com. Pres. Harriet Lainer; Exec. Dir. Dorothy Leffler. Maintains centers in Haifa, Tel Aviv, Jerusalem, Natanya. Projects include Family Therapy and Training, Centers for the Prevention of Domestic Violence, Meeting Places (supervised centers for noncustodial parents and their children), DROR (supporting families at risk), Yachdav-"Together" (long-term therapy for parents and children), the National Library for Social

Work, and the Hebrew University Blind Students' Unit.

WORLD CONFEDERATION OF UNITED ZIONISTS (1946; REORG.1958). 130 E. 59 St., NYC 10022. (212)371-1452. FAX: (212) 371-3265. Co-Pres. Marlene Post & Kalman Sultanik. Promotes Zionist education, sponsors nonparty youth movements in the Diaspora, and strives for an Israel-oriented creative Jewish survival in the Diaspora. *Zionist Information Views (in English and Spanish).*

WORLD ZIONIST ORGANIZATION-AMERICAN SECTION (1971). 633 Third Ave., 21ˢᵗ fl., NYC 10017. (212)688-3197. Chmn. Kalman Sultanik. As the American section of the overall Zionist body throughout the world, it operates primarily in the field of aliyah from the free countries, education in the Diaspora, youth and Hechalutz, organization and information, cultural institutions, publications; conducts a worldwide Hebrew cultural program including special seminars and pedagogic manuals; disperses information and assists in research projects concerning Israel; promotes, publishes, and distributes books, periodicals, and pamphlets concerning developments in Israel, Zionism, and Jewish history. *Midstream.*

——, DEPARTMENT OF EDUCATION AND CULTURE (1948). 633 Third Ave., 21ˢᵗ fl., NYC 10017. (212)339-6001. FAX: (212) 826-8959. Renders educational services to boards and schools: study programs, books, AV aids, instruction, teacher-in-training service. Judaic and Hebrew subjects. Annual National Bible Contest; Israel summer and winter programs for teachers and students.

——, ISRAEL ALIYAH CENTER (1993). 633 Third Ave., 21ˢᵗ fl., NYC 10017. (212)339-6060. FAX: (212)832-2597. Exec. Dir. N. Amer. Aliyah Delegation, Kalman Grossman. Through 26 offices throughout N. Amer., staffed by *shlichim* (emissaries), works with potential immigrants to plan their future in Israel and processes immigration documents. Through Israel Aliyah Program Center provides support, information, and programming for olim and their families; promotes long-term programs and fact-finding trips to Israel. Cooperates with Tnuat Aliyah in Jerusalem and serves as American contact with Association of Americans and Canadians in Israel.

YOUTH RENEWAL FUND. 488 Madison Ave., 10ᵗʰ fl., NYC 10022. (212)207-3195. FAX: (212)207-8379. E-mail: info@youthrenewal fund.org. Pres. Samuel L. Katz; Exec. Dir. Karen L. Berman. The Youth Renewal Fund was established in 1989 to provide supplemental education to disadvantaged youth in Israel. Since inception, YRF has implemented over $10 million in programs that have benefited over 19,500 Israeli children. (WWW.YOUTHRENEWAL FUND.ORG)

ZIONA. 641 Lexington Ave., 24ᵗʰ Floor, New York, NY 10022. (212) 688-2890. FAX: (212) 688-1327. Email: thezionist@aol. com. Pres. Arnie T. Goldfarb; Ex. Vice Pres. Rev. Salomon L. Vaz Dias. ZIONA is a volunteer organization whose members are motivated and inspired to strengthen their partnership with Israel, ensure Jewish continuity, and realize their potential as a dynamic force in American society. In Israel, ZIONA initiates and supports education and youth institutions, and land development to meet the country's changing needs; helps to restore the ancient cemetery on the Mount of Olives in Jerusalem. *The Zionist Update* (WWW.ZIONA.ORG)

ZIONIST ORGANIZATION OF AMERICA (1897). ZOA House, 4 E. 34 St., NYC 10016. (212)481-1500. FAX: (212)481-1515. E-mail: email@zoa.com. Natl. Pres. Morton A. Klein; Exec. Dir. Robert Jancu, Esq. Strengthens the relationship between Israel and the U.S. through Zionist educational activities that explain Israel's importance to the U.S. and the dangers that Israel faces. Works on behalf of pro-Israel legislation; combats anti-Israel bias in the media, textbooks, travel guides, and on campuses; promotes *aliyah.* Maintains the ZOA House in Tel Aviv, a cultural center, and the Kfar Silver Agricultural and Technical High School in Ashkelon, which provides vocational training for new immigrants. *ZOA Report; Israel and the Middle East: Behind the Headlines.*(WWW.ZOA.ORG)

OVERSEAS AID

AMERICAN FRIENDS OF THE ALLIANCE ISRAÉLITE UNIVERSELLE, INC. (1946). 420 Lexington Ave., Suite 1731, NYC 10170.

(212)808-5437. FAX: (212)983-0094. E-mail: afaiu@onsiteaccess.com. Pres. Albert Sibony; Asst. Batya Minkowitz. Participates in educational and human-rights activities of the AIU and supports the Alliance system of Jewish schools, teachers' colleges, and remedial programs in Israel, North Africa, the Middle East, Europe, and Canada. *Alliance Review.*

AMERICAN JEWISH JOINT DISTRIBUTION COMMITTEE, INC.—JDC (1914). 711 Third Ave., NYC 10017-4014. (212)687-6200. FAX: (212)370-5467. E-mail: newyork @jdcny.org. Pres. Ellen Heller; Exec. V.-Pres. Steven Schwager. Provides assistance to Jewish communities in Europe, Asia, Africa, and the Mideast, including welfare programs for Jews in need. Current concerns include: Rescuing Jews from areas of distress, facilitating community development in the former Soviet Union; helping to meet Israel's social service needs by developing innovative programs that create new opportunities for the country's most vulnerable populations; youth activities in Eastern Europe and nonsectarian development and disaster assistance. *Annual Report; Snapshots: JDC's Activities in the Former Soviet Union; JDC: One People, One Heart.* (www. JDC.ORG).

AMERICAN JEWISH PHILANTHROPIC FUND (1955). 122 E. 42 St., 12th fl., NYC 10168-1289. (212)755-5640. FAX: (212)644-0979. Pres. Charles J. Tanenbaum. Provides college scholarship assistance to Jewish refugees through pilot programs being administered by the Jewish Family Service in Los Angeles and NYANA in New York.

AMERICAN JEWISH WORLD SERVICE (1985). 45 West 36th Street., NYC 10018. (212) 736-2597. FAX: (212)736-3463. E-mail: jws@ajws.org. Chmn. Marty Friedman; Pres. Ruth W. Messinger. Provides non-sectarian, humanitarian assistance and emergency relief to people in need in Africa, Asia, Latin America, Russia, Ukraine, and the Middle East; works in partnership with local nongovernmental organizations to support and implement self-sustaining grassroots development projects; serves as a vehicle through which the Jewish community can act as global citizens. *AJWS Reports (newsletter).* (WWW.AJWS.ORG)

AMERICAN ORT, INC. (1922). 817 Broadway, NYC 10003. (212)353-5800/(800)364-9678. FAX: (212)353-5888. E-mail: infor@ aort.org. Pres. Robert L. Sill; Exec. Dir. Paul B. Firstenburg. American ORT coordinates all ORT operations in the U.S., in cooperation with Women's American ORT; promotes and raises funds for ORT, a nonpolitical organization and the largest non-governmental global education and training organization in the world. With past and present activities in over 100 countries, ORT has educated nearly 4 million people in a global network of high schools, colleges, apprenticeship programs and teacher training institutes. This year, ORT's global network enables its 300,000 students in more than 60 countries to pursue fruitful careers and live lives of hope. Students at ORT schools everywhere around the world rely on funds raised by American ORT to help them meet tuition costs, build the most up-to-date learning facilities and furnish them with cutting-edge learning tools, computers, laboratories and other equipment. In Israel, 100,000 students attend 145 schools and training centers; there are 47 ORT schools and centers in the CIS (the former Soviet Union) and in the Baltic States; and in the U.S., over 15,000 students are served by ORT's Technical Institutes in Chicago, Los Angeles, and New York, and in Jewish day school programs in Atlanta, Chicago, Cleveland, Detroit, Florida, Los Angeles, and the National Capital Area (Washington, D.C.). Jewish day school students are served by ORT compute technology programs in Atlanta, Cleveland and Miami. (WWW.AORT.ORG)

———, **WOMEN'S AMERICAN ORT** (1927). 250 Park Ave. S., NYC 10003-1494. (212)505-7700; (800)51-WAORT. FAX: (212)674-3057. E-mail: waort@waort. org. Pres. Judy Menikoff; Exec. V.P. & Dir. Hope Kessler. Strengthens the worldwide Jewish community by empowering people to achieve economic self-sufficiency through technological and vocational training; educates 290,000 students in 60 countries including the United States, Israel and the former Soviet Union; supports ORT programs through membership, fundraising and leadership development; domestic agenda promotes quality public education, women's rights and literacy. *Women's American ORT Re-*

porter; Women's American ORT Annual Report.(WWW.WAORT.ORG)

CONFERENCE ON JEWISH MATERIAL CLAIMS AGAINST GERMANY, INC. (1951). 15 E. 26 St., Rm. 906, NYC 10010. (212)696-4944. FAX: (212)679-2126. E-mail: info@ claimscon.org. Pres. Dr. Israel Singer; Exec. V.-Pres. Gideon Taylor. Represents Jewish survivors in negotiations for compensation from the German government and other entities once controlled by the Nazis. Also an operating agency that administers compensation funds, recovers Jewish property and allocates funds to institutions that serve Holocaust survivors. The Claims Conference—made up of the conference on Jewish Material Claims Against Germany and the Committee for Jewish Claims on Austria—is one of the founders of the World Jewish Restitution Organization, Memorial Foundation for Jewish Culture and the United Restitution Organization. *Newsletter; Annual Report; Guide to Restitution and Compensation; Special Update.* (WWW.CLAIMSCON.ORG)

HIAS, INC. (HEBREW IMMIGRANT AID SOCIETY) (1880; reorg. 1954). 333 Seventh Ave., NYC 10001-5004. (212)967-4100. FAX: (212)967-4483. E-mail:public@ hias.org. Chair Jerome S. Teller; Pres. & CEO Neil Greenbaum. The oldest international migration and refugee resettlement agency in the United States, dedicated to assisting persecuted and oppressed people worldwide and delivering them to countries of safe haven. As the migration arm of the American Jewish community, it also advocates for fair and just policies affecting refugees and immigrants. Since its founding in 1881, the agency has rescued more than four and a half million people. *Bi-Annual report.*

JEWISH FOUNDATION FOR THE RIGHTEOUS (1986). 305 Seventh Ave., 19th fl., NYC 10001. (212)727-9955. FAX: (212) 727-9956. E-mail: jfr@jfr.org. Pres. Paul Goldberger; Exec. V.P. Stanlee J. Stahl. Provides monthly support to 1,700 aged and needy Righteous Gentiles living in 30 countries who risked their lives to save Jews during the Holocaust. The Foundation's education program focuses on educating teachers and their students about the history of the Holocaust and the significance of altruistic behavior for our so-

ciety. *Newsletter (3 times a year).* (WWW. JFR.ORG)

NORTH AMERICAN CONFERENCE ON ETHIOPIAN JEWRY (NACOEJ) (1982). 132 Nassau St., Suite 412, NYC 10038. (212)233-5200. FAX: (212)233-5243. E-mail: nacoej@aol.com. Pres. Judith L. Wolf; Exec. Dir. Barbara Ribakove Gordon. Provides programming for Ethiopian Jews in Israel in the areas of education (elementary school, high school and college) and cultural preservation. Assists Ethiopian Jews remaining in Ethiopia. National speakers bureau offers programs to synagogues, schools, and Jewish and non-Jewish organizations. Exhibits of Ethiopian Jewish artifacts, photos, handicrafts, etc. available. *Lifeline (newsletter).* (WWW.NACOEJ.ORG)

RE'UTH WOMEN'S SOCIAL SERVICE, INC. (1937). 130 E. 59 St., Suite 1200, NYC 10022. (212)836-1570. FAX: (212)836-1114. Chmn. Ursula Merkin; Pres. Rosa Strygler. Maintains, in Israel, subsidized housing for self-reliant elderly; old-age homes for more dependent elderly; Lichtenstadter Hospital for chronically ill and young accident victims not accepted by other hospitals; subsidized meals; Golden Age clubs. Recently opened a wing for chronically ill children. *Annual dinner journal.*

THANKS TO SCANDINAVIA, INC. (1963). The American Jewish Committee, 165 East 56th Street, 8th Fl., NYC 10022. (212)891-1403. FAX: (212)838-2120. Email: tts@ ajc.org. Pres. Richard Netter; Exec. Dir. Rebecca Neuwirth. Provides scholarships and fellowships at U.S. universities and medical centers and Israeli educational institutions to students/teachers/medical professionals from Denmark, Finland, Norway, and Sweden in lasting appreciation of the rescue of Jews during World War II and to build friendships based on those examples of courage and humanity in history. *(WWW.THANKSTOSCANDIAIVIA. ORG)*

UJA FEDERATION OF NORTH AMERICA. (1939). (*see* UNITED JEWISH COMMUNITIES)

UNITED JEWISH COMMUNITIES (1999). 111 Eighth Ave., 11th fl., NYC 10011-5201. (212)284-6500. FAX: (212)284-6822. Chmn. Robert Goldberg; Pres./CEO Howard Rieger. Formed from the merger of the United Jewish Appeal, the Council of Jewish Federations and United Israel Appeal, is the dominant fundraising arm for North American Jewry, and represents 189 Jewish Federations and 400 independent communities across the continent. It reflects the values and traditions of education, leadership, advocacy and social justice, and continuity of community that define the Jewish people.

RELIGIOUS AND EDUCATIONAL ORGANIZATIONS

AGUDATH ISRAEL OF AMERICA (1922). 42 Broadway, NYC, 10004. (212)797-9000. FAX: (646)254-1600. E-mail: shafran@agudathisrael.org. Exec. V.-Pres. Rabbi Shmuel Bloom; Exec. Dir. Rabbi Boruch B. Borchardt. Mobilizes Orthodox Jews to cope with Jewish problems in the spirit of the Torah; speaks out on contemporary issues from an Orthodox viewpoint; sponsors a broad range of projects aimed at enhancing religious living, education, children's welfare, protection of Jewish religious rights, outreach to the assimilated and to arrivals from the former Soviet Union, and social services. *Jewish Observer; Dos Yiddishe Vort; Coalition.*

———, AGUDAH WOMEN OF AMERICA-N'SHEI AGUDATH ISRAEL (1940). 42 Broadway, NYC 10004. (212)363-8940. FAX: (212)747-8763. Presidium Aliza Grund & Rose Isbee; Dir. Hannah Kalish, Esq. Organizes Jewish women for philanthropic work in the U.S. and Israel and for intensive Torah education. Its new division, N'shei C.A.R.E.S., (Community, Awareness, Responsibility, Education, & Support), conducts seminars and support groups promoting the health and well-being of Jewish women and their families.

———, BOYS' DIVISION-PIRCHEI AGUDATH ISRAEL (1925) 42 BROADWAY, NYC 10004 (212)797-9000. Natl. Coord. Rabbi Shimon Grama. Educates Orthodox Jewish children in Torah; encourages sense of communal responsibility. Branches sponsor weekly youth groups and Jewish welfare projects. National Mishnah contests, rallies, and conventions foster unity on a national level. *Leaders Guides.*

———, GIRLS' DIVISION—BNOS AGUDATH ISRAEL (1921). 42 Broadway, NYC 10004. (646)254-1600. Natl. Dir. Leah Zagel-baum. Sponsors regular weekly programs on the local level and unites girls from throughout the Torah world with extensive regional and national activities. *Kol Bnos.*

———, YOUNG MEN'S DIVISION—ZEIREI AGUDATH ISRAEL (1921) . . . 42 Broadway, NYC 10004. (212)797-9000, ext. 57. Dir. Rabbi Labish Becker. Educates youth to see Torah as source of guidance for all issues facing Jews as individuals and as a people. Inculcates a spirit of activism through projects in religious, Torah-educational, and community-welfare fields. *Am Hatorah; Daf Chizuk.*

AGUDATH ISRAEL WORLD ORGANIZATION (1912) 42 BROADWAY, 14ᵀᴴ FLOOR, NYC 10004. (212)797-9000. FAX: (212)254-1650. Chmn. Rabbi Yehudah Meir Abramowitz; U.N. Rep. Prof. Harry Reicher, Esq. Represents the interests of Orthodox Jewry on the national and international scenes. Sponsors projects to strengthen Torah life worldwide.

ALEPH: ALLIANCE FOR JEWISH RENEWAL (1963; REORG. 1993). 7000 Lincoln Drive, #B2, Philadelphia, PA 19119-3046. (215)247-9700. FAX: (215)247-9703. E-mail: alephajr@aol.com. Bd. Chmn. David Steinmetz; Rabbinic Dir. Rabbi Daniel Siegel. Serving the worldwide grassroots movement for Jewish spiritual renewal, ALEPH organizes and nurtures communities, trains lay and rabbinic leaders, creates new liturgy and adult learning resources, sponsors conferences, retreats and seminars and works for social and environmental justice. *New Menorah online journal and KolAleph/Or Hador combined quarterly newsletter of the Aleph and the Network of Jewish Renewal Communities (NJRC).* (WWW.ALEPH.ORG)

AM KOLEL JUDAIC RESOURCE CENTER (1990). 15 W. Montgomery Ave., Rockville, MD 20850. (301)309-2310. FAX: (301)309-2328. E-mail: amkolel@aol.com. Pres. David Shneyer. An independent Jewish resource center, providing a progressive Jewish voice in the community. Activities include: religion, educational and cultural programs; classes, workshops and seminars; interfaith workshops and programs; tikkun olam (social action) opportunities. The staff provides training and resources to emerging and independent communities throughout N. America. Am Kolel sponsors Jews United for Justice, the Center for Inclusiveness in Jewish Life (CIJL) and Yedid DC. *Directory of Independent Jewish Communities and Havurot in Maryland, DC and Virginia; Rock Creek Haggadah.*

AMERICAN ASSOCIATION OF RABBIS (1978). 350 Fifth Ave., Suite 3304, NYC 10118. (212)244-3350, (516)244-7113. FAX: (516)344-0779. E-mail: tefu@aol.com. Pres. Rabbi Jeffrey Wartenberg; Exec. Dir. Rabbi David L. Dunn. An organization of rabbis serving in pulpits, in areas of education, and in social work. *Quarterly bulletin; monthly newsletter.*

AMERICAN STUDENTS TO ACTIVATE PRIDE (ASAP/OU College Affairs) (1993). 11 Broadway, 14th fl., NYC 10004. (212) 563-4000. FAX: (212)564-9058. E-mail: davidfel@ix.netcom.com. Pres. Zelda Goldsmith; Natl. Dir. Rabbi David Felsenthal; Chmn. Bernard Falk. A spiritual fitness movement of Jewish college students promoting Torah learning and discussion. Supports 100 learning groups at over 65 campuses as well as regional and national seminars and shabbatonim. *Good Shabbos (weekly); Rimon Discussion Guide (monthly); Jewish Student College Survival Guide (yearly).*

ASSOCIATION FOR JEWISH STUDIES (1969). Center for Jewish History, 15 W. 16 St., NYC 10011. (917)606-8249. FAX: (917) 606-8222. E-mail: ajs@ajs.cjh.org. Pres. Judith R. Baskin; Exec. Dir. Rona Sheramy. Seeks to promote, maintain, and improve the teaching of Jewish studies in colleges and universities by sponsoring meetings and conferences, publishing a newsletter and other scholarly materials, aiding in the placement of teachers, coordinating research, and cooperating with other scholarly organizations. *AJS Review; AJS Perspectives.* (WWW.BRANDEIS. EDU/AJS)

ASSOCIATION FOR THE SOCIAL SCIENTIFIC STUDY OF JEWRY (1971). c/o Prof. Carmel U. Chiswick, Department of Economics (m/c 144), University of Illinois at Chicago, 601 S. Morgan Street, Chicago, Il 60607-7121. (312)996-2683. FAX: (312) 996-3344. E-mail: exec@assj.org. Pres. Sherry Israel; V.-Pres. Riv-Ellen Prell; Sec.-Treas. Carmel Chiswick. Journal Ed. Samuel Heilman; Mng. Ed. Uriel Heilman. Arranges academic sessions and facilitates communication among social scientists studying Jewry through meetings, journal, newsletter and related materials and activities. *Contemporary Jewry; Newsletter (electronic).*

ASSOCIATION OF HILLEL/JEWISH CAMPUS PROFESSIONALS (*see* TEKIAH: ASSOCIATION OF HILLEL/JEWISH CAMPUS PROFESSIONALS)

ASSOCIATION OF ORTHODOX JEWISH SCIENTISTS (1948). 25 W. 45St., Suite 1405, NYC 10036. (212)840-1166. FAX: (212)840-1514. E-mail: aojs@jerusalemail.com. Pres. Allen J. Bennett, M.D.; Bd. Chmn. Rabbi Nachman Cohen. Seeks to contribute to the development of science within the framework of Orthodox Jewish tradition; to obtain and disseminate information relating to the interaction between the Jewish traditional way of life and scientific developments—on both an ideological and practical level; to assist in the solution of problems pertaining to Orthodox Jews engaged in scientific teaching or research. Two main conventions are held each year. *Intercom; Proceedings; Halacha Bulletin; newsletter.*

B'NAI B'RITH HILLEL FOUNDATIONS (*see* HILLEL)

B'NAI B'RITH YOUTH ORGANIZATION (1924, Became Independent in 2002). 2020 K Street, NW, 7th Floor, Washington, DC 20006. (202)857-6633. FAX: (212)857-6568. Chmn. Lynn Schusterman; Intl. Dir. Brian Greene. Organized in local chapters, BBYO is a youth led international organization offering leadership opportunities and Jewish programming, which helps Jewish teenagers achieve self-fulfillment and contribute to the community. Assists members acquire a greater knowledge and appreciation for the Jewish religion, culture and the State of Israel. (WWW.BBYO.ORG)

CANTORS ASSEMBLY (1947). 3080 Broadway, Suite 613, NYC 10027. (212)678-8834. FAX: (212)662-8989. E-mail: caoffice @aol.com. Pres. Sheldon Levin; Exec. V.-Pres. Stephen J. Stein. Seeks to unite all cantors who adhere to traditional Judaism and who serve as full-time cantors in bona fide congregations to conserve and promote the musical traditions of the Jews and to elevate the status of the cantorial profession. *Annual Proceedings;*

Journal of Synagogue Music. (www.CANTORS.ORG)

CENTER FOR CHRISTIAN-JEWISH UNDERSTANDING OF SACRED HEART UNIVERSITY (1992). 5151 Park Ave., Fairfield, CT 06825. (203)365-7592. FAX: (203)365-4815. E-mail: jhe@sacredheart.edu. Pres. Dr. Anthony J. Cernera; Exec. Dir. Rabbi Joseph H. Ehrenkranz. An educational and research division of Sacred Heart University; brings together clergy, laity, scholars, theologians, and educators with the purpose of promoting interreligious research, education, and dialogue, with particular focus on current religious thinking within Christianity and Judaism. *CCJU Perspective.*

CENTRAL CONFERENCE OF AMERICAN RABBIS (1889). 355 Lexington Ave., NYC 10017. (212)972-3636. FAX: (212)692-0819. E-mail: info@ccarnet.org. Pres. Rabbi Harry Danziger; Exec. V.-Pres. Rabbi Paul J. Menitoff. Seeks to conserve and promote Judaism and to disseminate its teachings in a liberal spirit. The CCAR Press provides liturgy and prayerbooks to the worldwide Reform Jewish community. *CCAR Journal: A Reform Jewish Quarterly; CCAR Yearbook.* (WWW.CCARNET.ORG)

CLAL—NATIONAL JEWISH CENTER FOR LEARNING AND LEADERSHIP (1974). 440 Park Ave. S., 4th fl., NYC 10016-8012. (212)779-3300. FAX: (212)779-1009. E-mail: info@clal.org. Pres. Rabbi Irwin Kula; Chmn. Thomas O. Katz; Exec. V.-Chmn. Donna M. Rosenthal. Provides leadership training for lay leaders, rabbis, educators, and communal professionals. A faculty of rabbis and scholars representing all the denominations of Judaism make Judaism come alive, applying the wisdom of the Jewish heritage to help shape tomorrow's Jewish communities. Offers seminars and courses, retreats, symposia and conferences, lecture bureau and the latest on-line information through CLAL web site. *Sacred Days calendar; monographs; holiday brochures; CLAL Update.* (WWW.CLAL.ORG)

COALITION FOR THE ADVANCEMENT OF JEWISH EDUCATION (CAJE) (1977). 261 W. 35 St., #12A, NYC 10001. (212)268-4210. FAX: (212)268-4214. E-mail: cajeny@caje.org. Pres. Alan Wiener; Exec. Dir. Dr. Eliot G. Spack. The Coalition for the Advancement of Jewish Education (CAJE), the largest membership organization of Jewish educators in North America, hosts annual conferences and offers outreach programming, teacher recruitment, and mentoring, a Job Bank, and a Curriculum Response Service. CAJE has established an Early Childhood Department. Though its Hanukat CAJE Committee, CAJE advocates on behalf of Jewish educators. *Jewish Education News; CAJE Page; timely curricular publications; Hanukat CAJE series.* (WWW.CAJE.ORG)

CONGRESS OF SECULAR JEWISH ORGANIZATIONS (1970). 19657 Villa Dr. N., Southfield, MI 48076. (248)569-8127. FAX: (248)569-5222. E-mail: csjd@csjd.org. Chmn. Alan J. Wiener; V.-Chmn. Karen Knecht; Exec. Dir. Dr. Eliot G. Spack. An umbrella organization of schools and adult clubs; facilitates exchange of curricula and educational programs for children and adults stressing the Jewish historical and cultural heritage and the continuity of the Jewish people. *New Yorkish (Yiddish literature translations); Haggadah; The Hanuka Festival; Mame-Loshn.*

CONVERSION TO JUDAISM RESOURCE CENTER (1997). 74 Hauppauge Rd., Rm. 53, Commack, NY 11725. (631) 462-5826. E-mail: inform@convert.org. Pres. Dr. Lawrence J. Epstein; Exec. Dir. Susan Lustig. Provides information and advice for people who wish to convert to Judaism or who have converted. Puts potential converts in touch with rabbis from all branches of Judaism.

COUNCIL FOR JEWISH EDUCATION (1926) 11 Olympia Lane, Monsey, NY 10952-2829. (845)368-8657, Fax (845)369-6583. E-mail: mjscje@aol.com. Pres. Dr. Morton J. Summer; Editor Rabbi Irwin E. Witty. Fellowship of Jewish education professionals-administrators, supervisors, and teachers in Hebrew high schools and Jewish teachers colleges-of all ideological groupings; conducts national and regional conferences; represents the Jewish education profession before the Jewish community; cooperates with Jewish Agency Department of Education in promoting Hebrew culture and studies. *Journal of Jewish Education.*

EDAH (1996) 47 W. 34 St., Suite 700, NYC 10001. (212) 244-7501. FAX: (212)

244-7855. Pres. Morton Landowne; Dir. Rabbi Saul J. Berman. Gives voice to the ideology and values of modern Orthodoxy, valuing open intellectual inquiry and expression in both secular and religious arenas, engagement with the social, political, and technological realities of the modern world, the religious significance of the State of Israel, and the unity of Clal Yisrael. *Monograph series.* (www. EDAH.ORG)

FEDERATION OF JEWISH MEN'S CLUBS (1929). 475 Riverside Dr., Suite 832, NYC 10115. (212)749-8100; (800)288-FJMC. FAX: (212)316-4271. E-mail: international @fjmc.org. Intl. Pres. Bob Levine; Exec. Dir. Rabbi Charles E. Simon. Promotes principles of Conservative Judaism; develops family education and leadership training programs; offers the Art of Jewish Living series and Yom HaShoah Home Commemoration; sponsors Hebrew literacy adult-education program; presents awards for service to American Jewry. Latest innovation-"The Ties that Bind," a motivational and instructional video about Tefillin. *Torchlight; Hearing Men's Voices.* (WWW.FJMC.ORG)

FEDERATION OF RECONSTRUCTIONIST CONGREGATIONS AND HAVUROT (*see* JEWISH RECONSTRUCTIONIST FEDERATION)

HILLEL: THE FOUNDATION FOR JEWISH CAMPUS LIFE (Formerly B'NAI B'RITH HILLEL FOUNDATIONS) (1923). Charles and Lynn Schusterman International Center, Arthur and Rochelle Belfer Building, 800 Eight Street, NW, Washington, DC 20001-3724. (202)449-6500. FAX: (202)449-6600. E-mail: info@hillel.org. Chmn. Randall R. Kaplan; Pres. Avraham Infeld. The largest Jewish campus organization in the world, Hillel: The Foundation for Jewish Campus Life, is committed to creatively empowering and engaging Jewish students through its network of over 500 regional centers, campus-based foundations, program centers and affiliates. *The Hillel Annual Report; Shavua Tov. Israel Update.* (www. HILLEL.ORG)

INSTITUTE FOR COMPUTERS IN JEWISH LIFE (1978). 7074 N. Western Ave., Chicago, IL 60645. (773)262-9200. FAX: (773)262-9298. E-mail: rosirv@aol.com. Pres. Thomas Klutznick; Exec. V.-Pres. Dr. Irving J. Rosenbaum. Explores, develops, and disseminates applications of computer technology to appropriate areas of Jewish life, with special emphasis on Jewish education; creates educational software for use in Jewish schools; provides consulting service and assistance for national Jewish organizations, seminaries, and synagogues.

INTERNATIONAL FEDERATION OF SECULAR HUMANISTIC JEWS (1983). 224 West 35th Street, Suite 410, NYC 10024. (212)564-6711. FAX: (212)564-6721. E-mail: info @ifshj.org. Co-Ch. Felix Posen (Europe), Yair Tzaban (Israel) & Sherwin Wine (USA). The International Federation of Secular Humanistic Jews provides a voice for secular Jews worldwide in their common goal to foster Secular Humanistic Judaism as an option for modern Jewish identity. The IFSHJ develops awareness of Secular and Humanistic Judaism by serving as a resource and for general information, and developing literature, conferences, and communications that promote philosophy of Secular and Humanistic Judaism in the world community. *Newsletter (Hofesh); Contemplate: International Journal of Secular Jewish Thought.*

INTERNATIONAL INSTITUTE FOR SECULAR HUMANISTIC JUDAISM (1985). 28611 West Twelve Mile Rd., Farmington Hills, MI 48334. (248)476-9532. FAX: (248)476-8509. E-mail: iishj@iishj.org. Chmn. Rabbi Sherwin T. Wine. Established in 1985 in Jerusalem to serve the needs of a growing movement, its two primary purposes are to commission and publish educational materials and to train rabbis, leaders, teachers, and spokespersons for the movement. The Institute has two offices-one in Israel (Jerusalem) and one in N. America and offers educational and training programs in Israel, N. America, and the countries of the former Soviet Union. The N. American office, located in a suburb of Detroit, offers the Rabbinic Program, the Leadership Program, and the Adult Education Program. *Brochure, educational papers, and projects.*

JEWISH CHAUTAUQUA SOCIETY, INC. (sponsored by NORTH AMERICAN FEDERATION OF TEMPLE BROTHERHOODS) (1893). 633 Third Ave., NYC 10017. (212)650-4100/(800)765-6200. FAX: (212)650-4189. E-mail: jcs@urj.org. Pres. Irving B. Shnaider; Chancellor Stuart J. Aaronson;

Exec. Dir. Doug Barden. Works to promote interfaith understanding by sponsoring accredited college courses and one-day lectures on Judaic topics, providing book grants to educational institutions, producing educational videotapes on interfaith topics, and convening interfaith institutes. A founding sponsor of the National Black/Jewish Relations Center at Dillard University. *ACHIM Magazine.*

JEWISH EDUCATION IN MEDIA (1978). PO Box 180, Riverdale Sta., NYC 10471. (212)362-7633. FAX: (203)359-1381. Pres. Ken Asher; Exec. Dir. Rabbi Mark S. Golub. Devoted to producing television, film, and video-cassettes for a popular Jewish audience, in order to inform, entertain, and inspire a greater sense of Jewish identity and Jewish commitment. "L'Chayim," JEM's weekly half-hour program, which is seen nationally on NJT/National Jewish Television, features outstanding figures in the Jewish world addressing issues and events of importance to the Jewish community. (www.LCHAYIM.COM)

JEWISH EDUCATION SERVICE OF NORTH AMERICA (JESNA) (1981). 111 Eighth Ave., 11th fl., NYC 10011. (212)284-6950. FAX: (212)284-6951. E-mail: info@jesna. org. Pres. Jonathan S. Woocher; Bd. Ch. Joseph Kanfer. The Jewish Federation system's educational coordinating, planning, and development agency. Promotes excellence in Jewish education by initiating exchange of ideas, programs, and materials; providing information, consultation, educational resources, and policy guidance; and collaborating with partners in N. America and Israel to develop educational programs. *Agenda: Jewish Education; planning guides on Jewish Renaissance; research reports; Jewish Educators Electronic Toolkit.* (WWW.JESNA.ORG)

JEWISH OUTREACH INSTITUTE (1987). 1270 Broadway, Ste. 609, NYC 10001. (212) 760-1440. FAX: (212)760-1569. E-mail: info@joi.org. Pres. Terrence A. Elkes; Exec. Dir. Rabbi Kerry Olitzky. An independent national organization that conducts programs and services to empower and assist the Jewish community in welcoming and fully embracing all members of interfaith families—and anyone else looking to explore connections to the Jewish heritage—into Jewish life. *The In-*

clusive, The Inclusive Professional. (www. JOI.ORG)

JEWISH RECONSTRUCTIONIST FEDERATION (Formerly FEDERATION OF RECONSTRUCTIONIST CONGREGATIONS AND HAVUROT) (1954). 7804 Montgomery Ave., Suite 9, Elkins Park, PA 19027-2649. (215)782-8500. Fax: (215)782-8805. E-mail: info@ jrf.org. Pres. Daniel Cedarbaum; Exec. V.-Pres. Carl Sheingold. Provides educational and consulting services to affiliated congregations and havurot; fosters the establishment of new Reconstructionist communities. Publishes *Kol Haneshamah*, an innovative series of prayer books, including a new mahzor and haggadah; provides programmatic materials. Regional offices in NewYork, Los Angeles, Chicago, Philadelphia, and Washington DC. *Reconstructionism Today.* (WWW.JRF. ORG)

———, RECONSTRUCTIONIST RABBINICAL ASSOCIATION (1974). 1299 Church Rd., Wyncote, PA 19095. (215)576-5210. FAX: (215)576-8051. E-mail: info@therra.org. Pres. Rabbi Brant Rosen; Exec. Dir. Rabbi Richard Hirsh. Professional organization for graduates of the Reconstructionist Rabbinical College and other rabbis who identify with Reconstructionist Judaism; cooperates with Jewish Reconstructionist Federation in furthering Reconstructionism in the world. *Newsletters; position papers.* (WWW.THERRA.ORG)

———, RECONSTRUCTIONIST RABBINICAL COLLEGE (*see* p. 588)

JEWISH TEACHERS ASSOCIATION—MORIM (1931). 45 E. 33 St., Suite 310, NYC 10016-5336. (212)684-0556. Pres. Phyllis L. Pullman; V.-Pres. Ronni David; Sec. Helen Parnes; Treas. Mildred Safar. Protects teachers from abuse of seniority rights; fights the encroachment of anti-Semitism in education; offers scholarships to qualified students; encourages teachers to assume active roles in Jewish communal and religious affairs. *Morim JTA Newsletter.*

KULANU, INC. (formerly AMISHAV USA) (1993). 11603 Gilsan St., Silver Spring, MD 20902. (301)681-5679. FAX: (301)681-1587. Email: jdzeller@umich. edu. Pres. Jack Zeller; Sec. Karen Primack. Engages in outreach to dispersed Jewish communities around the world who wish to return to their Jewish roots.

Current projects include the formal conversion of Shinlung-Menashe tribesmen in India currently practicing Judaism, and supplying materials and rabbis for conversos/marranos in Mexico and Brazil. *Newsletter.*

NATIONAL COMMITTEE FOR FURTHERANCE OF JEWISH EDUCATION (1941). 824 Eastern Pkwy., Brooklyn, NY 11213. (718) 735-0200; (800)33-NCFJE. FAX: (718) 735-4455. Pres. Dr. Steven Rubel; Bd. Chmn. Rabbi Shea Hecht; Chmn. Exec. Com. Rabbi Sholem Ber Hecht. Seeks to disseminate the ideals of Torah-true education among the youth of America; provides education and compassionate care for the poor, sick, and needy in U.S. and Israel; provides aid to Iranian Jewish youth; sponsors camps and educational functions, family and vocational counseling services, family and early intervention, after-school and preschool programs, drug and alcohol education and prevention; maintains schools in Brooklyn and Queens. Every year distributes 25,000 toys/gifts through Toys for Hospitalized children; runs the Release-time program of Greater NY, offers classes FT/PT through Hadar Hatorah Rabbinal Seminary. *Panorama; Cultbusters; Intermarriage; Brimstone & Fire; Focus; A Life Full of Giving.*

NATIONAL COUNCIL OF YOUNG ISRAEL (1912). 3 W. 16 St., NYC 10011. (212)929-1525. FAX: (212)727-9526. E-mail: ncyi@youngisrael.org. Pres. Shlomo Mostofsky; Exec. V.-Pres. Rabbi Pesach Lerner. Through its network of member synagogues in N. America and Israel maintains a program of spiritual, cultural, social, and communal activity aimed at the advancement and perpetuation of traditional, Torah-true Judaism; seeks to instill in American youth an understanding and appreciation of the ethical and spiritual values of Judaism. Sponsors rabbinic and lay leadership conferences, synagogue services, rabbinic services, rabbinic and lay leader training, rabbinic placement, women's division, kosher dining clubs, and youth programs. *Viewpoint Magazine; Divrei Torah Bulletin; NCYI Suggestion Box; The Rabbi's Letter.* (WWW.YOUNGISRAEL.ORG)

———, AMERICAN FRIENDS OF YOUNG ISRAEL IN ISRAEL—YISRAEL HATZA'IR (1926). 3 W. 16 St., NYC 10011. (212)929-1525. FAX: (212)727-9526. E-mail: ncyi@youngisrael.org. Pres. Meir Mishkoff. Promotes Young Israel synagogues and youth work in Israel; works to help absorb Russian and Ethiopian immigrants.

———, YOUNG ISRAEL DEPARTMENT OF YOUTH AND YOUNG ADULTS ACTIVITIES (REORG. 1981). 3 W. 16 St., NYC 10011. (212)929-1525; (800)617-NCYI. FAX: (212)243-1222. Email: youth@yiyouth.org. Dir. Bradley Karasik. Fosters varied program of activities for the advancement and perpetuation of traditional Torah-true Judaism; instills ethical and spiritual values and appreciation for compatibility of ancient faith of Israel with good Americanism. Runs leadership training programs and youth shabbatonim; support programs for synagogue youth programs; annual national conference of youth directors; ACHVA summer programs for teens IN Israel and U.S.; Nachala summer program in Israel for Yeshiva H.S. girls and Natzach summer program for Yeshiva H.S. boys. *Torah Kidbits; Shabbat Youth Manual; Y.I. Can Assist You; Synagogue Youth Director Handbook.* (WWW.YIYOUTH.ORG)

NATIONAL HAVURAH COMMITTEE (1979). 7135 Germantown Ave., Philadelphia, PA 19119-1720. (215)248-1335. FAX: (215) 248-9760. E-mail: institute@havurah.org. Ch. Neil Zatz Litt. A center for Jewish renewal devoted to spreading Jewish ideas, ethics, and religious practices through havurot, participatory and inclusive religious mini-communities. Maintains a directory of N. American havurot and sponsors a weeklong summer institute, regional weekend retreats. *Havurah! (newsletter).* (WWW.HAVURAH.ORG)

NATIONAL JEWISH CENTER FOR LEARNING AND LEADERSHIP (*see* Clal)

NATIONAL JEWISH COMMITTEE ON SCOUTING (Boy Scouts of America) (1926). 1325 West Walnut Hill Lane, PO Box 152079, Irving, TX 75015-2079. (972)580-2000. FAX: (972)580-7870. Chmn. Rabbi Peter Hyman. Assists Jewish institutions in meeting their needs and concerns through use of the resources of scouting. Works through local Jewish committees on scouting to establish Tiger Cub groups (1st grade), Cub Scout packs, Boy Scout troops, and coed venturer crews in synagogues, Jewish community centers, day schools, and other Jewish organizations wishing to draw Jewish youth. Support materials and resources on request.

NATIONAL JEWISH GIRL SCOUT COMMITTEE (1972). 33 Central Dr., Bronxville, NY 10708. (914)738-3986, (718)252-6072. FAX: (914)738-6752. E-mail: njgsc@aol. com. Chmn. Rabbi Herbert W. Bomzer; Field Chmn. Adele Wasko. Serves to further Jewish education by promoting Jewish award programs, encouraging religious services, promoting cultural exchanges with the Israel Boy and Girl Scouts Federation, and extending membership in the Jewish community by assisting councils in organizing Girl Scout troops and local Jewish Girl Scout committees. *Newsletter.*

NATIONAL JEWISH HOSPITALITY COMMITTEE (1973; REORG. 1993). PO Box 53691, Philadelphia, PA 19105. (800)745-0301. Pres. Rabbi Allen S. Maller; Exec. Dir. Steven S. Jacobs. Assists persons interested in Judaism-for intermarriage, conversion, general information, or to respond to missionaries. *Special reports.*

NORTH AMERICAN ALLIANCE FOR JEWISH YOUTH (199650 WEST 58TH STREET, NYC, NY, 10019 (212)494-1023. FAX: (212)906-9371. E-mail: info@naajewishyouth.org. Chmn. Joseph E. Brenan; Dir. Heather Kibel. Serves the cause of informal Jewish and Zionist education in America; provides a forum for the professional leaders of the major N. American youth movements, camps, Israel programs, and university programs to address common issues and concerns, and to represent those issues with a single voice to the wider Jewish and Zionist community. Sponsors annual Conference on Informal Jewish Education for Jewish youth professionals from across the continent.

OZAR HATORAH, INC. (1946). 625 Broadway, 11th Fl. NYC, 10012. (212)253-7245. FAX: (212) 437-4773. E-mail: agutman @ozarhatorah.org. Pres. Henry Shalom; Sec. Sam Sutton; Exec. Dir. Rabbi Jean Paul Amoyelle. An international educational network which builds Sephardic communities worldwide through Jewish education.

PARDES PROGRESSIVE ASSOCIATION OF REFORM DAY SCHOOLS (1990). 633 Third Ave., NYC 10017-6778. (212)650-4000. FAX: (480)951-0829. E-mail: educate@

urj.org. Pres. Zita Gardner; Chmn. Carol Nemo. An affiliate of the Union for Reform Judaism; brings together day schools and professional and lay leaders committed to advancing the cause of fulltime Reform Jewish education; advocates for the continuing development of day schools within the Reform movement as a means to foster Jewish identity, literacy, and continuity; promotes cooperation among our member schools and with other Jewish organizations that share similar goals. *Visions of Excellence (manual).*

P'EYLIM-LEV L'ACHIM (1951). 1034 E. 12 St. Brooklyn, NY 11230. (718)258-7760. FAX: (718)258-4672. E-mail: joskarmel @aol.com. Natl. Dir. Rabbi Joseph C. Karmel; Exec. V.-Pres. Rabbi Nachum Barnetsky. Seeks to bring irreligious Jews in Israel back to their heritage. Conducts outreach through 12 major divisions consisting of thousands of volunteers and hundreds of professionals across the country; conducts anti-missionary and assimilation programs; operates shelters for abused women and children; recruits children for Torah schools.

RABBINICAL ALLIANCE OF AMERICA (Igud Harabonim) (1942). 3 W. 16 St., 4th fl., NYC 10011. (212)242-6420. FAX: (212) 255-8313. Pres. Rabbi Abraham B. Hecht. Seeks to promulgate the cause of Torahtrue Judaism through an organized rabbinate that is consistently Orthodox; seeks to elevate the position of Orthodox rabbis nationally and to defend the welfare of Jews the world over. Also has Beth Din Rabbinical Court for Jewish divorces, litigation, marriage counseling, and family problems. *Perspective; Nahalim; Torah Message of the Week; Registry.*

RABBINICAL ASSEMBLY (1901). 3080 Broadway, NYC 10027. (212)280-6000. FAX: (212)749-9166. Pres. Rabbi Perry Rank; Exec. V.-Pres. Rabbi Joel H. Meyers. The international association of Conservative rabbis; actively promotes the cause of Conservative Judaism and works to benefit *klal yisrael*; publishes learned texts, prayer books, and works of Jewish interest; administers the work of the Committee on Jewish Law and Standards for the Conservative movement; serves the professional and personal needs of its members through publications, conferences, and benefit programs and administers the movement's Joint Placement Commission. *Conservative Judaism; Proceedings of the Rabbinical Assembly; Rabbinical Assembly Newsletter.*

RABBINICAL COUNCIL OF AMERICA, INC. (1923; reorg. 1935). 305 Seventh Ave., Suite 1200, NYC 10001. (212)807-7888. FAX: (212)727-8452. Pres. Rabbi Dale Polakoff; Exec. V.-Pres. Rabbi Basil Herring. Promotes Orthodox Judaism in the community; supports institutions for study of Torah; stimulates creation of new traditional agencies. *Hadorom; Tradition.* (WWW.RABBIS.ORG)

SOCIETY FOR HUMANISTIC JUDAISM (1969). 28611 W. Twelve Mile Rd., Farmington Hills, MI 48334. (248)478-7610. FAX: (248) 478-3159. E-mail: info@shj.org. Pres. Shari Gelber; Pres. Elect Phillip Gould; Exec. Dir. M. Bonnie Cousens. Serves as a voice for Jews who value their Jewish identity and who seek an alternative to conventional Judaism, who reject supernatural authority and affirm the right of individuals to be the masters of their own lives. Publishes educational and ceremonial materials; organizes congregations and groups. *Humanistic Judaism (quarterly journal); Humanorah (quarterly newsletter).* (WWW.SHJ.ORG)

TEKIAH: ASSOCIATION OF HILLEL/JEWISH CAMPUS PROFESSIONALS (1949). c/o Hillel Foundation of New Orleans, 912 Broadway, New Orleans, LA 70118. (504)866-7060. FAX: (504)861-8909. E-mail: president@tekiah.org. Pres. Rabbi Jeffrey Kurtz-Lendner. Seeks to promote professional relationships and exchanges of experience, develop personnel standards and qualifications, safeguard integrity of Hillel profession; represents and advocates before the Foundation for Jewish Campus Life, Council of Jewish Federations. *Handbook for Hillel Professionals; Guide to Hillel Personnel Practices.* (WWW.TEKIAH.ORG)

TEVA LEARNING CENTER/SHOMREI ADAMAH (1988). 307 Seventh Ave., #900, NYC 10001. (212)807-6376. FAX: (212)924-5112. E-mail: teva@tevacenter.org. Co-Dir. Nili Simhai; Asst. Dir., Noam Dolgin Exists to renew the ecological wisdom inherent in Judaism. Runs Jewish environmental education programs for Jewish day schools, synagogues, community centers, camps, university groups and other organized groups. *Let the Earth Teach*

You Torah, Ecology and the Jewish Spirit. (WWW.TEVACENTER.ORG)

TORAH SCHOOLS FOR ISRAEL–CHINUCH ATZMAI (1953). 40 Exchange Pl., NYC 10005. (212)248-6200. FAX: (212)248-6202. Exec. Dir. Rabbi Henach Cohen. Conducts information programs for the American Jewish community on activities of the independent Torah schools educational network in Israel; coordinates role of American members of international board of governors; funds special programs of Mercaz Hachinuch Ha-Atzmai B'Eretz Yisroel; funds religous education programs in America and abroad.

TORAH UMESORAH–NATIONAL SOCIETY FOR HEBREW DAY SCHOOLS (1944). 160 Broadway, NYC 10038. (212)227-1000. FAX: (212)406-6934. E-mail: umesorah@aol.com. Exec. V.-Pres. Rabbi Joshua Fishman. Establishes Hebrew day schools and Yeshivas in U.S. and Canada and provides a full gamut of services, including placement, curriculum guidance, and teacher training. Parent Enrichment Program provides enhanced educational experience for students from less Jewishly educated and marginally affiliated homes through parent-education programs and Partners in Torah, a one-on-one learning program. Publishes textbooks; runs shabbatonim, extracurricular activities; national PTA groups; national and regional teacher conventions. *Olomeinu-Our World.*

——, NATIONAL ASSOCIATION OF HEBREW DAY SCHOOL PARENT-TEACHER ASSOCIATIONS (1948). 160 Broadway, NYC 10038. (212)227-1000. FAX: (212)406-6934. Natl. PTA Coord. Bernice Brand. Acts as a clearinghouse and service agency to PTAs of Hebrew day schools; organizes parent education courses and sets up programs for individual PTAs. *Fundraising with a Flair; PTA with a Purpose for the Hebrew Day School.*

——, NATIONAL CONFERENCE OF YESHIVA PRINCIPALS (1956). 160 Broadway, NYC 10038. (212)227-1000. FAX: (212)406-6934. E-mail: umesorah@aol.com. Pres. Rabbi Rabbi Schneur Aisenstark; Exec. V.-Pres. Rabbi Joshua Fishman. Professional organization of elementary and secondary yeshivah/day school principals providing yeshivah/day schools with school evaluation and guidance, teacher and principal conferences-including a Mid-Winter Conference and a National Educators Convention; offers placement service for principals and teachers in yeshivah/day schools. *Directory of Elementary Schools and High Schools.*

———, NATIONAL YESHIVA TEACHERS BOARD OF LICENSE (1953). 160 Broadway, NYC 10038. (212)227-1000. Exec. V.-Pres. Rabbi Joshua Fishman; Dir. Rabbi Yitzchock Merkin. Issues licenses to qualified instructors for all grades of the Hebrew day school and the general field of Torah education.

UNION OF AMERICAN HEBREW CONGREGATIONS (see UNION FOR REFORM JUDAISM)

UNION FOR REFORM JUDAISM (Formerly UNION OF AMERICAN HEBREW CONGREGATIONS) (1873). 633 Third Ave., NYC 10017-6778. (212)650-4000. FAX: (212) 650-4169. E-mail: urj@urj.org. Pres. Rabbi Eric H. Yoffie; V.-Pres. Rabbi Lennard R. Thal; Bd. Chmn. Russell Silverman. Serves as the central congregational body of Reform Judaism in the Western Hemisphere; serves its approximately 900 affiliated temples and membership with religious, educational, cultural, and administrative programs. *Reform Judaism.* (WWW.URJ.ORG)

———, AMERICAN CONFERENCE OF CANTORS (1953). 5591 Chamblee Dunwoody Rd. Bldg. 1360, Ste. 200, Atlanta, GA 30338. (770)390-0006. FAX: (770)390-0020. E-mail: accantors@aol.com. Pres. Richard Cohen, Exec. V.-Pres. Scott E. Colbert Exec. VP; Dir. of Placement Barbara Ostfeld; Admin. Asst. Deborah Barber. Members are invested or certified by accredited seminaries, i.e., Hebrew Union College-Jewish Insitute of Religion School of Sacred Music. Through the Joint Cantorial Placement Commission, the ACC serves Reform congregations seeking cantors. Dedicated to creative Judaism, preserving the past, and encouraging new and vital approaches to religious ritual, liturgical music and ceremony. *Koleinu (monthly).*

———, COMMISSION ON SOCIAL ACTION OF REFORM JUDAISM (*see* p. 543)

———, COMMISSION ON SYNAGOGUE MANAGEMENT (URJ-CCAR) (1962). 633 Third Ave., NYC 10017-6778. (212)650-4040.

FAX: (212)650-4239. Chmn. Marshall Krolick; Dir. Dale A. Glasser. Assists congregations in management, finance, building maintenance, design, construction, and art aspects of synagogues; maintains the Synagogue Architectural Library.

———, NATA (NATIONAL ASSOCIATION OF TEMPLE ADMINISTRATORS) (1941). 6114 La Salle Ave., Box 731, Oakland, CA 94611. (800)966-6282. FAX: (925)283-7713. E-mail: nataorg@hotmail.com. FTA Elizabeth L. Hirsh. Professional organization for URJ synagogue administrators. Sponsors graduate training in synagogue management with Hebrew Union College; offers in-service training, workshops, and conferences leading to certification; provides NATA Consulting Service, NATA Placement Service for synagogues seeking advice or professional administrators; establishes professional standards. *NATA Journal.*

———, NATE (NATIONAL ASSOCIATION OF TEMPLE EDUCATORS) (1955). 633 Third Ave., 7th fl., NYC 10017-6778. (212)452-6510. FAX: (212)452-6512. E-mail: nateoff @aol.com. Pres. Julie A. Vanek; Exec. Dir. Rabbi Stanley T. Schickler. Represents educators within the general body of Reform Judaism; fosters the full-time profession of the Jewish educator; encourages the growth and development of Jewish religious education consistent with the aims of Reform Judaism; stimulates communal interest in and responsibility for Jewish religious education. *NATE NEWS.* (WWW.RJ.ORG/NATE)

———, NORTH AMERICAN FEDERATION OF TEMPLE BROTHERHOODS (1923). 633 Third Ave., NYC 10017. (212)650-4100. FAX: (212)650-4189. E-mail: nftb@urj. org. Pres.Irving B. Shnaider; JCS Chancellor Stuart J. Aaronson; Exec. Dir. Douglas Barden. Dedicated to enhancing the world through the ideal of brotherhood, NFTB and its 300 affiliated clubs are actively involved in education, social action, youth activities, and other programs that contribute to temple and community life. Supports the Jewish Chautauqua Society, an interfaith educational project. *ACHIM (formerly Brotherhood magazine)* (www. RJ.ORG/NFTB)

———, URJ DEPARTMENT OF JEWISH EDUCATION (1923). 633 Third Ave., 7th fl.,

NYC 10017. (212)650-4112. FAX: (212) 650-4229. E-mail: jkatzew@urj.org. Chmn. Dr. Rabbi Jan Katzew, Robert Heller; Dir. Dr. Rabbi Jan Katzew. Long-range planning and policy development for congregational programs of lifelong education; materials concerning Reform Jewish Outreach, Teacher Development and Reform Day Schools; activities administered by the URJ Department of Education. *V'Shinantam; Torah at the Center, Family Shabbat Table Talk, Galilee Diary, Jewish Parent Page.*

————, WOMEN OF REFORM JUDAISM—THE FEDERATION OF TEMPLE SISTERHOODS (1913). 633 Third Ave., NYC 10017. (212)650-4050. FAX: (212)650-4059. E-mail: wrj@urj.org. Pres. Helene H. Waranch; Exec. Dir. Shelley Lindauer. Serves more than 600 sisterhoods of Reform Judaism; promotes interreligious understanding and social justice; provides funding for scholarships for rabbinic students; founded the Jewish Braille Institute, which provides braille and large-type Judaic materials for Jewish blind; supports projects for Israel; is the women's agency of Reform Judaism, an affiliate of the URJ; works in behalf of the Hebrew Union College-Jewish Institute of Religion and the World Union for Progressive Judaism. *Notes for Now; Art Calendar; Windows on WRJ.* (WWW.RJ.ORG/WRJ)

————, YOUTH DIVISION AND NORTH AMERICAN FEDERATION OF TEMPLE YOUTH (1939). 633 Third Ave, NYC 10017-6778. (212)650-4070. FAX: (212)650-4199. E-mail: youthdivision@urj.org. Dir. URJ Youth Div. Rabbi Allan L. Smith; Assoc. Dir. URJ Youth Div. Rabbi Andrew Davids. Dedicated to Jewishly enhancing the lives of the young people of North America's Reform congregations through a program of informal education carried out in URJ Camp-Institutes (11 camps for grades 2 and up), URJ/NFTY Israel Programs (summer and semester), European and domestic teen travel, NFTY/Junior & Senior High School Programs (youth groups), and Kesher/College Education Department (Reform havurot on campuses).

UNION FOR TRADITIONAL JUDAISM (1984). 241 Cedar Lane, Teaneck, NJ 07666. (201)801-0707. FAX: (201)801-0449. Pres. Burton G. Greenblatt; Exec. V.-Pres. Rabbi Ronald D. Price. Through innova-

tive outreach programs, seeks to bring the greatest possible number of Jews closer to an open-minded observant Jewish lifestyle. Activities include Kashrut Initiative, Operation Pesah, the Panel of Halakhic Inquiry, Speakers Bureau, adult and youth conferences, and congregational services. Includes, since 1992, the Morashah rabbinic fellowship. *Hagahelet (quarterly newsletter); Cornerstone (journal); Tomeikh Kahalakhah (Jewish legal responsa).*

UNION OF ORTHODOX JEWISH CONGREGATIONS OF AMERICA (1898). 11 Broadway, 14th fl., NYC 10004. (212)563-4000. FAX: (212)564-9058. E-mail: ou@ou.org. Pres. Stephen J. Savitsky; Exec. V.-Pres. Rabbi Dr. Tzvi Hersh Weinreb. Serves as the national central body of Orthodox synagogues; national OU kashrut supervision and certification service; sponsors Institute for Public Affairs; National Conference of Synagogue Youth; National Jewish Council for the Disabled; Israel Center in Jerusalem; Torah Center in the Ukraine; New Young Leadership Division; Pardes; provides educational, religious, and organization programs, events, and guidance to synagogues and groups; represents the Orthodox Jewish community to governmental and civic bodies and the general Jewish community. *Jewish Action magazine; OU Kosher Directory; OU Guide to Kosher for Passover Foods; Keeping Posted (NCSY); Synagogue Trends; Our Way magazine; Yachad magazine; Luach & Limud Personal Torah Study, Leadership Briefing, Behind the Union Symbol.* (WWW.OU.ORG)

————, INSTITUTE FOR PUBLIC AFFAIRS (1989). 11 Broadway, 14th fl., NYC 10004. (212)613-8124. FAX: (212)613-0724. E-mail: ipa@ou.org. Pres. Stephen J. Savitsky; Chmn. Richard Stone; Dir. Nathan Diament; Dir. Intl. Affairs & Comm. Rel. Betty Ehrenberg. Serves as the policy analysis, advocacy, mobilization, and programming department responsible for representing Orthodox/traditional American Jewry. *IPA Currents (quarterly newsletter).*

————, NATIONAL CONFERENCE OF SYNAGOGUE YOUTH (1954). 11 Broadway, 14th fl., NYC 10004. (212)563-4000. E-mail: ncsy@ou.org. Interim Dir. Shira Reifman. Central body for youth groups of Orthodox congregations; provides educational guidance, Torah study groups, community service, program consultation, Torah library, Torah fund scholarships, Ben Zakkai Honor Society, Friends of NCSY, weeklong seminars, Israel Summer Experience for teens and Camp NCSY East Summer Kollel & Michlelet, Teen Torah Center. Divisions include Senior NCSY, Junior NCSY for preteens, Our Way for the Jewish deaf, Yachad for the developmentally disabled, Israel Center in Jerusalem, and NCSY in Israel. *Keeping Posted with NCSY; Darchei Da'at.*

———, WOMEN'S BRANCH (1923). 156 Fifth Ave., NYC 10010. (212)929-8857. Pres. Sophie Ebert. Umbrella organization of Orthodox sisterhoods in U.S. and Canada, educating women in Jewish learning and observance; provides programming, leadership, and organizational guidance, conferences, conventions, Marriage Committee and projects concerning mikvah, Shalom Task Force, and Welcoming Guests. Works with Orthodox Union Commissions and outreach; supports Stern and Touro College scholarships and Jewish braille publications; supplies Shabbat candelabra for hospital patients; NGO representative at UN. *Hachodesh; Hakol.*

UNION OF ORTHODOX RABBIS OF THE UNITED STATES AND CANADA (1902). 235 E. Broadway, NYC 10002. (212)964-6337(8). Dir. Rabbi Hersh M. Ginsberg. Seeks to foster and promote Torah-true Judaism in the U.S. and Canada; assists in the establishment and maintenance of yeshivot in the U.S.; maintains committee on marriage and divorce and aids individuals with marital difficulties; disseminates knowledge of traditional Jewish rites and practices and publishes regulations on synagogal structure; maintains rabbinical court for resolving individual and communal conflicts. *HaPardes.*

UNION OF SEPHARDIC CONGREGATIONS, INC. (1929). 8 W. 70 St., NYC 10023. (212)873-0300. FAX: (212)724-6165. Pres. Rabbi Marc D. Angel; Bd. Chmn. Edward Misrahi. Promotes the religious interests of Sephardic Jews; prints and distributes Sephardic prayer books. *Annual International Directory of Sephardic Congregations.*

UNITED LUBAVITCHER YESHIVOTH (1940). 841-853 Ocean Pkwy., Brooklyn, NY 11230. (718)859-7600. FAX: (718)434-1519. Supports and organizes Jewish day schools and rabbinical seminaries in the U.S. and abroad.

UNITED SYNAGOGUE OF CONSERVATIVE JUDAISM (1913). 155 Fifth Ave., NYC 10010-6802. (212)533-7800. FAX: (212)353-9439. E-mail: info@uscj.org. Pres. Judy Yudof; Exec. V.-Pres. Rabbi Jerome M. Epstein. International organization of 760 Conservative congregations. Maintains 17 departments and 15 regional offices to assist its affiliates with religious, educational, youth, community, and administrative programming and guidance; aims to enhance the cause of Conservative Judaism, further religious observance, encourage establishment of Jewish religious schools, draw youth closer to Jewish tradition. Extensive Israel programs. *United Synagogue Review; Art/Engagement Calendar; Program Suggestions; Directory & Resource Guide; Book Service Catalogue of Publications.* (WWW.USCJ. ORG)

———, COMMISSION ON JEWISH EDUCATION (1930). 155 Fifth Ave., NYC 10010. (212)533-7800. FAX: (212)353-9439. E-mail: education@uscj.org. Chmn. Temma Kingsley; Dir. Rabbi Robert Abramson. Develops educational policy for the United Synagogue of Conservative Judaism and sets the educational direction for Conservative congregations, their schools, and the Solomon Schechter Day Schools. Seeks to enhance the educational effectiveness of congregations through the publication of materials and in-service programs. *Tov L'Horot; Your Child; Shiboley Schechter, Advisories.*

———, COMMISSION ON SOCIAL ACTION AND PUBLIC POLICY (1958). 155 Fifth Ave., NYC 10010. (212)533-7800. FAX: (212)353-9439. Chmn. Hon. Jerry Wagner; Dir. Sarrae G. Crane. Develops and implements positions and programs on issues of social action and public policy for the United Synagogue of Conservative Judaism; represents these positions to other Jewish and civic organizations, the media, and government; and provides guidance, both informational and programmatic, to its affiliated congregations in these areas. *HaMa'aseh.*

————, JEWISH EDUCATORS ASSEMBLY (1951). 426 W. 58 St., NYC 10019. (212)765-3303. FAX: (212)765-3310. Pres. Dr. Mark S. Silk; Exec. Dir. Susan Mitrani Knapp. The Jewish Educators Assembly is the professional organization for the Jewish educators within the Conservative movement. The JEA provides a forum to discuss the trends and challenges within Conservative Jewish education as well as provides professional development and a sense of community for educational directors. Services offered: annual conference, placement service, career services, research grants, personal benefits and *V'Aleh Ha-Chadashot* newsletter.

————, KADIMA (reorg. 1968). 155 Fifth Ave., NYC 10010-6802. (212)533-7800. FAX: (212)353-9439. E-mail:kadima@uscj.org. Dir. Karen L. Stein; Dir. of Youth Activities Jules A Gutin. Involves Jewish preteens in a meaningful religious, educational, and social environment; fosters a sense of identity and commitment to the Jewish community and the Conservative movement; conducts synagogue-based chapter programs and regional Kadima days and weekends. *Mitzvah of the Month; Kadima Kesher; Chagim; Advisors Aid; Games; quarterly Kol Kadima magazine.*

————, NORTH AMERICAN ASSOCIATION OF SYNAGOGUE EXECUTIVES (1948). 155 Fifth Ave., NYC 10010. (212)533-7800, ext 2609. FAX: (631)732-9461. E-mail: office@naase.org. Pres. Judith Kranz, FSA, ATz; Hon. Pres. Amir Pilch, FSA; Exec. Dir. Harry Hauser. Aids congregations affiliated with the United Synagogue of Conservative Judaism to further the aims of Conservative Judaism through more effective administration (Program for Assistance by Liaisons to Synagogues—PALS); advances professional standards and promotes new methods in administration; cooperates in United Synagogue placement services and administrative surveys. *NAASE Connections Newsletter; NAASE Journal . . .*

————, UNITED SYNAGOGUE YOUTH (1951). 155 Fifth Ave., NYC 10010. (212) 533-7800. FAX: (212)353-9439. E-mail: youth@uscj.org. Pres. Jesse Olitzky; Exec. Dir. Jules A. Gutin. Seeks to strengthen identification with Conservative Judaism, based on the personality, development,

needs, and interests of the adolescent, in a mitzvah framework. *Achshav; Tikun Olam; A.J. Heschel Honor Society Newsletter; SATO Newsletter; USY Program Bank; Hakesher Newsletter for Advisors.*

VAAD MISHMERETH STAM (1976). 4907 16th Ave., Brooklyn, NYC 11204. (718) 438-4980. FAX: (718)438-9343. Pres. Rabbi David L. Greenfield. A nonprofit consumer-protection agency dedicated to preserving and protecting the halakhic integrity of Torah scrolls, tefillin, phylacteries, and mezuzoth. Publishes material for laymen and scholars in the field of scribal arts; makes presentations and conducts examination campaigns in schools and synagogues; created an optical software system to detect possible textual errors in stam. Teaching and certifying sofrim worldwide. Offices in Israel, Strasbourg, Chicago, London, Manchester, Montreal, and Zurich. Publishes *Guide to Mezuzah* and *Encyclopedia of the Secret Aleph Beth. The Jewish Quill; and many other publications.*

PANIM: THE INSTITUTE FOR JEWISH LEADERSHIP AND VALUES (Formerly WASHINGTON INSTITUTE FOR JEWISH LEADERSHIP & VALUES) (1988). 6101 Montrose Road, Suite 200, Rockville, MD 20852. (301) 770-5070. FAX: (301) 770-6365. E-mail: info@panim.org. Founder/Pres. Rabbi Sidney Schwarz; Bd. Chmn. Mark Levitt. Institute for Jewish Leadership and Values is a non-profit educational organization dedicated to the renewal of American Jewish life through the integration of Jewish learning, values and social responsibility. Our flagship program, *Panim el Panim*: High School in Washington, each year brings over 1,000 Jewish teens from across the country to Washington, D.C. to learn about political and social activism in the context of Jewish learning and values. We also sponsor the Jewish Civics Initiative, the largest national Jewish service/learning program for teens. The Institute also sponsors a Synagogue Transformation Project, and conducts leadership training. *Jewish Civics: A Tikkun Olam/World Repair Manual; Jews, Judaism and Civic Responsibility.*

WOMEN'S LEAGUE FOR CONSERVATIVE JUDAISM (1918). 475 Riverside Dr., NYC 10115. (212)870-1260. FAX: (212)772-3507. Email: womensleague@wlcj.org Pres. Gloria Cohen; Exec. Dir. Bernice

Balter. Parent body of Conservative (Masorti) women's synagogue groups in U.S., Canada, Puerto Rico, Mexico, and Israel; provides programs and resources in Jewish education, social action, Israel affairs, American and Canadian public affairs, leadership training, community service programs for persons with disabilities, conferences on world affairs, study institutes, publicity techniques; publishes books of Jewish interest; contributes to support of Jewish Theological Seminary of America. *Women's League Outlook* magazine; *Ba'Olam world affairs newsletter.*

WORLD COUNCIL OF CONSERVATIVE/ MASORTI SYNAGOGUES (1957). 155 Fifth Ave., NYC 10010. (212)533-7800, ext. 2014, 2018. FAX: (212)533-9439. E-mail: worldcouncil@compuserve.com. Pres. Rabbi Alan Silverstein; Rabbi of Council, Rabbi Benjamin Z. Kreitman. Organize and support Conservative/Masorti congregations in Latin America, Europe, Australia and South Africa. *World Spectrum.*

WORLD UNION FOR PROGRESSIVE JUDAISM (1926). 633 Third Ave. NYC 10017. (212) 650-4280. FAX: (212)650-4289. E-mail: arzawupjna@urj.org. Exec. Dir. Rabbi Uri Regev. International umbrella organization of Liberal Judaism; promotes and coordinates efforts of Liberal congregations throughout the world; starts new congregations, recruits rabbis and rabbinical students for all countries; organizes international conferences of Liberal Jews. *World News.*(WWW.WUPJ.ORG)

SCHOOLS, INSTITUTIONS

THE ACADEMY FOR JEWISH RELIGION (1956). 6301 Riverdale Avenue, Riverdale, NY 10471. (718)543-9360. FAX: (718)5431038. E-mail: admin@ajrsem. org. Acting Pres. Rabbi David Greenstein; Dean Rabbi Dr. Ora Horn Prouser. The pluralistic rabbinic and cantorial seminary uniting teachers and students from all streams of Judaism, passionately committed to their own paths, yet respectful and supportive of the paths of others. Emphasis on integrating learning, practice, and spirt through traditional and contemporary approaches. Training for congregations, chaplaincy, education, community work. (WWW.AJRSEM.ORG)

ANNENBERG RESEARCH INSTITUTE (*see* CENTER FOR JUDAIC STUDIES)

BALTIMORE HEBREW UNIVERSITY (1919). 5800 Park Heights Ave., Baltimore, MD 21215. (410)578-6900; (888)248-7420. FAX: (410)578-6940. E-mail: bhu@bhu. edu. Pres. Dr. Rela Mintz Geffen; Bd. Chmn. Erika Schon. Offers PhD and MA degrees in Jewish studies (MAJS); MA in Jewish education (MAJE), and Jewish communal service (MAJCS). Concentrations in biblical and ancient Near Eastern civilization, contemporary Jewish studies, Jewish thought and mysticism, literature, history, and rabbinics. Dual master's degree opportunities available as well as certificate programs in nonprofit management and education. Lifelong learning programs; Joseph Meyerhoff Library; distinguished lecture series. (www. BHU.EDU)

———, BERNARD MANEKIN SCHOOL OF UNDERGRADUATE STUDIES. Dean Dr. Barbara G. Zirkin. BA upper division Jewish studies; *LaDa'at* program for high school juniors and seniors.

———, PEGGY MEYERHOFF PEARLSTONE SCHOOL OF GRADUATE STUDIES. Dean Dr. Barbara G. Zirkin. PhD and MA programs: MA in Jewish studies; MAJE in Jewish education; PhD in Jewish studies; dual master's degrees, some jointly with the University of Maryland.

———, LEONARD AND HELEN R. STULMAN SCHOOL OF CONTINUING EDUCATION. Director of lifelong learning Elaine Eckstein. Noncredit programs open to the community, including Jewish studies and Hebrew language courses, trips, retreats, and seminars; *Me'ah,* an intensive group study program..

BRAMSON ORT COLLEGE (1977). 69-30 Austin St., Forest Hills, NY 11375. (718)261-5800. Dean of Academic Services Barry Glotzer. A two-year Jewish technical college offering certificates and associate degrees in technology and business fields, including accounting, computer programming, electronics technology, business management, office technology. Additional locations in Brooklyn.

BRANDEIS-BARDIN INSTITUTE (1941). 1101 Peppertree Lane, Brandeis, CA 93064. (805)582-4450. FAX: (805)526-1398. E-mail: info@thebbi.org. Pres. Dr. Lee T.

Bycel; Chair, Bd. Of Dir. Helen Zukin. A Jewish pluralistic, nondenominational educational institution providing programs for people of all ages: BCI (Brandeis Collegiate Institute), a summer leadership program for college-age adults from around the world; Camp Alonim, a summer Jewish experience for children 8-16; Gan Alonim Day Camp for children in kindergarten to 6th grade; weekend retreats for adults with leading contemporary Jewish scholars-in-residence; Jewish music concerts; Family Days and Weekends, Grandparents Weekends, Elderhostel, Young Adult programs, dance weekends, institute for newly marrieds. *Monthly Updates; BBI Newsletter.*

BRANDEIS UNIVERSITY (1948). 415 South St., Waltham, MA 02454. (781)736-2000. Pres. Jehuda Reinharz; Provost Irving Epstein; Exec. V.-Pres./CEO Peter B. French; Sr. V.-Pres. of Devel. Nancy Winship. Founded in 1948 by the American Jewish community, Brandeis University is a private, coeducational, and nonsectarian institution of higher learning and research located in Waltham, Massachusetts, enrolling approximately 3,100 undergraduate students and 1,200 graduate students. While Brandeis maintains a special relationship with the Jewish community, it welcomes students and faculty of all backgrounds and beliefs. The University's principal components are the undergraduate College of Arts and Sciences, the Graduate School of Arts and Sciences, The Heller School for Social Policy and Management, the Graduate School of International Economics and Finance, and the Rabb School of Summer and Continuing Studies. *Various newsletters, scholarly publications.*

———, NATIONAL WOMEN'S COMMITTEE (1948). MS 132, Waltham, MA 02454-9110. (781) 736-4160. FAX: (781)736-4183. E-mail: bunwc@brandeis.edu. Pres. Marcia F. Levy; Exec. Dir. Joan C. Bowen. Provides support for Brandeis University and its Libraries. It connects Brandeis, a non-sectarian university founded by the American Jewish community, to its members and their communities through programs that reflect the ideals of social justice and academic excellence. In addition to its fundraising activities, NWC offers its members opportunity for intellectual pursuit, contin-

uing education, community service, social interaction, personal enrichment and leadership development. Open to all, regardless of race, religion, nationality or gender. *Connecting.*

CENTER FOR JUDAIC STUDIES, SCHOOL OF ARTS AND SCIENCES, UNIVERSITY OF PENNSYLVANIA. 420 Walnut St., Philadelphia, PA 19106. (215)238-1290. FAX: (215) 238-1540. Dir. David B. Ruderman. *Jewish Quarterly Review.*

CLEVELAND COLLEGE OF JEWISH STUDIES (1964). 26500 Shaker Blvd., Beachwood, OH 44122. (216)464-4050. FAX: (216) 464-5827. Pres. David S. Ariel; Dir. of Student Services Diane M. Kleinman. Provides courses in all areas of Judaic and Hebrew studies to adults and college-age students; offers continuing education for Jewish educators and administrators; serves as a center for Jewish life and culture; expands the availability of courses in Judaic studies by exchanging faculty, students, and credits with neighboring academic institutions; grants bachelor's and master's degrees.

DROPSIE COLLEGE FOR HEBREW AND COGNATE LEARNING (*see* Center for Judaic Studies)

GRATZ COLLEGE (1895). 7605 Old York Rd., Melrose Park, PA 19027. (215)635-7300. FAX: (215)635-7320. Bd. Chmn. Dr. Matti K. Gershenfeld.; Pres. Dr. Jonathan Rosenbaum. Offers a wide variety of undergraduate and graduate degrees and continuing education programs in Judaic, Hebraic, and Middle Eastern studies. Grants BA and MA in Jewish studies, MA in Jewish education (joint program in special needs education with La Salle U.), MA in Jewish music, MA in Jewish liberal studies, MA in Jewish communal studies, certificates in Jewish communal studies (joint program with U. of Penna. School of Social Work and Temple U), Jewish education, Israel studies, Judaica librarianship (joint program with Drexel U.), and Jewish music. Joint graduate program with Reconstructionist Rabbinical College in Jewish education and Jewish music. Netzky Division of Continuing Education and Jewish Community High School. *Various newsletters, annual academic bulletin, scholarly publications, centennial volume, Gratz newsletter and occasional papers.*

HEBREW COLLEGE (1921). 160 Herrick Road, Newton Centre, MA 02459. (617) 559-8600. FAX: (617)559-8601. Pres. Dr. David M. Gordis; Ch. Bd. Dir. Mickey Cail; Hon. Ch. Bd. Trustees Ted Benard-Cutler. Through training in Jewish texts, history, literature, ethics, and Hebrew language, prepares students to become literate participants in the global Jewish community. Offers graduate and undergraduate degrees and certificates in all aspects of Jewish education, Jewish studies, and Jewish music; serves students of all ages through its Prozdor High School, Camp Yavneh, Ulpan Center for Adult Jewish Learning, and *Me'ah*–One Hundred Hours of Adult Jewish Learning. *Hebrew College Today; Likut.* (www. HEBREWCOLLEGE.EDU)

HEBREW SEMINARY OF THE DEAF (1992). 4435 W. Oakton, Skokie, IL 60076. (847) 677-3330. FAX: (847)677-7945. E-mail: hebrewsemdeaf@juno.com. Pres. Rabbi Douglas Goldhamer; Bd. Chmn. Alan Crane. Trains deaf and hearing men and women to become rabbis and teachers for Jewish deaf communities across America. All classes in the 5-year program are interpreted in Sign Language. Rabbis teaching in the seminary are Reform, Conservative, and Reconstructionist.

HEBREW THEOLOGICAL COLLEGE (1922). 7135 N. Carpenter Rd., Skokie, IL 60077. (847)982-2500. FAX: (847)674-6381. E-mail: htc@htcnet.edu. Chancellor Rabbi Dr. Jerold Isenberg; Rosh Hayeshiva Rabbi Shlomo Morgenstern. Hebrew Theological College, a fully accredited insitution, includes the Bet Midrash for Men, Blitstein Institute for Women, Kanter School of Liberal Arts and Sciences, Fasman Yeshiva High School, Community Service Devision, Silber Memorial Library, Bellows Kollel, Israel Experience Program and Yeshivas HaKayitz summer camp. *Likutei Pshatim, Or Shmuel, Academic Journal.* (www. HTCNET.EDU)

HEBREW UNION COLLEGE–JEWISH INSTITUTE OF RELIGION (1875). 3101 Clifton Ave., Cincinnati, OH 45220. (513)221-1875. FAX: (513)221-1847. Pres. Rabbi David Ellenson; Chancellor Dr. Alfred Gottschalk; V.-Pres. Finance Robert J. Goldsmith; V.-Pres. Devel. Erica S. Frederick; Chmn. Bd. Govs. Burton Lehman; Provost Dr. Norman J. Cohen; V.-Pres.

For Communal Dev. Dr Paul M. Steinberg. Academic centers: 3101 Clifton Ave., Cincinnati, OH 45220 (1875), Dean Rabbi Kenneth Ehrlich. 1 W. 4 St., NYC 10012 (1922), Dean Rabbi Aaron Panken. FAX: (212) 388-1720. 3077 University Ave., Los Angeles, CA 90007 (1954), Dean Rabbi Lewis Barth; FAX: (213)747-6128. 13 King David St., Jerusalem, Israel 94101 (1963), Dean Rabbi Michael Marmur; FAX: (972-2)6251478. Prepares students for Reform rabbinate, cantorate, Jewish education and educational administration, communal service, academic careers; promotes Jewish studies; maintains libraries, archives, and museums; offers master's and doctoral degrees; engages in archaeological excavations; publishes scholarly works through Hebrew Union College Press. *American Jewish Archives; Bibliographica Judaica; HUC-JIR Catalogue; Hebrew Union College Annual; Studies in Bibliography and Booklore; The Chronicle; Kesher.* (WWW.HUC.EDU)

———, AMERICAN JEWISH PERIODICAL CENTER (1957). 3101 Clifton Ave., Cincinnati, OH 45220. (513)221-1875, ext. 396. FAX: (513)221-0519. Dir. Herbert C. Zafren. Maintains microfilms of all American Jewish periodicals 1823-1925, selected periodicals since 1925. *Jewish Periodicals and Newspapers on Microfilm (1957); First Supplement (1960); Augmented Edition (1984).*

———, BLAUSTEIN CENTER FOR PASTORAL COUNSELING. 1 West 4th Street, NYC, 10012. (212)824-2238. FAX: (212)388-1720. Email: nwiener@huc.edu. Dir. Nancy Wiener. In partnership with CCAR, prepares spiritual leaderss to sensitively and capably help congregants to deal with the critical issues they face throughout their lives; enables rabbinical students to complete a variety of supervised clinical experiences, including a year of congregational workd as well as pastoral counseling internships, and an academic grounding in psychodynamics and pastoral counseling; and develops new approaches to teaching counseling skills, grounding reflections on practical field work experiences in the teachings of Jewish texts.

———, CENTER FOR HOLOCAUST AND HUMANITY EDUCATION. 3101 Clifton Ave., Cincinnati, OH 45220. (513)221-1875, ext. 355. FAX: (513)221-1842. Email:

holocaustandhumanity@huc.edu. Dir. Dr. Racelle R. Weiman. Co-sponsored by Hebrew Union College-Jewish Institute of Religion and Combined Generations of the Holocaust of Greater Cincinnati; offers graduate level courses for educational professionals and clergy; surveys and assesses Holocaust education needs in public and private sectors; innovates curriculum development and evaluation; provides teacher training, pedgogic resources, and programming for general public of all ages and faiths; convenes conferences and symposia; cooperates with university consortium on outreach initiatives; creates traveling exhibits; fosters tolerance education and prejudice reduction in the school system.

———, EDGAR F. MAGNIN SCHOOL OF GRADUATE STUDIES (1956). 3077 University Ave., Los Angeles, CA 90007. (213)749-3424. FAX: (213)747-6128. E-mail: magnin@huc.edu. Dir. Dr. Reuven Firestone. Supervises programs leading to DHS, DHL, and MA degrees; participates in cooperative PhD programs with U. of S. Calif.

———, GRADUATE STUDIES PROGRAM. 1 W. 4 St. NYC 10012. (212)824-2252. FAX: (212)388-1720. E-mail: nysgrad@huc. edu. Dir. Dr. Carol Ochs. Offers the DHL (doctor of Hebrew letters) degree in a variety of fields; the MAJS (master of arts in Judaic studies), a multidisciplinary degree; and is the only Jewish seminary to offer the DMin (doctor of ministry) degree in pastoral care and counseling.

———, HUC-UC CENTER FOR THE STUDY OF ETHICS AND CONTEMPORARY MORAL PROBLEMS (1986). 3101 Clifton Ave., Cincinnati, OH 45220. (513)221-1875, EXT. 367. FAX: (5130221-1842. Email: ethics@huc.edu. Dir. Dr. Jonathan Cohen. Co-sponsored by Hebrew Unon College-Jewish Institute of Religion and the University of Cincinnati; dedicated to the study of contemporary moral problems on the basis of valuews that are at the heart of Judeo-Christian and secular ethical traditions; provides forum for open discussion and reflection on important moral dilemmas that arise in modern life; promotes the incorporation of ethical values in personal life, professional practice, and community development; lauching MA and PhD programs in Jewish and Comparative Law and Applied

Ethics; offering development programs for legal, medical, and social work professionals; promoting cooperative research among academic institutions, social service, and not-for-profit organizations in Greater Cincinnati.

———, IRWIN DANIELS SCHOOL OF JEWISH COMMUNAL SERVICE (1968). 3077 University Ave., Los Angeles, CA 90007. (800)899-0925. FAX: (213)747-6128. E-mail: swindmueller@huc.edu. Dir. Dr. Steven F. Windmueller. Offers certificate and master's degree to those employed in Jewish communal services, or preparing for such work; offers joint MA in Jewish education and communal service with Rhea Hirsch School; offers dual degrees with the School of Social Work, the School of Public Administration, the Annenberg School for Communication, Marshall School of Business and the School of Gerontology of the U. of S. Calif. and with other institutions. Single master's degrees can be completed in 15 months and certificates are awarded for the completion of two full-time summer sessions. (WWW.HUC.EDU)

———, JACOB RADER MARCUS CENTER OF THE AMERICAN JEWISH ARCHIVES (see p. 549)

———, JEROME H. LOUCHHEIM SCHOOL OF JUDAIC STUDIES (1969). 3077 University Ave., Los Angeles, CA 90007. (213)749-3424. FAX: (213)747-6128. Dir. Dr. Reuven Firestone. Offers programs leading to MA, BS, BA, and AA degrees; offers courses as part of the undergraduate program of the U. of S. Calif.

———, NELSON GLUECK SCHOOL OF BIBLICAL ARCHAEOLOGY (1963). 13 King David St., Jerusalem, Israel 94101. (972) 2-6203333. FAX: (972)2-6251478. Dir. Avraham Biran. Offers graduate-level research programs in Bible and archaeology. Summer excavations are carried out by scholars and students. University credit may be earned by participants in excavations. Consortium of colleges, universities, and seminaries is affiliated with the school. Skirball Museum of Biblical Archaeology (artifacts from Tel Dan, Tel Gezer, and Aroer).

———, RHEA HIRSCH SCHOOL OF EDUCATION (1967). 3077 University Ave., Los Angeles, CA 90007. (213)749-3424. FAX: (213)747-6128. Dir. Sara Lee. Offers PhD and MA programs in Jewish and Hebrew education; conducts joint degree programs with U. of S. Calif.; offers courses for Jewish teachers, librarians, and early educators on a nonmatriculating basis; conducts summer institutes for professional Jewish educators.

———, SCHOOL OF EDUCATION (1947). 1 W. 4 St., NYC 10012. (212)824-2213. FAX: (212)388-1720. E-mail: nysed@huc.edu. Dir. Jo Kay. Trains teachers and principals for Reform religious schools; offers MA degree with specialization in religious education.

———, SCHOOL OF GRADUATE STUDIES (1949). 3101 Clifton Ave., Cincinnati, OH 45220. (513)221-1875, ext. 230. FAX: (513)221-0321. E-mail: gradschool@huc.edu. Dir. Dr. Adam Kamesar. Offers programs leading to MA and PhD degrees; offers program leading to DHL degree for rabbinic graduates of the college.

———, SCHOOL OF JEWISH STUDIES (1963). 13 King David St., Jerusalem, Israel 94101. (972)2-6203333. FAX: (972)2-6251478. E-mail: jerusalem@huc.edu. Acting Pres. Dr. Norman J. Cohen; Dean Rabbi Michael Marmur; Assoc. Dean Rabbi Shaul R. Feinberg. Offers first year of graduate rabbinic, cantorial, and Jewish education studies (required) for North American students; graduate program leading to ordination for Israeli rabbinic students; non-degree Beit Midrash/Liberal Yeshivah program of Jewish studies (English language); in-service educational programming for teachers and educators (Hebrew language); Hebrew Ulpan for immigrants and visitors; Abramov Library of Judaica, Hebraica, Ancient Near East and American Jewish Experience; Skirball Museum of Biblical Archaeology; public outreach programs (lectures, courses, concerts, exhibits).

———, SCHOOL OF SACRED MUSIC (1947). 1 W. 4 St., NYC 10012. (212)824-2225. FAX: (212)388-1720. Dir. Cantor Israel Goldstein. Trains cantors for congregations; offers MSM degree. *Sacred Music Press.*

———, SKIRBALL CULTURAL CENTER (*see* p. 552)

INSTITUTE OF TRADITIONAL JUDAISM (1990). 811 Palisade Ave., Teaneck, NJ 07666. (201)801-0707. FAX: (201)801-

0449. Rector (Reish Metivta) Rabbi David Weiss Halivni; Dean Rabbi Ronald D. Price. A nondenominational halakhic rabbinical school dedicated to genuine faith combined with intellectual honesty and the love of Israel. Graduates receive "yoreh yoreh" smikhah.

JEWISH THEOLOGICAL SEMINARY (1886; REORG. 1902). 3080 Broadway, NYC 10027-4649. (212)678-8000. FAX: (212) 678-8947. Chancellor Dr. Ismar Schorsch; Bd. Chmn. Gershon Kekst. Operates undergraduate and graduate programs in Judaic studies; professional schools for training Conservative rabbis, educators and cantors; the JTS Library; the Ratner Center for the Study of Conservative Judaism; Melton Research Center for Jewish Education; the Jewish Museum; Ramah Camps and the Ivry Prozdor high-school honors program. Other outreach activities include the Distance Learning Project, the Finkelstein Institute for Religious and Social Studies, and the Wagner Institute lay leadership program. *Academic Bulletin; JTS Magazine; Gleanings; JTS News.* (www. JTSA.EDU)

———, ALBERT A. LIST COLLEGE OF JEWISH STUDIES (formerly SEMINARY COLLEGE OF JEWISH STUDIES—TEACHERS INSTITUTE) (1909). 3080 Broadway, NYC 10027. (212)678-8826. Dean Dr. Shuly Rubin Schwartz. Offers complete undergraduate program in Judaica leading to BA degree; conducts joint programs with Columbia University and Barnard College enabling students to receive two BA degrees.

———, GRADUATE SCHOOL OF JTS (Formerly INSTITUTE FOR ADVANCED STUDY IN THE HUMANITIES) (1968). 3080 Broadway, NYC 10027-4649. (212)678-8024. FAX: (212)678-8947. E-mail: gradschool @jtsa.edu. Dean Dr. Stephen P. Garfinkel; Asst. Dean Dr. Bruce E. Nielsen. Programs leading to MA, DHL, and PhD degrees in Judaic studies; specializations include Ancient Judaism, Bible and Ancient Semitic Languages, Interdepartmental Studies, Jewish Art and Material Culture, Jewish Education, Jewish History, Jewish Literature, Jewish Philosophy, Jewish Women's Studies, Liturgy, Medieval Jewish Studies, Midrash, Modern Jewish Studies, Talmud and Rabbinics, and Dual Degree Program with

Columbia University School of Social Work.

——, H. L. MILLER CANTORIAL SCHOOL AND COLLEGE OF JEWISH MUSIC (1952). 3080 Broadway, NYC 10027. (212)678-8036. FAX: (212)678-8947. Dean Cantor Henry Rosenblum. Trains cantors, music teachers, and choral directors for congregations. Offers full-time programs in sacred music leading to degree of MSM, and diploma of *Hazzan*.

——, JEWISH MUSEUM (*see* p. 000)

——, LIBRARY OF THE JEWISH THEOLOGICAL SEMINARY. 3080 Broadway, NYC 10027. (212)678-8075. FAX: (212)678-8998. E-mail: library@jtsa.edu. Librarian Dr. Mayer E. Rabinowitz. Contains one of the largest collections of Hebraica and Judaica in the world, including manuscripts, incunabula, rare books, and Cairo Geniza material. The 320,000-item collection includes books, manuscripts, periodicals, sound recordings, prints, broadsides, photographs, postcards, microform, videos and CD-ROM. Exhibition of items from the collection are ongoing. Exhibition catalogs are available for sale. The Library is open to the public for on-site use (photo identification required). *Between the Lines.* (WWW.JTSA.EDU/LIBRARY)

——, LOUIS FINKELSTEIN INSTITUTE FOR RELIGIOUS AND SOCIAL STUDIES (1938). 3080 Broadway, NYC 10027. (212)870-3180. FAX: (212)678-8947. E-mail: finkelstein@jtsa.edu. Dir. Dr. Alan Mittleman. Since 1938 has maintained an innovative interfaith and intergroup relations program, pioneering new approaches to dialogue across religious lines. Through scholarly and practical fellowship, highlights the relevance of Judaism and other contemporary religions to current theological, ethical, and scientific issues, including the emerging challenge of bioethics.

——, MELTON RESEARCH CENTER FOR JEWISH EDUCATION (1960). 3080 Broadway, NYC 10027. (212)678-8031. E-mail: stbrown@jtsa.edu. Dir. Dr. Steven M. Brown; Admin. Lisa Siberstein-Weber. Develops new curricula and materials for Jewish education; prepares educators through seminars and in-service programs; maintains consultant and supervisory relationships with a limited number of pilot schools; develops and implements research initiatives; sponsors "renewal" retreats. *Gleanings; Courtyard: A Journal of Research and Reflection on Jewish Education.*

——, NATIONAL RAMAH COMMISSION (1947). 3080 Broadway, NYC 10027. (212)678-8881. FAX: (212)749-8251. Pres. Alan H. Silberman; Natl. Dir. Mitchell Cohen. Sponsors an international network of 16 summer camps located in the US, Canada, S. America, Russia, and Israel, emphasizing Jewish education, living, and culture; offers opportunities for qualified college students and older to serve as counselors, administrators, specialists, etc., and programs for children with special needs (Tikvah program); offers special programs in U.S. and Israel, including National Ramah Staff Training Institute, Ramah Israel Seminar, Ulpan Ramah Plus, and Tichon Ramah Yerushalayim. Family and synagogue tours to Israel and summer day camp in Israel for Americans.

——, PROJECT JUDAICA (1992). 3080 Broadway, NYC 10027. (212)678-8983. Dir. Dr. David Fishman. Students in this intensive, five year program sponsored with YIVO and the Russian State University for the Humanities in Moscow pursue the university's general curriculum while majoring in Jewish history and culture taught by JTS faculty and advanced students. Graduates receive a diploma (the equivalent of an MA) or a candidate of sciences degree (the equivalent of a PhD) from RSUH.

——, RABBINICAL SCHOOL (1886). 3080 Broadway, NYC 10027. (212)678-8817. Dean Allan Kensky. Offers a program of graduate and professional studies leading to the degree of Master of Arts and ordination; includes one year of study in Jerusalem and an extensive field-work program.

——, RADIO AND TELEVISION (1944). 3080 Broadway, NYC 10027. (212)678-8020. Produces radio and TV programs expressing the Jewish tradition in its broadest sense, including hour-long documentaries on NBC and ABC. Distributes cassettes of programs at minimum charge.

——, REBECCA AND ISRAEL IVRY PROZDOR (1951). 3080 Broadway, NYC 10027.

(212)678-8824. E-mail: prozdor@jtsa. edu. Principal Rhonda Rosenheck; Community Advisory Board Chmn. Michael Katz. The Hebrew high school of JTS, offers a program of Jewish studies for day school and congregational school graduates in classical texts, Hebrew, interdisciplinary seminars, training in educational leadership, and classes for college credit. Classes meet one evening a week and on Sundays in Manhattan and at affiliated programs. *High School Curricula.*

———, SAUL LIEBERMAN INSTITUTE FOR TALMUDIC RESEARCH (1985). 3080 Broadway, NYC 10027. (212)678-8994. FAX: (212)678D8947. E-mail: liebinst@ jtsa.edu. Dir. Shamma Friedman; Coord. Jonathan Milgram. Engaged in preparing for publication a series of scholarly editions of selected chapters of the Talmud. The following projects support and help disseminate the research: Talmud Text Database; Bibliography of Talmudic Literature; Catalogue of Geniza Fragments.

———, SCHOCKEN INSTITUTE FOR JEWISH RESEARCH (1961). 6 Balfour St., Jerusalem, Israel 92102. (972)2-5631288. FAX: (972) 2-5636857. E-mail: sjssg@vms.huji.ac.il. Dir. Dr. Shmuel Glick. Comprises the Schocken collection of rare books and manuscripts and a research institute dedicated to the exploration of Hebrew religious poetry (*piyyut*). *Schocken Institute Yearbook (P'raqim).*

———, WILLIAM DAVIDSON GRADUATE SCHOOL OF JEWISH EDUCATION (1996). 3080 Broadway, NYC 10027. (212) 678-8030. E-mail: edschool@jtsa.edu. Dean Dr. Aryeh Davidson. Offers master's and doctoral degrees in Jewish education; continuing education courses for Jewish educators and Jewish communal professionals; and programs that take advantage of the latest technology, including distance learning and interactive video classrooms.

MAALOT–A SEMINARY FOR CANTORS AND JUDAISTS (1987). 15 W. Montgomery Ave., Suite 204, Rockville, MD 20850. (301)309-2310. FAX: (301)309-2328. Pres./Exec. Off. David Shneyer. An educational program established to train individuals in Jewish music, the liturgical arts, and the use, design, and application of Jewish customs and ceremonies. Offers

classes, seminars, and an independent study program.

MESIVTA YESHIVA RABBI CHAIM BERLIN RABBINICAL ACADEMY (1905). 1605 Coney Island Ave., Brooklyn, NY 11230. (718)377-0777. Exec. Dir. Y. Mayer Lasker. Maintains fully accredited elementary and high schools; collegiate and postgraduate school for advanced Jewish studies, both in America and Israel; Camp Morris, a summer study retreat; Prof. Nathan Isaacs Memorial Library; Gur Aryeh Publications.

NER ISRAEL RABBINICAL COLLEGE (1933). 400 Mt. Wilson Lane, Baltimore, MD 21208. (410)484-7200. FAX: (410)484-3060. Rosh Hayeshiva, Rabbi Aharon Feldman; Pres. Rabbi Herman N. Neuberger. Trains rabbis and educators for Jewish communities in America and worldwide. Offers bachelor's, master's, and doctoral degrees in talmudic law, as well as teacher's diploma. College has four divisions: Israel Henry Beren High School, Rabbinical College, Teachers Training Institute, Graduate School. Maintains an active community-service division. Operates special programs for Iranian and Russian Jewish students. *Ner Israel Update; Alumni Bulletin; Ohr Hanair Talmudic Journal; Iranian B'nei Torah Bulletin.*

RABBINICAL COLLEGE OF TELSHE, INC. (1941). 28400 Euclid Ave., Wickliffe, OH 44092. (216)943-5300. Roshei Hayeshiva and Pres. Rabbi Zalman Gifter and Rabbi Yitzchok Sorotzkin ; V.-Pres. Rabbi Abba Zalka Gewirtz. College for higher Jewish learning specializing in talmudic studies and rabbinics; maintains a preparatory academy including a secular high school, postgraduate department, teacher-training school, and teachers' seminary for women. *Pri Etz Chaim; Peer Mordechai; Alumni Bulletin.*

RECONSTRUCTIONIST RABBINICAL COLLEGE (1968). 1299 Church Rd., Wyncote, PA 19095. (215)576-0800. FAX: (215)576-6143. E-mail: rrcinfo@rrc.edu. Pres. Dan Ehrenkranz; Bd. Chmn. Donald L. Shapiro; Genl. Chmn. Aaron Ziegelman. Coeducational. Trains rabbis and cantors for all areas of Jewish communal life: synagogues, academic and educational positions, Hillel centers, federation agencies, and chaplaincy for hospitals, hospices, and geriatric centers; confers title of rabbi and cantor and grants degrees of Master and Doctor of Hebrew Letters and Master of Arts in Jewish Studies. *RRC Report; Reconstructionist.* (WWW.RRC.EDU)

SPERTUS INSTITUTE OF JEWISH STUDIES (1924). 618 S. Michigan Ave., Chicago, IL 60605. (312)922-9012. FAX: (312)922-6406. Pres. Howard A. Sulkin; Dean Dr. Dean Bell; Museum Dir. Rhoda Rosen; Lib. Dir. Glenn Ferdman. An accredited institution of higher learning offering one doctor of Jewish studies degree; master's degree programs in Jewish studies, Jewish education, Jewish communal service, and human-services administration; plus an extensive program of continuing education. Major resources of the college encompass Spertus Museum, Asher Library, Chicago Jewish Archives, and Spertus College of Judaica Press.

———, SPERTUS MUSEUM (*see* p. 553)

TOURO COLLEGE (1970). Executive Offices: 27 West 23rd Street., NYC 10010. (212)4630400. FAX: (212)627-9049. Pres. Dr. Bernard Lander; Bd. Chmn. Mark Hasten. Non-profit comprehensive college with Judaic Studies, Liberal Arts and professional programs leading to BA, BS, MA, MS and JD degrees at campuses in NYC and Long Island; emphasizes relevance of Jewish heritage to Western civilization. Undergraduate and graduate degree programs in Moscow and Jerusalem. California campuses offer DO degree and distance learning BS, MS, MBA and PhD degrees.

———, COLLEGE OF LIBERAL ARTS AND SCIENCES. 27-33 W. 23 St., NYC 10010. (212)463-0400. FAX: (212)627-9144. Exec. Dean Stanley Boylan. Offers comprehensive Jewish studies along with studies in the arts, sciences, humanities, and preprofessional studies in health sciences, law, accounting, business, computer science, education, and finance. Women's Division, 160 Lexington Ave., NYC 10016. (212)213-2230. FAX: (212)683-3281. Dean Sara E. Freifeld.

———, INSTITUTE OF JEWISH LAW. (631) 421-2244, ext. 335. A constituent of Touro College Jacob D. Fuchsberg Law Center, the Institute of Jewish Law provides an intellectual framework for the study and teaching of Jewish law. Coedits *Dinei Israel* (Jewish Law Journal) with Tel Aviv University Law School.

———, JACOB D. FUCHSBERG LAW CENTER (1980). Long Island Campus, 300 Nassau Rd., Huntington, NY 11743. (516) 421-2244. Dean Howard A. Glickstein. Offers studies leading to JD degree.

———, MOSCOW BRANCH. Oztozhenka #38, Moscow, Russia 119837. Offers BS program in business and BA program in Jewish studies.

———, SCHOOL OF GENERAL STUDIES. Midtown Main Campus, 27 W. 23 St., NYC 10010. (212)463-0400; Harlem Main Campus, 240 E. 123 St., NYC 10035; Sunset Park extension, 475 53rd St., Brooklyn, NY 11220; Flushing Extension, 133-35 Roosevelt Ave., Queens, NY 11374. Dean Stephen Adolphus. Associate and bachelor degree programs in human services, education N-6, computing, business and liberal arts; special emphasis on service to non-traditional students.

———, TOURO COLLEGE FLATBUSH CENTER (1979). 1602 Ave. J, Brooklyn, NY 11230. (718)252-7800. Dean Robert Goldschmidt. A division of the College of Liberal Arts and Sciences; options offered in accounting and business, education, mathematics, political science, psychology, special education and speech. Classes are given on weeknights and during the day on Sunday.

———, TOURO COLLEGE ISRAEL. 20 Pierre Koenig St., Jerusalem, Israel. (02) 6796666. FAX: (02)6796688. V-Pres., Israel, Matityahu Adler; Dean of Faculty, Israel, Prof. Moshe Lieberman. Touro College Israel offers both undergraduate and graduate degrees in management, marketing, economics, finance, and accounting. Touro College also offers a graduate degree in Jewish Studies. Courses in both these programs are given in Hebrew. In addition undergraduate courses in our one year program are offered in English. (WWW.TOURO.AC.IL)

———, TOURO COLLEGE SCHOOL OF HEALTH SCIENCES (1986). 1700 Union Blvd, Bay Shore, NY 11706. (516)665-1600. FAX: (516)665-6902. E-mail: edwarda@touro. edu. Pres. Dr. Bernard Lander; Dean Dr. Joseph Weisberg. Offers the following programs: MS/MD with Faculty of Medicine, Technion Institute, Israel; BS/MS Occupational Therapy; BS/MS Physical Therapy; MS Public Health; Advanced MS Orthopedic Physical Therapy; MS Forensic Examination; MS Clinical Engineering; MS Early Intervention; MS Gerontology; BS Physician Assistant; AAS Occupational Therapy Assistant; AAS Physical Therapists Assistant.

———, TOURO GRADUATE SCHOOL OF JEWISH STUDIES (1981). 160 Lexington Ave., NYC 10016. (212)213-2230. FAX: (212) 683-3281. E-mail: moshesh@touro.edu. Pres. Bernard Lander; Dean Michael A. Shmidman. Offers courses leading to an MA in Jewish studies, with concentrations in Jewish history or Jewish education. Students may complete part of their program in Israel through MA courses offered by Touro faculty at Touro's Jerusalem center.

UNIVERSITY OF JUDAISM (1947). 15600 Mulholland Dr., Los Angeles, CA 90077. (310)476-9777. FAX: (310)476-0347. E-mail: gleuenthal@uj.edu. Pres. Dr. Robert D. Wexler. The College of Arts and Sciences is an accredited liberal arts college for undergraduates offering a core curriculum of Jewish, Western, and non-Western studies, with majors including bioethics (a premedical track in partnership with Cedars-Sinai Medical Center), business, English, Jewish studies, journalism, literature & politics, political science, psychology, and U.S. public policy. Accredited graduate programs in nonprofit business administration (MBA), and Jewish education. The Ziegler School of Rabbinic Studies provides an intensive four-year program with Conservative ordination. Home of the Whizin Center for the Jewish Future, a research and programming institute. Offers the largest adult Jewish education program in the U.S., cultural-arts programs, and a variety of outreach services for West Coast Jewish communities. *Vision.* (WWW.UJ.EDU)

WEST COAST TALMUDICAL SEMINARY (Yeshiva ohr Elchonon Chabad) (1953). 7215 Waring Ave., Los Angeles, CA 90046. (323)937-3763. FAX: (323)937-9456. Dean Rabbi Ezra Schochet. Provides facilities for intensive Torah education as well as Orthodox rabbinical training on the West Coast; conducts an accredited college preparatory high school combined with a full program of Torah-talmudic training and a graduate talmudical division on the college level. *Torah Quiz; Kovetz Migdal Ohr; Kovetz Ohr HaMigdal.*

YESHIVA TORAH VODAATH AND MESIVTA TORAH VODAATH RABBINICAL SEMINARY (1918). 425 E. 9 St., Brooklyn, NY 11218. (718)941-8000. Bd. Chmn. Chaim Leshkowitz. Offers Hebrew and secular education from elementary level through rabbinical ordination and postgraduate work; maintains a teachers institute and community-service bureau; maintains a dormitory and a nonprofit camp program for boys. *Chronicle; Mesivta Vanguard; Thought of the Week; Torah Vodaath News; Ha'Mesifta.*

———, YESHIVA TORAH VODAATH ALUMNI ASSOCIATION (1941). 425 E. 9 St., Brooklyn, NY 11218. (718)941-8000. Pres. George Weinberger. Promotes social and cultural ties between the alumni and the schools through classes and lectures and fund-raising; offers vocational guidance to students; operates Camp Ohr Shraga; sponsors research fellowship program for boys. *Annual Journal; Hamesivta Torah periodical.*

YESHIVA UNIVERSITY (1886). Wilf Campus, 500 W. 185 St., NYC 10033-3201. (212) 960-5400. FAX: (212)960-0055. Chancellor Dr. Norman Lamm; Pres. Richard Joel; Chmn. Bd. of Trustees Ronald P. Stanton. The nation's oldest and most comprehensive independent university founded under Jewish auspices, with 18 undergraduate and graduate schools, divisions, and affiliates; widespread programs of research and community outreach; publications; and a museum. A broad range of curricula lead to bachelor's, master's, doctoral, and professional degrees. Undergraduate schools provide general studies curricula supplemented by courses in Jewish learning; graduate schools prepare for careers in medicine, law, social work, Jewish education, psychology, Jewish studies, and other fields. It has seven undergraduate schools, seven graduate and professional schools, and four affiliates. *Yeshiva University Review; Yeshiva University Today.* (WWW.YU.EDU)

Yeshiva University has four campuses in Manhattan and the Bronx: Wilf Campus, 500 W. 185 St., NYC 10033-3201; Midtown Campus, 245 Lexington Ave.,

NYC 10016-4699; Brookdale Center, 55
Fifth Ave., NYC 10003-4391; Jack and
Pearl Resnick Campus, Eastchester Rd. &
Morris Pk. Ave., Bronx, NY 10461-1602.
Undergraduate schools for men at Wilf
Campus (212)960-5400: Yeshiva College
(Bd. Chmn. Joshua L. Muss; Dean Dr.
Norman T. Adler) provides liberal arts
and sciences curricula; grants BA degree.
Isaac Breuer College of Hebraic Studies
(Dean Dr. Michael D. Shmidman) awards
Hebrew teacher's diploma, AA, BA,
and BS. James Striar School of General
Jewish Studies (Dean Dr. Michael D.
Shmidman) grants AA degree. Yeshiva
Program/Mazer School of Talmudic
Studies (Max and Marion Grill Dean
Rabbi Zevulun Charlop) offers advanced
course of study in Talmudic texts and
commentaries. Irving I. Stone Beit Mid-
rash Program (Dean Dr. Michael D.
Shmidman) offers diversified curriculum
combining Talmud with Jewish studies.
Undergraduate school for women at
Midtown Campus (212)340-7700: Stern
College for Women (Bd. Chmn. Marjorie
Diener Blenden; Dr. Monique C. Katz;
Dean Dr. Karen Bacon) offers liberal arts
and sciences curricula supplemented by
Jewish studies programs; awards BA, AA,
and Hebrew teacher's diploma.
Sy Syms School of Business at Wilf
Campus and Midtown Campus (Bd.
Chmn. Bernard L. Madoff; Dean Dr.
Charles Snow) offers undergraduate busi-
ness curricula in conjunction with study
at Yeshiva College or Stern College;
grants BS degree.
Universitywide programs serving the
community and the nation include the S.
Daniel Abraham Israel Program; Joseph
Alexander Foundation Program for En-
hancemant of Science Education; Samuel
H. and Rachel Golding Center for Judaic
Studies; Samuel H. and Rachel Golding
Institute for Biomedical Education; Carl
C. Icahn Foundation Institutes for Child
Protection; Irving and Hanni Rosenbaum
Aliyah Incentive Fund; Holocaust Stud-
ies Program; Yeshiva University Press;
Yeshiva University Museum.

———, ALBERT EINSTEIN COLLEGE OF
MEDICINE (1955). Eastchester Rd. &
Morris Pk. Ave., Bronx, NY 10461-1602.
(718)430-2000. Pres. Richard Joel; Ch-
pers. Bd. of Overseers Robert A. Belfer;
Marilyn and Stanley M. Katz Dean Dr.
Dominick P. Purpura. Prepares physi-
cians and conducts research in the health
sciences; awards MD degree; includes Sue
Golding Graduate Division of Medical
Sciences (Dir. Dr. Anne M. Etgen), which
grants PhD degree. Einstein's clinical fa-
cilities and affiliates encompass Jack D.
Weiler Hospital of Albert Einstein Col-
lege of Medicine, Jacobi Medical Center,
Montefiore Medical Center, Long Island
Jewish Medical Center, Beth Israel Med-
ical Center, Bronx-Lebanon Hospital
Center, and Rose F. Kennedy Center for
Research in Mental Retardation and De-
velopmental Disabilities. *Einstein; Ein-
stein Today; Einstein Quarterly Journal of
Biology and Medicine.*

———, ALUMNI OFFICE, 500 W. 185 St.,
NYC 10033-3201. (212)960-5373. FAX:
(212)960-5336. E-mail: alumdesk@ymail.
yu.edu. University Dir. Alumni Affairs
Robert R. Saltzman. Seeks to foster a
close allegiance of alumni to their alma
mater by maintaining ties with all alumni
and servicing the following associations:
Yeshiva College Alumni; Stern College
for Women Alumnae; Sy Syms School of
Business Alumni; Albert Einstein College
of Medicine Alumni; Ferkauf Graduate
School of Psychology Alumni; Wurzweiler School of Social Work Alumni;
Rabbinic Alumni; Benjamin N. Cardozo
School of Law Alumni. *Yeshiva University Review; AECOM Alumni News; Ferkauf Progress Notes; Wurzweiler Update;
Jewish Social Work Forum.*

———, AZRIELI GRADUATE SCHOOL OF
JEWISH EDUCATION AND ADMINISTRA-
TION (1945). 245 Lexington Ave., NYC
10016-4699. (212)340-7705. FAX: (212)
340-7787. Pres. Richard Joel; Chmn. Bd.
of Dirs. Moshael J. Straus; Dir. Dr.
Yitzchak S. Handel. Offers MS degree in
Jewish elementary and secondary education; specialist's certificate and EdD in
administration and supervision of Jewish
education. Block Education Program,
subsidized by a grant from the Jewish
Agency's Joint Program for Jewish Education, provides summer course work to
complement year-round field instruction
in local communities.

———, BELFER INSTITUTE FOR ADVANCED
BIOMEDICAL STUDIES (1978). Eastchester
Rd. & Morris Pk. Ave., Bronx, NY 10461-
1602. (718)430-2801. Dir. Dr. Dennis
Shields. Integrates and coordinates the
Albert Einstein College of Medicine's

postdoctoral research and training-grant programs in the basic and clinical biomedical sciences. Awards certificate as research fellow or research associate on completion of training.

——, BENJAMIN N. CARDOZO SCHOOL OF LAW (1976). 55 Fifth Ave., NYC 10003-4391. (212)790-0200. E-mail:lawinfo@ymail.yu.edu. Pres. Richard Joel; Chmn. Bd. Of Directors Earle I. Mack; Dean Paul R. Verkuil. Offers a rigorous and enriched legal education leading to juris doctor (JD) degree and two LLM programs—in intellectual property and in general law. Programs and services include Jacob Burns Institute for Advanced Legal Studies; Jacob Burns Center for Ethics in the Practice of Law; Bet Tzedek Legal Services Clinic, including the Herman J. Stich Program for the Aged and Disabled; Cardozo International Institute/Uri and Caroline Bauer Israel Program; Leonard and Bea Diener Institute of Jewish Law; Floersheimer Center for Constitutional Democracy; Ford Foundation Program in International Law and Human Rights; Samuel and Ronnie Heyman Center on Corporate Governance; Kukin Program for Conflict Resolution; Romie Shapiro Program in International Law and Human Rights; Stephen B. Siegel Program in Real Estate Law; Sol S. Singer Research Program in Real Property Law; Howard M. Squadron Program in Law, Media, and Society; Center for Professional Development. *Cardozo Life; Cardozo Law Review; Cardozo Arts and Entertainment Law Journal; Cardozo Women's Law Journal; Cardozo Journal of International and Comparative Law; Cardozo Studies in Law and Literature; Post-Soviet Media Law and Policy Newsletter; New York Real Estate Reporter.*

——, BERNARD REVEL GRADUATE SCHOOL OF JEWISH STUDIES (1935). 500 W. 185 St., NYC 10033-3201. (212)960-5253. Pres. Richard Joel; Chmn. Bd. Of Directors Mordecai D. Katz; Dean Dr. Arthur Hyman. Offers graduate programs in Bible, Talmudic studies, Jewish history, and Jewish philosophy; confers MA and PhD degrees. Harry Fischel Summer Program offers the Revel program during the summer.

——, FERKAUF GRADUATE SCHOOL OF PSYCHOLOGY (1957). Eastchester Rd. & Morris Pk. Ave., Bronx, NY 10461-1602.

(718)430-3941. FAX: (718)430-3960. E-mail: gill@aecom.yu.edu. Pres. Richard Joel; Chair Bd. of Governors. Dr. Jayne G. Beker; Dean Dr. Lawrence J. Siegel. Offers MA in applied psychology; PsyD in clinical and school-clinical child psychology; and PhD in developmental and clinical health psychology. Programs and services include the Leonard and Muriel Marcus Family Project for the Study of the Disturbed Adolescent; Max and Celia Parnes Family Psychological and Psychoeducational Services Clinic.

——, (AFFILIATE) PHILIP AND SARAH BELZ SCHOOL OF JEWISH MUSIC (1954). 560 W. 185 St., NYC 10033-3201. (212) 960-5353. FAX: (212)960-5359. Dir. Cantor Bernard Beer. Provides professional training of cantors and courses in Jewish liturgical music; conducts outreach; publishes *Journal of Jewish Music and Literature;* awards associate cantor's certificate and cantorial diploma.

——, (AFFILIATE) RABBI ISAAC EL-CHANAN THEOLOGICAL SEMINARY (1896). 2540 Amsterdam Ave., NYC 10033-9986. (212)960-5344. FAX: (212)960-0061. Chmn. Bd. of Trustees Julius Berman; Max and Marion Grill Dean Rabbi Zevulun Charlop. Leading center in the Western Hemisphere for Torah study and rabbinic training. RIETS complex encompasses 15 educational entities and a major service and outreach center with some 20 programs. Grants semikhah (ordination) and the degrees of master of religious education, master of Hebrew literature, doctor of religious education, and doctor of Hebrew literature. Includes Rabbi Joseph B. Soloveitchik Center of Rabbinic Studies; Gabriel Levine Post-Graduate School for Rabbinic Studies; Morris and Nellie L. Kawaler Rabbinic Training Program; Irving I. Stone Rabbinic Internship Program; Aaron, Martha, Isidore N., and Blanche Rosansky Foundation Contemporary Halakhah Program.

Kollelim include Marcos and Adina Katz Kollel (Institute for Advanced Research in Rabbinics); Kollel l'Horaah (Yadin Yadin) and External Yadin Yadin; Israel Henry Beren Institute for Higher Talmudic Studies (HaMachon HaGavohah L'Talmud); Bella and Harry Wexner Kollel Elyon and Semikhah Honors Program; Ludwig Jesselson Kollel Chaverim;

Caroline and Joseph S. Gruss Institute in Jerusalem.
RIETS sponsors one high school for boys (Manhattan) and one for girls (Queens).
The Max Stern Division of Communal Services (Acting Dir. Rabbi David A. Israel), provides personal and professional service to the rabbinate and related fields, as well as educational, consultative, organizational, and placement services to congregations, schools, and communal organizations around the world; coordinates a broad spectrum of outreach programs, including Association of Modern Orthodox Day Schools and Yeshiva High Schools, Stone-Sapirstein Center for Jewish Education, Gertrude and Morris Bienenfeld Department of Rabbinic Services, Gindi Program for the Enhancement of Professional Rabbinics, Continuing Rabbinic Education Initiatives, Leadership Education and Development Program (LEAD), Kiruv College Outreach Program, Community Kollel and Beit Midrash and Boardroom Learning Programs, Project Kehillah, Myer and Pauline Senders Off-Campus Lecture Series, Jewish Medical Ethics Consultation Service, National Commission on Torah Education.The Torah U-Madda Project, supported by the Joseph J. and Bertha K. Green Memorial Fund, includes the Orthodox Forum and publishes the *The Torah U-Madda Journal and Ten Da'at*.
Sephardic components are Jacob E. Safra Institute of Sephardic Studies and the Institute of Yemenite Studies; Sephardic Community Program; Dr. Joseph and Rachel Ades Sephardic Outreach Program; Maybaum Sephardic Fellowship Program.

———, SIMON WIESENTHAL CENTER (*see* p. 552)

———, WOMEN'S ORGANIZATION (1928). 500 W. 185 St., NYC 10033-3201. (212) 960-0855. Chmn. Natl. Bd. Dinah Pinczower. Supports Yeshiva University's national scholarship program for students training in education, community service, law, medicine, and other professions. Its Torah Chesed Fund provides monthly stipends to needy undergraduate students.

———, WURZWEILER SCHOOL OF SOCIAL WORK (1957). 500 W. 185 St., NYC 10033-3201. (212)960-0800. FAX: (212) 960-0822. Pres. Richard Joel; Chair Bd. of

Governors David I. Schachne; Dorothy and David I. Schachne Dean Dr. Sheldon R. Gelman. Offers graduate programs in social work and Jewish communal service; grants MSW and PhD degrees and certificate in Jewish communal service. MSW programs are: Concurrent Plan, 2-year, full-time track, combining classroom study and supervised field instruction; Plan for Employed Persons (PEP), for people working in social agencies; Block Education Plan (Dir. Dr. Adele Weiner), which combines summer course work with regular-year field placement in local agencies; Clergy Plan, training in counseling for clergy of all denominations; Silvia and Irwin Leiferman Center for Professional Training in the Care of the Elderly. *Jewish Social Work Forum*.

———, (AFFILIATE) YESHIVA OF LOS ANGELES (1977). 9760 W. Pico Blvd., Los Angeles, CA 90035-4701. (310)772-2424. FAX: (310)772-7661. E-mail: mhmay@ wiesenthal.com. Dean Rabbi Marvin Hier; Bd. Chmn. Samuel Belzberg; Dir. Academic Programs Rabbi Sholom Tendler. Affiliates are Yeshiva University High Schools of Los Angeles, Jewish Studies Institute and Kollel Torah MiTzion.

———, YESHIVA UNIVERSITY MUSEUM (*see* p. 554)

YESHIVAT CHOVEVEI TORAH (2002). 20 West End Ave., NYC 10023. (212)666-0036. FAX: (212) 666-5633. Dean Rabbi Avi Weiss. Dedicated to the training of open Orthodox rabbis who will lead the Jewish community and shape its spiritual and intellectual character in consonance with modern and open Orthodox values and commitments, emphasizing the encounter with classical Jewish texts not just as an intellectual exercise but as a form of divine service. (WWW.YCTORAH.ORG)

SOCIAL, MUTUAL BENEFIT

ALPHA EPSILON PI FRATERNITY (1913). 8815 Wesleyan Rd., Indianapolis, IN 46268-1171. (317)876-1913. FAX: (317)876-1057. E-mail: office@aepi.org. Internatl. Pres. Dr. Jay Levine; Exec. V.-Pres. Sidney N. Dunn. International Jewish fraternity active on over 100 campuses in the U.S. and Canada; encourages Jewish students to remain loyal to their heritage and to assume leadership roles in the community;

active in behalf of the State of Israel and Magen David Adom among other causes. *The Lion of Alpha Epsilon Pi (quarterly magazine).*

AMERICAN ASSOCIATION OF JEWS FROM THE FORMER USSR, INC. (AAJFSU) (1989). 100 Church Street, Suite 1608, NYC 10007. (212) 964-1946. FAX: (212) 964-1946. E-mail: GeorgeZilberman@ yahoo.com. Pres. Yury Zilberman; Bd. Chmn. Mark Gurevich. National not-for-profit, grassroots mutual assistance and refugee advocacy organization, which unites and represents interests of over 600,000 Russian speaking Jewish refugees and legal immigrants from the former Soviet Union. It has chapters and independent associations in seven states, including New York, Ohio, Colorado, New Jersey, Massachusetts, Wisconsin and Maryland. The national organization is a member of the National Immigration Forum and it is affiliated with the United Jewish Communities, Washington Action Office. It has become a founding member of the Jewish Community Relations Council of New York and the New York Immigration Coalition. Local Chapters work in cooperation with Jewish Federation and New York Chapter works in cooperation with JCRC, NYANA, HIAS and UJA-Federation of New York. The AAJFSU assists newcomers in their resettlement and vocational and cultural adjustment, fosters their Jewish identity and involvement in American civic and social affairs, fights anti-Semitism and violation of human rights in the FSU and the U.S. through cooperation with other human rights organizations and advocacy organizations, supports struggle of Israeli Jews for sustainable peace, collects money for Israeli victims of terror, provides assistance in social safety net and naturalization of the elderly and disabled, provides advocacy in cases of political asylum for victims of anti-Semitism in the FSU. *Chronicles of Anti-Semitism and Nationalism in Republics of the Former USSR (in English, annually); Information Bulletin (in Russian, quarterly).*

AMERICAN FEDERATION OF JEWS FROM CENTRAL EUROPE, INC. (1938). 570 Seventh Ave., NYC 10018. (212)921-3871. FAX: (212) 575-1918. Pres. Fritz Weinschenk; Exec. Asst. Dennis E. Rohrbaugh. Seeks to safeguard the rights and interests of American Jews of German-speaking Central European descent, especially in reference to restitution and indemnification; through its affiliate Research Foundation for Jewish Immigration sponsors research and publications on the history, immigration, and acculturation of Central European émigrés in the U.S. and worldwide; through its affiliate Jewish Philanthropic Fund of 1933 supports social programs for needy Nazi victims in the U.S.; undertakes cultural activities, publications; member, Council of Jews from Germany, London.

AMERICAN VETERANS OF ISRAEL (1951). 136 E. 39 St., NYC 10016. E-mail: spielgelsi @aol.com. Pres. Samuel Z. Klausner; V-Pres. David Kaplan. Maintains contact with American and Canadian volunteers who served in Aliyah Bet and/or Israel's War of Independence; promotes Israel's welfare; holds memorial services at grave of Col. David Marcus; is affiliated with World Mahal. *Newsletter.*

ASSOCIATION OF YUGOSLAV JEWS IN THE UNITED STATES, INC. (1941). 130 E. 59 St., Suite 1202, NYC 10022. (212)371-6891. V.-Pres. & Chmn. Emanuel Salom; Sec. Dr. Joseph Stock. Assistance to all Jews originally from Yugoslavia—Bosnia, Serbia, Croatia—and new settlers in Israel. *Bulletins.*

BNAI ZION–THE AMERICAN FRATERNAL ZIONIST ORGANIZATION (1908). 136 E. 39 St., NYC 10016. (212)725-1211. FAX: (212)684-6327. Pres. Michael J. Lazar; Exec. V.-Pres. Mel Parness. Fosters principles of Americanism, fraternalism, and Zionism. The Bnai Zion Foundation supports various humanitarian projects in Israel and the USA, chiefly the Bnai Zion Medical Center in Haifa and homes for retarded children-Maon Bnai Zion in Rosh Ha'ayin and the Herman Z. Quittman Center in Jerusalem Ahava Project. Also supports building of new central library in Ma'aleh Adumim. In U.S. sponsors program of awards for excellence in Hebrew for high school and college students. Chapters all over U.S. *Bnai Zion Voice* (quarterly). (WWW.BNAIZION.ORG)

BRITH ABRAHAM (1859; REORG. 1887). 136 E. 39 St., NYC 10016. (212)725-1211. FAX: (212)684-6327. Grand Master Robert Freeman. Protects Jewish rights and combats anti-Semitism; supports Soviet and Ethiopian emigration and the safety and dignity of Jews worldwide; helps to support Bnai Zion Medical Center in Haifa and other Israeli institutions; aids and supports various programs and projects in the U.S.: Hebrew Excellence Program-Gold Medal presentation in high schools and colleges; Camp Loyaltown; Brith Abraham and Bnai Zion Foundations. *Voice.*

BRITH SHOLOM (1905). 3939 Conshohocken Ave., Philadelphia, PA 19131. (215)878-5696. FAX: (215) 878-5699. Pres. Seymour Rose; Exec. Dir. Roy Shenberg; Exec. V. P., Jerome Verlin. Fraternal organization devoted to community welfare, protection of rights of Jewish people, and activities that foster Jewish identity and provide support for Israel. Through its philanthropic arm, the Brith Sholom Foundation (1962), sponsors Brith Sholom House in Philadelphia, nonprofit senior-citizen apartments; and Brith Sholom Beit Halochem in Haifa, Israel, rehabilitation, social, and sports center for disabled Israeli veterans, operated by Zahal. Chmn. Martin Winit; Exec. Dir. Saundra Laub. *Brith Sholom Digest; monthly news bulletin.*

FREE SONS OF ISRAEL (1849). 250 Fifth Ave., Suite 201, NYC 10001. (212)725-3690. FAX: (212)725-5874. Grand Master Arlene Hoberman Kyler; Grand Sec. Ronald J. Laszlo. Oldest Jewish fraternal-benefit society in U.S. Affordable membership men & women (18+). Supports Israel, UJA projects, non-sectarian toy drives/philanthropies. Social Action fights anti-Semitism, supports human rights. Member benefits-IBM Metro Credit Union, scholarships, cemetery, discounted Long Term Care Insurance, educational and social functions, Free Model Seder. *Free Sons Reporter.* (WWW.FREESONS.ORG)

JEWISH LABOR BUND (Directed by WORLD COORDINATING COMMITTEE OF THE BUND) (1897; Reorg. 1947). 25 E. 21 St., NYC 10010. (212)475-0059. FAX: (212) 473-5102. Acting Pres. Motl Zelmanowics; Sec. Gen. Benjamin Nade. Coordinates activities of Bund organizations throughout the world and represents them in the Socialist International; spreads the ideas of socialism as formulated by the Jewish Labor Bund; publishes books and periodicals on world problems, Jewish life, socialist theory and policy,

and on the history, activities, and ideology of the Jewish Labor Bund. *Unser Tsait* (U.S.); *Lebns-Fragn* (Israel); *Unser Gedank* (Australia).

SEPHARDIC JEWISH BROTHERHOOD OF AMERICA, INC. (1915). 97-45 Queens Blvd., Rm. 610, Rego Park, NY 11374. (718)459-1600. Pres. Bernard Ouziel; Sec. Irving Barocas. A benevolent fraternal organization seeking to promote the industrial, social, educational, and religious welfare of its members. *Sephardic Brother.*

SIGMA ALPHA MU FRATERNITY (1909). 9245 No. Meridian St., Ste. 105, Indianapolis, IN 46260. (317)846-0600. FAX: (317)846-9462. E-mail:samhq@sam.org. Sup. Prior Leland P.Manders; Exec. Dir. Aaron M. Girson. Founded at the City College of NY as a fraternity of Jewish men, currently active on 70 campuses across North America. Encourages students to take an active role on campus, offers leadership opportunities and financial aid to members and scholarships to leaders of Jewish youth groups. *Octogonian of Sigma Alpha Mu (quarterly).*

THE WORKMEN'S CIRCLE/ARBETER RING (1900). 45 E. 33 St., NYC 10016. (212) 889-6800. FAX: (212)532-7518. E-mail: member@circle.org. Pres. Martin Krupnick; Exec. Dir. Robert Kestenbaum. Fosters Jewish identity and participation in Jewish life through Jewish, especially Yiddish, culture and education, friendship, mutual aid, and the pursuit of social and economic justice. Offices are located throughout the U.S. and Canada. Member services include: Jewish cultural seminars, concerts, theater, Jewish schools, children's camp and adult resort, fraternal and singles activities, a Jewish Book Center, public affairs/social action, health insurance plans, medical/dental/legal services, life insurance plans, cemetery/funeral benefits, social services, geriatric homes and centers, and travel services. *The Call.* (WWW.CIRCLE.ORG)

ZETA BETA TAU FRATERNITY (1898). 3905 Vincennes Rd., Suite 300, Indianapolis, IN 46268. (317)334-1898. FAX: (317)334-1899. E-mail: zbt@zbtnational.org. Pres. Kenneth L. Simon, M.D.; Exec. Dir. Jonathan I. Yulish. Oldest historically Jewish fraternity; promotes intellectual awareness, social responsibility, integrity, and brotherhood among over 5,000 undergrads and 110,000 alumni in the U.S. and Canada. Encourages leadership and diversity through mutual respect of all heritages; nonsectarian since 1954. A brotherhood of Kappa Nu, Phi Alpha, Phi Epsilon Pi, Phi Sigma Delta, Zeta Beta Tau. *The Deltan (quarterly).* (www. zbt.org)

SOCIAL WELFARE

AMC CANCER RESEARCH CENTER (Formerly JEWISH CONSUMPTIVES' RELIEF SOCIETY, 1904; Incorporated as American Medical Center at Denver, 1954). 1600 Pierce St., Denver, CO 80214. (303)233-6501. FAX: (303)239-3400. E-mail: edelmanj@amc. org. Pres./CEO Bob R. Baker; Exec. V-Pres. Research Dr. Tom Slaga. A nationally recognized leader in the fight against cancer; employs a three-pronged, interdisciplinary approach that combines laboratory, clinical, and community cancer-control research to advance the prevention, early detection, diagnosis, and treatment of the disease. The exclusive scientific focus of our work is the prevention and control of cancer and other major diseases. *The Quest for Answers; Annual Report.* (WWW.AMC.ORG)

AMCHA FOR TSEDAKAH (1990). 9800 Cherry Hill Rd., College Park, MD 20740. (301) 937-2600. Pres. Rabbi Bruce E. Kahn. Solicits and distributes contributions to Jewish charitable organizations in the U.S. and Israel; accredits organizations which serve an important tsedakah purpose, demonstrate efficiency and fiscal integrity, and also support pluralism. Contributors are encouraged to earmark contributions for specific organizations; all contributions to General Fund are forwarded to the charitable institutions, as operating expenses are covered by a separate fund. *Newspaper supplement.*

AMERICAN JEWISH CORRECTIONAL CHAPLAINS ASSOCIATION, INC. (formerly NATIONAL COUNCIL OF JEWISH PRISON CHAPLAINS) (1937). 10 E. 73 St., NYC 10021-4194. (212)879-8415. FAX: (212) 772-3977. (Cooperates with the New York Board of Rabbis.) Supports spiritual, moral, and social services for Jewish men and women in corrections; stimulates support of correctional chaplaincy; provides spiritual and professional fellowship for Jewish correctional chaplains; promotes sound standards for correctional chaplaincy; schedules workshops and research to aid chaplains in counseling and with religious services for Jewish inmates. Constituent, American Correctional Chaplains Association. *Chaplains Manual.*

AMERICAN JEWISH SOCIETY FOR SERVICE, INC. (1950). 15 E. 26 St., Rm. 1029, NYC 10010. (212)683-6178. Email: aud1750 @aol.com. Founder/Chmn. Henry Kohn; Pres. Lawrence G. Green; Exec. Dirs. Carl & Audrey Brenner. Conducts voluntary work-service camps each summer to enable high school juniors and seniors to perform humanitarian service.

ASSOCIATION OF JEWISH AGING SERVICES (Formerly NORTH AMERICAN ASSOCIATION OF JEWISH HOMES AND HOUSING FOR THE AGING) (1960). 316 Pennsylvania Ave., SE, Suite 402, Washington, DC 20003. (202) 543-7500. FAX: (202)543-4090. E-mail: ajas@ajas.org. Pres. Jodi L. Lyons; Chmn. Michael Ellentuck. Represents nearly all the not-for-profit charitable homes and housing for the Jewish aging; promotes excellence in performance and quality of service through fostering communication and education and encouraging advocacy for the aging; conducts annual conferences and institutes. *Directory; The Scribe (quarterly newsletter).*

ASSOCIATION OF JEWISH CENTER PROFESSIONALS (1918). 15 E. 26 St., NYC 10010-1579. (212)532-4949. FAX: (212) 481-4174. E-mail: ajcp@jcca.org. Pres. Susan Bender; Exec. Dir. Harvey Rosenzweig. Seeks to enhance the standards, techniques, practices, scope, and public understanding of Jewish community center professionals and kindred agency work. *Kesher.*

ASSOCIATION OF JEWISH COMMUNITY ORGANIZATION PERSONNEL (AJCOP) (1969). 14619 Horseshoe Trace, Wellington, FL 33414. (561)795-4853. FAX: (561)798-0358. E-mail: marlene@ajcop.org. Pres. Rabbi Daniel Allen; Exec. Dir. Louis B. Solomon. An organization of professionals engaged in areas of fund-raising, endowments, budgeting, social planning, financing, administration, and coordination of services. Objectives are to develop and enhance professional practices in

Jewish communal work; to maintain and improve standards, practices, scope, and public understanding of the field of community organization, as practiced through local federations, national agencies, other organizations, settings, and private practitioners. *Prolog (quarterly newspaper); Proceedings (annual record of papers and speeches).* (WWW.AJCOP.ORG)

ASSOCIATION OF JEWISH FAMILY AND CHILDREN'S AGENCIES (1972). 557 Cranbury Rd., Suite 2, E. Brunswick, NJ 08816-5419. (800) 634-7346. FAX: (732)432-7127. E-mail: ajfca@ajfca.org. Pres. Bert J. Goldberg; Bd. Chair. Lawrence Abramson. The national service organization for Jewish family and children's agencies in the U.S. and Canada. Reinforces member agencies in their efforts to sustain and enhance the quality of Jewish family and communal life. Operates the Elder Support Network for the national Jewish community. *Tachlis (quarterly); Professional Opportunities Bulletin; Executive Digest (monthly).* (WWW.AJFCA.ORG)

AVODAH: THE JEWISH SERVICE CORPS (1996). 443 Park Ave. So., 11th floor, NYC 10016. (212)545-7759. FAX: (212)686-1353. E-mail: info@avodah.net. Exec. Dir. Rabbi David Rosenn. Combines direct antipoverty work in NYC and Washington D.C. with Jewish study and community-building; corps members live together and work full-time for a year on housing, welfare, and education, and other matters. (WWW.AVODAH.NET)

BARON DE HIRSCH FUND (1891). 130 E. 59 St., 12th fl., NYC 10022. (212)836-1358. FAX: (212)453-6512. Pres. Jenny Morgenthal; Mng. Dir. Lauren Katzowitz. Aids Jewish immigrants in the U.S. and Israel by giving grants to agencies active in resettlement, focusing on educational, community development, and vocational training.

B'NAI B'RITH (1843). 1640 Rhode Island Ave., NW, Washington, DC 20036. (202)857-6600. FAX: (202)857-1099. Pres. Joel S. Kaplan; Exec. V.-Pres. Daniel S. Mariaschin. International Jewish organization, with affiliates in 58 countries. Offers programs designed to ensure the preservation of Jewry and Judaism: Jewish education, community volunteer service, expansion of human rights, assistance to Israel, housing for the elderly, leadership training, rights of Jews in all countries to study their heritage. *International Jewish Monthly; B'nai B'rith Today.*

———, ANTI-DEFAMATION LEAGUE OF (*see* p. 542)

———, HILLEL (*see* p. 573)

———, KLUTZNICK MUSEUM (*see* p. 547)

———, YOUTH ORGANIZATION (*see* p. 571)

CITY OF HOPE NATIONAL MEDICAL CENTER AND BECKMAN RESEARCH INSTITUTE (1913). 1500 E. Duarte Rd., Duarte, CA 91010. (626)359-8111. FAX: (626) 301-8115. E-mail: dhalper@coh.org. Exec. V. P. Krontiris; Medical and Scientific Affairs Theodore. City of Hope is one of the world's leading research and treatment centers for cancer and other life-threatening diseases, including diabetes and HIV/AIDS. A pioneer in the fields of bone marrow transplantation and genetics, City of Hope is a Comprehensive Cancer Center, the highest designation bestowed by the National Cancer Institute, and a founding member of the National Comprehensive Cancer Network. *City of Hope Cancer Research Center Report.*

CONFERENCE OF JEWISH COMMUNAL SERVICE (*see* JEWISH COMMUNAL SERVICE ASSOCIATION OF N. AMERICA)

COUNCIL OF JEWISH FEDERATIONS (*see* UNITED JEWISH COMMUNITIES)

INTERNATIONAL ASSOCIATION OF JEWISH VOCATIONAL SERVICES (Formerly JEWISH OCCUPATIONAL COUNCIL) (1939). 1845 Walnut St., Suite 640, Philadelphia, PA 19103. (215) 854-0233. FAX: (215)854-0212. E-mail: coheng@iajvs.org. Exec. Dir. Genie Cohen; Vivian Seigel, President.Not-for-profit membership association of Jewish-sponsored social service agencies in the U.S., Canada, and Israel. Provides member agencies with technical, informational, and communications support; researches funding opportunities, develops collaborative program models, and represents Jewish vocational network nationally and internationally. Sponsors annual conference for members. Member agencies provide a wide range of educational, vocational, and rehabilitation services to both the Jewish and non-Jewish communities. *Executive quarterly newsletter.* (WWW.IAJVS.ORG)

INTERNATIONAL COUNCIL ON JEWISH SOCIAL AND WELFARE SERVICES (1961). c/o American Jewish Joint Distribution Committee, 711 Third Ave., NYC 10017. (NY liaison office with UN headquarters.) (212)687-6200. FAX: (212)370-5467. E-mail: newyork@jdcny.org. Pres. Eugene J. Ribokoff; Exec. V. P. Steven Schwager. Provides assistance to Jewish communities in Europe, Asia, Africa, and the Mideast, including welfare programs for Jews in need. Current concerns include: Rescuing Jews from areas of distress, facilitating community development in the former Soviet Union; helping to meet Israel's social service needs by developing innovative programs that create new opportunities for the country's most vulnerable populations; youth activities in Eastern Europe and nonsectariean development and disaster assistance. *Annual Report, JDC's Activities in the Former Soviet Union; JDC: One People One Heart, Crisis in Argentina Monthly Update.*

JBI INTERNATIONAL (FOUNDED IN 1931 AS THE JEWISH BRAILLE INSTITUTE OF AMERICA, INC.) (1931). 110 E. 30 St., NYC 10016. (212)889-2525. FAX: (212)689-3692. E-mail: sradinsky@jbilibrary.org. Pres. Barbara B. Friedman; Exec. V.-Pres. Dr. Ellen Isler. Provides Jewish books for the visually impaired, blind and reading-disabled on tape, in large print, and in Braille. International program serves clients in more than 50 countries; sponsors special programs in Israel and Eastern Europe. Periodical and journals available to our subscribers include *Moment, Tikkun, the Jerusalem Reporter and Commentary.* (WWW.JBILIBRARY.ORG)

JEWISH CHILDREN'S ADOPTION NETWORK (1990). PO Box 147016, Denver, CO 80214-7016. (303)573-8113. FAX: (303) 893-1447. E-mail: jcan@qwest.net. Pres. Stephen Krausz; Exec. Dir. Vicki Krausz. An adoption exchange founded for the primary purpose of locating adop-tive families for Jewish infants and children. Works with some 200 children a year, throughout N. Amer., 85-90% of whom have special needs. No fees charged for services, which include birth-parent and adoptive-parent counseling. *Quarterly newsletter.* (WWW.USERS.QWEST.NET/JCAN)

JEWISH COMMUNAL SERVICE ASSOCIATION OF N. AMERICA (1899; formerly CONFERENCE OF JEWISH COMMUNAL SERVICE). 15 E. 26 St., Suite 917, NYC 10010-1579. (212)532-0167. FAX: (212)532-1461. E-mail: info@jcsana.org. Pres. Dr. Audrey S. Weiner; Exec. Dir. Brenda Gevertz. Serves as forum for all professional philosophies in community service, for testing new experiences, proposing new ideas, and questioning or reaffirming old concepts; umbrella organization for 7 major Jewish communal service groups. Concerned with advancement of professional personnel practices and standards. *Journal of Jewish Communal Service; Concurrents.*

JEWISH COMMUNITY CENTERS ASSOCIATION OF NORTH AMERICA (Formerly JWB) (1917). 15 E. 26 St., NYC 10010-1579. (212)532-4949. FAX: (212)481-4174. E-mail: info@jcca.org. Chair Edward H. Kaplan; Pres. Allan Finkelstein. The leadership network of, and central agency for, the Jewish Community Center movement, comprising more than 275 JCCs, YM-YWHAs, and camps in the U.S. and Canada, which annually serve more than one million members and an additional million non-member users. JCC Association offers a wide range of services and resources to strengthen the capacity of its affiliates to provide educational, cultural, social, Jewish identity-building, and recreational programs to enhance the lives of North American Jews of all ages and backgrounds. Additionally, the movement fosters and strengthens connections between North American Jews and Israel as well as with world Jewry. JCC Association is also the only U.S. government-accredited agency for serving the religious and social needs of Jewish military personnel, their families, and patients in VA hospitals through JWB Chaplains Council. *JCC Circle; Chaplines; other newsletters for JCC professionals.* (WWW.JCCA.ORG)

———, JEWISH WELFARE BOARD JEWISH CHAPLAINS COUNCIL (Formerly COMMISSION ON JEWISH CHAPLAINCY) (1940). 15 E. 26 St., NYC 10010-1579. (212)532-4949. FAX: (212)481-4174. E-mail: nathanlandman@jcca.com. Chmn. Rabbi David S. Goldstein; Dir. Rabbi David Lapp; Dep. Dir. Rabbi Nathan M. Landman. Recruits, endorses, and serves Jewish military and Veterans Administration chaplains on behalf of the American Jewish community and the major rabbinic bodies; trains and assists Jewish lay leaders where there are no chaplains, for service to Jewish military personnel, their families, and hospitalized veterans. *CHAPLINES newsletter.*

JEWISH FAMILY AND CHILDREN'S PROFESSIONALS ASSOCIATION (*see* Jewish Social Services Professionals Association)

JEWISH FUND FOR JUSTICE (1984). 260 Fifth Ave., Suite 701, NYC 10001. (212) 213-2113. FAX: (212)213-2233. E-mail: jfjustice@jfjustice.org. Bd. Chmn. John Levy; Exec. Dir. Marlene Provizer. The Jewish Fund for Justice is the only national Jewish organization solely committed to fighting the injustice of poverty in America. By assisting on a nondenominational basis grassroots organizations struggling for decent housing, schools and jobs, and by helping Jews develop community-based, social justice partnerships, the Jewish Fund for Justice brings to life the core Jewish values of *tikkun olam* (repair of the world) and *tzedakah* (righteous giving). Giving opportunities include general support, family, wedding, and youth endowment funds and planned giving. *Annual report, newsletter.* (WWW.JFJUSTICE.ORG)

JEWISH FUNDERS NETWORK (1990). 15 E. 26 St., Suite 1038, NYC 10010. (212) 726-0177. FAX: (212) 726-0195. E-mail: jfn@jfunders.org. Pres. Mark Charendoff. International agency providing leadership, programs and services to help Jewish grantmakers be more effective and strategic in their philanthropy. JFN members collaborate and plan so that their money can be used to effectively change the world. Key initiatives: International Conference, regional programs, publications, strategic partnerships, web site, consultation, resources and referral. *Quarterly Newsletter, Reports on Philanthropy.*

JEWISH SOCIAL SERVICES PROFESSIONALS ASSOCIATION (JSSPA) (1965). c/o AJFCA, 557 Cranbury Rd., Suite 2, E. Brunswick, NJ 08816-0549. (800) 634-7346. FAX: (732)432-7127. E-mail: ajfca @ajfca.org. Chmn. Jaclynn Faffer; Chair Elect Norman Keane. Brings together executives, supervisors, managers, caseworkers, and related professionals in Jewish Family Service and related agencies. Seeks to enhance professional skills, improve personnel standards, further Jewish continuity and identity, and strengthen Jewish family life. Provides a national and regional forum for professional discussion and learning; functions under the auspices of the Association of Jewish Family and Children's Agencies. *Newsletter.* (WWW.AJFCA.ORG)

JEWISH WOMEN INTERNATIONAL (1897). 1828 L St., NW, Suite 250, Washington, DC 20036. (202)857-1300. FAX: (202) 857-1380. E-mail: jwi@jwi.org. Pres. Barbara Rabkin; Exec. Dir. Gail Rubinson. Jewish Women International breaks the cycle of violence by developing emotionally healthy adults, empowering women and strengthening families. Jewish Women International accomplishes its goals through direct service programs, education, advocacy and the promotion of "best practice" models. Offers programs in the United States, Canada, and Israel. *Jewish Woman Magazine (quarterly).* (WWW.JEWISHWOMEN.ORG)

JWB (*see* JEWISH COMMUNITY CENTERS ASSOCIATION OF NORTH AMERICA)

LEVI HOSPITAL (1914). 300 Prospect Ave., Hot Springs, AR 71901. (501)624-1281. FAX: (501) 622-3500. E-mail: levihospital @hsnp.com. Pres. Philip M. Clay; Admin. Patrick G. McCabe. Offers outpatient rehab, including therapy sessions in large thermal heated pool. Other programs: adult/geriatric inpatient and outpatient psychiatric program, child/adolescent psychiatric clinic, hospice care, home health care, osteoporosis clinic, Levi Rehabilitation Unit, a cooperative effort of Levi and St. Joseph's hospitals (inpatient rehab). *The Progress Chart; The Legacy.*

MAZON: A JEWISH RESPONSE TO HUNGER (1985). 1990 S. Bondy Drive, Suite 260, Los Angeles, CA 90025. (310)442-0020. FAX: (310)442-0030. Email:mazonmail@mazon. org. Exec. Dir. Eric Schockman, PhD. A grant-making and fund-raising organization that raises funds in the Jewish community and provides grants to nonprofit 501©(3) organizations which aim to prevent and alleviate hunger in the United States and abroad. Grantees include food pantries, food banks, multi-service organizations, advocacy, education and research projects, and international relief and development organizations. *Annual Report, 2 newsletters each year.*

NATIONAL ASSOCIATION OF JEWISH CHAP-LAINS (1988). 901 Route 10, Whippany, NJ 07981. (973)929-3168. FAX: (973) 736-9193. E-mail: cecille3@juno.com. Pres. Rabbi Stephen Roberts; Natl. Coord. Cecille Allman Asekoff. A professional organization for people functioning as Jewish chaplains in hospitals, nursing homes, geriatric, psychiatric, correctional, and military facilities. Provides collegial support, continuing education, professional certification, and resources for the Jewish community on issues of pastoral and spiritual care. *The Jewish Chaplain.*

NATIONAL COUNCIL OF JEWISH PRISON CHAPLAINS, INC. (*see* AMERICAN JEWISH CORRECTIONAL CHAPLAINS ASSOCIATION, INC.)

NATIONAL COUNCIL OF JEWISH WOMEN (1893). 53 W. 23 St., NYC 10010. (212) 645-4048. FAX: (212)645-7466. E-mail: actionline@ncjw.org. Pres. Phyllis Snyder. Works to improve the lives of women, children, and families in the United States and Israel; strives to insure individual rights and freedoms for all. NCJW volunteers deliver vital services in 500 U.S. communities and carry out NCJW's advocacy agenda through a powerful grassroots network. *NCJW Journal; Washington Newsletter.* (WWW.NCJW.ORG)

NATIONAL INSTITUTE FOR JEWISH HOSPICE (1985). PO Box 48025, Los Angeles, CA 90048. (800)446-4448. 330 Broad Ave., Englewood, NJ 07631. (201)816-7324. FAX: (201)816-7321. Pres. Rabbi Maurice Lamm; Exec. Dir. Shirley Lamm. Serves as a national Jewish hospice resource center. Through conferences, research, publications, referrals, and counseling services offers guidance, training, and information to patients, family members, clergy of all faiths, professional caregivers, and volunteers who work with the Jewish terminally ill. *Jewish Hospice Times.*

NATIONAL JEWISH CHILDREN'S LEUKEMIA FOUNDATION (1990). 172 Madison Avenue, NYC 10016. (212)686-2722. FAX: (212)686-2750. E-mail: leukemia@erols. com. Pres./Founder Zvi Shor. Dedicated to saving the lives of children. Programs:

Bone Marrow Donor Search, Stem Cell Banking-freezing cells from babies' umbilical cords for long-term storage, in case of need for bone marrow; Make-A-Dream-Come True-granting wishes for terminally ill children; Referral Service; Patient Advocacy. (WWW.LEUKEMIA FOUNDATION.ORG)

NATIONAL JEWISH MEDICAL AND RESEARCH CENTER (Formerly NATIONAL JEWISH HOS-PITAL/NATIONAL ASTHMA CENTER) (1899). 1400 Jackson St., Denver, CO 80206. (800)222-LUNG. E-mail: lungline@njc. org. Pres./CEO Lynn M. Taussig, MD; Bd. Chmn. Lawrence Gelfond. The only medical and research center in the United States devoted entirely to respiratory, allergic, and immune system diseases, including asthma, tuberculosis, emphysema, severe allergies, AIDS, and cancer, and autoimmune diseases such as lupus. Dedicated to enhancing prevention, treatment, and cures through research, and to developing and providing innovative clinical programs for treating patients regardless of age, religion, race, or ability to pay. *New Directions; Medical Scientific Update.* (WWW.NATIONAL JEWISH.ORG)

NORTH AMERICAN ASSOCIATION OF JEWISH HOMES AND HOUSING FOR THE AGING (*see* ASSOCIATION OF JEWISH AGING SERVICES)

UNITED JEWISH COMMUNITIES (*see* p. 569)

UNITED ORDER TRUE SISTERS, INC. (UOTS) (1846). 100 State St., Suite 1020, Albany, NY 12207. (518)436-1670, Fax (518) 436-1573. Pres. Marian S. Cohen; Fin. Sec. Betty Peyser; Treas. Rose Goldberg. Charitable, community service, especially home supplies, etc., for indigent cancer victims; supports camps for children with cancer. *Inside UotS.* (WWW.UOTS.ORG)

WORLD COUNCIL OF JEWISH COMMUNAL SERVICE (1966; REORG. 1994). 711 Third Ave., 10th fl., NYC 10017. (212)687-6200. FAX: (212)370-5467. Pres. Howard Charish; Assoc. Pres. Dr. Jack Habib; Exec. V.-Pres. Theodore Comet. Seeks to build Jewish community worldwide by enhancing professional-to-professional connections, improving professional practice through interchange of experience and sharing of expertise, fostering professional training programs, and stimulating research. Conducts quadrennial conferences in Jerusalem and periodic regional meetings. *Proceedings of international conferences; newsletters.*

PROFESSIONAL ASSOCIATIONS*

AMERICAN ASSOCIATION OF RABBIS (Religious, Educational)

AMERICAN CONFERENCE OF CANTORS, UNION FOR REFORM JUDAISM (Religious, Educational)

AMERICAN JEWISH CORRECTIONAL CHAPLAINS ASSOCIATION, INC. (Social Welfare)

AMERICAN JEWISH PRESS ASSOCIATION (Cultural)

AMERICAN JEWISH PUBLIC RELATIONS SOCIETY (Community Relations)

ASSOCIATION OF HILLEL/JEWISH CAMPUS PROFESSIONALS (Religious, Educational)

ASSOCIATION OF JEWISH CENTER PROFESSIONALS (Social Welfare)

ASSOCIATION OF JEWISH COMMUNITY ORGANIZATION PERSONNEL (Social Welfare)

ASSOCIATION OF JEWISH COMMUNITY RELATIONS WORKERS (Community Relations)

CANTORS ASSEMBLY (Religious, Educational)

CENTRAL CONFERENCE OF AMERICAN RABBIS (Religious, Educational)

COUNCIL OF JEWISH ORGANIZATIONS IN CIVIL SERVICE (Community Relations)

INTERNATIONAL JEWISH MEDIA ASSOCIATION (Cultural)

JEWISH CHAPLAINS COUNCIL, JWB (Social Welfare)

JEWISH COMMUNAL SERVICE ASSOCIATION OF N. AMERICA (Social Welfare)

JEWISH EDUCATORS ASSEMBLY, UNITED SYNAGOGUE OF CONSERVATIVE JUDAISM (Religious, Educational)

JEWISH SOCIAL SERVICES PROFESSIONALS ASSOCIATION (Social Welfare)

JEWISH TEACHERS ASSOCIATION–MORIM (Religious, Educational)

NATIONAL ASSOCIATION OF HEBREW DAY SCHOOL ADMINISTRATORS, TORAH UMESORAH (Religious, Educational)

NATIONAL ASSOCIATION OF JEWISH CHAPLAINS (Social Welfare)

NATIONAL ASSOCIATION OF TEMPLE ADMINISTRATORS, UNION FOR REFORM JUDAISM (Religious, Educational)

NATIONAL ASSOCIATION OF TEMPLE EDUCATORS, UNION FOR REFORM JUDAISM (Religious, Educational)

NATIONAL CONFERENCE OF YESHIVA PRINCIPALS, TORAH UMESORAH (Religious, Educational)

NORTH AMERICAN ASSOCIATION OF SYNAGOGUE EXECUTIVES, UNITED SYNAGOGUE OF CONSERVATIVE JUDAISM (Religious, Educational)

RABBINICAL ALLIANCE OF AMERICA (Religious, Educational)

RABBINICAL ASSEMBLY (Religious, Educational)

RABBINICAL COUNCIL OF AMERICA (Religious, Educational)

RECONSTRUCTIONIST RABBINICAL ASSOCIATION (Religious, Educational)

UNION OF ORTHODOX RABBIS OF THE U.S. AND CANADA (Religious, Educational)

WORLD CONFERENCE OF JEWISH COMMUNAL SERVICE (Community Relations)

WOMEN'S ORGANIZATIONS*

AMIT WOMEN (Israel-Related)

BRANDEIS UNIVERSITY NATIONAL WOMEN'S COMMITTEE (Educational)

EMUNAH WOMEN OF AMERICA (Israel-Related)

HADASSAH, THE WOMEN'S ZIONIST ORGANIZATION OF AMERICA (Israel-Related)

JEWISH WOMEN INTERNATIONAL (Social Welfare)

NA'AMAT USA, THE WOMEN'S LABOR ZIONIST ORGANIZATION OF AMERICA (Israel-Related)

NATIONAL COUNCIL OF JEWISH WOMEN (Social Welfare)

UOTS (Social Welfare)

WOMEN OF REFORM JUDAISM—FEDERATION OF TEMPLE SISTERHOODS, UNION

---

*For fuller listings see under category in parentheses

FOR REFORM JUDAISM (Religious, Educational)

WOMEN'S AMERICAN ORT, AMERICAN ORT FEDERATION (Overseas aid)

WOMEN'S BRANCH OF THE UNION OF ORTHODOX JEWISH CONGREGATIONS OF AMERICA (Religious, Educational)

WOMEN'S DIVISION OF POALE AGUDATH ISRAEL OF AMERICA (Israel-Related)

WOMEN'S LEAGUE FOR CONSERVATIVE JUDAISM (Religious, Educational)

WOMEN'S LEAGUE FOR ISRAEL, INC. (Israel-Related)

WOMEN'S ORGANIZATION, YESHIVA UNIVERSITY (Religious, Educational)

YOUTH AND STUDENT ORGANIZATIONS*

AGUDATH ISRAEL OF AMERICA (Religious, Educational)

B'NAI B'RITH YOUTH ORGANIZATION (Religious, Educational)

BNEI AKIVA OF NORTH AMERICA, RELIGIOUS ZIONISTS OF AMERICA (Israel-Related)

HABONIM—DROR NORTH AMERICA (Israel-Related)

HASHOMER HATZAIR, SOCIALIST ZIONIST YOUTH MOVEMENT (Israel-Related)

HILLEL (Religious, Educational)

KADIMA, UNITED SYNAGOGUE OF CONSERVATIVE JUDAISM (Religious, Educational)

NATIONAL CONFERENCE OF SYNAGOGUE YOUTH, UNION OF ORTHODOX JEWISH CONGREGATIONS OF AMERICA (Religious, Educational)

NATIONAL JEWISH COMMITTEE ON SCOUTING (Religious, Educational)

NATIONAL JEWISH GIRL SCOUT COMMITTEE (Religious, Educational)

NORTH AMERICAN ALLIANCE FOR JEWISH YOUTH (Religious, Educational)

NORTH AMERICAN FEDERATION OF TEMPLE YOUTH, UNION FOR REFORM JUDAISM (Religious, Educational)

STUDENT STRUGGLE FOR SOVIET JEWRY— see Center for Russian Jewry (Community Relations)

YOUNG JUDAEA/HASHACHAR, HADASSAH (Israel-Related)

YUGNTRUF–YOUTH FOR YIDDISH (Cultural)

CANADA

AISH HATORAH (1981). 949 Clark Ave., W., Thornhill, ONT L4J8G6. (905)764-1818. FAX: (905)764-1606. E-mail: www. Aish. com.Edu. Dir. Rabbi Ahron Hoch; Dr. Allan Seidenfeld. An educational center, a community center, and a network of synagogues throughout Toronto; seeks to reawaken Jewish values, ignite Jewish pride and promote Jewish unity through education; reaches out to Jews from all backgrounds in a friendly, warm and non-judgmental environment. *Shabbat Shalom Fax, Monthly newsletter-Village Shul, Winter, Sping, Summer, Fall Calendars.* (WWW.AISH.EDU)

B'NAI BRITH CANADA (1875). 15 Hove St., Downsview, ONT M3H 4Y8. (416)633-6224. FAX: (416)630-2159. E-mail: fdimant@bnaibrith.ca. Pres. Rochelle Wilner; Exec. V.-Pres. Frank Dimant. Canadian Jewry's major advocacy and service organization; maintains an office of Government Relations in Ottawa and co-sponsors the Canada Israel Committee; makes representations to all levels of government on matters of Jewish concern; promotes humanitarian causes and educational programs, community projects, adult Jewish education, and leadership development; dedicated to the preservation and unity of the Jewish community in Canada and to human rights. *The Jewish Tribune.*

——, INSTITUTE FOR INTERNATIONAL AFFAIRS (1987). E-mail: institute@bnaibrith.ca. Ch. Rochelle Wilner; Natl. Dir. Ruth Klein. Identifies and protests the abuse of human rights worldwide. Advocates on behalf of Israel and Jewish communities in distress. Monitors national and international legislation dealing with war crimes. Activities include briefs and consultations with governmental and non-governmental organiza-

*For fuller listings see under category in parentheses

tions, research and public education, advocacy and community mobilization, media monitoring, and international conferences and fact-finding missions. *Ad hoc publications on human rights issues.*

——, LEAGUE FOR HUMAN RIGHTS (1964). Co-Chmn. Marvin Kurz & Dr Harriet Morris. National volunteer association dedicated to combating racism, bigotry, and anti-Semitism. Educational programs include multicultural antiracist workshops, public speakers, Holocaust education, Media Human Rights Awards; legal and legislative activity includes government submissions, court interventions, monitoring hate-group activity, responding to incidents of racism and anti-Semitism; community liaison includes intergroup dialogue and support for aggrieved vulnerable communities and groups. Canadian distributor of ADL material. *Heritage Front Report: 1994; Anti-Semitism on Campus; Skinheads in Canada; Annual Audit of Anti-Semitic Incidents; Holocaust and Hope Educators' Newsletter; Combatting Hate: Guidelines for Community Action.*

——, NATIONAL FIELD SERVICES DEPARTMENT. Natl. Dir. Pearl Gladman. Services community affordable housing projects, sports leagues, food baskets for the needy; coordinates hands-on national volunteer programming, Tel-Aide Distress Line; responsible for lodge membership; direct-mail campaigns, annual convention and foundation dinners.

CANADIAN FRIENDS OF CALI & AMAL (1944). 7005 Kildare Rd., Suite 14, Côte St. Luc, Quebec, H4W 1C1. (514)484-9430. FAX: (514)484-0968. Pres. Harry J.F. Bloomfield, QC; Exec. Dir. Fran Kula. Incorporates Canadian Association for Labour Israel (Histadrut) and Canadian Friends of Amal; supports comprehensive health care and education in Israel. Helps to provide modern medical and surgical facilities and the finest vocational, technical education to the Israeli people of all ages.

CANADIAN FRIENDS OF THE HEBREW UNIVERSITY OF JERUSALEM (1944). 3080 Yonge St., Suite 5024, Toronto, ONT M4N 3N1. (416) 485-8000. FAX: (416)485-8565. E-mail: inquiry@cfhu.org. Pres. Ronald Appleby; Natl. Dir.

Charles S. Diamond. Represents the Hebrew University of Jerusalem in Canada; serves as fund-raising arm for the university in Canada; recruits Canadian students and promotes study programs for foreign students at the university; sponsors social and educational events across Canada.

CANADIAN JEWISH CONGRESS (1919; REORG. 1934). 100 Sparks Street, Suite 650, Ottawa, Ontario K1P 5B7. (613)233-8703. FAX: (613)233-8748. E-mail: canadian jewishcongress@cjc.ca. Pres. Ed Morgan. The community's national voice on public affairs, Canadian Jewish Congress works with governments, community organizations and other partners to fight antisemitism and racism, to promote positive links to Israel and to other Jewish communities, and to support humanitarian and human rights efforts. *DAIS; National Archives Newsletter; regional newsletters.*

CANADIAN YOUNG JUDAEA (1917). 788 Marlee Ave., Suite 205, Toronto, ONT M6B 3K1. (416)781-5156. FAX: (416) 787-3100. E-mail: cyj@idirect.com. Natl. Exec. Dir. Risa Epstein. Strives to attract Jewish youth to Zionism, with goal of aliyah; educates youth about Jewish history and Zionism; prepares them to provide leadership in Young Judaea camps in Canada and Israel and to be concerned Jews. *Judaean L'Madrich; Young Judaean.*

CANADIAN ZIONIST FEDERATION (1967). 5151 Côte St. Catherine Rd., #206, Montreal, PQ H3W 1M6. (514)739-7300. FAX: (514)739-9412. Pres. Kurt Rothschild; Natl. Sec. Florence Simon. Umbrella organization of distinct constituent member Zionist organizations in Canada; carries on major activities in all areas of Jewish life through its departments of education and culture, aliyah, youth and students, public affairs, and small Jewish communities, for the purpose of strengthening the State of Israel and the Canadian Jewish community. *Canadian Zionist.*

——, BUREAU OF EDUCATION AND CULTURE (1972). Pres. Kurt Rothschild. Provides counseling by pedagogic experts, in-service teacher-training courses and seminars in Canada and Israel; national pedagogic council and research center; distributes educational material and teaching aids; supports annual Bible contest and Hebrew-language courses for adults; awards scholarships to Canadian high-school graduates studying for one year in Israel.

HADASSAH–WIZO ORGANIZATION OF CANADA (1917). 1310 Greene Ave., Suite 900, Montreal, PQ H3Z 2B8. (514)937-9431. FAX: (514)933-6483. E-mail:natoff @canadian-hadassah-wizo.org. Natl. Pres. Rochelle Levinson; Natl. Exec. V.-Pres. Lily Frank. Largest women's volunteer Zionist organization in Canada, located in 43 Canadian cities; dedicated to advancing the quality of life of the women and children in Israel through financial assistance and support of its many projects, day-care centers, schools, institutions, and hospitals. In Canada, the organization promotes Canadian ideals of democracy and is a stalwart advocate of women's issues. *Orah Magazine.*

HASHOMER HATZAIR (1913). 1111 Finch Ave. W., #456, Downsview, ONT M3J 2E5. (416)736-1339. FAX: (416)736-1405. E-mail: mail@givathaviva.ca. Shlicha-Ora Merin; Pres. Sheryl Neshel; Sec. Lipa Roth. A Zionist youth movement established over 80 years ago with centers all over the world. In Toronto, there are weekly meetings during the school year where children get a strong sense of their Jewish identity and connection to Israel, celebrate Jewish holidays together and learn to be contributing members of the community. Hashomer Hatzair runs a 6-day residential winter camp and a 6-week summer camp for youth ranging from 7-16 on Otty Lake.

INTERNATIONAL JEWISH CORRESPONDENCE (IJC) (1978). c/o Canadian Jewish Congress, 1590 Dr. Penfield Ave., Montreal, PQ H3G 1C5.9 (514)931-7531. FAX: (514)931-0548. E-mail: barrys@cjc.ca. Founder/Dir. Barry Simon. Aims to encourage contact between Jews of all ages and backgrounds, in all countries, through pen-pal correspondence. Send autobiographical data and stamped self-addressed envelope or its equivalent (to cover cost of Canadian postage) to receive addresses.

JEWISH IMMIGRANT AID SERVICES OF MONTREAL (JIAS) (1922). 5500 Westbury, 2nd Floor, Montreal, Quebec H3W-2W8. (514)342-9351. FAX: (514)342-0287.

E-mail: jiasmail@aol.com. Pres. Joe Kislowicz; Exec. Dir. Shellie Ettinger. JIAS is a national organization assisting the lawful entry of Jews into Canada, as well as their settlement and integration . . . *JIAS News for Clients.*

JEWISH NATIONAL FUND OF CANADA (KEREN KAYEMETH LE'ISRAEL, INC.) (1901). 1980 Sherbrooke St. W., Suite 500, Montreal, PQ H3H 1E8. (514)934-0313. FAX: (514)934-0382. E-mail: mtl@jnf. canada.org. Natl. Pres. Sandra Posluns; Exec. V.-Pres. Joe Rabinovitch. Fundraising organization affiliated with the World Zionist Organization; involved in afforestation, soil reclamation, and development of the land of Israel, including the construction of roads and preparation of sites for new settlements; provides educational materials and programs to Jewish schools across Canada.

LABOUR ZIONIST ALLIANCE OF CANADA (1909). 272 Codsell Ave., Downsview, ONT M3H 3X2. (416)630-9444. FAX: (416) 630-9451. Pres. Josef Krystal; City Committee Chmn. Montreal-Harry Froimovitch. Associated with the World Labor Zionist movement and allied with the Israel Labor party. Provides recreational and cultural programs, mutual aid, and fraternal care to enhance the social welfare of its membership; actively promotes Zionist education, cultural projects, and forums on aspects of Jewish and Canadian concern.

MERETZ CANADA (1950s). 1111 Finch Ave. W., Suite 456, Downsview, ONT M3J 2E5. (416)736-1339. FAX: (416)736-1405. Pres. Joseph Podemski., Vice Pres. Lipa Roth. Acts as a voice of Socialist-Democratic and Zionist points of view within the Jewish community and a focal point for progressive Zionist elements in Canada; affiliated with Hashomer Hatzair and the Givat Haviva Educational Center.

MIZRACHI ORGANIZATION OF CANADA (1941). 296 Wilson Ave., North York, ONT M3H 1S8. (416)630-9266. FAX: (416)630-2305. Pres. Jack Kahn. Promotes religious Zionism, aimed at making Israel a state based on Torah; maintains Bnei Akiva, a summer camp, adult education program, and touring department; supports Mizrachi-Hapoel Hamizrachi and other religious Zionist institutions in

Israel which strengthen traditional Judaism. *Mizrachi Newsletter.*

NATIONAL COMMUNITY RELATIONS COMMITTEE OF CANADIAN JEWISH CONGRESS (1936). 4600 Bathurst St., Toronto, ONT M2R 3V2. (416)631-5673. FAX: (416) 635-1408. E-mail: mprutschi@ujafed. org. Chmn. Ellen T. Cole; Pres. Keith M. Landy; Dir. Manuel Prutschi. Seeks to safeguard the status, rights, and welfare of Jews in Canada; to combat antisemitism, and promote understanding and goodwill among all ethnic and religious groups.

NATIONAL COUNCIL OF JEWISH WOMEN OF CANADA (1897). 118-1588 Main St., Winnipeg, MAN R2V 1Y3. (204)339-9700. FAX: (204)334-3779. E-mail: info@ncjwc. org. Chmn. Carol Slater; Natl. V.-Pres. Roz Fine & Brenlee Gurvey Gales. Dedicated to furthering human welfare in the Jewish and general communities, locally, nationally, and internationally; through an integrated program of education, service, and social action seeks to fulfill unmet needs and to serve the individual and the community. *National ByLines.*

ORT CANADA (1948). 3101 Bathurst St., Suite 604, Toronto, ONT M6A 2A6. (416)787-0339. FAX: (416) 787-9420. E-mail: info@ort-toronto.org. Pres. Arthur Silber; Exec. Dir. Joel Shapiro. Chapters in 11 Canadian cities raise funds for ORT's nonprofit global network of schools where Jewish students learn a wide range of marketable skills, including the most advanced high-tech professions. *Focus Magazine.*

STATE OF ISRAEL BONDS (CANADA-ISRAEL SECURITIES, LTD.) (1953). 970 Lawrence Ave. W., Suite 502, Toronto, ONT M6A 3B6. (416)789-3351. FAX: (416)789-9436. Pres. Norman Spector; Bd. Chmn. George A. Cohon. An international securities organization offering interest-bearing instruments issued by the government of Israel. Invests in every aspect of Israel's economy, including agriculture, commerce, and industry. Israel Bonds are RRSP-approved.

UIA FEDERATIONS OF CANADA (1998). 4600 Bathurst St., Suite 315, Toronto, ONT M2R 3V3. (416)636-7655. FAX: (416)636-9897. E-mail: info@uiafed. org.Exec. V.-Pres. Maxyne Finkelstein. The national Jewish fund-raising orgnazation and community-planning body for Canada.

Jewish Federations, Welfare Funds, Community Councils

UNITED STATES

ALABAMA

BIRMINGHAM

BIRMINGHAM JEWISH FEDERATION (1936; reorg. 1971); Box 130219 (35213-0219); (205)879-0416. FAX: (205)803-1526. E-mail: federation@bjf.org. Exec. Dir. Richard Friedman. (WWW.BJF.ORG)

MOBILE

MOBILE JEWISH WELFARE FUND, INC. (INC. 1966); One Office Park, Suite 219 (36609); (334)343-7197. FAX: (334)343-7197. E-mail: mjwf123@aol.com. Pres. Eileen Susman.

MONTGOMERY

JEWISH FEDERATION OF MONTGOMERY, INC. (1930); 2820 Fairlane Dr. (36120-0058); (334)277-5820. FAX: (334)277-8383. E-mail: jfedmgm@aol.com. Pres. Alan Weil; Admin. Dir. Susan Mayer Bruchis.

ARIZONA

PHOENIX

JEWISH FEDERATION OF GREATER PHOENIX (1940); 12701 N. Scottsdale Rd., Suite 201 (85254); (480)634-4900. FAX: (480)634-4588. E-mail: info@jewishphoenix.org. Pres. Neil Hiller; Exec. Dir. Arthur Paikowsky. (WWW.JEWISHPHOENIX.ORG)

TUCSON

JEWISH FEDERATION OF SOUTHERN ARIZONA (1946); 3822 East River Rd., Suite 100 (85718); (520)577-9393. FAX: (520)577-0734. E-mail: gbarnhill@jfsa.org. Pres. Linda Tumarkin; Exec. Dir. Stuart Mellan. (WWW.JEWISHTUCSON.ORG)

ARKANSAS

LITTLE ROCK

JEWISH FEDERATION OF ARKANSAS (1911); 425 N. University (72205); (501)663-3571. FAX: (501)663-7286. E-mail: jflar@aristotle.net. Pres. Doris Krain; Exec. Dir. Ziva Starr. (WWW.JEWISHARKANSAS.ATFREEWEB.COM)

CALIFORNIA

EAST BAY

JEWISH FEDERATION OF THE GREATER EAST BAY (INCLUDING ALAMEDA & CONTRA COSTA COUNTIES) (1917); 401 Grand Ave., Oakland (94610-5022); (510)839-2900. FAX: (510)839-3996. E-mail: admin@jfed.org. Pres. Marjorie Wolf; Exec. V-Pres. Ami Nahshon. (WWW.JFED.ORG)

FRESNO

JEWISH FEDERATION OF FRESNO; 295 W. Cromwell Ave., Suite 111 (93711-6161); (559)432-2162. FAX: (559)432-0425.

LONG BEACH

JEWISH FEDERATION OF GREATER LONG BEACH AND W. ORANGE COUNTY (1937; inc. 1946); 3801 E. Willow St. (90815); (562)426-7601. FAX: (562)424-3915. E-mail: kgibbs@jewishlongbeach.org. Pres. Richard Lipeles; Exec. Dir. Michael S. Rassler. (WWW.JEWISHLONGBEACH.ORG)

LOS ANGELES

JEWISH FEDERATION COUNCIL OF GREATER LOS ANGELES (1912; reorg. 1959); 6505 Wilshire Blvd., 8th fl. (90048); (323)761-

8000. FAX: (323)761-8235. E-mail: web-coordinator@jewishla.org. Pres. John R. Fishel. (WWW.JEWISHLA.ORG)

ORANGE COUNTY

JEWISH FEDERATION OF ORANGE COUNTY (1964; inc. 1965); 250 E. Baker St., Suite A, Costa Mesa (92626); (714)755-5555. FAX: (714)755-0307. E-mail: info@jfoc.org. Pres. Charles Karp; Exec. Dir. Bunnie Mauldin. (WWW.JFOC.ORG)

PALM SPRINGS

JEWISH FEDERATION OF PALM SPRINGS AND DESERT AREA (1971); 255 N. El Cielo, Suite 430 (92262-6990); (760)325-7281. FAX: (760)325-2188. E-mail: msjfedps@gte.net. Pres. Larry Pitts; Exec. Dir. Mitzi Schafer. (WWW.JEWISHPALMSPRINGS.ORG)

SACRAMENTO

JEWISH FEDERATION OF THE SACRAMENTO REGION (1948); 2351 Wyda Way (95825); (916)486-0906. FAX: (916)486-0816. E-mail: jfed2@juno.com. Pres. Skip Rosenbloom; Exec. Dir. Phillis Helene Cohen. (www.JEWISHSAC.ORG)

SAN DIEGO

UNITED JEWISH FEDERATION OF SAN DIEGO COUNTY (1936); 4950 Murphy Canyon Rd. (92123); (858)571-3444. FAX: (858)571-0701. E-mail: fedujf@ujfsd.org. Pres. Gary Jacobs; Exec. V-Pres. Stephen M. Abramson. (WWW.JEWISHINSANDIEGO.ORG)

SAN FRANCISCO

JEWISH COMMUNITY FEDERATION OF SAN FRANCISCO, THE PENINSULA, MARIN, AND SONOMA COUNTIES (1910; reorg. 1955); 121 Steuart St. (94105); (415)777-0411. FAX: (415)495-6635. E-mail: info@sfjcf.org. Pres. Adele Corvin; Exec. V-Pres. Thomas Dine. (WWW.SFJCF.ORG)

SAN GABRIEL AND POMONA VALLEY

JEWISH FEDERATION OF THE GREATER SAN GABRIEL AND POMONA VALleys; 258 W. Badillo St. (91723-1906); (626)967-3656. FAX: (626)967-5135. E-mail: sgpvfed@aol. com. (WWW.SGPV.ORG)

SAN JOSE

JEWISH FEDERATION OF GREATER SAN JOSE (incl. Santa Clara County except Palo Alto and Los Altos) (1930; reorg. 1950); 14855 Oka Rd., Suite 2, Los Gatos (95030); (408)358-3033. FAX: (408)356-0733. E-mail: federation@jfgsj.org. Pres. Bonnie Slavitt Moore; Interim Exec. Dir. Janet Berg. (www.jewishsiliconvalley.org)

SANTA BARBARA

SANTA BARBARA JEWISH FEDERATION (1974); 524 Chapala St. (93190); (805)957-1115. FAX: (805)957-9230. E-mail: sbjfed @silcom.com. Exec. Dir. Shelly Katz. (WWW.JEWISHSANTABARBARA.ORG)

VENTURA COUNTY

JEWISH FEDERATION OF VENTURA COUNTY; 7620 Foothill Rd. (93004); (805)647-7800. FAX: (805)647-0482. E-mail: ujavtacty@ worldnet.att.net.

COLORADO

DENVER/BOULDER

ALLIED JEWISH FEDERATION OF COLORADO (1936); 300 S. Dahlia St., Denver (80222); (303)321-3399. FAX: (303)322-8328. E-mail: ajfcolo@aol.com. Pres. & CEO: Doug Seserman. (WWW.JEWISHCOLORADO.ORG)

CONNECTICUT

BRIDGEPORT

JEWISH FEDERATION OF EASTERN FAIR-FIELD COUNTY. (1936; reorg. 1981); 4200 Park Ave. (06604-1092); (203)372-6567. FAX: (203)374-0770. E-mail: jccs@snet.net. Chmn. Stanley Strouch; Pres. & CEO Daniel P. Baker. (www.JCCS.ORG)

DANBURY

THE JEWISH FEDERATION OF GREATER DANBURY, INC. (1945); 105 Newton Rd. (06810); (203)792-6353. FAX: (203)748-5099. E-mail: info@thejf.org. Pres. Daniel Wolinsky; Exec. Dir. Judy Prager. (WWW.THEJF.ORG)

EASTERN CONNECTICUT

JEWISH FEDERATION OF EASTERN CON-NECTICUT, INC. (1950; inc. 1970); 28 Channing St., New London (06320); (860)442-8062. FAX: (860)443-4175. E-mail: jfec@ worldnet.att.net. Pres. Myron Hendel; Exec. Dir. Jerome E. Fischer.

GREENWICH

GREENWICH JEWISH FEDERATION (1956); One Holly Hill Lane (06830-6080); (203) 622-1434. FAX: (203)622-1237. E-mail: pezmom3@aol.com. Pres. Martin J. Flashner; Exec. Dir. Pamela Ehrenkranz.

HARTFORD

JEWISH FEDERATION OF GREATER HART-
FORD (1945); 333 Bloomfield Ave., W. Hartford (06117); (860)232-4483. FAX: (860)
232-5221. E-mail: aperrault@jewish
hartford.org. Pres. Robert Nabolchek; Acting Exec. Dir. Steven Bayer. (WWW.JEWISH
HARTFORD.ORG)

NEW HAVEN

JEWISH FEDERATION OF GREATER NEW
HAVEN (1928); 360 Amity Rd., Woodbridge
(06525); (203)387-2424. FAX: (203)387-
1818. E-mail: marinak@megahits.com Pres.
David Schaefer; Exec. Dir. Neil Berro.
(WWW.JEWISHNEWHAVEN.ORG)

NORWALK

(See Westport)

STAMFORD

UNITED JEWISH FEDERATION (INC. 1973);
1035 Newfield Ave., PO Box 3038 (06905);
(203)321-1373. FAX: (203)322-3277. E-mail:
office@ujf.org. Pres. Corrine Lotstein; Dir.
of Dev. Edith Samers. (WWW.UJF.ORG)

WESTERN CONNECTICUT

JEWISH FEDERATION OF WESTERN CON-
NECTICUT (1938); 444 Maine St. N., South-
bury (06488); (203)267-5121. FAX: (203)
267-3392. E-mail: jfedwtby@aol.com. Pres.
Dan Goodman; Exec. Dir. Rob Zwang.
(WWW.JFED.NET)

WESTPORT-WESTON-WILTON-NORWALK

UJA/FEDERATION OF WESTPORT—
WESTON—WILTON—NORWALK (inc. 1980);
431 Post Road E., Suite 22, Westport
(06880); (203)226-8197. FAX: (203)226-
5051. E-mail: rkessler@optonline.net. Pres.
Ed Goldstein; Exec. Dir. Robert Kessler.
(WWW.UJAFEDERATION.ORG)

DELAWARE

WILMINGTON

JEWISH FEDERATION OF DELAWARE, INC.
(1934); 100 W. 10th St., Suite 301 (19801-
1628); (302)427-2100. FAX: (302)427-2438.
E-mail: delawarejfd@jon.cjfny.org. Pres.
Barry Kayne; Exec. V. Pres. Samuel H.
Asher. (WWW.SHALOMDEL.ORG)

DISTRICT OF COLUMBIA

WASHINGTON

THE JEWISH FEDERATION OF GREATER
WASHINGTON, INC. (1935); 6101 Montrose
Rd., Rockville, MD (20852); (301)230-7200.
FAX: (301)230-7265. E-mail: info@jewish
fedwash.org. Pres. Michael C. Gelman;
Exec. V.-Pres. Misha Galperin. (WWW.JEWISH
FEDWASH.ORG)

FLORIDA

BREVARD COUNTY

JEWISH FEDERATION OF BREVARD (1974);
108-A Barton Ave., Rockledge (32955);
(407)636-1824. FAX: (407)636-0614. E-mail:
jfbrevard@aol.com. Pres. Gary Singer; Exec.
Dir. Joanne Bishins.

BROWARD COUNTY

JEWISH FEDERATION OF BROWARD COUNTY
(1943; 1968); 5890 S. Pine Island Rd., Davie
(33351-7319); (954)252-6900. FAX: (954)
252-6892. E-mail: info@jewishfedbroward.
org. Pres. David B. Schulman; Exec. Dir.
Gary N. Rubin. (WWW.JEWISHFEDBROWARD.
ORG)

COLLIER COUNTY

JEWISH FEDERATION OF COLLIER COUNTY
(1974); 1250 Tamiami Trail N., Suite 202,
Naples (33940); (941) 263-4205. FAX: (941)
263-3813. E-mail: jfccfl@aol.com. Pres.
Ann Jacobson. (WWW.JEWISHNAPLES.ORG)

DAYTONA BEACH

(See Volusia & Flagler Counties)

FT. LAUDERDALE

(See Broward County)

GAINESVILLE

JEWISH COUNCIL OF NORTH CENTRAL
FLORIDA; 1861 NW 21 St. (32604); (352)
371-3846. E-mail: oberger@gnv.fdt.net.

JACKSONVILLE

JACKSONVILLE JEWISH FEDERATION, INC.
(1935); 8505 San Jose Blvd. (32217); (904)
448-5000. FAX: (904)448-5715. E-mail: jax-
jewishfed@jon.cjfny.org. Pres. Guy Ben-
rubi; Exec. V.-Pres. Alan Margolies. (www.
JAXJEWISH.ORG)

LEE COUNTY

JEWISH FEDERATION OF LEE AND CHAR-
LOTTE COUNTIES (1974); 6237-E Presidential
Court, Ft. Myers (33919-3568); (941)
481-4449. FAX: (941)481-0139. E-mail:
jfedswfl@aol.com. Pres. Rozzi Osterman;
Exec. Dir. Annette Goodman. (WWW.JEWISH
FEDERATIONSWFL.ORG)

MIAMI

GREATER MIAMI JEWISH FEDERATION, INC.
(1938); 4200 Biscayne Blvd. (33137); (305)

576-4000. FAX: (305)573-4584. E-mail: info @gmjf.or. Pres. Michael M. Adler; Exec. V.-Pres. Jacob Solomon.(WWW.JEWISHMIAMI. ORG)

ORLANDO

JEWISH FEDERATION OF GREATER ORLANDO (1949); 851 N. Maitland Ave.; PO Box 941508, Maitland (32794-1508); (407)645-5933. FAX: (407)645-1172. Pres. James S. Grodin; Exec. Dir. Eric Geboff. (www. ORLANDOJEWISHFED.ORG)

PALM BEACH COUNTY

JEWISH FEDERATION OF PALM BEACH COUNTY, INC. (1962); 4601 Community Dr., W. Palm Beach (33417-2760); (561)478-0700. FAX: (561)478-9696. E-mail: info@ jfedpbco.org. Pres. Norman P. Goldblum; Exec. V.-Pres. Jeffrey L. Klein. (WWW.JEWISH PALMBEACH.ORG)

JEWISH FEDERATION OF SOUTH PALM BEACH COUNTY, INC. (1979); 9901 Donna Klein Blvd. Boca Raton (33428-1788); (561)852-3100. FAX: (561)852-3136. E-mail: dstern @jewishboca.org. (WWW.JEWISHBOCA.ORG)

PENSACOLA

PENSACOLA JEWISH FEDERATION; 800 No. Palafox (32501); (850)434-7992.

PINELLAS COUNTY

JEWISH FEDERATION OF PINELLAS COUNTY, INC. (incl. Clearwater and St. Petersburg) (1950; reincorp. 1974); 13191 Starkey Rd., #8, Largo (33773-1438); (727) 530-3223. FAX: (727)531-0221. E-mail: pinellas@ jfedpinellas.org. Pres. David Abelson; Interim Exec. Dir. Bonnie Friedman. (www. JFEDPINELLAS.ORG)

SARASOTA-MANATEE

SARASOTA-MANATEE JEWISH FEDERATION (1959); 580 S. McIntosh Rd. (34232-1959); (941)371-4546. FAX: (941)378-2947. E-mail: jlederman@smjf.org. Pres. Scott Gordon; Exec. Dir. Jan C. Lederman. (WWW.SMJF.ORG)

TALLAHASSEE

APALACHEE FEDERATION OF JEWISH CHARITIES; PO Box 14825 (32317-4825); (850) 877-3989; FAX: (850)877-7989. E-mail: mdlevy@pol.net.

TAMPA

TAMPA JEWISH FEDERATION (1941); 13009 Community Campus Dr. (33625-4000); (813)264-9000. FAX: (813)265-8450. E-mail: tjfjcc@aol.com. Pres. Lili Kaufman; Exec. V.-Pres. Howard Borer. (WWW.JEWISHTAMPA. ORG)

VOLUSIA & FLAGLER COUNTIES

JEWISH FEDERATION OF VOLUSIA & FLAGLER COUNTIES, INC. (1980); 733 S. Nova Rd., Ormond Beach (32174); (904)672-0294. FAX: (904)673-1316. Pres. Steven I. Unatin; Exec. Dir. Gloria Max.

GEORGIA

ATLANTA

JEWISH FEDERATION OF GREATER ATLANTA, INC. (1905; reorg. 1967); 1440 Spring St., NW (30309-2837); (404)873-1661. FAX: (404) 874-7043/881-4027. E-mail: kkaplan@jfga. org. Pres. Dr. Arnold Rubenstein; Exec. Dir. David I. Sarnat. (WWW. SHALOMATLANTA. ORG)

AUGUSTA

AUGUSTA JEWISH FEDERATION (1937); 898 Weinberger Way, Evans (30809-3636); (706) 228-3636. FAX: (706)868-1660/823-3960. E-mail: augustafed1@knology.net. Exec. Dir. Leah Ronen.

COLUMBUS

JEWISH FEDERATION OF COLUMBUS, INC. (1944); PO Box 6313 (31906); (706)568-6668. Pres. Murray Solomon; Sec. Irene Rainbow.

SAVANNAH

SAVANNAH JEWISH FEDERATION (1943); 5111 Abercorn St. (31403); (912)355-8111. FAX: (912)355-8116. E-mail: jrgreen4@juno.com. Pres. Dr. Paul Kulbersh; Exec. Dir. Moises Paz. (WWW.SAVJ.ORG)

ILLINOIS

CHAMPAIGN-URBANA

CHAMPAIGN-URBANA JEWISH FEDERATION (1929); 503 E. John St., Champaign (61820); (217)367-9872. FAX: (217)344-1540. E-mail: cujf@shalomcu.org. Pres. Anthony E. Novak; Exec. Dir. Lee Melhado. (www. SHALOMCU.ORG)

CHICAGO

JEWISH FEDERATION OF METROPOLITAN CHICAGO/JEWISH UNITED FUND OF METROPOLITAN CHICAGO (1900); Ben Gurion Way, 1 S. Franklin St. (60606-4694); (312)346-6700. FAX: (312)444-2086. E-mail: webinfo@juf.org. Chmn. Fred Bondy; Pres. Steven B. Nasatir. (WWW.JUF.ORG)

JOLIET

JOLIET JEWISH WELFARE CHEST (1938); 250 N. Midland Ave. at Campbell St. (60435); (815)741-4600.

PEORIA

JEWISH FEDERATION OF PEORIA (1933; inc. 1947); 2000 W. Pioneer Pwky., Suite 10B (61615-1835); (309)689-0063. FAX: (309) 689-0575. Pres. Larry Seitzman; Exec. Dir. Susan Katz.

QUAD CITIES

JEWISH FEDERATION OF QUAD CITIES (1938; comb. 1973); 1705 2nd Ave., Suite 405, Rock Island (61201); (309)793-1300. FAX: (309) 793-1345. E-mail: qcfederation@juno.com. Pres. Paul Light; Exec. Dir. Ida Kramer.

ROCKFORD

JEWISH FEDERATION OF GREATER ROCK-FORD (1937); 1500 Parkview Ave. (61107); (815)399-5497. FAX: (815)399-9835. E-mail: rockfordfederation@juno.com. Pres. Sterne Roufa; Exec. Dir. Marilyn Youman.

SOUTHERN ILLINOIS

JEWISH FEDERATION OF SOUTHERN ILLI-NOIS, SOUTHEASTERN MISSOURI, AND WEST-ERN KENTUCKY (1941); 6464 W. Main, Suite 7A, Belleville (62223); (618)398-6100. FAX: (618)398-0539. E-mail: silfed@simokyfed. com. Co-Pres. Harvey Cohen & Carol Rudman; Exec. Dir. Steven C. Low. (www. SIMOKYFED.COM)

SPRINGFIELD

SPRINGFIELD JEWISH FEDERATION (1941); 2815 Old Jacksonville Rd., Ste 103A (62704); (217)787-7223. FAX: (217)787-7470. E-mail: sjf@springnet1.com. Pres. Rita Victor; Exec. Dir. Gloria Schwartz.

INDIANA

FORT WAYNE

FORT WAYNE JEWISH FEDERATION (1921); 227 E. Washington Blvd. (46802-3121); (219) 422-8566. FAX: (219)422-8567. E-mail: fwjewfed@aol.com. Pres. Larry Adelman; Exec. Dir. Jeff Gubitz.(www.SHALOMFW. ORG)

INDIANAPOLIS

JEWISH FEDERATION OF GREATER INDI-ANAPOLIS, INC. (1905); 6705 Hoover Rd. (46260-4120); (317)726-5450. FAX: (317) 205-0307. E-mail controljfg@aol.com. Pres. Richard Leventhal; Exec. V.-Pres. Harry Nadler. (WWW.JFGI.ORG)

LAFAYETTE

JEWISH FEDERATION OF GREATER LAFAYETTE (1924); PO Box 3802, W. Lafayette (47906); (765)426-4724. E-mail:

jfgl1@aol.com. Pres.Earl Prohofsky; Admin. Judy Upton.

NORTHWEST INDIANA

JEWISH FEDERATION OF NORTHWEST INDI-ANA (1941; reorg. 1959); 2939 Jewett St., Highland (46322); (219)972-2250. FAX: (219)972-4779. E-mail: defwej@aol.com. Pres. Carol Karol; Exec. Dir. David Tein. (WWW.JFEDOFNWI.COM)

ST. JOSEPH VALLEY

JEWISH FEDERATION OF ST. JOSEPH VALLEY (1946); 3202 Shalom Way, South Bend (46615); (219)233-1164. FAX: (219)288-4103. E-mail: mgardner@fedsjv.org. Pres. Dr. Douglas H. Barton; Exec. V.-Pres. Marilyn Gardner. (WWW.JFEDSJV.ORG)

IOWA

DES MOINES

JEWISH FEDERATION OF GREATER DES MOINES (1914); 910 Polk Blvd. (50312); (515)277-6321. FAX: (515)277-4069. E-mail: jcrc@dmjfed.org. Pres. Robert M. Pomerantz; Exec. Dir. Elaine Steinger. (www. DMJFED.ORG)

SIOUX CITY

JEWISH FEDERATION OF SIOUX CITY (1921); 815 38th St. (51104-1417); (712)258-0618. FAX: (712)258-0619. Pres. Michele Ivener; Admin. Dir. Doris Rosenthal.

KANSAS

KANSAS CITY

See listing under Missouri

WICHITA

MID-KANSAS JEWISH FEDERATION, INC. (serving South Central Kansas) (1935); 400 N. Woodlawn, Suite 8 (67208); (316)686-4741. FAX: (316)686-6008. E-mail: jpress@ mkjf.org. Pres. Jill S. Docking; Exec. Dir. Judy Press. (WWW.MKJF.ORG)

KENTUCKY

CENTRAL KENTUCKY

CENTRAL KENTUCKY JEWISH FEDERATION (1976); 340 Romany Rd., Lexington (40502-2400); (606)268-0672. FAX: (606)268-0775. E-mail: ckjf@jewishlexington.org. Pres. Martin Barr; Exec. Dir. Daniel Chejfec. (www. JEWISHLEXINGTON.ORG)

LOUISVILLE

JEWISH COMMUNITY FEDERATION OF LOUISVILLE, INC. (1934); 3630 Dutchmans

Lane (40205); (502)451-8840. FAX: (502) 458-0702. E-mail: jfed@iglou.com. Pres. Gerald D. Temes MD; Exec. Dir. Alan S. Engel. (WWW.JEWISHLOUISVILLE.ORG)

LOUISIANA

BATON ROUGE

JEWISH FEDERATION OF GREATER BATON ROUGE (1971); 3354 Kleinert Ave. (70806); (504) 387-9744. FAX: (504)387-9487. E-mail: jfedofbr@postoffice.att.net. Pres. Harvey Hoffman.

NEW ORLEANS

JEWISH FEDERATION OF GREATER NEW OR-LEANS (1913; reorg. 1977); 3747 W. Esplanade Ave., Metairie (70002-3524); (504) 780-5600. FAX: (504)780-5601. E-mail: shalom@jewishnola.com. Pres. Hugo Kahn; Exec. Dir. Eli Skora. (WWW.JEWISHNEW ORLEANS.ORG)

SHREVEPORT

NORTHERN LOUISIANA JEWISH FEDERATION (1941; inc. 1967); 4700 Line Ave., Suite 117 (71106-1533); (318)868-1200. FAX: (318)868-1272. E-mail: nljfed@bellsouth.net. Pres. Rick Murov; Exec. Dir. Howard L. Ross. (WWW.NLJFED.ORG)

MAINE

LEWISTON-AUBURN

LEWISTON-AUBURN JEWISH FEDERATION (1947); 74 Bradman St., Auburn (04210); (207) 786-4201. FAX: (207)783-1000. Pres. Scott Nussinow.

PORTLAND

JEWISH COMMUNITY ALLIANCE OF SOUTH-ERN MAINE (1942); 57 Ashmont St. (04103); (207)773-7254. FAX: (207)772-2234. E-mail: info@mainejewish.org. Pres. Charlie Miller. (WWW.MAINEJEWISH.ORG)

MARYLAND

BALTIMORE

THE ASSOCIATED: JEWISH COMMUNITY FED-ERATION OF BALTIMORE (1920; reorg. 1969); 101 W. Mt. Royal Ave. (21201-5728); (410) 727-4828. FAX: (410)752-1327. E-mail: information@associated.org. Chmn. Barbara L. Himmelrich; Pres. Darrell D. Friedman. (WWW.ASSOCIATED.ORG)

COLUMBIA

JEWISH FEDERATION OF HOWARD COUNTY; 8950 Rte. 108, Suite 115, Columbia (21045); (410)730-4976; FAX: (410)730-9393. E-mail: jfohc@starpower.net. Pres. Toby Knopf; Exec. Dir. Roberta Greenstein. (WWW.EROLS. COM/JFOHC)

MASSACHUSETTS

BERKSHIRE COUNTY

JEWISH FEDERATION OF THE BERKSHIRES (1940); 235 East St., Pittsfield (01201); (413)442-4360. FAX: (413)443-6070. E-mail: jreichbaum@berkshire.net. Pres. Stephen Rudin; Exec. Dir. Jaquelynne Reichbaum. (WWW.BERKSHIREWEB.COM/JEWISHFEDER)

BOSTON

COMBINED JEWISH PHILANTHROPIES OF GREATER BOSTON, INC. (1895; inc. 1961); 126 High St. (02110-2700); (617)457-8500. FAX: (617)988-6262. E-mail: info@cjp.org. Chmn. Robert Beal; Pres. Barry Shrage. (WWW.CJP.ORG)

MERRIMACK VALLEY

MERRIMACK VALLEY JEWISH FEDERATION (Serves Andover, Haverhill, Lawrence, Lowell, Newburyport, and 22 surrounding communities) (1988); PO Box 937, Andover (01810-0016); (978)688-0466. FAX: (978) 688-1097. E-mail: jan@mvjf.org. Pres. James H. Shainker; Exec. Dir. Jan Steven Brodie. (WWW.MVJF.ORG)

NEW BEDFORD

JEWISH FEDERATION OF GREATER NEW BEDFORD, INC. (1938; inc. 1954); 467 Hawthorn St., N. Dartmouth (02747); (508) 997-7471. FAX: (508)997-7730. Co-Pres. Harriet Philips, Patricia Rosenfield; Exec. Dir. Wil Herrup.

NORTH SHORE

JEWISH FEDERATION OF THE NORTH SHORE, INC. (1938); 21 Front St., Salem (01970-3707); (978)598-1810. FAX: (978)741-7507. E-mail: mail@jfns.org. Pres. Shepard M. Remis; Exec. Dir. Neil A. Cooper. (WWW.JFNS.ORG)

SPRINGFIELD

JEWISH FEDERATION OF GREATER SPRING-FIELD, INC. (1925); 1160 Dickinson St. (01108); (413)737-4313. FAX: (413)737-4348. E-mail: cfschwartz@jewishspringfield. org. Pres. Jeffrey Mandell. (WWW.JEWISH SPRINGFIELD.ORG)

WORCESTER

JEWISH FEDERATION OF CENTRAL MASSA-CHUSETTS (1947; inc. 1957); 633 Salisbury St. (01609); (508)756-1543. FAX: (508)798-0962. E-mail: info@jfcm.org. Pres. Bruce Hertzberg; Exec. Dir. Howard Borer. (WWW. JFCM.ORG)

MICHIGAN

ANN ARBOR

JEWISH FEDERATION OF WASHTENAW COUNTY/UJA (1986); 2939 Birch Hollow Dr. (48108); (734)677-0100. FAX: (734)677-0109. E-mail: info@jewishannarbor.org. Pres. Morley Witus; Exec. Dir. Nancy N. Margolis. (WWW.JEWISHANNARBOR.ORG)

DETROIT

JEWISH FEDERATION OF METROPOLITAN DE-TROIT (1899); 6735 Telegraph Rd., Suite 30, PO Box 2030, Bloomfield Hills (48301-2030); (248)642-4260. FAX: (248)642-4985. E-mail: jfmd@jfmd.org. Pres. Larry Jackier; Exec. V.-Pres. Robert Aronson. (WWW.THISIS FEDERATION.ORG)

FLINT

FLINT JEWISH FEDERATION (1936); 619 Wallenberg St. (48502); (810)767-5922. FAX: (810)767-9024. E-mail: fjf@tm.net. Pres. Dr. Steve Burton; Exec. Dir. Joel B. Kaplan. (http://users.tm.net/flint)

GRAND RAPIDS

JEWISH COMMUNITY FUND OF GRAND RAPIDS (1930); 4127 Embassy Dr. SE (49546-2418); (616)942-5553. FAX: (616) 942-5780. E-mail: jcfgr@iserv.net. Pres. Richard Stevens; Admin. Dir. Rosalie Stein; V.P. Maxine Shapiro. (WWW.JFGGR.ORG)

MINNESOTA

MINNEAPOLIS

MINNEAPOLIS JEWISH FEDERATION (1929; inc. 1930); 13100 Wayzata Blvd., Suite 200, Minnetonka (55305); (612)593-2600. FAX: (612) 593-2544. E-mail: webmaster@ujf.org. Pres. Michael Horovitz; Exec. Dir. Joshua Fogelson. (WWW.JEWISHMINNESOTA.ORG)

ST. PAUL

UNITED JEWISH FUND AND COUNCIL (1935); 790 S. Cleveland, Suite 227 (55116); (651) 690-1707. FAX: (651)690-0228. E-mail: webmaster@ujfc.org. Pres. James Stein; Exec. Dir. Eli Skora. (WWW.JEWISHMINNESOTA.ORG)

MISSOURI

KANSAS CITY

JEWISH FEDERATION OF GREATER KANSAS CITY MO/KS (1933); 5801 W. 115 St., Overland Park, KS (66211-1824); (913)327-8100. FAX: (913)327-8110. E-mail: jessical@ jewishkc.org. Pres. Howard Jacobson; Exec.

Dir. Todd Stettner. (WWW.JEWISHKANSAS CITY.ORG)

ST. JOSEPH

UNITED JEWISH FUND OF ST. JOSEPH (1915); 1816 Walnut (64503); (816)233-1186. FAX: (816)233-9399. Elliot Zidell; Exec. Sec. Sherri Ott.

ST. LOUIS

JEWISH FEDERATION OF ST. LOUIS (INCL. ST. LOUIS COUNTY) (1901); 12 Millstone Campus Dr. (63146-9812); (314)432-0020. FAX: (314)432-1277. E-mail: jfedstl@jfedstl.org. Pres. Heschel Raskas; Exec. V.-Pres. Barry Rosenberg. (WWW.JEWISHSTLOUIS.ORG)

NEBRASKA

LINCOLN

JEWISH FEDERATION OF LINCOLN, INC. (1931; inc. 1961); PO Box 67218 (68506); (402)489-1015. FAX: (402)476-8364. Pres. Herb Friedman; Exec. Dir. Karen Sommer.

OMAHA

JEWISH FEDERATION OF OMAHA (1903); 333 S. 132nd St. (68154-2198); (402)334-8200. FAX: (402)334-1330. E-mail: pmonsk@top. net. Pres. Steven Pitlor; Exec. Dir. Jan Goldstein. (WWW.JEWISHOMAHA.ORG)

NEVADA

LAS VEGAS

JEWISH FEDERATION OF LAS VEGAS (1973); 3909 S. Maryland Pkwy. # 400 (89119-7520); (702)732-0556. FAX: (702)732-3228. Bd. Chr. Michael Unger; Exec. Dir. Meyer Bodoff. (WWW.JEWISHLASVEGAS.COM)

NEW HAMPSHIRE

MANCHESTER

JEWISH FEDERATION OF GREATER MAN-CHESTER (1974); 698 Beech St. (03104-3626); (603)627-7679. FAX: (603) 627-7963. Exec. Dir. Adam M. Solender (WWW.JEWISHNH. ORG)

NEW JERSEY

ATLANTIC AND CAPE MAY COUNTIES

JEWISH FEDERATION OF ATLANTIC AND CAPE MAY COUNTIES (1924); 3393 Bargaintown Rd., Box 617, Northfield (08225-0196); (609)653-3030. FAX: (609)653-8881. E-mail: jfedacm@cyberenet.net. Pres.

Joseph Rodgers; Exec. V.-Pres. Bernard Cohen. (WWW.JFEDACM.COM)

BERGEN COUNTY

UJA FEDERATION OF NORTHERN NEW JERSEY (MERGED 2004); 111 Kinderkamack Rd., River Edge (07661); (201)488-6800. FAX: (201)488-1507. E-mail: contact@jewish bergen.org. Pres. Dr. Leonard Cole; Exec. V.-Pres. Howard E. Charish. (WWW.JEWISH BERGEN.ORG)

CENTRAL NEW JERSEY

JEWISH FEDERATION OF CENTRAL NEW JERSEY (1940; merged 1973); 1391 Martine Ave., Scotch Plains (07076); (908)889-5335. FAX: (908)889-5370. E-mail: community@jfedcnj.org. Pres. Mark Wilf; Exec. V.-Pres. Stanley Stone. (WWW.JFEDCNJ.ORG)

CLIFTON-PASSAIC

JEWISH FEDERATION OF GREATER CLIFTON-PASSAIC (1933); 199 Scoles Ave., Clifton (07012-1125). (973)777-7031. FAX: (973) 777-6701. E-mail: yymuskin@jfedclifton passaic.com. Pres. George Kramer; Exec. V.-Pres. Yosef Y. Muskin.

CUMBERLAND COUNTY

JEWISH FEDERATION OF CUMBERLAND COUNTY (INC. 1971); 1063 E. Landis Ave. Suite B, Vineland (08360-3752); (856)696-4445. FAX: (856)696-3428. E-mail: questions@jfedcc.org. Pres. Edward Roth; Exec. Dir. Kirk Wisemayer. (WWW.JFEDCC.ORG)

METROWEST NEW JERSEY

UNITED JEWISH FEDERATION OF METROWEST (1923); 901 Route 10, Whippany (07981-1156); (973)929-3000. FAX: (973) 884-7361. E-mail: webmail@ujfmetrowest. org. Pres. Kenneth R. Heyman; Exec. V.-Pres. Max L. Kleinman. (WWW.UJFMETRO WEST.ORG)

MIDDLESEX COUNTY

JEWISH FEDERATION OF GREATER MIDDLESEX COUNTY (ORG. 1948; reorg. 1985); 230 Old Bridge Tpk., S. River (08882-2000); (732)432-7711. FAX: (732)432-0292. E-mail: middlesexfed@aol.com. Pres. Roy Tanzman; Exec. Dir. Gerrie Bamira. (WWW.JFGMC.ORG)

MONMOUTH COUNTY

JEWISH FEDERATION OF GREATER MONMOUTH COUNTY (1971); 100 Grant Ave., PO Box 210, Deal (07723-0210); (732)531-6200-1. FAX: (732)531-9518. E-mail: info@ jewishmonmouth.org. Exec. Dir. Howard Gases. (WWW.JEWISHMONMOUTH.ORG)

OCEAN COUNTY

OCEAN COUNTY JEWISH FEDERATION (1977); 301 Madison Ave., Lakewood (08701); (732)363-0530. FAX: (732)363-2097. Pres. Dr. Bernie Grabelle; Exec. Dir. Danny Goldberg.

PRINCETON MERCER BUCKS

UNITED JEWISH FEDERATION OF PRINCETON MERCER BUCKS (MERGED 1996); 3131 Princeton Pike, Bldg. 2A, Lawrenceville (08648-2207); (609)219-0555. FAX: (609) 219-9040. E-mail: mailbox@ujfpmb.org. Pres. Carol Pollard; Exec. Dir. Andrew Frank. (WWW.UJFPMB.ORG)

SOMERSET COUNTY

JEWISH FEDERATION OF SOMERSET, HUNTERDON & WARREN COUNTIES (1960); 775 Talamini Rd., Bridgewater (08807); (908) 725-6994. FAX: (908)725-9753. E-mail: info@jfedshaw.org. Pres. Jo Ann Chase; Exec. Dir. Diane S. Naar. (WWW.JFEDSHAW.ORG)

SOUTHERN NEW JERSEY

JEWISH FEDERATION OF SOUTHERN NEW JERSEY (INCL. CAMDEN, BURLINGTON, AND GLOUCESTER COUNTIES) (1922); 1301 Springdale Rd., Suite 200, Cherry Hill (08003-2769); (856)751-9500. FAX: (856) 751-1697. E-mail: imorrow@jfedsnj.org. Pres. Dr. Robert Belafsky; Exec. V.-Pres. Stuart Alperin. (WWW.JFEDSNJ.ORG)

NEW MEXICO

ALBUQUERQUE

JEWISH FEDERATION OF GREATER ALBUQUERQUE (1938); 5520 Wyoming Blvd., NE (87109-3167); (505)821-3214. FAX: (505) 821-3351. E-mail: nmjfga@nmjfga.org. Pres. Steven Sanders; Exec. Dir. Sam Sokolove. (WWW.JEWISHNEWMEXICO.ORG)

NEW YORK

ALBANY

(See Northeastern New York)

BROOME COUNTY

JEWISH FEDERATION OF BROOME COUNTY; 500 Clubhouse Rd., Vestal (13850); (607) 724-2332; FAX: (607)724-2311. (WWW.TOER. NET/JFEDERATION)

BUFFALO (INCL. NIAGARA FALLS)

JEWISH FEDERATION OF GREATER BUFFALO, INC. (1903); 787 Delaware Ave. (14209);

(716)886-7750. FAX: (716)886-1367. Exec. Dir. Daniel G. Kantor.(WWW.JFEDBFLO.COM)

DUTCHESS COUNTY

JEWISH FEDERATION OF DUTCHESS COUNTY; 110 Grand Ave., Poughkeepsie (12603); (845) 471-9811. FAX: (845) 471-3233. E-mail: info@jewishdutchess.org. Exec. Dir. Bonnie Meadow. (WWW.JEWISHDUTCHESS.ORG)

ELMIRA-CORNING

JEWISH CENTER AND FEDERATION OF THE TWIN TIERS (1942); Grandview Ave. Extension, Elmira (14905-0087); (607)734-8122. FAX: (607)734-8123. Pres. John Spiegler; Admin. Diane Huglies.

NEW YORK

UJA-FEDERATION OF JEWISH PHILANTHROPIES OF NEW YORK, INC. (incl. Greater NY, Westchester, Nassau, and Suffolk counties) (Fed. org. 1917; UJA 1939; merged 1986); 130 E. 59 St. (10022-1302); (212)980-1000. FAX: (212)888-7538. E-mail: contact@ujafedny.org. Pres. Morris Offit; Exec. V.-Pres. & CEO John Ruskay. (WWW.UJAFED NY.ORG)

NORTHEASTERN NEW YORK

UNITED JEWISH FEDERATION OF NORTHEASTERN NEW YORK (1986); Latham Circle Mall, 800 New Loudon Rd., Latham (12110); (518)783-7800. FAX: (518)783-1557. E-mail: info@jewishfedny.org. Pres. Dr. Lewis Morrison; Exec. Dir. Rodney Margolis. (WWW.JEWISHFEDNY.ORG)

ORANGE COUNTY

JEWISH FEDERATION OF GREATER ORANGE COUNTY (1977); 68 Stewart Ave., Newburgh (12550); (845)562-7860. FAX: (914)562-5114. E-mail: jfogoc@aol.com. Pres. Mona Rieger; Admin. Dir. Joyce Waschitz.

ROCHESTER

JEWISH COMMUNITY FEDERATION OF GREATER ROCHESTER, NY, INC. (1939); 441 East Ave. (14607-1932); (716)461-0490. FAX: (716)461-0912. E-mail: info@jewishrochester. org. Pres. Howard Grossman; Exec. Dir. Lawrence W. Fine. (WWW.JEWISHROCHESTER. ORG)

ROCKLAND COUNTY

JEWISH FEDERATION OF ROCKLAND COUNTY (1985); 900 Route 45, Suite 1, New City (10956-1140); (914)362-4200. Fax: (914) 362-4282.

SCHENECTADY

(See Northeastern New York)

SYRACUSE

SYRACUSE JEWISH FEDERATION, INC. (1918); 5655 Thompson Rd. So., DeWitt (13214-0511); (315)445-2040. FAX: (315)445-1559. Pres. Gershon Vincow; Exec. V.-Pres. Richard Friedman. (WWW.SJFED.ORG)

TROY

(See Northeastern New York)

ULSTER COUNTY

JEWISH FEDERATION OF ULSTER COUNTY (1951); 159 Green St., Kingston (12401); (845)338-8131. FAX: (845)338-8131. E-mail: ucjf@ulster.net. Pres. Michelle Tuchman; Exec. Dir. Joan Plotsky. (WWW.UCJF. ORG)

UTICA

JEWISH COMMUNITY FEDERATION AND CENTER OF UTICA (1950; reorg. 1994); 2310 Oneida St. (13501-6009); (315)733-2343. FAX: (315)733-2346. E-mail: jcc1@borg. com. Pres. Ann Siegel; Exec. Dir. Barbara Ratner-Gantshar.

NORTH CAROLINA

ASHEVILLE

WESTERN NORTH CAROLINA JEWISH FEDERATION (1935); 236 Charlotte St. (28801-1434); (828)253-0701. FAX: (828)254-7666. Pres. Stan Greenberg; Exec. Dir. Marlene Berger-Joyce.

CHARLOTTE

THE JEWISH FEDERATION OF GREATER CHARLOTTE (1938); 5007 Providence Rd. (28226-5849); (704)366-5007. FAX: (704) 944-6766. E-mail: jfgc@shalomcharlotte. org. Pres. Jill Newman; Exec. Dir. Randy Czarlinsky. (WWW.JEWISHCHARLOTTE.ORG)

DURHAM-CHAPEL HILL

DURHAM-CHAPEL HILL JEWISH FEDERATION & COMMUNITY COUNCIL (1979); 3700 Lyckan Pkwy., Suite B, Durham (27707-2541); (919)489-5335. FAX: (919)489-5788. E-mail: federation@shalomdch.org. Pres. Lew Margolis; Interim Exec. Dir. David Sclove. (http://shalomdch.org)

GREENSBORO

GREENSBORO JEWISH FEDERATION (1940); 5509C W. Friendly Ave. (27410-4211);

(336)852-5433. FAX: (336)852-4346. E-mail: mchandler@shalomgreensboro.org. Pres. Nancy Brenner; Exec. Dir. Marilyn Chandler. (WWW.SHALOMGREENSBORO.ORG)

RALEIGH

RALEIGH-CARY JEWISH FEDERATION (1987); 8210 Creedmoor Rd., Suite 104 (27613); (919)676-2200. FAX: (919)676-2122. E-mail: info@rcjf.org. Pres. Jim Maass; Exec. Dir. Judah Segal. (WWW.RCJF.ORG)

OHIO

AKRON

AKRON JEWISH COMMUNITY FEDERATION (1935); 750 White Pond Dr. (44320-1128); (330)869-CHAI (2424). FAX: (330)867-8498. Pres. David Kock; Exec. Dir. Michael Wise. (WWW.JEWISHAKRON.ORG)

CANTON

CANTON JEWISH COMMUNITY FEDERATION (1935; reorg. 1955); 2631 Harvard Ave., NW (44709-3147); (330)452-6444. FAX: (330) 452-4487. E-mail: cantonjcf@aol.com. (jewishcanton.org)

CINCINNATI

JEWISH FEDERATION OF CINCINNATI (1896; reorg. 1967); 4380 Malsbary Rd., Suite 200 (45242-5644); (513) 985-1500. FAX: (513) 985-1503. E-mail: jfed@jfedcin.org. Pres. Harry B. Davidow; Chief Exec. Officer Rabbi Michael R. Zedek. (WWW.JEWISH CINCINNATI.ORG)

CLEVELAND

JEWISH COMMUNITY FEDERATION OF CLEVELAND (1903); 1750 Euclid Ave. (44115-2106); (216)566-9200. FAX: (216) 861-1230. E-mail: info@jcfcleve.org. Exec. V.-Pres. & CEO Joel Fox. (WWW.JEWISH CLEVELAND.ORG)

COLUMBUS

COLUMBUS JEWISH FEDERATION (1926); 1175 College Ave. (43209); (614)237-7686. FAX: (614)237-2221. E-mail: cjf@tcjf.org. Pres. & CEO Marsha Hurwitz. (WWW.JEWISH COLUMBUS.ORG)

DAYTON

JEWISH FEDERATION OF GREATER DAYTON (1910); 4501 Denlinger Rd. (45426-2395); (937)854-4150. FAX: (937)854-2850. Pres. Joseph Bettman; Exec. V.-Pres. Peter H. Wells. (WWW.JEWISHDAYTON.ORG)

STEUBENVILLE

JEWISH COMMUNITY COUNCIL (1938); 300 Lovers Lane (43952); (614)264-5514. FAX: (740)264-7190. Pres. Curtis L. Greenberg; Exec. Sec. Jennie Bernstein.

TOLEDO

JEWISH FEDERATION OF GREATER TOLEDO (1907; reorg. 1960); 6505 Sylvania Ave., Sylvania (43560-3918); (419)885-4461. FAX: (419)885-3207. E-mail: jftoledo@cjfny.org. CEO Joel Beren. (WWW.JEWISHTOLEDO.ORG)

YOUNGSTOWN

YOUNGSTOWN AREA JEWISH FEDERATION (1935); 505 Gypsy Lane (44504-1314); (330) 746-3251. FAX: (330)746-7926. E-mail: samkoopl@juno.com. Pres. Dr. Ronald Roth; Dir. Bonnie Deutsch-Burdman.

OKLAHOMA

OKLAHOMA CITY

JEWISH FEDERATION OF GREATER OKLAHOMA CITY (1941); 710 W. Wilshire, Suite C (73116-7736). (405)848-3132. FAX: (405) 848-3180. E-mail: okcfed@flash.net. Pres. Harriet Carson; Exec. Dir. Edie S. Roodman. (WWW.JFEDOKC.ORG)

TULSA

JEWISH FEDERATION OF TULSA (1938); 2021 E. 71 St. (74136); (918)495-1100. FAX: (918)495-1220. E-mail: federation@jewishtulsa.org. Pres. Andrew M. Wolov; Exec. Dir. David Bernstein. (WWW.JEWISHTULSA. ORG)

OREGON

PORTLAND

JEWISH FEDERATION OF PORTLAND (INCL. NORTHWEST OREGON AND SOUTHWEST WASHINGTON COMMUNITIES) (1920; reorg. 1956); 6651 SW Capitol Hwy. (97219); (503) 245-6219. FAX: (503)245-6603. E-mail: charlie@jewishportland.org. Pres. Rob Shlachter; Exec. Dir. Charles Schiffman. (WWW.JEWISHPORTLAND.ORG)

PENNSYLVANIA

BUCKS COUNTY

(See Jewish Federation of Greater Philadelphia)

ERIE

JEWISH COMMUNITY COUNCIL OF ERIE (1946); 1611 Peach St., Suite 405 (16501-2123); (814)455-4474. FAX: (814)455-4475.

618

E-mail: jcceri@erie.net. Pres. Robert Cohen; Admin. Dir. Cynthia Penman; Dir. Barbara Singer. (WWW.JCCERI.ORG)

HARRISBURG

UNITED JEWISH COMMUNITY OF GREATER HARRISBURG (1941); 3301 N. Front St. (17110-1436); (717)236-9555. FAX: (717) 236-8104. E-mail: communityreview@ desupernet.net. Pres. Raphael Aronson; Exec. Dir. David Weisberg. (WWW.HBG JEWISHCOMMUNITY.COM)

LEHIGH VALLEY

JEWISH FEDERATION OF THE LEHIGH VALLEY (1948); 702 N. 22nd St., Allentown (18104); (610)821-5500. FAX: (610)821-8946. E-mail: ivfed@enter.net. Exec. Dir. Mark Goldstein.

PHILADELPHIA

JEWISH FEDERATION OF GREATER PHILADELPHIA (INCL. BUCKS, CHESTER, DELAWARE, MONTGOMERY, AND PHILADELPHIA COUNTIES) (1901; reorg. 1956); 2100 Arch St. (19103); (215)832-0500. FAX: (215) 832-1510. E-mail: lyouman@philjnet.org. Pres. Dr. Harold Goldman. (WWW.JEWISH PHILLY.ORG)

PITTSBURGH

UNITED JEWISH FEDERATION OF GREATER PITTSBURGH (1912; reorg. 1955); 234 McKee Pl. (15213-3916); (412)681-8000. FAX: (412) 681-3980. E-mail: information@ujf.net. Chmn. Barbara Burstin. (WWW.UJF.NET)

READING

JEWISH FEDERATION OF READING, PA., INC. (1935; reorg. 1972); 1700 City Line St. (19604); (610)921-2766. FAX: (610)929-0886. E-mail: stanr@epix.net. Pres. Sheila Lattin; Exec. Dir. Stanley Ramati. (WWW. READINGJEWISHCOMMUNITY.COM)

SCRANTON

JEWISH FEDERATION OF NORTHEASTERN PENNSYLVANIA (1945); 601 Jefferson Ave. (18510); (570)961-2300. FAX: (570)346-6147. E-mail: jfednepa@epix.net. Pres. Louis Nivert; Exec. Dir. Mark Silverberg. (WWW.JFEDNEPA.ORG)

WILKES-BARRE

JEWISH FEDERATION OF GREATER WILKES-BARRE (1950); 60 S. River St. (18702-2493); (570)822-4146. FAX: (570)824-5966. E-mail: wbreport@aol.com. Pres. Murray Ufberg; Exec. Dir. Don Cooper.

RHODE ISLAND

PROVIDENCE

JEWISH FEDERATION OF RHODE ISLAND (1945); 130 Sessions St. (02906); (401)421-4111. FAX: (401)331-7961. E-mail: shalom @jfri.org. Pres. Edward D. Feldstein; Exec. Dir. Steven A. Rakitt. (WWW.JFRI.ORG)

SOUTH CAROLINA

CHARLESTON

CHARLESTON JEWISH FEDERATION (1949); 1645 Raoul Wallenberg Blvd., PO Box 31298 (29407); (843)571-6565. FAX: (843) 852-3547. E-mail: ellenk@jewishcharleston. org. Co-Pres. Wendy Goer and Paul Saltzman; Exec. Dir. Ellen J. Katzman. (www. JEWISHCHARLESTON.ORG)

COLUMBIA

COLUMBIA JEWISH FEDERATION (1960); 4540 Trenholm Rd., PO Box 6968 (29206-4462); (803)787-2023. FAX: (803)787-0475. E-mail: ternercjf@hotmail.com. Pres. Stephen Serbin; Exec. Dir. Steven Terner.

SOUTH DAKOTA

SIOUX FALLS

JEWISH WELFARE FUND (1938); 510 S. First Ave. (57102-1003); (605)332-3335. FAX: (605)334-2298. E-mail: asnh94@prodigy. com. Pres. Laurence Bierman; Exec. Sec. Stephen Rosenthal.

TENNESSEE

CHATTANOOGA

JEWISH COMMUNITY FEDERATION OF GREATER CHATTANOOGA (1931); 3601 Ringgold Rd. (37412); PO Box 8947 (37412); (423)493-0270. FAX: (423)493-9997. E-mail: mdzik@jcfgc.com. Pres. Michael Lebovitz; Exec. Dir. Michael Dzik. (WWW.JCFGC.COM)

KNOXVILLE

KNOXVILLE JEWISH FEDERATION, INC. (1939); 7800 Deane Hill Dr. (37919); (865) 693-5837. FAX: (865)694-4861. E-mail: ajc-ckjf@aol.com. Pres. Marilyn Lieberman; Exec. Dir. Dr. Bernard Rosenblatt. (www. JEWISHKNOXVILLE.ORG)

MEMPHIS

MEMPHIS JEWISH FEDERATION (INCL. SHELBY COUNTY) (1935); 6560 Poplar Ave. (38138-3614); (901)767-7100. FAX: (901) 767-7128. E-mail: jfeld@memjfed.org. Pres.

Louise Sklar; Exec. Dir. Jeffrey Feld. (www.KORRNET.ORG/MJF)

NASHVILLE

NASHVILLE JEWISH FEDERATION (1936); 801 Percy Warner Blvd. (37205-4009); (615)356-3242. FAX: (615)352-0056. E-mail: jnashjfed @aol.org. Pres. Fred Zimmerman; Exec. Dir. Steven J. Edelstein. (WWW.JNASHFED.ORG)

TEXAS

AUSTIN

JEWISH COMMUNTY ASSOCIATION OF AUSTIN (1939; reorg. 1956); 7300 Hart Lane (78731); (512)735-8000. FAX: (512)735-8001. E-mail: austinjfed@jfaustin.org. Pres. Linda Millstone; Exec. Dir. Sandy Sack. (WWW.JFAUSTIN.ORG)

BEAUMONT

BEAUMONT JEWISH FEDERATION; PO Box 1891 (77704-1981); (409)832-2881.

CORPUS CHRISTI

COMBINED JEWISH APPEAL OF CORPUS CHRISTI; 750 Everhart Rd. (78411-1906); (512)855-6239. FAX: (512)853-9040.

DALLAS

JEWISH FEDERATION OF GREATER DALLAS (1911); 7800 Northaven Rd. (75230-3226); (214)369-3313. FAX: (214)369-8943. E-mail: jharburger@jfgd.org. Pres. Donald Schaffer; Exec. Dir. Gary Weinstein. (WWW.JEWISH DALLAS.ORG)

EL PASO

JEWISH FEDERATION OF EL PASO, INC. (1937); 405 Wallenberg Dr. (79912-5605); (915)584-4437. FAX: (915)584-0243. Pres. Gary Weiser; Exec. Dir. Larry Harris. (WWW.JEWISHFED.HUNTLEIGH.NET)

FORT WORTH

JEWISH FEDERATION OF FORT WORTH AND TARRANT COUNTY (1936); 4255 Bryant Irvin Rd. #209 (76008); (817)569-0892. FAX: (817)569-0895. E-mail: jfed@tarrant federation.org. Pres. Harold Gernsbacher; Exec. Dir. Naomi Rosenfield.

HOUSTON

JEWISH FEDERATION OF GREATER HOUSTON (1936); 5603 S. Braeswood Blvd. (77096-3907); (713)729-7000. FAX: (713)721-6232. E-mail: lwunsch@houstonjewish.org. Pres. Marvin Woskow; Exec. V.-Pres. Lee Wunsch. (WWW.HOUSTONJEWISH.ORG)

SAN ANTONIO

JEWISH FEDERATION OF SAN ANTONIO (incl. Bexar County) (1922); 12500 NW Military Hwy., Suite 200 (78231); (210)302-6960. FAX: (210)408-2332. E-mail: markfreedman @jfsatx. Pres. Alan Petlin; Exec. Dir. Mark Freedman. (WWW.JFSATX.ORG)

WACO

JEWISH FEDERATION OF WACO & CENTRAL TEXAS (1949); PO Box 8031 (76714-8031); (817)776-3740. FAX: (817)776-4424. E-mail: debhersh@aol.com. Pres. Harry Smith; Exec. Sec. Deborah Hersh. (WWW.AGUDATH-JACOB.ORG/FED.HTM)

UTAH

SALT LAKE CITY

UNITED JEWISH FEDERATION OF UTAH (1936); 2 North Medical Drive (84113); (801)581-0102. FAX: (801) 581-1334. Pres. Robert Wolff; Exec. Dir. Donald Gartman.

VIRGINIA

RICHMOND

JEWISH COMMUNITY FEDERATION OF RICHMOND (1935); 5403 Monument Ave., PO Box 17128 (23226-7128); (804)288-0045. FAX: (804)282-7507. E-mail: executivedirector@jewishrich.org. Pres. Stewart Kasen; Exec. Dir. Ellen Chernack. (WWW.JEWISH RICHMOND.ORG)

TIDEWATER

UNITED JEWISH FEDERATION OF TIDEWATER (INCL. NORFOLK, PORTSMOUTH, AND VIRGINIA BEACH) (1937); 5000 Corporate Woods Dr., Suite 200, Virginia Beach (23462-4370); (757)965-6100. FAX: (757) 965-6102. E-mail: ujft@ujft.org. Pres. David Brand; Exec. V.-Pres. Harry Graber. (www.JEWISHVA.ORG)

VIRGINIA PENINSULA

UNITED JEWISH COMMUNITY OF THE VIRGINIA PENINSULA, INC. (1942); 2700 Spring Rd., Newport News (23606); (757)930-1422. FAX: (757)930-3762. E-mail: unitedjc@ erols.com. Pres. Roy H. Lasris; Exec. Dir. Rodney J. Margolis. (WWW.UJCVP.ORG)

WASHINGTON

SEATTLE

JEWISH FEDERATION OF GREATER SEATTLE (INCL. KING COUNTY, EVERETT, AND BREMERTON) (1926); 2031 Third Ave. (98121);

(206)443-5400. FAX: (206)443-0306. E-mail: wendyj@jewishinseattle.org. Pres. and CEO Barry M. Goren. (WWW.JEWISHINSEATTLE. ORG)

WEST VIRGINIA

CHARLESTON

FEDERATED JEWISH CHARITIES OF CHARLESTON, INC. (1937); PO Box 1613 (25326); (304)345-2320. FAX: (304)345-2325. E-mail: mzltov@aol.com. Pres. Stuart May; Exec. Sec. Lee Diznoff.

WISCONSIN

MADISON

MADISON JEWISH COMMUNITY COUNCIL, INC. (1940); 6434 Enterprise Lane (53719-

1117); (608)278-1808. FAX:(608)278-7814. E-mail: mjcc@mjcc.net. Pres. Diane Seder; Exec. Dir. Steven H. Morrison. (www. JEWISHMADISON.ORG)

MILWAUKEE

MILWAUKEE JEWISH FEDERATION, INC. (1902); 1360 N. Prospect Ave. (53202); (414)390-5700. FAX: (414)390-5782. E-mail: info@milwaukeejewish.org. Pres. Stephen L. Chernof; Exec. V.-Pres. Richard H. Meyer. (WWW.MILWAUKEEJEWISH.ORG)

CANADA

ALBERTA

CALGARY

CALGARY JEWISH COMMUNITY COUNCIL (1962); 1607 90th Ave. SW (T2V 4V7); (403)253-8600. FAX: (403)253-7915. E-mail: cjcc@cjcc.ca. Pres. Nate Feldman; Exec. Dir. Myrna Linder. (WWW.CJCC.CA)

EDMONTON

JEWISH FEDERATION OF EDMONTON (1954; reorg. 1982); 7200 156th St. (T5R 1X3); (780)487-5120. FAX: (780)481-1854. E-mail: edjfed@net.com.ca. Pres. Stephen Mandel; Exec. Dir. Lesley A. Jacobson.

BRITISH COLUMBIA

VANCOUVER

JEWISH FEDERATION OF GREATER VANCOUVER (1932; reorg. 1987); 950 W. 41st Ave., Suite 200 (V5Z 2N7); (604)257-5100. FAX: (604)257-5110. E-mail: jfed@jfgv.com. Pres. Sondra Green; Exec. Dir. Mark Gurvis. (WWW.JFGV.COM)

MANITOBA

WINNIPEG

JEWISH FEDERATION OF WINNIPEG/COMBINED JEWISH APPEAL(1938; reorg. 1973); 123 Doncaster St., Suite C300 (R3N 2B2); (204)477-7400. FAX: (204)477-7405. E-mail: bfreedman@aspercampus.mb.ca. Pres.Neil

Dubroff; Exec. V.-Pres. Robert Freedman. (WWW.JEWISHWINNIPEG.ORG)

ONTARIO

HAMILTON

UJA/JEWISH FEDERATION OF HAMILTON/ WENTWORTH & AREA (1932; merged 1971); PO Box 7258, 1030 Lower Lions Club Rd., Ancaster (L9G 3N6); (905)648-0605 #305. FAX: (905)648-8350. E-mail: hamujajf@ interlynx.net. Pres. Bonnie Loewith; Exec. Dir. Gerald Fisher. (WWW.JEWISHHAMILTON. ORG)

LONDON

LONDON JEWISH FEDERATION (1932); 536 Huron St. (N5Y 4J5); (519)673-3310. FAX: (519)673-1161. Pres. Ron Wolf; Off. Mgr. Debra Chatterley. (WWW.JEWISHLONDON.CA)

OTTAWA

UNITED JEWISH APPEAL OF OTTAWA (1934); 21 Nadolny Sachs Private (K2A 1R9); (613)798-4696. FAX: (613)798-4695. E-mail: uja@jccottawa.com. Pres. Barbara Farber; Exec. Dir. Jack Silverstein. (WWW.JEWISH OTTAWA.ORG)

TORONTO

UJA FEDERATION OF GREATER TORONTO (1917); 4600 Bathurst St. (M2R 3V2); (416)635-2883. FAX: (416)631-5715. E-mail:

webmaven@feduja.org. Pres. Joseph Steiner; Exec. V.-Pres. Allan Reitzes. (WWW.JEWISH TORONTO.NET)

WINDSOR

JEWISH COMMUNITY FEDERATION (1938); 1641 Ouellette Ave. (N8X 1K9); (519)973-1772. FAX: (519)973-1774. Pres. Jay Armeland; Exec. Dir. Harvey Kessler. (www. JEWISHWINDSOR.ORG)

QUEBEC

MONTREAL

FEDERATION CJA (formerly Allied Jewish Community Services) (1965); 1 Carrie Cummings Square (H3W 1M6); (514)735-3541. FAX: (514)735-8972. E-mail: dcantor@ federationcja.org. Pres. Steven Cummings; Exec. V.-Pres. Danyael Cantor. (www. FEDERATIONCJA.ORG)

Jewish Periodicals*

UNITED STATES

ALABAMA

DEEP SOUTH JEWISH VOICE (1990). PO Box 130052, Birmingham, 35213. (205)595-9255. FAX: (205)595-9256. E-mail: dsjvoice@aol.com. Lawrence M. Brook. Monthly. (WWW.DEEPSOUTHJEWISHVOICE. COM)

ARIZONA

ARIZONA JEWISH POST (1946). 2601 N. Campbell Ave., #205, Tucson, 85719. (520) 319-1112. FAX: (520) 319-1118. E-mail: pbraun@azjewishpost.com. Editor Phyllis Braun. Fortnightly. Jewish Federation of Southern Arizona.

JEWISH NEWS OF GREATER PHOENIX (1948). 1625 E. Northern Ave., Suite 106, Phoenix, 85020. (602)870-9470. FAX: (602)870-0426. E-mail: editor@jewishaz.com. Editor Rabbi Barry Cohen. Weekly. (www. JEWISHAZ.COM)

CALIFORNIA

THE AMERICAN RABBI (1968). 22711 Cass Ave., Woodland Hills, 91364. (818)225-9631. E-mail: amrabbi@pacbell.net. Ed.-in-Ch./Pub. David Epstein; Ed. Harry Essrig. Quarterly.

CENTRAL CALIFORNIA JEWISH HERITAGE (1914). 20201 Sherman Way, Winnetka, 91306. (818) 576-9000. FAX: (818) 576-9910. E-mail: heritagepub@earthlink.net. Dan Brin. Six times a year. Heritage Group.

HERITAGE-SOUTHWEST JEWISH PRESS (1914). 20201 Sherman Way, Suite 204,

Winnetka, 91306. (818) 576-9000. FAX: (818) 576-9910. E-mail: heritagepub@ earthlink.net. Dan Brin. Weekly. Heritage Group.

JEWISH BULLETIN OF NORTHERN CALIFORNIA (1946). 225 Bush St., Suite 1480, San Francisco, 94104-4281. (415)263-7200. FAX: (415)263-7223. E-mail: info@jbnc. com. Marc S. Klein. Weekly. San Francisco Jewish Community Publications, Inc.

JEWISH COMMUNITY CHRONICLE (1947). 3801 E. Willow St., Long Beach, 90815. (562)426-7601, ext. 1021. FAX: (562)595-5543. E-mail: jchron@surfside.net. Harriette Ellis. Fortnightly except January, July & August/ once per month 21 issues a year. Jewish Federation of Greater Long Beach & West Orange County.

JEWISH COMMUNITY NEWS (1976). 14855 Oka Rd., Suite 2, Los Gatos, 95030. (408)358-3033, ext. 31. FAX: (408)356-0733. E-mail: jcn@jfgsj.org. Eileen Goss; Adv. Lindsay Greensweig (408)286-6669. Monthly. Jewish Federation of Greater San Jose.

JEWISH JOURNAL OF GREATER LOS ANGELES (1986). 3660 Wilshire Blvd., Suite 204, Los Angeles, 90010.(213)368-1661. FAX: (213) 368-1684. E-mail:jjla@aol.com. Gene Lichtenstein. Weekly.

JEWISH NEWS (1973). 15060 Ventura Blvd., Suite 210, Sherman Oaks, CA 91403. (818)786-4000. FAX: (818)380-9232. Phil Blazer. Monthly. (Also weekly Sunday TV

---

* The information in this directory is based on replies to questionnaires circulated by the editors. For organizational bulletins, see the directory of Jewish organizations.

and radio broadcasts in LA, NY, and Miami.)

JEWISH SOCIAL STUDIES: HISTORY, CULTURE, AND SOCIETY (1939). c/o Program in Jewish Studies, Bldg. 240, Rm. 103, Stanford University, Stanford, 94305-2190. (650)725-0829. FAX: (650)725-2920. E-mail: jss@stanford.edu. Steven J. Zipperstein, Aron Rodrigue. Three times a year. Conference on Jewish Social Studies, Inc.

JEWISH SPORTS REVIEW. 1800 S. Robertson Blvd., #174, Los Angeles, 90035. (800)510-9003. E-mail: shel@jewishsportsreview. com. Shel Wallman/Ephraim Moxson. Bimonthly. (WWW.JEWISHSPORTSREVIEW.COM)

LOS ANGELES JEWISH TIMES (FORMERLY B'NAI B'RITH MESSENGER) (1897). 5455 Wilshire Blvd., Suite 903, Los Angeles, 90036. (323)933-0131. FAX: (323)933-7928. E-mail: lajtart@aol.com. Ed.-in-Chief Joe Bobker; Mng. Ed. Jane Fried. Weekly.

ORANGE COUNTY JEWISH HERITAGE. 24331 Muirlands Blvd., Suite D-347, Lake Forest, 92630. Phone/FAX: (949)362-4446. E-mail: ocnews@hotmail.com. Stan Brin. Biweekly.

SAN DIEGO JEWISH PRESS HERITAGE (1914). 3615 Kearny Villa Rd., #111, San Diego, 92123. (619)265-0808. FAX: (619)265-0850. E-mail: sdheritage@home.com. Donald H. Harrison. Weekly.

SAN DIEGO JEWISH TIMES (1979). 4731 Palm Ave., La Mesa, 91941. (619)463-5515. FAX: (619) 463-1309. E-mail: jewish times@earthlink.net. Editor Michael Sirota. Fortnightly.

SHALOM L.A. (1988). 16027 Ventura Blvd., #400, Encino, 91436. (818)783-3090. FAX: (818)783-1104. E-mail: news@sholomla. net. Gal Shor. Weekly. Hebrew.

TIKKUN MAGAZINE (1986). 2342 Shattuck Ave., Suite 1200, Berkeley, 94704. (510) 644-1200. FAX: (510)644-1255. E-mail: magazine@tikkun.org. Michael Lerner. Bimonthly. Institute for Labor & Mental Health. (WWW.TIKKUN.ORG)

WESTERN STATES JEWISH HISTORY (1968). 22711 Cass Ave., Woodland Hills, 91364. (818)225-9631. E-mail: amrabbi@pac-bell.net. Ed.-in-Ch. Gladys Sturman; Ed. David Epstein. Quarterly. Western States Jewish History Association.

COLORADO

INTERMOUNTAIN JEWISH NEWS (1913). 1275 Sherman St., Suite 214, Denver, 80203-2299. (303)861-2234. FAX: (303)832-6942. E-mail: email@ijn.com. Exec. Ed. Rabbi Hillel Goldberg; Pub. Miriam Goldberg. Weekly.

CONNECTICUT

CONNECTICUT JEWISH LEDGER (1929). 740 N. Main St., W. Hartford, 06117. (860) 231-2424. FAX: (860)231-2428. E-mail: editorial@jewishledger.com. Lisa Lenkiewicz. Weekly.

JEWISH LEADER (1974). 28 Channing St., PO Box 1468, New London, 06320. (860) 442-7395. FAX: (860)443-4175. E-mail jfecmim@aol.com. Ed. Mimi Perl. Biweekly. Jewish Federation of Eastern Connecticut.

DELAWARE

JEWISH VOICE. 100 W. 10th St., Suite 301, Wilmington, 19801. (302) 427-2100. FAX: (302) 427-2438. E-mail: jewishvoic @aol.com. Lynn Edelman. 22 times per year. Jewish Federation of Delaware.

DISTRICT OF COLUMBIA

AZURE (1996). 5505 Connecticut Ave., NW, Suite 1140, Washington, 20015. (877)298-7300. Fax: (888)766-1506. E-mail: patrick @shalemcenter.org. Dan Polisar. Quarterly. Hebrew/English. The Shalem Center. WWW.AZURE.ORG.IL

B'NAI B'RITH INTERNATIONAL JEWISH MONTHLY (1886, under the name Menovah). 2020 K Street, NW, 7th Floor, Washington, DC 20006. (202)857-2708. FAX: (202)857-2781. E-mail: ijm@bnaibrith. org. Editor Elana Harris. Quarterly. B'nai B'rith International.

CAPITAL COMMUNIQUÉ (1991). 777 N. Capital St., NE, Suite 305, Washington, 20002. (202)216-9060. FAX: (202)216-9061. Jason Silberberg. Biannually. National Jewish Democratic Council.

THE JEWISH VETERAN (1896). 1811 R St., NW, Washington, 20009-1659. (202)265-6280. FAX: (202)234-5662. E-mail: jwv@ jwv.org. Seymour "Sy" Brody. 5 times per year. Jewish War Veterans of the U.S.A. Quarterly

MOMENT (1975). 4710 41 St., NW, Washington, 20016. (202)364-3300. FAX:

(202)364-2636. E-mail: editor@moment-mag.com. Hershel Shanks. Bimonthly. Jewish Educational Ventures, Inc.

FSU MONITOR (1990). 1819 H Street, NW, Suite 230, Washington, 20006. (202)775-9770. FAX: (202)775-9776. E-mail: ucsj@ucsj.com. Nickolai Butkevich. Quarterly. Union of Councils for Soviet Jews.

NEAR EAST REPORT (1957). 440 First St., NW, Suite 607, Washington, 20001. (202) 639-5254. FAX: (202) 347-4916. Dr. Raphael Danziger. Fortnightly. Near East Research, Inc.

SECURITY AFFAIRS (1976). 1717 K St., NW, Suite 800, Washington, 20006. (202)833-0020. FAX: (202)296-6452. E-mail: info@jinsa.org. Jim Colbert. Quarterly. Jewish Institute for National Security Affairs.

WASHINGTON JEWISH WEEK. *See under* MARYLAND

FLORIDA

THE CHRONICLE (1971). 580 S. McIntosh Rd., Sarasota, 34232. (941)371-4546. FAX: (941)378-2947. Barry Millman. Fortnightly. Sarasota-Manatee Jewish Federation.

HERITAGE FLORIDA JEWISH NEWS (1976). PO Box 300742, Fern Park, 32730. (407) 834-8787. FAX: (407)831-0507. E-mail: heritagefl@aol.com. Pub. Jeffrey Gaeser; Asst. Ed. Uim Fischer. Weekly.

JACKSONVILLE JEWISH NEWS (1988). 8505 San Jose Blvd., Jacksonville, 32217. (904)448-5000, (904)262-1971. FAX: (904)448-5715. E-mail: srgnews@aol.com. Susan R. Goetz. Monthly. Jacksonville Jewish Federation.

JEWISH JOURNAL (PALM BEACH-BROWARD-DADE) (1977). 601 Fairway Dr., Deerfield Beach, 33441. (954)698-6397. FAX: (954) 429-1207. Alan Gosh. Weekly. South Florida Newspaper Network.

JEWISH PRESS OF PINELLAS COUNTY (CLEARWATER-ST.PETERSBURG) (1985). PO Box 6970, Clearwater, 33758-6970; 1101 S. Belcher Road, Suite H, Largo, FL 33771. (727)535-4400. FAX:(727)530-3039. E-mail: jewishpress@aol.com. Karen Wolfson Dawkins. Biweekly. Jewish Press Group of Tampa Bay (FL), Inc. in cooperation with the Jewish Federation of Pinellas County.

JEWISH PRESS OF TAMPA (1987). PO Box 6970, Clearwater 33758-6970; 1101 S. Belcher Road, Suit H, Largo, FL 33771. (727)535-4400. FAX: (727)530-3039. E-mail: jewishpress@aol.com. Karen Wolfson Dawkins. Biweekly. Jewish Press Group of Tampa Bay (FL), Inc.

SHALOM TODAY (1994) JEWISH FEDERATION OF BROWARD COUNTY, 5890 S. Pine Island Road, Davie, FL 33328. (954)352-6900. FAX: (954) 252-6893. Editor Ray Levi. Weekly. Jewish Federation of Broward County.

GEORGIA

ATLANTA JEWISH TIMES (1925). 6065 Roswell Rd., Suite 700, Atlanta 30328. (404) 252-1600. FAX: (404)252-1172. E-mail: bmenaker@atlantajewishtimes.com. Bob Menaker. Weekly.

ILLINOIS

CHICAGO JEWISH NEWS (1994). 5301 W. Dempster, Skokie, Ill 60077. (847)966-0606. FAX: (847)966-1656. E-mail: info@chicagojewishnews.com. Joseph Aaron. Weekly.

CHICAGO JEWISH STAR (1991). PO Box 268, Skokie, 60076-0268. (847)674-7827. FAX: (847)674-0014. E-mail: chicago-jewish-star@mcimail.com. Ed. Douglas Wertheimer; Assoc. Ed. Gila Wertheimer. Fortnightly.

JEWISH COMMUNITY NEWS (1941). 6464 W. Main, Suite 7A, Belleville, 62223. (618)398-6100/ (877)714-6103. FAX: (618)398-0539. E-mail: silfed@simokyfed.com Steve Low. Quarterly. Jewish Federation of Southern Illinois. (WWW.SIMOKYFED.COM)

JUF NEWS & GUIDE TO JEWISH LIVING IN CHICAGO (1972). One S. Franklin St., Rm. 701G, Chicago, 60606. (312)357-4848. FAX: (312)855-2470. E-mail: jufnews@juf.org. Aaron B. Cohen. Monthly (Guide, annually). Jewish United Fund/Jewish Federation of Metropolitan Chicago.

INDIANA

ILLIANA JEWISH NEWS (1975). 2939 Jewett St., Highland, 46322. (219)972-2250. FAX: (219)972-4779. E-mail: defwej@aol.com. Editor Carol Karol. Quarterly (except July/Aug.). Jewish Federation of Northwest Indiana, Inc.

INDIANA JEWISH POST AND OPINION (1935). 238 S. Meridian St., #502, Indianapolis, 46225. (317)972-7800. FAX: (317)972-7807. E-mail: jpost@surf-ici.com. Gabriel Cohen. Weekly.

NATIONAL JEWISH POST AND OPINION (1932). 238 S. Meridian St., Indianapolis, 46225. (317)972-7800. FAX: (317)972-7807. E-mail: jpost@surf.ici.com. Gabriel Cohen. Weekly.

PROOFTEXTS: A JOURNAL OF JEWISH LITERARY HISTORY (1980). Indiana University Press, 601 N. Morton St., Bloomington, 47404. (812)855-9449. FAX: (812)855-8507. E-mail: journals@indiana.edu. Editorial address (for contributors): Dept. of Hebrew Language, Box 46, Jewish Theological Seminary, 3080 Broadway, NY, NY 10027-4649. Alan Mintz, David G. Roskies. Three times a year.

KANSAS

KANSAS CITY JEWISH CHRONICLE (1920). 7373 W. 107 St., Overland Park, 66212. (913)648-4620. FAX: (913)381-1402. E-mail: chronicle@sunpublications.com. Rick Hellman. Weekly. Sun Publications.

KENTUCKY

COMMUNITY (1975). 3630 Dutchmans Lane, Louisville, 40205-3200. (502) 451-8840. FAX: (502) 458-0702. E-mail: jfed@iglou.com. Shiela Steinman Wallace. Biweekly. Jewish Community Federation of Louisville.

KENTUCKY JEWISH POST AND OPINION (1931). 3701 Bardatown Road, Sommerville, KY 40205. (502)459-1914. Gabriel Cohen. Weekly.

LOUISIANA

JEWISH CIVIC PRESS (1965). 804 Main Street, Suite A-2, Forest Park, GA 30297. (404)231-2194. E-mail: jewishcivicpress @yahoo.com. Claire & Abner Tritt, eds. and pubs. Monthly.

JEWISH NEWS (1995). 3747 W. Esplanade Avenue, Suite 307, Metairie, LA 70002. (504)780-5600. FAX: (504)780-5601. E-mail: jewishnews@jewishnola.com. Gail Naron Chalew. Fortnightly. Jewish Federation of Greater New Orleans.

MARYLAND

BALTIMORE JEWISH TIMES (1919). 2104 N. Charles St., Baltimore, 21218. (410)752-3504. FAX: (410)752-2375. Phil Jacobs. Weekly.

WASHINGTON JEWISH WEEK (1930, as the National Jewish Ledger). 1500 East Jefferson St., Rockville, 20852. (301) 230-2222. FAX: (301)881-6362. E-mail: wjweek@aol.com. Debra Rubin. Weekly.

MASSACHUSETTS

AMERICAN JEWISH HISTORY (1892). 160 Herrick Road, Newton Centre, MA 02459. (671)559-8880. FAX: (671)559-8881. E-mail: ajhs@ajhs.org. Eli Faber. Quarterly. American Jewish Historical Society.

THE JEWISH ADVOCATE (1902). 15 School St., Boston, 02108. (617)367-9100. FAX: (617)367-9310. E-mail: editorial@the jewishadvocate.com. David Nathan. Weekly.

THE JEWISH CHRONICLE (1927). 131 Lincoln St., Worcester, 01605. (508)752-2512. E-mail: chronicle.editor@verizon.net. Pub. Sondra Shapiro; Ed. Ellen Weingart. Fortnightly.

JEWISH GUIDE TO BOSTON & NEW ENGLAND (1972). 15 School St., Boston, 02108. (617)367-9100. FAX: (617)367-9310. Rosie Rosenzweig. Irregularly. The Jewish Advocate.

THE JEWISH JOURNAL/NORTH OF BOSTON (1976). 201 Washington St., PO Box 555, Salem, 01970. (978)745-4111 .FAX: (978) 745-5333. E-mail: editorial@jewishjournal. org. Judith Klein. Biweekly. Russian section. North Shore Jewish Press Ltd.

THE JEWISH NEWS OF WESTERN MASSACHUSETTS (see Jewish Advocate)

MetroWest Jewish Reporter (1970). 76 Salem End Rd., Framingham, 01702. (508)872-4808. FAX: (508)879-5856. Marcia T. Rivin. Monthly. Combined Jewish Philanthropies of Greater Boston.

PAKN-TREGER (1980). 1021 West St., Amherst, 01002. (413)256-4900. FAX: (413)256-4700. E-mail: pt@bikher.org. Nancy Sherman. Three times a year. National Yiddish Book Center.

SH'MA (1970). 90 Oak Street, 4th Floor, Newton MA 02459. (781)449-9894. FAX: (781) 449-9825. E-mail: susanb@jflmedia.com. Susan Berrin. Monthly. Jewish Family & Life.

MICHIGAN

DETROIT JEWISH NEWS (1942). 29200 Northwestern Highway, Ste. 110, Southfield, 48034. (248)354-6060. FAX: (248) 304-8885. E-mail: rsklar@thejewish news.com. Robert Sklar. Weekly.

HUMANISTIC JUDAISM (1968). 28611 W. Twelve Mile Rd., Farmington Hills, 48334. (248)478-7610. FAX: (248)478-3159. E-mail: info@shj.org. M. Bonnie Cousens, Ruth D. Feldman. Quarterly. Society for Humanistic Judaism.

WASHTENAW JEWISH NEWS (1978). 2935 Birch Hollow Dr., Ann Arbor, 48108. (734)971-1800. FAX: (734)971-1801. E-mail: wjna2@aol.com. Susan Kravitz Ayer. Monthly.

MINNESOTA

AMERICAN JEWISH WORLD (1912). 4509 Minnetonka Blvd., Minneapolis, MN 55416. (952)259-5280. FAX: (952)920-6205. E-mail: amjewish@isd.net. Mordecai Specktor. Weekly.

MISSISSIPPI

DEEP SOUTH JEWISH VOICE (see Alabama)

MISSOURI

Kansas City Jewish Chronicle. See under KANSAS

ST. Louis Jewish Light (1947; reorg. 1963). 12 Millstone Campus Dr., St. Louis, 63146. (314)432-3353. FAX: (314)432-0515. E-mail: stlouislgt@aol.com. Robert A. Cohn. Weekly. St. Louis Jewish Light.

NEBRASKA

JEWISH PRESS (1920). 333 S. 132 St., Omaha, 68154. (402)334-6450. FAX: (402)334-5422. E-mail: ckatzman@jewishomaha.org. Carol Katzman. Weekly. Jewish Federation of Omaha.

NEVADA

JEWISH REPORTER (1976). 3909 S. Maryland Pkwy., Suite 400, Las Vegas, 89119-7520. (702)948-5129. FAX: (702)967-1082. E-mail: lvjewishreporter@aol.com. Terri Herman. Bimonthly. Jewish Federation of Las Vegas.

LAS VEGAS ISRAELITE (1965). PO Box 14096, Las Vegas, 89114. (702)876-1255. FAX: (702)364-1009. Michael Tell. Bimonthly.

NEW JERSEY

AVOTAYNU (1985). 155 N. Washington Ave., Bergenfield, 07621. (201)387-7200. FAX: (201)387-2855. E-mail: info@avotaynu.com. Sallyann Amdur Sack. Quarterly.

JEWISH CHRONICLE (1982). 1063 East Landis Ave.,Suite B, Vineland, 08360.

(856)696-4445. FAX: (856)696-3428. E-mail: jfedcc@aol.com. Ann Lynn Lipton. Bimonthly. The Jewish Federation of Cumberland County.

JEWISH COMMUNITY NEWS. 1086 Teaneck Rd., Teaneck, 07666. (201) 837-8818. FAX: (201) 833-4959. E-mail: jewish std2@aol.com. Rebecca Kaplan Boroson. Fortnightly. Jewish Federation of North Jersey and Jewish Federation of Greater Clifton-Passaic.

JEWISH COMMUNITY VOICE (1941). 1301 Springdale Rd., Suite 250, Cherry Hill, 08003-2762. (856)751-9500, ext. 217. FAX: (856)489-8253. E-mail: jvcheditor @aol.com. Harriet Kessler. Biweekly. Jewish Federation of Southern NJ.

THE JEWISH JOURNAL (OF OCEAN COUNTY) (1999). 320 Raritan Ave., Suite 203, Highland Park, 08904. (732)393-0023. FAX: (732)393-0026. E-mail: jewish@castle.net. Ron Ostroff. Monthly. Published in cooperation with the Jewish Federation of Ocean County.

JEWISH STANDARD (1931). 1086 Teaneck Rd., Teaneck, 07666. (201)837-8818. FAX: (201)833-4959. Rebecca Kaplan Boroson. Weekly.

JEWISH STAR (1985). 230 Old Bridge Turnpike, South River, 08882-2000. (732)432-7711. FAX: (732)432-0292. E-mail: jfgmc @aol.com. Marlene A. Heller. Fortnightly. Jewish Federation of Greater Middlesex County.

THE JEWISH STATE – THE WEEKLY NEWSPAPER FOR CENTRAL JERSEY'S JEWISH COMMUNITIES (1996). 320 Raritan Ave., Suite 203, Highland Park, 08904. (732)393-0023. FAX: (732)393-0026. E-mail: jewish@castle.net. Ron Ostroff. Weekly.

JEWISH VOICE & OPINION (1987). 73 Dana Place, Englewood, 07631. (201) 569-2845. FAX: (201)569-1739. Susan L. Rosenbluth. Monthly.

JEWISH VOICE OF GREATER MONMOUTH COUNTY (1971). 100 Grant Ave., Deal Park, 07723. (732)531-6200. FAX: (732)531-9518. E-mail: pfdnuss@msn.com. Lauren Silver. Monthly. Jewish Federation of Greater Monmouth County and Ocean County Jewish Federation.

JOURNAL OF JEWISH COMMUNAL SERVICE (1899). 3084 State Hwy. 27, Suite 9, Kendall Pk., 08824-1657. (732)821-1871.

FAX: (732)821-5335. E-mail: jcsana@aol. com. Gail Naron Chalew. Quarterly. Jewish Communal Service Association of North America.

NEW JERSEY JEWISH NEWS (1947). 901 Route 10, Whippany, 07981-1157. (973) 887-3900. FAX: (973)887-5999. E-mail: 6853202@mcimail.com. Andrew Silow-Carroll. Weekly. United Jewish Federation of MetroWest.

THE SPEAKER (1999). 320 Raritan Ave., Suite 203, Highland Park, 08904. (732)393-0023. FAX: (732)393-0026. E-mail: jewish@castle.net. Ron Ostroff. Monthly. Published in cooperation with the Jewish Federation of Somerset, Hunterdon & Warren Counties.

NEW MEXICO

NEW MEXICO JEWISH LINK (1971). 5520 Wyoming NE, Albuquerque, 87109. (505)821-3214. FAX: (505)821-3351. E-mail: nmjlink@aol.com. Tema Milstein. Monthly. Jewish Federation of Greater Albuquerque.

NEW YORK

AFN SHVEL (1941). 200 W. 72 St., Suite 40, NYC, 10023. (212)787-6675. E-mail: yidleague@aol.com. Mordkhe Schaechter. Quarterly. Yiddish. League for Yiddish, Inc.

AGENDA: JEWISH EDUCATION (1949; FORMERLY PEDAGOGIC REPORTER). JESNA, 111 Eighth Ave., Suite 11E, NYC, 10011-5201. (212)284-6950. FAX: (212)284-6951. E-mail: info@jesna.org. Amy Stein. Twice a year. Jewish Education Service of North America, Inc.

ALGEMEINER JOURNAL (1972). 225 E. Broadway, NYC, 10002. (212)267-5561. FAX: (212)267-5624. E-mail: Algemeiner @aol.com. Gershon Jacobson. Weekly. Yiddish-English.

AMERICAN JEWISH YEAR BOOK (1899). 165 E. 56 St., NYC, 10022. (212)751-4000. FAX: (212)751-4017. E-mail: research @ajc.org. David Singer, Lawrence Grossman. Annually. American Jewish Committee.

AMIT (1925). 817 Broadway, NYC, 10003. (212)477-4720. FAX: (212)477-5213. E-mail: amitmag@amitchildren.org. Rita Schwalb. Quarterly. AMIT (formerly American Mizrachi Women).

AUFBAU (1934). 2121 Broadway, NYC, 10023. (212)873-7400. Voice mail: (212) 579-6578. FAX: (212)496-5736. E-mail: aufbau2000@aol.com. Monika Ziegler/Andreas Mink/Irene Armbruster. Fortnightly. German-English. New World Club, Inc.

BUFFALO JEWISH REVIEW (1918). 15 E. Mohawk St., Buffalo, 14203. (716)854-2192. FAX: (716)854-2198. E-mail: buffjewrev @aoc.com. Harlan C. Abbey. Weekly. Kahaal Nahalot Israel.

THE CALL (1933). 45 E. 33 St., NYC, 10016. (212)749-9000, ext. 225. FAX: (212)532-7518. E-mail: socolove@circle.org. Emily Socolov. Three times a year. The Workmen's Circle/Arbeter Ring.

CCAR JOURNAL: A REFORM JEWISH QUARTERLY (formerly Journal of Reform Judaism) (1953). 355 Lexington Ave., NYC, 10017. (212)972-3636. FAX: (212)692-0819. Ed. Stephen Pearce. Mng. Ed. Elliot Stevens. Quarterly. Central Conference of American Rabbis.

CIRCLE (1943). 15 E. 26 St., NYC, 10010-1579. (212)532-4949. FAX: (212)481-4174. E-mail: info@jcca.org. Miriam Rinn. JCC Circle Quarterly. Jewish Community Centers Association of North America (formerly JWB).

COMMENTARY (1945). 165 E. 56 St., NYC, 10022. (212)751-4000. FAX: (212)891-6700. E-mail: mail@commentarymagazine. com. Ed. Neal Kozodoy; Ed.-at-Large Norman Podhoretz. Monthly. American Jewish Committee.

CONGRESS MONTHLY (1933). 825 Third Ave., Ste. 1800, NYC, 10022. (212)879-4500. Rochelle Mancini. Six times a year. American Jewish Congress.

CONSERVATIVE JUDAISM (1945). 3080 Broadway, NYC, 10027. (212)280-6065. FAX: (212)749-9166. E-mail: rapubs@jtsa.edu. Rabbi Martin S. Cohen. Quarterly. Rabbinical Assembly and Jewish Theological Seminary of America.

FORVERTS (YIDDISH FORWARD) (1897). 45 E. 33 St., NYC, 10016. (212)889-8200. FAX: (212)684-3949. Boris Sandler. Weekly. Yiddish. Forward Association, Inc.

FORWARD (1897). 45 E. 33 St., NYC, 10016. (212)889-8200. FAX: (212)447-6406. E-mail: newsdesk@forward.com. J. J.

Goldberg. Weekly. Forward Newspaper, L.L.C.

HADAROM (1957). 305 Seventh Ave., NYC, 10001. (212)807-7888. FAX: (212)727-8452. Rabbi Gedalia Dov Schwartz. Annual. Hebrew. Rabbinical Council of America.

HADASSAH MAGAZINE (1914). 50 W. 58 St., NYC, 10019. (212)688-0227. FAX: (212) 446-9521. Alan M. Tigay. Monthly (except for combined issues of June-July and Aug.-Sept.). Hadassah, the Women's Zionist Organization of America.

I.A.J.E. NEWSLETTER (1999). (718)339-0337. E-mail: sanuav@stjohns.edu. Victor D. Sanua. International Association of Jews from Egypt.

JBI VOICE (1978). 110 E. 30 St., NYC, 10016. (212)889-2525, (800)433-1531, FAX (212) 689-3692. Email: dbarbara @jbilibrary.org. Dena Barbara. Ten times a year in U.S. (audiocassettes). English. Jewish Braille Institute of America.

JEWISH ACTION (1950). 11 Broadway, NYC, 10004. (212)613-8146. FAX: (212)613-0646. E-mail: ja@ou.org. Nechama Carmel. Quarterly. Orthodox Union.

JEWISH BOOK ANNUAL (1942). 15 E. 26 St., 10th fl., New York, NY 10010. (212)532-4949, ext. 297. E-mail: jbc@jewish books.org. Dr.Stephen H. Garrin. Hebrew & English with bibliography in Yiddish. Jewish Book Council, Jewish Book Annual published by Jewish Book Council.

JEWISH BOOK WORLD (1945). 15 E. 26 St., NYC, 10010. (212)532-4949, ext. 297. FAX: (212)481-4174. E-mail: jbc@jewish books.org. Esther Nussbaum. Three times annually. Jewish Book Council.

JEWISH BRAILLE REVIEW (1931). 110 E. 30 St., NYC, 10016. E-mail:dbarbara@ jbilibrary.org. (212)889-2525, (800)433-1531. Dena Barbara. 10 times a year in U.S. (braille). English. Jewish Braille Institute of America.

JEWISH CURRENTS (1946) 22 E. 17St., Suite 601, NYC, 10003-1919. (212)924-5740. FAX: (212)414-2227. Bimonthly. Association for Promotion of Jewish Secularism, Inc.

JEWISH EDUCATION NEWS (1980). 261 W. 35 St., Fl. 12A, NYC 10001. (212) 268-4210.

FAX: (212)268-4214. E-mail: publications@caje.org. Mng. Ed. Judi Resnick. Triannually. Coalition for the Advancement of Jewish Education.

JEWISH FRONTIER (1934). P.O. Box 4013, Amity Station, New Haven, CT 06525. (203)397-4903. FAX: (212)675-7685. E-mail: jewish-frontier@yahoo.com. Nahum Guttman-Graff. Bimonthly. Labor Zionist Letters, Inc. Managing Editor Bennett Lovett-Graff

JEWISH HERALD (1984). 1689 46 St., Brooklyn, NY 11204. (718)972-4000. E-mail: jewishherald@aol.com. Leon J. Sternheim. Weekly.

JEWISH JOURNAL (1969). 11 Sunrise Plaza, Valley Stream, 11580. (516)561-6900. FAX: (516)561-6971. Ed. Paul Rubens; Pub. Harold Singer. Weekly.

JEWISH LEDGER (1924). 2535 Brighton-Henrietta Town Line Rd., Rochester, 14623. (716)427-2434. FAX: (716)427-8521. Barbara Morgenstern. Weekly.

THE JEWISH OBSERVER (1963). 42 Broadway, NYC, 10004. (212)797-9000. FAX: (646)254-1600. E-mail: nwolpin@aol. com. Rabbi Nisson Wolpin. Monthly (except July and Aug.). Agudath Israel of America.

JEWISH OBSERVER OF CENTRAL NEW YORK (1978). 5655 Thompson Road, DeWitt, NY 13214. (315)445-2040 ext. 116 FAX: (315)445-1559. E-mail: jocny@aol.com. Bette Siegel. Biweekly. Syracuse Jewish Federation, Inc.

JEWISH POST OF NY (1993). 262 West 38th St., NYC, 10018. (212)398-1313. FAX: (212)398-3933. E-mail: jpost@nais.com. Ed. Gad Nahshon. Monthly. Link Marketing & Promotion, Inc.

JEWISH PRESS (1950). 338 Third Ave., Brooklyn, 11215. (718)330-1100. FAX: (718)935-1215. E-mail: editor@jewish press.com. Jerry Greenwald. Weekly.

JEWISH TELEGRAPHIC AGENCY COMMUNITY NEWS REPORTER (1962). 330 Seventh Ave., 11th fl., NYC, 10001-5010. (212)643-1890. FAX: (212)643-8498. Email: www.jta.org/info@jta.org. Lisa Hostein. Monthly.

JEWISH TELEGRAPHIC AGENCY DAILY NEWS BULLETIN (1917). 330 Seventh Ave., 11th fl., NYC, 10001-5010. (212)643-1890.

FAX: (212)643-8498. Exec. Ed. Mark Joffe; Ed. Lisa Hostein. Daily.

JEWISH TELEGRAPHIC AGENCY WEEKLY NEWS DIGEST (1933). 330 Seventh Ave., 11th fl., NYC, 10001-5010. (212)643-1890. FAX: (212)643-8498. E-mail: www.jta.org/info@jta.org. Exec. Ed. Mark Joffe; Ed. Lisa Hostein. Weekly.

JEWISH TRIBUNE. PMB #372, 169 South Main St., New City, 10956; Exec. off. (mailing address): 115 Middle Neck Rd., Great Neck, 11021. (845)352-5151. FAX: (516)829-4776. E-mail: lijeworld@aol.com. Jerome W. Lippman. Weekly. Jewish Tribune; Long Island Jewish World; Manhattan Jewish Sentinel.

JEWISH WEEK (1876; REORG. 1970). 1501 Broadway, NYC, 10036-5503. (212)921-7822. FAX: (212)921-8420. E-mail: editor @jewishweek.org. Gary Rosenblatt. Weekly.

JEWISH WORLD (1965). 3 Vatrano Road, Albany, 12205. (518)459-8455. FAX: (518) 459-5289. E-mail: news@jewishworld-news.org. Sam S. Clevenson. Weekly.

JOURNAL OF JEWISH EDUCATION-CJE (FORMERLY JEWISH EDUCATION) (1929). 11 Olympia Lane, Monsey, NY 10952. (845) 368-8657. FAX: (845)369-6538. E-mail: mjscje@aol.com. Rabbi Irwin E. Witty. Three times a year. Council for Jewish Education.

JOURNAL OF REFORM JUDAISM. See CCAR Journal

JTS PUBLICATIONS (1991). 3080 Broadway, NYC 10027. (212)678-8950. FAX: (212) 864-0109. E-mail: jowerner@jtsa.edu. Three times a year. The Jewish Theological Seminary. Asst. Dir. of Pub. Jodi Werner.

JUDAISM (1952). 825 Third Ave., Ste. 1800, NYC, 10022. (212)360-1500. FAX: (212)249-3672. Editor's address: Kresge Col., U. of California, Santa Cruz, CA, 95064. (831)459-2566. FAX: (831)459-4872. E-mail: judaism@cats.ucsc.edu. Prof. Murray Baumgarten. Quarterly. American Jewish Congress.

KASHRUS MONTHLY-YOUR UUDATE ON KOSHER (1990). PO Box 204, Brooklyn, 11204. (718)336-8544. Rabbi Yosef Wikler. Monthly. Kashrus Institute. (editorial@kashrusmagazin.com)

KASHRUS MAGAZINE-THE PERIODICAL FOR THE KOSHER CONSUMER (1980). PO Box 204, Brooklyn, 11204. (718)336-8544. E-mail: editorial@kashrusmagazine.com. Rabbi Yosef Wikler. Five times per year (January, March, May, July, October). Kashrus Institute. (WWW.KASHRUS MAGAZINE.COM)

KOL HAT'NUA (VOICE OF THE MOVEMENT) (1975). c/o Young Judaea, 50 W. 58 St., NYC, 10019. (212)303-4576. FAX: (212)303-4572. E-mail: info@young judaea.org. Dov Wilker. Quarterly. Hadassah Zionist Youth Commission-Young Judaea.

KULTUR UN LEBN-CULTURE AND LIFE (1960). 45 E. 33 St., NYC, 10016. (212)889-6800. FAX: (212)532-7518. E-mail: wcfriends@aol.com. Joseph Mlotek. Quarterly. Yiddish. The Workmen's Circle.

LAMISHPAHA (1963). 426 W. 58 St., NYC, 10019. (212)957-6658/9/8862-HEBREW. FAX: (212)957-5811 .E-mail: general@ hist-ivrit.org. Dr. Vered Cohen-Raphaeli. Illustrated. Monthly (except July and Aug.). Hebrew. Histadruth Ivrith of America. (WWW.HEBREWUSA.ORG)

LIKUTIM (1981). 110 E. 30 St., NYC, 10016. (212)889-2525. Joanne Jahr. Two times a year in Israel (print and audiocassettes). Hebrew. Jewish Braille Institute of America.

LILITH-THE INDEPENDENT JEWISH WOMEN'S MAGAZINE (1976). 250 W. 57 St., #2432, NYC, 10107. (212)757-0818. FAX: (212)757-5705. E-mail: lilithmag @aol.com. Susan Weidman Schneider. Quarterly. (WWW.LILITHMAG.COM)

LONG ISLAND JEWISH WORLD (1971). 115 Middle Neck Rd., Great Neck, 11021. (516)829-4000. FAX: (516)829-4776. E-mail: lijeworld@aol.com. Jerome W. Lippman. Weekly.

MANHATTAN JEWISH SENTINEL (1993). 115 Middle Neck Rd., Great Neck, 11021. (212)244-4949. FAX: (212)244-2257. E-mail: lijeworld@aol.com. Jerome W. Lippman. Weekly.

MARTYRDOM AND RESISTANCE (1974). 500 Fifth Ave., 42nd Floor, NYC, 10110-4299. (212)220-4304. FAX:(212)220-4308. E-mail: yadvashem@aol.com. Ed. Dr. Harvey Rosenfeld; Ed.-in-Chief Eli

Zborowski. Bimonthly. International Society for Yad Vashem.

MIDSTREAM (1954). 633 Third Ave., 21st fl., NYC, 10017. (212)339-6020. FAX: (212)318-6176. E-mail: midstreamthf@aol. com. Leo Haber. Eight times a year. Theodor Herzl Foundation, Inc.

NA'AMAT WOMAN (1925). 350 Fifth Ave., Suite 4700, NYC, 10118-4799. (212)563-5222. FAX: (212)563-5710. Judith A. Sokoloff. Quarterly. English-Yiddish-Hebrew. NA'AMAT USA, the Women's Labor Zionist Organization of America.

OLOMEINU-OURWORLD (1945). 5723 18th Ave., Brooklyn, 11204. (718)259-1223. FAX: (718)259-1795. Email: mail@tu publications.com. Rabbi Yaakov Fruchter. Monthly. English-Hebrew. Torah Umesorah-National Society for Hebrew Day Schools.

PASSOVER DIRECTORY (1923). 11 Broadway, NYC, 10004. (212)613-8135. FAX: (212)613-0772. Email: lieberd@ou.org Deborah Lieber. Annually. Union of Orthodox Jewish Congregations of America.

PROCEEDINGS OF THE AMERICAN ACADEMY FOR JEWISH RESEARCH (1920). 51 Washington Sq. South, NYC, 10012-1075. (212)998-3550. FAX: (212)995-4178. Dr. Nahum Sarna. Annually. English-Hebrew-French-Arabic-Persian-Greek. American Academy for Jewish Research.

RCA RECORD (1953). 305 Seventh Ave. NYC, 10001. (212)807-7888. FAX: (212) 727-8452. Rabbi Mark Dratch. Quarterly. Rabbinical Council of America.

REFORM JUDAISM (1972; FORMERLY DIMENSIONS IN AMERICAN JUDAISM). 633 Third Ave., 6th fl., NYC, 10017. (212)650-4240. Aron Hirt-Manheimer. Quarterly. Union for Reform Judaism. (urj.org/rjmag)

THE REPORTER (1971). 500 Clubhouse Rd., Vestal, 13850. (607)724-2360. FAX: (607) 724-2311. E-mail: TReporter@aol.com. Judith S. Huober. Weekly. Jewish Federation of Broome County, Inc.

THE REPORTER (1966). 315 Park Ave. S., NYC 10010. (212)505-7700. FAX: (212) 674-3057. E-mail; editor@waort.org. Marlene A. Heller. Semi-Annual. Women's American ORT, Inc.

RESPONSE: A CONTEMPORARY JEWISH REVIEW (1967). Columbia University Post Office, PO Box 250892, NYC, 10025. E-mail: response@panix.com. Chanita Baumhaft. Annual.

RUSSIAN FORWARD (1995). 45 E. 33 St., NYC, 10016. (212)889-8200. FAX: (212)448-9124. E-mail: rforward99@ yahoo.com. Leonid Shkolnik. Weekly. Russian.

SYNAGOGUE LIGHT AND KOSHER LIFE (1933). 47 Beekman St., NYC, 10038. (212)227-7800. Rabbi Meyer Hager. Quarterly. The Kosher Food Institute.

TRADITION (1958). 305 Seventh Ave., NYC, 10001. (212)807-7888. FAX: (212)727-8452. Rabbi Michael Shmidman. Quarterly. Rabbinical Council of America.

UNITED SYNAGOGUE REVIEW (1943). 155 Fifth Ave., NYC, 10010. (212)533-7800. FAX: (212)353-9439. E-mail: info@uscj. org. Lois Goldrich. Semiannually. United Synagogue of Conservative Judaism.

UNSER TSAIT (1941). 25 E. 21 St., 3rd fl., NYC, 10010. (212)475-0059. Bimonthly. Yiddish. Jewish Labor Bund.

VIEWPOINT MAGAZINE (1952). 3 W. 16 St., NYC, 10011. (212)929-1525, ext. 131. E-mail: ncyi@youngisrael.org. Esther Altman. Quarterly. National Council of Young Israel.

VOICE OF THE DUTCHESS JEWISH COMMUNITY (1989). 110 Grand Ave., Poughkeepsie, 12603. (845)471-9811. FAX: (845)471-3233. E-mail: jfeddutchess@ mindspring.com. Business off.:500 Clubhouse Rd., Vestal, 13850. (607)724-2360. FAX: (607)724-2311. Sandy Gardner and Judith Huober. Monthly. Jewish Federation of Dutchess County, Inc.

WOMEN'S LEAGUE OUTLOOK MAGAZINE (1930475 475 Riverside Drive, Suite 820, New York, 10115. (212)870-1260. FAX: (212)870-1261. E-mail: rkahn@wlcj.org. Janet Arnowitz. Quarterly. Women's League for Conservative Judaism.

WORKMEN'S CIRCLE CALL. See The Call

WYOMING VALLEY JEWISH REPORTER (formerly WE ARE ONE) (1995). 500 Clubhouse Rd., Vestal, 13850. (607)724-2360. FAX: (607)724-2311. E-mail: TReporter @aol.com. Judith S. Huober. Every other week. Wilkes-Barre Jewish Community Board.

YEARBOOK OF THE CENTRAL CONFERENCE OF AMERICAN RABBIS (1890). 355 Lexington Ave., NYC, 10017. (212)972-3636. FAX: (212)692-0819. Rabbi Elliot L. Stevens. Annually. Central Conference of American Rabbis.

YIDDISH (1973). Queens College, NSF 350, 65-30 Kissena Blvd., Flushing, 11367. (718)997-3622. Joseph C. Landis. Quarterly. Queens College Press.

DI YIDDISHE HEIM (1958). 770 Eastern Pkwy.,

BROOKLYN, 11213. (718)735-0458. Rachel Altein, Tema Gurary. Twice a year. English-Yiddish. Neshei Ub'nos Chabad-Lubavitch Women's Organization.

YIDDISHE KULTUR (1938). 1133 Broadway, Rm. 820, NYC, 10010. (212)243-1304. FAX (212)243-1305. E-mail: mahosu@ aol.com. Itche Goldberg. Bimonthly. Yiddish. Yiddisher Kultur Farband, Inc.— YKUF.

DOS YIDDISHE VORT (1953). 84 William St., NYC, 10038. (212)797-9000. Joseph Friedenson. Bimonthly, (November-December monthly). Yiddish. Agudath Israel of America.

YIDDISHER KEMFER (1900). 275 Seventh Ave., NYC, 10001. (212)675-7808. FAX: (212) 675-7685. Dr. Jacob Weitzney. Bimonthly. Yiddish. Labor Zionist Alliance.

YIDISHE SHPRAKH (1941). 15 W. 16 St., NYC, 10011. (212)246-6080, ext. 6139. FAX: (212) 292-1892. Dr. Mordkhe Schaechter. Irregularly. Yiddish. YIVO Institute for Jewish Research.

YIVO BLETER (1931). 15 W. 16 St., NYC, 10011. (212)246-6080. FAX: (212)292-1892.E-mail: yivomail@yivo.cjh.org. Dr. David E. Fishman. Biannually. Yiddish. YIVO Institute for Jewish Research.

THE YOUNG JUDAEAN (1909). 50 W. 58 St., NYC, 10019. (212)303-4588. FAX: (212)303-4572. Email: ugoldflam@young judaea.org. Uri Goldflam. Quarterly. Young Judaea Zionist Youth Movement/Hadassah.

YUGNTRUF: YIDDISH YOUTH MAGAZINE (1964). 200 W. 72 St., Suite 40, NYC, 10023. (212)787-6675. FAX: (212)799-1517. E-mail: yugntruf@yugntruf.org. Elinor Robinson. Two to four times a year. Yiddish. Yugntruf Youth for Yiddish.

ZUKUNFT (THE FUTURE) (1892). 25 E. 21 St., NYC, 10010. (212)505-8040. FAX: (212)505-8044. Chaim Beider & Yonia Fain. Quarterly. Yiddish. Congress for Jewish Culture.

NORTH CAROLINA

CHARLOTTE JEWISH NEWS (1978). 5007 Providence Rd., Charlotte, 28226. (704) 944-6765. FAX: (704) 365-4507. E-mail: amontoni@shalomcharlotte.org. Amy Krakovitz. Monthly (except July). Jewish Federation of Greater Charlotte.

JEWISH FEDERATION NEWS (1986). 8210 Creedmoor Rd., Suite 104, Raleigh, 27613. (919)676-2200. FAX: (919)676-2122. Sarah Falk. Monthly. Wake County Jewish Federation.

MODERN JUDAISM (1980). Oxford University Press, 2001 Evans Rd., Cary, 27513. (919)677-0977. FAX: (919)677-1714. E-mail: jnlorders@oup-usa.org. (Editorial address: Center for Judaic Studies, Boston University, 745 Commonwealth Ave., Boston, 02215. (617)353-8096. FAX: (617)353-5441.) Steven T. Katz. Three times a year.

OHIO

AKRON JEWISH NEWS (1929). 750 White Pond Drive, Akron, 44320. (330)869-2424. FAX: (330)867-8498.E-mail: Toby__Liberman@ jewishakron.org. Paula Maggio. Fortnightly. Fifteen times a year. Jewish Community Board of Akron.

AMERICAN ISRAELITE (1854). 906 Main St., Rm. 508, Cincinnati, 45202-1371. (513) 621-3145. FAX: (513)621-3744. E-mail: amisralite@aol.com. Stanley H. Bard. Weekly.

AMERICAN JEWISH ARCHIVES JOURNAL (1948). 3101 Clifton Ave., Cincinnati, 45220-2488. (513)221-1875. FAX: (513) 221-7812. E-mail: aja@cn.huc.edu. Ed. Dr. Gary P. Zola; Mng. Ed. Dr. Frederic Krome. Twice a year. Jacob Rader Marcus Center, American Jewish Archives, HUC-JIR.

CLEVELAND JEWISH NEWS (1964). 3645 Warrensville Center Rd., Suite 230, Cleveland, 44122. (216)991-8300. FAX: (216)991-2088. E-mail: editorial@cjn.org. Cynthia Dettelbach. Weekly. Cleveland Jewish News Publication Co.

INDEX TO JEWISH PERIODICALS (1963). PO Box 18525, Cleveland Hts., 44118. (216)381-4846. FAX: (216)381-4321. E-mail: index@jewishperiodicals.com. Lenore Pfeffer Koppel. Annually. Available in book and CD-ROM form. (WWW.JEWISHPERIODICALS.COM)

JEWISH JOURNAL (1987). 505 Gypsy Lane, Youngstown, 44504-1314. (330)744-7902. FAX: (330)746-7926. Email: yojjournal @aol.com Sherry Weinblatt. Biweekly (except July/Aug.). Youngstown Area Jewish Federation. (WWW.JEWISHJOURNAL PLUS.COM)

OHIO JEWISH CHRONICLE (1922). 2862 Johnstown Rd., Columbus, 43219. (614)337-2055. FAX: (614)337-2059. Email: ojc@insight.rr.com. Judy Franklin. Weekly.

STARK JEWISH NEWS (1920). 2631 Harvard Ave. NW, Canton, 44709. (330)452-6444. FAX: (330)452-4487. E-mail: cantonjcf @aol.com. Linda Sirak. Monthly. Canton Jewish Community Federation;

STUDIES IN BIBLIOGRAPHY AND BOOKLORE (1953). 3101 Clifton Ave., Cincinnati, 45220. (513)221-1875. FAX: (513)221-0519. E-mail: lwolfson@huc.edu. Editor David J. Gilner; Managing Editor Laurel S. Wolfson. Irregularly. English-Hebrew-etc. Library of Hebrew Union College-Jewish Institute of Religion.

TOLEDO JEWISH NEWS (1951). 6505 Sylvania Ave., Sylvania, 43560. (419)724-0363. FAX: (419)724-0423. E-mail: meira@jewish toledo.org. Laurie Cohen. Monthly. United Jewish Council of Greater Toledo.

OKLAHOMA

TULSA JEWISH REVIEW (1930). 2021 E. 71 St., Tulsa, 74136. (918)495-1100. FAX: (918)495-1220. Ed Ulrich. Monthly. Jewish Federation of Tulsa.

OREGON

BRIDGES: A JOURNAL FOR JEWISH FEMINISTS AND OUR FRIENDS (1990). PO Box 24839, Eugene, 97402. (541)343-7617. FAX: (541)343-7617. E-mail: clare@bridges journal.org. Mng. Ed. Clare Kinberg.

JEWISH REVIEW (1959). 6680 SW Capitol Highway, Portland, OR 97219. Edit.:(503) 245-4340. FAX: (503) 245-4342. Adv.: (503) 546-9883. FAX: (503) 620-3433. E-mail: news@jewishreview.

org. Paul Haist. Regular column in Russian. Fortnightly. Jewish Federation of Portland. (WWW.JEWISHREVIEW.ORG)

PENNSYLVANIA

COMMUNITY REVIEW (1925). 3301 N. Front St. Annex, Harrisburg, 17110. (717)236-9555, ext.3402. FAX:(717)236-2552. E-mail: communityreview@dcsupernet. net. Carol L. Cohen. Fortnightly. United Jewish Community of Greater Harrisburg.

CONTEMPORARY JEWRY (1974), under the name JEWISH SOCIOLOGY AND SOCIAL RESEARCH). Graduate Center CUNY, Room 6112-13, 365 Fifth Avenue, New York, NY 10016. (212) 817-8772. FAX: (914) 235-6717. E-mail: heilman@qc.edu. Samuel C. Heilman. Annually. Association for the Social Scientific Study of Jewry.

JERUSALEM LETTER/VIEWPOINTS (1978). 1515 Locust St., Suite 703, Philadelphia, 19102. (215)772-0564. FAX: (215)772-0566. Zvi R. Marom. Fortnightly. Jerusalem Center for Public Affairs.

JEWISH CHRONICLE OF PITTSBURGH (1962). 5600 Baum Blvd., Pittsburgh, 15206. (412)687-1000. FAX:(412)687-5119. E-mail: news@pittchron.com. Lee Chottiner. Weekly. Pittsburgh Jewish Publication and Education Foundation.

JEWISH EXPONENT (1887). 2100 Arch St., Philadelphia, 19103. (215)832-0740. FAX: (215)569-3389. E-mail: jexponent @aol.com. Jonathan S. Tobin. Weekly. Jewish Federation of Greater Philadelphia.

JEWISH POLITICAL STUDIES REVIEW (1989). 1515 Locust St., Suite 703, Philadelphia, 19102. (215)772-0564. FAX: (215)772-0566. Mark Ami-El. Twice a year. Jerusalem Center for Public Affairs.

JEWISH QUARTERLY REVIEW (1910). 420 Walnut St., Philadelphia, 19106. (215) 238-1290. FAX: (215)238-1540. E-mail: jqroffice@sas.upenn.edu. Ed. David M. Goldenberg; Mng. Ed. Bonnie L. Blankenship. Quarterly. Center for Advanced Jewish Studies, University of Pennsylvania.

NEW MENORAH (1978). 7318 Germantown Ave., Philadelphia, 19119-1793. (215)247-9700. FAX: (215)247-9703. Rabbi Arthur Waskow, PhD. Quarterly. Aleph: Alliance for Jewish Renewal.

RECONSTRUCTIONISM TODAY (1993). Beit Devora, 7804 Montgomery Ave., Suite 9, Elkins Park, 19027-2649. (215)782-8500. FAX: (215)782-8805. E-mail: jrfnatl@aol.com. Lawrence Bush. Quarterly. Jewish Reconstructionist Federation.

THE RECONSTRUCTIONIST (1935). 1299 Church Rd., Wyncote, 19095-1898. (215) 576-5210. FAX: (215)576-8051. E-mail: rhirsh@therra.org. Rabbi Richard Hirsh. Semiannually. Reconstructionist Rabbinical College.

RHODE ISLAND

JEWISH VOICE AND HERALD (formerly JEWISH VOICE OF RHODE ISLAND) (1973). 130 Sessions St., Providence, 02906. (401)421-4111. FAX: (401)331-7961. E-mail: voiceherald@jfri.org. Jonathan Rubin. Biweekly. Jewish Federation of Rhode Island.

RHODE ISLAND JEWISH HERALD (1930). 99 Webster St., Pawtucket, 02860. (401)724-0200. FAX: (401)726-5820. Luke O'Neill. Weekly. Herald Press Publishing Company.

RHODE ISLAND JEWISH HISTORICAL NOTES (1951). 130 Sessions St., Providence, 02906. (401)331-1360. FAX: (401)272-6729. E-mail: rjhist@aol.com. Leonard Moss. Annually. Rhode Island Jewish Historical Association.

SOUTH CAROLINA

CHARLESTON JEWISH VOICE (2001). 1645 Wallenberg Blvd., Charleston, 29407. (843)571-6565. FAX: (843)556-6206. Ellen Katzman. Monthly. Charleston Jewish Federation.

TENNESSEE

HEBREW WATCHMAN (1925). 4646 Poplar Ave., Suite 232, Memphis, 38117. (901) 763-2215. FAX: (901)763-2216. Herman I. Goldberger. Weekly.

OBSERVER (1934). 801 Percy Warner Blvd., Suite 102, Nashville, 37205. (615)354-1637. FAX: (615)352-0056. E-mail: judy@jewishnashville.org. Judith A. Saks. Biweekly (except July). Jewish Federation of Nashville.

SHOFAR. PO Box 8947, Chattanooga, 37414. (423)493-0270, Ext. 12. FAX: (423) 493-9997. E-mail: shofar@jcfgc.com. Rachel Schulson. Ten times a year. Jewish Federation of Greater Chattanooga.

TEXAS

JEWISH HERALD-VOICE (1908). 3403 Audley Street, Houston, 77098-1923. (713)630-0391. FAX: (713)630-0404. E-mail: jhvht@aol.com. Jeanne Samuels. Weekly. Four special issues: Rosh Hashanah; Passover; Wedding Planner; Bar/Bat Mitzvah Planner.

JEWISH JOURNAL OF SAN ANTONIO (1973). 8434 Ahern, San Antonio, 78213. (210)828-9511. FAX: (210)342-8098. Barbara Richmond. Monthly (11 issues). Jewish Federation of San Antonio.

TEXAS JEWISH POST (1947). 3120 S. Freeway, Fort Worth, 76110. (817)927-2831. FAX: (817)429-0840. 11333 N. Central Expressway, Suite 213, Dallas, 75243. (214)692-7283. FAX: (214)692-7285. Weekly.

VIRGINIA

RENEWAL MAGAZINE (1984). 5041 Corporate Woods Drive, Suite 150, Virginia Beach, 23462. (757)671-1600. FAX: (757)671-7613. E-mail: news@ujft.org. Reba Karp. Quarterly. United Jewish Federation of Tidewater.

SOUTHEASTERN VIRGINIA JEWISH NEWS (1959). 5041 Corporate Woods Drive, Suite 150, Virginia Beach, 23462. (757) 671-1600. FAX: (757)671-7613. E-mail: news@ujft.org. Reba Karp. 22 issues yearly. United Jewish Federation of Tidewater.

WASHINGTON

JEWISH TRANSCRIPT (1924). 2041 Third Ave., Seattle, 98121. (206)441-4553. FAX: (206)441-2736. E-mail: jewishtran@aol.com. Donna Gordon Blankinship. Fortnightly. Jewish Federation of Greater Seattle.

WISCONSIN

WISCONSIN JEWISH CHRONICLE (1921). 1360 N. Prospect Ave., Milwaukee, 53202. (414)390-5888. FAX: (414)271-0487. E-mail: milwaukeej@aol.com. Vivian M. Rothschild. Weekly. Milwaukee Jewish Federation.

INDEXES

INDEX TO JEWISH PERIODICALS (1963). PO Box 18525, Cleveland Hts., OH 44118. (216)381-4846. FAX: (216)381-4321. E-mail: index@jewishperiodicals.com.

Lenore Pfeffer Koppel. Annually. Available in book and CD-ROM form. (www.JEWISHPERIODICALS.COM)

NEWS SYNDICATES

JEWISH TELEGRAPHIC AGENCY, INC. (1917). 330 Seventh Ave., 17th fl., NYC., 10001-5010. (212)643-1890. FAX: (212)643-8498. Mark J. Joffe, Lisa Hostein. Daily.

CANADA

CANADIAN JEWISH HERALD (1977). 17 Anselme Lavigne, Dollard des Ormeaux, PQ H9A 1N3. (514)684-7667. FAX: (514)684-7667. Ed./Pub. Dan Nimrod. Irregularly. Dawn Publishing Co., Ltd.

THE CANADIAN JEWISH NEWS (1971). 1500 Don Mills Rd., Suite 205, North York, ONT M3B 3K4. (416)391-1836. FAX: (416)391-0829 (Adv.); (416)391-1836. FAX: (416)391-0829. Mordechai Ben-Dat. 50 issues a year. Some French.

CANADIAN JEWISH OUTLOOK (1963). #3-6184 Ash St., Vancouver, BC V5Z 3G9. (604)324-5101. FAX:(604)325-2470. E-mail: cjoutlook@telus.net. Carl Rosenberg. Six times per year. Canadian Jewish Outlook Society.

DAIS (1985) (FORMERLY INTERCOM). 100 Sparks St., #650, Ottawa, ONT KIP 5B7. (613)233-8703. FAX: (613)233-8748. E-mail: canadianjewishcongress@cjc.ca. Jack Silverstone. Three times a year. Canadian Jewish Congress.

DIRECTIONS (1998) (FORMERLY DIALOGUE (1988)). 1 Carré Cummings, Suite 202, Montreal, Quebec H3W 1M6. (514)345-64111. FAX: (514)345-6412. E-mail: etay@cjc.ca. Eta Yudin. Quarterly. French-English. Canadian Jewish Congress, Quebec Region.

JEWISH FREE PRESS (1990). 8411 Elbow Dr., SW Calgary, AB. T2V 1K8. (403)252-9423. FAX: (403)255-5640. E-mail: jewishfp@telus.net. Judy Shapiro. Fortnightly.

JEWISH POST & NEWS (1987). 113 Hutchings St., Winnipeg, MAN R2X 2V4. (204)694-3332. FAX: (204)694-3916. E-mail: jewishp@mts.net. Matt Bellan. Weekly.

JEWISH STANDARD (1928). 1912A Avenue Road, Suite E5, Toronto, ONT M5M 4A1. (416)537-2696. FAX: (416)789-3872.

Email: thejewishstandardasympatico.ca. Ed./Pub. Michael Hayman. Monthly.

JEWISH STANDARD (1928). 5184, Chemin de la Cote-des-Neiges, Suite 407, Montreal, Quebec H3T 1X8. Email: thejewishstandardasympatico.ca. Ed./Pub. Michael Hayman. Monthly

THE JEWISH TRIBUNE (1950). 15 Hove St., Toronto, ONT M3H 4Y8. (416)633-6224. FAX: (416)633-6299. E-mail: carla@jewishtribune.ca . Carla Lancit. B'nai Brith Canada, Bimonthly.

JEWISH WESTERN BULLETIN (1930). 301, 68 E. Second Ave., Vancouver, BC V5T 1B1. (604)689-1520. FAX: (604)689-1525. E-mail: jbeditor@istar.ca. Baila Lazarus. Weekly. 57786 BC Ltd.

JOURNAL OF PSYCHOLOGY AND JUDAISM (1976). 1747 Featherston Dr., Ottawa, ONT K1H 6P4. (613)731-9119. Reuven P. Bulka. Quarterly. Center for the Study of Psychology and Judaism.

OTTAWA JEWISH BULLETIN (1954). 21 Nadolny Sachs Private., Ottawa, ONT K2A 1R9. (613)798-4696. FAX: (613)798-4730. E-mail: bulletin@jccottawa.com. Barry Fishman. Nineteen times a year. Ottawa Jewish Bulletin Publishing Co. Ltd.

SHALOM (1975). 5670 Spring Garden Rd., Suite 508, Halifax, NS, B3J 1H1. (902)422-7491. FAX: (902)425-3722. E-mail: jgoldberg@theajc.ns.ca. Jon M. Goldberg. Quarterly. Atlantic Jewish Council.

LA VOIX SÉPHARADE (1975). 5151 Chemin de la Cote, St. Catherine, Montreal, PQ H3W 1M6. (514)733-4998, FAX: (514)733-3158. E-mail: elieb@fedcjamtl.org. Ed. James Dahan; Pub. Elie Benchitrit. Bimonthly (five times a year). French and occasional Spanish and English. Communauté Sépharade du Québec.

NEWS AND VIEWS (1942) (formerly WINDSOR JEWISH FEDERATION). 1641 Ouellette Ave., Windsor, ONT N8X 1K9. (519)973-1772. FAX: (519)973-1774. Exec. Dir. Harvey Kessler. Quarterly. Windsor Jewish Federation.

THE WORLD OF LUBAVITCH (1980). 770 Chabad Gate, Thornhill, ONT L4J 3V9. (905)731-7000. FAX: (905)731-7005. Rabbi Moshe Spalter. Quarterly. English. Chabad Lubavitch of Southern Ont.

Obituaries: United States*

ABRAMOVITZ, MAX, architect; b. Chicago, Ill., May 23, 1908; d. Pound Ridge, N.Y., Sept. 12, 2004. Educ.: U. Ill. (BS); Columbia U. (MS); École Des Beaux Arts, Paris. Served U.S. Army Engineers Corps, 1942–45; special asst., asst. sec. U.S. Air Force, 1950–52. Assoc., Harrison & Fouilhoux architects, 1935–41; assoc. prof., School of Fine Arts, Yale U., 1939–42; partner, Harrison, Fouilhoux & Abramovitz, 1941–45, Harrison & Abramovitz, 1945–76, Abramovitz-Harris-Kingsland, 1976–85. Responsible for designing such landmark buildings as CIA Headquarters (Langley, Va.), U.S. Steel Building (Pittsburgh), Avery Fisher Hall, Mobil, Corning Glass, Time & Life, McGraw-Hill, Exxon, Celanese buildings (NYC); involved in planning of UN headquarters, Brandeis U., U.S. foreign embassies, U.S. World War II airfields, Jewish chapel at U.S. Military Acad. (West Point). Mem., officer, architectural and regional planning assns.; trustee, Mt. Sinai Medical Center, NYC. "The Troubled Search: The Work of Max Abramovitz," a retrospective, held at Columbia U., Sept. 15–Dec. 11, 2004.

BERMAN, MURIEL, civic worker, philanthropist; b. Pittsburgh, Pa., June 21, 1924; d. Allentown, Pa., Apr. 13, 2004. Educ.: U. Pittsburgh; Carnegie Tech U.; Pa. State Coll. (BS in optometry). Practiced optometry, Pittsburgh; sec., dir., Fleetways, Inc.; sec.-treas., dir., Philip and Muriel Berman Found., which donated significant sums to Philadelphia Museum of Art, Amer. Jewish Com., Jewish Publ. Society, Hadassah Medical Org., Hebrew U., numerous other causes; established Philip and Muriel Berman Center for Jewish Studies, Lehigh U., Center for Biblical Archaeology, Hebrew U. Producer, TV shows "College Speak-Out," "Guest Spot." NGO delegate to internat'l. UNICEF confs., 1964, 1966; mem., Pa. Council on Status of Women, 1968–73; U.S. State Dept. delegate to UN Internat'l. Women's Year Conf., Mexico City, 1975; delegate, Democratic natl. conventions, 1972, 1976; trustee of numerous museums, educational institutions. Rec.: Woman of Valor, State of Israel; Mt. Scopus Award, State of Israel Bonds; Woman of the Year Award, Amer. Friends of Hebrew U.

BERNSTEIN, ELMER, composer; b. NYC, Apr. 4, 1922; d. Ojai, Calif., Aug. 18, 2004. Educ.: NYU (Bachelor of Musical Educ.). Served U.S. Army Air Corps, WWII, writing scores for propaganda films. Concert pianist, 1946–50; composer of over 200 movie scores beginning 1950, including *The Man With the Golden Arm* (1955), *The Ten Commandments* (1956), *Sweet Smell of Success* (1957), *The Mag-*

---

*Including American Jews who died between January 1 and December 31, 2004.

nificent Seven (1960), *Walk on the Wild Side* (1962), *To Kill a Mockingbird* (1962), *Birdman of Alcatraz* (1962), *The Great Escape* (1963), *Hud* (1963), *Thoroughly Modern Millie* (1967), *True Grit* (1969), *Animal House* (1978), *Airplane!* (1980), *Ghostbusters* (1984), *My Left Foot* (1989), *The Grifters* (1990), *The Age of Innocence* (1993); also several TV scores. Rec.: Acad. Award (1967) and 14 nominations; Motion Picture Exhibitor Laurel Award (1956, 1957, 1962); Emmy, best music for TV ("Making of a President, 1964").

BOORSTIN, DANIEL, historian; b. Atlanta, Ga., Oct. 1, 1914; d. Washington, D.C., Feb. 28, 2004. Educ.: Harvard U. (AB); Rhodes Scholar, Oxford U. (BA, BCL); Inner Temple, England (barrister-at-law); Yale U. (JSD). Instr., hist. and lit., Harvard Coll., Radcliffe Coll., 1938–42; instr., legal hist., Harvard Law School, 1939–42; sr. attorney, Lend-Lease Admin., 1942; asst. prof., hist., Swarthmore Coll., 1942–44; asst. prof., U. Chicago, 1944–49, assoc. prof., 1949–56, prof., 1956-64, Preston and Sterling Morton distinguished service prof., 1964–69; dir., Natl. Museum of Hist. and Technology, Smithsonian Inst., 1969–73, snr. historian, 1973–75; librarian of Cong., 1975–87, emer., 1987–; Fulbright visiting lect., U. Rome, 1950–51, Kyoto U., 1957; first occupant of chair in Amer. hist., U. Paris, 1961–62; Pitt prof., Amer. hist., Cambridge U., 1964–65. Au.: *The Mysterious Science of the Law* (1941); *The Genius of American Politics* (1953); *The Americans: The Colonial Experience* (1958); *America and the Image of Europe* (1960); *The Image: or What Happened to the American Dream* (1962); *The Americans: The National Experience* (1965); *The Decline of Radicalism* (1969); *The Americans: The Democratic Experience* (1973); *The Discoverers* (1983); *The Creators* (1992); *The Seekers* (1995). Ed.: Amer. hist. textbooks and source books; Encyclopaedia Britannica, Amer. hist. Rec.: Bancroft Award (1959); Francis Parkman Prize (1966); Pulitzer Prize (1974); Natl. Book Award (1989); numerous others.

CANTOR, NORMAN F., historian; b. Winnipeg, Canada, Nov. 19, 1929; d. Miami, Fla., Sept. 18, 2004; in U.S. since 1957. Educ.: U. Manitoba (BA); Princeton U. (MA. PhD); Oxford U. (Rhodes Scholar).

Instr., hist., Princeton U., 1955–59, asst. prof., 1959–60; assoc. prof., Columbia U., 1960–65, prof., 1965–66; Leff prof., Brandeis U., 1966–70; distinguished prof., SUNY Binghamton, 1970–76, provost, graduate studies, 1974–75, v.-pres. academic affairs, 1975–76; vice chancellor, academic affairs, U. Ill., Chicago, 1976–78; dean, faculty of arts and sciences, NYU, 1978–81, prof., hist., sociology, and comparative lit., 1981–87, emer., 1999–, dir., inst. for cultural analysis, 1981–87, affiliated prof., NYU law school, 1982–88; Fulbright prof., Tel Aviv U., 1987–88; lect., Inst. for Secular Jewish Humanism, 1996–. Au.: *Church, Kingship, and Lay Investiture* (1958); *Medieval History* (1963); *The English* (1968); *Western Civilization* (1972); *Twentieth Century Culture* (1988); *Inventing the Middle Ages* (1991); *The Civilization of the Middle Ages* (1993); *Medieval Lives* (1994); *The Sacred Chain: The History of the Jews* (1994); *In the Wake of the Plague* (2002); *The Last Knight* (2004). Ed.: *The Medieval Reader* (1994); *The Jewish Experience* (1997); *Encyclopedia of the Middle Ages* (1999).

COLEMAN, CY (SEYMOUR KAUFFMAN), composer; b. NYC, June 14, 1929; d. NYC, Nov. 18, 2004. Educ.: N.Y Coll. of Music (diploma). Began piano lessons at age four and made Carnegie Hall debut three years later; performed on TV shows from 1947 and in night clubs from 1948; appeared with major orchestras around the U.S.; wrote music for Broadway shows *Wildcat* (1960), *Little Me* (1962), *Sweet Charity* (1963), *See-Saw* (1973), *I Love My Wife* (1977), *On the Twentieth Century* (1978), *Barnum* (1980), *City of Angels* (1989), *The Will Rogers Follies* (1991), *The Life* (1997); composer of popular songs such as "Witchcraft," "Firefly," "Hey Look Me Over," "Big Spender," "The Best Is Yet to Come." Rec.: Tony Award (1978, 1990, 1991); Grammy Award (1992); Emmy Award (1974, 1975).

CULLMAN, JOSEPH F., III, business exec.; b. NYC, Apr. 9, 1912; d. NYC, Apr. 30, 2004. Educ.: Yale U. (AB). Served U.S. Navy as gunnery officer in Pacific, WWII. Worked in cigar manufacturing, 1933–41; mgr., Benson & Hedges tobacco co., 1945–54, where he pioneered the filter-tip Parliament brand; v.-pres., Phillip Morris Co., 1954–55, exec. v.-pres.,

1955–57, pres., CEO, 1957-67, chmn., CEO, 1967–78. Made Phillip Morris most successful tobacco co. in U.S., partly through replacement of Phillip Morris "bellhop" icon by Marlboro cowboy image; beginning in 1969, acquired non-tobacco products such as Miller Beer, Genl. Foods, Kraft Foods, Nabisco, Maxwell House, Oscar Meyer; the parent company, called the Altria Group, was the largest producer of consumer products in the world; appeared before congressional panels in 1960s to oppose imposition of health warnings on tobacco products. Both personally and on behalf of Phillip Morris, donated generously to Dance Theater of Harlem, Brooklyn Acad. of Music, Guggenheim, Whitney, and Metropolitan art museums; created Virginia Slims women's professional tennis tour, 1970. Commissioner, Port Authority of N.Y., 1976–83. Chmn., U.S. Open Tennis Championship, Tennis Hall of Fame; trustee, N.Y. State Nature and Historical Preserve Trust, Amer. Museum of Natural Hist.; pres., Atlantic Salmon Fed.; founder, Gomez Found. for Mill House. Rec.: Natl. Urban League Equal Employment Opportunity Award, 1972.

DANE, MAXWELL, advertising exec.; b. Cincinnati, Ohio, June 7, 1906; d. NYC, Aug. 8, 2004. Advertising dept., Stern Brothers, NYC, 1928–32; retail promotion mgr., N.Y. *Evening Post,* 1933–36; account exec., Dorland Internat'l., 1937–39; advertising promotion mgr., *Look* magazine, 1939–41; sales promotion mgr., WMCA radio, 1941–44; pres., Maxwell Dane Inc., 1944–49; founder, exec. v.-pres., sec.-treas., Doyle Dane Berbach, Inc., 1949–71; chmn., exec. com., 1969–71, dir., 1949–1985. Innovated low-key, humorous advertising, such as "Avis, We Try Harder"; responsible for the famous "daisy" commercial aimed against Barry Goldwater in 1964 presidential campaign; one of the original 20 names on Richard Nixon's "enemies list," 1971. V. chmn., N.Y. Civil Liberties Union, 1960–66, bd. dirs., 1966–89; chmn., advertising and publicity div., United Jewish Appeal, 1969–71; chmn., exec. com., N.Y. *Jewish Week,* 1976–81, pres., 1982–92; chmn, natl. program com., Anti-Defamation League, 1969–76, hon. v. chmn., 1976–. Rec.: Karl Menninger Award, Fortune Society, 1983.

DANGERFIELD, RODNEY (JACOB COHEN), comedian; b. Babylon, N. Y., Nov. 22, 1921; d. Los Angeles, Calif., Oct. 5, 2004. Worked as Borscht Belt comedian under the name Jack Roy, 1941–51; successful paint and siding salesman, Englewood, N.J., 1951–63; comedian, 1963–; attained recognition with appearance on "Ed Sullivan Show," 1967, with portrayal of self-deprecating everyman, later the man who "gets no respect"; opened his own club, Dangerfield's, NYC, 1969; appeared on numerous TV comedy specials and other shows, including 70 times on "Tonight Show," and in films such as *Caddyshack* (1980), *Back to School* (1986), *Ladybugs* (1992), *Natural Born Killers* (1994), *Casper* (1995); several record albums. Au.: *I Couldn't Stand My Wife's Cooking So I Opened a Restaurant* (1972); *I Don't Get No Respect* (1973); *It's Not Easy Bein' Me* (2004). Rec.: Grammy Award for record album "No Respect," 1984; Lifetime Creative Achievement Award, 1994 Amer. Comedy Awards.

DASH, SAMUEL, lawyer; b. Camden, N.J., Feb. 27, 1925; d. Washington, D.C., May 29, 2004. Educ.: Temple U. (BS); Harvard U. Law School (JD). Served U.S. Army Air Force, 1943–46. Teaching fellow, Northwestern U., 1950–51; trial attorney, criminal div., U.S. Dept. of Justice, 1951–52; asst. district attorney, Philadelphia, 1952–55, district attorney, 1955–56; partner, Bland and Rudenko, Philadelphia, 1956–58, Dash & Levy, 1958–63; dir., Philadelphia Council for Community Advancement, 1963–65; prof., dir., Inst. of Criminal Law and Procedure, Appellate Litigation Clinic, Georgetown U. Law School, 1965–; chief counsel, U.S. Senate Select Com. on Presidential Campaign Activities (Watergate Com.), 1973–74; consultant to several other inquiries into alleged crimes in govt., including independent counsel investigating Pres. Clinton and Whitewater, 1994–98. Au.: *The Eavesdroppers* (1959); *Chief Counsel* (1976); *The Intruders: Unreasonable Searches and Seizures from King John to John Ashcroft* (2004). Pres., Natl. Assn. Criminal Lawyers, 1958; regional chmn., Anti-Defamation League, 1960–63; mem., Human Relations Council of Philadelphia, 1957–65; exec. com., Community Relations Council, Philadelphia, 1960–65; bd. dirs., Hebrew U., 1975–, Philadelphia Fed. of Jewish Agencies,

1960–65, Albert Einstein Medical Center, 1962–65. Rec. numerous awards and commendations.

DAVIS, MARVIN, business exec.; b. Newark, N.J., Aug. 31, 1925; d. Beverly Hills, Calif., Sept. 25, 2004. Educ.: NYU (BSCE). Entered his father's garment business, then joined him in Davis Oil Co. (now Davis Petroleum Corp.), based in Denver, 1950s, becoming owner upon his father's death; became known as "Mr. Wildcatter," drilling thousands of wells and making a fortune during boom period of 1970s, then selling off most of his holdings in 1981, just before the market dropped; together with financier Marc Rich, bought Twentieth-Century Fox in one of the first successful leveraged buyouts, 1981, selling it at huge profit in 1984; subsequent Davis acquisitions were Pebble Beach Co., Aspen Skiing Co., Beverly Hills Hotel, and other properties around the country; ranked by *Forbes* in 2004 as 30th richest person in U.S., with assets of $5.8 billion. After their child was diagnosed with juvenile diabetes in 1977, Davis and his wife, Barbara, founded Children's Diabetes Found., Barbara Davis Center for Childhood Diabetes (the largest facility of its kind), and hosted biennial Carousel Ball (later Carousel of Hope) to raise funds for this cause.

GOLDSTINE, HERMAN, mathematician; b. Chicago, Ill., Sept. 13, 1913; d. Bryn Mawr, Pa., June 16, 2004. Educ.: U. Chicago (BS, MS, PhD). Served U.S. Army, 1942–46. Research asst., U. Chicago, 1936–37, instr., 1937–39; instr., U. Mich., 1939–42, asst. prof., 1942–50; assoc. project dir., electronic computer project, Inst. for Advanced Study, Princeton, N.J., 1946–55, acting project dir., 1954–57, permanent mem., 1952–; dir., mathematical sciences dept., IBM Research, 1960–65; dir., scientific devel., IBM Data Processing Headquarters, 1965–67; consultant to IBM research dir., 1967–69, fellow, 1969–; exec. officer, Amer. Philosophical Soc., 1984–97; consultant, various govt. and military agencies, 1946–84. As army ordnance mathematician in WWII, worked on top-secret Eniac, the earliest electronic computer, afterwards working on "second-generation" Edvac computer, introduced 1952. Au.: *The Computer from Pascal to von Neumann* (1952); *New and*

Full Moons: 1001 B.C. to A.D. 1651 (1973); *A History of Numerical Analysis from the 16th to the 19th Century* (1977). Rec.: Natl. Medal of Science (1983); Outstanding Civilian Service Award, U.S. Army (1984); Hall of Fame, Army Ordnance Dept. (1997).

HECHT, ANTHONY, poet; b. NYC, Jan. 16, 1923; d. Washington, D.C., Oct. 20, 2004. Educ.: Bard Coll. (BA); Kenyon Coll. (studied with John Crowe Ransom); Columbia U. (MA). Served U.S. Army, WWII, witnessing liberation of the concentration camps, an experience that deeply influenced his poetry. Teacher, Smith Coll., 1956–59; assoc. prof. English, Bard Coll., 1961; faculty, U. Rochester, 1967; Hurst Prof., Washington U., 1971; visiting prof., Harvard U., 1973, Yale U., 1977; university prof., Georgetown U., 1985–93; consultant in poetry, Library of Cong., 1982–84; trustee, Amer. Acad. in Rome, 1983–; chancellor, Amer. Acad. of Poets, 1971–95. Au.: *A Summoning of Stones* (1954); *The Seven Deadly Sins* (1958); *A Bestiary* (1960); *The Hard Hours* (1968); *Millions of Strange Shadows* (1977); *The Venetian Vespers* (1979); *Obbligati: Essays in Criticism* (1986); *The Transparent Man* (1990); *Collected Earlier Poems* (1990). Rec.: Pulitzer Prize (1968); Bollingen Prize (1983); Tanning Prize for Lifetime Achievement, Acad. of Amer. Poets (1997); Robert Frost Medal (2000).

KING, ALAN (IRWIN ALAN KNIBERG), comedian; b. Brooklyn, N.Y., Dec. 26, 1927; d. NYC, May 9, 2004. Educ.: Brooklyn public schools. Performed at hotels, cafes, army bases, theaters, U.S. and Great Britain, 1940s and 1950s; numerous TV appearances, 1950s and 1960s, including "Garry Moore Show," "Ed Sullivan Show" (56 times), "Perry Como Show," "The Tonight Show," panel shows, specials; appeared onstage in *The Impossible Years* (1965), *The Investigation* (1966), *Dinner at Eight* (1966), *Something Different* (1967); acted in films *Anderson Tapes* (1971), *Just Tell Me What You Want* (1979), *Author Author* (1982), *Lovesick* (1983), *Enemies, A Love Story* (1989), *Bonfire of the Vanities* (1990), *Night and the City* (1992), *Mr. Goldwyn* (2002); exec. producer, Toyota Comedy Festival, NYC, 1992–2002; founder, Alan King Tennis Classic, Las Vegas. Donated time and money for Nassau Center for Emotionally Disturbed Children, Long Island, N.Y.; endowed chair in dramatic arts, Brandeis U., Alan King Diagnostic Medical Center, Jerusalem; abbot, Friars club. Au.: *Name-Dropping: The Life and Lies of Alan King* (1996); *Matzo Balls for Breakfast and Other Memories of Growing Up Jewish* (2005). Rec.: first annual award for Amer. Jewish humor, Natl. Found. for Jewish Culture, 1999.

LAUDER, ESTÉE (JOSEPHINE ESTHER MENTZER LAUDER), cosmetics exec.; b. Queens, N.Y., July 1, 1908; d. NYC, Apr. 24, 2004. Educ.: NYC public schools. Developed interest in cosmetics during 1920s from an uncle who concocted facial creams in his kitchen; financed by a Dutch-born industrialist, Lauder launched Estée Lauder Inc., 1946, which sold its products through prestigious depart. stores; basing her business on the promise of enabling women to stay young-looking, Lauder ultimately created five companies (one, Aramis, was for men) and marketed about 2,000 individual products; by 1995, when Estée Lauder Companies went public, it was worth $5 billion. Her Lauder Found. helped support many causes, including three playgrounds in Central Park and the creation, in 1983, of the Joseph H. Lauder Inst. of Mgmt. and Internat'l. Studies at U. Pa. Au.: *Estée: A Success Story* (1995). Rec.: numerous fashion industry awards; decorated chevalier of French Legion of Honor, 1978.

MAYER, EGON, sociologist; b. Switzerland, Dec. 23, 1944; d. Laurel Hollow, N.Y., Jan. 30, 2004; in U.S. since 1956. Educ.: Brooklyn Coll. (BA); New School for Social Research (MA); Rutgers U. (PhD). Asst. prof., sociology, Brooklyn Coll., 1970–75, assoc. prof., 1979–84, prof., 1984–, dept. chmn, 2002–; dir., CUNY Graduate Center for Jewish Studies, 1990s; pres., Assn. for the Sociological Study of Jewry, 1983–85; founding dir., Jewish Outreach Inst., 1989–; managing ed., *Contemporary Jewry*, 1998–. Mem., Natl. Technical Adv. Com., Natl. Jewish Population Surveys, 1990, 2000–01. Au.: *From Suburb to Shtetl: The Jews of Boro Park* (1979); *Love and Tradition: Marriage Between Jews and Christians* (1985); *American Religious Identification Survey 2001* (with Barry Kosmin, 2002); and many others, including a series of monographs done for the Amer. Jewish Com.: *Intermarriage and the Jewish Future* (1979); *Children of Intermarriage* (1983); *Conversion Among the Intermarried* (1987); *Intermarriage and Rabbinic Officiation* (1989).

MERRILL, ROBERT (MOISHE MILLSTEIN), opera singer (baritone), b. Brooklyn, N.Y., June 4, 1917; d. NYC, Oct. 23, 2004. Educ.: public schools, private voice lessons. Sang at hotels, weddings, and bar mitzvahs, 1930s; after failing first audition at Metropolitan Opera in 1941, sang at Radio City Music Hall and with NBC Concert Orchestra; shared first prize at Metropolitan Opera auditions, 1944; performed with the Met in NYC and on tour, 1945–76, singing all the major baritone roles of the standard operatic repertoire (marked his 500th Met performance in 1973); featured soloist, RCA Victor Show (radio), beginning 1946; numerous recordings for RCA, including two complete operas under Arturo Toscanini, *La Traviata* (1946), *Un Balla in Maschera* (1953); performed for nine U.S. presidents; only singer to perform for both Houses of Cong.; official singer, N.Y. Yankees, 1969– (a recording of his recital of the Natl. Anthem at Yankee Stadium was used for years to open Yankee home games). Au.: *Once More From the Beginning* (1965); *Between Acts* (1976); *The Divas* (1978).

MORGENBESSER, SIDNEY, philosopher, educator; b. NYC, Sept. 22, 1921; d. NYC, Aug. 1, 2004. Educ.: CCNY (BA); Jewish Theol. Sem. (ordination); U. Pa. (MA, PhD). Instr., philosophy, Swarthmore Coll., New School for Social Research; lect., asst. prof., assoc. prof, Columbia U., 1954–66, prof., 1966–99, John Dewey prof., 1975–99, emer., 1997–; visiting prof., Princeton U., Rockefeller U., Brandeis U., Hebrew U.; mem., Columbia U. faculty com. to propose reforms after student riots, 1968. Au.: more than 50 scholarly articles; ed., six anthologies; book review ed., *Journal of Philosophy;* mem., editorial bd., *Nation*. Rec.: Society of Columbia Graduates Great Teacher Award (1982); Guggenheim Fellowship.

NAPARSTEK, ARTHUR J., urban planner, communal worker; b. NYC, June 1, 1938; d. Cleveland, Ohio, Apr. 24, 2004. Educ.: Ill. Wesleyan U. (BS); NYU (MSW); Brandeis U. (PhD); Columbia U. Senior health educator, U.S. Public Health Service, Chicago, 1962–65; dir., Urban Devel. Inst., Purdue U., 1965–69; asst. to Mayor Richard Hatcher, Gary Ind., 1967–69; dir. of research, Catholic U. Natl. Center for Ethnic Affairs, 1972–76; dir., prof., Washington Public Affairs Center, U. Southern Calif., Washington, D.C., 1976–83; dean, Coyle prof. of social work, Mandel School of Applied Social Science, Case Western Reserve U., Cleveland, 1983–88, Coyle prof., 1988–; dir., Cleveland Found. Comm. on Poverty, 1990–93, which issued a report that became the basis for federal HUD legislation called HOPE IV, 1993; appointed by Pres. Carter to Natl. Comm. on Neighborhoods (1979), by Pres. Clinton to Corp. for Natl. Service (1994); chmn., Cleveland Jewish Community Fed. Partnership 2000 (to develop the Beit She'an Valley in Israel); senior v.-pres., chmn., Israel and Overseas Pillar, United Jewish Communities, 2001–; founder, Ethiopian Natl. Project (to acculturate Ethiopian Jews in Israel), 2003–. Au.: *Neighborhood Networks* (1982); *Community Support Systems and Mental Health* (1982); *HOPE IV: Community Building Making a Difference* (2000).

NEWFIELD, JACK, journalist; b. Brooklyn, N.Y., Feb. 18, 1938; d. NYC, Dec. 20, 2004. Educ.: Hunter Coll. (BA). Copyboy, N.Y. *Daily Mirror*, ed., *West Side News*, 1960–64; staff writer, *Village Voice*, 1964–88; columnist, N.Y. *Daily News*, 1988–89, N.Y. *Post*, 1989–2001, N.Y. *Sun*, 2001–. His journalism focused on support for the underdog and the exposure of corruption. Au.: *The Prophetic Minority* (1966); *The Abuse of Power: The Permanent Government and the Fall of New York* (1977); *City for Sale* (1988); *Only in America* (1995); *Somebody's Gotta Tell It: The Upbeat Memoir of a Working-Class Journalist* (2002).

ORBACH, JERRY, actor; b. NYC, Oct. 20, 1935; d. NYC, Dec. 28, 2004. Educ.: U. Ill.; Northwestern U., studied acting and music, NYC. Played small parts in stock company productions, 1952–54; N.Y. debut as understudy in *The Threepenny Opera*, 1955, eventually playing the lead role, Mack the Knife, through 1959; achieved fame playing the original El Gallo in *The Fantasticks*, 1960, which, when it closed in 1992, was the longest-running N.Y. musical in history; also appeared on stage in many productions, including *The Cradle Will Rock* (1964), *Guys and Dolls* (1965), *Scuba Duba* (1967), *Promises Promises* (1968), *Chicago* (1975), *Forty-Second Street* (1980); film performances included *Please Come Home* (1964), *The Gang That Couldn't Shoot Straight* (1971), *Prince of the City* (1981), *Brewster's Millions* (1985), *Dirty Dancing* (1987), *Last Exit to Brooklyn* (1989), *Crimes and Misdemeanors* (1989); appeared in a number of TV dramas, most notably as Detective Lenny Briscoe in the immensely popular series "Law & Order." Rec.: Tony Award, best actor, 1968.

POLLACK, MILTON, lawyer, judge; b. Brooklyn, N.Y., Sept. 29, 1906; d. NYC, Aug. 13, 2004. Educ.: Columbia U. (AB, JD). Assoc., Gilman & Unger, NYC, 1929–38; partner, Unger and Pollack, NYC, 1938–44; Milton Pollack, NYC, 1945–67; judge, U.S. District Court, southern district, 1967–, sr. status, 1983–; mem., Judicial Conf. Com. on Court Admin., 1968–87, Judicial Panel on Multi-District Litigation, 1983–. Presided over several high-profile federal trials, including prosecution of Jane Alpert of the Weather Underground (1975); litigation over whether the Concorde could be barred from landing at Kennedy Internat'l. Airport (1977); Drexel Burnham Lambert bankruptcy case (1992); and class-action lawsuits against Merrill Lynch (2003). Chmn., lawyers div., N.Y. Fed. of Jewish Philanthropies, 1957–61; vice chmn., lawyers div., Amer. Jewish Com., 1954–57, chmn., 1964–66; trustee, Temple Emanu-El, 1977–, v.-pres., 1978–; pres., Columbia U. Law School Alumni Assn., 1970–72. Rec.: Learned Hand Award, Amer. Jewish Com., 1967; Proskauer Medal, N.Y. Fed. of Jewish Philanthropies, 1968; Distinguished Service Medal, Assn. of the Bar of NYC, 1991.

RANDALL, TONY (LEONARD ROSENBERG), actor; b. Tulsa, Okla., Feb. 26, 1920; d. NYC, May 17, 2004. Educ.: Northwestern U.; Neighborhood Playhouse School of the Theater, NYC. Served U.S. Army, 1942–46. Had parts in radio mysteries and soap operas, 1940s; acted in *Circle of Chalk* (1941), *Candida* (1941), *The Corn Is Green* (1942), *The Barretts of Wimpole Street* (1947), *Antony and Cleopatra*

(1948), *Caesar and Cleopatra* (1950), *Oh Men, Oh Women* (1954), *Inherit the Wind* (1955), *M. Butterfly* (1988); TV series included "Mr. Peepers," 1952–55, "The Odd Couple," 1970–75, "The Tony Randall Show," 1976–77, "Love Sydney," 1981–83; films included *Will Success Spoil Rock Hunter?* (1957), *The Mating Game* (1959), *Pillow Talk* (1959), *Lover Come Back* (1962), *Bang, Bang, You're Dead* (1966), *Huckleberry Finn* (1974), *The King of Comedy* (1983). Founder, artistic dir., Natl. Actors Theater, NYC, 1991–. Rec.: Emmy Award, 1975.

SCHAPPES, MORRIS U. (MOISE SHAPSHILE-VICH), scholar, political activist; b. Kamenets-Podolsk, Ukraine, May 3, 1907; d. NYC, June 3, 2004; in U.S. since 1914. Educ.: CCNY (BA); Columbia U. (MA). Instr., English, CCNY, 1928–41, where he was a well-known communist, having joined the party in 1934, and was dismissed from his post after a perjury conviction for testimony to Rapp-Coudert Com. investigating CCNY; served 13-and-a-half months in prison where he studied Hebrew and developed an interest in Jewish culture; upon release, worked in a war-production factory on Long Island; taught Jewish studies, Jefferson School of Social Sciences, 1948–57, School of Jewish Knowledge, 1958–69; adj. prof., Queens Coll., 1972–76; mem., editorial bd., *Jewish Life*, 1946–58; ed., *Jewish Currents*, 1958–99. Au.: *Letters from the Tombs* (1943); *Prose and Poetry of Emma Lazarus* (1944); *Letters of Emma Lazarus* (1949); *A Documentary History of the Jews in the United States, 1654–1875* (1950). Rec.: Torchbearer Award, Amer. Jewish Historical Society, 1993. In 1981, the CCNY faculty senate apologized to him and to 50 others for their dismissals 40 years earlier.

SHAW, ARTIE (ARTHUR JACOB ARSHAWSKY), Musician, bandleader; b. NYC, May 23, 1910; d. Newbury Park, Calif., Dec. 30, 2004. Educ.: Columbia U. Served U.S. Navy as bandleader, 1942–44. Played clarinet professionally with major jazz bands, 1920s; achieved fame with original composition, "Interlude in B Flat," performed at Imperial Theater, NYC, 1935; formed his own band that performed at Roseland-State Ballroom, Boston; recording of Cole Porter's "Begin the Beguine," 1938, made his band pre-

eminent "swing" band in U.S.; also known for his versions of "Lady Be Good," Star Dust," "Frenesi"; retired 1954 while still considered by many to be the greatest American clarinet player, spending the rest of his life as cattle farmer, film producer, lect., and competitive shooter of high-powered rifles. Married eight times, including to Lana Turner, Ava Gardner. Au.: *The Trouble with Cinderella* (an autobiography, 1952); *The Best of Intentions and Other Stories* (1989). Rec.: Hall of Fame Award, Natl. Acad. of Recording Arts and Sciences, 1977; Presidential Award, Amer. Society of Music Arrangers, 1990.

SHEINKMAN, JACK, labor leader, lawyer; b. NYC, Dec. 6, 1926; d. NYC, Jan 29, 2004. Educ.: Cornell U. (BS, LLB); Oxford U. (certificate in economics). Served U.S. Navy, WWII. Attorney, Natl. Labor Relations Bd., 1952–53; attorney, Amalgamated Clothing Workers, 1953–58, genl. counsel, 1958–72, v.-pres., 1968–72, sec.-treas., 1972–76; sec.-treas., Amalgamated Clothing and Textile Workers, 1976–87, pres., 1987–95; pres. emer., Union of Needle Trades, Industrial and Textile Employees, 1995–; pres., Jewish Labor Com., 1970s; chmn., Americans for Democratic Action, 1995–98. Pioneered the use of consumer boycotts and coalitions with civil-rights groups to unionize workers; the successful 1980 unionization of the J.P. Stevens, which he largely engineered, was portrayed in the 1979 movie *Norma Rae;* rallied workers against U.S. intervention in Latin America in opposition to leadership of AFL-CIO, 1980s.

SONTAG, SUSAN, writer, critic; b. NYC, Jan. 16, 1933; d. NYC, Dec. 28, 2004. Educ.:U. Calif. Berkeley; U. Chicago (BA); Harvard U. (MA, English, MA, philosophy); St. Anne's Coll., Oxford U.; U. Paris. Ed., *Commentary*, instr., CCNY, Sarah Lawrence Coll., 1959–60, Columbia U., 1960–64. Au.: *The Benefactor* (1963); *Against Interpretation* (1966), which included her celebrated essay "Notes on Camp"; *Death Kit* (1967); *Styles of Radical Will* (1969); essays on photography collected in *On Photography* (1977); short stories collected in *I, etcetera* (1978); *Illness as Metaphor* (1978); *Under the Sun of Saturn* (1980); *A Susan Sontag Reader* (1982); *AIDS and its Metaphors* (1988);

The Volcano Lover (1992); *In America* (2000); *Regarding the Pain of Others* (2003). Wrote and directed films *Duet for Cannibals* (1969); *Brother Carl* (1971). Pres., PEN, Amer. branch, 1987–89. Rec.: Natl. Book Critics Circle Award, 1978; McArthur Found. genius grant, 1990; Natl. Book Award, 2000.

SPITZER, JACK, banker, communal leader; b. NYC, Sept. 11, 1917; d. Seattle, Wash., July 31, 2004. Educ.: UCLA (BA). Served U.S. Army, WWII. District field dir., B'nai B'rith, 1940–42, district exec., 1942; assoc. dir. for Southern Calif., Natl. Conf. of Christian and Jews, 1947–49; assoc. exec. dir., Los Angeles Jewish Community Council, 1949–50; partner., Spitzer Co. Real Estate, Los Angeles, 1951–59; chmn., CEO, Brentwood Savings and Loan, Los Angeles, 1959–66; Sterling Savings and Loan, Riverside, Calif., 1966–72, Security Savings and Loan, Seattle, 1972–78; bd. chmn., CEO, Covenant Mortgage, Mercer Island, Wash., 1982–. District pres., B'nai B'rith, 1968–69, chmn., natl. fund-raising cabinet, 1971–78, cochmn., internat'l. council, 1976–78, pres., 1978–82, hon. life pres., 1982–; exec. com., Amer. Jewish Joint Distrib. Com., 1978–; v.-pres., treas., Conf. on Jewish Material Claims Against Germany, 1980–; vice-chmn., bd. of govs., Ben-Gurion U. of the Negev, 1984–, which named its Spitzer Dept. of Social Work in his honor; together with his wife, established Charlotte B. and Jack J. Spitzer B'nai B'rith Hillel Forum on Public Policy.

STRAUS, ROGER W., JR., publisher; b. NYC, Jan. 3, 1917; d. NYC, May 25, 2004. Educ.: Hamilton Coll.; U. Mo. School of Journalism (BJ). Served U.S. Navy office of public relations, WWII. Reporter, *White Plains Daily Reporter,* 1936, feature writer, 1939–40; editorial writer, reporter, *Columbia Missourian,* 1937–39; editorial asst., *Current History,* 1940, assoc. ed., 1940–45; assoc. ed., *Forum,* 1940–45; pres., Book Ideas, Inc. 1943–46; founder, Farrar, Straus & Co. (later Farrar, Straus & Giroux), 1946–87; kept title of pres. after sale of the firm to a German media giant in 1987. Responsible for the publication of works of Joseph Brodsky, T.S. Eliot, Nadine Gordimer, Robert Lowell, Bernard Malamud, Czeslaw Milosz, Flannery O'Connor, Philip Roth, Isaac Bashevis Singer, Aleksandr Solzhenitsyn, Susan Sontag, Edmund Wilson, Tom Wolfe, and other prize-winning authors. Chmn., publ. bd., *American Judaism,* 1955–65.

TISHMAN, MARGARET "PEGGY," Philanthropist, communal leader; b. NYC, Dec. 5, 1919; d. NYC, Mar. 5, 2004. Educ.: Wellesley Coll. (BA); Fairfield U. (MA). V.-pres., Tishman East Mgmt. Corp; dir., Bank Leumi; psychologist, Conn. public schools. Founder, Jewish Assn. for Services for the Aged (JASA), 1968; pres., N.Y. Jewish Community Relations Council, 1983–86; pres., N.Y. Fed. of Jewish Philanthropies, 1986–89, the first woman to lead a major Jewish federation, played key role in securing its merger with UJA, elected pres. of the combined entity. Bd. mem., Amer. Jewish Joint Distrib. Com., Jewish Home and Hosp. for the Aged; twice selected delegate to White House Conf. on Aging.

ZUCKOFF, MURRAY, editor; b. NYC, Dec. 5, 1925; d. NYC, Dec. 26, 2004. Educ.: NYC public schools. While working in a variety of jobs, including trolley driver, became active in Young Communist League, then Socialist Workers Party; ed., *The Militant* (Trotskyist newspaper), 1950s; reporter, *Morning Call* (Paterson, N.J.), *Bergen Evening Record,* 1960s; taught English, Lehman Coll., 1950s–60s; adopting left-Labor Zionist perspective, active in Jewish Liberation Project, Americans for Progressive Israel, Meretz U.S.A., 1968–; editor-in-chief, Jewish Telegraphic Agcy., 1969–87, known especially for coverage of Israel, black-Jewish relations, Jewish poverty, Timerman case in Argentina; ed., *Midstream* magazine, 1988–90.

Calendars

SUMMARY JEWISH CALENDAR, 5765–5769 (Sept. 2004–Aug. 2009)

HOLIDAY	5765 (2004)			5766 (2005)			5767 (2006)			5768 (2007)			5769 (2008)		
Rosh Ha-shanah, 1st day	Th	Sept.	16	T	Oct.	4	Sa	Sept.	23	Th	Sept.	13	T	Sept.	30
Rosh Ha-shanah, 2nd day	F	Sept.	17	W	Oct.	5	S	Sept.	24	F	Sept.	14	W	Oct.	1
Fast of Gedaliah	S	Sept.	19	Th	Oct.	6	M	Sept.	25	S	Sept.	16	Th	Oct.	2
Yom Kippur	Sa	Sept.	25	Th	Oct.	13	M	Oct.	2	Sa	Sept.	22	Th	Oct.	9
Sukkot, 1st day	Th	Sept.	30	T	Oct.	18	Sa	Oct.	7	Th	Sept.	27	T	Oct.	14
Sukkot, 2nd day	F	Oct.	1	W	Oct.	19	S	Oct.	8	F	Sept.	28	W	Oct.	15
Hosha'na' Rabbah	W	Oct.	6	M	Oct.	24	F	Oct.	13	W	Oct.	3	M	Oct.	20
Shemini 'Azeret	Th	Oct.	7	T	Oct.	25	Sa	Oct.	14	Th	Oct.	4	T	Oct.	21
Simhat Torah	F	Oct.	8	W	Oct.	26	S	Oct.	15	F	Oct.	5	W	Oct.	22
New Moon, Heshwan, 1st day	F	Oct.	15	W	Nov.	2	S	Oct.	22	F	Oct.	12	W	Oct.	29
New Moon, Heshwan, 2nd day	Sa	Oct.	16	Th	Nov.	3	M	Oct.	23	Sa	Oct.	13	Th	Oct.	30
New Moon, Kislew, 1st day	S	Nov.	14	F	Dec.	2	T	Nov.	21	S	Nov.	11	F	Nov.	28
New Moon, Kislew, 2nd day							W	Nov.	22						
Hanukkah, 1st day	W	Dec.	8	M	Dec.	26	Sa	Dec.	16	W	Dec.	5	M	Dec.	22
New Moon, Tevet, 1st day	M	Dec.	13	Sa	Dec.	31	Th	Dec.	21	M	Dec.	10	Sa	Dec.	27
New Moon, Tevet, 2nd day				S	Jan.	1	F	Dec.	22				S	Dec.	28
Fast of 10th of Tevet	W	Dec.	22	T	Jan. (2006)	10	S	Dec.	31	W	Dec.	19	T	Jan. (2009)	6

	2004	2005	2006	2007	2008	2009
New Moon, Shevat	Sa Jan. 24	T Jan. 11	M Jan. 30	Sa Jan. 20	T Jan. 8	M Jan. 26
Hamishshah-'asar bi-Shevat	Sa Feb. 7	T Jan. 25	M Feb. 13	Sa Feb. 3	T Jan. 22	M Feb. 9
New Moon, Adar I, 1st day	S Feb. 22	W Feb. 9	T Feb. 28	S Feb. 18	W Feb. 6	T Feb. 24
New Moon, Adar I, 2nd day	M Feb. 23	Th Feb. 10	W Mar. 1	M Feb. 19	Th Feb. 7	W Feb. 25
New Moon, Adar II, 1st day		F Mar. 11			F Mar. 7	
New Moon, Adar II, 2nd day		Sa Mar. 12			Sa Mar. 8	
Fast of Esther	Th Mar. 4	Th Mar. 24	M Mar. 13	Th Mar. 1	Th Mar. 20	M Mar. 9
Purim	S Mar. 7	F Mar. 25	T Mar. 14	S Mar. 4	F Mar. 21	T Mar. 10
Shushan Purim	M Mar. 8	Sa Mar. 26	W Mar. 15	M Mar. 5	Sa Mar. 22	W Mar. 11
New Moon, Nisan	T Mar. 23	S Apr. 10	Th Mar. 30	T Mar. 20	S Apr. 6	Th Mar. 26
Passover, 1st day	T Apr. 6	S Apr. 24	Th Apr. 13	T Apr. 3	S Apr. 20	Th Apr. 9
Passover, 2nd day	W Apr. 7	M Apr. 25	F Apr. 14	W Apr. 4	M Apr. 21	F Apr. 10
Passover, 7th day	M Apr. 12	Sa Apr. 30	W Apr. 19	M Apr. 9	Sa Apr. 26	W Apr. 15
Passover, 8th day	T Apr. 13	S May 1	Th Apr. 20	T Apr. 10	S Apr. 27	Th Apr. 16
Holocaust Memorial Day	S Apr. 18	F May 6*	T Apr. 25	S Apr. 15	F May 2*	T Apr. 21
New Moon, Iyar, 1st day	W Apr. 21	M May 9	F Apr. 28	W Apr. 18	M May 5	F Apr. 24
New Moon, Iyar, 2nd day	Th Apr. 22	T May 10	Sa Apr. 29	Th Apr. 19	T May 6	Sa Apr. 25
Israel Independence Day	M Apr. 26	Sa May 14†	W May 3	M Apr. 23	Sa May 10†	W Apr. 29
Lag Ba-'omer	S May 9	F May 27	T May 16	S May 6	F May 23	T May 12
Jerusalem Day	W May 19	M June 6	F May 26	W May 16	M June 2	F May 22
New Moon, Siwan	F May 21	W June 8	S May 28	F May 18	W June 4	S May 24
Shavu'ot, 1st day	W May 26	M June 13	F June 2	W May 23	M June 9	F May 29
Shavu'ot, 2nd day	Th May 27	T June 14	Sa June 3	Th May 24	T June 10	Sa May 30
New Moon, Tammuz, 1st day	Sa June 19	Th July 7	M June 26	Sa June 16	Th July 3	M June 22
New Moon, Tammuz, 2nd day	S June 20	F July 8	T June 27	S June 17	F July 4	T June 23
Fast of 17th of Tammuz	T July 6	S July 24	Th July 13	T July 3	S July 20	Th July 9
New Moon, Av	M July 19	Sa Aug. 6	W July 26	M July 16	Sa Aug. 2	W July 22
Fast of 9th of Av	T July 27	S Aug. 14	Th Aug. 3	T July 24	S Aug. 10	Th July 30
New Moon, Elul, 1st day	T Aug. 17	S Sept. 4	Th Aug. 24	T Aug. 14	S Aug. 31	Th Aug. 20
New Moon, Elul, 2nd day	W Aug. 18	M Sept. 5	F Aug. 25	W Aug. 15	M Sept. 1	F Aug. 21

*Observed Thursday, a day earlier, to avoid conflict with the Sabbath.

†Observed Thursday, two days earlier, to avoid conflict with the Sabbath.

CONDENSED MONTHLY CALENDAR
(2004–2007)

2004, Jan. 24–Feb. 22]   SHEVAṬ (30 DAYS)   [5764

Civil Date	Day of the Week	Jewish Date	SABBATHS, FESTIVALS, FASTS	PENTATEUCHAL READING	PROPHETICAL READING
Jan. 24	Sa	Shevaṭ 1	Wa-'era'; New Moon	Exod. 6:2–9:35 Num. 28:9–15	Isaiah 66: 1–24
31	Sa	8	Bo'	Exod. 10:1–13:16	Jeremiah 46:13–28
Feb. 7	Sa	15	Be-shallaḥ (Shabbat Shirah) Ḥamishar 'asar bi-Shevaṭ	Exod. 13:17–17:16	Judges 4:4–5:31 *Judges 5:1–31*
14	Sa	22	Yitro	Exod. 18:1–20:23	Isaiah 6:1–7:6; 9:5–6 *Isaiah 6: 1–13*
21	Sa	29	Mishpaṭim (Shabbat Sheḳalim)	Exod. 21:1–24:18 30:11–16	1 Samuel 20: 18–42
22	S	30	New Moon, first day	Num. 28: 1–15	

*Italics are for
Sephardi Minhag.*

2004, Feb. 23– Mar. 22]   ADAR (29 DAYS)   [5764

Civil Date	Day of the Week	Jewish Date	SABBATHS, FESTIVALS, FASTS	PENTATEUCHAL READING	PROPHETICAL READING
Feb. 23	M	Adar 1	New Moon, second day	Num. 28:1–15	
28	Sa	6	Terumah	Exod. 25:1–27:19	I Kings 5:26–6:13
Mar. 4	Th	11	Fast of Esther	Exod. 32:11–14 Exod. 34:1–10 (morning and afternoon)	Isaiah 55:6–56:8 (afternoon only)
6	Sa	13	Teẓawweh (Shabbat Zakhor)	Exod. 27:20–30:10 Deut. 25:17–19	I Samuel 15:2–34 *I Samuel 15:1–34*
7	S	14	Purim	Exod. 17:8–16	Book of Esther (night before and in the morning)
8	M	15	Shushan Purim		
13	Sa	20	Ki tissa' (Shabbat Parah)	Exod. 30:11–34:35 Num. 19: 1–22	Ezekiel 36:16–38 *Ezekiel 36:16–36*
20	Sa	27	Wa-yaḳhel, Peḳude (Shabbat Ha-ḥodesh)	Exod. 35:1–40:38 Exod. 12:1–20	Ezekiel 45:16–46:18 *Ezekiel 45:18–46:15*

Italics are for
Sephardi Minhag.

Civil Date	Day of the Week	Jewish Date	SABBATHS, FESTIVALS, FASTS	PENTATEUCHAL READING	PROPHETICAL READING
Mar. 23	T	Nisan 1	New Moon	Num. 28:1–15	
27	Sa	5	Wa-yiḳra'	Levit. 1:1–5:26	Isaiah 43:21–44:24
Apr. 3	Sa	12	Ẓaw (Shabbat Ha-gadol)	Levit. 6:1–8:36	Malachi 3:4–24
5	M	14	Fast of Firstborn		
6	T	15	Passover, first day	Exod. 12:21–51 Num. 28:16–25	Joshua 5:2–6:1, 27
7	W	16	Passover, second day	Levit. 22:26–23:44 Num. 28:16–25	II Kings 23:1–9, 21–25
8	Th	17	Ḥol Ha-mo'ed, first day	Exod. 13:1–16 Num. 28:19–25	Ezekiel 37:1–14
9	F	18	Ḥol Ha-mo'ed, second day	Exod. 22:24–23:19 Num. 28:19–25	
10	Sa	19	Ḥol Ha-mo'ed, third day	Exod. 33:12–34:26 Num. 28:19–25	
11	S	20	Ḥol Ha-mo'ed, fourth day	Num. 9: 1–14 Num. 28:19–25	
12	M	21	Passover, seventh day	Exod. 13:17–15:26 Num. 28:19–25	II Samuel 22:1—51
13	T	22	Passover, eight day	Deut. 15:19–16:17 Num. 28:19–25	Isaiah 10:32–12:6
17	Sa	26	Shemini	Levit. 9:1–11:47	II Samuel 6:1–7:17 *II Samuel 6:1–19*
18	S	27	Holocaust Memorial Day		
21	W	30	New Moon, first day	Num. 28:1–15	

Italics are for Sephardi Minhag.

2004, Apr. 22– May 20]   **IYAR (29 DAYS)**   [5764

Civil Date	Day of the Week	Jewish Date	SABBATHS, FESTIVALS, FASTS	PENTATEUCHAL READING	PROPHETICAL READING
Apr. 22	Th	Iyar 1	New Moon, second day	Num. 28:1–15	
24	Sa	3	Tazria', Meẓora'	Levit. 12:1–15:33	II Kings 7:3–20
26	M	5	Israel Independence Day		
May 1	Sa	10	Aḥare Mot, Ḳedoshim	Levit. 16:1–20:27	Amos 9:7–15 *Ezekiel 20:2–20*
8	Sa	17	Emor	Levit. 21:1–24:23	Ezekiel 44:15–31
9	S	18	Lag Ba-'omer		
15	Sa	24	Be-har, Be-ḥuḳḳotai	Levit. 25:1–27:34	Jeremiah 16:19–17:14
19	W	28	Jerusalem Day		

*Italics are for
Sephardi Minhag.*

2004, May 21–June 19]   SIWAN (30 DAYS)   [5764

Civil Date	Day of the Week	Jewish Date	SABBATHS, FESTIVALS, FASTS	PENTATEUCHAL READING	PROPHETICAL READING
May 21	F	Siwan 1	New Moon	Num. 28:1–15	
22	Sa	2	Be-midbar	Num. 1:1–4:20	Hosea 2:1–22
26	W	6	Shavu'ot, first day	Exod. 19:1–20:23 Num. 28:26–31	Ezekiel 1:1–28, 3:12
27	Th	7	Shavu'ot, second day	Deut. 15:19–16:17 Num. 28:26–31	Habbakuk 3:1–19 *Habbakuk 2:20–3:19*
29	Sa	9	Naso'	Num. 4:21–7:89	Judges 13:2–25
June 5	Sa	16	Be-ha'alotekha	Num. 8:1–12:16	Zechariah 2:14–4:7
12	Sa	23	Shelaḥ lekha	Num. 13:1–15:41	Joshua 2:1–24
19	Sa	30	Koraḥ; New Moon, first day	Num. 16:1–18:13 Num. 28:9–15	Isaiah 66:1–24 *Isaiah 66:1–24* *I Samuel 20:18, 42*

Italics are for Sephardi Minhag.

2004, June 20– July 18]   TAMMUZ (29 DAYS)   [5764

Civil Date	Day of the Week	Jewish Date	SABBATHS, FESTIVALS, FASTS	PENTATEUCHAL READING	PROPHETICAL READING
June 20	S	Tammuz 1	New Moon, second day	Num. 28:1–15	
26	Sa	7	Ḥuḳḳat	Num. 19:1–22:1	Judges 11:1–33
July 3	Sa	14	Balaḳ	Num. 22:2–25:9	Micah 5:6–6:8
6	T	17	Fast of 17th of Tammuz	Exod. 32:11–14 Exod. 34: 1–10 (morning and afternoon)	Isaiah 55:6–56:8 (afternoon only)
10	Sa	21	Pineḥas	Num. 25:10–30:1	Jeremiah 1:1–2:3
17	Sa	28	Maṭṭot Masʻe	Num. 30:2–36:13	Jeremiah 2:4–28 Jeremiah 3:4 *Jeremiah 2:4–28* *Jeremiah 4:1–2*

Italics are for
Sephardi Minhag.

Civil Date	Day of the Week	Jewish Date	SABBATHS, FESTIVALS, FASTS	PENTATEUCHAL READING	PROPHETICAL READING
July 19	M	Av 1	New Moon	Num. 28:1–15	
24	Sa	6	Devarim (Shabbat Ḥazon)	Deut. 1:1–3:22	Isaiah 1:1–27
27	T	9	Fast of 9th of Av	Morning: Deut. 4:25–40 Afternoon: Exod. 32:11–14 Exod. 34:1–10	(Lamentations is read the night before) Jeremiah 8:13–9:23 (morning) Isaiah 55:6–56:8 (afternoon)
31	Sa	13	Wa-etḥannan (Shabbat Naḥamu)	Deut. 3:23–7:11	Isaiah 40:1–26
Aug. 7	Sa	20	ʻEḳev	Deut. 7:12–11:25	Isaiah 49:14–51:3
14	Sa	27	Re'eh	Deut. 11:26–16:17	Isaiah 54:11–55:5
17	T	30	New Moon, first day	Numbers 28:1–15	

Italics are for Sephardi Minhag.

2004, Aug. 18–Sept. 15]   ELUL (29 DAYS)   [5764

Civil Date	Day of the Week	Jewish Date	SABBATHS, FESTIVALS, FASTS	PENTATEUCHAL READING	PROPHETICAL READING
Aug. 18	W	Elul 1	New Moon, second day	Num. 28:1–15	
21	Sa	4	Shofeṭim	Deut. 16:18–21:9	Isaiah 51:12–52:12
28	Sa	11	Ki teẓe'	Deut. 21:10–25:19	Isaiah 54:1–10
Sept. 4	Sa	18	Ki tavo'	Deut. 26: 1–29:8	Isaiah 60:1–22
11	Sa	25	Niẓẓavim, Wa-yelekh	Deut. 29:9–31:30	Isaiah 61:10–63:9

Italics are for
Sephardi Minhag.

Civil Date	Day of the Week	Jewish Date	SABBATHS, FESTIVALS, FASTS	PENTATEUCHAL READING	PROPHETICAL READING
Sept. 16	Th	Tishri 1	Rosh Ha-shanah, first day	Gen. 21:1–34 Num. 29:1–6	I Samuel 1:1–2:10
17	F	2	Rosh Ha-shana, second day	Gen. 22:1–24 Num. 29:1–6	Jeremiah 31:2–20
18	Sa	8	Ha'azinu (Shabbat Shuvah)	Deut. 32:1–52	Hosea 14:2–10 Micah 7:18–20 Joel 2:15–27 *Hosea 14:2–10* *Micah 7:18–20*
19	S	3	Fast of Gedaliah	Exod. 32:11–14 Exod. 34:1–10 (morning and afternoon)	Isaiah 55:6–56:8 (afternoon only)
25	Sa	10	Yom Kippur	Morning: Levit. 16:1–34 Num. 29:7–11 Afternoon: Levit. 18:1–30	Isaiah 57:14–58:14 Jonah 1:1–4:11 Micah 7:18–20
30	Th	15	Sukkot, first day	Levit. 22:26–23:44 Num. 29:12–16	Zechariah 14:1–21
Oct. 1	F	16	Sukkot, second day	Levit. 22:26–23:44 Num. 29:12–16	I Kings 8:2–21
2	Sa	17	Ḥol Ha-mo'ed, first day	Exod. 33:12–34:26 Num. 29:17–22	Ezekiel 38:18–39:16
3–5	S–T	18–20	Ḥol Ha-mo'ed, second to fourth days	S: Num. 29:20–28 M: Num. 29:23–31 T: Num. 29:26–34	
6	W	21	Hosha'na' Rabbah	Num. 29:26–34	
7	Th	22	Shemini 'Aẓeret	Deut. 14:22–16:17 Num. 29:35–30:1	I Kings 8:54–66
8	F	23	Simḥat Torah	Deut. 33:1–34:12 Gen. 1:1–2:3 Num. 29:35–30:1	Joshua 1:1–18 *Joshua 1:1–9*
9	Sa	29	Be-re'shit	Gen. 1:1–6:8	Isaiah 42:5–43:10 *Isaiah 42:5–21*
15	F	30	New Moon, first day	Num. 28: 1–15	

Italics are for Sephardi Minhag.

2004, Oct. 16–Nov. 13]   ḤESHWAN (29 DAYS)   [5765

Civil Date	Day of the Week	Jewish Date	SABBATHS, FESTIVALS, FASTS	PENTATEUCHAL READING	PROPHETICAL READING
Oct. 16	Sa	Ḥeshwan 1	Noaḥ; New Moon, second day	Gen. 6:9–11:32 Num. 28:1–15	Isaiah 66:1–24
23	Sa	8	Lekh lekha	Gen. 12:1–17:27	Isaiah 40:27–41:16
30	Sa	15	Wa-yera'	Gen. 18:1–22:24	II Kings 4:1–37 *II Kings 4:1–23*
Nov. 6	Sa	22	Ḥayye Sarah	Gen. 23:1–25:18	I Kings 1:1–31
13	Sa	29	Toledot	Gen. 25:19–28:9	I Samuel 20:18–42

Italics are for
Sephardi Minhag.

2004, Nov. 14–Dec. 12]   KISLEW (29 DAYS)   [5765

Civil Date	Day of the Week	Jewish Date	SABBATHS, FESTIVALS, FASTS	PENTATEUCHAL READING	PROPHETICAL READING
Nov. 14	S	Kislew 1	New Moon,	Num. 28:1–15	
20	Sa	7	Wa-yeẓe'	Gen. 28:10–32:3	Hosea 12:13–14:10 *Hosea 11:7–12:12*
27	Sa	14	Wa-yishlaḥ	Gen. 32:4–36:43	Hosea 11:7–12:12 *Obadiah 1:1–21*
Dec. 4	Sa	21	Wa-yeshev;	Gen. 37:1–40:23	Amos 2:6–3:8
8–10	W–F	25–27	Ḥanukkah, first to third days	W: Num. 7:1–17 Th: Num. 7:18–29 F: Num. 7:24–35	
11	Sa	28	Mi-ḳeẓ Ḥanukkah, fourth day	Gen. 41:1–44:17 Num. 7:30–35	Zechariah 2:14–4:7
12	S	29	Ḥanukkah, fifth day	Num. 7:36–47	

Italics are for Sephardi Minhag.

2004, Dec. 13–Jan. 20, 2005]   ṬEVET (29 DAYS)   [5765

Civil Date	Day of the Week	Jewish Date	SABBATHS, FESTIVALS, FASTS	PENTATEUCHAL READING	PROPHETICAL READING
Dec. 13	M	Ṭevet 1	New Moon; Ḥanukkah, sixth day	Num. 28:1–15 Num. 7:42–47	
14–15	T–W	2–3	Ḥanukkah, seventh and eight days	T: Num. 7:48–53 W: Num. 7:54–8:4	
18	Sa	6	Wa-yiggash	Gen. 44:18–47:27	Ezekiel 37:15–28
22	W	10	Fast of 10th of Ṭevet	Exod. 32:11–14 Exod. 34:1–10 (morning and afternoon)	Isaiah 55:6–56:8 (afternoon only)
25	Sa	13	Wa-yeḥi	Gen. 47:28–50:26	I Kings 2:1–12
Jan. 1 2005	Sa	20	Shemot	Exod. 1:1–6:1	Isaiah 27:6–28:13 Isaiah 29:22–23 *Jeremiah 1:1–2:3*
8	Sa	27	Wa-'era'	Exod. 6:2–9:35	Ezekiel 28:25–29:21

Italics are for Sephardi Minhag.

2005, Jan. 11–Feb. 9]   SHEVAṬ (30 DAYS)   [5765

Civil Date	Day of the Week	Jewish Date	SABBATHS, FESTIVALS, FASTS	PENTATEUCHAL READING	PROPHETICAL READING
Jan. 11	T	Shevaṭ 1	New Moon	Num. 28:1–15	
15	Sa	5	Bo'	Exod. 10:1–13:16	Jeremiah 46:13–28
22	Sa	12	Be-shallaḥ (Shabbat Shirah)	Exod. 13:17–17:16	Judges 4:4–5:31 *Judges 5:1–31*
25	T	15	Ḥamisha 'asar bi-Shevaṭ		
29	Sa	19	Yitro	Exod. 18:1–20:23	Isaiah 6:1–7:6; 9:5–6 *Isaiah 6: 1–13*
Feb. 5	Sa	26	Mishpaṭim	Exod. 21:1–24:18	Jeremiah 34:8–22 33:25–26
9	W	30	New Moon, first day	Num. 28: 1–15	

Italics are for Sephardi Minhag.

2005, Feb. 10– Mar. 11]   ADAR I (30 DAYS)   [5765

Civil Date	Day of the Week	Jewish Date	SABBATHS, FESTIVALS, FASTS	PENTATEUCHAL READING	PROPHETICAL READING
Feb. 10	Th	Adar 1	New Moon, second day	Num. 28:1–15	
12	Sa	3	Terumah	Exod. 25:1–27:19	I Kings 5:26–6:13
19	Sa	10	Teẓawweh	Exod. 27:20–30:10	Ezekiel 43:10–27
26	Sa	17	Ki tissa'	Exod. 30:11–34:35	I Kings 18:1–39 *I Kings 18:20–39*
Mar.	Sa	24	Wa-yaḵhel	Exod. 35:1–38:20	I Kings 7:40–50
11	F	30	New Moon first day	Num. 28:1–15	

Italics are for
Sephardi Minhag.

2005, Mar. 10–Apr. 9]   ADAR II (29 DAYS)   [5765

Civil Date	Day of the Week	Jewish Date	SABBATHS, FESTIVALS, FASTS	PENTATEUCHAL READING	PROPHETICAL READING
Mar. 12	Sa	Adar II 1	Peḳude (Shabbat Sheḳalim), New Moon, second day	Exod. 38:21–40:38 Num. 28:9–15 Exod. 30:11–16	II Kings 12:1–17 *II Kings 11:17–12:17* Isaiah 66:1, 24
19	Sa	8	Wa-yiḳra' (Shabbat Zakhor)	Levit. 1:1–5:26 Deut. 25:17–19	I Samuel 15:2–34 *I Samuel 15:1–34*
24	Th	13	Fast of Esther	Exod. 32:11–14 Exod. 34:1–10 (morning and afternoon)	Isaiah 55:6–56:8 (morning and afternoon)
25	F	14	Purim	Exod. 17:8–16	Book of Esther (night before and morning)
26	Sa	15	Ẓaw (Shushan Purim)	Levit. 6:1–8:36	Jeremiah 7:21–8:3; 9:22–23
Apr. 2	Sa	22	Shemini (Shabbat Parah	Levit. 9:1–11:47 Exod. 12:1–20	Ezekiel 36:16–38 *Ezekiel 36:16–36*
9	Sa	29	Tazria' (Shabat Ha-ḥodesh)	Levit. 12:1–13:59 Exod. 12:1–20	Ezekiel 45:16–46:1 *Ezekiel 45:18–46:15* I Samuel 20:18, 42

Italics are for
Sephardi Minhag.

2005, Apr. 10– May 9] NISAN (30 DAYS) [5765

Civil Date	Day of the Week	Jewish Date	SABBATHS, FESTIVALS, FASTS	PENTATEUCHAL READING	PROPHETICAL READING
Apr. 10	S	Nisan 1	New Moon	Num. 28:1–15	
16	Sa	7	Meẓora‘	Levit. 14:1–15:33	II Kings 7:3–20
21	Th	12	Fast of Firstborn		
23	Sa	14	Aḥare Mot Shabbat Ha-gadol	Levit. 16:1–18:30	Malachi 3:4–24
24	S	15	Passover, first day	Exod. 12:21–51 Num. 28:16–25	Joshua 5:2–6:1, 27
25	M	16	Passover, second day	Levit. 22:26–23:44 Num. 28:16–25	II Kings 23:1–9, 21–25
26	T	17	Ḥol Ha-mo‘ed, first day	Exod. 13:1–16 Num. 28:19–25	Ezekiel 37:1–14
27	W	18	Ḥol Ha-mo‘ed, second day	Exod. 22:24–23:19 Num. 28:19–25	
28	Th	19	Ḥol Ha-mo‘ed, third day	Exod. 33:12–34:26 Num. 28:19–25	
29	F	20	Ḥol Ha-mo‘ed, fourth day	Num. 9: 1–14 Num. 28:19–25	
30	Sa	21	Passover, seventh day	Exod. 13:17–15:26 Num. 28:19–25	II Samuel 22:1—51
May 1	S	22	Passover, eighth day	Deut. 15:19–16:17 Num. 28:19 –25	Isaiah 10:32–12:6
6	F	27	Holocaust Memorial Day*		
7	Sa	28	Ḳedoshim	Levit. 16:1–20:27	Amos 9:7–15 *Ezekiel 20:2–20*
9	M	30	New Moon, first day	Num. 28:1–15	

*Observed May 5, to avoid conflict with the Sabbath.

*Italics are for
Sephardi Minhag.*

2005, May 10– June 7]   **IYAR (29 DAYS)**   [5765

Civil Date	Day of the Week	Jewish Date	SABBATHS, FESTIVALS, FASTS	PENTATEUCHAL READING	PROPHETICAL READING
May. 10	T	Iyar 1	New Moon second day	Num. 28:1–15	
14	Sa	5	Emor, Israel Independence Day*	Levit. 21:1–24:23	Ezekiel 44:15–31
21	Sa	12	Be-har	Levit. 25:1–26:2	Jeremiah 32:6–27
27	F	18	Lag Ba-'omer		
28	Sa	19	Be-ḥukkotai	Levit. 26:3–27:34	Jeremiah 16:19–17:14
June 4	Sa	26	Be-midbar	Num 1:1–4:20	Hosea 2:1–22
6	M	28	Jerusalem Day		

*Independence Day celebrated May 12, to avoid conflict with the Sabbath.

*Italics are for
Sephardi Minhag.*

2005, June 8–July 7]   SIWAN (30 DAYS)   [5765

Civil Date	Day of the Week	Jewish Date	SABBATHS, FESTIVALS, FASTS	PENTATEUCHAL READING	PROPHETICAL READING
June 8	W	Siwan 1	New Moon	Num. 28:1–15	
11	Sa	4	Naso'	Num. 4:21–7:89	Judges 13:2–25
13	M	6	Shavu'ot, first day	Exod. 19:1–20:23 Num. 28:26–31	Ezekiel 1:1–28, 3:12
14	T	7	Shavu'ot, second day	Deut. 15:19–16: 17 Num. 28:26–31	Habbakuk 3:1–19 *Habbakuk 2:20–3:19*
18	Sa	11	Be-ha'alotekha	Num. 8:1–12:16	Zechariah 2:14–4: 7
25	Sa	18	Shelaḥ lekha	Num. 13:1–15:41	Joshua 2:1–24
July 2	Sa	25	Ḳoraḥ	Num. 16:1–18:13	I Samuel 11:14–12:23
7	Th	30	New Moon, first day	Num. 28:9–15	

Italics are for
Sephardi Minhag.

TAMMUZ (29 DAYS)

Civil Date	Day of the Week	Jewish Date	SABBATHS, FESTIVALS, FASTS	PENTATEUCHAL READING	PROPHETICAL READING
July 8	F	Tammuz 1	New Moon, second day	Num. 28:1–15	
9	Sa	2	Ḥuḳḳat	Num. 19:1–22:1	Judges 11:1–33
16	Sa	9	Balaḳ	Num. 22:2–25:9	Micah 5:6–6:8
23	Sa	16	Pineḥas	Num. 25:10–30:1	II Kings 18:46–19:2
24	S	17	Fast of 17th of Tammuz	Exod. 32:11–14 Exod. 34: 1–10 (morning and afternoon)	Isaiah 55:6–56:8 (afternoon only)
30	Sa	23	Maṭṭot	Num. 30:2–32:42	Jeremiah 1:1–2:3

Italics are for Sephardi Minhag.

2005, Aug. 6–Sept. 4] AV (30 DAYS) [5765

Civil Date	Day of the Week	Jewish Date	SABBATHS, FESTIVALS, FASTS	PENTATEUCHAL READING	PROPHETICAL READING
Aug. 6	Sa	Av 1	Mas'e, New Moon	Num. 33:1–36:13 Num. 28:9–15	Jeremiah 2:4–28; 3:4 *Jeremiah 2:4–28* *Jeremiah 4:1–2* Isaiah 66:1, 23
13	Sa	8	Devarim (Shabbat Ḥazon)	Deut. 1:1–3:22	Isaiah 1:1–27
14	S	9	Fast of 9th of Av	Morning: Deut. 4:25–40 Afternoon: Exod. 32:11–14 Exod. 34:1–10	(Lamentations is read the night before) Jeremiah 8:13–9:23 (morning) Isaiah 55:6–56:8 (afternoon)
20	Sa	15	Wa-ethannan (Shabbat Naḥamu)	Deut. 3:23–7:11	Isaiah 40:1–26
27	Sa	22	'Eḳev	Deut. 7:12–11:25	Isaiah 49:14–51:3
Sept. 3	Sa	29	Re'eh	Deut. 11:26–16:17	Isaiah 54:11–55:5 *Isaiah 54:11–55:5* *I Samuel 20:18, 42*
4	S	30	New Moon, first day	Numbers 28:1–15	

Italics are for
Sephardi Minhag.

2005, Sept. 5–Oct. 3] ELUL (29 DAYS) [5765

Civil Date	Day of the Week	Jewish Date	SABBATHS, FESTIVALS, FASTS	PENTATEUCHAL READING	PROPHETICAL READING
Sept. 5	M	Elul 1	New Moon, second day	Num. 28:1–15	
10	Sa	6	Shofeṭim	Deut. 16:18–21:9	Isaiah 51:12–52:12
17	Sa	13	Ki teze'	Deut. 21:10–25:19	Isaiah 54:1–10
24	Sa	20	Ki tavo'	Deut. 26: 1–29:8	Isaiah 60:1–22
Oct. 1	Sa	27	Niẓẓavim,	Deut. 29:9–30:20	Isaiah 61:10–63:9

Italics are for
Sephardi Minhag.

2005, Oct. 4–Nov. 2]   TISHRI (30 DAYS)   [5766

Civil Date	Day of the Week	Jewish Date	SABBATHS, FESTIVALS, FASTS	PENTATEUCHAL READING	PROPHETICAL READING
Oct. 4	T	Tishri 1	Rosh Ha-shanah, first day	Gen. 21:1–34 Num. 29:1–6	I Samuel 1:1–2:10
5	W	2	Rosh Ha-shana, second day	Gen. 22:1–24 Num. 29:1–6	Jeremiah 31:2–20
6	Th	3	Fast of Gedaliah	Exod. 32:11–14 Exod. 34:1–10 (morning and afternoon)	Isaiah 55: 6–56:8 (afternoon only)
8	Sa	5	Wa-yelekh (Shabbat Shuvah)	Deut. 31:1–30	Hosea 14:2–10 Micah 7:18–20 Joel 2:15–27 *Hosea 14:2–10* *Micah 7:18–20*
13	Th	10	Yom Kippur	Morning: Levit. 16:1–34 Num. 29:7–11 Afternoon: Levit. 18:1–30	Isaiah 57:14–58:14 Afternoon: Jonah 1:1–4:11 Micah 7:18–20
15	Sa	12	Ha'azinu	Deut. 32:1–52	II Samuel 22:1–51
18	T	15	Sukkot, first day	Levit. 22:26–23:44 Num. 29:12–16	Zechariah 14:1–21
19	W	16	Sukkot, second day	Levit. 22:26–23:44 Num. 29:12 –16	I Kings 8:2–21
20-21	Th-F	17-18	Ḥol Ha-mo'ed; first and second days	Th: Num. 29:17–25 F: Num. 29:20–28	
22	Sa	19	Shabbat Ḥol Ha-mo'ed, third day	Exod. 33:12–26 Num. 29:23–28	Ezekiel 38:18–39:16
23	S	20	Ḥol Ha-mo'ed, fourth day	Num. 29:26–31	
24	M	21	Hosha'na' Rabbah	Num. 29:26–34	
25	T	22	Shemini 'Aẓeret	Deut. 14:22–16:17 Num. 29:35–30:1	I Kings 8:54–66
26	W	23	Simḥat Torah	Deut. 33:1–34:12 Gen. 1:1–2:3 Num. 29:35–30:1	Joshua 1:1–18 *Joshua 1:1–9*
29	Sa	26	Be-re'shit	Gen. 1:1–6:8	Isaiah 42:5–43:10 *Isaiah 42:5–21*
Nov. 2	W	30	New Moon, first day	Num. 28: 1–15	

Italics are for
Sephardi Minhag.

2005, Nov. 3–Dec. 1] HESHWAN (29 DAYS) [5766

Civil Date	Day of the Week	Jewish Date	SABBATHS, FESTIVALS, FASTS	PENTATEUCHAL READING	PROPHETICAL READING
Nov. 3	Th	Heshwan 1	New Moon, second day	Num. 28:1–15	
5	Sa	3	Noah	Gen. 6:9–11:32	Isaiah 54:1–55:5 *Isaiah 54:1–10*
12	Sa	10	Lekh lekha	Gen. 12:1–17:27	Isaiah 40:27–41:16
19	Sa	17	Wa-yera'	Gen. 18:1–22:24	II Kings 4:1–37 *II Kings 4:1–23*
26	Sa	24	Hayye Sarah	Gen. 23:1–25:18	I Kings 1:1–31

Italics are for Sephardi Minhag.

2005, Dec. 2–31] KISLEW (30 DAYS) [5766

Civil Date	Day of the Week	Jewish Date	SABBATHS, FESTIVALS, FASTS	PENTATEUCHAL READING	PROPHETICAL READING
Dec. 2	F	Kislew 1	New Moon	Num. 28:1–15	
3	Sa	2	Toledot	Gen. 25:19–28:9	Malachi 1:1–2:7
10	Sa	9	Wa-yeẓe'	Gen. 28:10–32:3	Hosea 12:13–14:10
17	Sa	16	Wa-yishlaḥ	Gen. 32:4–36:43	Hosea 11:7–12:12 *Obadiah 1:1–21*
24	Sa	23	Wa-yeshev	Gen. 37:1–40:23	Amos 2:6–3:8
26	M	25	Hanukkah, first day	Num. 7:1–17	
27-30	T–F	26–29	Hanukkah, second to fifth days	T: Num. 7:18–29 W: Num. 7:24–35 Th: Num. 7:30–41 F: Num. 7:36–41	
31	Sa	30	Mi-ḳeẓ, Hanukkah, sixth day; New Moon, first day	Gen. 41:1–44:17 Num. 28:9–15 Num. 7:48–53	Zechariah 2:14–4:7

Italics are for Sephardi Minhag.

2006, Jan. 1–29] TEVET (29 DAYS) [5766

Civil Date	Day of the Week	Jewish Date	SABBATHS, FESTIVALS, FASTS	PENTATEUCHAL READING	PROPHETICAL READING
Jan. 1	S	Tevet 1	New Moon, second day; Hanukkah, seventh day	Num. 28:1–15 Num. 7:48–53	
2	M	2	Hanukkah, eighth day	Num. 7:54–8:4	
7	Sa	7	Wa-yiggash	Gen. 44:18–47:27	Ezekiel 37:15–28
10	T	10	Fast of 10th of Tevet	Exod. 32:11–14 Exod. 34:1–10 (morning and afternoon)	Isaiah 55:6–56:8 (afternoon only)
14	Sa	14	Wa-yehi	Gen. 47:28–50:26	I Kings 2:1–12
21	Sa	21	Shemot	Exod. 1:1–6:1	Isaiah 27:6–28:13 Isaiah 29:22–23 *Jeremiah 1:1–2:3*
28	Sa	28	Wa-'era'	Exod. 6:2–9:35	Ezekiel 28:25–29:21

*Italics are for
Sephardi Minhag.*

2006, Jan. 30–Feb. 28]　　　SHEVAṬ (30 DAYS)　　　[5766

Civil Date	Day of the Week	Jewish Date	SABBATHS, FESTIVALS, FASTS	PENTATEUCHAL READING	PROPHETICAL READING
Jan. 30	M	Shevaṭ 1	New Moon	Num. 28:1–15	
Feb. 5	Sa	6	Bo'	Exod. 10:1–13:16	Jeremiah 46:13–28
11	Sa	13	Be-shallaḥ (Shabbat Shirah)	Exod. 13:17–17:16	Judges 4:4–5:31 *Judges 5:1–31*
13	M	15	Ḥamisha 'asar bi-Shevaṭ		
18	Sa	20	Yitro	Exod. 18:1–20:23	Isaiah 6:1–7:6; 9:5–6 *Isaiah 6: 1–13*
25	Sa	27	Mishpaṭim (Shabbat Sheḳalim)	Exod. 21:1–24:18 30:11–16	II Kings 12:1–17 *II Kings 11:17–12:17*
28	T	30	New Moon, first day	Num. 28: 1–15	

Italics are for Sephardi Minhag.

ADAR (29 DAYS)

Civil Date	Day of the Week	Jewish Date	SABBATHS, FESTIVALS, FASTS	PENTATEUCHAL READING	PROPHETICAL READING
Mar. 1	W	Adar 1	New Moon, second day	Num. 28:1–15	
4	Sa	4	Terumah	Exod. 25:1–27:19	I Kings 5:26–6:13
11	Sa	11	Teẓawweh (Shabbat Zakhor)	Exod. 27:20–30:10 Deut. 25:17–19	I Samuel 15:2–34 *I Samuel 15:1–34*
13	M	13	Fast of Esther	Exod. 32:11–14 Exod. 34:1–10 (morning and afternoon)	Isaiah 55:6–56:8 (morning and) afternoon)
14	T	14	Purim	Exod. 17:8–16	Book of Esther (night before and morning)
15	W	15	Shushan Purim		
18	Sa	18	Ki tissa' (Shabbat Parah)	Exod. 30:11–34:35 Num. 19:1–22	Ezekiel 36:16–38 *Ezekiel 36:16–36*
25	Sa	25	Wa-yaḵhel, Peḵude (Shabbat Ha-ḥodesh)	Exod. 35:1–40:38 Exod. 12:1–20	Ezekiel 45:16–46:1 *Ezekiel 45:18–46:15*

Italics are for Sephardi Minhag.

2006, Mar. 30–Apr. 28]   NISAN (30 DAYS)   [5766

Civil Date	Day of the Week	Jewish Date	SABBATHS, FESTIVALS, FASTS	PENTATEUCHAL READING	PROPHETICAL READING
Mar. 30	Th	Nisan 1	New Moon	Num. 28:1–15	
Apr. 1	Sa	3	Wa-yiḳra'	Levit. 1:1–5:26	Isaiah 43:21–23
8	Sa	10	Ẓaw (Shabbat Ha-gadol)	Levit. 6:1–8:36	*Malachi 3:4–24*
12	W	14	Fast of Firstborn		
13	Th	15	Passover, first day	Exod. 12:21–51 Num. 28:16–25	Joshua 5:2–6:1, 27
14	F	16	Passover, second day	Levit. 22:26–23:44 Num. 28:16–25	II Kings 23:1–9, 21–25
15	Sa	17	Ḥol Ha-mo'ed, first day	Exod. 33:12–34:26 Num. 28:19–25	Ezekiel 37:1–14
16	S	18	Ḥol Ha-mo'ed, second day	Exod. 13:1–16 Num. 28:19–25	
17	M	19	Ḥol Ha-mo'ed, third day	Exod. 22:24–23:19 Num. 28:19–25	
18	T	20	Ḥol Ha-mo'ed, fourth day	Num. 9: 1–14 Num. 28:19–25	
19	W	21	Passover, seventh day	Exod. 13:17–15:26 Num. 28:19–25	II Samuel 22:1—51
20	Th	22	Passover, eighth day	Deut. 15:19–16:17 Num. 28:19 –25	Isaiah 10:32–12:6
22	Sa	24	Shemini	Levit. 9:1–11:47	Isaiah 10:32–12:6
25	T	27	Holocaust Memorial Day		
28	F	30	New Moon, first day	Num. 28:1–15	

Italics are for Sephardi Minhag.

Civil Date	Day of the Week	Jewish Date	SABBATHS, FESTIVALS, FASTS	PENTATEUCHAL READING	PROPHETICAL READING
Apr. 29	Sa	Iyar 1	Tazria', Mezora' New Moon, second day	Levit. 12:1–15:33 Num. 28:1–15	Isaiah 66:1–24
May 3	W	5	Israel Independence Day		
6	Sa	8	Aḥare Mot, Ḳedoshim	Levit. 16:1–20:27	Amos 9:7–15 *Ezekiel 20:2–20*
13	Sa	15	Emor	Levit. 21:1–24:23	Ezekiel 44:15–31
16	T	18	Lag Ba-'omer		
20	Sa	22	Be-har, Be-ḥukkotai	Levit. 25:1–27:34	Jeremiah 16:19–17:14
26	F	28	Jerusalem Day*		
27	Sa	29	Be-midbar	Num. 1:1–4:20	Hosea 2:1–22

*Jerusalem Day celebrated May 25, to avoid conflict with the Sabbath.

*Italics are for
Sephardi Minhag.*

2006, May 28–June 26] SIWAN (30 DAYS) [5766

Civil Date	Day of the Week	Jewish Date	SABBATHS, FESTIVALS, FASTS	PENTATEUCHAL READING	PROPHETICAL READING
May 28	S	Siwan 1	New Moon	Num. 28:1–15	
June 2	F	6	Shavu'ot, first day	Exod. 19:1–20:23 Num. 28:26–31	Ezekiel 1:1–28, 3:12
3	Sa	7	Shavu'ot, second day	Deut. 15:19–16:17 Num. 28:26–31	Habbakuk 3:1–19 *Habbakuk 2:20–3:19*
10	Sa	14	Naso'	Num. 4:21–7:89	Judges 13:2–25
17	Sa	21	Be-ha'alotekha	Num. 8:1–12:16	Zechariah 2:14–4:7
24	Sa	28	Shelaḥ lekha	Num. 13:1–15:41	Joshua 2:1–24
26	M	30	New Moon, first day	Num. 28:1–15	

Italics are for Sephardi Minhag.

2006, June 27–July 25] TAMMUZ (29 DAYS) [5766

Civil Date	Day of the Week	Jewish Date	SABBATHS, FESTIVALS, FASTS	PENTATEUCHAL READING	PROPHETICAL READING
June 27	T	Tammuz 1	New Moon, second day	Num. 28:1–15	
July 1	Sa	5	Ḳoraḥ	Num. 16:1–18:32	I Samuel 11:14–12:23
8	Sa	12	Ḥuḳḳat, Balaḳ	Num. 19:1–25:9	Micah 5:6–6:8
13	Th	17	Fast of 17th of Tammuz	Exod. 32:11–14 Exod. 34: 1–10 (morning and afternoon)	Isaiah 55:6–56:8 (afternoon only)
15	Sa	19	Pineḥas	Num. 25:10–30:1	Jeremiah 1:1–2:3
22	Sa	26	Maṭṭot Mas'e	Num. 30:2–36:13	Jeremiah 2:4–28; 3:4 *Jeremiah 2:4–28; 4:1–2*

Italics are for Sephardi Minhag.

2006, July 26–Aug. 24]　　　AV (30 DAYS)　　　[5766

Civil Date	Day of the Week	Jewish Date	SABBATHS, FESTIVALS, FASTS	PENTATEUCHAL READING	PROPHETICAL READING
July 26	W	Av 1	New Moon	Num. 28:1–15	
29	Sa	4	Devarim (Shabbat Ḥazon)	Deut. 1:1–3:22	Isaiah 1:1–27
Aug. 3	Th	9	Fast of 9th of Av	Morning: Deut. 4:25–40 Afternoon: Exod. 32:11–14 Exod. 34:1–10	(Lamentations is read the night before) Jeremiah 8:13–9:23 (morning) Isaiah 55:6–56:8 (afternoon)
5	Sa	11	Wa-etḥannan (Shabbat Naḥamu)	Deut. 3:23–7:11	Isaiah 40:1–26
12	Sa	18	ʿEḳev	Deut. 7:12–11:25	Isaiah 49:14–51:3
19	Sa	25	Re'eh	Deut. 11:26–16:17	Isaiah 54:11–55:5
24	Th	30	New Moon, first day	Numbers 28:1–15	

Italics are for Sephardi Minhag.

2006, Aug. 25–Sept. 22]   ELUL (29 DAYS)   [5766

Civil Date	Day of the Week	Jewish Date	SABBATHS, FESTIVALS, FASTS	PENTATEUCHAL READING	PROPHETICAL READING
Aug. 25	F	Elul 1	New Moon, second day	Num. 28:1–15	
26	Sa	2	Shofeṭim	Deut. 16:18–21:9	Isaiah 51:12–52:12
Sept. 2	Sa	9	Ki teẓe'	Deut. 21:10–25:19	Isaiah 54:1–10
9	Sa	16	Ki tavo'	Deut. 26: 1–29:8	Isaiah 60:1–22
16	Sa	23	Niẓẓavim, Wa-yelekh	Deut. 29:9–31:30	Isaiah 61:10–63:9

Italics are for
Sephardi Minhag.

2006, Sept. 23–Oct. 22]   TISHRI (30 DAYS)   [5767

Civil Date	Day of the Week	Jewish Date	SABBATHS, FESTIVALS, FASTS	PENTATEUCHAL READING	PROPHETICAL READING
Sept. 23	Sa	Tishri 1	Rosh Ha-shanah, first day	Gen. 21:1–34 Num. 29:1–6	I Samuel 1:1–2:10
24	S	2	Rosh Ha-shana, second day	Gen. 22:1–24 Num. 29:1–6	Jeremiah 31:2–20
25	M	3	Fast of Gedaliah	Exod. 32:11–14 Exod. 34:1–10 (morning and afternoon)	Isaiah 55:6–56:8 (afternoon only)
30	Sa	8	Ha'azinu (Shabbat Shuvah)	Deut. 32:1–52	Hosea 14:2–10 Micah 7:18–20 Joel 2:15–27 *Hosea 14:2–10* *Micah 7:18–20*
Oct. 2	M	10	Yom Kippur	Morning: Levit. 16:1–34 Num. 29:7–11 Afternoon: Levit. 18:1–30	Isaiah 57:14–58:14 Afternoon: Jonah 1:1–4:11 Micah 7:18–20
7	Sa	15	Sukkot, first day	Levit. 22:26–23:44 Num. 29:12–16	Zechariah 14:1–21
8	S	16	Sukkot, second day	Levit. 22:26–23:44 Num. 29:12–16	I Kings 8:2–21
9–12	M–Th	17–20	Ḥol Ha-mo'ed, first through fourth days	M: Num. 29:17–25 T: Num. 29:20–28 W: Num. 29:23–28 Th: Num. 29:26–34	
13	F	21	Hosha'na' Rabbah	Num. 29:26–34	
14	Sa	22	Shemini 'Aẓeret	Deut. 14:22–16:17 Num. 29:35–30:1	I Kings 8:54–66
15	S	23	Simḥat Torah	Deut. 33:1–34:12 Gen. 1:1–2:3 Num. 29:35–30:1	Joshua 1:1–18 *Joshua 1:1–9*
21	Sa	29	Be-re'shit	Gen. 1:1–6:8	1 Samuel 20:18–42
22	S	30	New Moon, first day	Num. 28: 1–15	

Italics are for
Sephardi Minhag.

2006, Oct. 23–Nov. 21]   ḤESHWAN (29 DAYS)   [5767

Civil Date	Day of the Week	Jewish Date	SABBATHS, FESTIVALS, FASTS	PENTATEUCHAL READING	PROPHETICAL READING
Oct. 23	M	Ḥeshwan 1	New Moon, second day	Num. 28:1–15	
28	Sa	6	Noaḥ	Gen. 6:9–11:32	Isaiah 54:1–55:5 *Isaiah 54:1–10*
Nov. 4	Sa	13	Lekh lekha	Gen. 12:1–17:27	Isaiah 40:27–41:16
11	Sa	20	Wa-yera'	Gen. 18:1–22:24	II Kings 4:1–37 *II Kings 4:1–23*
18	Sa	27	Ḥayye Sarah	Gen. 23:1–25:18	I Kings 1:1–31
21	T	30	New Moon, first day	Num. 28:1–15	

Italics are for
Sephardi Minhag.

2006, Nov. 22–Dec. 21] KISLEW (29 DAYS) [5767

Civil Date	Day of the Week	Jewish Date	SABBATHS, FESTIVALS, FASTS	PENTATEUCHAL READING	PROPHETICAL READING
Nov. 22	W	Kislew 1	New Moon, second day	Num. 28:1–15	
25	Sa	4	Toledot	Gen. 25:19–28:9	Malachi 1:1–2:7
Dec. 2	Sa	11	Wa-yeẓe'	Gen. 28:10–32:3	Hosea 12:13–14:10
9	Sa	18	Wa-yishlaḥ	Gen. 32:4–36:43	Hosea 11:7–12:12 *Obadiah 1:1–21*
16	Sa	25	Wa-yeshev; Ḥanukkah, first day	Gen. 37:1–40:23 Num. 7:1–17	Zechariah 2:14–4:7
17–20	S–W	26–29	Ḥanukkah, second to fifth days	S: Num. 7:18–29 M: Num. 7:24–35 T: Num. 7:30–41 W: Num. 7:36–47	
21	Th	30	New Moon, first day; Ḥanukkah, sixth day	Num. 28:1–15 Num. 7:42–47	

Italics are for Sephardi Minhag.

2006, Dec. 22–Jan. 19, 2007]   ṬEVET (29 DAYS)   [5766

Civil Date	Day of the Week	Jewish Date	SABBATHS, FESTIVALS, FASTS	PENTATEUCHAL READING	PROPHETICAL READING
Dec. 22	F	Ṭevet 1	New Moon, second day; Ḥanukkah, seventh day	Num. 28:1–15 Num. 7:48–53	
23	Sa	2	Mi-ḳeẓ; Ḥanukkah, eighth day	Gen. 41:1–44:17 Num. 7:54–8:4	Zechariah 2:14–4:7
30	Sa	9	Wa-yiggash	Gen. 44:18–47:27	Ezekiel 37:15–28
31	S	10	Fast of 10th of Ṭevet	Exod. 32:11–14 Exod. 34:1–10 (morning and afternoon)	Isaiah 55:6–56:8 (afternoon only)
Jan. 6	Sa	16	Wa-yeḥi	Gen. 47:28–50:26	I Kings 2:1–12
13	Sa	23	Shemot	Exod. 1:1–6:1	Isaiah 27:6–28:13 Isaiah 29:22–23 *Jeremiah 1:1–2:3*

Italics are for
Sephardi Minhag.

Index

Taubman, Craig, 44, 45
Tausky, Vilem, 335
Taylor, Elizabeth, 302, 303
Taylor, Kate, 313
Taylor, Nat, 314
Tekiah, 577
Tel Aviv University: American Council, 565
Teleki, Pal, 473
Teller, Harvey, 526
Temple, Jack, 334
Tenenbaum, Inez, 131
Teodori, Massimo, 401
Teutsch, David, 56n
Teva Learning Center/Shomrei Adamah, 577
Texas Jewish Post, 631
Thanks to Scandinavia, 569
The Holocaust Museum and Learning Center in Memory of Gloria Goldstein, 548
Theodor Herzl Foundation, 566
Theodorakis, Mikis, 470
Thientthong, Uraiwan, 251
Thierse, Wolfgang, 426, 428
Thompson, John, 287
Thompson, Mark, 323
Thune, John, 132, 133
Tietz, Oscar, 439
Tikkun, 621
Tisch, James, 193
Tishman, Margaret, 640
Tiso, Jozef, 495
To Save a Life, 566
Toben, Frederick, 521
Tobin, Gary A. 22n
Toibin, Colin, 313
Toledo Jewish News, 630
Toledo, Avraham, 444, 445

Tolts, Mark, 87n, 95n, 112n, 113n, 117n
Tonge, Jenny, 320
Tonino, Joost, 368
Toomey, Pat, 131
Torah Schools for Israel–Chinuch Atzmai, 577
Torah Umesorah, 577
Torczyner, Jim, 314
Touro College, 589
Touro National Heritage Trust, 553
Towarnicky, Carol, 57n
Tradition, 628
Trajkovski, Boris, 478
Tratner, Tiferet, 258
Tree, Stephen, 439
Trimbobler, Larissa, 280
Trostinky, Vladimir, 254
Troy, Gil, 297
Tsien, Roger, 283
Tsitsiashvili, Gotcha, 281
Tsomet-Techiya USA, 566
Tubul, Maurice, 255
Tucker, Raymond, 538
Tudjman, Franjo, 460
Tudor, Corneliu Vadim, 488, 489
Tulsa Jewish Review, 630
Tumarkin, Yigael, 282
Turgeman, Shalom, 232
Turgemann, Nisim, 259
Turnbull, Malcolm, 517
Turok, Ben, 527
Tutu, Desmond, 532
Tyagnybok, Oleg, 510
Tyndall, John, 325
Tyrah, Oded, 273

UIA Federations of Canada, 605
Ukeles, Jacob, 29n